Reading Latin

Grammar, vocabulary and exercises

SENATVS
POPVLVSQVEROMANVS
IMP CAESARI DIVI F AVGVSTO
COS VIII DEDIT CLVPEVM
VIRTVTIS CLEMENTIAE
IVSTITIAE PIETATIS ERGA
DEOS PATRIAMQVE

Marble copy of the Clupeus Virtutis of Augustus, found at Arles (see p. xvi and p. 297 ll. 6–8)

PETER V. JONES AND KEITH C. SIDWELL

Reading Latin

GRAMMAR, VOCABULARY
AND EXERCISES

CAMBRIDGE
UNIVERSITY PRESS

PUBLISHED BY THE PRESS SYNDICATE OF THE UNIVERSITY OF CAMBRIDGE
The Pitt Building, Trumpington Street, Cambridge, United Kingdom

CAMBRIDGE UNIVERSITY PRESS
The Edinburgh Building, Cambridge CB2 2RU, UK
40 West 20th Street, New York, NY 10011–4211, USA
477 Williamstown Road, Port Melbourne, VIC 3207, Australia
Ruiz de Alarcón 13, 28014 Madrid, Spain
Dock House, The Waterfront, Cape Town 8001, South Africa

http://www.cambridge.org

First published 1986
Nineteenth printing 2004

Printed in the United Kingdom at the University Press, Cambridge

Library of Congress catalogue card number: 85–11682

British Library Cataloguing in Publication data
Jones, Peter V.
Reading latin: grammar, vocabulary and exercises.
1. Latin language
I. Title   II. Sidwell, Keith C.
470   PA2057

ISBN 0 521 28622 0 paperback

SE

CONTENTS

Note. In Sections 1A–4C the order of items is as follows: Vocabulary (Running, Learning), Grammar and Exercises, *Dēliciae Latīnae*. From 4D to 5G there is an additional 'Reading' section before *Dēliciae Latīnae*. Sections 6A and 6D have Vocabulary (Running, Learning) and Grammar and Exercises; Sections 6B–C have only Vocabulary; there are no additional 'Reading' sections or *Dēliciae Latīnae*.

This list gives the contents of Running Grammar in detail, by Section number, but only general headings for the Reference Grammar. For detailed references to the latter see Index, pp. 602–10.

v

Contents

A–G Verbs   A Active   B Passive   C Deponent
D Semi-deponent   E Irregular verbs   F Defective verbs,
impersonal verbs   G Principal parts of irregular verbs

H–I Nouns, pronominal nouns/adjectives

J–K Adjectives, adverbs and prepositions

L–V Constructions   L The cases   M The infinitive
N Gerund   O Gerundive   P Participles   Q Relative

Contents

ACKNOWLEDGEMENTS

The poem by Giovanni Cotta on p. 76 and that by Elio Giulio Crotti on
p. 287 are reproduced from A. Perosa and J. Sparrow, eds., *Renaissance
Latin Verse* (Duckworth 1979). 'St Columba subdues the Loch Ness
Monster' (p. 270) is reproduced from Sidney Morris, ed., *Fons Perennis*
(Harrap 1962). The authors thank the publishers concerned.

PREFACE

ūsus magister est optimus
(Cicero, *Rab. Post* 4.9.)

This volume accompanies *Reading Latin* (*Text*), C.U.P. 1986 and is to be used in conjunction with it. For an introduction to the *Reading Latin* course – its aims, methodology and future development – and our acknowledgements of all the help we have received in its production, please refer to the Introduction of the *Text* volume.

Notes to *Grammar, Vocabulary and Exercises*

1 All dates are B.C., unless otherwise specified.
2 The running grammar for each section comes in four parts:

(a) Running vocabulary.
(b) Learning vocabulary. Words set to be learnt will not be glossed in running vocabularies again, unless they occur in the *Text* with a different meaning. On p. 557 there is a total vocabulary of all words set to be learnt with their full range of meanings given in this course, and a note of where they should have been learnt (teachers should use this information when devising their own tests).
(c) Grammar and exercises. It is extremely important to note that the exercises should be regarded as a pool out of which the teacher/students should choose what to do, and whether in or out of class. Some of the simpler exercises we have already split into necessary and optional sections, but this principle should be applied to all of them.
(d) *Dēliciae Latīnae* / further reading.

3 On p. 448 there is a full reference grammar, based on the running grammar explanations, but in many cases adding further information to that given in the running explanations.

4 On p. 548 there is an Appendix on the Latin language.

5 On p. 557 there is the total learning vocabulary, and on p. 578 an English–Latin vocabulary for those doing the English–Latin sentence and prose exercises.

6 At the end of the book, p. 593, there is a supplementary Latin–English vocabulary, containing important words which have been met, but not learnt in this course. Those who wish to continue with their Latin studies should attempt to learn them.

7 In cross-references, superior figures appended to a section number indicate *Notes*, e.g. **139**[4]. If the reference is in the form '**140.1**', the last digit indicates a numbered sub-section.

8 Linking devices are used occasionally in passages of original Latin poetry to indicate words that should be taken together. ⌐——links words next to each other, ⌐ ⌐ links words separated from each other. Where such words are glossed, they will be found in separate entries in close proximity to one another. In later sections, a longer linking device ———— shows the limits of a larger phrase.

9 The case which follows an adjective or a verb is usually indicated by e.g. '(+ acc.)'. But occasionally you will meet e.g. '(x: acc.)'.

10 In places where standard beginners' texts print *v* (i.e. consonantal *u*), we have in accordance with early MS practice printed *u*. But in some later Latin texts we have reverted to *v*, which is commonly found in early printed books.

11 In learning vocabularies, where a new meaning is listed for a word already learned, the meaning(s) previously met are placed in brackets after the new meaning(s). E.g. at **2A**: *bene* good! fine! (well, thoroughly, rightly).

12 Bold numbers in pageheads, e.g. **15**, refer to sections of the Running Grammar. Where these numbers have an arrow, e.g. ←**15 16**→, the arrow shows the direction to go to find the section indicated.

Peter V. Jones
28 Akenside Terrace,
Newcastle upon Tyne,
NE2 1TN, UK

Keith C. Sidwell
Dept. of Ancient Classics,
University College, Cork,
IRELAND

ABBREVIATIONS

abl.(ative)
abs.(olute)
acc.(usative)
act.(ive)
adj.(ective)
adv.(erb)
cf. (= *cōnfer* (Latin), 'compare')
comp.(arative)
conj.(ugation, ugated)
dat.(ive)
decl.(ension)
dep.(onent)
dir.(ect)
f.(eminine)
fut.(ure)
gen.(itive)
imper.(ative)
impf./imperf. (= imperfect)
indecl.(inable)
ind.(icative)
indir.(ect)
inf.(initive)
intrans.(itive)
irr.(egular)
l(l.) line(s)
lit.(erally)
m.(asculine)
neg.(ative)
n.(euter)
nom.(inative)
part.(iciple)
pass.(ive)

perf./pf. (= perfect)
pl.(ural)
plupf./plup. (= pluperfect)
p.p. (= principal part)
prep.(osition)
pres.(ent)
prim.(ary)
pron.(oun)
q.(uestion)
rel.(ative)
s.(ingular)
sc.(= *scīlicet* (Latin), 'presumably')
sec.(ondary)
seq.(uence)
sp.(eech)
subj.(unctive)
sup.(erlative)
trans.(itive)
tr.(anslate)
vb (= verb)
voc.(ative)
1st, 2nd, 3rd refer to persons of the verb, i.e.
   1st s. = 'I'
   2nd s. = 'you'
   3rd s. = 'he', 'she', 'it'
   1st pl. = 'we'
   2nd pl. = 'you'
   3rd pl. = 'they'
1f., 2m. etc. refer to declension and
gender of nouns

PRONUNCIATION

'English' refers throughout to the standard or 'received' pronunciation of southern British English unless otherwise qualified.

a as English 'c*u*p', or '*a*ha' (cf. 'c*a*t', or Italian or French '*a*-')

ā as English 'f*a*ther' (roughly)

ae as in English 'h*i*gh' (roughly)

au as in English 'h*o*w'

b as English

c as English 'c' in 'cat' (not 'cider', 'cello')

ch as English 'pa*ck-h*orse'

d as English

e as in English 'p*e*t'

ē as in 'fianc*é*e' (French pronunciation)

ei as in English 'd*a*y'

eu 'e-oo' (cf. Cockney 'b*e*lt')

f as English

g as English 'g*o*t'; but 'gn' = 'ngn' as in 'ha*ng*nail'

h as English

i as in English 'd*i*p'

ī as in English 'd*ee*p'

i consonant (sometimes written as a 'j'); as English 'y*o*u'

k as English

l as English

m as English at the beginning and in the middle of words (cf. 'm*a*t', 'ca*m*p'); a final 'm' expresses nasalisation of the preceding vowel (cf. French 'parfu*m*')

n as English

o as in English 'p*o*t'

ō as in French 'b*eau*'

oe as in English 'b*o*y'

p as English

ph as in English

qu as in English '*qu*ick'

r as Scottish 'rolled' 'r'

s as s in English '*s*ing' (never as in 'ro*s*es')

t as t in English 't*i*n' (cleanly pronounced, with no 'h' sound)

th as in English 'po*t-h*ouse'

u as in English 'p*u*t'

ū as in English 'f*oo*l'

u (pronounced as a consonant) as in English 'w' (sometimes written as 'v')

x as English

y as French 'u'

z as English.

Rules of word stress (accent)

1 A word of two syllables is stressed on the first syllable, e.g. *ámō, ámās.*
2 A word of more than two syllables is stressed on the penultimate (i.e. second syllable from the end) if that syllable is HEAVY, e.g. *astútus, audiúntur* (see p. 318 for the terms 'heavy', 'light').
3 In all other cases, words of more than two syllables are stressed on the antepenultimate (i.e. third syllable from the end), e.g. *amábitis, pulchérrimus.*
4 Words of one syllable (monosyllables) always have the stress, e.g. *nóx.* But prepositions *before* a noun are not accented, e.g. *ad hóminem.*
5 Some words, e.g. *-que, -ne* and *-ue,* which are appended to the word which precedes them, cause the stress to fall on the last syllable of that word, e.g *uírum* but *uirúmque.*

For a clear account of Classical Latin pronunciation see W. S. Allen, *Vox Latina* (2nd edition), Cambridge 1975.

NOTES ON ILLUSTRATIONS

Cover   Villa by the sea. Wall-painting from Stabiae; 1st century A.D. Naples, Museo Nazionale 9409. Photo: DAI (R).

Frontispiece   The *clupeus aureus* of Augustus. Marble copy of the gold original set up in the senate house (*cūria*): SENATVS POPVLVSQVE ROMANVS IMP(ERATORI) CAESARI DIVI F(ILIO) AVGVSTO CO(N)S(VLI) VIII DEDIT CLVPEVM VIRTVTIS CLEMENTIAE IVSTITIAE PIETATIS ERGA DEOS PATRIAMQVE.

Arles, Musée Lapidaire, Photo: Giraudon.

GLOSSARY OF ENGLISH–LATIN GRAMMAR

This explains the most important terminology of Latin grammar, with examples in English. To make it as practically useful as possible, we provide simple definitions with down-to-earth examples of each term. Students should bear in mind, however, that (1) there is only a limited 'fit' between English grammar and Latin grammar, and (2) brevity and simplicity lead to technical inaccuracy (grammatical terms are notoriously difficult to define). So this index should be regarded as a simplified guide to the subject, for use when you forget the definition of a term used in the grammar or to refresh your memory of grammatical terms before you begin the course.

Before beginning the course, you should be acquainted with the following terms: noun, adjective, pronoun, conjunction, preposition, verb, person, number, tense, gender, case, singular, plural.

ablative: name of a case of the noun, pronoun and adjective. Functions defined at Reference Grammar **L**.

accidence: grammar which deals with variable forms of words, e.g. declensions, conjugations.

accusative: name of a case of the noun, pronoun or adjective. Function defined at Reference Grammar **L**.

active: a verb is active when the subject is doing the action, e.g. 'she (subject) *runs*', 'Thomas Aquinas (subject) *reads* his book'.

adjective: words which define the quality of a noun or pronoun by describing it, e.g. '*steep* hill', '*red* house', '*clever* me'. There are also adjectival clauses, for which see *relative clauses*. Possessive adjectives are 'my', 'your', 'our', 'his', 'her', 'their'. In Latin adjectives must agree with nouns or pronouns in case, number and gender.

adverb: word which defines the quality of a verb by showing how the action of the verb is carried out, e.g. 'she ran *quickly*', 'she works *enthusiastically*'.

Adverbial clauses do the same job, e.g. 'she ran *as quickly as she was able*'. Adverbs in Latin are indeclinable.

agree(ment): an adjective agrees with a noun when it adopts the same case, number and gender as the noun. E.g. if a noun is nominative singular masculine, an adjective which is to describe it must also be nominative singular masculine.

apposition: nouns or noun–plus–adjective phrases which add further information about a noun already mentioned are said to be 'in apposition' to it, e.g. 'the house, a red-brick building, was placed on the side of a hill' – here 'a red-brick building' is 'in apposition' to 'the house'.

article: the definite article is the word 'the', the indefinite article the word 'a'.

aspect: whether the action of the verb is seen as a simple statement, as continuing or repeated, e.g. 'I run', 'I am running' (or, in English, emphasised 'I *do* run').

auxiliary (verb): in 'she will love', 'she does love', 'she has loved', the verbs 'will', 'does' and 'have' are auxiliary verbs, brought in to help the verb 'love' (*auxilium* = help), defining its tense and aspect. 'May', 'might', 'would', 'should' are auxiliaries indicating the mood of the verb to which they are attached. Latin only uses auxiliary verbs in the perfect, pluperfect and future perfect deponent and passive.

case: form of the noun, pronoun or adjective which defines the relationship between that word and the rest of the sentence, e.g. a Latin word adopting the form which shows that it is in the nominative case (e.g. *serua*) might show that the word is the subject of its clause; a Latin word adopting the form which shows that it is in the accusative case (e.g. *seruam*) might show that it is the object of the sentence. There are six cases in Latin: nominative, vocative, accusative, genitive, dative and ablative. Most have more than one function.

causal clause: clause expressing the reason why something has happened or will happen, e.g. clauses beginning 'because . . .', 'since . . .'

clause: part of a sentence containing a subject and finite verb. E.g. main clause 'she had finished', 'she hated it', 'she may succeed'; subordinate clause 'when she had finished', 'which she hated', 'so that she may succeed'. Cf. *phrase*. (See *adjective, adverb, noun*.)

comparative: form of adjective or adverb which implies a comparison, e.g. 'hotter', 'better', 'more slowly'.

complement: when a subject is said *to be* something, or *to be called, to be thought*, or *to seem* something, the 'something' is the complement of the verb, e.g. 'she is *intelligent*', 'it seems *OK*', 'she is thought to be *a promising scholar*'.

concessive clause: clause introduced by the word 'although', e.g. '*although it is raining*, we shall go to the shops'.

conditional clause: clause introduced by the word 'if', e.g. '*If it rains today*, I shall not go to the shops.' The technical term for the 'if' clause is '*protasis*', and for the main clause '*apodosis*' ('pay-off').

conjugation (conjugate): the parts of a verb are its conjugation, e.g. the conjugation of 'I love' in the present indicative active is 'I love, you love, he/she/it loves, we love, you love, they love'.

conjunction: words (indeclinable in Latin) which link clauses or phrases or sentences, e.g. '*When* the light was out *and* she went up to have dinner, the burglar entered *and* took the piano. *But* he was not unseen . . .' Co-ordinating conjunctions link together units (i.e. clauses, sentences, phrases) of equal grammatical value e.g. 'He went *and* stood *and* laughed out loud; *but* she sulked *and* stalked off *and* had a drink.' Subordinating conjunctions, words like 'when', 'although', 'if', 'because', 'since', 'after', introduce units of different grammatical value compared with the main clause. See *main verb*.

consecutive clause: see *result clause*.

consonant: a letter which is not a vowel, e.g. 'b', 'c', 'd', 'f', 'g', 'h', etc.

dative: name of case of the noun, pronoun and adjective. For function, see Reference Grammar **L**.

declension (decline): the forms of a noun, pronoun or adjective. To decline a noun is to list all its forms (i.e. nominative, vocative, accusative, genitive, dative, ablative) in both singular and plural.

deponent: a verb whose dictionary form (1st person singular) ends in *-or* e.g. *minor, hortor, sequor* etc., and whose meaning is always *active*.

diphthong: see *vowel*.

direct speech: speech which is quoted in the exact words of the speaker, e.g. 'Give me that book' (cf. *indirect speech*).

final clause: a clause which expresses the idea '(in order) to', i.e. it expresses purpose. E.g. '*in order to* swim the river, she took off her shoes', '*to* cross the railway, use the bridge'.

finite (verb): a verb which has a defined number and person, e.g. 'she runs' (third person, singular). Contrast 'to run', 'running', which are examples of the infinite verb (cf. *infinitive*).

future perfect tense: a verb form of the type 'I shall have —ed', e.g. 'I shall have tried', 'you will have gone', 'he will have spoken'.

future tense: a verb form of the type 'I shall/will —', e.g. 'I shall go', 'you will be', 'they will run'.

gender: whether a noun, pronoun or adjective is masculine, feminine or neuter.

genitive: a case of the noun, pronoun, or adjective. Function defined at Reference Grammar **L**.

historic sequence (also called 'secondary sequence'): when the main verb of a sentence is in a past tense ('I have —ed' counts as a present tense for the purposes of sequence).

imperative: the form of a verb which gives a command, e.g. 'run!'

imperfect tense: verb form of the type 'I was —ing', 'I used to —', 'I kept on —ing'. It indicates continued or repeated action in the past.

indeclinable: a word which has only one form.

indicative: a verb form which states something as a fact, not as a wish or command, e.g. 'she runs'. Compare 'run!', 'may she run!', etc.

indirect object: term for the person *to whom* something is given or said, e.g. 'she said *to him*, "Give it *to me*" '; 'she told *him* to give *her* the book'.

indirect speech: words which are reported, not, as in direct speech, stated exactly as the speaker said or thought them, e.g. direct command 'let me go', indirect command 'she told them to let her go'; direct statement 'he has gone', indirect statement 'he said that he had gone'; direct question 'where am I?', indirect question 'she wondered where she was'. Any verb of speaking or thinking can introduce indirect speech.

infinitive: verb form prefixed in English by 'to', e.g. 'to run', 'to have walked' etc.

inflexion: the different endings that a word takes to express its meaning in a sentence, e.g. 'he' (subject), 'him' (object) indicate case and may be said to be 'inflected'. Cf. 'they *say*', 'we *said*', indicating tense.

interrogative: asking a question, e.g. 'who?' is an interrogative pronoun.

intransitive (verb): a verb is intransitive when it does not require a direct object to complete its meaning, e.g. 'I stand', 'I sit'. In English such words can, at a stretch, be used transitively as well, when they adopt a different meaning, e.g. 'I sit (= take) an exam'; 'I cannot stand (= endure) that man'.

jussive (subjunctive): related to giving orders. The form of the jussive subjunctive in English is 'let him/them/me/us'.

locative case: the case used to indicate where something is at. It is used in Latin with names of towns and one-town islands, e.g. 'at Rome', 'on Malta'.

main verb: the main verb(s) of a sentence is(are) the verb(s) left when all other verbs have been cut out (e.g. infinitives, participles, verbs in subordinating clauses), e.g. '(Although being something of a bibliophile) (who loved nothing more than a good read) (if she could get one), she *sold* her books (when the examinations were over) and *lived* in misery the rest of her life with her friends (who were totally illiterate)'. Main verbs – 'sold' and 'lived'.

mood: whether a verb is indicative, subjunctive or imperative.

morphology: study of the forms which words take.

nominative: a case of the noun, pronoun or adjective. For function, see **6.2,4**.

noun: name of a person ('woman', 'child'), place ('London'), thing ('table', 'chair', 'mountain') or abstraction ('virtue', 'courage', 'thought', 'quality').

Noun clauses are clauses which do the job of a noun in the sentence, e.g. all indirect speech (e.g. 'he says words'; 'words' = noun, object: 'he says *that she is divine*'; 'that she is divine' = noun-clause, object), constructions following 'I fear that/lest, I doubt that, I prevent x from' and 'it happened that . . .'

number: whether something is singular or plural; 'table' and 'he' are singular, 'tables' and 'they' are plural.

object: a direct object is that onto which the action of the subject and verb directly move, e.g. 'she hits *the ball*', 'they love *books*', 'we can see *Rome*'. Cf. *indirect object*.

participle: a verb-form with the qualities and functions of an adjective, e.g. 'a *running* sore', 'a woman *thinking* . . .' In Latin there are present participles active (meaning ' —ing'), future participles active (meaning 'about to —; on the point of —ing'), and perfect participles active (meaning 'having —ed') and passive (meaning 'having been —ed').

passive: a verb is passive when the subject is not doing the action, but having the action done to it. The same *action* may be described in both the active and the passive 'voice', e.g. 'she hit the ball' (active), 'the ball was hit by her' (passive); 'we visited Rome' (active), 'Rome was visited by us' (passive).

perfect tense: verb-form of the type 'I —ed', 'I have —ed', 'I did —', expressing a simple action in the past, e.g. 'I walked', 'she has gone', 'we did see it'.

person: the persons are expressed by the pronouns 'I', 'we' (first persons, singular and plural); 'you' (second person singular and plural); 'he'/'she'/'it', 'they' (third persons singular and plural).

phrase: part of a sentence not having a finite verb, often introduced by a preposition, e.g. 'in the house' (prepositional phrase); '*going to work*, he —' (participle phrase); 'I wish *to do it*' (infinitive phrase).

pluperfect tense: a verb-form of the type 'I had —ed', e.g. 'I had walked', 'they had gone'.

plural: more than one, e.g. 'tables' is plural, 'table' is singular.

predicate: what is said about the subject of a sentence, e.g. 'The man', (subject) 'wore blue socks' (predicate).

predicative: to predicate something of someone is to say something new about them. So when adjectives (including participles) and nouns say something new, i.e. not previously acknowledged, about a person or thing, they are being used 'predicatively'. In English, predicative adjectives and participles usually come *after* the nouns they go with, e.g. 'I saw the man *working*', 'the woman went away *happy*', 'Caesar became *consul*', 'she is a *help* to them' (the last two are predicative nouns). Contrast 'I saw the working man', 'the happy woman went away', in which the adjectives describe what is already understood or acknowledged, adding nothing new (such adjectives are technically called 'attributive').

prefix: a small addition to the front of a word, which alters the basic meaning, e.g. fix, re fix, pre fix; ex port, im port; embark, dis embark, redis embark.

preposition: word coming before a noun or pronoun which (in Latin) affects the noun/pronoun's case, e.g. '*into* the house', '*from* the pot', '*from* the hill', '*with* my friend', '*by* train'. Such expressions are called 'prepositional phrases'.

present tense: verb-form of the type 'I —', 'I am —ing', 'I do —', e.g. 'I love', 'I am loving', 'I do love'.

primary sequence: when the main verb of a sentence is present, future, or perfect in the form 'I have —ed'.

principal parts: (in Latin) the four parts of an active verb (present, infinitive, perfect and perfect participle) from which all other parts are formed; deponent verbs have only three such parts (present, infinitive, and perfect participle).

pronoun: this refers to a noun, without naming it, e.g. 'he' (as against 'the man', or 'Caesar'), 'they' (as against 'the women', or 'the Mitfords'), 'we', 'you', 'who', 'which'.

question (direct): a sentence ending in '?' (see also *indirect speech*).

reflexive: a pronoun or adjective is reflexive when it refers to (i.e. is the same person or thing as) the subject of the clause in which it stands, e.g. 'they warmed *themselves* by the fire', 'when they had checked *their* equipment, the leader gave them (*not* reflexive, since 'leader' is the subject) orders'.

regular: a 'regular' verb, noun, or adjective follows the pattern of the type to which it belongs, without deviation.

relative clause: a clause introduced by a relative pronoun such as 'who', 'which', 'what', 'whose', 'whom', 'that'; the relative pronoun refers back to a previous noun or pronoun (sometimes it refers forward to it) and the whole clause helps to describe or define the noun or pronoun referred to (hence it is an adjectival clause) e.g. 'the book *which I am reading* is rubbish', 'she presented the man *whom she had brought*', '*Who* dreads, yet undismayed/Dares face his terror . . . *Him* let saint Thomas guide'.

reported speech: see *indirect speech*.

result clause: a clause which expresses the result or consequence of an action. It takes the form 'so . . . that / as to . . .' e.g. 'they were *so* forgetful *that they left (as to leave) all their money behind*'.

secondary sequence: see *historic sequence*.

semi-deponent: a verb which takes active forms in present, future and imperfect tenses, but deponent forms in perfect, future perfect and pluperfect.

sequence: see *primary* and *historic*.

singular: expresses *one* of something, e.g. 'table' is singular, 'tables' is plural; 'he' (singular), 'they' (plural).

statement: an utterance presented as a fact, e.g. 'I am carrying this pot'. Cf. question 'Am I carrying this pot?', command 'Carry this pot!'

subject: the subject of a sentence is, in the case of active verbs, the person/thing doing the action or being in the state (e.g. '*Gloria* hits out'; '*Gloria* is champion'); in the case of passive verbs, the subject is the person or thing on the receiving end of the action, e.g. '*the ball* was hit by Gloria'.

subjunctive: the mood of the verb used in certain main and subordinate clauses in Latin and English, often expressing wishes or possibilities or commands, e.g. 'may I win!', 'let him think!', 'she left in order that she *might* catch the bus'.

subordinating clause (sub-clause): any clause which is not the main one (e.g. see *noun, relative clause, result clause, final clause, adverb, temporal clause, causal clause, concessive clause, conditional clause, participle, infinitive*). Cf. *phrase*. Also see *main verb*.

suffix: a small addition to the end of a word which changes its meaning, e.g. 'act', 'act*or*', 'act*ion*', 'act*ive*'.

superlative: the form of an adjective or adverb which expresses its highest degree, e.g. 'the *fastest* horse', 'he jumped *very high*', 'she worked *extremely hard*'.

syllable: a vowel or a vowel + consonant combination, pronounced without interruption as a word or part of a word, e.g. 'the' (one syllable), 'Julius' (three syllables), 'antidisestablishmentarianism' (eleven syllables).

syntax: grammar which deals with the constructions of a sentence (e.g. indirect speech, result clauses, temporal clauses, participle phrases etc.).

temporal clause: a clause expressing the time *when* something happened in relation to the rest of the sentence, e.g. 'when . . .', 'after . . .', 'while . . .', 'before . . .', 'as soon as . . .'.

tense: the time at which the action of a verb is meant to take place. See under *present tense, future tense, imperfect tense, perfect tense, future perfect tense, pluperfect tense*.

transitive (verb): a verb which takes a direct object to complete its meaning, e.g. 'I put *the book* on the table', 'I make *a chart*' (it is very difficult to think of a context in which 'I put' and 'I make' could make a sentence *on their own*. This is not the case with *intransitive* verbs, e.g. 'I sit').

verb: a word expressing action or state, e.g. 'run', 'jump', 'stand', 'think', 'be', 'say'. (See under *active* and *passive*). Every complete sentence has at least one.

vocative: a case of the noun, pronoun or adjective, used when addressing someone (e.g. 'you too, Brutus?', '*et tū, Brūte?* ').

voice: whether a verb is active or passive.

vowel: 'a', 'e', 'i', 'o', 'u'. Diphthongs are two vowels pronounced as a single syllable (e.g. 'ou', 'ae').

Introduction

Running vocabulary for Introduction

aedēs house
auārus greedy, miserly
cum fīliā with (his) daughter
ego I
es you are (in question: are you?)
est is; he/she/it is; there is
estis you (pl.) are (in question: are you?)
et and; too
Eucliō Euclio
Eucliōnis of Euclio, Euclio's
Eucliōnis familia Euclio's household

familia household
fīlia daughter
fīlia Eucliōnis the daughter of Euclio
habitant (they) live
habitat (he/she/it) lives
in aedibus in the house
in familiā Eucliōnis in Euclio's household
omnēs all (pl.)
paterfamiliās head of the family
pater Phaedrae father of Phaedra
Phaedra Phaedra
Phaedrae of Phaedra

quī who? (pl.)
quis who? (s.)
scaena stage
senex old man
serua (woman) slave
serua Eucliōnis Euclio's slave
seruae nōmen the name of the slave
Staphyla Staphyla
sum (I) am
sumus we are
sunt are; they are; there are
tū you

Learning vocabulary for Introduction

Nouns
Eucliō Euclio
famili-a household

fīli-a daughter
Phaedr-a Phaedra

seru-a slave-woman
Staphyl-a Staphyla

Verbs
habit-ō I dwell

Others
et and; also, too, even

1

General notes

1 All vowels are pronounced *short* unless marked with a ⁻ (macron) over them. So observe different vowel length of '*i*' in, e.g., *fīlia*, etc. It may be helpful, but is not essential, to mark macra in your exercises.

2 ´ above a vowel indicates *stress*. Stress marks are included in all tables and throughout the Reference Grammar.

3 You should learn the learning vocabulary for each section *before* attempting the exercises. Please see *Text*, p. viii for suggested methodology.

Grammar for Introduction – *familia Euclīōnis*

---

1   *sum* 'I am'

1st person singular	*(1st s.)*	su–m	'I am'
2nd person singular	*(2nd s.)*	es[1]	'you are'
3rd person singular	*(3rd s.)*	es–t	'he/she/it is' 'there is'
1st person plural	*(1st pl.)*	sú–mus	'we are'
2nd person plural	*(2nd pl.)*	és–tis	'you (*pl.*) are'
3rd person plural	*(3rd pl.)*	su–nt	'they/there are'

[1] Really *es-s*

Notes

1 *sum* is the most common verb in Latin.

2 Whereas English takes two words to express 'I am', Latin takes *one*. This is because the *endings* of the verb – *m, -s, -t, -mus, -tis, -nt* – indicate the person doing the action. Thus in full:

> ⁻*m* = I[1]
> ⁻*s* = you (s.)
> ⁻*t* = he, she, it, there
> ⁻*mus* = we
> ⁻*tis* = you (pl.)
> ⁻*nt* = they, there

[1] In other verbs ⁻*ō* = 'I'

3 *sum* is irregular because, as you can see, the stem changes from *su-* to *es-*. If it is any consolation, all verbs meaning 'to be' are irregular, e.g. English 'I *am*', 'you *are*', 'he *is*'; French (deriving from Latin) 'je *suis*', 'tu *es*', 'il *est*' etc.

2

4 In the 3rd s. and 3rd pl., *est* and *sunt* mean only 'is' and 'are' if the subject is named, e.g. *senex est* = 'he is an old man'; *Eucliō senex est* = 'Euclio is an old man'; *seruae sunt* = 'they are slave-women'; *omnēs seruae sunt* = 'all are slave-women'.

5 Note the following points about word-order in sentences with *sum*:

(a) Where subject and complement are stated

    (i) the unemphatic order is: subject complement *sum*. E.g.

      Eucliō senex est 'Euclio is an old man'.

    (ii) other orders place emphasis on the first word, e.g.

      senex est Eucliō (complement *sum* subject)
      senex Eucliō est (complement subject *sum*)

      Both mean 'an old man, that's what Euclio is.'

NB   The order 'subject *sum* complement' emphasizes the subject.

    (iii) The verb *sum* may come first and is then emphatic, e.g. *est enim Eucliō auārus* (*sum* subject complement) 'for Euclio *is* (in fact) a miser.'

(b) Where the subject is not stated in Latin, the usual order is: complement *sum*. E.g.

    Staphyla est 'it's Staphyla'.

(c) *est/sunt* at the beginning of a sentence commonly indicate the *existence* of something, and are often best translated 'there is/ there are'. E.g.

    est locus . . . 'there is a place . . .'

In such sentences, more information will be expected e.g. 'there is a place, where roses grow', 'there are people, who like Latin.'

NB   In (a) (i) and (ii) and (b) observe how complement + *sum* usually stick together to form the predicate, e.g.

Eucliō senex-est
senex-est Eucliō

sum is likely to go closely with the word preceding it, except where the order has been altered for special emphasis (as in e.g. *senex Eucliō est*).

Exercises

Morphology

1 *Translate into Latin*: you (*s.*) are; there are; he is; there is; you (*pl.*) are; they are; it is; I am; she is.

2 *Change s. to pl. and vice versa*: sum; sunt; estis; est; sumus; es.

Reading

Using Note 5 in the grammar section, give the correct translation of these sentences:

   (a)   familia est.
   (b)   serua Staphyla est.
   (c)   est enim aula aurī plēna (aula, *pot*; aurī plēna, *full of gold*).
   (d)   coquus est seruus (coquus, *cook*; seruus, *slave*).
   (e)   Phaedra fīlia est.
   (f)   in aedibus sunt Eucliō, Phaedra et serua (in aedibus, *in the house*).
   (g)   auārus est senex (auārus, *miser*; senex, *old man*).
   (h)   est prope flūmen paruus ager (prope flūmen, *near the river*; paruus, *small*; ager, *field*).

English–Latin

Translate the Latin sentences into English. Then translate the English sentences into Latin, using the pattern of the Latin ones to help you arrange the word-order correctly.

   (a)   sunt in familiā Eucliō, Phaedra, Staphyla.
         There is in the household a slave-girl.
   (b)   Eucliō et Phaedra in aedibus sunt.
         The slave-girl is in the house.
   (c)   Eucliō sum.
         You (*s.*) are a slave.
   (d)   fīlia Eucliōnis Phaedra est.
         Euclio's slave is Staphyla.
   (e)   quis es?
         I am Euclio.
   (f)   quī estis?
         We are Euclio and Phaedra.

SECTION ONE

Section 1A

Running vocabulary for 1A

Important notes

1 nom. is short for nominative and indicates the subject or complement of a sentence.

acc. is short for accusative and indicates the object (direct) of a sentence. See Glossary of English–Latin Grammar p. xxi.

2 Where a 3rd s. verb is glossed '(he/she/it)', select the appropriate pronoun where there is no stated subject.

ad focum to the hearth
ad iānuam to the door
ad Larem to the Lar
ad nūptiās (fīliae tuae) to the wedding (of your daughter)
ad tē to you (s.)
adest (he/she/it) is present
aedēs (nom. pl.) house
ante iānuam Dēmaenetī before Demaenetus' door
aperīs (you) (s.) open
aperit (he/she/it) opens
appropinquat (he/she/it) approaches
appropinquō I approach
at but
aula (nom.) pot
aulam (acc.) pot
aurī plēna (nom.) ⎫ full of
aurī plēnum (acc.) ⎭ gold

aurum (nom., acc.) gold
autem but
bene good!
bonam (acc.) good
cēlat (he/she/it) hides
cēlō I hide away, secrete
circumspectat (he/she/it) looks around
clam secretly
clāmās (do) you (s.) shout
clāmat (he/she/it) shouts, is shouting
clāmātis you (pl.) shout; are you shouting?
clausa (nom.) closed, shut
cognōuī I know
contrā in return
coquī (nom.) cooks
coquōrum et tībīcinārum of cooks and pipe-girls
coquōs (acc.) cooks
coquum (acc.) cook

coquus (nom.) cook
corōnam(que) (acc.) (and) a garland
corōnō I garland
cūncta (nom.) the whole
cūnctī (nom.) everyone
cūr why?
cursitant (they) run about
cursitō (I) run about
dās you (s.) give
dat he gives, offers
Dāue (voc.) O Davus
Dāuus (nom.) Davus
dē aulā about the pot
deinde then
Dēmaenetus (nom.) Demaenetus
dō I give
dominus (nom.) master
dominus seruī et seruae master of the slave-man and slave-woman

5

ecce look!
ecquis (nom.) anyone?
ego I
enim for, because
Eucliōnis auus Euclio's grandfather
familiae Eucliōnis of Euclio's household
festīnat (he/she/it) hurries about
fīliae tuae of your daughter
fīliam (acc.) daughter
Fortūnam (acc.) luck
fouea hole, pit
furcifer rascal
fūrem (acc.) thief
fūrēs (nom.) thieves
fūrum plēnae full of thieves
habeō I have
habēs you have
heu alas
heus hey!
hodiē today
hominum of men
homo (nom.) man
honōrem (acc.) respect
hūc here
iānua (nom.) door
iānuam (acc.) door
igitur therefore
ignōrat (he/she/it) is ignorant
illūc there
immō more precisely
in aedīs Dēmaenetī into the house of Demaenetus
in aedīs (meās) into (my) house
in fouea in the pit, hole
in mātrimōnium dat (he/she/it) gives in marriage
in scaenam onto the stage
intrant (they) enter
intrat (he/she/it) enters
intrātis you (pl.) enter

Lar (voc.) O Lar (household god)
Larī to the Lar
latet (it) lies hidden
mē (acc.) me
meus mine, my
mōnstrat (he/she/it) shows, reveals
nam for, because
nēminem (acc.) no-one
nēmo (nom.) no-one
nōn no, not
nūllam (acc.) \
nūllum (acc.) ∫ no
nunc now
nūptiae (nom.) (*fīliae meae*) marriage-rites (of my daughter)
nūptiās (acc.) (*fīliae meae*) marriage-rites (of my daughter)
ō O (addressing someone)
obsecrō I beseech
occupāta busy
olet (it) gives off a smell
olfactant (they) sniff out
ōrō I beg
ōtiōsī idle
ōtiōsus idle
Pamphila (nom., voc.) Pamphila
parant (they) prepare
parātis you (pl.) prepare
parō I prepare
perditissimus the most done for
perditus lost, done for
plēnae (nom. pl.) full
portat (he/she/it) carries
portō I carry
prius first, beforehand
prope focum near the hearth
puellae (nom.) girls
puerī (nom.) boys
pulsat (he/she/it) beats on, pounds
pulsō (I) beat on, pound

quī who?
quid what?
quis who?
quod because
quoque also, too
sacrificium (acc.) sacrifice
saluum safe
saluus safe
sed but
semper always
senex (nom.) old man
serua (nom., voc.) slave (-woman)
seruā save!, protect!
.seruae nōmen the name of the slave
seruam (acc.) slave-woman
seruī nōmen the name of the slave
seruus (nom.) slave
seruus Dēmaenetī senis slave of Demaenetus the old man
sī if
sōlus alone
spectat (he/she/it) does look at, looks at
stat (he/she/it) stands
stātis you (pl.) stand, are you standing?
sub terrā beneath the earth
sub ueste under my clothes
supplicō I pray (to)
tē (acc.) you (s.)
tibi to you (s.)
tībīcina (nom.) pipe-girl
tībīcinae (nom.) pipe-girls
tībīcinam (acc.) pipe-girl
tībīcinās (acc.) pipe-girls
timeō I fear, am afraid
tū (nom.) you (s.)
tūtēla meae familiae protector (lit. protection) of my household
ualdē very much

6

uenīmus we come	*uocās* (do) you (s.) call	*uōs* (nom., voc., acc.) you
uidet (he/she/it) sees	*uocat* (he/she/it) calls	(pl.)
unguentum (acc.) ointment	*uocō* I call, summon	

Learning vocabulary for 1A

Nouns

aul-a ae 1f. pot	*ego* I	*scaen-a ae* 1f. stage
aur-um ī 2n. gold	*Lar Lar-* Lar (household	*seru-us ī* 2m. male slave
coqu-us ī 2m. cook	god)	*tē* you (s.)
corōn-a ae 1f. garland	*mē* me	*tū* you (s.)

Adjectives

plēn-us a um full
(of) + gen.

Verbs

cēl-ō I hide	*port-ō* I carry	*time-ō* I fear, am afraid
clām-ō I shout	*uoc-ō* I call	(of)
intr-ō I enter	*habe-ō* I have	

Others

ad (+ acc.) to(wards); at	translated 1st word in	*nōn* no(t)
autem but (2nd word in	English)	*nunc* now
Latin, to be translated	*igitur* therefore (usually	*quoque* also
first word in English)	2nd word in Latin);	*sed* but
cūr why?	*in* (+ acc.) into, onto	*semper* always
deinde next	(+ abl.) in, on	*sī* if
enim for, because (2nd	*nam* for, because (1st	*sub* (+ abl.) under,
word in Latin, to be	word in Latin)	beneath

Grammar and exercises for 1A

(Please see *Text*, p. vi for a suggested methodology. Most importantly, make a SELECTION from the exercises.)

2   Present indicative active (1st conjugation): *amō* 'I love', 'I am loving', 'I do love'

1st s.	ám-ō	'I love' 'I am loving' 'I do love'
2nd s.	ámā-s	'you love' *etc.*
3rd s.	áma-t	'he/she/it loves'

1st pl.	amā́-mus	'we love'
2nd pl.	amā́-tis	'you (*pl.*) love'
3rd pl.	áma-nt	'they love'

3   Present indicative active (2nd conjugation): *habeō* 'I have', 'I am having', 'I do have'

1st s.	hábe-ō	'I have' 'I am having' 'I do have'
2nd s.	hábē-s	'you have' *etc.*
3rd s.	hábe-t	'he/she/it has'
1st pl.	habḗ-mus	'we have'
2nd pl.	habḗ-tis	'you (*pl.*) have'
3rd pl.	hábe-nt	'they have'

Notes

1   All verbs called 1st conjugation conjugate in the present like *am-ō*, e.g. *habit-ō* 'I live', *intr-ō* 'I enter', *uoc-ō* 'I call', *clām-ō* 'I shout', *par-ō* 'I prepare', *cēl-ō* 'I hide'.

   All verbs called 2nd conjugation, which all end in -*eō*, conjugate like *habe-ō*, e.g. *time-ō* 'I fear'.

2   Observe that these regular verbs are built up out of a *stem + endings*. The stem gives the *meaning* of the verb (*ama-* 'love', *habe-* 'have'), the endings give the *person*, i.e.:

-ō	'I' (cf. su-m)
-s	'you'
-t	'he/she/it; there'
-mus	'we'
-tis	'you (*pl.*)'
-nt	'they/there'

3   Observe that the 'key' vowel of 1st conjugation verbs is *A* (*amA-*), of 2nd conjugation is *E* (*habE-*). The only exception is the 1st s. *amō* 'I love', though this was originally *amaō*.

4   Terminology

Conjugation means 'the setting out of a verb in all its persons' as illustrated in **2** and **3**. Thus to conjugate a verb means to set it out as at **2** and **3**.

   Indicative means that the action is being presented as a fact (though it need not be actually true). E.g.:

'I speak to you' (fact, true)

'The pig flies past the window' (presented as a fact, but not true!)

Active means the subject is performing the action, e.g. '*Euclio* runs'; '*Staphyla* sees the daughter'.

Tense means the time at which the action is taking place. Thus 'present' means 'present tense', i.e. the action is happening in the present, e.g. 'I am running'. Cf. future tense 'I will run', etc.

5 Meaning

The present indicative active of e.g. *amō* has three meanings, i.e. 'I love, I am loving, I do love'. Each of these three 'aspects' (as they are called) of the present tense represents the actions in a slightly different way. 'I love' is the plainest statement of fact, 'I am loving' gives a more vivid, 'close-up', continuous picture (you can see it actually going on), 'I do love' is emphatic. You must select *by context* which meaning suits best. Remember, however, that in general the emphatic meaning is indicated in Latin by the verb being put first in the sentence.

Exercises

Morphology

1 *Conjugate:* cēlō; timeō; portō; habeō; (*optional:* habitō; clāmō; intrō; uocō; sum).

2 *Translate, then change pl. to s. and vice versa:* clāmās; habent; intrat; uocō; sumus; portāmus; timēs; habētis; est; timet; uocant; cēlātis; timēmus; habeō; sunt.

3 *Translate into Latin:* you (*pl.*) have; I do hide; we are carrying; they call; you (*s.*) are afraid of; she is dwelling; there are; it has; there enters; she is.

6 The cases in Latin: terminology and meaning

The terms 'nominative', 'accusative', 'genitive', 'dative' and 'ablative' are the technical terms for five of the six so-called 'cases' of Latin nouns and adjectives. (The sixth case, the vocative, is used to address people, e.g. 'welcome, *friend*', but since its form is the same as the nominative in almost all instances, we have left it out of the charts.) The cases will be referred to as nom., acc., gen., dat., and abl. When laid out in this form the cases are called a 'declension'. 'Declining' a noun means to go through all its cases. *The different forms of the cases are of absolutely vital importance in Latin and must be learned by heart till you know them to perfection.* The reason is as follows. In English, we determine the meaning of a sentence by the order in which the words come. The sentence 'man bites dog' means something quite different from 'dog bites man', for no other reason than that the words come in a different order. A Roman would have been bewildered by this, because in Latin word-order does not determine the grammatical functions of the words in the sentence (though it plays its part in emphasis): what is vital is the *form* the words take. In 'daughter calls the slave', 'daughter' is the subject of the sentence, and 'slave' the object. A Roman used the *nom.* form to indicate a subject, and the *acc.* form to indicate an object. Thus when he wrote or said the word for daughter, *fīlia*, he indicated not only what the word meant, but also its function in the sentence – in this case, subject; likewise, when he said 'slave', *seruum*, the form he used would tell him that slave was the object of the sentence. Thus, hearing *fīlia seruum*, a Roman would conclude at once that a daughter was doing something to a slave. Had the Roman heard *fīliam seruus*, he would have concluded that a slave, *seruus*, which is here in the nom. case, was doing something to a daughter, *fīliam*, here in the acc. case. WORD-ORDER IN LATIN IS OF SECONDARY IMPORTANCE since its function relates not to grammar or syntax so much as to emphasis, contrast and style. To English-speakers word-order is, of course, the critical indicator of meaning. In Latin, grammar or syntax is indicated by WORD FORM. WORD FORM IS VITAL.

We can note here that English has a residual case system left. E.g., 'I like beer', not 'me like beer'; 'he loves me', not 'him loves I'; and cf. he, him / she, her, hers / they, them, theirs.

1 *Noun*: the name of something (real or abstract), e.g. 'house', 'door', 'idea', 'intelligence'.
2 *Nominative case*: the most important functions are (i) as subject of a sentence, and (ii) as complement after the verb 'to be'. Nominative means 'naming' (*nōminō* 'I name'). In Latin, the subject of a sentence is 'in the verb', e.g.

>   *habeō* means 'I have'
>   *habet* means 'he/she/it has'

If one wants to 'name' the subject, it goes into the nom. case, e.g.

habeō serua 'I (the slave) have'
habet serua 'she (the slave) has', 'the slave has'
habet uir 'he (the man) has', 'the man has'

3 *Accusative case*: the most important function is as object of a verb. The acc. case denotes the person or thing on the receiving end of the action, e.g. 'the man bites <u>the dog</u>'. One may also look at it as limiting or defining the extent of the action, e.g. 'the man bites' (what does he bite? A bullet? A jam sandwich? No –) 'the dog'. So the accusative case can also limit or define the extent of a description, e.g. <u>*nūdus*</u> <u>*pedēs*</u> 'naked <u>in respect of</u> the feet', 'with naked feet'.

4 NB The verb 'to be' is NEVER followed by a direct object in the acc., but frequently by a 'complement', in the NOM. E.g. 'Phaedra is the <u>daughter</u>' *Phaedra fīlia est*. This is perfectly reasonable, since 'daughter' obviously describes Phaedra. They are both the same person, and will be in the same case.

5 *Genitive case*: this case expresses various senses of the English 'of'. Its root is the same as *genitor*, 'author', 'originator'; 'father'. Thus it denotes the idea 'belonging to' (possession), e.g. 'slave *of Euclio*', and origin, e.g. 'son *of Euclio*'. Cf. English 'dog's dinner' (= 'dinner of dog') and 'dogs' dinner' (= 'dinner of the dogs'), where *dog's* and *dogs'* are genitive forms.

Dative and ablative cases: these will only be used in very limited ways in the *Text* at the moment, but you should attempt to learn their forms *now*. Dative and ablative forms will appear in exercise work.

6 *Word-order*: the usual word-order in English for a simple sentence consisting of subject, verb and object is: (i) subject (ii) verb (iii) object, e.g. 'The man (subj.) bites (verb) the dog (obj.).'
   In Latin the usual order is (i) subject (ii) object (iii) verb. See **1**[5] above and Reference Grammar **W** for a full discussion.

7 Singular and plural; masculine, feminine and neuter

As well as having 'case', nouns can be either singular (s.), when there will be one of the persons or things named, or plural (pl.), when there will be more than one. This feature is called the 'number' of a noun. Nouns also possess 'gender', i.e. are masculine (m.), feminine (f.) or neuter (n.).

8 1st declension nouns: *seru-a ae* 1 feminine (f.) 'slave-woman'

The pattern which nouns follow is called 'declension'. Nouns 'decline'.

		case	*s.*	
nominative	(*nom.*)	séru-a	'slave-woman'
accusative	(*acc.*)	séru-am	'slave-woman'
genitive	(*gen.*)	séru-ae (-áī)	'of the slave-woman'
dative	(*dat.*)	séru-ae	
ablative	(*abl.*)	séru-ā	

		case	*pl.*	
nominative	(*nom.*)	séru-ae	'slave-women'
accusative	(*acc.*)	séru-ās	'slave-women'
genitive	(*gen.*)	seru-árum	'of the slave-women'
dative	(*dat.*)	séru-īs	
ablative	(*abl.*)	séru-īs	

Notes

1 Since it is only in special circumstances that Latin uses a word corresponding to 'the' and 'a', *serua* can mean 'slave-woman', 'the slave-woman', or 'a slave-woman'. The same applies to all nouns in Latin.

2 All 1st decl. nouns end in -*a* in the nom. s. This is called the 'ending', the rest of the noun is called the 'stem'. So the stem of *serua* is *seru-*, the ending -*a*. The same applies to all 1st decl. nouns. Cf. *fīli-a, famili-a, Phaedr-a, Staphyl-a, aul-a, corōn-a, scaen-a.*

3 Most 1st decl. nouns are f. in gender (common exceptions are e.g. *agricol-a* 'farmer', *naut-a* 'sailor', both m.).

4 Note ambiguities:

    (a)   *seru-ae* can be gen. s., dat. s., or nom. pl.

    (b)   *seru-a* is nom. s., but *seru-ā* = abl. s. (not ambiguous if you note vowel length carefully: -*a* nom. / -*ā* abl.)

    (c)   *seru-īs* can be dat. or abl. pl.

5 Nouns of this declension you should have learned are: *famili-a* 'household', *fīli-a* 'daughter', *Phaedr-a* 'Phaedra', *seru-a* 'slave-woman', *Staphyl-a* 'Staphyla', *aul-a* 'pot', *corōn-a* 'garland', *scaen-a* 'stage', 'scene'.

9   2nd decl. nouns: *seru-us ī* 2 masculine (m.) 'male slave'

	s.			*pl.*	
nom.	séru-us	'male slave'		séru-ī	'male slaves'
acc.	séru-um	'male slave'		séru-ōs	'male slaves'

gen.	séru-ī	'of the male slave'	seru-órum	'of the male slaves'
dat.	séru-ō		seru-īs	
abl.	séru-ō		séru-īs	

Notes

1 The vocative case, used when addressing people (e.g. 'hello, Brutus'), ends in -*e* in the 2nd decl. m., e.g. 'you too, Brutus?' *et tū, Brūte?* (see **17A** for full discussion).

2 Observe ambiguities:

(a) *seru-ō* can be dat. or abl. s.
(b) *seru-īs* can be dat. or abl. pl.
(c) *seru-ī* can be gen. s. or nom. pl.
(d) Watch -*um* endings of acc. s. and gen. pl.

3 The other noun of this decl. you should have learned is *coqu-us* 'cook'.

Exercises

1 *Decline*: coquus; aula; (*optional*: seruus, familia, corōna, scaena).

2 *Name the case or cases of each of these words*: seruārum; coquō; corōnam; seruōs; scaenae; fīliā; coquus; seruī; coquum; fīliae; scaenās; seruō; coquōrum; aula; seruīs.

3 *Translate each sentence, then change noun(s) and verb to pl. or s. as appropriate. E.g.* coquus seruam uocat: *the cook calls the slave-girl.* coquī seruās uocant.

(a) sum seruus.
(b) aulam portō.
(c) corōnās habent.
(d) serua timet seruum.
(e) seruās uocātis.
(f) seruae aulās portant.
(g) cēlāmus aulās.
(h) seruās cēlant coquī.
(i) familia corōnam habet.
(j) uocat seruus seruam.

13

10   Prepositions

Prepositions (*praepositus* 'placed in front') are the little words *placed in front* of nouns e.g. *in* 'into', *ad* 'towards' etc. Learn the following important prepositions.

in, ad + *acc.*

> *in* 'into', 'onto', e.g. *in scaenam intrat* 'he enters onto (i.e. right onto) the stage'
> *ad* 'to(wards)' e.g. *ad scaenam aulam portat* 'he carries the pot towards (not necessarily onto) the stage'

Observe that the acc. denotes direction *towards which* something moves. Compare the next preposition.

in + *abl.*

> *in* 'in', 'on', e.g. *in scaenā est* 'he is on the stage'

Observe that *in* + abl. denotes position *at.*

Exercise

Write the Latin for: onto the stage; in the pot; onto the garlands; into the pots; in the household; towards the slave-woman; in the slaves; towards the daughter.

Translation hint
It is extremely important that Latin words be taken in the order in which they appear in a sentence, but that judgement about the final meaning of the sentence be suspended until all the necessary clues have been provided. Take, for example, the following sentences:

> (a)   *aulam igitur clam sub terrā cēlō*

One should approach it as follows:

> *aulam* 'pot': *-am* = accusative case, so something is happening to it
> *igitur* 'therefore' (fixed)
> *clam* 'secretly' (fixed)

sub 'underneath'

terrā 'earth', so probably 'underneath the earth'

cēlō something to do with 'hide', person ending -*ō*, so 'I hide'. That gives us subject and verb; *aulam* must be object, so 'I hide the pot under the earth'. Add 'therefore' and 'secretly' in aptest place.

(b)   *in aedīs intrant seruus et serua et nūptiās parant*

in 'in' or 'into', depending on case of following noun

aedīs = plural, so 'house'. Accusative, so 'into the house'

intrant = something to do with entering. -*ant* = 'they', so 'they enter'

seruus = something to do with a slave. But -*us* shows subject, so the slave must be doing something. Can he be 'entering'? But *intrant* is plural, 'they enter'. Oh dear!

et 'and'. Ah. Perhaps another subject about to appear

serua 'slave-woman', -*a* ending shows subject. Excellent: 'The slave and the slave-woman are entering into the house'

et 'and'. More people entering? Or another clause?

nūptiās 'marriage-rites'. -*ās* shows object. So something being done to the marriage-rites

parant: something about preparing. -*ant* shows 'they'. So 'they prepare the marriage-rites'. Presumably 'they' are the two slaves of the earlier clause. So 'The slave and slave-woman enter the house and prepare the marriage-rites.'

This is the best way to approach a Latin sentence. A number of the exercises will encourage you to do this kind of analysis.

Reading exercise

1   *Read each of these sentences, then without translating, say what the subject of the second verb is (in Latin). Finally, translate each sentence into English.*

(a)   seruus in scaenam intrat. corōnās portat.

(b)   coquī in aedibus sunt. seruās uocant.

(c)   est in familiā Eucliōnis serua. Staphyla est.

(d)   in scaenam intrat Dēmaenetus. aulam aurī plēnam habet.

(e)   coquus et serua clāmant. seruum enim timent.

2   *Take each word as it comes and define its 'job' in the sentence (e.g.* Dēmaenetus coquum . . . – *Demaenetus is subject, so Demaenetus is doing*

15

something. coquum *is object, so Demaenetus is doing something to a cook).
Then add an appropriate verb in the right form (e.g. Demaenetus calls a cook –*
Dēmaenetus coquum uocat).

(a)   aulam seruus . . .
(b)   serua corōnam, aulam seruus . . .[1]
(c)   seruās seruī . . .
(d)   familia coquōs . . .
(e)   Lar seruōs . . .
(f)   aurum ego . . .
(g)   Eucliō familiam . . .
(h)   aulās aurī plēnās et corōnās seruae . . .

[1] The verb must be s.

3 *Define subject, verb, object and prepositional phrases in the following
passages and answer the questions:*

(a)   And now the sun had stretched out all the hills,
      And now was dropped[1] into the western bay;
      At last he rose, and twitched his mantle blue:
      Tomorrow to fresh woods and pastures new.
                                    (*Milton, Lycidas 190–3*)

[1] What 'was dropped'?

(b)   Still green[1] with bays each ancient Altar stands,
      Above the reach of sacrilegious hands;
      Secure[1] from Flames, from Envy's fiercer rage,
      Destructive War, and all-involving Age.
      See from each clime the learn'd their incense bring!
                                    (*Pope, Essay on Criticism 181–5*)

[1] What is 'green' and 'secure'?

4 *With the help of the running vocabulary for 1A, work through the Latin
passage 'Dēmaenetus . . .', following these steps:*

(a)   *As you meet each word, ask*

      (i) its meaning
      (ii) its job in the sentence (i.e. subject or object? part of a phrase?).
      e.g.
      Dēmaenetus coquōs et tībīcinās uidet.

      Dēmaenetus *'Demaenetus', subject;* coquōs *'cooks', object;* et
      'and' almost certainly joining something to coquōs; tībīcinās *'pipe-*

girls', object – part of a phrase coquōs et tībīcinās: uidet '*(he) sees'*,
verb: '*Demaenetus the cooks and pipe-girls (he) sees'*.

(b)   *Next produce a version in good English, e.g. 'Demaenetus sees the*
      cooks and pipe-girls'.

(c)   *When you have worked through the whole passage, go back to the Latin*
      and read the piece aloud, taking care to phrase correctly, thinking
      through the meaning as you read.

Dēmaenetus coquōs et tībīcinās uidet. ad nūptiās fīliae ueniunt. in aedīs
Dēmaenetī intrant et nūptiās parant. nunc aedēs Dēmaenetī coquōrum et
tībīcinārum plēnae sunt. Dēmaenetus autem timet. aulam enim aurī
plēnam habet. nam sī aula Dēmaenetī in aedibus est aurī plena, fūrēs ualdē
timet Dēmaenetus. aulam Dēmaenetus cēlat. nunc aurum saluum est.   5
nunc saluus Dēmaenetus. nunc salua aula. Lar enim aulam habet plēnam
aurī. nunc prope Larem Dēmaenetī aula sub terrā latet. nunc igitur ad
Larem appropinquat Dēmaenetus et supplicat. 'ō Lar, ego Dēmaenetus tē
uocō. ō tūtēla meae familiae, aulam ad tē aurī plēnam portō. fīliae nūptiae
sunt hodiē. ego autem fūrēs timeō. nam aedēs meae fūrum plēnae sunt. tē   10
ōrō et obsecrō, aulam Dēmaenetī aurī plēnam seruā.'

English–Latin

Translate the Latin sentences into English. Then translate the English sentences
into Latin, using the pattern of the Latin ones to help you arrange the word-order
correctly.

(a)   coquus aulam Dēmaenetī portat.
      The slave has the cooks' garlands.

(b)   tū clāmās, ego autem aulās portō.
      The slave girl is afraid. Therefore I am calling the cook.

(c)   cūr scaena plēna est seruōrum?
      Why is the household full of cooks?

(d)   ego Lar tē uocō. cūr mē timēs?
      (It is) I, Phaedra (who)[1] enter. Why are you (*pl.*) hiding the pot?

(e)   sī aurum habet, Dēmaenetus timet.
      If they hide the pot, the slaves are afraid.

(f)   corōnās et aulās portant seruī.
      (It is)[1] a cook and a slave-girl Demaenetus is summoning.

[1] Put stressed words first in the sentence.

17

Section 1B

Running vocabulary for 1B

a ha!
ab illō from that (former self of his) [The whole phrase is a quotation from Virgil *Aeneid* 2.274, used by Aeneas of the ghost of Hector.]
ab īnferīs from the dead
adhūc so far
aedēs (nom.) house
aedīs (acc.) house
aggerō I pile, heap up
amō 1 I love
an? or?
anxius worried
appāreō 2 I appear
appropinquō 1 I go up to, approach
ār-a ae 1f. altar
auārus greedy
au-us ī 2m. grandfather
bene good! well
bona (nom.) ⎫
bonam (acc.) ⎪
⎬ good
bonum (acc.) ⎪
bonus (nom.) ⎭
cēlā hide!
celeriter quickly
circumspectō 1 I look around
clam secretly
collocō 1 I place
cōnsilium plan
crēdō I believe
cūr-a ae 1f. care, devotion, worry, concern
cūrō 1 I care for, look after, am concerned about
dē (+ abl.) concerning

dēcipit (he/she/it) deceives
Dēmaenete O Demaenetus
Dēmaenet-us ī 2m. Demaenetus
de-us ī 2m. god
dī (nom. pl.) gods; (voc. pl.) O gods!
dīues (nom.) rich (man)
dīuitum (gen.) of rich (men)
dō 1 I give
dormiō I am asleep
dormit (he/she/it) sleeps
dōtem (acc.) dowry
dūcit (he) leads
dum while
ē out of, from
ecce look!
ecquis (does) anyone?
eheu what a pity! oh dear!
Eucliōnem (acc.) Euclio
Eucliōnī (dat.) to Euclio
Eucliōnis (gen.) of Euclio
euge ⎫ hoorah!
eugepae ⎭ yippee!
explicō 1 I explain, tell
fābul-ae ae 1f. story
facis you (s.) make, do
facit (he/she/it) makes, does
falsa ⎫ false
falsum ⎭
familiāris of the household
festīnō 1 I hurry about
foue-a ae 1f. pit, hole
fūrēs (nom., acc.) thieves
fūrum (gen.) of thieves
hem what's this?
hercle by Hercules!
heu oh dear!

hodiē today
hominum (gen.) of men
homo (nom.) man, fellow
honōrem (acc.) respect
ignōrō 1 I do not know
imāginem (acc.) vision
imāgō (nom.) vision
in aedīs into the house
in aedibus in the house
in somniō in a dream
intrō (l. 151) inside
iterum again
iuxtā (+ acc.) next to
Larem (acc.) Lar
Laris (gen.) of the Lar
lateō 2 I lie hidden
magnī (voc. pl.) great
magnus great (amount of)
malus evil, wicked
maneō 2 I remain
meī (of) my
meum my
mihi (to) me
mīrum amazing
miserum miserable, unhappy
mōnstrō 1 show, reveal
moueō 2 I move
multam (acc.) ⎫
multās (acc.) ⎪ many,
multī (nom.) ⎬ much
multōrum (gen.) ⎪
multum (acc.) ⎭
murmurō 1 I mutter
mutātus changed
nēminem (acc.) no-one
nempe clearly, no doubt
nūllam ⎫
nūllās ⎬ (acc.) no, none
nūllum ⎭

numquam never
pauper (nom.) poor (man)
pecūni-a ae 1f. money
perditissimus most done
   for
possideō 2 I possess, have,
   hold
praetereā besides
quantum how (much)
quārē why?
quia because
quid what?
quod because
saluē welcome!
saluum safe
scīlicet evidently
sēcum with himself
senex old man

seruā keep safe!
seruō 1 I keep
simul at the same time
somnia (acc.) dreams
somnium dream
spectō 1 I look at, see
spectātōrēs spectators,
   audience
stupeō 2 I am amazed,
   astonished
sub pedibus under (your)
   feet
sub (+abl.) under
sub ueste under (my)
   cloak
subitō suddenly
super (+acc.) above
supplicō 1 I make prayers (to)

tamen however, but
tandem at length
teneō 2 I hold, possess,
   keep
terr-a ae 1f. earth
thēsaur-us ī 2m. treasure
tum then
ualdē greatly
uērum true
uexō 1 I annoy, worry
uideō 2 I see
uidēte see! look!
uigilō 1 I am awake
uīsō I visit
unguentum ointment
ut how!

Learning vocabulary for 1B

Nouns

cūr-a ae 1f. care, worry,
   concern
de-us ī 2m. god
thēsaur-us ī 2m. treasure

unguent-um ī 2n. ointment
aedis aed-is 3f. temple; pl.
   aed-ēs ium house

fūr fūr-is 3m. thief
honor honōr-is 3m. respect
senex sen-is 3m. old man

Adjectives

mult-us a um much, many

nūll-us a um no, none

Verbs

am-ō 1 I love
cūr-ō 1 I look after, care
   for
d-ō 1 I give

explic-ō 1 I tell, explain
supplic-ō 1 I make prayers
   (to)

posside-ō 2 I have, hold,
   possess
uide-ō 2 I see

Others

clam secretly
quārē why?

quod because
tamen however, but

tandem at length

Grammar and exercises for 1B

11 **3rd declension nouns (consonant stem): *fūr fūr-is* 3m. 'thief'**

	s.		pl.	
nom.	fūr	'thief'	fúr-ēs	'thieves'
acc.	fúr-em	'thief'	fúr-ēs	'thieves'
gen.	fúr-is	'of the thief'	fúr-um	'of thieves'
dat.	fúr-ī		fúr-ibus	
abl.	fúr-e		fúr-ibus	

NB. This is the standard pattern of endings for 3rd decl. nouns whose stems end in a consonant. There are, however, slight changes of pattern in nouns whose stem ends in the vowel -*i*- (the so-called '*i*-stem' nouns) as follows.

12 **3rd declension nouns (*i*-stem) *aedis aed-is* 3f. 'room', 'temple'; in plural 'temples', 'house'**

	s.	
nom.	aéd-is	'room', 'temple'
acc.	aéd-em	'room', 'temple'
gen.	aéd-is	'of the room', 'of the temple'
dat.	aéd-ī	
abl.	aéd-e (aéd-ī)	

	pl.	
nom.	aéd-ēs	'temples' / 'house'
acc.	aéd-īs (-ēs)	'temples' / 'house'
gen.	aéd-ium	'of temples' / 'of the house'
dat.	aéd-ibus	
abl.	aéd-ibus	

Notes

1 *aed-is* in the s. means 'room', 'temple'; in the pl. usually 'house'.
2 Observe acc. pl. in -*īs*, gen. pl. in -*ium*, and alternative abl. s. in -*ī*. This dominance of -*i*- is the mark of *i*-stem nouns of the third declension. In fact originally *all* the cases would have had the -*i*-, since it is part of the stem. The s. of *turris* 3f. 'tower', which keeps the old forms even in classical Latin, will demonstrate this: *turri-s, turri-m, turri-s, turrī, turrī.*

20

Note that we indicate in the grammar sections which nouns and adjectives are *i*-stem, but for practical reasons we present the endings as for consonant stems, i.e. *aed-is*, not (the technically correct) *aedi-s*.

13 Stems and endings of 3rd decl. nouns

1 3rd decl. nouns have a great variety of endings in the nom. s. What unites them all is that their gen. s. has the same ending, e.g. *Euclio Euclion-is, senex sen-is*. You must therefore learn both the decl. and the gen. s. as well as the gender of these 3rd decl. nouns, i.e. not *aedis* 'temple', pl. 'house', but *aedis aed-is* 3f. 'temple', pl. 'house'.

2 The gen. s. is doubly important, because it gives you the STEM OF THE NOUN to which the endings are added to make the declension. Thus when you have learned *senex sen-is* 3m., you know that the stem is *sen-*. IT IS THE GEN. S. WHICH GIVES YOU THIS.

3 You also need to be able to work back from the stem to the nom. s. in order to find the word in a dictionary. E.g. if you see *pācem* in the text, you MUST be able to deduce that the nom. s. is *pāx*, otherwise you will not be able to look the word up. Observe the following common patterns of CONSONANT STEMS:

(a) stems ending in *-l-* or *-r-* keep *l* and *r* in the nom., e.g.

cōnsul-is→nom. *cōnsul* 'consul'
fūr-is→nom. *fūr* 'thief'

(b) stems ending in *-d-* or *-t-* end in *-s* in the nom., e.g.

ped-is→nom. *pēs* 'foot'
dōt-is→nom. *dōs* 'dowry'

(c) stems ending in *-c-* or *-g-* end in *-x* in the nom., e.g.

rēg-is→nom. *rēx* 'king'
duc-is→nom. *dux* 'general'

(d) stems ending in *-ōn* or *-iōn* end in *-ō* or *-iō* in the nom., e.g.

Scīpiōn-is→nom. *Scīpiō* 'Scipio'
praedōn-is→nom. *praedō* 'pirate'

Exercises

1 *Decline*: honor, fūr, (*optional*: Eucliō (*s*.), Lar, aedis).
2 *Name the case of each of these words*: Ecliōnis, fūrem, aedium, honōrēs, Lar, senum, aedīs, honōrem, fūr, Laris.
3 *Translate each sentence, then change noun(s) and verb(s) to s. or pl. as appropriate*, *e.g.* fūrem seruus timet – *the slave is afraid of a thief* – fūrēs seruī timent.

    (a)   deinde thēsaurum senis fūr uidet.
    (b)   Lar honōrem nōn habet.
    (c)   igitur senem deus nōn cūrat.
    (d)   quārē tamen supplicātis, senēs?
    (e)   unguentum senex tandem possidet.
    (f)   in aedibus senex nunc habitat.
    (g)   fūr aulam aurī plēnam semper amat.
    (h)   honōrem tamen non habet fūr.
    (i)   quārē in aedīs nōn intrās, senex?
    (j)   seruam clam amat senex.

14   **1st/2nd declension adjectives: *mult-us a um* 'much', 'many'**

s.

	m.	*f.*	*n.*
nom.	múlt-us	múlt-a	múlt-um
acc.	múlt-um	múlt-am	múlt-um
gen.	múlt-ī	múlt-ae	múlt-ī
dat.	múlt-ō	múlt-ae	múlt-ō
abl.	múlt-ō	múlt-ā	múlt-ō

pl.

	m.	*f.*	*n.*
nom.	múlt-ī	múlt-ae	múlt-a
acc.	múlt-ōs	múlt-ās	múlt-a
gen.	mult-órum	mult-árum	mult-órum
dat.	múlt-īs	múlt-īs	múlt-īs
abl.	múlt-īs	múlt-īs	múlt-īs

Notes

1 Adjectives (from the stem *adiectus* 'added to') give additional information about a noun, e.g. *fast* horse, *steep* hill (adjectives are often called 'describing words').

2 Since nouns can be m., f. or n., adjectives need to have m., f. and n. forms so that they can 'AGREE' grammatically with the noun they describe. So adjectives must agree with nouns in *gender*.

3 Adjectives must also 'AGREE' with nouns in *number*, s. or pl.

4 Finally, they must 'AGREE' with nouns in *case* (nom., acc., gen., dat. or abl.). A noun in the acc. can only be described by an adjective in the acc.

5 In summary, if a noun is to be described by an adjective in Latin, the adjective will have to agree with it in *gender, number and case*. Here are three examples:

(a) 'I see *many* temples' – 'temples' are the object, and plural; the word we shall use in Latin is *aedīs*, which is f. So if 'many' is to agree with 'temples', it will need to be acc., pl. and f. Answer: *multās aedīs*.

(b) 'He shows *much* respect' – 'respect' is object, s. The word we shall use, *honor honōr-is*, is m. So 'much' will have to be acc. s. m. Answer: *multum honōrem*.

(c) 'I hear the voice of *many* slaves' – 'slaves' is gen. and pl.; the word we shall use, *serua*, is f. So 'many' will be gen. pl. f. Answer: *multārum seruārum*.

6 It is worth emphasising here that an adjective does not necessarily describe a noun it is standing next to. It describes a noun it *agrees with* in case, number and gender, e.g.:

(a) *multum fīlia servat thēsaurum. multum* = acc. s. m.; *fīlia* = nom. s. f.; *thēsaurum* = acc. s. m. I.e. 'It's a great deal of treasure the daughter keeps.'

(b) *nūllum fūrum cōnsilium placet. nūllum* = acc. s. m. or nom./acc. s. n.; *fūrum* = gen. pl.; *cōnsilium* = nom./acc. s. n. I.e. 'No scheme of thieves is pleasing.'

multus usually precedes its noun, e.g. *multī seruī* 'many slaves'. When it follows its noun it is emphatic, e.g. *seruōs multōs habeō* 'I really do have lots of slaves'.

7 Adjectives can be used on their own as nouns, when *gender* will indicate meaning, e.g. *bonus* (m.) 'a good man', *bonum* (n.) 'a good thing'.

15 2nd declension neuter nouns: *somni-um ī* 2n. 'dream'

	s.		pl.	
nom.	sómni-um	'dream'	sómni-a	'dreams'
acc.	sómni-um	'dream'	sómni-a	'dreams'
gen.	sómnī *or* sómni-ī	'of the dream'	somni-órum	'of dreams'
dat.	sómni-ō		sómni-īs	
abl.	sómni-ō		sómni-īs	

Notes

1 There is only one neuter noun type of the 2nd decl.; they all end in *-um* in nom. s. Cf. *aur-um* 'gold', *unguent-um* 'ointment'.
2 As with other neuters, the nom. and acc. s. and pl. are the same (see **26**).
3 Do not confuse the neuter s. forms with the acc. s. of 2nd decl. m. nouns like *seru-us* (*seru-um*) or gen. pl. of 3rd decl. nouns like *aedis* (*aedium*). Be sure that you learn nouns like *somnium* as type 2 *neuter*.
4 As with all neuters, there is a danger of confusing the pl. forms in *-a* with 1st decl. f. nouns like *serua*.
5 Note the gen. s. *somnī* or *somniī*. Nouns of the 2nd decl. ending in *-ius* (e.g. *fīlius* 'son') usually have gen. s. in *-ī* (e.g. *fīlī*) and nom. pl. always in *-iī* (e.g. *fīliī*).
6 Gen., dat., abl. s. and pl. endings are the same as for *seruus* (**9**).

Exercises

1 *Here to learn is a list of 2nd decl. neuter nouns like* somnium:

  exiti-um ī 2n. 'death', 'destruction'
  ingeni-um ī 2n. 'talent', 'ability'
  perīcul-um ī 2n. 'danger'

2 *Pick out the gen. pls. from the following list. Say what nouns they come from, with what meaning (e.g.* perīculōrum = *gen. pl. of* perīcul-um ī *danger*): honōrum, ingenium, aedibus, fūrum, exitiō, seruum, unguentōrum, aurum, senum, thēsaurīs.
3 *Pick out, and give the meanings of, the pl. nouns in the following list*: scaena, serua, ingenia, familia, cūra, unguentīs, fīliā, somnia, corōna, perīcula.

16 2nd declension noun (irregular): *de-us ī* 2m. 'god'

	s.		*pl.*		
nom.	dé-us	'god'	dī		'gods'
acc.	dé-um	'god'	déōs		'gods'
gen.	dé-ī	'of the god'	de-órum (dé-um)		'of the gods'
dat.	dé-ō		dīs		
abl.	dé-ō		dīs		

7A Vocatives

The vocative case (*uocō* 'I call') is used when addressing a person. Its form is the same as the nominative in all nouns, except 2nd declension m., where *-us* of nom. s. becomes *-e* (e.g. *Dēmaenete* 'Demaenetus!', *serue* 'O slave') and the *-ius* of nom. s. becomes *-ī* (e.g. *fīlius* 'son'; *fīlī* 'son!').

NB.   The vocative s. of *meus* 'my' is *mī*, e.g. *mī fīlī* 'O my son'.

7B Apposition

Consider this sentence:

> *sum Dēmaenetus, Eucliōnis auus* 'I am Demaenetus, Euclio's grandfather'

The phrase *Eucliōnis auus* gives more information about Demaenetus. It is said to be 'in apposition' to *Dēmaenetus* (from *adpositus* 'placed near'). Note that *auus*, the main piece of information, is the same case as *Dēmaenetus*.

Note
Appositional phrases may be added to a noun in any case. E.g. *sum seruus Dēmaenetī senis* 'I am the slave of Demaenetus the old man'. *senis* (gen.) is in apposition to *Dēmaenetī* (gen.).

Exercises

1   *Attach the correct form of* multus *to these nouns (in ambiguous cases, give all possible alternatives):* cūrās, aurum, fūrēs, senem, honōris, aedem, seruōrum, senum, aedīs, corōnae, (*optional:* seruum, unguenta, aedis, familiam, aedium, honor, aedēs).

25

2 *Pair the given form of* multus *with the nouns with which it can agree*:

> multus: senex, cūra, Larem, familiae, seruus
> multī: honor, aedēs, Laris, senēs, seruī
> multīs: honōribus, aedīs, cūram, seruum, deum, senibus, aurum
> multās: senis, honōrēs, aedīs, cūram, familiās
> multae: seruae, aedī, cūram, senēs, dī
> multa: aedēs, unguenta, senem, cūra, corōnārum
> (*optional*:
> multōs: aedīs, unguentum, cūrās, seruōs, fūrēs
> multō: aurum, Larem, cūram, honōrī, aedem
> multōrum: aedium, unguentōrum, seruum, senum, deōrum,
> corōnārum
> multārum: fūrum, aurum, honōrem, seruārum, aedium)

3 *Translate into Latin*: many slave-girls (*nom.*); of much respect; of many garlands; much gold; many an old man (*acc.*); of many thieves; many old men (*acc.*).

4 *Translate these sentences*:

> (a) multī fūrēs sunt in aedibus.
> (b) multās cūrās multī senēs habent.
> (c) multae seruae plēnae sunt cūrārum.
> (d) multum aurum Eucliō, multās aulās aurī plēnās habet.
> (e) seruōs senex habet multōs. (*See* **14**[6].)

5 *Translate these sentences*:

> (a) nūlla potentia longa est. (*Ovid*)
> (b) uīta nec bonum[1] nec malum[1] est. (*Seneca*)
> (c) nōbilitās sōla est atque ūnica uirtūs. (*Juvenal*)
> (d) longa est uīta sī plēna est. (*Seneca*)
> (e) fortūna caeca est. (*Cicero*)

[1] See **14**[7].

potenti-a ae 1f. power	bon-us a um good	ūnic-us a um unique,
long-us a um long, long-	mal-us a um bad	unparalleled
lived	nōbilitās nōbilitāt-is 3f.	uirtūs uirtūt-is 3f. goodness
uīt-a ae 1f. life	nobility	fortūn-a ae 1f. fortune
nec . . . nec neither . . .	sōl-us a um only	caec-us a um blind
nor	atque and	

Optional exercises

1 *Identify the case (or cases, where ambiguities exist) of the following words, say what they mean, and then turn s. into pl. and pl. into s.:* seruae, honōrī, thēsaurīs, familiā, deum, fīliā, dīs, corōna, senum.
2 *Give the declension and case of each of the following words:* thēsaurum, honōrum, deōrum, seruārum, aedium.
3 *Case work*

(a) *Group the following words by case (i.e. list all nominatives, accusatives, genitives etc.). When you have done that, identify s. and pl. within each group:* Eucliōnem, senī, thēsaurō, fīliae, familia, deī, corōna, scaenās, dī, aedēs, honōribus, seruārum, multīs.

(b) *Identify the following noun forms by showing:*

> *what case they are*
> *whether s. or pl.*
> *their nom. s. form, gen. s. form and gender*
> *their meaning*

e.g. senem *is acc. s. of* senex sen-is, *m. 'old man'. Remember ambiguities!*

(i) *3rd declension:* aedēs, patris, senibus, honōrum, senem, aedibus, honōrī, sene, aedium, honōris, senēs, aedīs
(ii) *1st declension f.:* Phaedrae, aulārum, corōnās, scaenā, cūrīs, fīliārum, familiae, Staphylam, seruīs, aulam, corōnae, scaenās
(iii) *2nd declension m.:* seruī, coquus, thēsaurum, seruīs, coquī, seruō, deōs, thēsaurīs, coquō, deī
(iv) *Various declensions:* sene, seruīs, patris, coquīs, honōrī, aedīs, aulārum, honōrum, deum, seruārum

Reading exercises

1 *English and Latin*

Pick out subject(s), verb(s) and object(s) in the following English sentences. Identify also adjectives, and say with what nouns they agree.

(a) In the long echoing streets the laughing dancers throng. (*Keats*)
(b) And the long carpets rose along the gusty floor. (*Keats*)
(c) I bring you with reverent hands
   The books of my numberless dreams. (*Yeats*)

27

(d)   'Tis no sin love's fruit to steal
      But the sweet theft to reveal. (*Jonson*)
(e)   His fair large Front and Eye sublime declar'd
      Absolute Rule. (*Milton, describing Adam*)
(f)   Gazing he spoke, and kindling at the view
      His eager arms around the goddess threw.
      Glad earth perceives, and from her bosom pours
      Unbidden herbs and voluntary flowers.

                    (*Pope, translating Homer's* Iliad, *where
                      Zeus makes love to his wife Hera*)

2 *In each of these sentences, the verb comes first or second. Say in each case
whether the subject is s. or pl., then, moving on, say in order as they come
whether the following words are subjects or objects of the verb. Next, translate
into English. Finally read out the sentences in Latin with the correct phrasing.*

(a)   clāmant seruī, senex, seruae.
(b)   dat igitur honōrem multum Phaedra.
(c)   nunc possidet Lar aedīs.
(d)   amant dī multum honōrem.
(e)   dat aurum multās cūrās.
(f)   habitant quoque in aedibus seruī.
(g)   est aurum in aulā multum.
(h)   timent autem fūrēs multī senēs.
(i)   quārē intrant senex et seruus in scaenam?
(j)   tandem explicat Lar cūrās senis.

3 *In order of appearance, translate each word and say whether it is the subject or
the object or genitive. Then supply a suitable verb in the correct person and
translate the sentence into English.*

(a)   senem seruus . . .
(b)   aedīs deus . . .
(c)   honōrēs Lar . . .
(d)   fūr aurum . . .
(e)   Eucliōnis fīliam dī . . .
(f)   fīliae senum honōrēs . . .
(g)   aedem deus . . .
(h)   unguenta dī . . .
(i)   Larem Phaedra, Phaedram Lar . . .[1]
(j)   seruōs Phaedra et seruās . . .

[1] The verb must be s.

28

4 *Take the Latin as it comes and say, as you translate, what the function of each word is (subject, object, verb etc.), grouping words into phrases where necessary. Translate into English. Then read out the Latin correctly phrased, thinking through the meaning as you read.*

(a) aulās enim habet multās Eucliō senex.
(b) aedīs fūrum plēnās multī timent senēs.
(c) thēsaurum Eucliōnis clam uidet serua.
(d) nūllus est in aedibus seruus.
(e) Phaedram, fīliam Eucliōnis, et Staphylam, fīliae Eucliōnis seruam, Lar amat.
(f) deinde Eucliō aulam, quod fūrēs ualdē timet, cēlat.
(g) mē igitur Phaedra amat, Phaedram ego.
(h) nam aurum Eucliō multum habet, corōnās multās, multum unguentum.
(i) senex autem fūrēs, quod multum habet aurum, ualdē timet.
(j) multum seruī unguentum ad Larem, multās corōnās portant.

Reading exercise / Test exercise

*Read through this passage, as for Reading Exercise no. 4 in **1A** (p. 16). For an adjective, say (i) what it belongs with (if it follows its noun) (ii) what sort of noun you will expect with it (if it precedes). Use the running vocabulary for **1B** for any words you do not know. At the end, after translating the passage, read it out in Latin, correctly phrased.*

Lar in scaenam intrat. deus est Eucliōnis familiae. seruat Lar sub terrā thēsaurum Dēmaenetī. multus in aulā thēsaurus est. ignōrat autem dē thēsaurō Eucliō, quod Larem nōn cūrat. nam nūllum dat unguentum, nūllās corōnās, honōrem nūllum. Phaedram autem, senis auārī fīliam, Lar amat. dat enim Eucliōnis fīlia multum unguentum, multās corōnās,   5
multum honōrem. Lar igitur Dēmaenetī aulam, quod bona est Eucliōnis fīlia, Eucliōnī dat. Eucliō autem aulam, quod auārus est, sub terrā iterum collocat. nam fūrēs ualdē timet Eucliō! cūrās habet multās! uexat thēsaurus senem auārum et anxium. plēnae enim fūrum sunt dīuitum   10
hominum aedēs.

English–Latin

Translate the Latin sentences into English. Then translate the English sentences into Latin, using the pattern of the Latin ones to help you arrange the word-order correctly.

(a)   Lar igitur Eucliōnem, quod honōrem nōn dat, nōn amat.
      The gods therefore care for Phaedra, my son, because she cares
      for the Lar.
(b)   senex autem cūrās habet multās, quod aurum habet multum.
      The slaves however are carrying many garlands, because they
      are bestowing much respect.
(c)   Eucliōnis aedēs fūrum sunt plēnae, quod aulam aurī plēnam
      habet senex.
      The temple of the gods is full of gold, because the daughters of
      the rich give pots full of gold.
(d)   ego multum unguentum, corōnās multās, multum honōrem
      habeō.
      You (*s.*) have much worry and much treasure.
(e)   tē, Dēmaenete, nōn amō.
      I'm not carrying *gold*, my son.
(f)   clāmant seruī, supplicant seruae, timet senex.
      The daughter is praying, the old men shouting and the slave-
      girls are afraid.

Deliciae Latinae

These sections, which will occur at the end of Grammar and Exercise
sections, will consist of a mixture of hints on word-building, word
exercises, Latin words and phrases in everyday use, and easy pieces of
original Latin for translation. The title means 'Latin delights'.

NB.   The vocabulary help in *Dēliciae Latīnae* sections is aimed at
helping you to translate as quickly and easily as possible. Consequently,
we do not always give full grammatical information about words.

Derivations

The Roman Empire extended over modern Italy, Spain, Portugal and
France, all of whose languages are descended directly from Latin. Britain
was part of the Roman Empire, but it was overrun by Anglo-Saxons in
the years following the end of Roman rule, so that there was no major
Latin influence on the language at this stage – Anglo-Saxon was the
predominant tongue. Latin was, however, still the language of the

church in Britain so all interaction was not wholly lost. (Bede (*Baeda*), the eighth-century monk from Jarrow near Newcastle upon Tyne, wrote his history of the English church in Latin.) The turning-point for the English language came in 1066 when the Norman Duke William the Conqueror took England. French-speaking kings ruled England for some 300 years (till Agincourt (1415), when English again became the official language of royalty). The Latin-based French language became incorporated into Middle English, adding enormous richness to it, e.g. Middle English gives us 'kingly', French/Latin adds 'regal', 'royal', 'sovereign'. It is largely through French that English has the Latin component that it does.

Consequently, Latin is very useful to anyone who wants to learn the Romance languages (i.e. languages descended from the language of the Romans), and vice versa knowledge of Romance languages can help you to understand Latin. Four hints:

(a) Identify the stem of the Latin word as well as its nom. s. form, e.g. *senex* gives us 'senile' (from the Latin adjective *senīlis*, formed from *sen-* the stem of *senex*).

(b) Many English words ending in -ion come from Latin via French.

(c) Many English words ending in -ate, -ance, -ent, -ence come from Latin, again via French.

(d) English derivatives have 'j' and 'v' where the Latin words from which they come have *i* and *u* used as consonants (i.e. before or between vowels). So *Iānuārius* produces 'January' and *uideō* produces 'video'. The reverse process will help you to see whether a word has a Latin root, e.g. 'juvenile' comes from Latin *iuuenīlis*.

Note

English has taken some of its Latin-based words direct from Latin rather than through an intermediary language such as French, e.g. 'wine' from *uīnum*, 'wall' from *uallum* (see Appendix p. 554). Other English words look similar to Latin not because they have been taken from Latin, but because both English and Latin share a common linguistic ancestor, Indo–European, the vocabulary of which is preserved in different ways in the various derivative tongues. Thus the Indo–European word for 'two', which can be reconstructed as **duō*, emerges in English as *two*, German *zwei*, Sanskrit *dvau*, and Latin as *duo* (whence French *deux*, Italian *due*, Spanish *dos*).

Word-building

(a) Stems

The stem of one word gives the clue to the meaning of many other words, e.g. *seru-* in the form *seru-us* or *seru-a* means 'slave'; as a verb, with a verb-ending, *seruiō*, it means 'I am a slave to'.

> *coqu-* in the noun form *coquus* = 'a/the cook'; in the verb form *coquō* = 'I cook'
>
> *aed-* in the form *aedēs* = 'a/the house'; with the suffix *-ficō* (= 'make'): *aedificō* = 'I build'; in the form *aedīlis*, it means 'aedile', a Roman state official originally with a particular responsibility for building

(b) Prefixes

A 'prefix' (*prae* 'in front of', *fīxus* 'fixed') is a word fixed in front of another. Most prepositions (see **10**), e.g. *in* 'into', 'in', 'on', *ad* 'towards' etc., can also be used as prefixes, and as such slightly alter the meaning of the 'root' word to which they are fixed, e.g.

> root word *sum* 'I am': *adsum* 'I am near'; *īnsum* 'I am in'
> root word *portō* 'I carry': *importō* 'I carry in'; *apportō* 'I carry to'
> (observe that *inp-* becomes *imp-* and *adp-* becomes *app-*)

Note the following prepositions which are commonly used as prefixes:

> *cum* (*con-*) 'with'
> *prae* 'before, in front of, at the head of'
> *post* 'after'

Exercise

Split the following Latin words up into prefix and root, and say what they might mean: conuocō, inhabitō, inuocō, praeuideō, comportō, praesum, posthabeō.

(c) Verb-stems different from the present stem

As you will soon discover, Latin verbs have a number of different 'stems'. So far you have learnt the present stem, e.g. *uoc-ō* 'I call'. But most 1st conjugation verbs have another stem in *-āt-* i.e. *uoc-āt-*. This stem was very fruitful in forming other Latin words, and so French words, and so English words, particularly those in -ate or -ation. Thus vocation, convocation, invocation, invocate etc.

Exercise

Give an English word in -ate or -ation from the following Latin words, and say what it means: supplicō, explicō, importō, dō, habitō.

uideō *has another stem,* uīs-, *and* possideō *has* possess- − *giving us what English nouns, by the addition of what letters?*

Word exercises

1 *Give English words connected with the following Latin words:* familia, corōna, scaena, timeō, deus, multus, uideō.
2 *With what Latin words are the following connected?* pecuniary, honorific, amatory, thesaurus, porter, clamorous, filial, edifice (*Latin* ae *becomes* e), unguent, furtive, servile, nullify.

Everyday Latin

We use Latin words and phrases every day of our lives:

> a.m. = *ante merīdiem.* What does *ante* mean?
> p.m. = *post merīdiem.* What does *post* mean? What is a *post mortem?* What is a *post scrīptum?*
> *iānua* = 'door'. *Iānus* (Janus) was a Roman god who had two faces, so that he could look out and in like a door and, like the month January, forward to the new year and back to the old
> *tandem* = 'at length', just like the bicycle made for two (introduced originally as a learned joke; the Latin word was never used of space)
> *uōx* (= 'voice') *populī, uōx deī* – meaning? Cf. *agnus* ('lamb') *deī*

Frequently in English we give Latin words their correct Latin plurals, e.g. we talk of termini, pl. of the Latin *terminus.* What would you say of someone who gave the plural of 'ignoramus' as 'ignorami' (*ignōr-ō* 1)?

Consider the following plurals: *data* ('given things'), *agenda* ('things to be done'), *media* ('things in the middle'). They are neuter plurals, declining like *multus,* directly from Latin. What are their singular forms?

Real Latin

Vulgate
(*Taken from the Vulgate, Jerome's fourth–fifth-century A.D. translation of the Bible into Latin. Called 'Vulgate' from its title* ēditiō uulgāta *'popular edition'. Cf. 'vulgar' in English.*)

et (Deus) ait (*said*) 'ego sum Deus patris tuī, Deus (*of*) Abraham, Deus (*of*) Isaac, et Deus (*of*) Jacob.' (*Exodus 3.6*) 'ego sum quī (*who*) sum.' (*Exodus 3.14*)

Conversational Latin

Contrary to popular belief, Latin always has been a spoken as well as a written language. Most of our texts from ancient times, of course, reflect the literary, written, form. But in Plautus, Terence and the letters of Cicero we do hear the voice of Romans. Here are some common conversational gambits:

> *saluē* or *saluus sīs* or *auē* (or *hauē*) 'Hello!' (lit. 'Greetings', 'May you be safe', 'Hail!')
> *ualē* 'Goodbye!' (lit. 'Be strong')
> *sīs* or *sī placet* or *nisi molestum est* or *grātum erit sī . . .* or *amābō tē* 'Please' (lit. 'If you will', 'If it pleases', 'If it's no trouble', 'It would be nice if . . .', 'I will like you (if you . . .)')
> *grātiās tibi agō* 'Thank you' (lit. 'I give thanks to you')
> *ut ualēs?* or *quid agis?* or *quid fit?* 'How are you?' (lit. 'Are you strong?', 'What are you doing?', 'What is happening?')
> *est* or *est ita* or *etiam* or *ita* or *ita uērō* or *sānē* or *certē* 'Yes' (lit. 'It is', 'It is so', 'Even', 'Thus', 'Thus indeed', 'Certainly', 'Surely')
> *nōn* or *nōn ita* or *minimē* 'No' (lit. 'Not', 'Not so', 'Least')
> *age* or *agedum* 'Come on'
> *rēctē* 'Right' (lit. 'Correctly')
> *malum* 'Damn!' (lit. 'A bad thing')
> *dī tē perdant!* 'Damn you!' (Lit. 'May the gods destroy you')
> *īnsānum bonum* 'Damned good' (Lit. 'A crazy good thing')

Latin conversation did not die out with the end of the Roman Empire. Erasmus of Rotterdam, the great Dutch humanist, originally wrote his *Colloquia Familiāria* (first published in 1518) partly as an aid to teaching Latin conversation. The first 'Colloquy' introduces the pupil to various modes of greeting. These are the formulae recommended to lovers ('Greetings my . . .'):

	mea *Cornēliola*	('little Cornelia')
	mea *uīta*	('life')
	mea *lūx*	('light')
	meum *dēlicium*	('darling', 'delight')
	meum *suāuium*	('sweetheart', lit. 'kiss')
saluē	mel *meum*	('honey')
	mea *uoluptās ūnica*	('only joy')
	meum *corculum*	('sweetheart', lit. 'little heart')
	mea *spēs*	('hope')
	meum *sōlātium*	('comfort')
	meum *decus*	('glory')

Section 1C

Running vocabulary for 1C

abeō I go away
abī go away!
abit (he/she/it) goes away
adeunt (they) approach, come up
adit (he/she/it) approaches, comes up
anim-us ī 2m. mind
aqu-a ae 1f. water
arāne-a ae 1f. cobweb
audī listen!
Bona (bon-us a um) good
clāmatque and shouts
cōgitō 1 I think, reflect, ponder
cōnsili-um ī 2n. plan
cōnsistunt they stand around
cultrum (acc.) knife
dīuidit he divides
dīuitum of rich (men)
domī at home

domin-us ī 2m. lord, master
dormit (he/she/it) sleeps
ē Lycōnidē, uīcīnō 'by Lyconides, the neighbour'
ē, ex (+ abl.) from, out of
egone am I?
eō I go
etiam nunc further still
exī get out!
exīs you (s.) go/come out
exit (he/she/it) goes out
expellis you (s.) drive out
expellit (he/she/it) drives out
exstingue put out!
facis you (s.) make, do
Fortūn-a ae 1f. luck
for-um ī 2n. forum
grauid-us a um pregnant
hem well!

hercle by Hercules!
hīc here
hodiē today
homo homin-is 3m. man, fellow
iānu-a ae 1f. door
ignis ign-is 3m. fire
ignōrō 1 I do not know
īmus we go
in uirōs among the men
ineunt (they) enter
inquiunt (they) say
īnsān-us a um mad
intrō inside
inuīt-us a um unwilling(ly)
īs you (s.) go
istīc there
it he goes
iterum again
mal-us a um evil, wicked, bad
manē! wait!

maneō 2 I wait
me-us a um my, mine
mī 'O my'
miser miser-a um unhappy
moneō 2 I advise, warn
murmurō 1 I mutter
neque neither, and . . . not
nimis too (much)
nōs (nom., acc.) we, us
numquam never
occidī I'm done for!
occipiti-um ī 2n. back of head
occlūde shut!
ocul-us ī 2m. eye
ohē stop!
operam dā! pay attention!
pauper (nom.) poor (man)

pecūni-a ae 1f. money
per diem by day
per noctem by night
periī I'm lost!
peruigilō 1 I stay awake
praetor praetōr-is 3m. praetor
prohibē stop (her)!
quid what?
quid agis? what are you (s.) up to?
quō where?
redeō I return
redit (he/she/it) returns
respondē reply!
rogō 1 I ask (for)
salu-us a um safe
sēcum with himself/herself

sēdulō carefully
seruā keep!
seruō 1 I keep, preserve
sollicitō 1 I worry
stā! stand (still)!
statim at once
tacē shut up!
taceō 2 I am silent
tam so
tu-us a um your
uerberō 1 I flog, beat
uexō 1 I annoy, trouble
uīcīn-us ī 2m. neighbour
ut how!
ut ualēs? how are you? (s.)

Learning vocabulary for 1C

Nouns
aqu-a ae 1f. water

domin-us ī 2m. master, lord

ocul-us ī 2m. eye
uīcīn-us ī 2m. neighbour(ing)

ignis ign-is 3m. fire

Adjectives
mal-us a um bad, evil, wicked

me-us a um my, mine (voc. *mī* 'O my')

salu-us a um safe
tu-us a um your(s)

Verbs
cōgit-ō 1 I ponder, reflect, consider
rog-ō 1 I ask
seru-ō 1 I save, keep

st-ō 1 I stand
uerber-ō 1 I flog, beat
uex-ō 1 I annoy, trouble, worry

mane-ō 2 I remain, wait
mone-ō 2 I advise, warn
tace-ō 2 I am silent

Others
ē, ex (+abl.) out of, from
neque neither; and . . . not; nor

numquam never
quid? what?
statim at once

ut how!

New forms: adjectives
miser miser-a um miserable, unhappy, wretched

36

New forms: verbs

eō I go, come; cf. *exeō*
  I come, go out; *abeō*
  I come, go away; *adeō*
  I go, come to,
  approach; *redeō* I return

Grammar and exercises for 1C

---

18 **Present imperative active 1st and 2nd conjugation**

	1st conj.		*2nd conj.*	
2nd s.	ámā	'love!'	hábē	'have!'
2nd pl.	amá-te	'love!'	habé-te	'have!'

Notes

1 These forms express a command in Latin.
2 The understood subject is 'you' (s. or pl.).
3 The s. form is the bare stem of the verb; the pl. adds *-te*.

Exercises

1 *Construct and translate the s. and pl. imperatives of these verbs*: timeō, rogō, taceō, cōgitō, moneō, cūrō, possideō, (*optional*: habeō, stō, explicō, cēlō, amō, uideō, maneō).
2 *Translate into English*: dā corōnam!; portā aquam!; in aedibus manēte!; tacē!; thēsaurum seruā!; monēte fīliam!
3 *Translate into Latin*: see! (*pl.*); ask Euclio! (*s.*); be quiet! (*pl.*); hide the pot! (*pl.*).

---

19 ***eō* 'I go', 'I come' (irregular): present indicative active**

1st s.	e-ō	'I go', 'I come', 'I am going/coming', 'I do go/come'
2nd s.	ī-s	'you go', 'you come' etc.
3rd s.	i-t	
1st pl.	í-mus	
2nd pl.	í-tis	
3rd pl.	é-u-nt	

Imperatives

2nd s.	ī	'go!' etc
2nd pl.	í-te	

Notes

1 The stem of the verb is simply *i-* (as shown by the imperative s.).
2 There are many compound words based on *eō*, e.g. *adeō* 'I approach', 'I go up to' (cf. *ad* 'towards', 'near'); see learning vocabulary for **1C**.

Exercises

1 *Translate into English and then turn s. into pl. and vice versa:* ī; eunt; ītis; eō; it; īmus; exītis; abīmus; abītis; redeunt; redītis; īte; redeō; exeunt.
2 *Translate into Latin:* we are going away; they return; go away! (*s.*); you (*pl.*) are approaching; she is coming out; I am going; go back! (*pl.*); you (*s.*) go.

20 1st and 2nd declension adjectives: *meus, tuus*

me-us a um 'my', 'mine', and *tu-us a um* 'your(s)' decline exactly like *mult-us a um*, and agree with their nouns in the same way. Observe that *tu-us* means 'your(s)' when you are *one* person.

NB.   The vocative of *meus* is *mī* (cf. **17A**), e.g. *mī fīlī* 'O my son'.

21 1st and 2nd declension adjectives: *miser miser-a miser-um*

s.

	m.	*f.*	*n.*
nom.	míser	míser-a	míser-um
acc.	míser-um	míser-am	míser-um
gen.	míser-ī	míser-ae	míser-ī
dat.	míser-ō	míser-ae	míser-ō
abl.	míser-ō	míser-ā	míser-ō

pl.

	m.	*f.*	*n.*
nom.	míser-ī	míser-ae	míser-a
acc.	míser-ōs	míser-ās	míser-a

gen.	miser-ṓrum	miser-ā́rum	miser-ṓrum
dat.	← míser-īs →		
abl.	← míser-īs →		

NB.   Arrows indicate that the form shown is the same for all genders.

Exercises

1   *Add the appropriate forms of* meus *and* tuus *to the following nouns (see 20) and say what case they are:* igne; aedīs; honōris; familiā; oculōrum; dominō; aquae; Eucliōnem; senex.
2   *Add the appropriate form of* miser *to the following nouns and say what case they are:* Eucliōnī; Phaedrā; deus; fīliam; aedibus; dominī; seruārum; coquīs; senum.

22   Personal pronouns: *ego* 'I' and *tū* 'you'

nom.	égo	'I'	tū	'you'
acc.	mē		tē	
gen.	méī		túī	
dat.	míhi (mī)		tíbi	
abl.	mē		tē	

Notes

1   *tū* is used when one person is being referred to (cf. *tuus*).
2   When 'I' or 'you' are subject of a verb, we have seen that Latin does not need to express them separately, since the verb itself indicates the person by its personal endings -ō, -s, -t etc. But Latin does use *ego*, *tū* when the speaker wants to stress the identity of the person talking or draw a specific contrast between one person and another. E.g.

(a)   *ego Eucliōnem amō, tū Phaedram* '*I* like Euclio, whereas *you* like Phaedra'
(b)   *ego deum cūrō, tū senem uexās* '*I* care for the god, *you* simply annoy the old man'

It is a matter of emphasis, especially when a contrast is involved.
3   *meī* and *tuī* are 'objective' genitives, i.e. 'of me', 'of you' means 'directed at me/you'. For example, *amor tuī* means 'love of/for you' in the sense 'love directed at you'. The idea 'belonging to me/you' is performed by the adjectives *meus, tuus* e.g. *pater meus* = 'my father', i.e. 'the father belonging to me'.

Exercises

1 *Translate these sentences, then change nouns and their adjectives and verb to the s. or pl. as appropriate:*

(a) manent in dominī meī aedibus neque seruae neque seruī.
(b) malī senis mala serua dominum meum uexat.
(c) tuus uīcīnus uīcīnum meum uidet.
(d) senis miserī seruus in aedibus numquam manet.
(e) seruae miserae ad Larem meum numquam adeunt neque supplicant.
(f) dominus malus seruās statim uerberat miserās.

2 *In these sentences, most adjectives are not directly next to the noun they qualify. Read through each sentence, predicting the gender, number and case of the noun you await (where the adjective comes first) and indicating when the adjective is 'solved'. Then translate.*

(a) malus igitur senex nōn multum habet honōrem.
(b) meā est tuus ignis in aulā.
(c) meīs tamen in aedibus multī habitant patrēs.
(d) malōs enim senēs Lar nōn amat meus.
(e) meusne tuum seruat pater ignem? (–ne = ?)

3 *Translate these sentences:*

(a) sōla pecūnia rēgnat. (*Petronius*)
(b) uēritās numquam perit. (*Seneca*)
(c) semper auārus eget. (*Horace*)
(d) nōn dēterret sapientem mors. (*Cicero*)
(e) in fugā foeda mors est, in uictōriā glōriōsa. (*Cicero*)

sōl-us a um alone	*auār-us ī* 2m. miser	*mors mort-is* 3f. death
pecūni-a ae 1f. money	*egeō* 2 I am in need	*fug-a ae* 1f. rout, flight
rēgnō 1 I rule, am king	*dēterreō* 2 I frighten off,	*foed-us a um* disgraceful
uēritās uēritāt-is 3f. truth	deter	*uictōri-a ae* 1f. victory
pereō (conjugates like *eō*) I	*sapiēns sapient-is* 3m. wise	*glōriōs-us a um* glorious
die	man	

23 Prepositions

Note that *ā*, *ab* '(away) from' and *ē*, *ex* 'out of', 'from' take the ablative (cf. *in* + abl. at **10**).

NB. *ab* and *ex* are the forms used before following vowels, e.g. *ab aulā*, *ex igne*.

Exercise

Translate into Latin: out of the water; into the eye; away from the fire; towards the masters; away from the house; onto the stage (*optional*: out of the pot; towards the thieves; from the old men; into the house.)

Reading exercises

1 *Take the Latin as it comes and, as you translate, say what each word is doing in the sentence, taking care to ascribe adjectives to the correct nouns (if they follow them) or to predict the number, gender and case of the noun (if the adjective precedes). Then supply a suitable verb in the correct person and translate into correct English.*

   (a)   uīcīnum senex miser . . .
   (b)   dominus enim meus tuum ignem . . .
   (c)   neque ego meum neque tū tuum seruum . . .[1]
   (d)   deinde mē seruī malī . . .
   (e)   seruōs malōs uīcīnus meus . . .
   (f)   aulam, mī domine, serua mala . . .
   (g)   fūrem miserum ego quoque . . .
   (h)   ignem tū, ego aquam . . .[2]
   (i)   oculōs meōs serua tua semper . . .
   (j)   quārē aurum et unguentum et corōnās Eucliō miser numquam
       . . .?

[1] Verb 2nd s.
[2] Verb 1st s.

2 *Analyse noun-functions, adjectives, and verbs:*

   (a)   Close up the casement, draw the blind,
        Shut out that stealing moon,
     She wears too much the guise she wore
        Before our lutes were strewn
     With years-deep dust, and names we read
        On a white stone were hewn. (*Thomas Hardy*)

   (b)   Hail, native language, that by sinews weak
     Didst move my first endeavouring tongue to speak,
     And mad'st imperfect words with childish trips,
     Half unpronounced, slide through my infant lips . . .

                                  (*Milton*)

(c)   Know then thyself, presume not God to scan;
The proper study of Mankind is Man. (*Pope*)

Reading exercise / Test exercise

Read the following passage carefully, translating each word as it comes and analysing its function. Identify word-groups and anticipate, as far as you can, what is to come. When you have done this, translate into correct English. Finally read out the passage in Latin with the correct phrasing, thinking out the meaning as you read. Use the running vocabulary of **1C**.

EUCLIŌ (*clāmat*) exī! exī ex aedibus, serua.
(*serua in scaenam intrat*)
SERVA quid est, mī domine? quārē tū mē ex aedibus uocās? (*Eucliō seruam uerberat*) ō mē miseram. ut dominus meus mē uexat. nunc enim mē uerberat. sed tū, mī domine, quārē mē uerberās?
EUC. ō mē miserum. tacē. ut mala es! ut mē miserum uexās! manē istīc, Staphyla, manē! stā! moneō tē.
(*in aedīs intrat Eucliō*)
SER. ō mē miseram. ut miser dominus meus est.
(*Eucliō ex aedibus in scaenam intrat*)
EUC. saluum est. tū tamen quārē istīc stās? quārē in aedīs nōn īs? abī! intrā in aedīs! occlūde iānuam!
(*serua in aedīs intrat*)
nunc abeō ad praetōrem, quod pauper sum. ut inuītus eō! sed sī hīc maneō, uīcīnī meī 'hem' inquiunt 'senex miser multum habet aurum.'

English–Latin

Translate the Latin sentences into English. Then translate the English sentences into Latin, using the pattern of the Latin ones to help you arrange the word-order correctly.

(a)   Staphyla, abī et aquam portā!
Slave-women, go out and ask for fire!
(b)   tū autem, mī domine, quārē cūrās malās habēs?
But why do you, my Euclio, love a wretched slave-woman?
(c)   ut aurum multum senēs uexat miserōs!
How the evil old man beats his unhappy slaves!
(d)   ō mē miseram! ut oculī meī mē uexant!
O dear me! How wretched an old man I am!

42

(e)   malōs dominōs miserī seruī habent.
      (It is) a wretched old man the unhappy daughter loves.
(f)   malōrum seruōrum oculī dominī miserī cūrās nōn uident.
      The eyes of a bad slave-woman do not see the worry of the
      unhappy daughter.

Deliciae Latinae

Word-building

Prefixes

> *in-* can = 'into', 'in' (e.g. *ineō* 'I go in', *īnsum* 'I am in'), but it can
> equally well be a negative, e.g. *īnsānus* = *in* + *sānus* 'not sane',
> 'mad'
> *ē, ex* usually means 'out of', 'out', e.g. *exit* 'he goes out', *exstinguō*
> 'I put out', *expellō* 'I push out'
> *ā, ab* = 'away (from)', e.g. *abeō* 'I go away'
> *re-* (only used as a prefix) = 'back', 'again', e.g. *redit* 'he returns'.
> (Observe that *re-* becomes *red-* before vowels)

Exercise

1 *Give the Latin derivation (prefix and root) of the following English words:*
  cogitate, excogitate, instate, reinstate, reverberate, export, revoke,
  abrogate, reserve, explicate (*plicō* 'fold').
2 *Give English words, with meanings, formed from the following stems* māns-
  (maneō); monit- (moneō). *Use prefixes as necessary.*

Word exercises

1 *What do the following English words mean?* vexatious, admonish,
  aquatic, dominant, impecunious, inexplicable.
2 *Give English words from:* ignis, oculus, maneō, malus, saluus.

Everyday Latin

> *notā bene* (NB) 'note well!' What conjugation is *notō*?
> *vidē*[1] *infrā* (or simply *vidē*, abbreviated *v.*) 'see below'

43

adeste, fidēlēs 'be present, faithful!' 'O come, all ye faithful'
exit '(s)he goes out'; *exeunt* 'they go out'

¹ See n. 10 on p. xii.

Real Latin

Vulgate
honōrā patrem tuum et mātrem tuam. (*Exodus 20.12*)
uōs estis sal ('salt') terrae . . . uōs estis lūx ('light') mundī. (*Matthew 5.13*)

Sayings of Cato
parentēs amā.
datum (= *what you are given*) seruā.
uerēcundiam (= *modesty*) seruā.
familiam cūrā.
iūsiūrandum (= *oath*) seruā.
coniugem (= *wife*) amā.
deō supplicā.

These are from a collection of *dicta Catōnis* 'Sayings of Cato', (= Marcus
Cato, 234–149 B.C.), written in the third or fourth century A.D. but
ascribed to that grand old man who epitomised Roman wisdom and
tradition to later generations. They were firm favourites from the
Middle Ages till the seventeenth century in England.

Beginning of an epitaph
sepulcrum hau pulcrum pulcrāī fēminae . . .

sepulcr-um ī 2n. tomb
hau not (archaic for *haud*)
pulc(h)r- beautiful, fine
pulcrāī : note ancient f.s.
   genitive ending

We know the woman buried there was called Claudia – perhaps one of
the family called Claudii Pulchri?

Section 1D

Running vocabulary for 1D

ā, ab (+abl.) away from
adstant (they) hang about
anim-us ī 2m. mind
arculāri-us ī 2m. chest-
  maker
audiō I hear, listen
aurifex aurific-is 3m.
  goldsmith
aurīque and (of) gold
calceolāri-us ī 2m.
  shoemaker
caupō caupōn-is 3m.
  shopkeeper
clāmor clāmōr-is 3m. shout
dīc say! tell!
dīcis you (s.) say, are
  saying, mean
dīcō I say
dīues dīuit-is rich (man)
domī at home
domum (to) the home
domum dūc marry!
domum nōn dūcis you (s.)
  do not marry
dōs dōt-is 3f. dowry
dōtemque and a dowry
drāma drāmat-is 3n. play
dūcis you (s.) lead, take
dūcit (he/she/it) leads,
  takes
dūcō I lead, take
eburāt-us a um adorned
  with ivory
ecce look!
egone I?
Eunomi-a ae 1f. Eunomia
faciunt (they) make, do
fēmin-a ae 1f. woman
fīli-us ī 2m. son
flammāri-us ī 2m. maker
  of bridal veils

for-um ī 2n. forum
frāter frātr-is 3m. brother
fullō fullōn-is 3m. fuller
habeō 2 I hold, regard as
imperi-um ī 2n. command,
  order
intolerābilis unendurable
ita so, thus
iubeō 2 I order
lānāri-us ī 2m. wool-
  worker
līber-ī ōrum 2m. (pl.)
  children
limbulāri-us a um
  concerned with
  making ornamental
  hems
linteō linteō-nis 3m. linen-
  weaver
Lycōnidēs Lyconid-is 3m.
  Lyconides
magn-us a um great, large
manuleāri-us ī 2m. maker
  of sleeves
manum (acc.) hand
Megadōr-us ī 2m.
  Megadorus
mihi (to) (for) me
moneōque 'and I warn'
monument-a ōrum 2n. (pl.)
  memorial(s)
nec and . . . not, neither
nimis (+gen.) too much
  (of)
nōmen name
nōmine by name
nūpti-ae ārum 1f. (pl.)
  marriage-rites
occidī I'm done for!
oper-a ae 1f. attention
optim-us a um best

pall-a ae 1f. garment
pater patr-is 3m. father
pauper pauper-is poor
  (man)
pecūni-a ae 1f. money
periī I'm lost!
persōn-a ae 1f. actor
phrygiō phrygiōn-is 3m.
  embroiderer
post (+acc.) after
potestās potestāt-is 3f.
  power
praetereā furthermore
propōl-a -ae 1m. retailer
puell-a ae 1f. girl
puellamne the girl?
pulcher pulchr-a um
  beautiful
purpur-a ae 1f. purple
quaesō please (lit. 'I ask')
quam (acc.) whom? what
  woman?
quamquam although
-que and
quis who?
quod because
rēctē rightly
satis enough (of)
sēcum with himself/herself
seruantque 'and they
  protect'
simul at the same time
sōnāri-us ī 2m. girdle-
  maker
soror sorōr-is 3f. sister
sororque and your sister
strophiāri-us ī 2m. seller of
  breast-bands
sūmptus extravagance,
  expense
textor textōr-is 3m. weaver

45

thȳlacist-a ae 1m. collector
  of offerings
tibi to you (s.)
tum then

tūne 'do you?' (s.)
ualē! goodbye!
uehicul-um ī 2n. waggon
uir uir-ī 2m. man,

  husband
uīs you (s.) wish, want
ut as
uxor uxōr-is 3f. wife

Learning vocabulary for 1D

Nouns
fēmin-a ae 1f. woman
pecūni-a ae 1f. money
puell-a ae 1f. girl
fīli-us ī 2m. son
uir uir-ī 2m. man,

  husband
dīues dīuit-is 3m.f. rich
  (person)
frāter frātr-is 3m. brother
pater patr-is 3m. father

pauper pauper-is 3m.f.
  poor (person)
soror sorōr-is 3f. sister
uxor uxōr-is 3f. wife

Adjectives
magn-us a um great, large
optim-us a um best, very
  good

Verbs
habe-ō 2 I hold, regard
  (have)[1]

iube-ō 2 *iuss-*[2] I order,
  command, tell

ualē goodbye!

Others
ā, ab (+ abl.) away from
ita so, thus; yes
nec and . . . not, neither;
  nor

nimis too much
  (of) + gen.
-que and
satis enough (of) + gen.
tum then

ut as, when (how!)[1]

New forms: nouns
nōmen nōmin-is 3n. name

domum to home

domī at home

New forms: adjectives
pulcher pulchr-a um
  beautiful

New forms: verbs
dūc-ō 3 *dūx-, duct-*[2] I lead
domum dūcō I take home,
  marry

dīc-o 3 *dīx-, dict-*[2] I speak,
  say

audi-ō 4 I hear, listen to

---

[1] See n. 11 on p. xii for the significance of the brackets.

[2] Learn these other stems *now*. They are irregular and used to form other tenses.

Grammar and exercises for 1D

**24 Present indicative active (3rd conjugation): *dīcō* 'I speak',
'I say'**

1st s.	dĭc-ō	'I say'
2nd s.	dĭc-i-s	'you say'
3rd s.	dĭc-i-t	'he/she/it says'
1st pl.	dĭc-i-mus	'we say'
2nd pl.	dĭc-i-tis	'you (*pl.*) say'
3rd pl.	dĭc-u-nt	'they say'

Imperatives

2nd s.	dĭc	'say!' (*irregular*)
2nd pl.	dĭc-i-te	'say!'

Notes

1 Note the key vowel in the 3rd conj. – the short -*i*- throughout (cf. *amō*, *habeō*). This -*i*- is *not* part of the stem in the way that -*e*- in *habeo* (stem *habe*-) was.

2 Observe that the 3rd pl. is *dīc-u-nt*.

3 A similar verb to this is *dūcō* 'I lead', 'I take'.

4 Normal imperatives of 3rd conj. verbs are -*e*, -*ite* (see **36**). Note that the vowels in these endings are all short. Cf. imperatives of *audiō* in **25**.

**25 Present indicative active (4th conjugation): *audiō* 'I hear',
'I listen to'**

1st s.	aúdi-ō	'I hear'
2nd s.	aúdī-s	'you hear'
3rd s.	aúdi-t	'he/she/it hears'
1st pl.	audī-mus	'we hear'
2nd pl.	audī-tis	'you (*pl.*) hear'
3rd pl.	aúdi-u-nt	'they hear'

Imperatives

2nd s.	aúdī	'listen!'
2nd pl.	audī-te	'listen!'

Notes

1 The key vowel in the 4th conj. is -*i*-, which follows the same pattern of long and short as the -*e*- of the 2nd conj., and is, like that, part of the

stem. So -*i*- appears throughout (contrast the -*i*- in *dīcō*).

2 Observe the 3rd pl. in *i-unt*; cf. *dīc-unt*.

Exercises

1 *Translate into Latin*: she says; they are leading; we hear; we say; you (*pl.*) hear; speak! (*s.*); listen! (*pl.*); lead! (*pl.*); you (*s.*) are saying; he hears; they are listening.

2 *Identify the conjugation (1, 2, 3 or 4) of the following verbs and translate them*: cūrō, cēlat, habētis, dūcunt, rogās, possidēmus, audiō, (*optional*: iubētis, supplicō, clāmāmus).

3 *Translate and turn s. into pl. and vice versa*: dīcitis, audiunt, supplicāmus, audīs, dīcō, dūcimus, audīmus, clāmant, tacēs, (*optional*: rogat, dīcit, cōgitō, manētis, amātis, dūcunt, moneō, uocās, dūcis).

26 3rd decl. nouns: *nōmen nōmin-is* 3n. 'name'

	s.	*pl.*
nom.	nṓmen	nṓmin-a
acc.	nṓmen	nṓmin-a
gen.	nṓmin-is	nṓmin-um
dat.	nṓmin-ī	nōmín-ibus
abl.	nṓmin-e	nōmín-ibus

Notes

1 All n. nouns have the same forms for the nom. and acc. in both s. and pl. (-*a*); cf. **15**. Only the context will tell you whether they are subject or object. Note that if verb is singular then a neuter pl. must be the object; if verb is plural, then neuter s. must be the object.

2 All 3rd decl. nouns in -*men* are neuter, and follow the pattern of *nōmen*.

3 *nōmen* is a consonant-stem noun. There are also 3rd decl. neuter *i*-stems. You will meet these later.

27 1st/2nd decl. adjectives: *pulcher pulchr-a pulchr-um* 'beautiful', 'handsome'

	s.		
	m.	*f.*	*n.*
nom.	púlcher	púlchr-a	púlchr-um
acc.	púlchr-um	púlchr-am	púlchr-um

gen.	púlchr-ī	púlchr-ae	púlchr-ī
dat.	púlchr-ō	púlchr-ae	púlchr-ō
abl.	púlchr-ō	púlchr-ā	púlchr-ō

pl.

	m.	*f.*	*n.*
nom.	púlchr-ī	púlchr-ae	púlchr-a
acc.	púlchr-ōs	púlchr-ās	púlchr-a
gen.	pulchr-ōrum	pulchr-árum	pulchr-ōrum
dat.		←púlchr-īs→	
abl.		←púlchr-īs→	

NB.   We have already met *miser* which, apart from the nom. s. m., declines like *multus* on the stem *miser-* (**21**). *pulcher* is identical, except that it declines on the stem *pulchr-*.

28   2nd decl. nouns: *puer puer-ī* 2m. 'boy', *uir uir-ī* 2m. 'man', *culter cultr-ī* 2m. 'knife'

puer puer-ī 2m. 'boy'[1]   *uir uir-ī* 2m. 'man'[1]

	s.	*pl.*			*s.*	*pl.*
nom.	púer	púer-ī		*nom.*	uir	uír-ī
acc.	púer-um	púer-ōs		*acc.*	uír-um	uír-ōs
gen.	púer-ī	puer-ōrum		*gen.*	uír-ī	uir-ōrum (uír-um – see **16**)
dat.	púer-ō	púer-īs		*dat.*	uír-ō	uír-īs
abl.	púer-ō	púer-īs		*abl.*	uír-ō	uír-īs

[1] These nouns decline exactly like *seru-us* on the stems *puer-* and *uir-*. Only nom. s. m. is different. Cf. *miser* (**21**).

culter cultr-ī 2m. 'knife'[1]

	s.	*pl.*
nom.	cúlter	cúltr-ī
acc.	cúltr-um	cúltr-ōs
gen.	cúltr-ī	cultr-ōrum
dat.	cúltr-ō	cúltr-īs
abl.	cúltr-ō	cúltr-īs

[1] This noun declines exactly like *seru-us* on the stem *cultr-*. Only nom. s. m. is different. Cf. *pulcher* (**27**).

Exercises

1 *Give the correct form of the adjectives* magnus, miser, pulcher *for these cases of* nōmen: nōmen, nōminis, nōmine, nōmina, nōminum.

2 *Give the correct form of* pulcher *and* miser *to describe each of these nouns (e.g.* senem *acc. s. m., so* senem pulchrum): uxōrum, sorōribus, uirō, uxōris, fēminae, frātrī, aedīs, Larem, seruā, aedēs, fēminīs, dominī, seruōs.

Optional exercise

Add the appropriate form of miser, *then of* pulcher, *to the following words and translate (e.g.* Euclionem = *acc. s. m.* – miserum/pulchrum *'unhappy/ handsome Euclio'):* sorōre, dīuitis, uir, uxōrī, fēminae, puellīs, fīliī, uīcīnō, Larem, frātrum, seruā.

29 Interrogative pronoun/adjective *quis/quī, quis/quae, quid/quod* 'who?', 'which?', 'what?'

		s.			*pl.*		
		m.	*f.*	*n.*	*m.*	*f.*	*n.*
nom.	*pron.*	quis	quis	quid ⎫	quī	quae	quae
	adj.	quī	quae	quod ⎭			
acc.	*pron.* ⎫	quem	quam	⎧ quid ⎫	quōs	quās	quae
	adj. ⎭			⎩ quod ⎭			
gen.		←cúius→			quórum	quárum	quórum
dat.		←cúi→			←quíbus (quīs)→		
abl.		quō	quā	quō	←quíbus (quīs)→		

Notes

1 'Interrogative' means 'asking a question'.

2 Observe that the endings are a mixture of 2nd and 3rd declension. You will meet this again (it is called the 'pronominal' declension).

3 Adjective and pronoun are identical except for nom. s. and the acc. s. n.

4 For the pronoun use, cf. 'who is calling?' *quis uocat?* 'what do I see?' *quid uideō?*; for the adjective 'what man is it?' *quī(quis) uir est?*, 'what gold do I see?' *quod aurum uideō?*

50

Exercises

1 *Translate into Latin the underlined words with the appropriate form of* quis *or* quī + *noun. You will need to ask whether the question word is a pronoun or an adjective, and then define its case.*

(a) <u>Whose</u> (*s. m.*) are these books?
(b) <u>Which</u> women do we see?
(c) <u>What</u> is this?
(d) <u>What</u> name is this?
(e) <u>Whom</u> (*m. s.*) do you hate most?
(f) <u>What</u> woman's are these?
(g) <u>Whom</u> (*f. s.*) should we persecute?
(h) <u>Which</u> man is guilty?

30 *domus* 'house', 'home'

domus used with prepositions means 'house'. But when it means 'home' it is used without the preposition in the following ways: *domum* '(to) home'; *domī* 'at home'; *domō* 'from home'. Cf. *aedēs* which means only 'house': *in aedīs* 'into the house', *in aedibus* 'in the house'.

31 *satis* 'enough', *nimis* 'too much', 'too many'

Both these words control nouns in the gen. case (the so-called 'partitive' genitive indicating *part of* a whole), e.g. *satis pecūniae* 'enough (of) money', *nimis honōris* 'too much (of) respect'. *satis* and *nimis* are fixed in form.

32 *-que*

-que means 'and' and either (i) links the noun it is joined to with the previous word e.g. *seruum patremque* 'slave <u>and</u> father' or (ii) in poetry indicates that a list is coming, e.g. *seruumque patremque sorōremque* 'both slave <u>and</u> father <u>and</u> sister'.

Exercises

1 *In each of these sentences, there is one adjective which precedes and does not stand next to the noun it qualifies. Read through each sentence, predicting the gender, number and case of the noun awaited, noting when the adjective is 'solved'. Then translate.*

    (a)   nōn multam possident pecūniam optimae uxōrēs.
    (b)   multī meās sorōrēs amant fīliī.
    (c)   seruōs miserōs optimī nōn uexant senēs.
    (d)   malī frātrēs pulchrās uerberant sorōrēs.
    (e)   multī fēminās pulchrās domum dūcunt senēs.

Before doing Exercises 2 and 3, revise carefully the ablative forms of nouns of the 1st, 2nd and 3rd declension.

2 *Translate into English*: in aedīs; in aulā; ad Larem; ab ignibus; in aquam; ex aulīs; in aedibus; in aquā; ā dominō; ex oculīs; (*optional*: ad dominum; in scaenam; in nōmine; ā seruā; in aulam; in scaenā).

3 *Translate into Latin*: in the house (*use* aedēs); towards the girl; towards the brothers; away from the wife; onto the stage; in the house; out of water; away from the fires; (*optional*: in the waters; from the stage; into the family; in the eye; towards the masters; out of the household).

4 *Translate*: nimis corōnārum; satis seruōrum; nimis aquae; satis nōminum; nimis sorōrum; satis ignis.

5 *Translate these sentences*:

    (a)   quem uirum audiō?
    (b)   cuius nōmen nunc dīcitis?
    (c)   in aedibus Eucliōnis satis aurī semper est.
    (d)   habet fīlia Eucliōnis misera nimis cūrārum.
    (e)   tū autem quam fēminam domum dūcis?
           (*optional*)
    (f)   puer pulcher est, uir tamen malus.
    (g)   pater meus nimis pecūniae habet, satis cūrārum.
    (h)   quārē pulchra fēmina pauperem numquam amat?
    (i)   optimī uirī satis aurī semper habent.

6 *Translate these sentences*:

    (a)   uir bonus est quis? (*Horace*)
    (b)   quis nōn paupertātem extimēscit? (*Cicero*)
    (c)   quis bene cēlat amōrem? (*Ovid*)

(d) quid est beāta uīta? sēcūritās et perpetua tranquillitās. (*Seneca*)
(e) mors quid est? aut fīnis aut trānsitus. (*Seneca*)
(f) immodica īra gignit īnsāniam. (*Seneca*)
(g) uītam regit fortūna, nōn sapientia. (*Cicero*)

bon-*us a um* good
paupertās paupertāt-*is* 3f.
  poverty
extimēscō 3 I am greatly
  afraid of
bene well
amor amōr-*is* 3m. love
beāt-*us a um* happy,
  blessed
uīt-*a ae* 1f. life

sēcūritās sēcūritāt-*is* 3f.
  freedom from worry
perpetu-*us a um* perpetual,
  continuous
tranquillitās tranquillitāt-*is*
  3f. peace
mors mort-*is* 3f. death
aut . . . aut either . . . or
fīn-*is fīn-is* 3m. end
trānsit-*us* (nom.)

transition
immodic-*us a um*
  immoderate
īr-*a ae* 1f. anger
gignō 3 I beget, cause
īnsāni-*a ae* 1f. madness
regō 3 I rule, direct
fortūn-*a ae* 1f. fortune
sapienti-*a ae* 1f. wisdom

Reading

1 *Observe the following*:

> ego tē uxōrem habeō = *I regard you as a wife.*
> ego tē pauperem faciō = *I make you poor / a poor man* (NB. faciō
> *conjugates like* audiō, *but* –i– *is short throughout*).

Supply a part of habeō *or* faciō *which will make sense of the following
combinations and translate. Then read out in Latin, phrasing correctly.*

(a) tandem uir mē fīlium . . .
(b) Eucliō uīcīnum dīuitem . . .
(c) Eucliōnem pauperem . . .
(d) Megadōrus fīliam Eucliōnis uxōrem . . .
(e) ego autem dīuitēs miserōs . . .
(f) dominus malōs seruōs miserōs . . .

2 *Analyse the following passage in terms of subject, object; genitive usages;
adjectives; prepositions.*

*Zeus, as he had promised, has Apollo remove the body of Sarpedon, 'the
breathless hero', from the battlefield.*

Apollo bows, and from Mount Ida's Height
Swift to the Field precipitates his Flight;
Thence, from the War, the breathless Hero bore,
Veil'd in a Cloud, to silver Simois' shore:
There bath'd his honourable wounds, and drest   5

His manly Members in th' Immortal Vest,
And with Perfumes of Sweet Ambrosial Dews,
Restores his Freshness, and his Form renews.
Then Sleep and Death, two twins of winged Race,
Of matchless swiftness, but of silent Pace,   10
Received Sarpedon, at the Gods' command,
And in a Moment reach'd the Lycian land;
The Corps amidst his weeping Friends they laid,
Where endless Honours wait the Sacred Shade.

(*Pope, translation of* Iliad *XVI*)

Reading exercise / Test exercise

Read the following passage carefully, translating in order of the words and analysing the function of each one, defining word-groups, and anticipating, as far as you can, what is to come. Then translate into correct English. Finally, read the passage aloud with the correct phrasing, thinking through the meaning as you read. Use the running vocabulary of **1D**.

Megadōrum, uirum dīuitem et Eucliōnis uīcīnum, soror Eunomia ex aedibus uocat. Eunomia enim anxia (*worried*) est, quod Megadōrus uxōrem nōn habet. Megadōrus autem uxōrem nōn uult (*wants*). nam uxōrēs uirōs dīuitēs pauperēs faciunt. habet satis aurī Megadōrus et fēminās pulchrās nōn amat. ut enim pulchra fēmina est, ita uirum uexat.   5
ut uir dīues est, ita uxor uirum pauperem facit. Eunomiam autem sorōrem optimam Megadōrus habet. ut igitur postulat (*demands*) soror, ita facit frāter. Phaedram enim, Eucliōnis fīliam, puellam optimam habet. ut tamen pauper Eucliō est, ita dōtem habet Phaedra nūllam. Megadōrus autem dōtem nōn uult (*wants*). nam sī dīuitēs uxōrēs sunt   10
magnamque habent dōtem, magnus est post nūptiās sūmptus, nimis dant uirī pecūniae.

English–Latin

Translate the Latin sentences into English. Then translate the English sentences into Latin, using the pattern of the Latin ones to help you arrange the word-order correctly.

(a)   ut ego soror optima sum, ita tū frāter optimus.
      Just as Phaedra is an excellent daughter, so Euclio is an excellent
      father.
(b)   dominus meus frātrem uirum optimum habet.

I consider beautiful women (to be) bad wives.
(c) quid nōmen uxōris est tuae?
Who is the brother of my neighbour?
(d) uir pauper uxōrem pauperem domum dūcit.
The best husbands marry beautiful wives.
(e) fēminae in aedibus stant.
The girls are going into the water.
(f) satis ego aurī habeō, satis pecūniae.
The rich man has too much money and too much worry.

Deliciae Latinae

Word exercises

1 *What do the following English words mean?* sorority, uxorious, fraternal, virile, optimise, pauper, pulchritude, duke (*also:* il duce; duchy; duchess; doge; ducat (*coin bearing the duke's image*)), audio-visual, magnify.
2 *Derive English words from the following Latin:* nōmen, domī, pecūnia, fēmina, uale, satis.

Everyday Latin

Where would one write *ex librīs* (*liber, libr-* 'book')?
What sort of statement comes *ex cathedrā*? (*cathedra* is a special papal seat – originally the bishop's seat in his church, hence 'cathedral')
Christ told the story of Dives and Lazarus. Who was Dives? (see Luke 16:19ff.)
Often things seem to go on *ad īnfīnītum* – explain. What is the force of the *in-* prefix?
in vīnō vēritās (= 'truth'). Where is truth found?
To 'ad lib' is to talk *ad libitum*, i.e. to whatever extent you want (*libet* 'it is pleasing, desirable').
ad nauseam – to what point?
deus ex māchinā. māchina is a stage crane. Explain how the phrase comes to refer to a miraculous ending to an event.
per ardua ad astra (Royal Air Force motto) 'Through the heights / through difficulties . . .' – where?

Word-building

dūcō has another stem, *duct-*. Use the 'pool' of prefixes (pp. 32, 43) and your knowledge of common endings to produce at least ten English derivatives, with meanings.

See how large a score you can make with *audiō, audīt-* and *dīcō, dict-* in the same way.

Real Latin

Martial

Martial (c. AD 40–104) was a Roman satirical epigrammatist.

Thāida Quīntus amat. 'quam Thāida?' Thāida luscam.
ūnum oculum Thāis nōn habet, ille duōs.

(3.8)

Thāis name of a very famous Roman courtesan (acc. = *Thāida*)	*quam* which? *lusc-us a um* one-eyed *ūn-us a um* one	*ille* 'but he' i.e. Quintus (sc. *nōn habet*) *duōs* two (eyes)

NB. The Romans thought of love as blind and lovers as 'blinded'.

habet Āfricānus mīliēns, tamen captat.
Fortūna multīs dat nimis, satis nūllī.

(12.10)

mīliēns 100 million sesterces	*captō* 1 I hunt legacies *multīs* to many	*nūllī* to no-one

Vulgate

Dominus regit mē. (*Psalm 23*)

Ordinary of the Mass

in nōmine Patris et Fīliī et Spīritūs Sānctī.

Section 1E

Running vocabulary for 1E

adsum I am near, at hand, present
aegrē hardly
aequ-us a um content
anim-us ī 2m. mind, heart, spirit
asin-us ī 2m. donkey
audī hear! listen!
audīsne: *ne* turns *audīs* into a question
bene well, thoroughly
blandē ingratiatingly
bon-us a um good
bōs bou-is 3m. ox
certē without doubt
cognōuī I know
cōnsili-um ī 2n. plan
dōs dōt-is 3f. dowry
dubi-us a um in doubt
dūc lead! take!
et ... et both ... and
exīsne: *ne* turns *exīs* into a question
fac do! make!
facile easily
facimus we do, make
facinora (nom.) schemes
facinus (nom., acc.) deed, scheme
facit (he/she/it) makes, does
fer carry! bring!
ferō I carry, endure
fers you (s.) carry, endure
fert (he/she/it) carries
for-um ī 2n. forum
grauid-us a um pregnant

hercle by Hercules!
heus hey!
hīc here
hodiē today
homo homin-is 3m. man, fellow
iaceō 2 I lie
immortālēs immortal
imperō 1 I order
irrīdeō 2 I laugh at (+*ne*=?)
lut-um ī 2n. mud
mihi (to) me
mox soon
nefāri-us a um wicked
nihil nothing
nūpti-ae ārum 1f. (pl.) marriage-rites
occidī I'm done for!
omnia (acc.) everything
onus (acc.) load, burden
oper-a ae 1f. attention
opus (nom.) need
ōrdō ōrdin-is 3m. rank, class
pateō 2 I am obvious, lie exposed
paupertās paupertāt-is 3f. poverty
periī I'm lost!
perspicu-us a um obvious
pol certainly (lit. 'by Pollux')
poscō 3 I demand, ask for (in marriage)
praetereā moreover

prōmitte promise!
prōmittō 3 I promise
quasi as if
quid cōnsilī what (of) plan?
quō to where?
respiciō 3/4 I give a second glance to
saluē hail!
salūtō 1 I greet, welcome
scelus (nom., acc.) crime; criminal, villain
scelera (nom., acc.) crimes; criminals, villains
sēcum with himself/herself
sīc thus, as follows
sine (+ abl.) without
stult-us a um stupid
subit-us a um suddenly
tibi to you
trānscendō 3 I cross over (to) (*ad*+acc.:= I become)
ualeō 2 I am well; I wield influence; *ualeō ā* (+abl.) I am well from the point of view of
ubi where?
uērō truly
uīs you (s.) wish, want
uolō I wish, want
uolumus we wish, want
uult (he/she/it) wishes, wants
uultis you (pl.) wish, want

Learning vocabulary for 1E

Nouns

nūpti-ae ārum 1f. pl.
  marriage-rites
anim-us ī 2m. mind,
  spirit, heart
cōnsili-um ī 2n. plan;

advice, judgement
dōs dōt-is 3f. dowry
homo homin-is 3m. man,
  fellow

Adjectives

bon-us a um good; brave;
  fit; honest

Verbs

irrīde-ō 2 I laugh at, mock

saluē welcome!
posc-ō 3 I demand

prōmitt-ō 3 *prōmīs- prōmiss-*
  I promise

Others

bene well; thoroughly;
  rightly
et ... et both ... and
hodiē today
-ne = ?

occidī I'm done for!
periī I'm lost!
quasi as if, like
quid cōnsilī? what (of)
  plan?

quō (to) where
sēcum with/to himself/
  herself
ubi where (at)?

New forms: nouns

facinus facinor-is 3n. deed;
  crime; endeavour

onus oner-is 3n. load,
  burden

scelus sceler-is 3n. crime,
  villainy; criminal,
  villain

New forms: verbs

faci-ō 3/4 *fēc-, fact-* I make,
  do

fer-ō 3 *tul-, lāt-* I bear,
  lead

uol-ō I wish, want

Grammar and exercises for 1E

---

33 **Present indicative active (3rd/4th conjugation): *capiō* 'I capture'**

1st s.   cápi-ō   'I capture' *etc.*
2nd s.   cápi-s
3rd s.   cápi-t

1st pl.	cápi-mus
2nd pl.	cápi-tis
3rd pl.	cápi-u-nt

Notes

1 There are a number of verbs which draw their forms from both 3rd and 4th conjs. You have met *faciō*, 'I make, do'.
2 *capiō* appears to be straight 4th conjugation in the pres. ind. act., but observe a difference. True, it keeps the -*i*- all the way through, but the -*i*- remains *short* as in the 3rd conj.

34 *uolō* **'I wish', 'I want' (irregular): present indicative active**

1st s.	uól-ō	'I wish', 'I want' *etc.*
2nd s.	uī-s	
3rd s.	uul-t (uol-t)	
1st pl.	uól-u-mus	
2nd pl.	uúl-tis (uól-tis)	
3rd pl.	uól-u-nt	

NB.   The stem of *uolō* is irregular but observe that the personal endings are regular, i.e. -*o*, -*s*, -*t* etc.

35 *ferō* **'I bear', 'I carry, 'I lead' (irregular): present indicative active**

1st s.	fér-ō	'I bear' *etc.*
2nd s.	fer-s	
3rd s.	fer-t	
1st pl.	fér-i-mus	
2nd pl.	fér-tis	
3rd pl.	fér-u-nt	

NB.   It is the absence of -*i*- between stem and ending in 2nd, 3rd s. and 2nd pl. that makes this irregular.

36 **Present imperatives active (all conjugations)**

1	2	3	4	3/4
ámā 'love!'	hábē 'have!'	pósc-e 'ask!'	aúdī 'hear!'	cáp-e 'take!'
amā́-te	habḗ-te	pósc-ite	audī́-te	cápi-te

Note

1 We use *poscō* for 3rd conj. as *dīco* has an irregular imperative, and *capiō* 'I take', 'I capture' should be learnt now, as it will exemplify 3rd/4th conj. throughout.

2 Note the similarity of 3rd and 3rd/4th conjugation imperative forms. Despite the presence of the *-i-* in *capiō*, the imperative form in the s. is still *cap-e*.

37 Irregular imperatives

sum	*eō*	*dīcō*	*dūcō*	*ferō*	*faciō*
es 'be!'	ī 'go!'	dīc 'say!'	dūc 'lead!'	fer 'bring!'	fac 'do', 'make!'
és-te	í-te	díc-i-te	dúc-i-te	fér-te	fáci-te

Notes

1 Herewith a mnemonic to help you remember four of the irregular imperatives: '*dīc* had a *dūc* with *fer* on its back, and that's a *fac*'.

2 Observe the lack of *-i-* in *ferte*.

Exercises

1 *Translate into Latin*: you (*s.*) make; hear! (*pl.*); they carry; bring! (*s., two verbs*); she wishes; we do; he bears; go! (*pl.*); you (*s.*) want; demand! (*s.*); I do; take (*s.*) the dowry (*optional*: we make; you (*s.*) endure; you (*pl.*) bring; you (*pl.*) wish; love your father! (*s.*)).

2 *Translate the following, then change s. to pl. and vice versa*: facimus; fert; uult; ferunt; dīc; ferte; uolumus; est; eunt; facis; dūcite; īte; capite (*optional*: fac; uīs; es; habent; dīcit; audīte; faciunt; fers).

38 3rd. decl. nouns: *onus oner-is* 3n. 'load', 'burden'

	s.	*pl.*
nom.	ónus	óner-a
acc.	ónus	óner-a
gen.	óner-is	óner-um
dat.	óner-ī	onér-ibus
abl.	óner-e	onér-ibus

NB. All 3rd decl. nouns in *-us, -eris* are n. (cf. *nōmen* **26**). Observe that, as usual, the nom. and acc. forms are the same; and that, like *nōmen*, the nom. and acc. pl. end in *-a*. It is vital to know the full categorisation (i.e. *onus oner-is* 3n.) of nouns like *onus*, for fear of confusing them with 2nd decl. m. nouns like *thēsaurus, dominus* etc. *onus* is a consonant-stem noun.

Exercises

1 *Give the correct form of* multus *for these cases of* onus: onus, oneris, onere, onera, oneribus.
2 *Find the words which agree with the given form of* pulcher:

> pulchrō: oneris, scelere, dominī, facinus, deī, dī
> pulchra: fēmina, facinora, scelera, seruae, senex
> pulchrum: opus, seruum, fēminam, senēs, Larem, scelus, facinoris
> pulchrōrum: nōminum, seruārum, deōrum, senum, scelerum

39 Questions in *-ne?*

-ne attached to the FIRST word of a sentence turns a statement into a question, e.g. *puerum amās* 'you love the boy' – *amāsne puerum?* 'do you love the boy?'

NB. Emphasis is placed on the first word in such questions. *puerumne amās?* means 'is it *the boy* you love?'

Exercise

Read out these sentences in Latin, correctly phrased. Then translate. Next turn each into a question, putting the word to be questioned first, and adding -ne *to it. Translate and read out the Latin again.*

(a) est bona puella.
(b) īmus ad aedīs Eucliōnis.
(c) fert bene onus serua.

(d)   optimum cōnsilium habent.
(e)   Eucliō fīliam statim prōmittit.
(f)   Megadōrus satis pecūniae habet.
(g)   soror frātrem bene audit.
(h)   scaenam uidētis.
(i)   Eucliō honōrem numquam dat.
(j)   uxōrēs nimis aurī semper habent.

40   *quid* + **gen.**

We have already met *satis* + gen. 'enough (of)', and *nimis* + gen. 'too much (of)'. *quid* + gen. = 'what (of)?', e.g. *quid cōnsilī est?* 'what (of) plan is there?' *quid negōtī est?* 'what (of) trouble is there?' 'what's the problem?' This is another example of the so-called 'partitive' genitive (cf. **31**).

Exercises

1   *Translate:* in aedīs; ē dōte; in animō; ad hominēs; ab aquā; ex ignibus; domī; ē perīculō; in exitium; ad aquās; in perīculum.
2   *Translate these sentences:*

(a)   ubi est Megadōrus? quid cōnsilī habet?
(b)   uxōremne pulchram uult uir dīues? quid negōtī est?
(c)   tē igitur bonum habeō.
(d)   seruī in aedibus nimis faciunt scelerum, nimis facinorum malōrum.
(e)   quid oneris fers? quō īs?

3   *Translate these sentences:*

(a)   festīnā lentē. (*Suetonius*)
(b)   uirtūs sōla uītam efficit beātam. (*Cicero*)
(c)   nihil inuītus facit sapiēns. (*Seneca*)
(d)   auctor opus laudat. (*Ovid*)
(e)   nihil in uulgō modicum. (*Tacitus*)
(f)   neque bonum est uoluptās neque malum. (*Aulus Gellius*)

festīnō 1 I hurry, hasten
lentē slowly
uirtūs uirtūt-is 3f. goodness
sōl-us a um alone, only
uīt-a ae 1f. life
efficiō 3/4 I make (x acc.,
   Y acc.)

beāt-us a um happy,
   blessed
nihil nothing
inuīt-us a um unwilling(ly)
sapiēns sapient-is 3m. wise
   man
auctor auctōr-is 3m. author

opus oper-is 3n. work
laudō 1 I praise
uulg-us ī 2n. crowd, mob
modic-us a um moderate
uoluptās uoluptāt-is 3f.
   pleasure

Reading exercises

1 *Read through each of these pairs of sentences. In each case (1) say whether the subject of the second sentence is m., f. or n., (2) say to what or whom the second sentence refers, (3) translate the sentences, (4) read aloud in Latin, correctly phrased.*

(a) Megadōrus fīliam Eucliōnis sine dōte domum dūcit. optimus igitur homo est.

(b) Megadōrus domī hodiē neque nūptiās parat neque coquōs uocat. malum est.

(c) Eunomia soror Megadōrī est. bona fēmina est.

(d) Eunomia frātrem habet. nōn dubium est.

(e) Eucliō fīliam amat. malus nōn est.

(f) Eucliō timet. nōn dubium est.

(g) Staphyla cōnsilium Eucliōnis audit. malum est.

(h) Staphyla in aedīs redit. cūrae enim plēna est.

2 *Analyse the following piece, stating, as you read, subject, verb, object, adjective.*

But anxious Cares the pensive Nymph oppress'd,
And secret Passions labour'd in her Breast.
Not youthful Kings in Battle seiz'd alive,
Not scornful Virgins who their Charms survive,
Not ardent Lovers robb'd of all their Bliss,   5
Not ancient Ladies when refused a Kiss,
Not Tyrants fierce that unrepenting die,
Not Cynthia when her Mantle's pinned awry,
E'er felt such Rage, Resentment and Despair,
As thou, sad Virgin! for thy ravish'd Hair. (*Pope*)   10

Reading exercise / Test exercise

Read carefully through this passage, translating in the order of the words, analysing the function of each and the groupings of the words, and anticipating the direction of the sentences. Translate into correct English. Then read aloud the passage with correct phrasing, thinking through the meaning as you read. Use the running vocabulary of **1E**.

Megadōrus Eucliōnem uīcīnum uidet. ā forō abit Euclio. anxius est. nam animus Eucliōnis, quod aurum nōn uidet, domī est, Euclio ipse (*himself*) forīs (*outside*). Eucliōnem blandē salūtat Megadōrus, homo dīues pauperem. timet autem Euclio, quod Megadōrus uir dīues est. perspicuum est. Megadōrus thēsaurum Eucliōnis uult. nōn dubium est.   5 Euclio in aedīs it, uidet aurum, saluum est. ex aedibus igitur exit. Megadōrus fīliam Eucliōnis uxōrem poscit. fīliam prōmittit Euclio, sed sine dōte. pauper enim est. dōtem igitur habet nūllam. Megadōrus dōtem uult nūllam. bonus est et dīues satis. nūptiae hodiē sunt. coquum igitur uocat Megadōrus in aedīs. timet autem Staphyla, quod Phaedra ē   10 Lycōnidē grauida est. Megadōrus uxōrem domum dūcit grauidam. malum est.

English–Latin

Translate the Latin sentences into English. Then translate the English sentences into Latin, using the pattern of the Latin ones to help you arrange the word-order correctly.

- (a) irrīdēsne mē, homo malus uirum optimum?
  Is he, a rich man, pouring scorn on Euclio, a poor man?
- (b) malum est. Megadōrus enim fīliam Eucliōnis uxōrem facit.
  There's no doubt. The old man considers the girl his daughter.
- (c) redīte ad Larem, seruī! corōnās ferte multās!
  Go into the house, slave-woman. Bring your burdens.
- (d) quid cōnsilī est? Megadōrusne dōtem uult? malum est.
  What's up? Do you want money? There's no doubt (of that).
- (e) quō abīs? īsne in aedīs? nūptiāsne parās hodiē? optimum est.
  What do they want? Are they going home? Are they carrying loads? They're good lads.
- (f) bonum habē animum, Megadōre. nam cōnsilium bonum est.
  Cheer up, master. The deed's a very good one.

Deliciae Latinae

Word-building

trāns means 'across'. Sometimes it appears as *trā-*, e.g. *trādō* 'I hand over', 'I hand across (the ages)' – whence 'tradition'.

prō means 'in front of', 'on behalf of', 'for'.

Learn three important stems:

> *mittō* has another stem *miss-* (thus *prō + mittō* 'send ahead', 'send in advance' gives 'promise')
>
> *faciō* has another stem *fact-*. When *faciō* has a prefix, it becomes *-ficiō*, stem *fect-*, e.g. *prae + faciō* becomes *praeficiō*, stem *praefect-*. Add *-ant/-ent* to your list of suffixes, e.g. efficient
>
> *ferō* has another stem *lāt-*

Exercise

Using the pool of prefixes and suffixes you have built up so far (pp. 32, 43), construct English words from the stems of mittō *(miss-),* faciō *(fact-),* ferō *(lāt-) and* dūcō *(duct-). Say how the English word gets its meaning. The final list should be on the long side.*

Word exercise

1 *Give the meaning and Latin connection of these English words*: nuptial, animate, hominid (-id = '*son of*'), voluntary, onus, fact.
2 *Observe how fruitful the* fer- *stem is in English. Give the meanings of*: igniferous, auriferous.
3 *What sort of people are those who are asinine and bovine?*
4 *Note that* ae- *in Latin becomes* e- *in mediaeval Latin and so, often, in English, e.g.* aequus – '*equal*'.

Everyday Latin

Cf. = *cōnfer* 'compare!' (*cum + ferō* 'bring together').

A 'recipe' in English is an imperative – *recipe!* 'take!', from *recipiō*. This is a useful way of remembering 3/4 imperatives.

A common neuter noun in *-us* in Latin is *corpus*. Remember it is neuter, with stem *corpor-*, through *mēns sāna in corpore sānō* 'a healthy mind in a healthy body' (Juvenal, Roman satirist, telling us what all men should pray for). Cf. corporeal, incorporate, corporation. Equally helpful may be the tag *habeās corpus* 'you may have the body'.

Real Latin

Martial

Tongiliānus habet nāsum: scio, nōn nego. sed iam
nīl praeter nāsum Tongiliānus habet. (*12.88*)

Tongilian-us ī 2m.	(*habeō nāsum* means 'I	*nego* 1 I deny
Tongilianus (based on	am critical' – lit. 'I	*iam* now
tongeō 2 'I know')	have a nose')	*nīl* nothing
nās-us ī 2m. discernment	*scio* I know	*praeter* + acc. except

nōn cēnat sine aprō noster, ⌐Tite, ⌐Caeciliānus.
bellum conuīuam Caeciliānus habet.[1] (*7.59*)

[1] See p. xii for an explanation of the linking devices used here.

cēnō 1 I dine	*Tite* = O Titus	*conuīu-a ae* 1m. guest,
sine + abl. without	*Caecilian-us ī* 2m.	table-companion
aper apr-ī 2m. wild boar	Caecilianus	
noster nostr-a um our	*bell-us a um* handsome	

NB.   Boar was a dish usually cooked for a party; Caecilianus ate it when dining alone.

Vulgate

saluum mē fac, domine (*Psalm 59*)
pater, sī uīs, trānsfer calicem istum ā mē. (*Luke 22.42*)

calicem istum this cup

Ordinary of the Mass

laudāmus tē, benedīcimus tē, adōrāmus tē, glōrificāmus tē, grātiās
agimus tibi propter magnam glōriam tuam: Domine Deus, rēx caelestis,
Deus pater omnipotēns.

laudō 1 I praise ('laud')	*glōrificō* 1 I glorify	*rēx* king
benedīcō 3 I bless	*grātiās agō* 3 I give thanks	*caelestis* in heaven
adōrō 1 I worship	*tibi* to you	*omnipotēns* all-powerful
(*ad* + *ōrō*)	*propter* (+ acc.) for the	
	sake of	

Section 1F

Running vocabulary for 1F

āmittere to lose
āmittō 3 I lose
anim-a ae 1f. breath
apud (+ acc.) at the home of
arāne-a ae 1f. cobweb
argente-us a um silver
ārid-us a um dry
attatae aaaargh!
auār-us a um greedy
audācēs (nom. pl.) ⎫ cocky,
audācīs (acc. pl.) ⎬ out-
audāx (nom. s.) ⎭ rageous
auferre to take away
auferō I take away
auid-us a um greedy
aut or
caput head, fount, source
cēn-a ae 1f. dinner
cīuis cīu-is 3m.f. citizen
cognōuistisne do you (pl.) know?
colligō 3 I collect
comprehendō 3 I seize
coquere to cook
coquō 3 I cook
culter cultr-ī 2m. knife
dē (+ abl.) from
difficile difficult
domō from the house
dormīre to sleep
dormiō 4 I sleep
dūcere to lead (in marriage)
dum while
dux duc-is 3m. leader

ergō so
facere to make, do
facile easy
follis foll-is 3m. bag
forās outside
fugiō 3/4 I flee
fūm-us ī 2m. smoke
hāc this
hercle by Hercules!
immortālēs immortal
impōnō 3 I place
ināni-a ae 1f. emptiness
ingēns (nom.) ⎫
ingentem (acc.) ⎬ s. ⎫ huge,
ingentēs (nom.) ⎫ ⎬ large,
ingentia (nom., ⎬ pl. ⎭ massive
acc.) ⎪
ingentīs (acc.) ⎭
inīre to enter
intrō inside
inuenīre to find
īre to go
istīc there
lapis lapid-is 3m. stone
lauō 1 I wash
manibus (abl.) hands
mēcum with me
mendāx (nom.) liar
mittō 3 I send
negōtium habēre to do business
nihil ⎫
nīl ⎬ nothing
nisi unless
nōs (nom., acc.) we, us
omne (nom., acc. s.) all

omnēs (nom. pl.), *omnīs* (acc. pl.) all
omnia (nom., acc. pl. n.) all, all things
opus oper-is 3n. work, job
ōs ōr-is 3n. mouth
pauper-tās paupertāt-is 3f. poverty
periit (it) has disappeared
portābō I will carry
praesegmin-a 3 (n. pl.) nail-clippings
praetor praetōr-is 3m. praetor (state official who tried criminal cases)
profundere to pour away
quid negōtī what (of) business?
sī quid 'if . . . anything' (obj.)
sciō 4 I know
scīre to know
stult-us a um stupid
tēcum with you
tōnsor tōnsōr-is 3m. barber
trīstis sad
turb-a ae 1f. crowd, mob; disturbance
ubi when
uās-um ī 2n. pot, vase
uerberāre to flog
uestis uest-is 3f. clothes
uester uestr-a um your(s)
uexō 1 annoy
ui-a ae 1f. road, way
uōs (nom., acc.) you (pl.)

Learning vocabulary for 1F

Nouns

cēn-a ae 1f. dinner
turb-a ae 1f. crowd, mob
cīuis cīu-is 3m. f. citizen

nihil (nīl) (indecl.)
nothing

Verbs

āmitt-ō 3 *āmīs- āmiss-*
I lose
aufer-ō auferre 3 *abstul-*
ablāt- I take away
coqu-ō 3 I cook
mitt-ō 3 *mīs- miss-* I send

dormi-ō 4 I sleep
inueni-ō inuenīre 4 I find
sci-ō 4 I know
fugi-ō 3/4 I escape, run
off, flee
habe-ō negōtium I conduct

business
ine-ō inīre I enter, go in

Others

apud + acc. at the house
of, in the hands of, in
the works of

aut or
quid negōtī? what (of)
business, problem,

trouble?
ubi when? (where (at)?)

New forms: adjectives

audāx audāc-is brave,
bold, resolute
facil-is e easy

ingēns ingent-is huge,
large, lavish
omn-is e all, every;
omnia everything

trīst-is e sad, gloomy,
unhappy

Grammar and exercises for 1F

---

41 Present infinitive active 'to —' (= second principal part): all conjugations

1	2	3	4	3/4
'to love'	*'to have'*	*'to say'*	*'to hear'*	*'to capture'*
amā-re	habē-re	dīc-e-re	audī-re	cáp-e-re

Notes

1 The infinitive commonly means 'to —', e.g. *amāre* 'to love'. It is, in fact, an indeclinable NOUN based on a verb (derivation = *in* 'no', *fīnis* 'ending'). Consider how 'I like *a run*' ('run', noun, object) means virtually the same as 'I like *to run*' ('to run' noun, object).

2 Note the long vowel in conjs. 1, 2 and 4, and the loss of *-i-* in the 3rd/ 4th conj. infinitive.

3 The infinitive is known as the second principal part (the first principal part being the dictionary form, i.e. *amō, habeō, dīcō, audiō, capiō*). At the moment it is important to learn because, in conjunction with the first principal part, it tells you infallibly what conjugation the verb is. Thus:

1st p.p.	2nd p.p.	
-ō	-āre	= 1st conj.
-eō	-ēre	= 2nd conj.
-ō	-ere	= 3rd conj.
-iō	-īre	= 4th conj.
-iō	-ere	= 3rd/4th conj.

42 Irregular infinitives: *sum, eō, uolō, ferō*

Learn the following irregular infinitives:

> *sum* – *és-se* 'to be'
> *eō* – *í-re* 'to go'
> *uolō* – *uél-le* 'to wish'
> *ferō* – *fér-re* 'to bear'

Exercise

Give the infinitive of these verbs and translate: habeō, explicō, cēlō, inueniō, maneō, redeō, dūcō, dīcō, poscō, stō, rogō, fugiō, āmittō, auferō, faciō, sum, (*optional*: uerberō, coquō, dormiō, seruō, uolō).

43 Personal pronouns: *ego, nōs; tū, uōs*

nom.	égo	'I'	nōs	'we'	tū	'you'	uōs	'you'
acc.	mē		nōs		tē		uōs	
gen.	méī		nóstrum ⎱		túī		uéstrum ⎱	
			nóstrī ⎰				uéstrī ⎰	
dat.	míhi (mī)		nóbīs		tíbi		uóbīs	
abl.	mē		nóbīs		tē		uóbīs	

Notes
1 You have already met the s. forms *ego, tū*. Here are their plurals, *nōs, uōs*. Note the gen. pl. forms.

2 *nostrum, uestrum* are the so-called 'partitive' genitives (**31**), e.g. *multī nostrum* 'many of us'. *nostrī, uestrī* are 'objective' genitives (see **22³**), e.g. *memor nostrī* 'mindful of us'.

44 3rd decl. adjectives: *omn-is e* 'all', 'every'

	s.		pl.	
	m./f.	*n.*	*m./f.*	*n.*
nom.	ómni-s	ómn-e	ómn-ēs	ómn-ia
acc.	ómn-em	ómn-e	ómn-īs (omn-ēs)	ómn-ia
gen.	←ómn-is→		←ómn-ium→	
dat.	←ómn-ī→		←ómn-ibus→	
abl.	←ómn-ī→		←ómn-ibus→	

Notes

1 Just as with 2nd decl. adjectives like *mult-us a um*, 3rd decl. adjectives must agree in *gender, number and case* with the nouns they describe (**14**).

2 M. and f. forms are the same as each other in s. and pl. – a useful saving of labour for the learner.

3 Generally, 3rd declension adjectives are *-i-* stems (cf. **12**) and have:

abl. s. in *-ī*, acc. pl. in *-īs*, n. pl. in *-ia*, gen. pl. in *-ium*

Contrast 3rd declension consonant-stem *nouns*, which have:

abl. s. in *-e*, acc. pl. in *-ēs*, n. pl. in *-a*, gen. pl. in *-um*

4 Similar to *omnis: trīst-is e* 'sad'; *facil-is e* 'easy'; *difficil-is e* 'difficult'.

45 3rd decl. adjectives: *ingēns ingēns* (*ingent-*) 'huge'

	s.		pl.	
	m./f.	*n.*	*m./f.*	*n.*
nom.	íngēns	íngēns	ingént-ēs	ingént-ia
acc.	ingént-em	íngēns	ingént-īs (ingént-ēs)	ingént-ia
gen.	←ingént-is→		←ingént-ium→	
dat.	←ingént-ī→		←ingént-ibus→	
abl.	←ingént-ī→		←ingént-ibus→	

NB.   Observe the stem change of this common type of adjective in *-ēns* and note that its n. s. form is the same as the m./f. form in the nom. Otherwise, its endings are identical to those of *omnis*.

46 **3rd decl. adjectives: *audāx audāx (audāc-)* 'bold', 'courageous'**

	s.		*pl.*	
	m./f.	*n.*	*m./f.*	*n.*
nom.	aúdāx	aúdāx	audāc-ēs	audāc-ia
acc.	audāc-em	aúdāx	audāc-īs (audāc-ēs)	audāc-ia
gen.	←audāc-is→		←audāc-ium→	
dat.	←audāc-ī→		←audāc-ibus→	
abl.	←audāc-ī→		←audāc-ibus→	

NB.   This very common 3rd decl. adjective type ends in -*x* in the nom.,
and has its stem in -*c*-. *audāx* follows the pattern of *ingēns* in the
relationship between the nom. s. m. and n. forms. Other endings
identical with *omnis, ingēns*.

Exercise

1 *Decline in full*: puer audāx; omnis aqua; ingēns perīculum.

2 *Construct a grid consisting of 7 columns with headings as follows*:

NOUN   CASE   NUMBER   GENDER   omnis   ingēns   audāx

Under the heading NOUN *write the following list of nouns down the column*:
seruae, thēsaurī, oculōs, dominus, nōminibus, cōnsilium, cēnā,
turbārum, cīuī, pecūniās, puellā, perīculō, ignis, animīs.

*Leave plenty of space between each noun. In the next three columns, define
exactly the case, number and gender of each of the nouns. In the last three columns
make* omnis, ingēns *and* audāx *agree with the noun. Where the form of the
noun indicates different possible cases, write down all the possibilities. E.g.*:

NOUN	CASE	NUMBER	GENDER	omnis	ingēns	audāx
fīliae	gen.	s.	f.	omnis	ingentis	audācis
	dat.	s.	f.	omnī	ingentī	audācī
	nom.	pl.	f.	omnēs	ingentēs	audācēs

3 *Determine which of the nouns is in agreement with the given adjective (the
answer may be one or more than one)*:

>   ingentem − nōminum, cōnsilium, deum, seruārum
>   audāx − puellā, cōnsilium, homo, dominus, ingenia
>   omnium − oculum, coquōrum, perīculum, honōrem

trīstēs − animōs, dominī, fīliae, familiam, aedīs
facilia − aqua, serua, puella, familia, scelera
difficilī − coquō, frāter, sorōris, dominus, fīliā, turba, exitiō

47   *dīues dīuit-is* **'wealthy', 'a wealthy man';** *pauper pauper-is*
'poor', 'a poor man'

	s.		*pl.*	
	m./f.	*n.*	*m./f.*	*n.*
nom.	dīues	dīues	dīuit-ēs	dīuit-a
acc.	dīuit-em	dīues	dīuit-ēs	dīuit-a
gen.	←dīuit-is→		←dīuit-um→	
dat.	←dīuit-ī→		←dīuít-ibus→	
abl.	←dīuit-e→		←dīuít-ibus→	

	s.		*pl.*	
	m./f.	*n.*	*m./f.*	*n.*
nom.	paúper	paúper	paúper-ēs	paúper-a
acc.	paúper-em	paúper	paúper-ēs	paúper-a
gen.	←paúper-is→		←paúper-um→	
dat.	←paúper-ī→		←paupér-ibus→	
abl.	←paúpere→		←paupér-ibus→	

When used to describe a noun, these two adjectives mean 'wealthy' or
'poor'. But they can be used *on their own*, when they act as *nouns*, and
mean 'a wealthy person', 'a poor person', e.g. *Eucliō dīuitēs amat* 'Euclio
adores the rich/rich people' (noun); but *Eucliō homo pauper est* 'Euclio is a
poor man' (adjective).

   The same principle applies to all adjectives in Latin. When used on
their own, they can stand as nouns. In such circumstances, it is very
important to pay close attention to the *gender* of the adjective, e.g. *multī*
(pl.) on its own would mean 'many men'; *multae* 'many women'; *multa*
'many things'. *omnēs* could mean 'all men' or 'all women'; but *omnia*
would mean 'all things', 'everything'.

NB.   These are consonant-stem adjectives. Contrast *omnis, ingēns,*
audāx **44–6**.

Exercises

1 *Translate into English:*

(a) cēnam igitur ingentem coquus audāx coquere uult.
(b) quārē omnia coquōrum nōmina scīre uīs?
(c) cōnsilium autem audāx in animō habēs.
(d) ubi in aedīs intrāre uultis, statim nōs uocāte.
(e) scelera audācia omnis pauper facere uult.
(f) turba hominum audācium ingēns ad aedīs Megadōrī adit.

2 *Translate into English:*

(a) multae neque dormiunt neque cēnam coquunt.
(b) bona aufert.
(c) omnia scīre uultis.
(d) pulchrī pulchrās amant.
(e) omnēs pecūniam habēre uolunt.
(f) multī fugiunt, multī autem stant.
(g) pauperem dīues nōn amat.
(h) omnēs bonī cīuīs cūrant.
(i) malī mala cōgitant.
(j) pecūnia omnīs uexat.

3 *Translate these sentences:*

(a) aeuum omne et breue et fragile est. (*Pliny*)
(b) senectūs īnsānābilis morbus est. (*Seneca*)
(c) īra furor breuis est. (*Horace*)
(d) ratiōnāle animal est homo. (*Seneca*)
(e) facilis est ad beātam uītam uia. (*Seneca*)
(f) difficile est saturam nōn scrībere. (*Juvenal*)
(g) difficile est longum subitō dēpōnere amōrem. (*Catullus*)
(h) nātūram quidem mūtāre difficile est. (*Seneca*)
(i)   uarium et mūtābile semper
     fēmina (*Virgil*)
(j) turpe senex mīles, turpe senīlis amor. (*Ovid*)

aeu-um ī 2n. age	*morb-us* ī 2m. disease	*animal animāl-is* 3n.
breu-is e short	*īr-a ae* 1f. anger	animal
fragil-is e brittle, frail	*furor furōr-is* 3m. madness	*beāt-us a um* happy,
senectūs senectūt-is 3f. old	*ratiōnāl-is* e possessing	blessed
age	reason	*uīt-a ae* 1f. life
īnsānābil-is e incurable		

ui-a ae 1f. road, way	*subitō* suddenly	*mūtō* 1 I change, alter
difficil-is e difficult	*dēpōnō* 3 I lay aside	*uari-us a um* variable
satur-a ae 1f. satire	*amor amōr-is* 3m. love	*mūtābil-is e* changeable
scrībō 3 I write	*nātūr-a ae* 1f. nature	*turp-is e* disgraceful
long-us a um long, long lasting	*quidem* indeed (emphasises preceding word)	*mīles mīlit-is* 3m. soldier *senīl-is e* in an old man

Reading exercises

1 *Analyse these examples, in the order of the words, determining subject, object, verb, infinitive.*

   (a)   The intellect of man is forced to choose
         Perfection of the life, or of the work. (*Yeats*)
   (b)   To err is human, to forgive divine. (*Pope*)
   (c)   And that same prayer doth teach us all to render
         The deeds of mercy. (*Shakespeare*)
   (d)   We'll teach you to drink deep. (*Shakespeare*)
   (e)   To make dictionaries is dull work. (*Johnson*)
   (f)   Love looks not with the eyes but with the mind,
         And therefore is wing'd Cupid painted blind. (*Shakespeare*)

2 *Say, as you translate in the order of the words, what the functions of the words and the word-groups are in these incomplete sentences. Complete them (with part of uolō) and translate into correct English. Then read them aloud, phrasing them correctly.*

   (a)   ubi pauper cēnam ingentem habēre . . .?
   (b)   quō tū inīre . . .?
   (c)   cūrās dīuitis ferre omnis pauper . . .
   (d)   amāre puellās pulchrās et aurum dominī auferre nōs seruī . . .
   (e)   facile ferre onus cīuēs omnēs . . .
   (f)   uōs apud Eucliōnem cēnam coquere numquam . . .

Reading exercise / Test exercise

Read this passage, translating in word-order, defining the function of each word and anticipating the construction. Translate into correct English. Then read the passage aloud in Latin, phrasing correctly, thinking through the meaning as you read. Use the running vocabulary of **1F**.

Megadōrus nūptiās facere uult. coquōs igitur uocat multōs ad aedīs. coquōrum opus est cēnam coquere ingentem. uxōrem domum dūcit

74

Megadōrus Phaedram, Eucliōnis fīliam. sed coquī Eucliōnem uirum pauperem habent et trīstem. nam nīl āmittere uult. follem enim ingentem, ubi dormīre uult, in ōs impōnit. ita animam, dum dormit, nōn 5 āmittit. apud tōnsōrem praesegmina, quod nihil uult āmittere, colligit omnia et domum dūcit. aquam dare nōn uult. ignem dare, quod āmittere timet, nōn uult. uir trīstis est. coquī igitur in aedīs inīre Megadōrī, uirī dīuitis et facilis, uolunt. perīculum autem in aedibus Megadōrī multum est, uāsa argentea ingentia, uestēs multae, multum aurum. sī quid seruī 10 āmittunt, coquōs fūrēs putant (*think*) et comprehendere uolunt. apud Eucliōnem autem coquī saluī sunt. uāsa argentea ex aedibus auferre Eucliōnis facile nōn est, quod uāsa nūlla habet!

English–Latin

Translate the Latin sentences into English. Then translate the English sentences into Latin, using the pattern of the Latin ones to help you arrange the word-order correctly.

(a) quārē in aedīs Megadōrī, uirī dīuitis, onus ferre uultis?
    Do you want to cook dinner in a poor man's, Euclio's, house?
(b) cīuēs omnēs ē perīculō exīre uolunt.
    Resolute slaves want to escape from the house.
(c) ingentem enim āmittere pecūniam quis uult?
    What woman doesn't want to find a bold slave?
(d) dīuitēs ubi nūptiās faciunt, coquōs in aedīs uocant.
    When they want a large dinner, masters ask for a good cook.
(e) omnēs coquī cultrōs portant ingentīs.
    A beautiful woman draws (*ferō*) a big crowd.
(f) apud tamen pauperem cēna trīstis est.
    At a rich man's house dinners are excellent.

Deliciae Latinae

Word-building

ā/ab appears as *au* as a prefix to *ferō*, i.e. *auferō* 'I take away'.
  in means 'into', 'upon' in *inueniō* 'I come upon', 'I find'.
  Observe the interesting combination of elements in *negōtium* 'business'. The word is built up of *nec(g)-* 'not' + *ōtium* 'leisure'.

Word exercises

1 *Give the meaning and Latin connection of:* civilised, nihilistic, cook, dormitory, fugitive, negotiate, initial, invention, science, emit.
2 *Give English words from the Latin:* facilis, audāx, omnis (*dat. pl.*), āridus, lapis (*NB stem*), tōnsor.

Real Latin

Sayings of Cato
quod (*an amount which*) satis est dormī.
āleam (*gambling*) fuge.
meretrīcem (*whore*) fuge.

Vulgate
beātī pauperēs quia uestrum est rēgnum deī. (*Luke 6.20*)

beātus blessed	*uestrum* yours	*rēgnum* kingdom
beatī pauperēs insert *sunt*		

Giovanni Cotta (1480–1510)[1]
amō, quod fateor, meam Lycōrim,
ut pulchrās iuvenēs amant puellās;
amat mē mea, quod reor, Lycōris,
ut bonae iuvenēs amant puellae.

quod fateor 'as I admit'	*iuuenis iuuen-is* 3m. young	*quod reor* 'as I think'
Lycōrim = acc. s. of	man	
Lycoris		

[1] Latin was the language of scholarship and international communication throughout the Renaissance (fifteenth and sixteenth centuries) and was still felt by and large to be the proper medium for literature also. These are the first four lines of a poem in which the poet's girl gives him some locks of her hair as a love-pledge. The poet burns them, since they have, he claims, 'burned' him – with love!

Mottoes[1]
fac rēctē et nīl timē. (*Hill*)
ā deō et patre. (*Thomas*)
amat uictōria cūram. (*Clark*)

rēctē rightly	*ā* on the side of	*uictōria* victory

[1] These mottoes originate in mediaeval times or later. Many families have several.

Word study

uestis means 'clothes' (*uestiō* 'I dress'), so English 'vest'. *uestiārium* 'dressing room' emerges in English as 'vestry'. *inuestīre* 'to put clothes on', 'surround' gives 'investiture' and 'invest' (clothing one's money with yet more?). *trāns* 'across' + *uest-* yields 'transvestite', one who crosses over to the clothes of the opposite sex, or simply one who disguises himself: hence 'travesty'. *dī-* (indicating separation) + *uest-* gives 'divest', 'take clothes off'.

Do not confuse with 'vestige', from *uestīgium* 'footprint', 'trace': hence e.g. 'investigate', which means 'following on someone's tracks'.

Section 1G

Running vocabulary for 1G

age! come!
alter alter-a um one or other (of two)
amb-ō ae ō both
amor amōr-is 3m. love
an or
animō aequō in a calm frame of mind, i.e. cool, collected
animō bonō in a cheerful frame of mind, i.e. cheerful
ante (+ acc.) before
auferō 3 I take x (acc.) away from y (dat.)
caec-us a um blind
certē without doubt
certō for a fact
crēdō 3 I believe x (dat.); entrust x (acc.) to y (dat.)
culp-a ae 1f. blame, guilt
cum (+ abl.) with

currō 3 I run
custōdiō 4 I guard
custōs custōd-is 3m.f. guard
dē (+ abl.) about, concerning
dextr-a ae 1f. right (hand)
domō (from) home
ēbriō (to) a drunkard
ecce look!
edepol by Pollux!
em here you are! there!
es! be! (s.)
esse to be
etiam still
fānō (to) the shrine
fān-um ī 2n. shrine
fateor I confess
Fidēs Faith
forās outside
heus hey!
hominī (from) the man
id quod that which
ignōscō 3 (+ dat.) I pardon

immō more precisely
immortāl-is e immortal
impudēns impudent, shameless (one)
inrēpō 3 I creep
īnsān-us a um mad
inueniō 4 I find
iuuenis iuuen-is 3m. youth
laeu-a ae 1f. left (hand)
licet it is permitted to (+ dat.)
loc-us ī 2m. place, site
lumbrīc-us ī 2m. worm
manum (acc.) hand
mēcum with me
melius better
mihi to/for me; from me
miserō (dat.) miserable
nesciō 4 I do not know
nisi except
noster nostr-a um our
nūllā continentiā of no self-restraint

ostendō 3 I show
perdō 3 I lose, destroy
plāg-a ae 1f. blow; *plāgās*
  dō (+ dat.) I beat
plōrō 1 I weep
prōferō 3 I show, hold out
prohibeō 2 I prevent, stop
propter (+ acc.) on
  account of
quiduīs whatever he likes
quod what, that which;
  which
reddō 3 I give back

referō 3 I hand back
rūrsum again
sit-us a um placed
spectātōribus (dat. pl.) to
  the audience
summā audāciā of great
  boldness
summā pulchritūdine of
  great beauty
summā uirtūte of great
  uprightness
tangō 3 I touch, lay hands
  on

terti-us a um third (hand)
tibi to/for you; from you
trifūr triple thief
tuō (dat.) your
uae shame on!
uerb-um ī 2n. word
uerberābilissim-us most
  floggable
uēr-us a um true
uīl-is e cheap
uīn-um ī 2n. wine

Learning vocabulary for 1G

Nouns

audāci-a ae 1f. boldness,
  cockiness
continenti-a ae 1f. self-
  control, restraint

fān-um ī 2n. shrine
iuuenis iuuen-is is 3m.
  young man

uirtūs uirtūt-is 3f.
  manliness, courage,
  goodness

Adjectives

aequ-us a um fair,
  balanced, equal

summ-us a um highest, top
  of

Verbs

age! come!
crēdō 3 *crēdid- crēdit-*
  I believe (+ dat.);
  I entrust x (acc.) to y
  (dat.)

ostendō 3 I show, reveal
reddō 3 *reddid- reddit-*
  I return, give back

tangō 3 *tetig- tāct-* I touch,
  lay hands on

Others

certē without doubt

certō for a fact

Grammar and exercises for 1G

---

48 The dative case: usage and meaning

1 The dative is in one sense only the 'giving' case (the word derives from
dō datus 'I give'). That is, if I give something *to* a person, the person who

receives it is in the dative case, e.g. *mihi aulam dat* 'he gives me the pot /
the pot to me'. But equally, it is the 'losing' case too, since if I take
something *from* a person, the person goes into the dative case, e.g.
hominī aulam auferō 'I take the pot from the man'. So one can say that
the dative is the case defining the gainer or the loser, the one *advantaged*
or *disadvantaged*.

2 Another 'advantage' sense is that of possession, expressed by
sum + dative, e.g. *est mihi pecūnia* 'there is money to me', 'I have
money'.

3 Another common usage of the dative is to denote the person spoken to
(also, in some sense, a gainer – a gainer of the words you have spoken),
e.g. *fēminae dīcit multa* 'he says many things to the woman'.

'To' (i.e. 'to the advantage of') and 'from' (i.e. 'to the disadvantage
of') (and sometimes 'for') will translate the dative best for the time
being. But you should note that the usages and meanings of the dative
are very wide, and that when they are all gathered together the
common idea behind them all seems to be that the person in the dative
is somehow *involved or interested* in *the action of the verb*: that action has
some consequences for the person, sometimes specific, sometimes
quite vague. So when you come across a dative, ask first 'how is the
person in the dative case affected by the verb?'

Distinguish between 'to' and 'from' indicating primarily *motion*
(when Latin uses *ad, ex, ab*) and the dative usages (indicating gain or
loss) outlined above.

Exercises

1 *Form the dative s. and pl. of these noun + adjective phrases:* senex miser;
puella audāx; puer ingēns; onus multum; cōnsilium audāx; (*optional:*
soror optima; nōmen meum; culter tuus; seruus omnis).

2 *Pick out the datives in this list:* cūram, animō, fāna, uirtūtī, audāciae,
hominis, animōs, dīuitibus, uxor, onerī, pecūniam, fīliīs, aquae,
dominō, ignibus, uīcīnum, dīs, honōrēs, fēminīs, corōnae, cōnsiliō.

3 *Give the Latin for:* to the huge slaves; for me; to the unhappy old man's
disadvantage; to the wicked wives; for us; belonging to you (s.);
(*optional:* to the advantage of the best citizen; belonging to the bold
slave-girl; to the good father's disadvantage; for every boy).

4 *Translate these sentences:*

(a) deinde Lar familiae aulam Eucliōnī dat aurī plēnam.
(b) senex miser tamen aurum omne fānō crēdit.
(c) sed seruus audāx senī miserō aurum auferre uult.
(d) Eucliō autem ita seruō clāmat malō; 'quid tibi negōtī est in fānō? quid mihi aufers?'
(e) seruus igitur timet et Eucliōnī aurum nōn aufert.
(f) Eucliō autem ā fānō aulam aufert, quod nunc deō aurum crēdere nōn uult.

49 The ablative of description

The ablative is used to *describe the qualities* people or things have which enable them to act as they do. This is the ablative of description, e.g. *uir summā uirtūte* 'a man with/of great courage', *iuuenis nūllā continentiā* 'a young man with/of no self-control'. Translate such ablatives as 'with' first time round, then adjust to produce a smooth English version.

Exercises

1 *Form the ablative s. and pl. of these noun + adjective phrases*: senex miser; puella audāx; puer ingēns; onus multum; cōnsilium audāx; (*optional*: soror optima; nōmen meum; culter tuus; seruus omnis).

2 *Pick out the ablatives in this list*: curā, animō, fānum, uirtūtis, audāciīs, homine, animī, dīuitī, uxōre, pecūniā, fīliīs, aquam, dominō, ignibus, uīcīnōs, deus, honōribus, fēminā, corōnīs, cōnsiliō, scelere.

3 *Give the Latin for*: in the shrine; away from the woman; out of the waters; in a crime; out of the mind; in the plans; out of the fires; (*optional*: away from worry; out of the pots; in the household; away from a brother; out of the names).

4 *Translate these sentences*:

(a) Eucliō uir est summā continentiā.
(b) Lycōnidēs iuuenis summā pulchritūdine est, nūllā continentiā.
(c) animō aequō es, mī fīlī.
(d) tū serua es summā audāciā, summā pulchritūdine, continentiā nūllā.
(e) animō bonō sum, quod fīliam meam summā uirtūte puellam habeō.

5 *Translate these sentences:*

(a) fortīs fortūna iuuat. (*Terence*)
(b) nēmo est in amōre fidēlis. (*Propertius*)
(c) omnis ars nātūrae imitātiō est. (*Seneca*)
(d) patet omnibus uēritās. (*Seneca*)
(e) omnī aetātī mors est commūnis. (*Cicero*)
(f) magna dī cūrant, parua neglegunt. (*Cicero*)
(g) Britannī capillō sunt prōmissō atque omnī parte corporis rāsā praeter caput et labrum superius. (*Caesar*)

fort-is e brave	*uēritās uēritāt-is* 3f. truth	*capill-us ī* 2m. hair
fortūn-a ae 1f. fortune	*aetās aetāt-is* 3f. age	*prōmiss-us a um* long
iuuō 1 I help	*mors mort-is* 3f. death	*atque* and
nēmo (nom.) no one	*commūn-is e* common (to: + dat.)	*pars part-is* 3f. part
amor amōr-is 3m. love	*paru-us a um* small	*corpus corpor-is* 3n. body
fidēl-is e faithful	*neglegō* 3 I neglect, do not bother with	*rās-us a um* shaved
ars art-is 3f. art	*Britann-ī ōrum* 2m. pl. Britons	*praeter* (+acc.) except
nātūr-a ae 1f. nature		*caput capit-is* 3n. head
imitātiō imitātiōn-is 3f. imitation		*labr-um ī* 2n. lip
pateō 2 I lie open		*superius* upper (n. s.)

Reading exercises

1 *Read through these sentences carefully. As you translate, in the order of the words, define the function of each word (making certain that you phrase the words correctly). When you meet a dative, if you have not yet had any clue to help define its function closely (e.g. a verb like* crēdō, reddō*), register dative as 'affecting* x' *and proceed until the precise meaning emerges, e.g.:*

crēdō (*I entrust – you expect an object + a dative*) tibi (*dative – to you, solved by* crēdō) aurum (*object – the gold, already anticipated*) aurum (*gold – subject or object*) tibi (*dative – with some effect on you; not solved yet – we expect a verb*) auferō ('*I take away*' – aurum *object,* tibi '*from you*', *solved by construction of* auferō).

(a) senī miserō seruus audāx multa dīcit mala.
(b) unguentum et corōnās et aurum mihi ostende.
(c) uxōrī meae domī nimis cūrārum est.
(d) quārē tū mihi meum aurum nōn reddis?
(e) ego tibi, quod uīcīnus es bonus, meam fīliam prōmittō.
(f) uxōrēs pulchrae dīuitibus, quod coquīs pecūniam multam dare uolunt, aurum semper auferunt.

(g) tibi multōs seruōs pecūniamque multam dō.

(h) seruō audācī et seruae pulchrae nihil umquam crēdō.

(i) uirō dīuitī, quod mihi dōs nūlla est, fīliam meam prōmittere uolō.

(j) nōbīs corōna, unguentum uōbīs domī est.

2 *In these sentences, the verb has been omitted. By doing as in the previous exercise, say what you anticipate. Then fill the gap (it may often be possible to insert verbs which alter the function of the dative completely). Translate.*

(a) hominibus bonīs cīuēs omnēs pecūniam . . .

(b) quārē mihi aurum . . .?

(c) nōbīs animus bonus . . .

(d) fānō, nōn hominī audācī, Eucliō aurum . . .

(e) tū nōbīs quārē corōnās omnīs et omne unguentum . . .?

(f) puellīs audācibus et iuuenibus pulchrīs nūlla continentia . . .

(g) ego fīliae meae dōtem ā uirō . . .

(h) quārē pater tuus mihi tē uxōrem nōn . . .?

(i) scelus, quid tibi negōtī in aedibus meīs . . .?

(j) omnī bonō iuuenī uirtūtem audācia . . .

Reading exercise / Test exercise

Read the following passage carefully, defining, as you translate, in word-order, the functions of the words and word-groups, and anticipating the following parts of the sentence. When you have done this, translate. Finally, read out the passage, phrasing correctly, thinking through the meaning as you read. Use the running vocabulary of 1G.

est Eucliōnī aula aurī plēna. Eucliō aulam ex aedibus portat. timet enim ualdē. omnibus enim bonīs fūrēs omne aurum auferre semper uolunt. uult igitur in fānō aulam cēlāre. ubi aurum in fānō cēlat Eucliō, Strobīlus uidet. ē fānō exit Eucliō. bonō animō est, quod nunc fūrem timet nūllum. Strobīlus autem ut lumbrīcus in fānum inrēpit. nam aulam Eucliōnī   5
miserō auferre uult. sed seruum audācem uidet Eucliō. seruō audācī mala multa dīcit et aurum poscit. seruus autem senī aurum reddere nōn uult, quod aurum nōn habet. Eucliōnī manum dextram seruus ostendit. deinde senī miserō ostendit laeuam. Eucliō autem manum tertiam rogat. seruus Eucliōnem īnsānum habet et exit. aulam Eucliō ā fānō aufert et   10
alterī (*dat. s. m.*) locō clam crēdit.

English–Latin

Translate the Latin sentences into English. Then translate the English sentences into Latin, using the pattern of the Latin ones to help you arrange the word-order correctly.

(a)   Eucliō uir summā uirtūtē est.
      Phaedra is an extremely beautiful girl.
(b)   bonō animō es et dā mihi pecūniam.
      Be calm (*s.*) and take the gold from the slave.
(c)   senex miser hominī malō aulam aurī plēnam crēdit.
      All the old men are returning the pots full of money to the good citizens.
(d)   uōs autem quārē senī aurum nōn redditis?
      But why are you taking the young man's garland from him?
(e)   quid tibi negōtī est in aedibus senis miserī?
      What business have you (*pl.*) in the shrine of my household god?
(f)   est mihi pater optimus, uir summā continentiā.
      I've an excellent son, a young man of the highest qualities.

Deliciae Latinae

Word building

(a) Prefixes

> *sub-* (sometimes appears as *su-*, *sus-*) 'under', 'from under'
> *dē-* 'down from'
> *per-* 'through', 'thoroughly', 'very'

Exercise
Divide each of the following words into their compound parts and suggest a meaning for each: ēuocō, circumdūcō, perfacilis, trānsmittō, redeō, prōuideō, efferō, praeficiō, āmittō, reddō, subdūcō, ēdūcō, subeō, permultus, anteferō, trādō, perficiō, circumdō, dēdūcō, referō, dēuocō, summittō, perstō.

(b) Noun formation
Many nouns are formed from verbs or adjectives. This is often done by placing a suffix (*sub-fīxus* 'fixed on under', i.e. at the end) onto the verb or

83

adjective stem. This suffix frequently gives a clue to the meaning of the noun, e.g.:

> *-sor* or *-tor* (gen. s. *-ōris* m.) means 'the person who', e.g. *amātor* 'lover'
>
> *-or* (gen. s. *-ōris* m.) means 'activity', 'state' or 'condition', e.g. *amor* 'the state of loving', 'love'
>
> *-iō, -tiō, -siō* (gen. s. *-iōnis* f.) means 'action or result of an action', e.g. *cōgitātiō* 'the act of thinking', 'thought'
>
> *-ium* n. means 'action or result of an action', e.g. *aedificium* 'the result of making a house', 'a building'
>
> *-men* (gen. s. *-minis* n.) means 'means, or result of an action', e.g. *nō-men* 'means of knowing', 'name'

Exercise

1 *Give the meaning of the following nouns:* audītor, cūrātor, uexātiō, inuentiō, cōnsilium, dictiō, turbātor, prōmissiō, maleficium, beneficium, habitātiō.

2 *Form the genitive singular of:* uexātiō, dictiō, habitātiō, inuentiō, audītor, turbātor.

Real Latin

Vulgate

pānem nostrum quotīdiānum dā nōbis hodiē et dīmittē nōbis peccāta nostra (*Luke 11.3–4*)

pānis pān-is 3m. bread	*quotīdiān-us a um* daily	*dīmittō* 3 I discharge
		peccāt-um ī 2n. sin

Mottoes (based on the dative)

nōn nōbis, sed omnibus. (*Ash, Ashe*)
nōn mihi, sed deō et rēgī. (*Booth, Warren*)
nōn mihi, sed patriae. (*Heycock, Jones-Lloyd, Lloyd, Whittingham*)
deō, rēgī et patriae. (*Irvine, Duncombe*)
deō, patriae, tibi. (*Lambard, Sidley*)
glōria deō. (*Challen, Henn*)

rēx rēg-is 3m. king	*patri-a ae* 1f. fatherland	*glōri-a ae* 1f. glory

SECTION TWO

Section 2A

Running vocabulary for 2A

abībis you (s.) will go off
ac and
accipiō 3/4 I take, receive
accumbō 3 I recline, lie
   down
adferam I shall bring (in)
adferēs you (s.) will bring
   (in)
adscrībam I shall write
   alongside
adscrībō 3 I write next to,
   alongside
adseruābit (he) will keep/
   guard
adseruō 1 I keep, guard
adiuuō 1 I help
aduertō: see *animum*
agam I shall deal / take
   action
agēmus: see *grātiās*
alter (nom. s. m.) one,
   another (of two)
alteram (acc. s. f.) a
   second
alterīus (gen. s. f.) of the
   one / of the other (of
   two)
amātor amātōr-is 3m. lover
amīc-a ae 1f. mistress
amīc-us ī 2m. friend

animum aduertō 3 I pay
   attention
antīqu-us a um ancient
astūti-a ae 1f. astuteness,
   (pl.) tricks
atque and
audiēs you (s.) will hear
auferam I shall take away
auferētis you (pl.) will
   take away
Bacchis Bacchid-is 3f.
   Bacchis (worshipper of
   Bacchus, god of wine)
ballist-a ae 1f. catapult
bell-us a um lovely,
   beautiful
bene good, fine
biclīni-um ī 2n. dining-
   couch (for two
   persons)
bis twice, a second time
capiam I (shall) capture
capiēs you (s.) will take
cauēbit (he) will be wary
caueō 2 I am wary
celerem (acc. s. f.) swift
celerēs (nom. pl. f.) swift
celeris (nom. s. f.) swift
celeriter quickly
cēr-a ae 1f. wax

Chrȳsal-us ī 2m.
   Chrysalus ('goldie')
citō quickly
cognōscet (he) will
   recognise
compōnō 3 I devise, put
   together
corbis corb-is 3m. or f.
   basket
crēdet (+ dat.) he will
   believe
cum (+ abl.) with
cūrābō I shall take care of
dabis you (s.) will give
dabit he will give
dabō I shall give
dē (+ abl.) about,
   concerning
dēbeō 2 I ought
dēcipiam I shall deceive
dēcipiō 3/4 I deceive
dēlēbit it destroys (actually
   future, 'it will destroy')
dīcam I shall say
dict-um ī 2n. word
diēs (nom. s. m.) day
difficil-is e difficult
doctē cleverly
doct-us a um clever
donec until

85

ducent-ī ae a 200
dum while
ecce look!
erit (it, there, she) will be
erunt (they) will be
etiam also
etiamsī even if
euax good!
exsurgō 3 I get up
faciam I shall do
faciēmus we will run up
faciēs you (s.) will do
fallō 3 I deceive, trick
foris for-is 3f. door
grātiās agēmus we will give thanks (to x: dat.)
grauitās grauitāt-is 3f. seriousness
habēbis you (s.) will have
habēbitis you (pl.) will have
habēbō I shall have
hercle by Hercules
iam now already
immō no; more precisely
imperātor imperātōr-is 3m. general
ingeni-um ī 2n. intelligence, brain
inquit (he) says
īnspiciō 3/4 I look in
intendam I shall aim
intrō inside
inuādam I shall assault, invade (*in* + acc.)
ioc-us -ī 2m. joke
ita uērō yes, indeed
iterum again
iubēbō I shall order, give instructions
leget he (will) read
līn-um ī 2n. thread
litter-a ae 1f. letter (of alphabet)
litter-ae ārum 1f. pl. letter
loc-us ī 2m. place
lūn-a ae 1f. moon
mālō I prefer

mālumus we prefer / would rather
manum (acc. s. f.) hand
manū (abl. s. f.) hand
manus (nom. s. f.) hand
manūs (nom. or acc. pl. f.) hands
māuīs you (s.) prefer
māuultis you (pl.) prefer
mēcum with me
mendāx mendāc-is untruthful, lying
mīles mīlit-is 3m. soldier
Mnēsiloch-us ī 2m. Mnesilochus ('remembers the ambush')
modo now
Nīcobūl-us ī 2m. Nicobulus ('victorious in judgement')
nesciō 4 I do not know
nisi except
nōli (s.)
nōlite (pl.) } don't (+ inf.)
nōlō I do not want / refuse
nōn uīs you (s.) do not want / refuse
nōnne surely?
noster nostra nostrum our
nox noct-is 3f. night
numm-us ī 2m. coin
obligābō I shall tie up
obligō 1 I tie up
obsecrō 1 I beseech, beg
obsignābō I shall seal
obsignō 1 I seal
offici-um ī 2n. duty, job
oppid-um ī 2n. town
per (+ acc.) through
pergō 3 I continue, go on
Pistoclēr-us ī 2m. Pistoclerus ('trusty with property')
plān-us a um smooth
port-a ae 1f. gate
possum I am able / can

post (+ acc.) after
posteā afterwards
poterō I shall be able
poteris you (s.) will be able
potes you (s.) are able
potest (he) is able
prīmō
prīmum } first
prō (+ abl.) for
prob-us a um good, excellent
prōpugnācul-um ī 2n. rampart
quam than
quantum (+ gen.) how much?
quia because
quōmodo how?
rem (acc. s. f.)
rēs (nom. s. f., nom. or acc. pl. f.) } the matter(s), things
salūtō 1 I greet
sapienti-a ae 1f. wisdom
scrībam I shall write
scrībēs you (s.) will write
scrībō 3 I write
semel once
sīc thus
sīcut just as
sign-um ī 2n. signal
sōl sōl-is 3m. sun
spērō 1 I hope
stil-us ī 2m. stylus (writing implement for wax tablet)
stultiti-a ae 1f. stupidity
stult-us a um stupid
sūmptus (nom. s. m.) expense
sūmptūs (acc. pl. m.) expenses
su-us a um his
tabell-ae ārum 1f. pl. writing tablets
tāl-is e such

tenēbis you (s.) will hold
turris turr-is 3f. tower
  (acc. s. *turrim*)
ūsus erit it will be of
  benefit

ueniō 4 I come
uērō indeed
uēr-us a um true
uester uestra uestrum your
  (pl.)

ui-a ae 1f. way, road
uictōri-a ae 1f. victory
uinciet (he) will bind
uinciō 4 I bind

Learning vocabulary for 2A

Nouns

amīc-a ae 1f. mistress
astūti-a ae 1f. astuteness;
  (pl.) tricks
cēr-a ae 1f. wax
lūn-a ae 1f. moon
tabell-ae ārum 1f. pl.
  writing tablets

ui-a ae 1f. way, road
numm-us ī 2m. coin; (pl.)
  money
offici-um ī 2n. duty, job
oppid-um ī 2n. town

stil-us ī 2m. stylus
  (writing implement for
  wax tablet)
nox noct-is 3f. night
sōl sōl-is 3m. sun

Adjectives

alter altera alterum one,
  another (of two: see
  Grammar 2B)
ducent-ī ae a 200

noster nostra nostrum our(s)
uester uestra uestrum
  your(s) (pl.)

difficil-is e difficult
mendāx mendāc-is lying,
  untruthful

Verbs

adiuuō 1 I help
adseruō 1 I keep, guard
obsecrō 1 I beseech, beg
adscrībō 3 I write in
  addition

scrībō 3 *scrīps- scrīpt-*
  I write
uinciō 4 *uīnx- uīnct-* I bind
capiō 3/4 *cēp- capt-* I take,
  capture

dēcipiō 3/4 I deceive
adferō 3 irr. *attul- allāt-* I
  bring to

Others

ac (*atque*) and
bene good! fine! (well,
  thoroughly, rightly)

cum (+ abl.) (in company)
  with
dē (+ abl.) about,
  concerning

dum while
iterum again
modo now

New forms: nouns

man-us ūs 4f. hand
sūmpt-us ūs 4m. expense(s)

New forms: adjectives

celer celeris celere swift

New forms: verbs

mālō mālle I prefer

nōlō nōlle I refuse, am
  unwilling

possum posse I am able,
  can

Grammar and exercises for 2A

50 Future indicative active 'I shall —' (all conjugations)

	1 'I shall love'	*2* 'I shall have'	*3* 'I shall say'
1st s.	amá-b-ō	habé-b-ō	díc-a-m
2nd s.	amá-bi-s	habé-bi-s	díc-ē-s
3rd s.	amá-bi-t	habé-bi-t	díc-e-t
1st pl.	amá-bi-mus	habé-bi-mus	dīc-ḗ-mus
2nd pl.	amá-bi-tis	habé-bi-tis	dīc-ḗ-tis
3rd pl.	amá-bu-nt	habé-bu-nt	díc-e-nt

	4 'I shall hear'	*3/4* 'I shall capture'
1st s.	aúdi-a-m	cápi-a-m
2nd s.	aúdi-ē-s	cápi-ē-s
3rd s.	aúdi-e-t	cápi-e-t
1st pl.	audi-ḗ-mus	capi-ḗ-mus
2nd pl.	audi-ḗ-tis	capi-ḗ-tis
3rd pl.	aúdi-e-nt	cápi-e-nt

Notes

1 The following rhythmic chant may help you to memorise future forms: '-*bō* -*bis* -*bit* in 1 and 2, and -*am* -*ēs* -*et* in 3 and 4'.
2 Note that in 1st and 2nd conjs., the endings -*bō* -*bis* -*bit* etc. follow the pattern of 3rd conj. present, i.e. *dūc-ō* -*is* -*it* etc. In 3rd and 4th conjs. the new 1st s. ending in -*am* needs to be learned.

51 Irregular futures: *sum* → *erō*; *eō* → *ībō*

1st s.	ér-ō 'I shall be' etc.	í-b-ō 'I shall go' etc.
2nd s.	ér-i-s	í-bi-s
3rd s.	ér-i-t	í-bi-t
1st pl.	ér-i-mus	í-bi-mus
2nd pl.	ér-i-tis	í-bi-tis
3rd pl.	ér-u-nt	í-bu-nt

Notes

1 The future of *sum* was originally *es-ō*. The *s* became *r* between vowels, hence *erō*.

2 *ferō* is regular in the future – *fer-am -ēs -et* etc.

Exercises

1 *Translate these futures, change s. to pl. and vice versa, and say to what conjugation each verb belongs*: cēlābunt, inueniet, āmittēs, habēbimus, coquent, iubēbit, uerberābis, crēdet, capiētis, scrībam, facient, audiētis, (*optional*: obsecrābunt, dormiet, fugiēs, habitābitis, clāmābit, timēbis, uidēbimus, poscēmus, prōmittam, ostendent, uexābō, tacēbitis, amābunt).

2 *Give the corresponding future form of each of these presents, then translate*: crēdunt, salūtat, scrībit, fers, estis, it, rogō, cūrant, (*optional*: uincīs, capiō, adfertis, sunt, adiuuant, dēcipimus, scītis, possidēs, exeō, portō, tangunt, reddis, irrīdēmus, dat).

3 *Form and translate 3rd s. and 3rd pl. of the future of the following verbs*: dō, clāmō, maneō, taceō, ducō, poscō, dormiō, uinciō, capiō, fugiō, sum, redeō, (*optional*: obsecrō, uocō, moneō, habeō, prōmittō, dīcō, sciō, inueniō, dēcipiō, faciō).

4 *Translate into Latin*: you (*s.*) will hear; they will call; I shall make; we will speak; you (*pl.*) will be silent; he will lead; we will love; (*optional*: they will deceive; you (*s.*) will fear; I shall keep; you (*pl.*) will cook; she will see).

5 *Pick out the futures in this list and translate*: ferunt, dūcent, uident, uerberābō, dīcis, possidēs, dūcēs, amābunt, iubētis, facimus, fugiēmus, timēmus, mittēs, manēs, tacēs, dēcipiēs.

52 Three irregular verbs: *possum, nōlō, mālō*

Present indicative

	possum 'I can', 'I am able'	nōlō 'I am unwilling', 'I do not want', 'I refuse'	mālō 'I prefer'
1st s.	pós-sum	nṓl-ō	mā́l-ō
2nd s.	pót-es	nōn uīs	mā́-uīs
3rd s.	pót-est	nōn uult	mā́-uult

1st pl.	pós-sumus	nṓl-u-mus	mā́l-u-mus
2nd pl.	pot-éstis	nōn uúltis	mā-uúltis
3rd pl.	pós-sunt	nṓl-u-nt	mā́l-unt
Infinitive	pós-se	nṓl-le	mā́l-le

Notes

1 *possum* is a combination of the stem *pot-* meaning 'power', 'capacity' + *sum*. Where *t* and *s* meet, the result is *-ss* e.g. *potsum→possum*.

2 *nōlō*, *mālō* are based on *uolō*. *nōlō* is a combination of *ne* + *uolō*. *mālō* is a combination of *magis* (*ma-*) 'more' + *uolō* 'I want (to do x) more (than y)'.

3 All three verbs control an infinitive, as they do in English, e.g. 'I am unwilling *to*', 'I am able *to*', 'I prefer *to*'. Note that *mālō* often controls two infinitives, separated by *quam* 'than', e.g. *mālō amāre quam pugnāre* 'I prefer to have love affairs rather than to fight'. The construction often has acc. nouns rather than infinitives.

4 The futures of *nōlō*, *mālō*, *uolō* are quite regular – note that *nōlam*, *mālam*, *mālēs* are not actually found; the future of *possum* is again a combination of *pot* + *sum*:

Future indicative

1st s.	póterō	uól-a-m	(nṓl-a-m)	(mā́l-a-m)
2nd s.	pót-eris	uól-ē-s	nṓl-ē-s	(mā́l-ē-s)
3rd s.	pót-erit	uól-e-t	nṓl-e-t	mā́l-e-t
1st pl.	pot-érimus	uol-ḗ-mus	nōl-ḗ-mus	māl-ḗ-mus
2nd pl.	pot-éritis	uol-ḗ-tis	nōl-ḗ-tis	māl-ḗ-tis
3rd pl.	pót-erunt	uól-e-nt	nṓl-e-nt	mā́l-e-nt

Exercises

1 *Translate into Latin:* you (*s.*) wish; we prefer; they refuse; he can; we will prefer; you (*pl.*) do not wish; you (*s.*) are able; they will refuse; (*optional:* he will wish; they can; we will be able; you (*s.*) prefer; we can; I shall be able).

2 *Translate and convert presents into futures, futures into presents:* est, possunt, uolēs, mālent, nōn uīs, erimus, nōlumus, (*optional:* erunt, uult, poterit, nōlet, māuultis, uīs, potes).

53 Adjectives in -er: noster, uester; celer; ācer

1st/2nd decl. adjectives: **noster, uester**
noster 'our(s)' and *uester* 'your(s)' decline like *pulcher pulchr-a um* (**27**). The difference between *uester* and *tuus* is that *uester* means 'your(s)' when 'you' are more than one person (cf. **20**).

3rd decl. adjectives ending in -er
(e.g. **celer celer-is celer-e** *'swift'*, *'fast')*

	s.			*pl.*	
	m.	*f.*	*n.*	*m./f.*	*n.*
nom.	céler	céler-is	céler-e	céler-ēs	celér-ia
acc.	céler-em	céler-em	céler-e	céler-īs(-ēs)	celér-ia
gen.	←céler-is→			←celér-ium→	
dat.	←céler-ī→			←celér-ibus→	
abl.	←céler-ī→			←celér-ibus→	

Notes
1 3rd decl. adjectives ending in -er (do not confuse with 2nd decl. adjectives like *miser*, *pulcher*) decline virtually identically with *omnis*, but do show a difference between the nom. s. m. (*celer*) and f. (*celeris*). They are *i*-stems (cf. **12**).
2 Note that, while *celer* keeps the -er throughout the declension (cf. *miser* of the 1/2nd declension), some -er adjectives drop the 'e' (cf. *pulcher* of the 1/2nd declension), e.g. *ācer*.

ācer ācris ācre *'keen'*, *'sharp'*

	s.			*pl.*	
	m.	*f.*	*n.*	*m./f.*	*n.*
nom.	ā́cer	ā́cr-is	ā́cr-e	ā́cr-ēs	ā́cr-ia
acc.	ā́cr-em	ā́cr-em	ā́cr-e	ā́cr-īs(-ēs)	ā́cr-ia
gen.	←ā́cr-is→			←ā́cr-ium→	
dat.	←ā́cr-ī→			←ā́cr-ibus→	
abl.	←ā́cr-ī→			←ā́cr-ibus→	

54 Cardinal numerals 1–10, 100–1,000

			s.		
			m.	*f.*	*n.*
1	I	*nom.*	ún-us	ún-a	ún-um
		acc.	ún-um	ún-am	ún-um
		gen.		←ūn-íus→	
		dat.		←ún-ī→	
		abl.	ún-ō	ún-ā	ún-ō

			pl.		
			ún-ī	ún-ae	ún-a (*like pl. of* multus)

			m.	*f.*	*n.*
2	II	*nom.*	dú-o	dú-ae	dú-o
		acc.	dú-ōs (dú-o)	dú-ās	dú-o
		gen.	du-ṓrum	du-ā́rum	du-ṓrum
		dat./abl.	du-ṓbus	du-ā́bus	du-ṓbus

			m./f.	*n.*
3	III	*nom.*	tr-ḗs	tr-ía
		acc.	tr-ḗs (tr-īs)	tr-ía
		gen.	←tr-íum→	
		dat.	←tr-íbus→	
		abl.	←tr-íbus→	

4	IV/IIII	quáttuor
5	V	quínque
6	VI	sex
7	VII	séptem
8	VIII	óctō
9	IX/VIIII	nóuem
10	X	décem
100	C	céntum
200	CC	ducént-ī ae a (*like pl. of* multus)
300	CCC	trecént-ī ae a
400	CD	quadringént-ī ae a
500	D	quīngént-ī ae a
1,000	M	mílle (*indecl. adj.*), *pl.* mília *gen.* mílium *dat./abl.* mílibus (*see* Note)

Note

Normally, *mīlle* is used as an adjective and *mīlia* as a noun, e.g.

mīlle mīlitēs = one thousand soldiers
duo mīlia mīlitum = two thousand(s) (of) soldiers
tria mīlia mīlitum = three thousand(s) (of) soldiers etc.

55   4th declension nouns: *manus man-ūs* 4f. 'hand'

	s.	*pl.*
nom.	mánu-s	mánū-s
acc.	mánu-m	mánū-s
gen.	mánū-s	mánu-um
dat.	mánu-ī	máni-bus
abl.	mánū	máni-bus

Notes

1 Most 4th decl. nouns are m. (*manus* is one of the few exceptions).
2 It is obviously very easy to confuse these with 2nd decl. nouns like,
   e.g., *thēsaurus*, so it is vital to learn the nom. and gen. s. together.
3 Care is needed with the *-ūs* ending, which might be gen. s., nom. or
   acc. pl. Note that the form *manus* can only be nom. s.

56   4th declension noun (irregular): *domus* 'house' 4f.

	s.	*pl.*
nom.	dómu-s	dómū-s
acc.	dómu-m	dómū-s *or* dómō-s
gen.	dómū-s *or* dom-ī	dom-ṓrum (dómu-um)
dat.	dómu-ī *or* dóm-ō	dóm-ibus
abl.	dóm-ō	dóm-ibus

Notes

1 See **30** above for *domum*, *domī* and *domō* meanings.
2 *domus* has a mixture of 2nd declension forms in with the 4th.

Exercises

1 *Give the Latin for:* beautiful hand; large hand; my hand; swift hand.
   Now decline noun and adjective together in all cases, s. and pl.
2 *Pick out datives and ablatives from this list (note where the form is
   ambiguous):* uiā, amīcae, mendācēs, oppida, lūnam, nocte, nummōs,
   tabellās, manuī, celerī, sūmptuum, officiō facilī, scelere audācī, stilōs
   bonōs, sōlī, nummīs ducentīs, astūtiae tuae, cēram meam, sūmptuī
   magnō.

57 3rd declension monosyllables

If a 3rd decl. noun is a *monosyllable* with *two consonants at the end of the stem*, gen. pl. is in *-ium*, e.g.

> *nox noct-is*, gen. pl. *noctium*
> *dōs dōt-is*, gen. pl. *dōtum*

Cf. the normal rule for consonant-stems at **11**. Nouns like *nox* are in fact *i*-stem.

Exercises

1 *Translate these sentences:*

   (a) nummōs senex noster ducentōs in manum tibi hodiē dabit.
   (b) quid uīs mē facere? mālō enim adiuuāre quam nīl facere.
   (c) sī senex mendācem mē habēbit, ego astūtiās magnās facere uolam.
   (d) ego meum officium faciam, uōs uestrum facere mālō.
   (e) amīcīs uestrīs, sī senī aurum auferre poterō, nummōs ducentōs dare poteritis.
   (f) dā mihi manum tuam, tē obsecrō; ego tibi meam dabō.
   (g) sī fēminae uīs crēdere, in aquā celerī scrībere uīs.
   (h) aurum sī senī auferre poteris, Chrȳsale, tē seruum magnā astūtiā habēbō.
   (i) dum tacet nox, fūrēs facinora facere mala quam dormīre mālunt.
   (j) cēram, tabellās, stilum aufer mihi: hodiē scrībere nōlō.

2 *Translate these sentences:*

   (a) ūsus magister est optimus. (*Cicero*)
   (b)   sed quis custōdiet ipsōs custōdēs? (*Juvenal*)
   (c) ācta deōs numquam mortālia fallunt. (*Ovid*)
   (d) īrācundia leōnēs adiuuat, pauor ceruōs, accipitrem impetus, columbam fuga. (*Seneca*)
   (e) potest ex casā uir magnus exīre, potest ex dēfōrmī humilīque corpusculō fōrmōsus animus et magnus. (*Seneca*)
   (f) beātus esse sine uirtūte nēmō potest. (*Cicero*)
   (g) sine imperiō nec domus ūlla nec cīuitās stāre potest. (*Cicero*)

ūs-us ūs 4m. experience
magister magistr-ī 2m.
  teacher
optim-us a um best
custōdiō 4 I guard
ipsōs (acc. pl. m.)
  themselves
custōs custōd-is 3m. guard
āct-um ī 2n. deed
mortāl-is e of human
  beings
fallō 3 I deceive, escape
  the notice of

īrācundi-a ae 1f. rage
leō leōn-is 3m. lion
pauor pauōr-is 3m. panic,
  fear
ceru-us ī 2m. stag
accipiter accipitr-is 3m.
  hawk
impet-us ūs 4m.
  vehemence; attack
columb-a ae 1f. dove
fug-a ae 1f. flight
cas-a ae 1f. cottage, hovel

dēfōrm-is e ugly,
  misshapen
humil-is e humble, lowly
corpuscul-um ī 2n. little
  body
fōrmōs-us a um beautiful
beāt-us a um happy,
  blessed
nēmo (nom.) no one
imperi-um ī 2n. control,
  authority
ūll-us a um any
cīuitās cīuitāt-is 3f. state

Reading

Infinitives may add a simple idea to verbs like *possum, uolō, nōlō, mālō* etc.; e.g. *uidēre possum* = I can see; *īre uolō* = I want to go. They may also introduce more complex ideas, since the infinitive may take its own object or prepositional phrase, e.g. *sōlem iterum uidēre uolō* = I want to see the sun again; *in aedīs Bacchidum inīre possum* = I can go into the house of the Bacchises. The limits of the infinitive phrase are marked by the underlining. In the case of *uolō, nōlō, mālō, iubeō*, the verb itself may also have an object, which becomes attached to the infinitive phrase: e.g. *tē* (obj.) *sōlem iterum uidēre uolō* = I want you (obj.) to see the sun again. *mālō* is more complex still, since it often outlines a preference between two things, which are compared by *quam* = 'than', e.g. *lūnam uidēre quam sōlem mālō* = I prefer to see the moon to seeing the sun.

1 *In the following sentences, translate in word-order and make explicit the boundaries of the infinitive phrase. Mark which word in the phrase is the object of the introductory verb.*

  (a) hominem bonum quam malum fīliam meam domum dūcere mālō.
  (b) seruum hominem esse magnā audāciā nōlō.
  (c) tē tuum officium, mē facere meum dominus iubet.
  (d) dominōs uerberāre seruōs audācīs cīuēs mālunt.
  (e) uxōrēs uirōs amāre iubeō.

2 *Now read out the sentences in Exercise 1 in Latin, phrasing so as to avoid any possible ambiguities. How would you read sentence (e) in response to these two questions?*

  (a) What do you tell husbands to do?
  (b) What do you tell wives to do?

3 *Here are some disembodied infinitive phrases. Translate in word-order, then add a part of* uolō, nōlō, mālō, iubeō *or* possum *to complete the sense. Translate into correct English. Finally, read out the Latin correctly phrased.*

(a) tē mihi crēdere . . .
(b) seruum ad senem uiam inuenīre alteram . . .
(c) nummōs ducentōs capere quam nīl habēre . . .
(d) amīcam mē amāre meam . . .
(e) stilōs et cēram et tabellās tē adferre . . .
(f) hominēs ex oppidō exīre audācīs . . .
(g) Chrȳsalum iterum patrem dēcipere meum . . .
(h) seruum unguentum, corōnās seruam adferre mihi . . .
(i) aurum Larī meō quam seruō audācī crēdere . . .
(j) amīcīs auferre audācibus nummōs tē ducentōs . . .

4 *In English, the following is normal:* 'I want to have the gold. Give it to me'. *But in Latin this would be:* aurum habēre uolō. dā mihi.
    Say in each of the following pairs of sentences which pronoun English inserts and Latin omits.

(a) aurum tibi crēdō, ō Lar. adseruā!
(b) tē dē fīliā timēre nōlō, senex. adseruābō.
(c) cēram et tabellās adferō. cape.
(d) ego lūnam uidēre possum. uidēsne tū?
(e) hodiē officium uōbīs difficile dabō. cūrāte.

Reading exercise / Test exercise

Read carefully this passage, translating in the order of the words and defining the function of each word and phrase and anticipating the direction of the sense. Then translate into correct English. Finally, read aloud the passage, phrasing correctly, thinking out the meaning as you read. Use the running vocabulary of 2A.

est Chrȳsalus, seruus audāx Nīcobūlī, homo magnō ingeniō, astūtiā summā. per (*through*) Chrȳsalum uult Mnēsilochus senem iterum dēcipere. officium difficile habet Chrȳsalus. neque Chrȳsalō senex neque fīliō crēdit. sed Chrȳsalus cōnsilium capit audāx. in aedīs Pistoclērum, Mnēsilochī amīcum, mittit. Pistoclērum cēram, tabellās, stilum, līnum   5 adferre iubet. Chrȳsalus, ubi redit amīcus, Mnēsilochum litterās ad patrem scrībere iubet. ita patrī scrībit fīlius probus: 'Chrȳsalus malus est, mī pater. hodiē enim ad tē adībit et in tē ballistam intendet magnam. nam tē oppidum habet, antīquum et aurī plēnum. sī turrim dēlēbit tuam et

prōpugnācula tua, per portam in oppidum tē statim inuādet. tum aurum   10
tuum in corbibus ex oppidō mē auferre iubēbit et meae dare amīcae. tē
cauēre, pater mī, iubeō. sūmptus enim magnus erit, sī tē iterum dēcipiet.
uale'.

English–Latin

Translate the Latin sentences into English. Then translate the English sentences into Latin, using the pattern of the Latin ones to help you arrange the word-order correctly.

(a)   tē fīliam meam statim domum dūcere iubeō.
      Mnesilochus will want Chrysalus to deceive the poor old man again.

(b)   pauperis hominis uirtūtem quam dīuitis audāciam semper mālō.
      He will always prefer the tricks of a bold slave to the boldness of a lying mistress.

(c)   Nīcobūlus, uir nūllā astūtiā, aurum seruō audācī numquam auferre poterit.
      Chrysalus, a man of great astuteness, will easily be able to remove the old man's two hundred coins.

(d)   amīcae sūmptus semper magnus est.
      The hand of a thief is always swift.

(e)   dīuitēs pauperibus nummōs dant nūllōs.
      The old men will give the young men a lot of money.

(f)   erit mihi magnus sūmptus, quod uxōrem habeō dīuitem.
      The young men will have large expenses, because they have pretty mistresses.

Deliciae Latinae

Word-building

dē + abl. = 'about', 'concerning', 'down from'.

dē as a prefix to verbs = 'away', 'down', e.g. *dēscendō* 'I go down' (see above p. 83), cf. *spērō* 'I hope', *dēspērō* 'I lose hope'. Sometimes it intensifies the word, e.g. *capiō* 'I catch', *dēcipiō* 'I catch out' (hence 'deceive').

If the simple verb has a short *ă* or *ĕ* as its first vowel, e.g. *căpiō*, *sĕdeō* ('sit'), that vowel will usually change to an *i* after a prefix, e.g.:

căpiō   dēcĭpiō

sĕdeō   obsĭdeō

făciō   perfĭciō

ob as a prefix means 'in front of', 'against' e.g. *sedeō* = 'sit', *obsideō* = 'sit in front of', 'besiege' (cf. obsession); *ob* + *ferō* = *offerō* 'put in someone's path', 'offer' (note *b*→*f* before *f*); *ob* + *eō* = *obeō* 'come face to face with', 'meet'. Romans said one came 'face to face' with death (*mortem obeō* – hence 'obituary'). Verbs compounded with *ob* often take the dative.

Word exercise

Give the meaning and Latin connection of: lunatic, style, official, adjutant (*adiuuō*), nocturnal, solar, manual, mendacious, credible, scribble, a posse, beneficial, reiterate, sumptuary (laws).

Everyday Latin

> A *possum* is the trade-name of an electronic typewriter for quadriplegics.
> If you go *via* somewhere, what does it mean?
> What is one's *alter ego*?

Word study

alter

alter means 'one, or the other, of two people'; so *alterō* 'I change', so 'alter'. It is from this stem that we get 'adultery', which is nothing to do with 'adult' (the word 'adult' derives from *adultus*, past participle of *adolēscō* 'I grow up'. An 'adolescent' is 'one growing up', and 'adult' is 'one having grown up'). 'Adultery' derives from *ad* + *alterō*, i.e. moving from one state to another, so changing a lot, so corrupting.

possum

As we saw, this word is a combination of *pot* + *sum*. The *pot*- root means 'ability', 'power', so *possum* means 'I am able', 'I can', the infinitive of which is *posse*, 'to be able'. Hence 'possibility', 'possible', 'impossible' etc.

A sheriff's posse derives from mediaeval Latin *posse comitātūs* 'the power of the county', i.e. a force with legal authority. The *pot-* root yields Latin *potentia* 'power', hence 'potential', 'potency' and the negative 'impotence'. With *omni-* 'all', we have 'omnipotence'.

sincere

It is a good story, but not true, that 'sincere' (Latin *sincērus*) derives from *sine* 'without' + *cēra* 'wax'. The false derivation springs from the Roman practice of mending broken statuary with wax and selling it off as if complete. In the heat of the day, however . . . Another 'folk' etymology derived the word from honey 'without wax', i.e. clean, pure, simple. Its true origin is uncertain.

Real Latin

Martial

nōn amo tē, Sabidī, nec possum dīcere quārē.
  hoc tantum possum dīcere, nōn amo tē. (*1.32*)

Sabidī = O Sabidius
hoc tantum this only

Cf. the famous version of Thomas Brown (1663–1704):

> I do not love thee, Dr Fell.
> The reason why I cannot tell.
> But this I know and know full well.
> I do not love thee, Dr Fell.

Veientāna mihī miscēs, ubi Massica pōtās:
  olfacere haec mālō pōcula, quam bibere. (*3.49*)

Veientāna (obj.) (name of cheap wine)	*Massica* (obj.) Massic (name of fine wine)	*haec pōcula* (obj.) these drinks (i.e. the Massica)
mihī for me	*pōtō* 1 I drink	*quam* than
misceō 2 I mix	*olfaciō* 3/4 I smell	*bibō* 3 I drink

Vulgate

God speaks to Moses in a cloud: 'nōn poteris uidēre faciem meam: nōn enim uidēbit mē homo et uīuet.' (*Exodus 33.20*)

faciem (acc. s. f.) face
uīuō 3 live

'nōn occīdēs ... nōn fūrtum faciēs ... nōn concupīscēs domum proximī tuī; nec dēsīderābis uxōrem eius, nōn seruum, nōn ancillam, nōn bouem, nōn asinum.' (*Exodus 20.13.*)

occīdō 3 I kill	*proxim-us ī* 2m.	*ancill-a ae* 1f. maidservant
fūrt-um ī 2n. theft	neighbour	*bōs bou-is* 3m. m. ox
concupīscō 3 I desire	*dēsīderō* 1 I long for	*asin-us ī* 2m. ass
	eius his	

et ego uōbīs dīcō . . . 'quaerite et inueniētis'. (*Luke 11.9*)

quaerō 3 I seek

Mottoes

omnia superat virtūs. (*Gardiner*)
omnia vincit amor. (*Bruce, Rogers*)
omnia vincit labor. (*Cook*)
omnia vincit vēritās. (*Eaton, Mann, Naish, Nash*)
omnia bona bonīs. (*Wenman*)

superō 1 I overcome	*labor labōr-is* 3m. work	*uēritās uēritāt-is* 3f. truth
uincō 3 I conquer		

Section 2B

Running vocabulary for 2B

a! ah!
abdūcō 3 I lead away
accipiō 3/4 I receive, take
accūsō 1 I accuse
adgredior I am going up to (*ad* + acc.)
adgreditur (he) goes up to (*ad* + acc.)
adulēscēns adulēscent-is 3m. young man
agō 3 I do
annōn or not (see *utrum*)
at but

Bellerophōn Bellerophont-is 3m. Bellerophon (who was given a letter to bear ordering his own death)
caput capit-is 3n. source (*scelerum caput* = scoundrel)
caueō 2 I am wary
cicer cicer-is 3n. chick-pea
cognōscō 3 I get to know, examine
column-a ae 1f. column

cōnāris you (s.) try
conuīui-um ī 2n. dinner-party
dīligō 3 I love
domō from home
ecce look!
ēgreditur (he) comes/goes out
ēgrediuntur (they) come out
eho ha!
etiam even
euge hurrah!

fīō I happen (*fit* 3rd s.)
fortiter vigorously
frīct-us a um roasted
fung-us ī 2m. mushroom
haud not
iam presently
id quod that which, what
immō more precisely
impingō 3 I thrust (x acc.)
    forward (sc. 'against
    him')
īnsan-us a um crazy
īnspiciō 3/4 I look in
intereā meanwhile
intrō inside
īrāscor I am getting angry
īrāt-us a um angry
lect-us ī 2m. couch
legō 3 I read
līberō 1 I free
lībertās lībertāt-is 3f.
    freedom
litter-ae ārum 1f. pl. letter
loquere speak! (s.)
loqueris you (s.) speak of,
    you say
loquī to talk
loquitur (he) speaks
loquor I am speaking,
    I say
loquuntur (they) say
lumbrīc-us ī 2m. worm
mē esse 'myself to be',
    'that I am'
mēcum with/to myself
mentīrī (to) lie
minārī (to) threaten
    (+ dat.)

mināris you (s.) are
    threatening (+ dat.)
minor I am threatening
    (+ dat.)
modo just
moritur (he) dies
mōs mōr-is 3m. way,
    habit; (pl.) character
mox soon
necesse est it is necessary
negōti-um ī 2n. business
nesciō 4 I do not know
nesci-us a um forgetful of
    (+ gen.)
nōlī don't (s.) (+ inf.)
nūntiō 1 I report
oblīuīsceris you (s.) forget
oblīuīscor I forget
obsignāt-us a um sealed
opīnor I think
opus oper-is 3n. job, work,
    task
perficiō 3/4 I finish,
    complete, carry out
pergō 3 I go on, go ahead
persequor I pursue
petō 3 I go after, seek
plūs more (+ gen.)
polliceor I promise
precārī (to) beg
precor I beg
prōgreditur (he) is coming
    / comes forward
prope nearby
propter (+ acc.) because of
pugn-us ī 2m. fist
pūtid-us a um rotten

quantī: see *tantī*
quem he whom
quia because
recordāris you (s.)
    remember
recordor I remember
rem (acc. s. f.) the matter
rērum (gen. pl. f.) (of)
    things
rēs (nom. s. f.) the matter
rēs (nom., acc. pl. f.)
    things
respondeō 2 I reply
saeu-us a um wild, angry
sapienti-a ae 1f. wisdom
scelest-us a um criminal
sequere follow! (s.)
sequiminī follow! (pl.)
sequitur (he) follows
sequor I follow
sīc thus
sign-um ī 2n. seal, mark
spectō 1 I look at
stult-us a um stupid
tam so
tam . . . quam as . . . as
tantī . . . quantī worth as
    much . . . as
tranquill-us a um calm
trāsenn-a ae 1f. trap
turd-us ī 2m. thrush
uerb-um ī 2n. word
uetustissim-us a um very
    old
utrum . . . annōn do . . .
    or not? (double
    question)

Learning vocabulary for 2B

Nouns

litter-ae ārum 1f. pl. letter
sapienti-a ae 1f. wisdom

lect-us ī 2m. couch, bed
uerb-um ī 2n. word

opus oper-is 3n. job, work,
    task

Adjectives

nesci-us a um ignorant of (+gen.)

saeu-us a um wild, angry

stult-us a um stupid

Verbs

caueō 2 I am wary
respondeō 2 I reply
agō 3 *ēg- āct-* I do, act
cognōscō 3 *cognōu- cognit-* I get to know, examine

dīligō 3 I love
legō 3 I read
pergō 3 I go on, go ahead, continue
nesciō 4 I do not know

īnspiciō 3/4 *īnspex-* inspect- I look into; inspect, examine
perficiō 3/4 *perfēc- perfect-* I finish, complete; carry out

Others

at but (often introduces a supposed objection)
domō from the home (cf. *domī, domum*)

ecce look!
intrō (to) inside
mēcum with/to myself (= *mē* abl., *cum* with)

mox soon
quia because
sīc thus, in this way, so
tam so

New forms: nouns

caput capit-is 3n. head; source

rēs rē-ī 5f. thing, matter, business, property, affair

diēs diē-ī 5m. or f. day

Verbs

minor 1 dep. I threaten (+dat.)
opīnor 1 dep. I think
precor 1 dep. I beg, pray
recordor 1 dep. I remember
polliceor 2 dep. I promise

loquor 3 dep. *locūt-* I talk, speak, say
oblīuīscor 3 dep. I forget
sequor 3 dep. *secūt-* I follow
mentior 4 dep. I lie

adgredior 3/4 dep. *adgress-* I approach
ēgredior 3/4 dep. *ēgress-* I go/ come out
prōgredior 3/4 dep. *prōgress-* I advance

Grammar and exercises for section 2B

---

58 **Present deponent (all conjugations): indicative, imperative, infinitive**

	1	*2*	*3*
	minor 'I threaten'	*polliceor* 'I promise'	*loquor* 'I speak'
Indicative			
1st s.	mín-o-r	pollíce-o-r	lóqu-o-r
2nd s.	miná-ris (-re)	pollicé-ris (-re)	lóqu-e-ris (-re)
3rd s.	miná-tur	pollicé-tur	lóqu-i-tur

1st pl.	minā́-mur	pollicḗ-mur	lóqu-i-mur
2nd pl.	minā́-minī	pollicḗ-minī	loqu-í-minī
3rd pl.	miná-ntur	pollicé-ntur	loqu-ú-ntur

Imperative

| 2nd s. | minā́-re | pollicḗ-re | lóqu-e-re |
| 2nd pl. | minā́-minī | pollicḗ-minī | loqu-í-minī |

| *Infinitive* | minā́-rī | pollicḗ-rī | lóqu-ī |

	4	*3/4*
Indicative	*mentior 'I lie'*	*prōgredior 'I advance'*
1st s.	ménti-o-r	prōgrédi-o-r
2nd s.	mentī́-ris (-re)	prōgréd-e-ris (-re)
3rd s.	mentī́-tur	prōgrédi-tur
1st pl.	mentī́-mur	prōgrédi-mur
2nd pl.	mentī́-minī	prōgredí-minī
3rd pl.	menti-ú-ntur	prōgredi-ú-ntur

Imperative

| 2nd s. | mentī́-re | prōgréd-e-re |
| 2nd pl. | mentī́-minī | prōgredí-minī |

| *Infinitive* | mentī́-rī | prṓgred-ī |

Notes

1 So far you have only met verbs in their 'active' forms. But there is another class of verb, called 'deponent'. It is this class you are now meeting for the first time. Deponents are identified by the different personal endings they take.

2 The personal endings of active verbs are, as we know, *-ō, -s, -t, -mus, -tis, -nt*. The personal endings of deponent verbs are *-r, -ris (-re), -tur, -mur, -minī, -ntur*. These new personal endings are of the highest importance as they are more widely used than just with deponents (as you will see). Consequently, if you learn them now, you will be saving yourself a great deal of learning in the future.

3 Given the new personal endings, deponent verbs are constructed exactly as active verbs are, i.e. stem with its key vowel + personal endings. E.g.

   1st conj.: *mına-* + endings (NB *minor* cf. *amō*).
   2nd conj.: *pollice-* + endings.
   3rd conj.: *loqu-* + *-i-* + endings. (NB *loquor* cf. *dīcō*; *loquuntur* cf.

dicunt. The really difficult one here is the 2nd s.: *loqueris* cf.
dīcis. Observe the pattern of short vowels.)
4th conj.: *mentī-* + endings.
3rd/4th conj.: *prōgredi-* + endings, except for 2nd s., where the *-i-*
of the stem alters to *-e-* (as in 3rd conj.). Note that the *-i-*
remains short (contrast 4th conj. *mentīris, mentītur* etc.).

4 Imperatives present a problem, in that the s. and pl. imperatives can be
   identical in form with the indicatives. For example, *mināminī* may
   mean 'you threaten' or 'threaten!' (pl.), and *mināre* could mean 'you
   threaten' or 'threaten!' (s.). The context will tell you which is right.
5 Do not confuse s. deponent forms in *-āre, -ere, -ēre,* and *-īre* with active
   infinitives like *amāre* etc.
6 The most difficult infinitive is the 3rd and 3rd/4th conj. infinitive,
   which ends in plain *-ī,* e.g. *loqu-ī, prōgred-ī.* All the rest end in stem
   (+ key vowel) + *-rī.*

Exercises

1 *Translate and convert s. to pl. and vice-versa*: precātur, mentīris,
   pollicēmur, sequuntur, mināris, loquiminī, mentior, opīnāre,
   prōgrediminī, loqueris, pollicēre, mināmur, (*optional*: recordor,
   ēgreditur, oblīuīscuntur, sequeris, precāre, opīnāmur, adgrederis,
   loquitur, mentiuntur, prōgrediuntur, mināmur).
2 *Give the Latin for*: we threaten; he promises; they forget; you (*pl.*)
   remember; you (*s.*) speak; I am following; advance! (*s.*); beg! (*s.*); talk!
   (*pl.*); promise! (*s.*); (*optional*: we are thinking; they advance; he comes
   out; she threatens; remember! (*pl.*); we are lying; they speak; you (*pl.*)
   promise; talk! (*s.*); you (*s.*) follow).
3 *Say whether each of the following is an infinitive or an imperative and
   translate*: amāre, mināre, pollicēre, sequere, uocāre, habēre, loquī,
   audī, inuenīre, prōgredī, dormī, mentīrī, precāre, opīnārī, inuenī,
   dūcere, loquere, inīre, iubēre, prōgredere.
4 *Give the meaning, infinitive and s. imperative of the following verbs:* habeō,
   cūrō, minor, loquor, audiō, dūcō, mittō, precor, fugiō, crēdō,
   (*optional*: opīnor, prōgredior, moneō, sequor, maneō, polliceor).

9 *nōlī* + infinitive

nōlī (pl. *nōlīte*), the imperative of *nōlō*, means in Latin 'don't!', and is followed by the infinitive (lit. 'do not wish to!', 'refuse to!'). E.g. *nōlī/nōlīte clāmāre* 'don't shout!', *nōlī/nōlīte loquī* 'don't speak!'

Exercise

Translate into Latin: don't follow (*s.*); don't (*pl.*) threaten me; don't (*s.*) be stupid (*m.*); don't (*pl.*) send the letter; don't (*s.*) hide the pot; don't (*pl.*) lead the slaves; (*optional*: don't (*s.*) advance; don't (*pl.*) mention; don't (*s.*) do the business today; don't (*pl.*) carry the garlands).

0 5th decl. nouns: *rēs rē-ī* 5f. 'thing', 'matter', 'business', 'affair'

	s.	pl.
nom.	rē-s	rē-s
acc.	re-m	rē-s
gen.	ré-ī	ré-rum
dat.	ré-ī	ré-bus
abl.	rē	ré-bus

NB. Most 5th decl. nouns are f. But *diēs* 'day' is normally m. (it is f. when it denotes a special day).

Exercise

Decline in full: omnis rēs; pulcher diēs; mea rēs; trīstis diēs.

1 3rd decl. n. noun: *caput capit-is* 'head'

	s.	pl.
nom.	cáput	cápit-a
acc.	cáput	cápit-a
gen.	cápit-is	cápit-um
dat.	cápit-ī	capít-ibus
abl.	cápit-e	capít-ibus

NB. Given the gen. s. *capit-is*, this noun follows the normal pattern of 3rd decl. n. nouns like e.g. *nōmen* **26**.

62 Special 1st/2nd decl. adjectives *nūll-us a um* 'no(ne)', 'not any'; *alter alter-a um* 'one' (of two), 'the one . . . the other'

	s.			pl.		
	m.	*f.*	*n.*	*m.*	*f.*	*n.*
nom.	nū́ll-us	nū́ll-a	nū́ll-um	nū́ll-ī	nū́ll-ae	nū́ll-a
acc.	nū́ll-um	nū́ll-am	nū́ll-um	nū́ll-ōs	nū́ll-ās	nū́ll-a
gen.	←——nūll-íus ——→			nūll-ṓrum	nūll-ā́rum	nūll-ṓrum
dat.	←——nū́ll-ī ———→			←——— nū́ll-īs———→		
abl.	nū́ll-ō	nū́ll-ā	nū́ll-ō	←——— nū́ll-īs———→		

	s.			pl.		
	m.	*f.*	*n.*	*m.*	*f.*	*n.*
nom.	álter	álter-a	álter-um	álter-ī	álter-ae	álter-a
acc.	álter-um	álter-am	álter-um	álter-ōs	álter-ās	álter-a
gen.	←—— alter-íus ——→			alter-ṓrum	alter-ā́rum	alter-ṓrum
dat.	←—— álter-ī———→			←—— álter-īs ——→		
abl.	álter-ō	álter-ā	álter-ō	←—— álter-īs ——→		

NB. Both these adjectives are entirely regular except that the gen. s. ends in *-īus*, e.g. *nūllīus, alterīus* and the dat. s. in *-ī*; cf. *quis* gen. s. *cuius* dat. s. *cui, ūnus* gen. s. *ūnīus* dat. s. *ūnī*.

Exercises

1 *Translate into English*:

(a) Nīcobūlus: nōlī mihi minārī, Chrȳsale.
Chrȳsalus: at ut rēs est, domine, sīc tibi loquor.

(b) seruus audāx caput habet astūtiārum plēnum.

(c) seruī ex aedibus mox ēgrediuntur atque senem sequuntur.

(d) at quis loquitur? ut opīnor, Chrȳsalus est.

(e) intrō īnspice, mī domine. quid in aedibus uidēs? rēs mala est, ut opīnor.

(f) Chrȳsalus dominum cauēre iubet et nescium rērum omnium uocat.

(g) rēs omnīs cognōsce. tē enim recordārī quam oblīuīscī mālō.

(h) ut pollicēris, sīc rem esse uolō.

(i) quid uōs opīnāminī? ecce! seruus mihi minātur, deinde mentītur, tum obsecrat mē et precātur.

(j) tū, mī Nīcobūle, prōgredere atque Chrȳsalō statim mināre.

2 *Translate these sentences*:

   (a) crēdula rēs amor est. (*Ovid*)
   (b) rēs est magna tacēre. (*Martial*)
   (c) uitia erunt dōnec hominēs. (*Tacitus*)
   (d) rēs hūmānae fragilēs cadūcaeque sunt. (*Cicero*)
   (e) dulce et decōrum est prō patriā morī. (*Horace*)
   (f) et facere et patī fortia Rōmānum est. (*Livy*)

crēdul-us a um confiding, unsuspecting
amor amōr-is 3m. love
uiti-um ī 2n. fault, crime
dōnec while, as long as (sc. there are)
hūmān-us a um human

fragil-is e brittle, frail
cadūc-us a um perishable
dulc-is e sweet
decōr-us a um fitting, seemly, honourable
prō (+ abl.) for, on behalf of

patri-a ae 1f. native land
morior 3/4 dep. I die
patior 3/4 dep. I suffer, endure
fort-is e brave
Rōmān-us a um Roman

Reading

When a sentence contains more than one clause, there are, in the conjunctions and other small words within previous clauses, signposts marking the direction of the sense. You have met ita . . . *leading up to* ut (*or vice versa*) *and in* **2B** (*Text*) *you saw* tam . . . quam = '*as . . . as*' *and* tantī . . . quantī = '*worth as much . . . as*'. *Ambiguities in the conjunction are often resolved in advance by markers, e.g.* tum, ubi . . . *shows* ubi *to mean 'when' rather than 'where'. More generally, you will know from seeing* sī, *that the sentence is conditional* ('*if* x, *then* y') *and* quod/quia *give the reason for something in another clause.*

Translate only the 'signposts' (markers like tum, tam *etc. and conjunctions like* sī, quod *etc.) and say what the basic structure of each of these sentences is. When you have done this, translate (in word-order first, then into correct English). Finally read aloud, phrasing correctly, thinking through the meaning as you read.*

   (a) tum rem cognōscēs omnem, mī domine, sī scīre uolēs, ubi fīlium tuum in aedibus uidēbis Bacchidum.
   (b) ut tū mihi rem dīcis, sīc ego, quod tibi crēdō, opīnor.
   (c) tantī est senex noster, ut opīnātur Chrȳsalus, quia seruus est summā audāciā, quantī fungus pūtidus.
   (d) tē īnspicere intrō, quod tē omnia scīre uolō, iubēbo in aedīs, ubi fīlium, sī oculōs habēs, cum amīcā mox uidēbis.
   (e) at sī senī litterās tum dare poterō, ubi ego uolam, tam erit frīctus, ut opīnor, quam est frīctum cicer.

Reading exercise / Test exercise

Read this passage carefully, translating in word-order. Define the function of each word as you go, grouping them into the correct phrases and anticipating the direction of the sense. Then translate into correct English. Finally, read aloud, with the correct phrasing, thinking out the meaning as you read. Use the running vocabulary of **2B**.

īnsānum negōtium Chrȳsalus, ut opīnātur, persequitur, quia senem dēcipere iterum uult. cōnsilium tamen satis audāx in animō est. Mnēsilochī enim litterās senī dabit. Chrȳsalus tum dominum saeuum esse uult, ubi litterās accipiet, quia tum mōrēs Mnēsilochī malōs nārrāre poterit. litterās in manūs senī tum dat seruus audāx, ubi ex aedibus ēgreditur. senex litterās legit, deinde seruōs uocat. tum ubi domō ēgrediuntur, seruōs Chrȳsalum uincīre iubet, Chrȳsalum tacēre. senem autem irrīdet Chrȳsalus ac rērum nescium omnium stultumque uocat. tantī habet dominum, ut dīcit, quantī fungum pūtidum. senex tam īrātus fit quam uult seruus. tum autem Chrȳsalus perīculum Mnēsilochī loquitur, senem in aedīs intrō īnspicere Bacchidum iubet. prōgreditur senex ad aedīs et intrō īnspicit. at conuīuium uidet et rem malam atque trīstem.

English–Latin

Translate the Latin sentences into English. Then translate the English sentences into Latin, using the pattern of the Latin ones to help you arrange the word-order correctly.

(a) nōlī uxōrem meam adgredī, Chrȳsale.
    Don't threaten the poor old man, slave.

(b) ubi litterās scrībis, rem in animō habē; uerba mox sequuntur.
    When you (*pl.*) recall the matter, remember the dangers; the mind never lies.

(c) dīues autem, uirtūtis nescius, pauperī minātur.
    The slaves, ignorant of everything, are forgetting their danger.

(d) cīuēs bonī in perīculum prōgrediuntur.
    All the girls are coming out of their house.

(e) ego tibi nōn minor, sed ita loquor, ut rēs est.
    We are not lying, but telling you how the matter stands.

(f) sequiminī mē, meī seruī, atque omnia oblīuīsciminī.
    Follow me, my son, into the house and pray to the gods.

Deliciae Latinae

Word-building

sub + abl./acc. = 'under', 'close up to'.

sub- as a prefix (sometimes appearing as *su-* or *sus-*) attaches the same meaning to the verb, e.g. *sub* + *capiō* = *suscipiō* 'undertake'; *sub* + *sequor* = *subsequor* 'follow closely'. Cf. submarine, subcutaneous etc. See above p. 83.

Word exercise

Give the meanings and Latin connection of: perfect, capital, verb, irate, maximise, legible, advent, opinion, loquacious, progressive, stultify, oblivious, record (*NB.* cor cordis *heart*), literate.

Everyday Latin

In logic, what does a *nōn sequitur* not do?

secundus 'second' is connected with *sequor*. It is, after all, what follows the first. Since a following wind was favourable to sailors, *secundus* also means 'favourable'.

Letters often say '*re* your bill for drinks now outstanding at . . .' This means 'in the matter of', the abl. of *rēs*. Something *ad rem* is 'to the point', 'relevant to the matter in hand' (also a motto of the Wright family).

If you see (*sic*), it indicates that what has just been written is intentionally writen (*sic*) like that.

Real Latin

Martial

cum tua nōn ēdās, carpis mea carmina, Laelī.
 carpere uel nōlī nostra, uel ēde tua.

cum since	*carpō* 3 I criticise	*uel . . . uel* either . . . or
tua = *tua carmina*	*carmen carmin-is* 3n. poem	*nostra, tua*: i.e. *carmina*
ēdō 3 I publish: *ēdās* 'you publish'	*Laelī* O Laelius	

Sayings of Cato
cum bonīs ambulā.
rem tuam custōdī (*guard*).
librōs (*books*) lege.
miserum nōlī irrīdēre.

Vulgate
The Lord to Moses: 'ingredere ad Pharaōnem, et loquere ad eum "haec dīcit dominus deus Hebraeōrum: dīmitte populum meum".' (*Exodus 9.1*)
Jesus to the disciples: 'sinite puerōs uenīre ad mē et nōlīte uetāre eōs; tālium enim est rēgnum deī.' (*Luke 18.16*)

Pharaō Pharaōn-is Pharaoh	*Hebrae-ī ōrum* 2m.	*sinō* 3 I allow
eum him	pl.Hebrews	*uetō* 1 I forbid
haec as follows	*dīmittō* 3 I let go	*tālium* of such a sort
	popul-us ī 2m. people	*rēgn-um ī* 2n. kingdom

Mottoes
nōlī irrītāre leōnem. (*Cooper, Walsh*)
nōlī mentīrī. (*Notley*)
nōlī mē tangere. (*Graeme, Graham, Willett*)
dum crēscō, spērō. (*Rider*)
dum spīrō, spērō. (*Anderson, Baker, Brook, Cutler, Davies, Gordon, Greaves, Hunter, Jacobs, Lee, Mason, Moore, Nicholls, Pearson, Roberts, Smith, Symonds, Taylor, Thomason, Walker, Whitehead, Young*)
dum vigilō, cūrō. (*Cranstoun*)
dum vīvō, spērō. (*Monteith*)
dum in arborem (?) (*Hamilton*)
fac et spērā. (*Armstrong, Arthur, Campbell, Morison, Richardson*)

irrītō 1 I annoy		
leō leōn-is 3m. lion	*spērō* 1 I hope	*arbor arbor-is* 3f. tree
tangō 3 I touch	*spīrō* 1 I breathe	(= the cross?; *dum*
crēscō 3 I grow	*uigilō* 1 I am on guard	then = 'until', i.e. 'as far
	uīuō 3 I live	as (onto)')

Word study

ambulō
ambulō means 'I walk', 'take a turn'. Hence 'amble', and 'preamble', the introductory stroll round a subject (*prae* 'in front of'). The French had an *hôpital ambulant*, i.e. 'touring hospital', 'field hospital', whence our

'ambulance'. 'Perambulate' means 'walk through or over' (*per* 'through'); hence the English derivation 'perambulator', which *should* mean 'one who walks over'. It is tempting to think that 'ramble' comes from *re + ambulō*, but this is disputed.

diēs

The Latin adjective *dīus* means 'divine', 'of the sky' and 'luminous'. It connects with *deus* 'god' (cf. Greek '*Zeus*'), whence *dīuus*, *dīuīnus*, the goddess Diana, English 'divine'. It also connects with *diēs* 'day' – so 'light' and 'god' appear to be closely connected semantically. (Cf. John 1.4: 'In Him was life and the life was the light of men'; I John 1.5: 'God is light and in Him there is no darkness at all'.) *Iuppiter* is cognate with Greek *zeu pater* 'O Zeus father'. Observe that Jupiter also appears in Latin as *diēspiter* (connected with *diēs + pater* 'father of day'), and that the gen. s. of *Iuppiter* is *Iouis*, in primitive Latin *Diouis*. Both *diēspiter* and *Diouis* bring us back to the *di-* root again. *Iou-* gives us 'jovial' (from the astrological influence of the planet Jupiter). There is also a connection between *Zeus*, *deus* and the Old English god of war Tīw, whence Tuesday!

　　diēs helps to give us 'dismal' (*diēs malī* 'unlucky days'), and 'diary' (*diārium* 'ration for the day'). From *diēs* Latin got the adjective *diurnus* 'daily', giving English 'diurnal' and (through French) 'journal'. Note that in France and Italy, *Thursday* is named after Jupiter (Fr. *jeudi*, It. *gióvedi*).

Section 2C

Running vocabulary for 2C

absum I am absent
accipiō 3/4 I receive
adloquor 3 dep. I address
admodum fairly, quite
aedis aed-is 3f. shrine, temple
amātor amātōr-is 3m. lover

ambō ambae both (*ambōs* acc. pl. m.; *ambās* acc. pl. f.)
ambulō 1 I walk
annōn or not?
arbitror 1 dep. I think
aure-us a um golden

bell-us a um pretty
Castor Castor-is 3m. Castor (brother of Pollux)
Ceres Cerer-is 3f. Ceres (goddess of crops)
citō immediately, at once

cognōuī I know
cognōuistī you (s.) know
cōnor 1 dep. I try
cōnspicor 1 dep. I catch
    sight of
conueniō 4 I meet
crux cruc-is 3f. cross (*in
    malam crucem* = to a bad
    death, to Hell)
cubō 1 I sleep
dēfendō 3 I defend
ergō therefore
errō 1 I am mistaken, err
exanim-us a um lifeless
exhērēs exhērēd-is
    disinherited
    (from + gen.)
exsoluō 3 I release
fīō I happen (3rd s. *fit*)
for-um ī 2n. forum
haud not
hercle by Hercules!
Herculēs Hercul-is 3m.
    Hercules
heus hey!
hic (nom. s. m.) this
    (adj.); this man, he
    (pron.)
hōs (acc. pl. m.) these
huic (dat. s. m.) to this
    man, to him
huius (gen. s. m.) of this
hunc (acc. s. m.) this man,
    him
iam now presently
illa (nom. s. f.) that (adj.);
    she (pron.); that
    woman
illā (abl. s. f.) her (pron.);
    that (adj.); that woman
illae (nom. pl. f.) those
    (adj.)
ille (nom. s. m.) that
    (adj.); he (pron.); that
    man
illī (dat. s. m./f.) (to) him,
    (to) that man

illīus (gen. s. m.) of that
    (adj.); of him, his
    (pron.)
illō (abl. s. m.) him; that
    man
illōrum (gen. pl. m.) of
    them, their
illōs (acc. pl. m.) them
    (pron.); those (adj.)
illud (acc. s. n.) that
illum (acc. s. m.) him,
    that man
immō yes; indeed
impūr-us a um vile, defiled
ingredior 3/4 dep. I enter
inquam I say
Iouem (acc. s.)
Iuppiter = Jupiter
īrāscor 3 dep. I get angry
īrāt-us a um angry
Iūnō Iūnōn-is 3f. Juno
iūrō 1 I swear
Lātōn-a ae 1f. Leto
lepid-us a um charming
manifestō openly
Mārs Mārt-is 3m. Mars
    (god of war)
Mercuri-us ī 2m. Mercury
    (messenger god)
meretrīx meretrīc-is 3f.
    prostitute
mīles mīlit-is 3m. soldier
Mineru-a ae 1f. Minerva
    (goddess of wisdom)
modo just
mōs mōr-is 3m. way,
    habit; (pl.) character
mulier mulier-is 3f.
    woman; wife
necō 1 I kill
nisi unless, if . . . not
nōnne surely? can't I?
nūpt-us a um married
nusquam nowhere
opprīmō 3 I surprise, catch
Ops Op-is 3f. Ops
    (goddess of plenty)

ōsculor 1 dep. I kiss
pacīscor 3 dep. I make a
    bargain
per (+ acc.) through, by
periūri-um ī 2n. perjury
Philipp-us ī 2m. a gold
    coin (struck by Philip
    of Macedon)
plānē obviously, clearly
Pollūx Pollūc-is 3m.
    Pollux (brother of
    Castor)
quam how! (with adj. or
    adv.); (rather) than
quid why?
quod whatever, in
    whatever way
retineō 2 I hold, detain
Sāturn-us ī 2m. Saturn
    (father of Jupiter)
scelest-us a um criminal
sēdulō zealously,
    assiduously
sermō sermōn-is 3m.
    conversation
Sōl Sōl-is 3m. the god of
    the sun
Spēs Spē-ī 5f. Hope
suāu-is e sweet
Summān-us ī 2m.
    Summanus (a Roman
    god who caused
    lightning at night)
suspicor 1 dep. I suspect
tempus tempor-is 3n. time
    (*ad tempus* = in time)
uel or
ueniō 4 I come
Venus Vener-is 3f. Venus
    (goddess of love)
uideor 2 dep. I seem
Virtūs Virtūt-is 3f. the
    goddess Virtue
uīs 3f. (irreg.) force (acc.
    uim)
uīsō 3 I visit
uīt-a ae 1f. life

Learning vocabulary for 2C

Nouns

meretrīx meretrīc-is 3f.
    prostitute
mīles mīlit-is 3m. soldier

mōs mōr-is 3m. way,
    habit, custom; (pl.)
    character

mulier mulier-is 3f.
    woman; wife

Adjectives

aure-us a um golden

īrāt-us a um angry

scelest-us a um criminal,
    wicked

Verbs

necō 1 I kill
dēfendō 3 I defend
opprimō 3 *oppress-*
    I surprise, catch; crush

arbitror 1 dep. I think,
    consider; give
    judgement
cōnor 1 dep. I try

uideor 2 dep. *uīs-* I seem
īrāscor 3 dep. *īrāt-*
    I grow angry

Others

citō quickly
ergō therefore
haud not

iam now, by now,
    already; presently
per (+acc.) through, by

plānē clearly
quam how! (+adj. or
    adv.)

New forms:
adjectives

hic haec hoc this; this
    person/thing; (pl.) these

ille illa illud that; that
    person/thing; (pl.)
    those

Grammar and Exercises for 2C

---

63 *hic haec hoc* 'this', 'this person', 'this thing', 'the latter', pl.
'these'

	s.			*pl.*		
	m.	*f.*	*n.*	*m.*	*f.*	*n.*
nom.	hic	haec	hoc	h-ī	h-ae	haec
acc.	hunc	hanc	hoc	h-ōs	h-ās	haec
gen.	←— húius —→			h-ōrum	h-árum	h-ōrum
dat.	←— huic —→			←——— h-īs———→		
abl.	hōc	hāc	hōc	←——— h-īs———→		

Notes

1 Describing a noun, *hic* means 'this' (pl. 'these'); on its own, it will mean 'this man', 'this woman', 'this thing', depending on gender and context. Often 'he', 'she', 'it' will suffice.

2 Its forms seem to be irregular, but note the *-ius* of the gen. s. (cf. *nūllus, alter* **62** and *quis* **29**), and the pl., except for *haec*, is just like *multus* on the stem *h-*.

3 NB. *hinc* 'from here'; *hīc* '(at) here'; *hūc* '(to) here'.

64 *ille illa illud* 'that', 'that person', 'that thing', 'the former'

	s.			pl.		
	m.	*f.*	*n.*	*m.*	*f.*	*n.*
nom.	ill-e	ill-a	ill-ud	ill-ī	ill-ae	ill-a
acc.	ill-um	ill-am	ill-ud	ill-ōs	ill-ās	ill-a
gen.	←——— ill-íus ———→			ill-órum	ill-árum	ill-órum
dat.	←——— ill-ī ———→			←——— ill-īs ———→		
abl.	ill-ō	ill-ā	ill-ō	←——— ill-īs ———→		

Notes

1 On its own, *ille* means 'that man', 'that woman', 'that thing', depending on gender and context; describing a noun, it means 'that', 'those'. Often it best translates as 'he', 'she', 'it'.

2 The forms at first glance seem irregular, but on closer inspection you will see that, apart from *ille, illud, illīus, illī* (cf. *nūllīus, nūllī; cuius, cui; alterīus, alterī*) they are simply the stem *ill-* with 2nd decl. adjective endings like *multus*.

3 From *ille* came French *le, la* and Italian *il, la*.

4 NB. *illinc* 'from there'; *illīc* (at) there' *illūc* '(to) there'. Cf. **63**³.

5 *ille . . . hic* are often used in contrast to mean 'the former' (i.e. *that one* over there, a long way away) and 'the latter' (i.e. *this one* here which is so close to us).

6 Ambiguities: note that *illī* can be dat. s. m. f. or n. or nom. pl. m. But *illae* can only be nom. pl. f., because gen. and dat. s. are *illīus, illī*.

Exercises

1 *Decline in all cases:* hic seruus; ille mīles; haec serua; illud perīculum; hoc uerbum; illa mulier.

2 *What case or cases are the following phrases in:* huius patris; hāc fīliā; hae uxōrēs; huic animō; hoc onus; hīs cenīs; (*optional:* hunc diem; hārum noctium; hōs seruōs; haec cōnsilia; hōc capite; huius perīculī); illī stilī; illō uerbō; illud opus; illōs diēs; illīs sceleribus; illī manuī; (*optional:* illam turbam; illa soror; illīus ignis; illī familiae; illōs honōrēs; illīus reī; illa domus; illā rē).

3 *Give the Latin for:* this soldier (*acc.*); to that old man; this girl's; those plans (*nom./acc.*); these dangers (*nom./acc.*); that woman's.

4 *Give the case of the following phrases, where the noun could be ambiguous, but where the form of* hic *or* ille *solves the problem:* hī thēsaurī; illīus thēsaurī; illās sorōrēs; hae sorōrēs; illa rēs; hās rēs; illae rēs; huius manūs; illae manūs; hae manūs; illās mulierēs; hae mulierēs; illī puerō; hōc puerō; illae fēminae; huic fēminae; illīus fēminae; hic diēs; illōs diēs; hī diēs.

5 *Join* hic *or* ille *to the word(s) with which it agrees, and translate:*

> huius: seruus, amīcī, mulierēs, lūnae, stilōs
> illum: cōnsilium, opus, puerum, diērum, frātrem, rem
> illā: uxōre, nox, manū, stilus, officia
> hoc: mīles, officium, nōmen, cīuem, aurum
> haec: aedēs, corōna, opera, manus, negōtia, rēs
> illōs: cīuīs, senem, facinus, deōs, domus

Optional revision

1 *Give the meaning, conjugation and infinitive of the following verbs:* cēlō, explicō, inueniō, audiō, dūcō, fugiō, mittō, ferō, mālō, sum, crēdō, scrībō, salūtō, legō, nesciō.

2 *Translate the following verbs, and then analyse them as follows:*

> *If an indicative, give person, number, tense (present or future) and voice (active or deponent), e.g.* amās – *2nd person singular present active of* amō *'love'*
> *If imperative, say whether s. or pl., active or deponent*
> *If infinitive, say whether active or deponent*
> *In all cases, end your analysis by saying what the verb is and what it means (see example above)*

amābis, habēre, dūc, minārī, dīcet, uelle, scrībitis, poterō, cape, dormiunt, prōgredere, dēfendis, opprimēs, necā, loquī, nōlumus, irrīdēre, stāte, rogās.

Exercises

1 *Translate*: cum hīs mulieribus; in illō capite; ad hanc rem; per illam turbam; cum hāc meretrīce; ex illō perīculō.
2 *Give the Latin for*: onto this stage; with that woman; through these fires; with those brothers; in this eye; into that town; through these dangers.
3 *Translate these sentences*:

(a) sī ille mīles Mnēsilochum cum Bacchide opprimet, illōs necābit.
(b) haec Bacchis amīca Mnēsilochī, illa Pistoclērī esse uīdētur.
(c) hanc mulierem ille iuuenis, illam hic amat.
(d) Nīcobūlus mīlitis illīus audit uerba, tum mōrēs fīlī plānē cognōscit.
(e) huic seruō omnēs meretrīcēs malae, illīs iuuenibus optimae esse uidentur.
(f) hunc senem seruus ille dēcipere cōnātur.

4 *Translate these sentences*:

(a) ūna salūs uictīs nūllam spērāre salūtem. (*Virgil*)
(b) praeterita mūtāre nōn possumus. (*Cicero*)
(c) nītimur in uetitum semper cupimusque negāta. (*Ovid*)
(d) semel ēmissum uolat irreuocābile uerbum. (*Horace*)

salūs salūt-is 3f. salvation, source of safety	*mūtō* 1 I change	we have been denied
uict-ī ōrum 2m. pl. the conquered	*nītor* 3 dep. I strive towards (*in* + acc.)	*semel* once
spērō 1 I hope for	*uetit-um ī* 2n. the forbidden	*ēmiss-us a um* spoken, sent forth
praeterit-a ōrum 2n. pl. the past	*cupiō* 3/4 I yearn for	*uolō* 1 I fly
	negāt-a ōrum 2n. pl. what	*irreuocābil-is e* beyond recall, irrevocable

Reading

Translate in word-order, defining which is subject (if one is quoted), which is object etc. in these incomplete sentences, then supply a verb to complete them and translate into correct English. Finally read out the sentences in Latin with correct phrasing, thinking through the meaning as you read.

(a) ille mīles hanc mulierem huic iuuenī crēdere . . .
(b) illum huius senis seruum . . .
(c) hoc aurum illī mīlitī hic seruus . . .
(d) cum hāc muliere illum iuuenem hic mīles mox . . .
(e) huic ille fēminae hōs nummōs omnīs dare . . .

Reading exercise / Test exercise

Read this passage carefully, translating in word-order as usual. You will need to choose from the bracketed words the one which makes sense of your suppositions about the direction of the sense so far. Translate into correct English; then, finally, read the passage aloud in Latin, phrasing correctly, thinking through the meaning as you read. Use the running vocabulary of **2C**.

Nīcobūlus fīlium et Bacchidem in aedibus (hanc, cōgitat, uidet). meretrīx Bacchis (ambās, arbitrātur, est). Chrȳsalō autem meretrīx esse (hanc, mīles, illa) nōn uidētur. nunc intrat Cleomachus mīles et illīus (uxōris, meretrīcis, fīliae) amātor. illum autem Chrȳsalus Bacchidis (uirum, fīlium, plānē) uocat. Chrȳsalī dominus nunc timet (amātor, citō, 5 ualdē), quod Bacchidem mīlitis (fīliam, nihil, uxōrem) arbitrātur. Chrȳsalī manūs seruōs statim (cūrāre, exsoluere, crēdere) iubet, Chrȳsalum cum hōc (fēminā, perīculō, mīlite) pacīscī, quod uult. huic mīlitī seruus statim nummōs (illum, fēminās, ducentī, multōs) pollicētur. sed illum tacēre ac uerba mala (dīcere, audīre, precārī) iubet, quod senem 10 (amāre, pollicērī, dēcipere) uult. deinde nummōs mīlitī (hunc, ille, magnō) prōmittit. Chrȳsalus autem mīlitī illī multa periūria dīcit (ad tempus, dē Mnēsilochō, in aedibus) et illum ad forum mittit.

English–Latin

1 *Translate these sentences into Latin, taking care to choose a word-order which gives the correct emphasis (see Reference Grammar* **W** *).*

(a) This man loves *that* man's daughter.
(b) This young man's father seems to be rich.
(c) Those women I consider as prostitutes.
(d) This is a great duty for good citizens.
(e) That soldier wants to defend this woman.

(f)   It's the character of these women I consider wicked.
(*Remember 'it's the' is just a way English has of emphasising something; Latin puts the emphatic words early in the sentence.*)

2   *Translate this passage (after rereading the text of **2C**):*

CHRYSALUS Who is this chap?
NICOBULUS He's my son Mnesilochus.
CHR. He appears to be with a pretty woman. What do you think?
NIC. She *is* pretty. But who is she? Tell me, I beg you.
CHR. Do you see that man?
NIC. Do you mean (*use* dīcō) that soldier?
CHR. Yes.
NIC. Go on.
CHR. I will. He is this woman's man.
NIC. What are you saying? But this woman's obviously a whore.
CHR. (Is) this (what) you think? You'll know everything soon.
NIC. What? Is she married (*use* nūpt-us a um)? I'm done for. O poor me!
    O wicked young man!

Deliciae Latinae

Word-building

Suffixes
Verbs often receive a change in their meaning from a suffix (or 'infix') which becomes part of their stem, e.g.

> -sc- indicates the beginning of an action. So *cognōscō* means 'I begin to know', 'I get to know'; *pacīscor* 'I begin/attempt to make a treaty'. All -scō verbs are 3rd conjugation.
> -it- denotes repetition. So *clāmitō* = 'I keep on shouting'. All verbs in -itō are 1st conjugation.

Word exercise

Give the meaning of these words and their connections with Latin: military; (*French*) le, la; (*Italian*) il, la; conative, arbitrate, meretricious, morals.

Everyday Latin

ad hoc 'for, directed at, this one occasion', i.e. unplanned.
post hoc, ergō propter hoc 'after this, therefore because of this'. A
famous logical trap into which it is only too easy to fall. After
you learned Latin you became a drunken layabout; therefore
it was because you learned Latin that . . . etc. Particularly
tempting for historians.

Real Latin

Martial

laudat amat cantat nostrōs⌐ mea Rōma ⌐libellōs,
  mēque sinūs omnēs mē manus omnis habet.
ecce rubet quīdam, pallet, stupet, ōscitat, ōdit.
  hoc uolo: nunc nōbīs carmina nostra placent. (*6.60*)

laudō 1 I praise	*ecce* but look!	*hoc, nunc,* are the
cantō 1 I sing up	*rubeō* 2 I blush	emphatic words here
libell-us ī 2m. book of	*quīdam* someone (subject)	*nōbīs* i.e. to me
poems	*palleō* I go pale	*carmen carmin-is* 3n. poem
sinūs (nom. pl.) pockets (a	*stupeō* I look bewildered	*placet* 2 it is pleasing
fold in the toga where	*ōscitō* 1 I yawn	
books kept)	*ōdit* 'he hates'	

Mottoes

hoc signum (*emblem*) nōn onus sed honor. (*Stoughton*)
hoc opus. (*Dee*)
hoc virtūtis opus. (*Collison*)

Word study

plānus

This means 'flat', 'level', so 'clear', 'obvious' in Latin. This becomes
English 'plane', a level surface, and the tool which makes a surface level.
Through French, we have English 'plain', a level surface, and plainsong
(as opposed to measured music, i.e. Gregorian chant as opposed to
polyphony). In Italian *plānus* emerges as *piano*, 'flat', hence in music,
'softly'. Combined with Italian *forte* 'loud' (cf. Latin *fortis* 'brave',
'strong'), it yields 'pianoforte', which can play both soft and loud.
'Explain' comes from *explānō* 'flatten', 'spread out', literally and before
the mind.

119

Do not confuse with the '-plain' of e.g. 'complain', which derives (again through French) from Latin *plangō*, 'mourn', 'lament' (cf. 'plangent', 'plaintiff').

Section 2D

Running vocabulary for 2D

Note. Places can be located by reference to the maps in *Text*. For this section see p. xiii. For places in later sections see also pp. xii, xiv, 64, 113, 136–7.

accipiō 3/4 I receive
adhūc up to now
adsum I am present, am at hand
aedificāuērunt (they) built
Agamemnōn Agamemnon-is 3m. Agamemnon (king of Argos, leader of expedition against Troy)
āmīsistī you (s.) have lost
annō year (see *decimō*)
ante (+acc.) in front of
arc-a ae 1f. money-chest
arm-a ōrum 2n. pl. arms
armāt-us a um armed
arx arc-is 3f. citadel
astūt-us a um clever, astute
Atrīd-ae um 1m. pl. the sons of Atreus (Agamemnon, Menelaus)
attulī (I) have brought
audīuī (I) have heard
audīuit he listened to
bīn-ī ae a two lots of, twice
castīgāuī I reprimanded
cēpērunt (they) captured

cēpī I captured; I have captured
coēgī I reduced
congredior 3/4 dep. I come to meet
cōnscrīpsit he wrote
cōnspicor 1 dep. I catch sight of, spot
contrā (+acc.) against
cūrāuī I have taken care of
dē (+abl.) according to
dēbeō 2 I ought
dēcēpī I deceived
decimō annō in the tenth year
dedit he gave
dēleō 2 I destroy
dīxistī you (s.) said
dīxit (he) said
ecferō I bring out
ēgī I have done
egistī you (s.) have done
equidem for my part
equ-us ī 2m. horse
euge hurrah!
eugepae yippee!
exercit-us ūs 4m. army
expugnō 1 I take by storm
fām-a ae 1f. story

fēcērunt (they) did
fēcit (he) did; he made
fīō happen (3rd s. *fit*)
for-um ī 2n. forum
fuērunt there were
fugāuī I put to flight / routed
fūgit (he) ran away
fuit (it/he) was
gessī I have conducted
gradior 3/4 dep. I come
Graec-us ī 2m. a Greek
hīc here
hōc tempore at this time
hōrā hour (see *ūnā hōrā*)
hūc (to) here
Īli-um ī 2n. Troy
illō tempore at that time
immō no; more precisely
impet-us ūs 4m. attack
in (+acc.) against
iussit he ordered
lacrim-a ae 1f. tear
Lāerti-us a um son of Laertes
ligne-us a um wooden
male badly
maledīxī I cursed
maxim-us a um very great

mīr-us a um amazing,
  surprising
miserē unhappily
misereor 2 dep. I feel pity
  for (+ gen.)
miserrim-us a um most
  wretched
mīsērunt (they) sent
multō tempore: haud multō
  tempore post = not long
  afterwards
necesse est it is necessary
nihilī of no value
nōscō 3 I examine
nōuī I know, recognise
obsideō 2 I besiege
obsignāt-us a um sealed
odiōsē odiously,
  annoyingly
ohē ho!
ōrātor ōrātōr-is 3m. orator,
  speaker
patri-a ae 1f. fatherland

Pergam-um ī 2n. Troy
periistī you (s.) have
  perished
perlegō 3 I read through
persuādeō 2 persuade
Philipp-us ī 2m. gold coin
  (minted by Philip of
  Macedon)
port-a ae 1f. gate
post afterwards
praed-a ae 1f. booty
Priam-us ī 2m. Priam
prōmīsit (he) has promised
pugnāuī I fought
quaesō 3 I beg
reueniō 4 I return
rēx rēg-is 3m. king
sententi-a ae 1f. opinion
seruāuī I saved
sign-um ī 2n. seal
simil-is e like (+ gen.)
sine (+ abl.) without
sollicitō 1 I bother, worry

soluō 3 I undo
spoli-a ōrum 2n. pl. spoils
suādeō 2 I advise,
  recommend
suspicor 1 dep. I suspect
tacit-us a um silent
tempore time (see *illō, hōc,*
  multō)
triumphō 1 I celebrate a
  triumph
Trōi-a ae 1f. Troy
uehementer violently
uērō indeed
uērum but
uetō 1 I forbid
uīcī I conquered
uīnxērunt (they) bound
Vlixēs Vlix-is 3m. Ulysses
  (= Odysseus, 'man of
  many wiles')
ūnā hōrā in one hour
urbs urb-is 3f. city

Learning vocabulary for 2D

Nouns

hōr-a ae 1f. hour
praed-a ae 1f. booty
ann-us ī 2m. year
equ-us ī 2m. horse

for-um ī 2n. forum
  (central business place
  of the city)
sign-um ī 2n. seal; signal,
  sign

tempus tempor-is 3n. time
urbs urb-is 3f. city
exercit-us ūs 4m. army

Adjectives

tacit-us a um silent

Verbs

pugnō 1 I fight
suspicor 1 dep. I suspect
dēbeō 2 I ought; owe
dēleō 2 I destroy (perf.
  dēlēuī)
gerō 3 *gessī gest-* I do,
  conduct

soluō 3 *soluī* I release,
  undo
uincō 3 *uīcī uict-*
  I conquer
adsum adesse adfuī I am
  present, am at hand

fīō fierī fact- I become, am
  done, am made

Others

ante (+ acc.) before, in
    front of
hīc here
immō more precisely, i.e.
    no or yes (a strong

agreement or
disagreement with
what precedes)
in (+ acc.) against (into,
onto)

post later, afterwards
sine (+ abl.) without
uērō indeed
uērum but

Grammar and exercises for section 2D

---

65 **Perfect indicative active: 'I —ed', 'I have —ed'**

	1	*2*	*3*
	'I loved'	*'I had'*	*'I said'*
	'I have loved'	*'I have had'*	*'I have said'*
1st s.	amā́-u-ī	háb-u-ī	díx-ī
2nd s.	amā-u-ístī (amā́stī)	hab-u-ístī	dīx-ístī (díxtī)
3rd s.	amā́-u-i-t	háb-u-i-t	díx-i-t
1st pl.	amā́-u-i-mus	hab-ú-i-mus	díx-i-mus
2nd pl.	amā-u-ís-tis (amā́stis)	hab-u-ís-tis	dīx-ís-tis
3rd pl.	amā-u-éru-nt (amāuére/amā́runt)	hab-u-éru-nt (habuére)	dīx-éru-nt (dīxére)

	4	*3/4*
	'I heard' 'I have heard'	*'I captured' 'I have captured'*
1st s.	audī́-u-ī	cḗp-ī
2nd s.	audī-u-ístī (audiístī/audī́stī)	cḗp-ístī
3rd s.	audī́-u-i-t	cḗp-i-t
1st pl.	audī́-u-i-mus	cḗp-i-mus
2nd pl.	audī-u-ís-tis (audī́stis)	cḗp-ís-tis
3rd pl.	audī-u-éru-nt (audīuére/audiérunt/ audiére)	cḗp-éru-nt (cēpére)

Notes

1 The perfect tense (*perfectus* 'completed', 'finished') has three basic
  meanings:

   (a) (by far the most common): completed action in past time, e.g.
        amāuī 'I loved'.

   (b) action in the past seen from the point of view of the present, e.g.
        amāuī 'I <u>have</u> loved'.

(c)   present state arising from past action, e.g. *periī* 'I am done for'
(i.e. 'I <u>have</u> perished and <u>therefore</u> am (now) done for').

Cf. Cicero's announcement that the conspirators involved with
Catiline had been executed – *uīxērunt* 'they have lived', i.e. 'they are
dead'. Generally speaking, the choice will be between (a) and (b),
according to context

2 Formation of the perfect tense:

(a)   The perfect active is formed for 1st and 4th conjugations by
adding *-uī* to the stem, e.g. *ama-uī, audī-uī*. 2nd conjugation verbs
only rarely add *-uī* to the stem (e.g. *dēleō dēlēre dēlēuī*); they drop
the *-e* of the stem as a rule, e.g. *habeō habēre habuī*. Note the *u* still
appears in the ending: this is the key to perfect active in
conjugations 1, 2 and 4. Third conjugation are unpredictable (see
Note 4).

(b)   Note, however, that in 1st and 4th conjugations, *-uī-/-ue-/-u-* is
sometimes dropped giving e.g. *amāstī* for *amāuistī*, *audiit* for
audīuit etc. See the bracketed forms in the chart.

3 BUT: *all* perfect actives have personal endings in:

-ī
-istī
-it
-imus
-istis
-ērunt (-ēre)

Note that, apart from 1st and 2nd s., the personal endings (*-t, -mus, -tis,
-nt*) are the normal active ones. Note variations on *-ērunt*; it can be *-ēre*
(do not confuse with infinitives, e.g. *habēre* and 2nd s. deponents, e.g.
pollicēre).

4 The perfect active stems of 3rd and 3rd/4th conjugation verbs, and
some irregular 1st and 2nd conj. verbs, are not as neatly predictable as
those of the other conjugations, but certain patterns do emerge, e.g.:

(a)   adding *-sī* to the stem, like:

   maneō 2 *mānsī* 'I stayed'
   irrīdeō 2 *irrīsī* 'I laughed at'
   iubeō 2 *iussī* 'I ordered'
   mittō mīsī 'I sent'

Note the effect on e.g.
dūcō dūxī 'I led'
dīcō dīxī 'I said'
uinciō uīnxī 'I bound'
scrībō scrīpsī 'I wrote'

(b)   doubling up ('reduplicating') the initial consonant and adding a vowel, like:

dō 1 *dedī* 'I gave'
tangō tetigī 'I touched'
poscō poposcī 'I demanded'

(c)   lengthening the vowel in the stem, like:

inueniō inuēnī 'I found'
fugiō fūgī 'I fled'
legō lēgī 'I read'

(d)   changing the vowel in the stem:

faciō fēcī 'I made', 'I did'
agō ēgī 'I did', 'I drove'
capiō cēpī 'I took'

(e)   no change in the stem at all:

dēfendō dēfendī 'I defended'
compounds of *-cendō -cendī*
verbs in *-uō -uī* e.g. *soluō soluī* 'I released'

(f)   stems ending in *lmnr* ('liquids', 'nasals') add *-uī*, e.g.:

uolō uoluī 'I wished'
aperiō aperuī 'I opened'

66   Irregular verbs

Irregular verbs learned to date are:

1   *adiuuō adiuuāre adiūuī* 'I help'
    dō dare dedī 'I give'
    stō stāre stetī 'I stand'

2   *caueō cauēre cāuī* 'I am wary', 'I look out'
    dēleō dēlēre dēlēuī 'I destroy'

irrīdeō irrīdēre irrīsī 'I laugh at'
iubeō iubēre iussī 'I order'
maneō manēre mānsī 'I remain'
possideō possidēre possēdī 'I possess'
respondeō respondēre respondī 'I reply'
uideō uidēre uīdī 'I see'

3 *adscrībō* see *scrībō*
agō agere ēgī 'I do', 'I act'
āmittō see *mittō*
cognōscō cognōscere cognōuī 'I get to know'
coquō coquere coxī 'I cook'
crēdō crēdere crēdidī 'I believe', 'I trust'
dēfendō dēfendere dēfendī 'I defend'
dīcō dīcere dīxī 'I say'
dīligō dīligere dīlēxī 'I love'
dūcō dūcere dūxī 'I lead'
gerō gerere gessī 'I do', 'I act' ('I wage')
legō legere lēgī 'I read'
mittō mittere. mīsī 'I send'; (ā-) 'I lose'
opprimō opprimere oppressī 'I surprise', 'I catch'; 'I crush'
ostendō ostendere ostendī 'I show'
pergō pergere perrēxī 'I carry on'
poscō poscere poposcī 'I demand'
prō-mittō -mittere -mīsī 'I promise'
reddō reddere reddidī 'I give back'
scrībō scrībere scrīpsī 'I write' (to)
soluō soluere soluī 'I release'
tangō tangere tetigī 'I touch'
uincō uincere uīcī 'I conquer'

4 *inueniō inuenīre inuēnī* 'I find'
uinciō uincīre uīnxī 'I bind'

3/4 *capiō capere cēpī* 'I capture'
dēcipiō dēcipere dēcēpī 'I deceive'
faciō facere fēcī 'I do', 'I make'
fugiō fugere fūgī 'I flee'
īnspiciō īnspicere īnspexī 'I inspect', 'I look into'
perficiō perficere perfēcī 'I complete'

Irregulars
(*ad*)*ferō ferre tulī* 'I bear, carry'
adsum 'I am present' see *sum*
auferō auferre abstulī 'I take away', 'I remove'
eō īre īuī or *i-ī* 'I go' (not really irregular, as the stem is -*i*)
mālō mālle māluī 'I prefer'
nōlō nōlle nōluī 'I do not want'
sum esse fuī 'I am'
uolō uelle uoluī 'I wish'

Exercises

1 *Form and then conjugate the perfect of these verbs*: clāmō, uideō, uincō, uinciō, abeō, sum, dō, capiō, ferō, faciō, (*optional*: pugnō, dēleō, gerō, dormiō, redeō, adsum, fugiō, adferō, dēcipiō).

2 *Translate each of these perfects. Change s. to pl. and vice versa*: dēlēuistī, gessērunt, uīcit, adfuistis, soluī, pugnāuimus, abiistis, (*optional*: amāuit, habuērunt, dēfendistī, necāuērunt, audīuī, cēpistis).

3 *What verbs are these perfects from? Translate them*: dedistī, crēdidit, attulērunt, fuit, dēbuistis, mānsī, oppressimus, scrīpsērunt, adiūuistis, tetigit, āmīsistī, dīximus, exiit, (*optional*: uīdit, mīsī, habitāuimus, timuistī, possēdistis, rogāuērunt, stetī, monuit, inuēnērunt, iniistī, abstulimus, reddidī, potuit, uoluī, māluērunt, cāuistis, perfēcimus, ēgit, dīlēxī, īnspexērunt).

4 *Give the Latin for*: I have given; we fought; you (*s.*) destroyed; he has loved; they were present; you (*pl.*) conquered; I went out; they have killed; he replied; you (*s.*) have acted; we completed; you (*pl.*) carried.

5 *Give present, future and perfect 3rd s. and pl. of these verbs*: dormiō, pugnō, dēleō, gerō, sum, auferō, redeō, dēcipiō.

6 *Locate the perfects in this list and translate them (say what tense the others are)*: stābit, dedērunt, crēdet, aderis, uīcistī, pugnābunt, soluunt, dēlent, gerent, mānsī, inuēnistis, perficiēs, dīligis, habēs, monuistis.

67 Ablatives: phrases of time

We have met two uses of the ablative to date: with prepositions (esp. of place, e.g. 'in', 'at', 'from'), and descriptive ('a man <u>of great arrogance</u>') (cf. **10**, **23**, **49**).

The ablative case is also used to show the time *at which* or *within which* something took place (cf. locational use), e.g. *illō tempore* 'at that time'; *prīmā hōrā* 'at the first hour'; *decem annīs* '(with)in ten years'.

Exercise

1 *Translate these sentences*:

(a) Mnēsilochus tacitus uerba Chrȳsalī audīuit.
(b) cum mīlite pugnāuī, iam cum sene pugnābō, nunc autem tacitus sum.
(c) magnō post tempore Graecī urbem Trōiam cēpērunt.
(d) hōc tempore noctis omnēs dormīre dēbent.
(e) fūrēs in aedīs nocte clam ineunt tacitī.
(f) ut Graecī equum illō tempore contrā[1] Trōiam mīsērunt, ita hodiē tabellās mittet contrā dominum Chrȳsalus.

[1] contrā (+ acc.) against

2 *Translate these sentences*:

(a) dēfēnsor culpae dīcit mihi 'fēcimus et nōs haec iuuenēs.' (*Juvenal*)
(b) dīc mihi, quid fēcī, nisi nōn sapienter amāuī? (*Ovid*)
(c) fuimus Trōes: fuit Īlium. (*Virgil*)
(d) lūsistī satis, ēdistī satis atque bibistī; tempus abīre tibi est. (*Horace*)
(e) nātūra sēmina nōbīs scientiae dedit; scientiam nōn dedit. (*Seneca*)

dēfēnsor defensōr-is 3m. defender	*Trōs Trō-is* 3m. Trojan	*bibō* 3 *bibī* I drink
culp-a ae 1f. fault	*Īli-um ī* 2n. Troy	*nātūr-a ae* 1f. nature
nisi except that	*lūdō* 3 *lūsī* I play, have	*sēmen sēmin-is* 3n. seed
sapienter wisely	fun	*scienti-a ae* 1f. knowledge
	ēdō ēsse ēdī I eat	

Reading exercise

Recognising the function of an ablative phrase is not always easy. So far you have met three types: (a) descriptive, e.g. uir summō ingeniō *'a very intelligent man', (b) prepositional, e.g.* cum illā muliere *'with that woman', (c) time when or within which, e.g.* hōc tempore *'at this time',* ūnā hōrā *'(with)in one hour'. Translate the following phrases and say to which category they belong:* uir

127

summā audāciā; illō tempore; hāc nocte; dē tuō perīculō; tacitā nocte; ā senibus miserīs; seruus multā astūtiā; mēcum; hōrīs multīs; magnō post tempore; fēmina summā pulchritūdine; ē forō; illō noctis tempore; cum meā uxōre; annīs decem.

Reading exercise / Test exercise

Read this passage carefully, translating in word-order. You will need to stop to group the ablative phrases and decide their function. Often the words in the phrase will not be next to one another. Attempt as you read to classify ablative adjectives and hold them in your mind without attempting to translate fully until the noun solves them. Translate into correct English, then read aloud in Latin, phrasing correctly, thinking through the meaning as you read.

Atrīdae longō post tempore Īlium cēpērunt. decimō enim annō urbem Trōiam tandem expugnāuērunt. nam illō tempore rēgēs in urbem equum mīsērunt ligneum. Epēus, uir astūtiā magnā, equum illum aedificāuit. mīlitēs in equō fuērunt armātī, summā audāciā uirī. hī ex equō illā exiērunt nocte et urbem mox dēlēuērunt. sīc illō diē Trōia urbs ūnā periit hōrā.

English–Latin

1 *Translate into Latin. Consult Reference Grammar **W** on word-order.*

   (a) The young man stood in the house silently.
   (b) Has the old man given the gold to the soldier?
   (c) They have sent the horses against the city of Troy.
   (d) On this night I have defeated my master and captured much booty.
   (e) At this time of year all people ought to stay at home.
   (f) The soldiers have seen the signal and will soon advance against the town.

2 *Translate this passage (after rereading the text of **2D**).*

NICOBULUS What ought I to do, Chrysalus? Tell me.
CHRYSALUS I don't want to say.
NIC. I beg you, speak. What shall I do? For I want to succeed (*use* rem bene gerere).
CHR. You will succeed, in my view, if you give the gold to your son. But I'm not giving an order.

NIC. I'll give him the money. Stay here! I'll be back soon.
(*Nicobulus goes into the house*)
CHR. The old man's destruction is nigh! How I've deceived him!
Now Mnesilochus will be able to give his mistress enough
money.

Deliciae Latinae

Real Latin

Vulgate

in prīncipiō creāuit Deus coelum et terram. (*Genesis 1.1*)
fōrmāuit igitur dominus Deus hominem dē līmō terrae et īnspīrāuit in
faciem eius spīrāculum uītae. (*Genesis 2.7*)
septimō autem diē sabbatum dominī Deī tuī est; nōn faciēs omne opus in
eō, tū et fīlius tuus et fīlia tua, seruus tuus et ancilla tua, iūmentum tuum
. . . sex enim diēbus fēcit dominus coelum et terram et mare. (*Exodus
20.10–11*)

prīncipi-um beginning	*īnspīrō* 1 I breathe	*sabbat-um* sabbath
creō 1 I make	*faciem* (acc.) face	*omne* = any (i.e. all *opus* is
coel-um heaven, sky	*eius* his	excluded)
terr-a earth	*spīrācul-um* breath	*in eō* in, during it
fōrmō 1 I form	*uīt-a* life	*ancill-a* maidservant
līm-us mud, clay	*septim-us* seventh	*iūment-um* ox
		mare sea

Mottoes

nīl sine Deō. (*Awdry*)
nīl sine labōre. (*Atkinson, Simpson*)
nīl sine causā. (*Brown*)
nōn sine Deō. (*Eliot*)
nōn sine causā. (*Drury*)
nōn sine industriā. (*Bevan*)
nōn sine iūre. (*Charter*)
nōn sine perīculō. (*Mackenzie, Walker*)

labor labōr-is 3m. work	*industri-a ae* 1f. effort	*iūs iūr-is* 3n. justice, right
caus-a ae 1f. reason, cause		

Word-building

Further suffixes

The following suffixes commonly form abstract nouns, 'the quality of',
'the condition of':

> -ia (gen. s. -iae f.) e.g. *audācia* 'boldness'
> -tās (gen. s. -tātis f.) e.g. *bonitās* 'goodness'
> -tūs (gen. s. -tūtis f.) e.g. *seruitūs* 'slavery'
> -tūdō (gen. s. -tūdinis f.) e.g. *multitūdō* 'manyness', 'crowd',
>   'plenty'

Exercise

1 *Derive and give the meaning of the following nouns:* iuuentūs, scientia,
timor, uirtūs, pulchritūdō, paupertās, praedictiō, facilitās, praetor,
malefactor, clāmor, cīuitās.
2 *Form the gen. s. of:* uirtūs, pulchritūdō, paupertās, facilitās, timor,
praetor.
3 *What are the nominatives of the following nouns, none of which you have met?*
Scīpiōnis, Cicerōnis, legiōnibus, longitūdinem, uictōrēs, cupiditātī,
ēruptiōne, iuuentūtis, lībertātem, explōratōrum.
4 *Can you guess the meaning of any of the nouns in 3?*

Adjective formation

Here is a list of common suffixes which form adjectives:

> -ilis ⎫
> -bilis ⎭ 'able to be', e.g. *ductilis* 'leadable', *mōbilis* 'mobile'
> -idus 'condition', e.g. *timidus* 'being in a condition of fear',
>   'afraid'
> -ōsus 'full of', e.g. *perīculōsus* 'full of danger', 'dangerous'
> -eus 'made of', e.g. *aureus* 'made of gold', 'golden'

The following list of suffixes may best be covered by the meaning
'pertaining to': -ālis, -ānus, -āris, -ārius, -icus, -īlis, -īnus, -īuus, -ius, e.g.
Rōm-ānus 'pertaining to Rome', *Lat-īnus* 'pertaining to Latium', *seru-īlis*
'pertaining to slaves', 'servile', *patr-ius* 'pertaining to one's father',
'paternal', 'ancestral' etc.

Exercise

Analyse the following adjectives etymologically, and reach a conclusion about their meaning: familiāris, facilis, audībilis, incrēdibilis, fertilis, scaenicus, fūrtīuus, senīlis, honōrābilis, igneus, oculeus (*used of monsters*), aquārius, pecūniōsus, uirīlis, uxōrius, domesticus, nōminātīuus, dōtālis, animōsus, cīuīlis, iuuenīlis.

Everyday Latin

Remember three important perfects with reference to Julius Caesar's famous words that he wrote on a placard at a huge triumph in Rome in 46 celebrating one of his quickest victories (at Zela in Asia Minor in 47):

uēnī, uīdī, uīcī 'I came, I saw, I conquered'

On tombstones *fl.* = *floruit* '(s)he flourished' and *ob.* = *obiit* '(s)he died' (cf. 'obituary') – both perfect tense.

Word exercise

Give the Latin connection of the following words: predatory, annuity, perennial, anniversary[1], millennium[2], temporary, urbane, tacit, pugnacious, delete, debt, solve, ante–chamber.

[1] *uers-* 'turn'.
[2] *mīlle* '1,000'.

Word study

sinecure (cūra)
This derives from *sine + cūra*, 'without the care', and *cūra*, through French, came to mean 'cure' in Middle English. In ecclesiastical language, *cūra* became the 'cure of souls', whence 'curate', one who cures souls (cf. French *curé*). So a 'sinecure' was a church office which paid a salary but did not involve work, the cure of souls. 'Secure' comes from *sē-* ('without') + *cūra*, 'without anxiety or care'; and *sēcūrus* became *seür* in Old French, whence English 'sure'. Late Latin *excūrō* 'I clean off' (Classical Latin 'I take great care') becomes, by a circuitous route, 'scour'! 'Curious' comes from *cūra* too. Latin *cūriōsus* means 'full of cares', 'anxious about', and so also 'inquisitive': hence 'curiosity', and in abbreviated form 'curio'. 'Accurate' comes from *ad + cūrō* 'give care to'.

aequus *and* **equus**

Since classical *ae-* became *e-* in mediaeval Latin, the derivations of these two words are easily confused! *aequus* 'even', 'equal' gives all the 'equality' words (and through French 'egalitarian'). 'Equations', of course, are supposed to balance and the 'equator' equates, i.e. makes equal, the two halves of the earth. 'Equitable' means 'fair', and its negative gives 'iniquity'. *adaequāre* means 'I make truly level' (i.e. 'at a suitable level'), so 'adequate'. 'Equilibrium' is 'even balance' (*lībra* 'scales'); 'equanimity' is the state of a balanced *animus* or 'mind'; and an 'equinox' occurs when night equals day.

   equus 'horse' (cf. *eques* 'cavalryman') gives us 'equine', 'equestrianism' etc.

arca

arca, 'box', 'coffer', comes from the same root as *arceō* 'I keep at a distance'. *arcānus* means 'boxed in', 'closed in', whence 'arcane', meaning 'secret'. In compounds, *arceō* becomes *-erceō*. So *coerceō* 'contain', 'restrain' gives English 'coerce'; *exerceō* 'drive out', 'keep someone moving' yields 'exercise' (cf. *exercitus* 'a trained force').

Section 2E

Running vocabulary for 2E

---

accipiō 3/4 I receive
accumbō 3 I lie down
addict-us ī 2m. debt-slave, bondman (a debtor who could not pay could become the slave of his creditor)
adgrediar I shall come up (to)
agn-us ī 2m. lamb
ais you (s.) say
aliquis (nom. s. m.) someone

alloquar I shall speak to
amātor amātōr-is 3m. lover
amb-ō ae both
amplexābor I shall embrace
amplexor 1 dep. I embrace
ante-eō -īre I beat, I am in advance of
aperiō 4 I open
appellō 1 I call
ariēs ariet-is 3m. ram
attōns-us a um shorn
audeō 2 I dare

bālitantēs (nom. pl. f.) bleating
bard-us a um dull
bene faciō 3/4 I do x (dat.) a favour
bis twice
blandiloqu-us a um persuasive, sweet-talking
blenn-us ī 2m. blockhead
buccō buccōn-is 3m. blabberer
castīgō 1 I rebuke

cōgō 3 I drive
colloquor 3 dep. I discuss together
cōnābimur we will try
cōnābor I shall try
conclūs-us a um shut in
condiciō condiciōn-is 3f. term
cōnspicor 1 dep. I catch sight of
cōnsultō 1 I deliberate
conuīui-um ī 2n. party
cupiō 3/4 I desire
dērīdeō 2 I mock
dīmidi-um ī 2n. half
dolor dolōr-is 3m. pain
effringō 3 I break down
ei alas!
eōdem (abl. s. n.) the same
etiam actually, then! (expresses indignation, impatience); still
ēueniō 4 I happen, turn out
euge hurrah!
ēuocō 1 I call out
exspectō 1 I wait for
fatu-us a um silly
feriō 4 I strike (*obscene*)
flāgiti-um ī 2n. disgrace
foris for-is 3f. door
fortūn-a ae 1f. fortune
fung-us ī 2m. mushroom
gerō 3 I conduct; *sē gerere* to behave oneself
hāc this way
heus! hey!
hūc (to) here
hūmān-us a um human
ibi there
improb-us a um abandoned, wicked
incursō 1 I charge into (*in* + acc.) (*obscene*)
indicō 1 I point to
īnfortūnāt-us a um down on his luck
ingrediēris you (s.) will enter

ingredior 3/4 dep. I enter
intereō interīre interiī I die
intus inside
lac lact-is 3n. milk
lacerō 1 I tear to pieces
lān-a ae 1f. wool
lēniō 4 I soothe, calm
lepidē charmingly, pleasantly
lepid-us a um charming
long-us a um long
loquar I shall speak
loquēris you (s.) will speak
lūdō 3 I play about, have a good time
magis more
mal-um ī 2n. trouble
mandō 1 I entrust (x acc. to y dat.)
maximē very much, especially
metuō 3 I am afraid
minimē not at all (lit. least)
modestē in moderation
molest-us a um nasty, irksome
moror 1 dep. I delay (NB. *haud moror* = I'm not bothered, I don't mind)
mors mort-is 3f. death
nārrō 1 I tell, relate
negō 1 I say no
nēquiti-a ae 1f. wickedness
nihilī worth nothing, of no value
nisi unless, if . . . not
niteō 2 I glisten, am in good condition
nōminō 1 I name
nōnne? surely?
oblīuīscētur he will forget
occāsiō occāsiōn-is 3f. chance, opportunity
ōrō 1 I beg
ouis ou-is 3f. sheep
pāstor pāstōr-is 3m. shepherd

patiar I shall endure
patiēmur we will endure
pecū pecūs 4n. flock
perdō 3 *perdidī* I destroy, ruin
pessim-us a um very bad, very wicked
Philipp-us ī 2m. gold coin (minted by Philip of Macedon)
Philoxen-us ī 2m. Philoxenus ('friend of strangers')
pol by Pollux!; indeed!
prō (+ abl.) for
procul far away
prōdigi-um ī 2n. miracle
prōdūcō 3 I lead out, bring out
prōgrediēmur we will advance
propter (+ acc.) on account of
pulsō 1 I knock at
pūtid-us a um rotten
quamquam although
quantī (see *tantī*)
quī (of) those who
quidem indeed
quid multa? lit. why (should I say) a lot? = to cut a long story short
quōmodo how?
regrediēmur we shall go back
sapienter wisely
sē himself
sē gerere to behave (himself)
sequar I shall follow
sequēminī you (pl.) will follow
sequēmur we will follow
sequēris you (s.) will follow
simil-is e alike, similar
sinō 3 I allow
soci-us ī 2m. ally

sollicitō 1 I bother, worry	*tantī . . . quantī* worth as	*uīn-um ī* 2n. wine
sōl-us a um alone	much . . . as	*uīt-a ae* 1f. life
sordid-us a um dirty	*tondeō* 2 *totondī* I shear,	*uīuō* 3 I live
spoliō 1 I despoil, strip	fleece	*uix* with difficulty
stolid-us a um senseless	*tranquill-us a um* calm	*ulcīscor* 3 dep. I take
stultissim-us a um stupidest	*ueniō* 4 I come	revenge on
stultiti-a ae 1f. stupidity	*uesper uesper-is* 3m.	*umquam* ever
tamquam like	evening	*unde* from where?
	uīctus ūs 4m. food	*uōx uōc-is* 3f. voice

Learning vocabulary for 2E

Nouns

uīt-a ae 1f. life	*foris for-is* 3f. door	*ouis ou-is* 3f. sheep
mal-um ī 2n. trouble; evil	*mors mort-is* 3f. death	*uōx uōc-is* 3f. voice; word

Adjectives

amb-ō ae both (like *duo*: see **54**)	*pūtid-us a um* rotten	*simil-is e* alike, similar; like x (gen.)

Verbs

castīgō 1 I rebuke	*audeō* 2 *aus-* I dare	*ingredior* 3/4 dep. *ingress-* I enter
sollicitō 1 I bother, worry	*accipiō* 3/4 *accēpī, accept-* I receive, welcome, learn, obtain	
amplexor 1 dep. I embrace		*patior* 3/4 dep. *pass-* I endure, suffer; allow
cōnspicor 1 dep. I catch sight of		

Others

hāc this way	*nisi* unless, if . . . not; except	*propter* (+ acc.) on account of
hūc (to) here	*prō* (+ abl.) for, in return for; on behalf of; in front of	*quamquam* although
ibi there		

Grammar and exercises for 2E

68 Future indicative deponent (all conjugations)

	1	*2*	*3*
	minābor	*pollicēbor*	*loquar*
	'I shall threaten'	'I shall promise'	'I shall speak'
1st s.	minā–bo–r	pollicē–bo–r	lóqu–a–r
2nd s.	minā–be–ris	pollicē–be–ris	loqu–ḗ–ris
	(minā–be–re)	(pollicē–be–re)	(loqu–ḗ–re)

3rd s.	minā́-bi-tur	pollicḗ-bi-tur	loqu-ḗ-tur
1st pl.	minā́-bi-mur	pollicḗ-bi-mur	loqu-ḗ-mur
2nd pl.	minā-bí-minī	pollicē-bí-minī	loqu-ḗ-minī
3rd pl.	minā-bú-ntur	pollicē-bú-ntur	loqu-é-ntur

	4	*3/4*
	mentiar 'I shall lie'	*prōgrediar* 'I shall advance'
1st s.	ménti-a-r	prōgrédi-a-r
2nd s.	menti-ḗ-ris (menti-ḗ-re)	prōgredi-ḗ-ris (progredi-ḗ-re)
3rd s.	menti-ḗ-tur	prōgredi-ḗ-tur
1st pl.	menti-ḗ-mur	prōgredi-ḗ-mur
2nd pl.	menti-ḗ-minī	prōgredi-ḗ-minī
3rd pl.	menti-é-ntur	prōgredi-é-ntur

Notes

1 We noticed the close relationship between present deponent and present active forms at **58**. There is an equally close relationship between future deponent and future active forms (for which see **50**).

2 While in the 3rd and 4th conjs. the *-am, -ēs, -et* of the active becomes regularly *-ar, -ēris (-ēre), -ētur*, in the 1st and 2nd conjs., the active *-bō, bīs, -bit* becomes *-bor, -beris (-bere), -bitur*. Cf. 3rd conjugation presents (*loquor, loqu-eris, loqu-itur*). Note in both the change of vowel *-i-* to *-e-* in 2nd s.

3 Observe the vowel-length of the 2nd s. future of *loquor – loquēris*. Contrast the 2nd s. present – *loqueris*.

Exercises

1 *Conjugate the future of*: opīnor, cōnspicor, uideor, īrāscor, oblīuīscor, mentior, ēgredior, patior, (*optional*: minor, precor, recordor, sequor, ingredior, suspicor).

2 *Translate and turn s. to pl. and vice versa*: opīnābor, mentiēris, precābitur, uidēbiminī, loquēris, pollicēbimur (*optional*: ingrediar, sequētur, uidēberis, cōnspicābuntur).

3 *Give the Latin for*: you (*s.*) will pray; she will threaten; they will seem; you (*pl.*) will talk; I shall advance; we shall think; they will try; he will follow.

4 *Turn the following presents into their future equivalents and translate*:

minātur, precantur, opīnor, uidēminī, cōnspicātur, sequitur, loquuntur (*optional*: īrāsceris, mentīris, ēgredior, prōgrediminī, precāmur, patimur).

5 *Turn these futures into their present equivalents and translate*: arbitrāberis, cōnābitur, patientur, loquēminī, sequēmur, adgrediēris, morābor, opīnābimur, prōgrediēminī, uidēbitur, mentiar.

6 *Name the tenses of these verbs*: dedit, conāberis, mentītur, uidēbitur, fēcērunt, amant, dēlent, dīcent, loquēris, tulistī (*optional*: fert, erit, īrāscar, fuistis, timet, dūcet, potest, mānsī).

69   Genitive of value

The genitive case is used to express the value put on a person or thing, e.g. *homo nihilī* 'a man of nothing' i.e. 'of no value', 'worth nothing'; *tantī es quantī fungus* 'you are of such (value) as a mushroom' (lit. 'you are of such value as of what value (is) a mushroom').

Exercises

1 *Translate these sentences*:

(a)   Nīcobūlus fīlium uocāuit iuuenem nihilī.

(b)   Philoxenus autem amīcās nīl nisi bonum habuit.

(c)   Nīcobūlus Bacchidī exitium minātur, nisi fīlium illa soluet.

(d)   Philoxenus Nīcobūlō, quod amat, tantī esse quantī fungus pūtidus uidētur.

(e)   Bacchis! tē illum senem amplexārī iubeō. ego hunc amplexar.

(f)   soror! ita agam dē sene, ut iussistī, quamquam malum mihi esse magnum uidētur mortem amplexārī.

(g)   senēs, ut opīnor, ambō mox ad forēs prōgredientur.

(h)   ita est, ut dīxī: ad forēs prōgrediuntur senēs.

2 *Translate these sentences*:

(a)   humilēs labōrant, ubi potentēs dissident. (*Phaedrus*)

(b)   dīuīna nātūra dedit agrōs, ars hūmāna aedificāuit urbīs. (*Varro*)

(c)   meminī enim, meminī neque umquam oblīuīscar noctis illīus. (*Cicero*)

(d)   hīc, ubi nunc Rōma est, orbis caput, arbor et herbae
        et paucae pecudēs et casa rāra fuit. (*Ovid*)

(e) rēligiō peperit scelerōsa atque impia facta. (*Lucretius*)
(f) nēmo repente fuit turpissimus. (*Juvenal*)

humil-is humil-is 3m.
  lowly person
labōrō 1 I have a hard
  time
potēns potent-is 3m.
  powerful man
dissideō 2 I disagree
dīuīn-us a um divine
nātūr-a ae 1f. nature
ager agr-ī 2m. field
ars art-is 3f. art, skill
hūmān-us a um human
aedificō 1 I build

meminī I remember
umquam ever
oblīuīscor 3 dep. (+ gen.) I
  forget
Rōm-a ae 1f. Rome
orb-is orb-is 3m. world
arbor arbor-is 3f. tree
herb-a ae 1f. grass
pauc-ī ae a a few
pecus pecud-is 3f. cattle
cas-a ae 1f. cottage, hovel
rārus a um few and far

between, scattered
rēligiō rēligiōn-is 3f.
  religion
pariō 3/4 *peperī* I bring
  forth, cause
scelerōs-us a um wicked
impi-us a um impious
fact-um ī 2n. deed
nēmo no one
repente suddenly
turpissimus (nom. m.) an
  utter scoundrel

Optional supplementary revision exercises

1 *Give the conjugation, infinitive and meaning of the following verbs:* adseruō, scrībō, salūtō, crēdō, perficiō, arbitror, nesciō, opprimō, reddō, dērīdeō, possum, mālō, agō, dēfendō, fugiō, dormiō, ferō, prōmittō, poscō, stō, sum, iubeō.

2 *Give the meaning, declension, gender and gen. s. of the following nouns:* serua, sōl, diēs, manus, officium, opus, scelus, stilus, ouis, caput, rēs, perīculum, nox, mulier, puer, cīuis.

3 *Pair the nouns of list A which agree with the adjectives of list B (often a noun will find agreement with more than one adjective). Identify the case, and translate, e.g.* familiam + hanc = *acc.* 'this household'; familiam + similem = *acc.* 'the same sort of household'.

A Nouns
familiam, deōs, uxōrī, nōminum, sorōre, frāter, onera, animō, cōnsilium, iuuenēs, manū, rēī, diēs, mīlitem, uōx.

B Adjectives
multī, illā, magnōs, omnium, ingentia, celerīs, haec, illud, hanc, similem, trīstis, facilēs, huic.

Reading and Reading exercise / Test exercise

1 *Below are given a number of main clauses and a pool containing an equal number of subordinate clauses or phrases to complete them. Read and translate*

each main clause, then, on the basis of sense, choose the subordinate clause which best fulfils your expectations.

(a) ego tē, homo pūtide, nihilī habeō propter hoc . . .
(b) uītam arbitror nīl . . .
(c) senēs mortem semper mālunt . . .
(d) magnum tibi malum, Bacchis, dabō . . .
(e) Nīcobūlus tamen aurum accipiet et in aedīs Bacchidum ingrediētur . . .
(f) tū tibi bene facere hōc tempore dēbēs . . .
(g) tum fīlium tuum cōnspicāberis . . .

dum uīuis
quod amātor senex fierī audēs
quamquam Mnēsilochum et Chrȳsalum ulcīscī māuult
nisi bonum
nisi nōbīs fīliōs nostrōs reddēs
quam uītam
ubi ad forēs Bacchidum adgrediēris et īnspiciēs

2 *Read the following passage carefully, translating in word-order, defining word function and phrasing word-groups, while anticipating what is to come. Then translate into correct English. Finally, read the passage aloud in Latin, phrasing correctly, thinking through the meaning as you read.*

Philoxenus, Pistoclērī pater, uir summā uirtūte, in scaenam intrāuit. ibi Nīcobūlum, Mnēsilochī patrem, uīdit. Philoxenō ille multa mala nārrāuit dē fīliīs. tandem ad aedīs Bacchidum adiērunt, pulsāuērunt forēs, meretrīcēs uocāuērunt. tum, ubi ex aedibus illae mulierēs exiērunt, fīliōs poposcērunt. tandem senēs in aedīs illae dūxērunt.

English–Latin

1 (a) If you (*s.*) don't give me back my money, I'll kill you.
   (b) Nothing bothers me except a lying slave.
   (c) That old man is worth as much as a wicked slave.
   (d) I will embrace my son, if he dares to approach me.
   (e) At that time I couldn't hear any[1] voice but[2] yours.
   (f) Although life is good,[3] death will approach the doors of rich and poor.

[1] Rephrase: 'I was able to hear no voice'.
[2] = *nisi*.
[3] Trans. 'a good thing'.

2 *Read the text of* **2E** *again carefully, then translate this passage*:

NICOBULUS Philoxenus, you are of no value. Although you are an
old man, yet you dare to become a lover.

PHILOXENUS Don't blame me, Nicobulus. And if you want to
rebuke your son, go inside. The women will look after you, if
you enter.

BACCHIS 1: I'll give back two hundred pieces, old man, if you'll
come in. And I'll embrace you.

NIC. I'm done for. It's difficult, because I want to upbraid the
scoundrels. Nevertheless, although I shall think myself a
scoundrel, I'll go in.

SOROR 2: Good. You are doing yourself a good turn, as you
should, while you're alive. In death no mistress will embrace
you.

Deliciae Latinae

Word exercise

Give the meaning and Latin connections of: vital, malicious, vociferous,
ambidextrous, castigate, solicitous, patience, mortal, accept.

Word-building

English suffixes
Note the common anglicisation of Latin suffixes (via French):

English	*Latin*	
–ry	*–ris, -rius, -ria*	
–an	*–ānus*	
–ious	*–ius*	'pertaining to'
–ic	*–icus*	
–ive	*–īuus*	
–able	*–ābilis*	'able to be'
–ible	*–ibilis*	
–ion	*–iō*	'action or result of action'
–ate, ite	*–ātus, -itus*	
–ty	*–tās*	'quality, condition of'
–nce	*–ntia*	
–tude	*–tūdo*	

Exercise

Say what you can about the derivation and meaning of the following English words.

Adjectives: legible, submersible, inaudible, irrevocable, military, captive, laudable, urban, scenic, nuptial, impecunious, filial, visible.

Nouns: fraternity, sorority, submission, nomination, audition, vicinity, admonition, station, visibility, vision, mission, longitude, instance (= *insto* I urge), arrogance (= *adrogō* I claim), replication, fugitive.

Word study

forum

forum, the legal and business centre of a town, basically means 'outdoors' and is connected with *forēs* 'doors' and the adverb *forās* 'out of doors'. *forum* yields the adjective *forēnsis* 'connected with the legal and business centre', hence English 'forensic', 'connected with the law'. *forestis* is a late Latin adjective often connected with *silua* 'a wood out of doors', whence 'forest'. From *forāneus* through Middle English *foreine* and Old French *forain* we eventually get 'foreign'.

Real Latin

Martial

praedia sōlus habēs, et sōlus, Candide, nummōs,
     aurea sōlus habēs, murrina sōlus habēs,
Massica sōlus habēs et Opīmī Caecuba sōlus,
     et cor sōlus habēs, sōlus et ingenium.
omnia sōlus habēs – nec mē puta uelle negāre!
     uxōrem sed habēs, Candide, cum populō. (*3.26*)

praedi-um ī 2n. farm	*Opīmī Caecub-um ī* 2n.	*cor cord-is* 3n. heart
sōl-us a um alone	Caecuban wine of	*ingeni-um ī* 2n. wit
Candide O Candidus	Opimius' vintage	*nec mē puta* 'do not
murrin-um ī 2n. expensive	(supposedly laid down	reckon that I' . . .
agate jar	121; cf. 'Napoleon	*negō* 1 I deny (it)
Massic-um ī 2n. fine wine	brandy')	*popul-us ī* 2m. people

Vulgate

sex diēbus operāberis, et faciēs omnia opera tua . . . nōn moechāberis . . .
nōn loquēris contrā proximum tuum falsum testimōnium. (*Exodus
20.9ff.*)

sex six	*contrā* + acc. against	*testimōni-um* ī 2n.
operor 1 dep. I am busy	*proxim-us* ī 2m. neighbour	evidence
moechor 1 dep. I commit	*fals-us* untrue	
adultery		

Mottoes

prō deō et − patriā (*Mackenzie*) / lībertāte (*Wilson*) / ecclēsiā. (*Bisshopp*)
prō Deō, prō rēge, prō patriā, prō lēge. (*Blakemore*)
prō fidē et patriā. (*Long*)
prō patriā et − lībertāte (*Michie*) / rēge (*Jones, Thomas*) / religiōne
(*Shanley*) / virtūte. (*Higgins*)
prō patriā vīvere et morī. (*Grattan*)
prō rēge et populō. (*Bassett*)
prō rēge, lēge, grege. (*Shield*)
prō lūsū et praedā. (*MacMoran*)

patri-a ae 1f. fatherland	*religiō religiōn-is* 3f.	*popul-us* ī 2m. people
ecclēsi-a ae 1f. church	religion	*grex greg-is* 3m. crowd,
rēx rēg-is 3m. king	*uīuō* 3 I live	mob
lēx lēg-is 3f. law	*morior* 3/4 I die	*lūs-us ūs* 4m. sport
fidēs fidē-ī 5f. faith		

SECTION THREE

Section 3A

Running vocabulary for 3A

---

abigō 3 I drive off
adpōt-us a um tipsy
Alcumēn-a ae 1f.
  Alcumena
amātor amātōr-is 3m. lover
ambulō 1 I walk
Amphitruō Amphitruōn-is
  3m. Amphitruo
appāreō 2 I appear
audācior bolder, cockier
audācissimus boldest,
  cockiest
bell-um ī 2n. war; *bellum*
  gerō I wage war
cael-um ī 2n. sky
commoueō 2 I move on
cōnfīdentior more
  undaunted
cōnfīdentissimus most
  undaunted
coniūnx coniug-is 3m. or f.
  husband/wife
cōnstanti-a ae 1f. loyalty
cubō 1 I lie down
dol-us ī 2m. trick
dux duc-is 3m. leader
ea (nom. s. f.) that
  (woman); (nom. pl. n.)
  those
eā (abl. s. f.) that, her

eae (nom. pl. f.) those (tr.
  that)
eam (acc. s. f.) that
eās (acc. pl. f.) those (tr.
  that)
ēbrior rather drunk
edepol by Pollux!
eī (dat. s. f.) to her
eīs (dat. pl. f.) those (tr.
  that)
eius (gen. s. m.) his
eō (abl. s. m.) him, that
  man
eōrum (gen. pl. m.) of
  them, their
eum (acc. s. m.) him, that
  man
expugnō 1 I storm
exsequor 3 dep. I carry
  out
fortior braver
fortissimus bravest
grauid-us a um pregnant
hostis host-is 3m. enemy
imāgo imāgin-is 3f.
  likeness, image
imperi-um ī 2n. order
intus inside
Ioue: see *Iuppiter*
is (nom. s. m.) that

Iugul-ae ārum 1f. pl.
  Orion
Iuppiter Iou-is 3m. Jupiter
legiō legiōn-is 3f. legion
līber līber-a um free and
  easy in (+ gen.)
long-us a um long
longior (nom. s. m.)
  longer
longiōrem (acc. s. m.)
  longer
longissima (nom. s. f.)
  longest
longissimam (acc. s. f.)
  longest
Lūn-a ae 1f. moon
meditor 1 dep. I think on,
  ponder, practise
meliōrem (acc. s. f.) better
meliōrī (dat. s. m.) better
Mercuri-us ī 2m. Mercury
mūtō 1 I change
nārrō 1 I tell, narrate
nigrior (nom. s. m.)
  blacker
nigriōrem (acc. s. f.)
  blacker
Nocturn-us ī 2m.
  Nocturnus, god of
  night

nōuī (perf.) I know
nūntiō 1 I announce,
  proclaim
nūnti-us ī 2m. messenger
ob (+ acc.) on account of,
  because of
occidō 3 I set
ōlim once upon a time
oper-a ae 1f. attention
ōrātiō ōrātiōn-is 3f. speech
paulisper briefly
pendō 3 *pependī* I hang
probē well and truly
pudīciti-a ae 1f. modesty,
  chastity
quam than
quōmodo how

reueniō 4 I return, come
  back
rēx rēg-is 3m. king
sē (acc.) himself;
  themselves; itself
*Septentriōnēs Septentriōn-
  um* 3f. pl. the seven
  stars of the Great Bear
sign-um ī 2n. constellation
sōl-us a um alone
Sōsi-a ae 1m. Sosia
statim (l. 35) stock still
stultior (nom. s. m.) more
  stupid
stultiōrem (acc. s. m.)
  more stupid
stultissimum (acc. s. m.)
  most stupid

stultissimus (nom. s. m.)
  most stupid
Tēlebo-ae (ār)um 1m. pl.
  the Teleboae
Thēb-ae ārum 1f. pl.
  Thebes
Thēbān-us a um Theban
tōt-us a um whole,
  complete
ueniō 4 I come
Vergili-ae ārum 1f. pl.
  Pleiades
Vesperūgō 3f. the Evening
  Star
uictōri-a ae 1f. victory
umquam ever
ūn-us a um one
utrimque on both sides

Learning vocabulary for 3A

Nouns

uictōri-a ae 1f. victory,
  triumph
bell-um ī 2n. war, conflict

imperi-um ī 2n. order,
  command
dux duc-is 3m. leader,
  general

Iuppiter Iou-is 3m. Jupiter,
  Jove
rēx rēg-is 3m. king,
  monarch

Adjectives

long-us a um long
līber lībera-a um free

niger nigr-a um black
fort-is e brave, courageous

is e-a id that; he, she, it

Verbs

ambul-ō 1 I walk
nūnti-ō 1 I announce,
  proclaim

medit-or 1 dep. I think on,
  reflect, ponder; practise
bellum gerō 3 *gessī gest-*
  I wage war

ueni-ō 4 *uēn-ī uent-*
  I come, arrive

Others

ob + acc. on account of,
  because of

quam than; (how!)

umquam ever

143

Grammar and exercises for 3A

70 *is ea id* 'that', 'those', 'that person', 'he', 'she', 'it'

	s.			*pl.*		
	m.	*f.*	*n.*	*m.*	*f.*	*n.*
nom.	is	é-a	id	é-ī[1]	é-ae	é-a
acc.	é-um	é-am	id	é-ōs	é-ās	é-a
gen.	←——é-ius——→			e-órum	e-árum	e-órum
dat.	←—— é-ī ——→			←—— é-īs[2] ———→		
abl.	é-ō	é-ā	é-ō	←—— é-īs[2] ———→		

[1] *éī* (nom. pl.) often becomes *íī.*
[2] *éīs* often becomes *íīs.*

Notes

1 This word works in the same way as *hic, ille*. On its own, it means 'that
man', 'that woman', 'that thing'; 'he', 'she', 'it' depending on gender
and context; describing a noun it means 'that'. The difference between
is and *ille* is that *is* = 'the one mentioned', while *ille* = 'that one over
there I'm pointing to' or 'the former one as opposed to this one'.

2 Apart from *is, id, eius, eī* (cf. *huius, illīus, illī*), the word declines exactly
like *mult-us a um* on the stem *e-*. This shows up most regularly in the pl.

71 **Accusative of time – 'throughout', 'for', 'during'**

Time 'for' or 'throughout' is expressed either by *per* + acc., or the plain
acc. without any preposition at all; e.g. *per eam noctem* or *eam noctem*
'through that night', 'for that night'. Distinguish between the accusative
and the plain ablative (**67**), which expresses time when or within which
e.g. *eā nocte* 'within that night', 'in that night'.

The accusative in time phrases may be graphically represented as a line
———— ; the ablative as a dot · or as a point *within* a circle ⊙.

Exercises

1 *Decline in all cases s. and pl.*: id bellum; ea urbs; is dux.
2 *What case(s) and number are the following phrases in?* eius rēgis; eī
exercitūs; eī uxōrī; iīs imperiīs; eam uxōrem; eōrum nōminum; ea
perīcula; ea nox; eum lectum; eōs mīlitēs.

3 *Give the Latin (using* is) *for:* (through) those days; that victory (*acc. s.*); of that war; for those kings; those generals (*acc.*); that command (*nom./ acc.*); to that mistress; those customs (*nom.*); his; to them; hers; to him; to her; on that night.

4 *Say with which of the words in each line the given part of* is *agrees (where there is ambiguity, explain the alternatives):*

> eī: mīlitem, uirī, fēminae, exercituī, puerō, patrēs
> eae: uxōrī, amīcae, noctis, uiās, rēs
> ea: imperia, astūtia, uirtūs, sōl, urbs, capita, manus
> eius: operis, puerī, reī, exercitūs, mōrēs, aedīs
> eīs: mīlitēs, signīs, meretrīcibus, ouīs, uirīs, mōribus

5 *Translate:* in eō oppidō; ob eam uirtūtem; apud eōs; eō tempore; per eam uiam; cum eā; eā nocte; in eam urbem; eās hōrās; ad eōs mīlitēs; eam noctem; multōs diēs; eō annō; id tempus.

6 *Give the Latin for (using* is*):* with those women; at that hour; at his house; onto that stage; in those cities; because of those dangers; on those nights; on account of that war; over those hours.

7 *Replace the English word in these sentences with the appropriate form of* hic, ille *or* is, *and translate:*

(a) (These) fēminae pulchrae sunt.
(b) uidēsne (those) mīlitēs?
(c) satis (of that) bellī est.
(d) (That man's) caput ingēns est.
(e) turba (of those) mulierum ingreditur.

72 Comparative adjectives: *longior longius* 'longer'

Comparative adjectives carry the meanings 'more . . .', 'rather . . .', '—er', 'quite . . .', 'too . . .'; e.g. *longior* 'longer', 'quite long', 'rather long'.
   Basic rule: look for the stem + *-ior-* (occasionally *-ius*).

	s.		*pl.*	
	m./f.	*n.*	*m./f.*	*n.*
nom.	lóng-ior	lóngius	long-iór-ēs	long-iór-a
acc.	long-iór-em	lóngius	long-iór-ēs	long-iór-a
gen.	←long-iór-is→		←long-iór-um→	
dat.	←long-iór-ī→		←long-iór-ibus→	
abl.	←long-iór-e→		←long-iór-ibus→	

Notes

1 To form the comparative, take the gen. s. of the positive adjective, remove the ending (leaving you with the stem) and add the endings for the comparative as indicated above. E.g. *ingēns ingent-is* – *ingentior*; *audāx audāc-is* – *audācior*.

2 Comparatives have consonant stems. This accounts for abl. in -*e*, n. pl. in -*a*, gen. pl. in -*um*. Note -*ius* in nom. and acc. n. s.

3 The original ending of the comparative was -*ios* (which becomes the neuter -*ius*). Then the *s* of -*ios* becomes *r* between vowels: so *longiōrem*, not *longiōsem* (cf. Reference Grammar **E5** *Note* 1 and **H3(d)** *Note*).

4 Note the Latin for 'than', used very frequently with comparatives – *quam*. The thing being compared in the *quam* clause adopts the same case as the thing it is being compared with e.g. 'Phaedra is more lovely than Euclio' – *Phaedra* (nom.) *pulchrior est quam Ecliō* (nom.); 'I hold you more foolish than him' – *habeō tē stultiōrem quam illum.*

73 Superlative adjectives: *longissim-us a um* 'longest'

Superlative adjectives carry the meanings '—est', 'most . . .' 'very . . .', 'extremely . . .'; e.g. *longissimus* 'longest', 'very long', 'extremely long'. Basic rule: look for -*ISSIM*- or -*ERRIM*-.

s.

	m.	*f.*	*n.*
nom.	long-íssim-us	long-íssim-a	long-íssim-um
acc.	long-íssim-um	long-íssim-am	long-íssim-um
gen.	long-íssim-ī	long-íssim-ae	long-íssim-ī
dat.	long-íssim-ō	long-íssim-ae	long-íssim-ō
abl.	long-íssim-ō	long-íssim-ā	long-íssim-ō

pl.

	m.	*f.*	*n.*
nom.	long-íssim-ī	long-íssim-ae	long-íssim-a
acc.	long-íssim-ōs	long-íssim-ās	long-íssim-a
gen.	long-issim-ōrum	long-issim-ārum	long-issim-ōrum
dat.	←———— long-íssim-īs ————→		
abl.	←———— long-íssim-īs ————→		

Notes

1 These superlatives are again based on the gen. s. stem of the positive adjective, to which the endings -*issimus* -*issima* -*issimum* (older spelling

146

-issum-us) are added, declining exactly like *multus*, e.g. *ingēns ingent-is ingentissimus a um.*

2 Adjectives ending in *-er* like *pulcher, celer, miser*, form their comparatives regularly (based on the stem of the gen. s.) but have superlatives in *-errimus a um*, e.g. *pulcher (pulchr-ī)* comp. *pulchrior*, sup. *pulcherrimus*; *celer (celer-is)* comp. *celerior*, sup. *celerrimus*; *miser (miser-ī)* comp. *miserior*, sup. *miserrimus.*

3 Two common irregular adjectives are *facilis, similis* (and their opposites *difficilis, dissimilis*). These have regular comparatives (*facilior, similior*), but irregular superlatives *facillimus, simillimus*. See Reference Grammar **J3**.

Exercise

Add the appropriate forms of both comparative and superlative degrees of the given adjective to the nouns:

> longus: diem, nocte
> celer: mīlitēs, oculō
> ingēns: aedēs, familiam
> pulcher: manūs, mulierum
> stultus: cōnsilia, hominī, operum

74 Irregular comparatives and superlatives: *bonus, malus, multus, magnus, paruus*

bon-us a um	melior (meliōr-is)	optim-us a um	'good', 'better', 'best' (*cf. ameliorate, optimise*)
mal-us a um	peior (peiōr-is)	pessim-us a um	'bad', 'worse', 'worst' (*cf. pejorative, pessimist*)
mult-us a um	plūs (plūr-is)	plūrim-us a um	'much', 'more', 'most' (*cf. plus*(+))
magn-us a um	maior (maiōr-is)	maxim-us a um	'big', 'bigger', 'biggest' (*cf. major, maximise*)

paru-us a um   minor (minōr-is)   minim-us a um   'small'/'few',
'smaller'/'fewer'/
'less', 'smallest'/
'fewest'/'least'
(*cf. minor, minimise*)

These decline quite regularly (see *longior longissimus*) except for *plūs*:

s.		*pl.*	
(*plūs plūr-is 3n., noun*)		(*plūrēs plūra, 3rd decl. adj.*)	
		m./f.	*n.*
nom.	plūs	plūrēs	plūra
acc.	plūs	plūr-īs (plūrēs)	plūra
gen.	plūris	←plūrium→	
dat.	—	←plūribus→	
abl.	plūre	←plūribus→	

Notes

1 Note: abl. s. in *-e*, n. pl. in *-a*: and then gen. pl. in *-ium*. *plūs* is consonant-stem, but *plūrēs* is *i*-stem (cf. **12**).

2 To express 'more . . .' in the s., *plūs* + gen. 'more *of* . . .' is used (cf. *satis, nimis, quid?*), e.g. *plūs pecūniae* 'more (of) money'. In the pl., *plūrēs* is an adjective and agrees regularly with its noun, e.g. *plūrēs hominēs* 'more men'.

Exercises

1 *Construct comparative and superlative of the following adjectives, giving their meanings when you have done so:* līber, fortis, bonus, niger, similis, magnus, celer, paruus, scelestus, stultus, malus, trīstis, facilis, multus, ingēns.

2 *Translate these sentences:*

(a) rēx deōrum et hominum eam noctem cum eā muliere in aedibus mānsit.

(b) eius uir, Amphitruō, domō fortissimō cum exercitū abiit.

(c) ea Iouem Amphitruōnem arbitrātur, quod is sē[1] illī similem fēcit.

(d) is deus eam tōtam[2] noctem amat, quod fēminam pulchriōrem numquam uīdit quam eam.

(e) is eam noctem propter Alcumēnam longiōrem fēcit.

(f) immō longissimam omnium fēcit noctium eam noctem.

(g) Mercurius, eius fīlius, deus summā est astūtiā. immō astūtior is est quam omnēs dī atque hominēs.

(h) is sē Sōsiae seruō simillimum fēcit.

(i) Amphitruō hāc nocte domum regrediētur, quod in bellō rem bene gessit et uictōriam tulit maximam.

(j) seruum quam Sōsiam stultiōrem, deum quam Mercurium scelestiōrem, numquam in scaenā uīdī.

¹ *sē* 'himself'.

² *tōt-us a um* 'whole'.

3 *Translate these sentences*:

(a) posteriōrēs cōgitātiōnēs, ut aiunt, sapientiōrēs solent esse. (*Cicero*)

(b) nōn faciunt meliōrem equum aureī frēnī. (*Seneca*)

(c) uideō meliōra probōque,
dēteriōra sequor. (*Ovid*)

(d) nūlla seruitūs turpior est quam uoluntāria. (*Seneca*)

(e) amā ratiōnem: huius tē amor contrā dūrissima armābit. (*Seneca*)

poster-ior ius later	*probō* 1 I approve	*ratiō ratiōn-is* 3f. reason
cōgitātiō cōgitātiōn-is 3f. thought	*dēter-ior ius* worse	*amor amōr-is* 3m. love
aiō I say	*seruitūs seruitūt-is* 3f. slavery	*contrā* (+ acc.) against
sapiēns sapient-is wise	*turp-is e* base, degrading	*dūr-us a um* hard, difficult
soleō 2 I am accustomed	*uoluntāri-us a um* voluntary, willing	*armō* 1 I arm, equip
frēn-ī ōrum 2m. pl. bridle		

Reading

Read (translating in word-order) each of these incomplete sentences (all containing a comparative idea) and choose from the pool below them the correct phrase to complete them. Then translate into correct English.

(a) noctem numquam uīdī longiōrem . . .

(b) hic seruus audācior est . . .

(c) eī senī aurī plūs dabō . . .

(d) hōc tempore nigrior est nox . . .

(e) is uir maiōre uirtūte est . . .

(f) seruum stultissimum mālō . . .

(g) numquam perīculum maius ferre poterō . . .

(h) mīlitēs numquam fuērunt fortiōrēs . . .
(i) uirumne deō similiōrem umquam uīdistis . . ?
(j) fēmināsne pulchriōrēs umquam cōnspicābor . . ?

quam hic; quam hoc; quam hanc; quam huic; quam eās; quam illī; quam eum; quam ille; quam mendācem; quam illō.

Reading exercise / Test exercise

Read this passage carefully, translating in word-order, defining the functions of words and the groups to which they belong, and stating at each point what you anticipate on the basis of the information you already have. Then translate into correct English. Finally, read out in Latin, phrasing correctly, thinking through the meaning as you read. Use the running vocabulary of **3A**.

Mercurius, deōrum astūtissimus, ad urbem Thēbās cum patre uenit, quod is fēminam pulcherrimam amat, uxōrem ducis legiōnum Thēbānārum. Iuppiter quamquam ea fēmina nūpta est, tamen cum eā tōtam noctem cubāre uult. hārum rērum, ut uidēmus, līberiōrēs esse quam hominēs dī possunt, quod habent imperium maximum,   5
mortemque numquam patiuntur. Alcumēna autem uirum ualdē amat. Mercurium igitur Iuppiter sēcum attulit, quod is dolōs plūrimōs atque astūtiās optimās scit. Mercurius igitur sē Sōsiae, Amphitruōnis seruō, similem, Iuppiter autem Amphitruōnī sē simillimum fecit. ita in aedīs Amphitruōnis dī intrāuērunt. Iuppiter, rēx hominum atque deōrum,   10
Alcumēnam clam tōtam noctem amāuit et grauidam fēcit. immō grauidiōrem eam fēcit, quod Amphitruō quoque eam grauidam fēcit eā nocte, ubi ad bellum abiit. nunc deus maximus, quod Alcumēnam ualdē amat, noctem longiōrem fēcit et Mercurium ante aedīs posuit.[1] mox Sōsia ad aedīs adgrediētur et intrāre cōnābitur, eum Mercurius ab aedibus   15
abiget.

[1] *posuit* 'has placed'.

English–Latin

1 *Translate into Latin:*

(a) This victory was greater than that (one).
(b) In those years because of the command of a rather stupid king, many very brave soldiers fought a very long war.
(c) There is nothing better than the duty of the best citizens.

(d) The wisdom of the gods is greater than (that) of men. (*Miss out the second 'that'*).

(e) My brother is more like my father than me.

(f) Nothing is worse than this trouble.

2 *Read the text of* **3A** *again, then translate this passage into Latin:*

SOSIA Who is (there) better than I?

MERCURY Who more rotten?

SOS. No, I'm truly the best of all slaves, the bravest of all men . . .

MER. And the most stupid of fools[1].

SOS. I'm rather bold because on this very long night I'm walking alone through these streets. And I've certainly never seen a blacker night or a longer (one) than this. Why is the moon not changing, nor these constellations[2] setting? Will the day never appear?

MER. I want you, night, to go on just as you are going on now. For you will never do a greater duty for my father than this.

[1] Use *stultus* as a noun.
[2] Use *signum*.

Deliciae Latinae

Word exercise

Give the Latin connections of: victory, bellicose, imperial, regal, urban, long, summit, liberal, meditate, fortitude.

Everyday Latin

The *ego* (and *superego*) and the *id* were terms used by Sigmund Freud to denote respectively the conscious and subconscious self

i.e. = *id est* 'that is'

An argument *ā fortiōrī* (alternative later form for the classical *fortiōre*) is one 'from a stronger case' e.g. 'Hercules cannot pick up this rock; *ā fortiōrī* a baby will not be able to'

Other useful comparatives are *posterior* ('further behind'), *superior* ('higher'), *iūnior* ('younger' from *iuuenis*, cf. English 'junior'), *senior* ('older' from *senex*)

ē plūribus ūnum 'from rather many (peoples), one' – the American motto

An important principle of law is *dē minimīs nōn cūrat lēx* – meaning?

Word study

summus

summus means 'the top', 'highest point' and gives us 'to sum', i.e. calculate the total of, since the Romans added columns of figures from the bottom up, till they reached the *summa līnea* 'the top line'. Hence a 'sum', especially of money. *summārius* is an accountant, one who does the sums, or sums up, whence English 'summary'. A 'summit' is the highest point of a hill. A 'consummation' is the complete (*con-*) summing up, so a completion or achievement.

Do not confuse with 'summon' – from *submoneō* 'warn secretly' – or words like 'consume', 'assume' from *sūmō* 'take up' 'take upon oneself' 'spend'.

fortis

fortis means 'strong' or 'brave'. The English 'force' derives ultimately from the n. pl. of *fortis*, i.e. *fortia*. English derivatives include 'fort', 'fortify' and 'fortitude'. They also include 'comfort' ('strengthen together' or 'strengthen considerably') and 'effort' (through Old French *esfors*, 'forcing oneself out' (*es-* = Latin *ex*)).

Section 3B

Running vocabulary for 3B

adeptī (m. pl. nom.)
   having gained, taken
adept-us (nom. s. m.)
   having gained
adeptī sunt (they) gained,
   took

adgressī sunt (they)
   attacked
adgressī (m. pl. nom.)
   having attacked
adlocūtus est (he) addressed
ager agr-ī 2m. territory,

land, field
Alcumēn-a ae 1f.
   Alcumena
ār-a ae 1f. altar
arbitri-um ī 2n.
   jurisdiction, power

Argīu-us a um Argive,
Greek
audācter courageously,
boldly
cael-um·ī 2n. sky
castr-a ōrum 2n. pl. camp
canō 3 *cecinī* I sound
caus-a ae 1f. reason
celeriter quickly
clāmor clāmōr-is 3m. shout
collocūtī (nom. pl. m.)
having discussed
collocūtī sunt (they)
discussed
condiciō condiciōn-is 3f.
terms
cōnsentiō 4 *cōnsēnsī* I reach
agreement
cōnsonō 1 *cōnsonuī* I roar
cōnspicātus (nom. s. m.)
having caught sight of
cōpi-ae ārum 1f. pl. troops
dēdō 3 *dēdidī* I hand over,
surrender
dēdūcō 3 I lead off
dēnique finally, at last
dirimō 3 *dirēmī* I break off,
end
dīuīn-us a um divine
domin-a ae 1f. mistress
ēdūcō 2 *ēdūxī* I lead out
ēgressī sunt they came out,
disembarked
ēgressī having
disembarked
equit-ēs um 3m. pl.
cavalry
exsecūtus (nom. s. m.)
having carried out
exsequor 3 I carry out
extrā (+ acc.) outside,
beyond
ferōci-ae ae 1f. fierceness
ferōciter fiercely

foc-us ī 2m. hearth
fortiter bravely
fug-a ae 1f. flight, escape
hortātus (nom. s. m.)
having encouraged
hortātus est (he)
encouraged
hostis host-is 3m. enemy
hūmān-us a um human
illūstr-is e famous
imperātor imperātōr-is 3m.
commander
ingressus (nom. s. m.)
having entered
iniūst-us a um unjust
īnstruō 3 *īnstrūxī* I draw
up
iūst-us a um just
lēgāt-us ī 2m. ambassador
legiō legiōn-is 3f. legion
līber-ī ōrum 2m. pl.
children
locūtī sunt (they) spoke
locūtī (nom. pl. m.)
having spoken
locūtus (nom. s. m.)
having spoken
man-us ūs 4m. band
medi-us a um middle
minātī (nom. pl. m.)
having threatened
miserē unhappily
nāu-is is 3f. ship
necesse necessary
oppugnō 1 I attack
ōrdō ōrdin-is 3m. rank
ōti-um ī 2n. peace,
freedom from war
pāx pāc-is 3f. peace
paulisper briefly
post (+ acc.) after
postrēmō finally
postrīdiē next day
pōnō 3 *posuī* I pitch, place

precātī (nom. pl. m.)
having prayed (to)
precātus (nom. s. m.)
having prayed to
precātus est (he) prayed to
prōdūcō 3 *prōdūxī* I lead
forward
proeli-um ī 2n. battle
profectī (nom. pl. m.)
having set out
prōgressī having advanced
prōgressī sunt (they)
advanced
prōterō 3 *prōtrīuī*
I trample down
pugnō 1 I fight
redūcō 3 I lead back
regressī sunt (they)
returned
sē himself, themselves
(nb. pl. at l. 84)
sēque and themselves
subitō suddenly
su-us a um his, her
superō 1 I gain the upper
hand
tant-us a um so much, so
great
terr-a ae 1f. land
tub-a ae 1f. trumpet
tul- perf. of *ferō*; note *mē*
ferō 'I bear myself,
charge'
tūtor 1 dep. I protect
uehementer ardently
uesper uesper-ī 2m. dusk,
evening
uict-ī ōrum 2m. the
defeated
uictor uictōr-is 3m.
conqueror
ulcīscor 3 I take revenge on
usque (*ad* + acc.) right up
to
utrimque on both sides

Learning vocabulary for 3B

Nouns

cōpi-ae ārum 1f. pl. troops
ferōci-a ae 1f. fierceness
terr-a ae 1f. land
lēgāt-us ī 2m. ambassador
ager agr-ī 2m. land, field, territory
castr-a ōrum 2n. pl. camp

ōti-um ī 2n. cessation of conflict, leisure; inactivity
proeli-um ī 2n. battle
eques equit-is 3m. horseman; (pl.), cavalry

hostis host-is 3m. enemy
legiō legiōn-is 3f. legion
nāuis nāu-is 3f. ship
pāx pāc-is 3f. peace
man-us ūs 4f. band; (hand)

Adjectives

illūstr-is e famous
su-us a um his, her(s), their(s)

Verbs

oppugnō 1 I attack
super-ō 1 I conquer, overcome, get the upper hand
hort-or 1 *hortāt-us* dep. I urge, encourage
dēd-ō 3 *dēdid-ī dēdit-* I surrender, hand over

dēdūc-ō 3 *dēdūx-ī dēduct-* I lead away, lead down
ēdūc-ō 3 *ēdūx-ī ēduct-* I lead out
redūc-ō 3 *redūx-ī reduct-* I lead back
adipīsc-or 3 *adept-us* dep. I get, gain, acquire

adloqu-or (alloqu-or) 3 *adlocūt-us (allocūt-us)* dep. I address
proficīsc-or 3 *profect-us* dep. I set out
mē fer-ō ferre tul-ī lāt- I charge, attack (lit. 'I bear myself')

Others

celeriter quickly
ferōciter fiercely

fortiter bravely

utrimque on both sides

Grammar and exercises for 3B

---

75 Perfect indicative deponent: 'I —ed', 'I have —ed'

	1 *minor* 'I threatened / have threatened'	2 *polliceor* 'I promised / have promised'	3 *loquor* 'I spoke / have spoken'
1st s.	minát-us a um sum	pollícit-us a um sum	locū́t-us a um sum
2nd s.	minát-us a um es	pollícit-us a um es	locū́t-us a um es
3rd s.	minát-us a um est	pollícit-us a um est	locū́t-us a um est

1st pl.	minā́t-ī ae a súmus	pollícit-ī ae a súmus	locū́t-ī ae a súmus
2nd pl.	minā́t-ī ae a éstis	pollícit-ī ae a éstis	locū́t-ī ae a éstis
3rd pl.	minā́t-ī ae a sunt	pollícit-ī ae a sunt	locū́t-ī ae a sunt

	4	3/4
	mentior	*prōgredior*
	'I lied / have lied'	'I advanced / have advanced'
1st s.	mentī́t-us a um sum	prōgréss-us a um sum
2nd s.	mentī́t-us a um es	prōgréss-us a um es
3rd s.	mentī́t-us a um est	prōgréss-us a um est
1st pl.	mentī́t-ī ae a súmus	prōgréss-ī ae a súmus
2nd pl.	mentī́t-ī ae a éstis	prōgréss-ī ae a éstis
3rd pl.	mentī́t-ī ae a sunt	prōgréss-ī ae a sunt

Notes

1 *Formation of perfect stem*

(a) The perfect stem of the deponent is regularly formed by adding -*t-us a um* to the stem of the verb. Thus:

> 1st conj.: *minā-t-us a um*
> 2nd conj.: *pollici-t-us a um* (note that -*e* changes to -*i*)
> 4th conj.: *mentī-t-us a um*

Standing on its own, it forms the perfect participle and means 'having —ed' (see **77**), e.g. *minātus* 'having threatened' etc.

(b) You have now met the three 'principal parts' of deponent verbs, i.e. the present indicative active (e.g. *minor*), the infinitive (e.g. *mināri*) and the perfect (e.g. *minātus*). Of regular deponent verbs, the principal parts are formed as follows:

> 1: *minor minārī minātus*
> 2: *polliceor pollicērī pollicitus*
> 4: *mentior mentīrī mentītus*

These are the bases for forming *all parts of the deponent*, and must be learned from now on.

(c) As we found with non-deponent verbs, however, 3rd and 3rd/4th conjugation deponent verbs are unpredictable in their formation of the perfect stem. Perfect stems of these verbs are formed in -*t-us a um* and -*s-us a um*. Here are the three 'principal parts' of the *irregular* deponents you have met so far (including one 2nd decl. verb):

in -*s*-*us a um*

2 *uideor uidērī uīsus* 'I seem'

3/4 (*ad-*)
(*ē-*)
(*in-*) } *gredior gredī gressus* 'I go', 'I come'
(*prō-*)

patior patī passus 'I endure', 'I undergo', 'I suffer'

in -*t*-*us a um*

3 (*ad-*) *loquor loquī locūtus* 'I speak (to)'
sequor sequī secūtus 'I follow'
oblīuīscor oblīuīscī oblītus 'I forget'
īrāscor īrāscī īrātus 'I get angry'
adipīscor adipīscī adeptus 'I gain', 'I get'
proficīscor proficīscī profectus 'I set out'

2 *Formation of deponent perfect indicative*
To form the perfect indicative deponent, the perfect stem ending in -*us*
-*a* -*um* (which means on its own 'having —ed') is combined with the
appropriate part of *sum es est sumus estis sunt*, e.g. *locūtus sum* (lit.) 'I am
(in a state of) having spoken', 'I spoke', 'I have spoken', 'I did speak'.
Since the perfect stem ending in -*us* -*a* -*um* acts as an adjective, it must
agree with the subject, e.g.

'I (= a woman) spoke' *locūta sum*
'they (= the men) promised' *pollicitī sunt*
'the boy lied' *puer mentītus est*
'you (= the women) set out' *profectae estis*

The perfect stem in -*us a um* will be in the *nominative*, since it is agreeing
with the subject of the sentence.

3 *Meaning*
The meaning, literally 'I am (in a state of) having —ed', can be treated
as identical with 'I —ed', 'I have —ed' and (in certain cases) 'I am —' –
a present state which results from a past action.

76 Semi-deponents: *audeō* and *fīō*

A number of verbs, called 'semi-deponents', adopt *active forms* in some
tenses, and *deponent forms* in others. Of the tenses you have met so far,

present and future forms of such verbs are active in form; the perfects, however, are deponent in form. Thus:

audeō 'I dare' *audēre* 'to dare' (no perfect active stem) *ausus* 'having dared'

Present		Future		Perfect	
aúde-ō	'I dare'	audé-b-ō	'I shall dare'	aús-us a um sum	'I dared'
aúdē-s		audé-bi-s		aús-us a um es	
aúde-t		audé-bi-t		aús-us a um est	
audé-mus		audé-bi-mus		aús-ī ae a súmus	
audé-tis		audé-bi-tis		aús-ī ae a éstis	
aúde-nt		audé-bu-nt		aús-ī ae a sunt	

fīō 'I become', 'I am made', 'I happen' *fierī* 'to become, be made' (no perfect active stem) *factus* 'having become', 'having been made'

Present	Future	Perfect
fī-ō 'I become' *etc.*	fī-a-m 'I shall become' *etc.*	fáct-us a um sum 'I became' *etc.*
fī-s	fī-ē-s	fáct-us a um es
fi-t	fī-e-t	fáct-us a um est
—[1]	fī-ē-mus	fáct-ī ae a súmus
—[1]	fī-ē-tis	fáct-ī ae a éstis
fī-unt	fī-e-nt	fáct-ī ae a sunt

[1] *fīmus* and *fītis* are not found.

Exercises

1 *Form and conjugate the perfect of*: meditor, cōnor, uideor, oblīuīscor, proficīscor, mentior, prōgredior, patior, (*optional*: cōnspicor, adipīscor, polliceor, hortor, sequor, recordor, ēgredior, īrāscor).

2 *Translate each perfect then change s. to pl. and vice versa*: locūtus sum; uīsum est; recordāta est; mentītī sumus; ingressae sunt, pollicita es; secūta sunt; adeptus est; (*optional*: īrāta est; oblītus sum; passa es; profectus est; meditātī estis; arbitrātī sunt; suspicātae sunt).

3 *Say what verbs these perfects come from and translate*: uīsus est; adepta est; oblītus sum; ingressae sumus; locūtī estis; profectī sunt; factum est.

4 *Give the Latin for*: she has threatened; they (*m.*) set out; I (*m.*) have

encouraged; you (*s. f.*) seemed; we (*f.*) forgot; he promised; it happened; you (*pl. m.*) have lied.

5 *Give 3rd s. and pl. present, future and perfect of these verbs and translate:* īrāscor, minor, polliceor, mentior, patior, (*optional:* profīciscor, ingredior, uideor, fīō, recordor.

77 Perfect participles deponent: 'having —ed'

A participle is an *adjective* which derives from a *verb* and shares the nature of both (from *pars* and *capiō* 'take a share/part in'). In English, it tends to be formed in '—ing' or 'having —ed', e.g. 'I saw the man <u>running</u>', 'the men, <u>having departed</u>, reached home'. The perfect stem of deponent verbs ending in *-us, -a, -um* is the *perfect participle* and means 'having —ed', e.g. *minātus* 'having threatened', *locūtus* 'having spoken', *ēgressus* 'having gone out'. These perfect participles decline like *multus a um* and, like any adjectives, agree with the person described as 'having —ed', e.g. 'the woman, <u>having spoken</u>, goes out' *mulier <u>locūta</u> ēgreditur,* 'the men, <u>having spoken</u>, go out' *hominēs <u>locūtī</u> ēgrediuntur,* 'I see the soldiers <u>having-gone-out</u> / the soldiers <u>when they have gone out</u>' *mīlitēs <u>ēgressōs</u> uideō.*

Participles are on the whole used predicatively, i.e. they say what people *do* rather than *describe* or *define* people. Thus *mulier locūta ēgreditur* should be translated 'the woman – after speaking/having spoken/when she has spoken/speaks and – goes out'. It is not accurate to translate it 'the woman *who has spoken* goes out'. See 'predicative', p. xxi.

Exercises

1 *Give the meaning of these words and say from what verb each comes:* locūtus, profectus, adeptus, īrātus, cōnātus, precātus, suspicātus, pollicitus, hortātus, uīsus, ēgressus, factus, (*optional:* arbitrātus, opīnātus, mentītus, secūtus, passus, adgressus).

2 *Translate these sentences:*

    (a)   mīlitem ingressum cēpit.
    (b)   hominēs paulum (*a little*) meditātī uēnērunt.
    (c)   ille multa mentītus abiit.
    (d)   exercitus celeriter ex urbe prōgressus mox castra posuit.
    (e)   haec locūta exiit.

'8 Translation hint

Deponent participles can, of course, control their own little clauses (and sometimes not so little), in the same way that infinitives do. Observe how infinitives and some direct objects in the following sentences depend on the participle, not on the main verb:

> *hominēs fugere cōnātōs necāuimus* 'we killed the men having-tried to escape', '... the men after they had tried to escape' (*fugere* depends on *cōnātōs*)
> *mulierēs hoc locūtās nōn amō* 'I do not like the women having-said / since they said this'
> *mīlitēs, multa minātī, ēgrediuntur* 'the soldiers, having threatened much, depart'

Observe the way in which the participles in such complex sentences gravitate towards the end of their clause, in the same way that main verbs and infinitives tend to. Often this results in a pleasing 'bracketing' effect rather like an equation, especially when the participle has a direct object, e.g. 'The priest, seeing the horse galloping down the street, gave chase.' A typical Latin order for this would be: 'The priest (nom.), the horse (acc.) down the street galloping (acc.) seeing (nom.), gave chase.'

Exercise

Select subject, verb, adjective and participle in these sentences:

(a) She writhed about, convulsed with scarlet pain. (*Keats*)
(b) Naked she lay, clasped in my longing arms. (*Rochester*)
(c) I saw three ships go sailing by on Christmas day. (*Do you place 'on Christmas day' with the 'I saw' clause or the 'go sailing by' clause?*)
(d) Know you not, / Being mechanical, you ought not walk / Upon a labouring day . . .? (*Shakespeare*)
(e) See! from the Brake the whirring Pheasant springs,
    And mounts exulting on triumphant Wings:
    Short is his Joy; he feels the fiery Wound,
    Flutters in Blood, and panting beats the Ground. (*Pope*)

79 Regular and irregular adverbs

A common way of forming adverbs in English is to add '-ly' to an adjective (e.g. 'slow-ly', 'quick-ly', 'passionate-ly'). In Latin, adverbs (which never change) are also regularly formed from adjectives as follows.

Adverbs based on 1st/2nd declension adjectives: add *-ē* to the stem, e.g. *stultus — stultē* 'foolishly'; *miser — miserē* 'unhappily'; *pulcher — pulchrē* 'beautifully'. A very few end in *-ter*.

Adverbs based on 3rd declension adjectives: add *-(i)ter* to the stem, e.g. *fortis — fortiter* 'bravely'; *audāx — audācter* 'boldly'; *celer — celeriter* 'swiftly'. But note an important exception: *facile* 'easily'.

Here are some irregularly formed adverbs:

> *bonus — bene* 'well'
> *paruus — paulum* '(a) little', 'slightly'
> *multus — multum* 'much'
> *magnus — magnopere* 'greatly' (= *magnō + opere*)

NB.   *longē* (regularly formed from *longus* 'long') 'far'.

Exercises

1 *Identify and translate the adverbs in this list*: hōrum, audācter, mulier, malum, multae, male, līberī, bene, omne, līberē, magnopere, multum, scelere, pater, celeriter, pulchrē, proelium, paulum.
2 *Form adverbs from these adjectives and translate*: stultus, bonus, fortis, longus, similis, saeuus, tacitus, magnus, celer, multus, miser.
3 *The Roman literary critic Quintilian here lists the sorts of styles an orator will need to develop to suit all occasions. Translate:*

dīcet . . . grauiter, seuērē, ācriter, uehementer, concitātē, cōpiōsē, amārē, cōmiter, remissē, subtīliter, blandē, lēniter, dulciter, breuiter, urbānē.

grauis serious	*cōmis* affable	*blandus* flattering
seuērus stern	*remissus* gentle	*lēnis* kind
concitātus passionate	*subtīlis* precise	*urbānus* witty
amārus bitter		

160

0   *sē; su-us a um*

So far you have met *ego* 'I' (pl. *nōs* 'we'), *tū* (pl. *uōs* 'you') and their possessive forms *meus* 'mine', *tuus* 'your(s)', *noster* 'our(s)', *uester* 'your(s)'. But we have not yet fully grappled with the reflexive forms for 'him, her, it, them' and their possessive forms 'his, her(s), its, their(s)'. Latin makes an important distinction between reflexive usage of such words (which means that the 'him, her' etc. being referred to is the same person as the *subject* of the clause) and non-reflexive (when the 'him, her' etc. being referred to is *not* the same person as the subject of the clause). When Latin uses a form of *sē*, the 'him, her, it, them' being referred to is *the same person as the subject of the verb of the particular clause*. Likewise, when Latin uses a form of *suus a um*, the person referred to in the 'his', 'her(s)', 'their(s)' is the *same as the subject of the verb*, e.g.:

> *Phaedra sē amat* 'Phaedra loves (*sē* MUST = Phaedra) herself'
> *Nīcobūlus suōs nummōs habet* 'Nicobulus has (*suōs* MUST refer to Nicobulus) his own (i.e. no-one else's) money'
> *Phaedra eam amat* 'Phaedra loves (*eam* CANNOT be Phaedra) her (i.e. some else)'
> *Nīcobūlus eius nummōs habet* 'Nicobulus has (*eius* CANNOT refer to Nicobulus) his (someone else's) money'.

sē declined

	s./pl.
nom.	—
acc.	sē
gen.	súī
dat.	síbi
abl.	sē

NB.   The forms are the same for s. and pl. and all genders. Reference to the subject of the verb will tell you whether to translate s. or pl., m., f. or n.

su-us a um

This possessive adjective 'his', 'hers', 'its', 'theirs' declines like *mult-us a um*.

Exercises

1 *Translate the following sentences*:

(a) hostem īrātum et multa minātum mīles audāx saeuē adgressus est.

(b) equitēs ē castrīs suīs ēgressī ad urbem celeriter prōgressī sunt.

(c) nauem adeptus celerem rēx longē ā terrā suā fūgit.

(d) uxōrī multa locūtae uir ferōciter respondit.

(e) ubi lēgātī hostīs adlocūti sunt, ad castra regressī uerba eōrum ducī nostrō nūntiāuērunt.

(f) dux mīlitēs hortātus audācter sē in proelium tulit.

(g) hostēs nostrōrum ferōciam equitum passī in oppidum suum fūgērunt et ibi sē cēlāuērunt.

2 *Translate these sentences*:

(a) nōn uīuere bonum est, sed bene uīuere. (*Seneca*)

(b) nēmo togam sūmit nisi mortuus. (*Juvenal*)

(c) multōrum opēs praepotentium exclūdunt amīcitiās fidēlīs: nōn enim sōlum ipsa fortūna caeca est, sed eōs etiam plērumque efficit caecōs quōs complexa est. (*Cicero*)

uīuō 3 I live	*exclūdō* 3 I exclude,	*caec-us a um* blind
tog-a ae 1f. toga	prevent	*plērumque* generally
sūmō 3 I put on	*amīciti-a ae* 1f. friendship	*efficiō* 3/4 I make (x acc.
morior 3/4 dep. *mortuus*	*fidēl-is e* loyal, faithful	Y acc.)
I die	*nōn sōlum . . . sed etiam*	*quōs* (acc. pl. m.) whom
op-ēs op-um 3f. pl. wealth	not only . . . but also	*complector* 3 dep.
praepotēns praepotent-is	*ipsa* herself (nom. s. f.)	*complexus* I embrace
3m. very powerful	*fortūn-a ae* 1f. fortune	
man		

Reading

1 *As you translate in word-order, determine the limits of the participle phrase in each of these sentences and say what function it has in the sentence (i.e. agreeing with and describing subject, object, indirect object etc.) Then translate into correct English, finally returning to the Latin to read it out correctly phrased. E.g. hanc praedam adeptī domum regressī sunt. Participle phrase: hanc . . . adeptī: agreeing with subject. 'When they had obtained this booty, they returned home'. Read out with a comma pause after adeptī.*

(a) Amphitruō igitur mīlitēs eō tempore hortātus in proelium sē tulit.

(b) dux mīlitēs allocūtus est et praedam post uictōriam pollicitus signum dedit.

(c) uxor Amphitruōnis uirum in uiā cōnspicāta domō ēgressa est.

(d) uxōrī multa precātae et cōnstantiam uirī recordātae Amphitruō tamen nīl respondit.

(e) seruus autem dominum multa mentītus facile dēcēpit.

2 *Read these participle phrases, translating in word-order, and decide their function in the sentence (NB. there are no ablatives). Then pair each with the correct ending from the list below. Finally, having translated into correct English, read aloud in Latin, phrasing correctly, and thinking through the meaning as you read.*

(a) cīuibus ōtium et pācem adeptīs . . .
(b) lēgātōs haec uerba locūtōs . . .
(c) manum seruōrum in castra hostium profectōrum . . .
(d) eī mulierī clam in bellum uirum secūtae . . .
(e) ducem ad exercitum hostium prōgressum . . .

mīlitēs mala uerba locūtī sunt
dux hostium castīgāuit
bellum malum uidētur maximum esse
legiōnēs secūtae sunt
dominī necāuērunt

Reading exercise / Test exercise

Read this passage carefully, translating in word-order, determining as you go the function of the words met and the groups in which they should be phrased and stating what each new item makes you anticipate. Translate into correct English, then read aloud in Latin, phrasing correctly, thinking through the meaning as you read.

Tēleboās praedam nostrā in terrā plūrimam adeptōs dux noster ulcīscī uoluit. cum exercitū igitur in terram Tēleboārum profectus bellum cum eīs gessit. Amphitruō autem, uir summā uirtūte, per lēgātōs locūtus Tēleboās praedam reddere iussit. sed Tēleboae, uirī summā ferōciā, multa ferōciter locūtī multaque exercituī nostrō minātī, Amphitruōnem 5 statim abīre iussērunt. ergō proelium factum est. dux noster deōs

precātus atque exercitum hortātus mīlitēs in proelium dūxit. hostīs
fortiter prōgressōs tandem uīcimus. Amphitruō autem lēgatōs hostium
postrīdiē in castra accēpit, hanc uictōriam adeptus tam illūstrem. lēgātī
hostium, ubi ex urbe profectī sunt et ad castra uēnērunt, ducem   1
uehementer precātī nostrum dēdidērunt sē in eius arbitrium.

English–Latin

1 *Translate into Latin*:

(a) Our general, after encouraging the army, gave the signal.
(b) Amphitruo addressed the enemy through ambassadors.
(c) All men when they have gained wisdom prefer peace and leisure to war.
(d) The enemy set out from the camp at that hour.
(e) Although I have tried to speak clearly to them, the enemy have threatened me fiercely.
(f) They killed the man when he had spoken thus.

2 *Read through the text of 3B again and then translate this passage*:

SOSIA When Amphitruo had spoken through ambassadors to
them, the Teleboans replied thus to him: 'You have attacked
our land. Go away at once. If you do not leave, we will fight.'
Thus they spoke. But Amphitruo, a man of very great
courage, after advancing with his army from the camp,
encouraged his men. Then he led them into battle. The battle
was (a) massive (one). However, our leader gained a famous
victory and has now returned home.

Deliciae Latinae

Word-building

Prefixes

The prefix *dī-* or *dis-* (or *dif-*) means 'apart', 'asunder', 'not' (occasionally
'exceedingly'), e.g.

> *distō* 1 'I stand apart' (cf. 'distant')
> *dissideō* 'I sit apart' (i.e. disagree) (cf. 'dissident')
> *differō* 'I scatter', 'I differ'

sē- as a prefix means 'apart', 'without', e.g. *sēcūrus* 'free from worry', *sēdūcō* 'I lead aside, astray', *sēditiō* 'a going (*eō, it-*) apart', *sēdulus* 'aside from tricks' (*dolus* 'trick'), *sēcrētus* 'separated apart' (cf. English 'secret' – something set apart; hence 'a secretary' deals with confidentialities). This *sē-* has nothing to do with *sē* reflexive.

Word exercise

Give the meaning and discuss the Latin connections of: copious, *terra firma*, legation, agrarian, otiose, hostile, naval, pacify, ferocious, invincible, exhort, illustrious, suicide (-cīd- – *simple verb* caedō '*I kill*').

Everyday Latin

> *per sē* 'through itself', 'because of its own nature'

Real Latin

Martial

difficilis facilis, iūcundus acerbus es īdem.
nec tēcum possum uīuere, nec sine tē. (*12.46*)

iūcundus sweet ⎫ NB Gender   *īdem* the same (nom.)
acerbus bitter ⎭   *uīuō* 3 I live

Motto

agnus in pāce, leō in bellō. (*Edmonds*)

agn-us ī 2m. lamb
leō leōn-is 3m. lion

Word study

castrum

castrum in the s. means a fortified post or settlement, in the pl. a camp. The '-caster', '-cester', '-chester' endings to the names of towns indicate 'camp' e.g. Lancaster, Worcester, Manchester and Chester. *castrum* has a diminutive *castellum*, whence 'castle' and in French *château* (a French circumflex accent often indicates a 'hidden' *s*; cf. Latin *fenestra* 'window', French *fenêtre*). Newcastle upon Tyne was so called because it had a *Novum Castellum* built by William Rufus in 1080.

castrum may be akin to *castrō*, 'I cut', i.e. *castrum* = 'a place cut off', 'entrenchment'. If so, *castrum* and English 'castrate' have similar origins!

sequor

sequor 'I follow' has a present participle *sequēns* 'following' and perfect participle *secūtus* 'having followed'. From these we get 'sequel' and 'sequence' and through the French *suivre* a 'suit', hence 'suitor', one who pursues a marriage partner, and 'sue', to chase someone at law. 'Pursue' derives from *prōsequor* (French *poursuivre*). *cōnsequor* 'I follow all together', gives 'consecutive' and 'consequence'. *exsequor* 'I follow out' gives 'execute' in the sense of 'carry out' or 'judicially put to death'. *obsequor* 'I follow on account of / in accordance with the wishes of' gives 'obsequious', while *persequor* 'I follow thoroughly' gives 'persecute'. *subsequor* 'I follow under', hence to succeed (as in a list), gives 'subsequent'.

Section 3C

Running vocabulary for 3C

abigō 3 I drive off
an or
astūtiīs (abl.) with cunning
astūt-us a um sharp, smart
barb-a ae 1f. beard
callid-us a um cunning
celerius more quickly
celerrimē very quickly
cēnō 1 I have dinner
cicātrīcōs-us a um scarred
coll-um ī 2n. neck
cōnsūtīs tunicīs with a second-hand tunic
Dāu-us ī 2m. Davus
dictūrus (nom. s. m.) about to say

dolīs (abl.) with tricks;
dolīs cōnsūtīs with your second-hand tricks
domō 1 I soften up
eadem (acc. pl. n.) ⎫
eandem (acc. s. f.) ⎬ the
eāsdem (acc. pl. f.) ⎭ same
edō 3 I eat
eōsdem (acc. pl. m.) the same
equidem for my part
etiam still
eundem (acc. s. m.) the same
exercitūrus (nom. s. m.) about to exercise
exossāt-us a um boned

exossō 1 I bone, fillet
fact-um ī 2n. deed
factūrus (nom. s. m.) about to do, make
fallāciīs (abl.) with deceptions
ferōcissimē most fiercely
ferōcius more fiercely
fōrm-a ae 1f. looks
fort-is e strong
habitō 1 I dwell, live in
hercle by Hercules
hospiti-um ī 2n. reception
īdem (nom. s. m.) the same
idem (nom. s. n.) the same
ingressūrus (nom. s. m.) about to enter

interrogō 1 I ask
intrātūrus (nom. s. m.)
    about to enter
itūrus (nom. s. m.) about
    to go
labr-um ī 2n. lip
māl-a ae 1f. cheek
malitiā (abl.) with evil
maximē most of all
ment-um ī 2n. chin
minimē no; least (of all)
miserrimē most
    wretchedly
modo just, recently
mūrēn-a ae 1f. eel
nārrātūrus (nom. s. m.)
    about to tell
nās-us ī 2m. nose
nēmo nēmin-is 3m. no-one
nescioquis (nom.) someone
    or other

nihilī of no value,
    worthless
nōnne surely?
nūntiātūrus (nom. s. m.)
    about to announce
obsecrō 1 I beg, beseech
optimē best of all; very
    well
ōs ōr-is 3n. face
pariēs pariet-is 3m. wall
pedibus with feet; on foot
pēs ped-is 3m. foot
perueniō 4 I reach
petas-us ī 2m. hat
placet it is pleasing
plūrimum very much, a
    great deal
ponderō 1 I weigh
pondus ponder-is 3n.
    weight

prīmō first
prohibeō 2 I prevent, stop
pugne-us a um fisty
pugnīs (abl.) with fists
pugn-us ī 2m. fist
quandō when, since
quis anyone
silenter silently
sinō 3 I allow
statūr-a ae 1f. height
tantī . . . quantī of such
    value . . . as; worth
    . . . as much as
tēcum with you(rself)
terg-um ī 2n. back
tōt-us a um whole, all
tunicīs with/on your tunic
uestīt-us ūs 4m. clothes
uī (abl.) with force

Learning vocabulary for 3C

Nouns

fōrm-a ae 1f. shape, looks;
    beauty
dol-us ī 2m. trick

pugn-us ī 2m. fist
nēmo nēmin-is 3m./f. no-
    one, nobody

pēs ped-is 3m. foot

Adjectives

uērus a um true

fort-is e strong; (brave,
    courageous)

ī-dem ea-dem i-dem (cf. *is
    e-a id*) the same

Verbs

interrog-ō 1 I ask, question

placet 2 *placu-it/placitum est*
    it is pleasing; x (dat.)
    votes (to)

sin-ō 3 *sīu-ī sit-us* I allow

Others

etiam still, even, as well;
    yes, indeed

nōnne surely?
quandō since, when

tēcum (pl. *uōbīscum*) with
    you, yourself; (pl. with
    yourselves)

Grammar and exercises for 3C

81 Future participles, active and deponent: 'about to / on the point of –ing'

Future participles of both deponent *and* active verbs are always active in *meaning*. They mean 'about to —', 'on the point of —ing', 'intending to —', and are formed by adding *-ūrus a um* to the stem of the perfect participle, e.g. *minātūrus* 'about to threaten', *amātūrus* 'about to love' etc. As with deponent perfect participles, these forms are *adjectives* and must agree in person, number and gender with the person 'about to . . .', e.g. *locūtūra* (fem.) *est* 'she is about to speak'; *ēgressūri sunt* 'they are about to go out'; *eōs prōgressūrōs uideō* 'I see them on the point of advancing'. Note the clue to form in the word 'fu<u>tu</u>re' – giving you *-ūr-us*.

82 The 4th principal part (perfect participle) of active verbs

You have already met three principal parts of active verbs, i.e. the dictionary form, the infinitive and the perfect (e.g. *amō, amāre, amāuī; habeō, habēre, habuī* etc.). The perfect participle is formed as follows:

Regular principal parts

	Present indicative	*Present infinitive*	*Perfect indicative*	*Perfect participle passive*
1st conj.	ámō	amā́re	amā́uī	amā́-t-us a um
2nd conj.	hábeō	habḗre	hábuī	hábi-t-us a um
4th conj.	aúdiō	audī́re	audī́uī	audī́-t-us a um

Notes

1 As you can see, the perfect participle is regularly formed by adding *-t-us a um* to the stem: *amā-t-us, audī-t-us* etc. Note *habi-t-us* (*-e-* changes to *-i-*). Thus the future participles of the three regular conjugations will be *amāt-ūr-us a um, habit-ūr-us a um, audīt-ūr-us a um*.

2 For the curious, the meaning of this participle on its own is 'having been —ed', e.g. *amātus* 'having been loved'. Cf. **77** for deponent and semi-deponent participles, which, as we have seen, mean 'having —ed'. The perfect participle meaning 'having been —ed' will not be met properly till **151**.

3 Unpredictable principal parts

The principal parts of all 3rd and 3/4th conj. verbs are best treated as
unpredictable, and need to be learned. Note, however, that stem + -*tus*
(sometimes + -*sus*) is one pattern, e.g. *dīc-o dic-tus*. Here are the full
principal parts of the active verbs of these conjugations which you have
learned so far, listed by *ending* of perfect participle, plus those of irregular
1st, 2nd and 4th conjugation verbs.

Present indicative	*Present infinitive*	*Perfect indicative*	*Perfect participle passive*	

Perfect participle ending in –ct-us a um

(*a*) –c(i)ō

dē- in- prō- re- ē- } dūcō	–dūcere	–dūxī	–ductus	'I lead'
dīcō	dīcere	dīxī	dictus	'I say'
faciō	facere	fēcī	factus	'I make', 'I do'
perficiō	perficere	perfēcī	perfectus	'I complete'

(*b*) –nc-ō

uincō	uincere	uīcī	uictus	'I conquer'

(*c*) –g-ō

agō	agere	ēgī	āctus	'I do', 'I drive'
legō	legere	lēgī	lēctus	'I read'

(*d*) –qu-ō

coquō	coquere	coxī	coctus	'I cook'

Perfect participle ending in –st-us a um

-r-ō

gerō	gerere	gessī	gestus	'I do', 'I act (wage)'

Present indicative	Present infinitive	Perfect indicative	Perfect participle passive	

Perfect participle ending in –pt–us a um

(*a*) –p(i)ō

| capiō | capere | cēpī | captus | 'I capture' |
| dēcipiō | dēcipere | dēcēpī | dēceptus | 'I deceive' |

(*b*) –b–ō

| (ad)scrībō | –scrībere | –scrīpsī | –scrīptus | 'I write (to)' |

Perfect participle ending in –(n)sus, –(s)sus

(*a*) –ttō

| mittō | mittere | mīsī | missus | 'I send' |

(*b*) –dō

| dēfendō | dēfendere | dēfendī | dēfēnsus | 'I defend' |

(*c*) –deō

uideō	uidēre	uīdī	uīsus	'I see'
irrīdeō	irrīdēre	irrīsī	irrīsus	'I laugh at'
possideō	possidēre	possēdī	possessus	'I hold', 'I keep'
respondeō	respondēre	respondī	respōnsum[1]	'I answer'

(*d*) –m–ō

| opprimō | opprimere | oppressī | oppressus | 'I surprise, catch, crush' |

(*e*) *other* –eō

| iubeō | iubēre | iussī | iussus | 'I order' |
| maneō | manēre | mānsī | mānsus | 'I wait', 'I remain' |

Perfect participle ending in –itus

(*a*) –d–ō

crēdō	crēdere	crēdidī	crēditum[1]	'I believe'
dēdō	dēdere	dēdidī	dēditus	'I surrender'
reddō	reddere	reddidī	redditus	'I return'

Present indicative	*Present infinitive*	*Perfect indicative*	*Perfect participle passive*	

Perfect participle ending in -ūtus, -ōtus

-u-(e)ō

soluō	soluere	soluī	solūtus	'I release, pay'
moueō	mouēre	mōuī	mōtus	'I move'
adiuuō	adiuuāre	adiūuī	adiūtus	'I help'

Perfect participle ending in -tus added to a plain stem

dō	dare	dedī	datus	'I give'
stō	stāre	stetī	statum[1]	'I stand'
(in)ueniō	-uenīre	-uēnī	-uentum	'I come'
uinciō	uincīre	uīnxī	uīnctus	'I bind'
fugiō	fugere	fūgī	fugitūrus[2]	'I flee'
sinō (*stem* si-)	sinere	sīuī	situs	'I allow'
dēleō	dēlēre	dēlēuī	dēlētus	'I destroy'
ad-⎫ prae-⎭ sum	esse	fuī	futūrus[2]	'I am' { 'present' / 'in charge of' }
ferō	ferre	tulī	lātus	'I carry, bear'
auferō	auferre	abstulī	ablātus	'I take away'
in-⎫ ab-⎪ ex-⎬eō red-⎭	īre	īuī *or* iī	itum[1]	'I go' { 'into' / 'away' / 'out of' / 'back' }

[1] Intransitive verbs have only the *-um* form of past participle, which we will give from now on. See Reference Grammar **A–G Intro (d) Note**.
[2] No past participle; in such cases we give the future participle, if it exists.

Note

As you attempt to learn these vital 4th principal parts, you will not fail to notice how extraordinarily fruitful they have been in the formation of English words. You will find that you can frequently form an English word by adding '-ion', '-ive', '-ure' and '-or' to the stem of the perfect participle (cf. p. 31): try the list above. For formation of the future participle see **81** and **82** above.

Exercises

1 *Translate these future participles and say what verb each is from*: intrātūrus,
   clāmātūrus, factūrus, habitūrus, monitūrus, mānsūrus, audītūrus,
   mentītūrus, ēgressūrus, ductūrus, captūrus, (*optional*: suspicātūrus,
   reditūrus, locūtūrus, datūrus, rogātūrus, precātūrus, dictūrus,
   dēfēnsūrus, dēlētūrus, solūtūrus, passūrus).
2 *Say which in this list are future participles and which past*: scrīptūrō,
   locūtae, āctūrīs, inuentūrī, secūtās, ēgressūra, acceptūrōrum, futūrā,
   morātārum, gestūrum, nūntiātūrōs, suspicātus, uictūram, hortātōs.
3 *Give the Latin for*: about to go; on the point of making; intending to
   defend; about to give back; on the point of laughing; about to place;
   about to see; intending to order; intending to deceive.

84 The ablative of instrument or means – 'by means of', 'with'

We have identified three areas of usage for the ablative:

(a) Locative, e.g. 'in', 'at', 'on', 'within' of place *and* time (cf. **10, 67**).
(b) Separation (cf. *auferō – ablātus* 'I take away') e.g. *ex, ab* + abl. (cf.
     23).
(c) The ablative of description, e.g. 'a woman *of/with great courage*'
     (cf. **49**).

We now meet the 'instrumental' usage of the ablative for the first time.
This shows the instrument *with which* or means *by which* an action is
carried out, e.g.

> *pugnīs mē uerberat* 'he beats me with his fists / by means of his
> fists' / using his fists as the instrument'.
> *pedibus hūc uenit* 'he comes here by means of his feet / on his feet'.

Exercises

1 *Translate*:

(a) at mē per omnem uītam miserrimam dolīs dēcēpit homo
     pessimus.
(b) quārē igitur eam pugnīs ferōciter uerberāuit?
(c) manibus meīs hās aedīs hōc annō perfēcī.

(d) neque astūtiīs neque dolīs cīuīs umquam dēcipiēs.

(e) facinoribus maximīs et sceleribus plūrimīs rem sibi optimē gessit homo pessimus.

(f) omnīs uxōrēs uirtūte et continentiā Alcumēna superāuit.

2 *Translate*:

(a) nōnne ille seruus in aedīs intrātūrus est?

(b) ego illum pugnīs meīs eōdem tempore uerberātūrus sum.

(c) nōnne Sōsia ille stultissimē āctūrus est, sī hās aedīs ingredī uolet?

(d) eum seruum ego maximē uolō meā fōrmā hanc noctem dēcipere.

(e) Sōsia suā uirtūte mē numquam uincet.

(f) quid futūrum arbitrātur? hāc enim hōrā illī nōmen meā astūtiā ablātūrus sum.

---

85 *nōnne?* ('doesn't . . .?')

nōnne? asks a question in such a way that the speaker wants the answer to it to be 'yes'. The best formula for translation is 'doesn't x happen?' (or 'x does happen, doesn't it?'); 'surely?' is also a safe translation. E.g.

> *nōnne eam amō?* 'don't I love her?', 'I do love her, don't I?', 'surely I love her?'

---

86 *īdem* 'the same' and *nēmo* 'no one'
īdem eadem idem *'the same'*

	s.			*pl.*		
	m.	*f.*	*n.*	*m.*	*f.*	*n.*
nom.	í-dem	éa-dem	í-dem	eí-dem[1]	eaé-dem	éa-dem
acc.	eún-dem	eán-dem	í-dem	eós-dem	eás-dem	éa-dem
gen.	←——— eiús-dem ———→			eōrún-dem	eārún-dem	eōrún-dem
dat.	←——— eí-dem ———→			←——— eís-dem[2] ———→		
abl.	eó-dem	eá-dem	eó-dem	←——— eís-dem[2] ———→		

[1] *īdem* also found.
[2] *īsdem* also found.

Note

This declines like *is ea id* + *dem* (but NB. ĭdem, where one might expect isdem, iddem). Note that where the forms of *is* end in -*m*, the -*m* becomes an -*n*- before the -*d*- of -*dem* e.g. *eum-dem* – *eun-dem*; *eārum-dem* – *eārundem*.

nēmo *3m.(f.)*

nom. nḗmo
acc. nḗmin-em
gen. nūll-íus (nḗmin-is)
dat. nḗmin-ī
abl. nū́ll-ō (nḗmin-e)

87 Comparative and superlative adverbs 'more —ly', 'most —ly'

Comparative and superlative adverbs are formed from the comparative and superlative adjectives.

	foolish(ly)	more foolish(ly)	most foolish(ly)
Adjective	stúlt-us	stúlt-ior	stultíssim-us
Adverb	stúlt-ē	stúlt-ius (*neut.*)	stultíssim-ē

	quick(ly)	more quick(ly)	most quick(ly)
Adjective	céler	celér-ior	celérrim-us
Adverb	celér-iter	celér-ius (*neut.*)	celérrim-ē

Irregular comparative and superlative adverbs
NB. Most of these are only irregular in as far as the corresponding adjective has irregular comparative and superlative forms. If you already know the adjective forms, most of these adverbs are formed quite regularly from the adjective:

béne	'well'	mélius	'better'	óptimē	'best'
mále	'badly'	péius	'worse'	péssimē	'worst', 'very badly'
paúlum	'a little'	mínus	'less'	mínimē	'very little'; 'no'
múltum	'much'	plūs	'more'	plū́rimum	'most'; 'a lot'
magnópere	'greatly'	mágis	'more'	máximē	'very much'; 'most'; 'yes'

Exercises

1 *Form and translate the comparative and superlative adverbs of:* stultē, bene, pūtidē, miserē, pulchrē, celeriter, audācter, male (*optional:* multum, paulum, plānē, magnopere, facile).

2 *Identify and translate the comparative and superlative adverbs in this list:* facillimē, malum, scelere, illīus, astūtius, uērō, optimē, stultē, opere, magnopere, fortius, alterīus, nimis, magis, minimē, hodiē, pulcherrimē.

3 *Translate each of these phrases:* uir summā uirtūte; summā uirtute; seruus summā astūtiā; astūtiā summā; manibus pedibusque; hōc annō; eādem fōrmā; meīs pugnīs; eōdem tempore.

4 *Give the Latin for:* on the same day; a wife of the utmost excellence; with the greatest courage; with my fist; in the same year; with the same hands; a slave of great boldness; with a trick.

5 *Translate these sentences:*

(a) omne futūrum incertum est. (*Seneca*)
(b) inter peritūra uīuimus. (*Seneca*)
(c) dē futūrīs rēbus semper difficile est dīcere. (*Cicero*)
(d) uirtūs eadem in homine ac deō est. (*Cicero*)
(e) fit uia uī. (*Virgil*)

incert-us a um uncertain   *pereō perīre periī peritus* I   *uīs* f. force, violence (abl.
inter (+ acc.) among   die   *uī*)
                uīuō 3 I live

Reading exercise / Test exercise

Read these passages, translating in word-order, defining the function of each word and phrase-group. Translate into correct English. Finally, read aloud the Latin, correctly phrased, thinking through the meaning as you read.

(a) mihi hōc tempore pater meus officium crēdidit maximum. nam dum eī fōrmā Amphitruōnis Alcumēnam dēcipere placet, ego seruum Sōsiam ab aedibus abāctūrus sum. ego igitur meīs pugnīs illī seruō exitium minātūrus in uiam ibō. meā illum astūtiā dēcipiam facile, quod mihi uir nūllā sapientiā esse uidētur. eī ego nōmen eōdem tempore meīs auferam dolīs. placēbit enim mihi   5
ad eum eādem fōrmā ac uōce eādem adgredī.
(b) Sōsiam in aedīs dominī ingressūrum Mercurius dolīs atque astūtiīs dēcēpit. Sōsiam enim ingredī nōn sīuit, quamquam eum Amphitruō Alcumēnae eō tempore omnia nārrāre iussit. Mercurius enim patrem suum, id est Iouem, cūrat. nam ille hīs in   10
aedibus hanc noctem Alcumēnam fōrmā uirī dēcēpit. Mercurius autem sē Sōsiae similem fēcit et eādem fōrmā et uōce eādem nōmen eius cēpit. Mercuriō tandem Sōsia uix (*hardly*) crēdidit, quandō sibi simillimum deum arbitrātus est. et hoc facilius opīnātus est seruus quod deus eundem habuit petasum, uestītum   15
eundem, eandem statūram, pedēs eōsdem, idem mentum, mālās eāsdem, eadem labra, barbam eandem, nāsum eundem, collum idem. sēmet (*himself: acc. s.*) uērō Sōsiam arbitrārī tandem Sōsiae placuit, quod sē bene cognōuit.

175

English–Latin

1 *Translate into Latin*:

   (a)   What is that slave intending to do?
   (b)   Surely he's going to relate the battle to Alcumena?
   (c)   I intend to fool him with my tricks and my fists at the same time.
   (d)   For I've come here intending to threaten him with death[1].
   (e)   I've decided[2] to take his name from him by this trick.
   (f)   I've done nothing more easily, nothing better, nothing more quickly.

[1] = 'threaten death to him'.
[2] Use *mihi placet* + infinitive.

2 *Read the text of **3C** again, then translate this passage*:

MERCURY Who's speaking? If I find him, I intend to attack him with my fists.

SOSIA I'd better keep quiet. If he touches me with those fists, surely I'll be worth as much as a flatfish.

MER. Where are you intending to go, criminal? Who are you? Are you a citizen?

SOS. I'm a slave.

MER. I want you to tell me more than this. What's your name?

SOS. My name is Sosia.

MER. You're lying. Are you intending to deceive me with your tricks? If you don't go away quickly, I'll kill you with these fists.

Deliciae Latinae

Word-building

(a) Suffixes

-fex fic-is as a suffix is connected with *faciō* 'I make', 'I do' and commonly expresses occupation. So *carnufex = carō* (*carn-*) 'meat' + *fex*, 'meat-maker', 'executioner', 'scoundrel'; *artifex = ars* (*art-*) 'skill', 'craft' + *fex*, 'craftsman'; *aurifex = aurum* + *fex*, 'goldsmith'.

    Nero said of himself on his death-bed *quālis artifex pereō* 'What an (*quālis*) artist perishes in me!'

(b) Perfect participle

The perfect participle is an enormously fruitful source of vocabulary (cf. p. 171). Many English words are formed by the addition of '-ion', '-ure', '-ive', '-or' to that stem, e.g. 'production', 'diction', 'factor', 'missive', 'capture', 'perfection', 'action', etc., etc. Consequently, you can use these words to help you determine what the perfect participle is. For example, what is the perfect participle of *scrībō*? *scrībitus*? No English word 'scribition'. But there is a word 'inscription'. Chances are, therefore, that the perfect participle is *scrīptus*. Likewise, for Latin-into-English translation, a word like *prōgressūrus* reminds one of 'progression', i.e. going forward.

   -ūr-a ae 1f. added to the stem of the 4th principal part generates abstract nouns denoting:

>   action: *scrīptūra* 'writing' (*scrībō* 'I write')
>   result: *nātūra* 'birth', 'nature' (*nāscor* 'I am born')
>   occupation: *mercātūra* 'trade' (*mercor* 'I sell, trade')

Word exercise

Give the meaning and Latin connection of these words: form, pedestrian, ameliorate, pejorative, interrogate, station, mansion, vision, retention, possession, position, verify, gesture, solution, concoction, elation, future, status, amateur.

Everyday Latin

>   *placebo* – the harmless pill or coloured water given to pacify hypochondriac patients
>   *id.* = *idem* 'the same' (usually, 'the same author')
>   *ibid.* = *ibidem* 'the same place in the same author already cited'
>   Those on their way to die in the gladiatorial arena saluted the emperor with the words *auē* ('hail'), *Caesar, moritūrī tē salūtant*
>   *auē atque uale* 'hail and farewell', 'hello goodbye' (common on tombstones)
>   One's *magnum opus* is one's 'great work' – usually referring to a book

The following phrases will help you revise the difference between *in* + acc. and *in* + abl.:

in locō parentis 'in the position of a parent'
in camerā 'in private', 'in secret' (*camera* = vaulted room, the
origin of our 'chamber'. The term refers to legal judgements
made privately by a judge in his rooms)
in propriā persōnā '(speaking) in one's own person'
in absentiā 'in one's absence'
in flagrante dēlictō '(caught) in flagrant (open) sin (crime)', i.e.
taken in the act, caught red-handed.
in memoriam 'to the memory'
in mediās rēs '(plunged) into the middle of the action'

Real Latin

The Vulgate

(*The last day*.) dē Siōn ēgrediētur lēx, et uerbum Dominī dē Hierusalem,
et iūdicābit inter populōs multōs, et corripiet gentēs fortēs usque in
longinquum; et concīdent gladiōs suōs in uōmerēs et hastās suās in
ligōnēs; nōn sūmet gēns aduersus gentem gladium; et nōn discent ultrā
belligerāre . . . quia omnēs populī ambulābunt unusquisque in nōmine
Dei suī; nōs autem ambulābimus in nōmine Dominī Deī nostrī in
aeternum et ultrā. (*Micah 4.2–5*)

Siōn (abl.) Sion	*concīdō* 3 I beat	*discō* 3 I learn
lēx lēg-is 3f. law	*gladi-us ī* 2m. sword	*ultrā* further, more,
Hierusalem (abl.)	*uōmer uōmer-is* 3m.	beyond
Jerusalem	ploughshare	*belligerō* 1 I fight
iūdicō 1 I judge	*hast-a ae* 1f. spear	*unusquisque* each and
popul-us ī 2n. people	*ligō ligōn-is* 3m. pruning	every one
corripiō 3/4 I control	hook	*in aeternum* for ever
gēns gent-is 3f. nation	*sūmō* 3 I take up	
usque in longinquum afar	*aduersus* + acc. against	
off		

Mottoes using the ablative

nōn vī, sed mente. (*Lincolne*)
nōn vī, sed virtūte. (*Burrowes, Ramsbotham*)
nōn vī sed voluntāte. (*Boucher*)
nōn gladiō sed grātiā. (*Charteris, Charters*)
nōn cantū sed āctū. (*Gillman*)
ingeniō ac labōre. (*Kerr*)
ingeniō et vīribus. (*Huddleston*)
igne et ferrō. (*Hickman*)
industriā et labōre. (*McGallock*)

industriā et spē. (*Warden*)
industriā et virtūte. (*Bolton*)
cōnsiliō ac virtūte. (*Rose-Lewin*)
cōnsiliō et animīs. (*Maitland, Ramadge*)
cōnsiliō et armīs. (*Stephens*)
fidē et amōre. (*Conway, Gardner, Hart, Seymour*)
fidē et clēmentiā. (*Martin*)
fidē et armīs. (*Fairquhar*)
fidē et cōnstantiā (*Dixon, James, Lee*)
fidē et dīligentiā. (*Crawford*)
fidē et fidūciā. (*Blackman, Gilchrist, Hogg, Wall, Watt*)
fidē et labōre. (*Allan*)
fidē et spē. (*Borthwick*)

uīs (pl.) *uīr-ēs* s. force; (pl.) strength	*āct-us ūs* 4m. deed, doing	*fidēs fidē-ī* 5f. faith
mēns ment-is 3f. mind	*labor labōr-is* 3m. effort, work	*clēmenti-a ae* 1f. mercy
uoluntās uoluntāt-is 3f. will	*ferr-um -ī* 2n. sword, iron	*cōnstanti-a ae* 1f. constancy
gladi-us ī 2m. sword	*industri-a ae* 1f. industry	*dīligenti-a ae* 1f. diligence
grāti-a ae 1f. grace	*spēs spē-ī* 5f. hope	*fidūci-a ae* 1f. trust
cant-us ūs 4m. song	*arm-a ōrum* 2n. pl. arms	

Word study

pēs

pēs ped-is means 'foot', and is akin to Greek *pous pod-os* 'foot' – cf. 'octopus' ('eight feet'); 'podium'; 'antipodes' ('people with their feet opposite'); 'tripod' ('three-feet'). The adjective *pedālis* gives 'pedal' and *pedester* gives 'pedestrian', 'of the feet', hence, 'lowly', 'earth-bound', 'using one's feet'. *pedō* is late Latin for 'foot-soldier', whence English 'pawn', via Old French *pion*.

expediō means 'I free my feet from a trap', whence 'expedient', meaning 'advantageous' and to 'expedite', meaning 'get things moving'. Conversely, 'impede' comes from *impediō* 'I put feet in shackles'; so *impedīmentum* 'hindrance'. *impedicō* 'I tangle someone's feet in a *pedica* ('foot-trap')' gives Middle French *empechier* and English 'impeach', meaning 'charge with an official crime'. Less obviously, *repudium*, meaning 'back-footing', yields 'repudiate'. Piedmont is the area at the foot of the mountains (*mōns mont-is*). Most fascinating of all, 'pedigree', a register of descent or lineage, comes from *pēs + dē + grūs*, Middle French *pié de grue* 'foot of a crane', the three-line mark like a bird's foot (人) which is used to show family succession.

Section 3D

Running vocabulary for 3D

---

aliquid something
amātor amātōr-is 3m. lover
astūt-us a um sharp
auxiliō (for) a help
breu-is e short, brief
callid-us a um cunning
card-ō cardin-is 3f. door-hinge
cār-us a um dear
complector 3 dep. *complexus* I embrace
crēdō 3 (+ dat.) I believe
crepō 1 I creak, groan
cui (after *sī*) (with) (to) anyone; (in question) to whom?
cūrae (for) a care, concern
dīmittō 3 I dismiss
exemplō (for) an example
faueō (+ dat.) I am favourable to
gratiās agō (+ dat.) I thank
impedīmentō (for) a hindrance

imperō (+ dat.) I give orders (to), command
imperātor imperātōr-is 3m. general
inquiet (he) will say
intereā meanwhile
īrātus (+ dat.) angry with, at
licet 2 *licuit* it is permitted for x (dat.) to y (inf.)
māne early in the morning
medi-us a um middle (of)
metuō 3 I fear, am afraid
mī = mihi (or 'O my')
necesse necessary
numquid anything?
obstō 1 *obstitī* (+ dat.) I stand in the way (of)
odiō (for) an object of hatred
operam dō (+ dat.) I pay attention to
opus est there is a need for

x (dat.) to y (inf.)
parcō 3 (+ dat.) I spare, go easy on
pāreō 2 (+ dat.) I obey
parturiō 4 I give birth
pater-a ae 1f. dish
paulum a little
plūs more
prae ahead
praesum (+ dat.) I am in charge of
quantō (by) how much
. . . *tantō* (by) so much
quibus (after *sī*) (to) any (pl.); (in question) to which (pl.)?
sī quid if anything, if in any respect, at all
sī quis if anyone
subitō suddenly
taediō (for) a source of boredom
teneō 2 I hold
uoluptātī (for) a source of pleasure

Learning vocabulary for 3D

Nouns
grāti-a ae 1f. thanks, recompense

auxili-um ī 2n. help
impedīment-um ī 2n. hindrance

uoluptās uoluptāt-is 3f. desire, love, passion

Adjectives
breu-is e short, brief

Verbs

imper-ō 1 (+dat.) I give orders (to), command

obst-ō 1 *obstit-ī* (+dat.) I stand in the way of, obstruct

operam d-ō 1 *ded-ī dat-us* (+dat.) I pay attention to

faue-ō 2 *fāu-ī faut-um* (+dat.) I do service to, favour

pāre-ō 2 (+dat.) I obey

tene-ō 2 I hold

licet 2 *licu-it/licitum est* it is permitted to x (dat.) to Y (infin.)

grātiās agō (+dat.) I thank

praesum praeesse praefu-ī praefutūr-us (+dat.) I am in charge of, at the head of

inquit (he) says (1st s. *inquam*, 2nd s. *inquis*, 3rd pl. *inquiunt*)

necesse est it is necessary

Others

subitō suddenly

Grammar and exercises for 3D

88 Datives

So far the dative case has been used to indicate the person *advantaged*[1] or *disadvantaged* by an action (*mī aurum dedit* 'he gave the gold *to me*', *mihi aurum abstulit* 'he took the gold *from me*'; this sense includes the possessor also, e.g. *est mihi pecūnia* 'I have money'), and to indicate the person spoken to (*mihi dīxit* 'he spoke to me'). But, as was said at the time, the range of the dative is far wider than that, and its root meaning seems to be that the person is in some way interested or involved in the action of the verb, and when faced by a dative one should ask 'In what way is the person in the dative affected by the verb?'

[1] Q. What is an *omnibus*? A. A vehicle 'for everyone' – 'to everyone's advantage'.

1 Possessive dative: further notes

Remember the two ways of expressing the idea of possession in Latin:

(a) *habeō* or *teneō* + acc. 'I have'. e.g. *seruum habeō* 'I have a slave'.

(b) *est/sunt* + person possessing in the dative (lit. 'there is/are to x . . .') e.g *est mihi seruus* 'there is a slave to me' 'I have a slave'; *sunt Amphitruōnī multī seruī* 'there are to Amphitruo many slaves', 'Amphitruo has many slaves'.

Note the idiom *nōmen Mercuriō est mihi* 'the name to me is Mercury' i.e. 'my name is Mercury'. Observe that *Mercuriō* agrees with *mihi* (see **17B**).

2 The sympathetic dative

This is used in place of the genitive to stress the involvement of the person, e.g. *oculī mihi splendent* 'the eyes for me are shining', i.e. 'my eyes are shining'.

3 Dative of judging

This means 'in the eyes of', e.g. *uir bonus mihi uidētur* 'he seems a good man to me', i.e. 'in my eyes'. Cf. *Quīntia fōrmōsa est multīs* (Catullus) 'Quintia is beautiful to many', i.e. 'in many people's eyes'.

4 Ethic dative

This usage indicates that the person in the dative is or should be especially concerned about the action, e.g. *quid mihi Celsus agit?* 'what is Celsus doing (I am especially interested in what it is)?' (Horace). The best translation might be 'what is Celsus doing, please?' *at tibi repente uēnit ad mē Caninius* 'but Caninius suddenly came to me (and this is especially interesting to you)', i.e. 'Listen! / Guess what? / Pay attention: Caninius suddenly came to me' (Cicero).

5 Verbs which take the dative

All the following verbs take the dative and have meanings related to usages of the dative outlined above:

> *crēdō* 'I have belief in', 'I trust': *eīs crēdit* 'he believes them'. (Cf. the meaning 'I entrust': *crēdō* x (acc.) to y (dat.), e.g. *deō aurum crēdit* 'he entrusts the gold to the god')
>
> *faueō* 'I favour', 'I give support to': *fēminae fauet* 'he favours the woman'
>
> *praesum* 'I am in charge of': *ille exercituī praeest* 'he is in charge of the army'
>
> *pāreō* 'I obey', 'I am obedient to': *Mercurius patrī pāret* 'Mercury obeys his father'
>
> *imperō* 'I give orders': *mulier nōbīs imperat* 'the woman gives us orders' (NB. *iubeō* takes the acc. + infin., e.g. *seruam exīre iubet* 'he orders the slave to go out'.)
>
> *obstō* 'I hinder' 'I stand in the way of': *hic mīlitibus obstat* 'he hinders the soldiers'
>
> *licet*[1] 'it is permitted': *uōbīs licet* 'it is permitted to you', 'you are allowed'
>
> *placet*[1] 'it pleases': *cīuibus placet* 'it is pleasing to the citizens', 'the

citizens agree/vote' (cf. *placet | nōn placet* as voting procedure at some universities)

minor 'I make a threat against': *dominus seruō minātur* 'the master threatens the slave'

adsum 'I am present with', 'I am close to', 'assist': *sociīs adest* 'he is present with his friends', 'he helps his friends'

supplicō 'I implore' 'I bow to': *dīs omnibus supplicat* 'he implores all the gods'

¹ For these 'impersonal verbs' see further **154** and Reference Grammar **F2**.

6 Non-personal uses of the dative

The dative case is used in certain circumstances to denote the *purpose* for which something is done, e.g.:

> *pecūniam dōtī dat* 'he gives money <u>for/as a dowry</u>'
> *mihi <u>auxiliō</u> it* 'he comes <u>for a help</u> to me' i.e. 'to help me'

Similar to this is the so-called *predicative dative*, where datives of purpose are used with the verb 'to be', e.g.

> *mīlitēs <u>salūtī</u> sunt cīuibus* 'the soldiers are <u>for a salvation</u> to the citizens', 'the soldiers save the citizens', '<u>the soldiers</u> are a salvation to the citizens'
> *<u>auxiliō</u> erimus oppidō* 'we shall be <u>for a help</u> to the town', 'we shall help the town'

Note the following predicative dative expressions:

> *uoluptātī sum* 'I am <u>a source of pleasure</u> to x (dat.)'
> *odiō sum* 'I am <u>a source of hatred</u> to x (dat.)', 'I am <u>hated by</u> x (dat.)'
> *impedīmentō sum* 'I am <u>a hindrance to</u> x (dat.)'

Revision exercises

1 *Give the meaning, and then form the dative s. and pl., of the following nouns:*

1st–2nd declension: familia, oculus, cōnsilium, animus, cēna, bellum, deus, turba, uictōria, oppidum, praeda, (*optional:* officium, cōpiae, stilus, lūna, serua, fōrma, lēgātus, grātia, proelium, cūra, auxilium).

3rd–5th declension: pater, honor, aedēs, frāter, soror, uxor, onus, homo, cīuis, manus, diēs, nox, opus, caput, (*optional:* rēs, mīles, scelus, uōx, urbs, rēx, exercitus, nāuis, legiō, hostis, equitēs, mōs, pēs, uolūptas).

2 *Give the meaning, and then form the dative s. and pl., of the following adjectives:*

1st/2nd declension (m. f. n. forms in the s., one form for the pl.): multus, miser, malus, meus, tuus, noster, uester, (*optional:* bonus, summus, longus, alter¹, nūllus¹, īrātus, optimus, pessimus).

3rd declension and others (one form for both dat. s. and pl.): omnis, trīstis, ingēns, breuis, audāx, hic, (*optional:* facilis, fortis, ille, illūstris, melior, is, peior, maior).

¹ NB. These are irregular in gen. and dat. s. See **62**.

3 *Principal parts:*

Give meaning and all four principal parts of: dō, stō, iubeō, possideō, sum, eō, ferō, uolō, dīcō, dūcō, capiō, gerō, ueniō, uincō.

Give meaning and all three principal parts of: adipīscor, adgredior, loquor, sequor, proficīscor, hortor, polliceor, mentior, cōnspicor, arbitror, cōnor.

Exercises

1 *Put the bracketed noun/pronoun in the correct case and translate the sentence (NB. not every example requires the dative).*

(a) (ego) licet ex aedibus exīre.
(b) (seruus) Mercurius pugnīs suīs aggressus est.
(c) (hic) seruus obstitit.
(d) (tū) nōn crēdō.
(e) (illa) uir maximē amat.
(f) (uōs) is seruus minātur.
(g) (pater) fīlius bonus semper pāret.
(h) (cēna) coquus nunc parat.
(i) (exercitus) dominus meus praeest.
(j) (tū) aedīs inīre iubeō.
(k) (is) dux hoc imperāuit.

2 *Translate:*

(a) equitēs legiōnī impedīmentō sunt.
(b) Alcumēna Iouī magnae cūrae est.
(c) cīuis hic malus omnibus bonīs odiō est.
(d) Amphitruō cīuibus suīs salūtī[1] fuit.
(e) urbī huic ego auxiliō erō.
(f) hoc officium mihi uoluptātī est.
(g) hoc tibi officiō est.
(h) mē miserum! ego omnibus meīs exitiō erō.
(i) hoc tibi malō erit.
(j) Amphitruōnis uictōria omnibus cīuibus bonō est.

[1] *salūs salūt-is* 3f. 'safety'.

3 *Translate (refer back to **48.2** and **88.1** for possessive dative):*

(a) fuit mihi fīlius bonus.
(b) uxōrī meae dōs maxima est.
(c) cīuibus nostrīs nūllum auxilium fuit.
(d) nēminī amīca bona est.
(e) sunt eīs fīlius et fīlia.

4 *Translate these sentences:*

(a) doctō hominī et ērudītō uīuere est cōgitāre. (*Cicero*)
(b) inuia uirtūtī nūlla est uia. (*Ovid*)
(c) iniūria sapientī nōn potest fierī. (*Seneca*)
(d) hominēs amplius oculīs quam auribus crēdunt. (*Seneca*)
(e) omne tulit pūnctum quī miscuit ūtile dulcī. (*Horace*)

doct-us a um learned	*sapiēns sapient-is* wise	*misceō* 2 I mix (x acc.
ērudīt-us a um educated	*amplius* more	with y dat.)
uīuō 3 I live	*auris aur-is* 3f. ear	*ūtil-is* e useful; profitable
inui-us a um impassable	*pūnct-um ī* 2n. vote	*dulc-is* e sweet,
iniūri-a ae 1f. harm,	*quī* (nom. s. m.) the man	pleasurable,
injury	(writer) who	entertaining

Reading exercise / Test exercise

Datives (or ablatives) placed early in a sentence are often difficult to tackle, until you come to the verb (or something else which solves the intransigent case). You must 'hold' the dative in these circumstances until you have information which will solve it. Read this passage and, as you translate it in word-order, say which are the datives and where the construction becomes clear. E.g.:

ille <u>mihi</u> pecūniam multam <u>auferre</u> uult

At mihi *there is no clue as to whether the idea is possession, advantage/ disadvantage or indirect object. So hold it as 'in relation to me', 'affecting me'. When you reach* auferre, *you can see that it is likely to be disadvantage, since that verb construes with accusative and dative meaning taking something away from someone.*

Note that mihi, tibi *and* sibi *are often to be found second word in their clauses, however far away the verb is.*

Sōsia tum dominō Amphitruōnī, ubi ad nāuem. eius ueniet, ita dīcet: 'uxōrī uerba tua nūntiāre nōn potuī, domine, quod mihi seruus ingēns pugnōs minātus est. mihi ille ferōciter obstitit. in aedīs igitur mihi intrāre nōn licuit. is enim seruus tuō seruō maximō fuit impedīmentō. necesse fuit igitur mihi ad tē regredī et eius imperiīs statim pārēre, quod mihi fōrma mea ita placet, ut est. officium hoc mihi nōn fuit, ut tū pollicitus es, uoluptātī, sed onerī magnō.' seruō autem ita respondēbit Amphitruō 'quid illī seruō ingentī nōmen est?' tum Sōsia 'eī nōmen Sōsiae est. nam mihi meum nōmen, fōrmam meam, meam uōcem, omnia is seruus abstulit. mihi nunc est nōmen nūllum, nisi nēmo.'   1(

English–Latin

1 *Translate into Latin:*

(a) A very large slave stood in my way.
(b) The old man has a pretty daughter.
(c) I am allowed to give orders to my soldiers.
(d) Money is a source of great pleasure to Euclio.
(e) A bad citizen is hated by everyone.
(f) I want everyone to obey my orders.
(g) This duty will be burdensome to my wife.
(h) (It is) the general (who) is in charge of the army, not the soldiers.
(i) You (*s.*) must return to your land very quickly.
(j) Lovers like things thus.

2 *Read the text of* **3D** *again and then translate this passage:*

JUPITER Goodbye, my wife. I must go back to my troops.
ALCUMENA What's up? Am I a bore to you already?

J U P. On the contrary, you are a great pleasure to me. But when the general is not at the head of his army, the soldiers do not pay attention to their duties.

A L C. Don't go away, my husband. I shall be able to love you more, if you obey me.

J U P. Don't get in my way. I shall return soon, just as you want. But now I have decided[1] to go. Goodbye.

[1] Use *mihi placet* (present).

Deliciae Latinae

Word-building

Prefix

You have already met *prae-* as a prefix = 'before', 'in front of', e.g. *praeeō* 'I go in front', 'I go ahead'; *praesum* 'I am in front of', 'I am in charge'; but *prae-* can also mean 'extremely', 'very', e.g. *praealtus* 'very high'.

Word exercise

Give the meaning and Latin connection of: gratitude, auxiliary, voluptuary, brevity, minus, favour, licence, obstinate, tenacious, emperor, impede, necessary.

Note that 'parent' comes from pariō parere *I procure, give birth to, not* pāreō *I obey.*

Everyday Latin

'Let there be sung *Non Nobis* and *Te Deum*' (Shakespeare, *Henry V*, IV.8.122: Henry V after the battle of Agincourt). *Non Nobis* is Psalm 115 (Vulgate, part of Ps. 113), which begins *nōn nōbis, Domine, nōn nōbis, sed nōminī tuō dā glōriam* (*glōria ae* 1f. 'glory'). *Te Deum* is the beginning of the canticle *tē deum laudāmus* (*laudō* 1 'I praise').

cui bonō? 'to whom (is it) for a benefit?' 'to whose advantage is it?' (NOT 'what use is it?').

urbī et orbī 'to the city and the world'. The papal pronouncement made from the Vatican at Easter to the crowds below.

Real Latin

Martial

Īliacō⌐ similem puerum, Faustīne, ⌐ministrō
lusca Lycōris amat. quam bene lusca uidet! (*3.39*)

Īliac-us a um Trojan [hold	*Faustīne* = O Faustinus
Īliacō: it depends on	*minister ministr-ī* 2m. slave
similem and agrees with	*lusc-us a um* one-eyed
ministrō]	*Lycōris (nom. f.)* Lycoris

NB. *The 'Trojan slave' is Ganymede, a beautiful young boy with whom Jupiter fell in love. He took him up to heaven to be his cup-bearer.*

Vulgate

Glōria in altissimīs Deō, et in terrā pāx hominibus bonae uoluntātis. (*Luke 2.14*)

alt-us a um high	*uoluntās uoluntāt-is* 3f. will

Word study

auxilium

The root of *auxilium* 'help' is *augeō* 'I enlarge', 'I increase', with its perfect participle *auctus*. Hence 'auction', an increasing, and 'author', originally an *auctor* 'increaser', hence 'founder', and so 'authority' etc. An augment is an increase, and *aug-silium* 'an increase (in forces)' 'an auxiliary' – hence 'help'. More strangely still, *augur* probably means 'one who predicts increase, i.e. success', so 'augury', 'inaugurate' (= 'give a start to', 'consecrate'). *augustus* signifies either 'consecrated by the augurs' or 'undertaken under favourable auspices'. This was the name given to Octavius Caesar in 27, who, as Augustus, was the first Roman emperor and gave his name to the month August. Note the following place-names which originate from the name Augustus: Val d'Aosta (Augusta Praetoria), Autun (Augustodunum), Zaragoza (Saragossa) = Caesar-augusta.

SECTION FOUR

Section 4A

Running vocabulary for 4A(i)

---

accurrō 3 *accurrī* I run up
Agrigentīn-us ī 2m. person
  from Agrigentum
  (town in Sicily)
apud (+ acc.) among
armāt-us a um armed
arripiō 3 *arripuī* ¹ seize,
  snatch
clāu-a ae 1f. club
commoueō 2 I shake free,
  shift
commouēbant 'they began
  to shift' (impf. of
  commoueō)
cōnābantur 'they tried'
  (impf. of *cōnor*)
concurrō 3 *concurrī* I make
  a charge, rush
custōs custōd-is 3m. guard
dīligentius (comparative
  adverb of *dīligenter*)
  carefully
effringō 3 *effrēgī* I break
  open
expugnābant 'they began
  to storm' (impf. of
  expugnō)

expugnō 1 I storm
fām-a ae 1f. rumour,
  report
fīēbat 'there occurred'
  (impf. of *fīō*)
Herculēs Hercul-is 3m.
  Hercules
ibi there
impetum faciō 3/4 *fēcī*
  I make an attack
intereā meanwhile
ips-e a um (him-, her-,
  it-)self (gen. s. *ipsīus*)
iūdex iūdic-is 3m. judge
lapidātiō lapidātiōn-is 3f.
  stoning
longē ā/ab (+ abl.) far
  from
num surely . . . not?
nūnti-us ī 2m. messenger
obsistō 3 (+ dat.) I resist,
  obstruct
percrēbrēscēbat 'it began to
  spread' (impf. of
  percrēbrēscō)
perueniō 4 *peruēnī* (*ad*)
  I reach, arrive at, come
  to

quīdam quaedam quoddam
  a, a certain, some (**92**)
repellō 3 *reppulī* I drive
  back, drive out
repente suddenly
seruōs . . . commouēre 'that
  slaves . . . were
  shifting'
seruōs . . . cōnārī 'that
  slaves . . . were trying'
seruōs . . . expugnāre 'that
  slaves . . . were
  storming'
simulācrum ī 2n. image
surgō 3 *surrēxī* I arise, rise
  up
tēl-um ī 2n. weapon,
  missile
templ-um ī 2n. temple
tōt-us a um (like *ūnus* (see
  54): gen. s. *tōt-īus*, dat.
  s. *tōt-ī*) whole,
  complete
ualu-a ae 1f. folding door
Verrēs Verr-is 3m. Verres
uīs irr. f. force, violence
  (acc. *uim*, abl. *uī*)

189

Learning vocabulary for 4A(i)[1]

Nouns

Agrigentīn-us ī 2m. person from Agrigentum (town in Sicily)
custōs custōd-is 3m. or f. guard
fāma ae 1f. rumour, report; reputation

impetus -ūs 4m. attack
nūnti-us ī 2m. messenger
simulācr-um ī 2n. image, copy
templ-um ī 2n. temple
Verrēs Verr-is 3m. Verres

uīs irr. f. force, violence (acc. *uim*, abl. *uī*); pl. *uīrēs, uīrium* 3f. strength, military forces

Adjectives

quīdam quaedam quoddam a, a certain, some

tōt-us a um (gen. s. *totīus*) whole, complete

Verbs

expugnō 1 I storm
impetum faciō 3/4 *fēcī factus* I make an attack

perueniō 4 *peruēnī peruentum* (*ad*) I reach, arrive at, come to

repellō 3 *reppulī repulsus* I drive back, drive out

Others

apud (+acc.) among; (at the house of, in the hands of, in the works of)

intereā meanwhile

repente suddenly

[1] From now on items are listed alphabetically in each category.

Running vocabulary for 4A(ii)

---

aēne-us a um bronze
Assōrīn-us ī 2m. person from Assorus
būcinā 'on the horn'
Chrȳs-as ae m. River Chrysas
colō 3 I worship
concurrēbant 'they began to rush' (impf. of *concurrō*)
dīcam 'should I say'
doctrīn-a ae 1f. learning
effringō 3 *effrēgī* I break down
Enguīn-us ī 2m. person from Engyum
erant 'there were' (impf. of *sum*)

fact-us a um made, constructed
fluō 3 I flow
fluui-us ī 2m. river
fortitūdō fortitūdinis 3f. bravery
gale-a ae 1f. helmet
Hierō Hierōn-is 3m. Hiero
hominēs . . . intrāre 'that men were entering'
hūmānitās hūmānitāt-is 3f. culture
hydri-a ae 1f. jar
imitor 1 *imitātus* I copy
īnscrībō 3 *īnscrīpsī* I inscribe

intellegēbat '(he) understood' (impf. of *intellegō*)
intellegō 3 I understand
iūdex iūdic-is 3m. judge
iūdicō 1 I judge, evaluate
lōrīc-a ae 1f. breastplate
marmor marmor-is 3n. marble
Māter Magna Mātris Magnae Great Mother (i.e. the goddess Cybele)
mātūre early, in time
monument-um ī 2n. monument
negōti-um ī 2n. business, job

pōnō 3 I place, put
posteā afterwards
quī 'which' (nom. s. m.)
quid why?
religiō religiōn-is 3f.
sanctity

religiōs-us a um sacred,
revered, holy,
awesome
relinquō 3 *relīquī* I leave
Scīpiō Scīpiōnis 3m. Scipio
sentiō 4 *sēnsī* I perceive,
realise

singulār-is e peculiar,
unique
sōl-us a um alone
Tlēpolem-us ī 2m.
Tlepolemus
ualu-a ae 1f. folding door
uidēlicet apparently
(sarcastic)

Learning vocabulary for 4A(ii)

Nouns
iūdex iūdic-is 3m. judge
negōti-um ī 2n. business,
work, duty

Adjectives
religiōs-us a um sacred,
revered, holy,
awesome

Verbs
colō 3 *coluī cultus* I
worship; cultivate, till;
inhabit

pōnō 3 *posuī positus* I
place, position, put
relinquō 3 *relīquī relictus* I
leave, abandon

sentiō 4 *sēnsī sēnsus* I feel,
understand, perceive,
realise

Others
posteā afterwards
quid why?

Running vocabulary for 4A(iii)

accūsō 1 I accuse
affirmō 1 I state strongly,
assert
aliquis someone (decl. like
quis)
amīc-us ī 2m. friend, ally
antīqu-us a um old
atrōx atrōc-is appalling,
shocking

audītūrōs esse 'to be about
to hear', (fut. inf. of
audiō)
audīuisse 'to have heard',
(perf. inf. of *audiō*)
Catinēnsis Catinēns-is 3m.
person from Catina
Cerēs Cerer-is 3f. Ceres
(goddess of corn)

cōnficiō 3/4 I carry out
cōnfirmō 1 I state clearly,
confirm
cōnspicātās esse 'to have
seen' (perf. inf. of
cōnspicor)
cōnstituō 3 *cōnstituī* I
decide
crīmen crīmin-is 3n. charge

dēferō dēferre dētulī I report
dēmoueō 2 I remove
erat 'there was' (impf. of *sum*)
eum . . . esse 'that he was'
fīct-us a um false
illum seruum . . . ingressum esse . . . sustulisse 'that that slave had entered . . . (and) removed'
ingressum esse 'to have entered' (perf. inf. of *ingredior*)
innocēns innocent-is guiltless
intrāuisse 'to have entered', (perf. inf. of *intrō*)
ist-e that person (i.e. Verres)
iūdicō 1 I judge
lēx lēg-is 3f. law

locus ī 2m. place
magistrāt-us ūs 4m. magistrate, state official
negō 1 I deny, say that x is not the case
nōlēbat '(he) did not want' (impf. of *nōlō*)
perantīqu-us a um very old
postrīdiē next day
putō 1 I think
reperiō 4 I find
sacr-a ōrum 2n. pl. rites
sacerdōs sacerdōt-is 3f. priestess
sacrāri-um ī 2n. shrine
sē . . . cōnspicātās esse 'that they had seen'
senāt-us ūs 4m. senate
seruōs . . . intrāuisse . . . sustulisse 'that the slaves had entered . . . (and) removed'

sign-um ī 2n. statue
soleō 2 I am accustomed, used
suspiciō suspiciōn-is 3f. suspicion
sustulisse 'to have removed' (perf. inf. of *tollō*)
testis test-is 3m. witness
tollō 3 *sustulī* I remove, take away
uidēbātur '(it) seemed' (impf. of *uideor*)
uirgō uirgin-is 3f. young girl, virgin
uolēbat 'he wished' (impf. of *uolō*)
uōs . . . audītūrōs esse 'that you will hear'
uōs . . . audīuisse 'that you have heard'

Learning vocabulary for 4A(iii)

Nouns

amīc-us ī 2m. friend, ally
ist-e a ud that over there / of yours (used especially when referring to opponents at a trial: *iste* here is always used to mean Verres)

loc-us ī 2m. place (pl. *loc-a ōrum* 2n. pl.)
magistrāt-us ūs 4m. magistrate, state official
sacerdōs sacerdōt-is 3m. f. priest(ess)

sacr-a ōrum 2n. pl. rites
senāt-us ūs 4m. senate
sign-um ī 2n. statue; (seal; signal, sign)
uirgō uirgin-is 3f. young girl, virgin

Adjectives

innocēns innocent-is guiltless

sacer sacr-a um holy, sacred

Verbs

accūsō 1 I accuse x (acc.) of y (gen.)
affirmō 1 I state strongly, assert
cōnfirmō 1 I state clearly, confirm

dēferō dēferre dētulī dēlātus I report, bring news of; accuse, denounce; transfer
iūdicō 1 I judge
negō 1 I deny, say that x is not the case

putō 1 I think
reperiō 4 *repperī repertus* I find
soleō 2 *solitus* (semi-dep.) I am accustomed, used
tollō 3 *sustulī sublātus* I lift; remove, take away

Running vocabulary for 4A(iv)

ampl-us a um important, prestigious
auctōritās auctōritāt-is 3f. influence, guidance
ausūrum esse 'to be about to dare' (fut. inf. of *audeō*)
clāmor clāmōr-is 3m. outcry
coniciō 3/4 I throw
creō 1 I choose
cuius 'whose'
dīcam 'should I say'
ēdūcō 3 I pick out
erat 'it was' (impf. of *sum*)
ēuent-us ūs 4m. outcome, result
exspectābant 'they awaited' (impf. of *exspectō*)
extrā (+acc.) outside
fās indecl. n. right
fās esse ⎫ 'that it
fās . . . esse ⎭ was right'
fīēbat 'there arose' (impf. of *fīō*)
genus gener-is 3n. tribe

hydri-a ae 1f. jar
id . . . posse 'that it could'
illō modō 'in that way'
iniciō 3/4 I throw in
īnscrīpt-us a um inscribed
laet-us a um happy (tr. 'happily')
lēx lēg-is 3f. law
negābant '(they) denied' (impf. of *negō*)
nōmine 'with the name'
oportet it is right, proper, necessary
perfectūrum esse 'to be about to achieve' (fut. inf. of *perficiō*)
praetereā besides, moreover
prīmō at first
quot however many; how many?
recitō 1 I read out
renūntiātus est '(he) was returned, selected'
renūntiō 1 I return, select, appoint

sacerdōti-um ī 2n. priesthood
sors sort-is 3f. lot-drawing; lot
sortior 4 dep. I draw lots
spērābant 'they were hoping' (impf. of *spērō*)
suffrāgi-um ī 2n. vote
Syrācūsān-us ī 2m. person from Syracuse, Syracusan
Syrācūsīs 'at Syracuse'
Theomnāst-us ī 2m. Theomnastus
tot so many
Verrem . . . ausūrum esse 'that Verres . . . would dare'
Verrem . . . perfectūrum esse 'that Verres would achieve'
uetō 1 uetuī I forbid
uidēbātur '(it) seemed' (impf. of *uideor*)

Learning vocabulary for 4A(iv)

Nouns

clāmor clāmōr-is 3m. shout; outcry; noise
lēx lēg-is 3f. law

Syrācūsān-us ī 2m. person from Syracuse, Syracusan

Adjectives

laet-us a um happy

Verbs

coniciō 3 coniēcī coniectus I throw

uetō 1 uetuī uetitus I forbid

Others

prīmō at first

praetereā besides, moreover

Grammar and exercises for 4A

89 **Imperfect indicative active 'I was —ing', 'I used to —', 'I began to —', 'I tried to —'**

	1	*2*	*3*
	'I was loving'	*'I was having'*	*'I was saying'*
1st s.	amā́-ba-m	habḗ-ba-m	dīc-ḗ-ba-m
2nd s.	amā́-bā-s	habḗ-bā-s	dīc-ḗ-bā-s
3rd s.	amā́-ba-t	habḗ-ba-t	dīc-ḗ-ba-t
1st pl.	amā-bā́-mus	habē-bā́-mus	dīc-ē-bā́-mus
2nd pl.	amā-bā́-tis	habē-bā́-tis	dīc-ē-bā́-tis
3rd pl.	amā́-ba-nt	habḗ-ba-nt	dīc-ḗ-ba-nt

	4	*3/4*
	'I was hearing'	*'I was capturing'*
1st s.	audi-ḗ-ba-m	capi-ḗ-ba-m
2nd s.	audi-ḗ-bā-s	capi-ḗ-bā-s
3rd s.	audi-ḗ-ba-t	capi-ḗ-ba-t
1st pl.	audi-ē-bā́-mus	capi-ē-bā́-mus
2nd pl.	audi-ē-bā́-tis	capi-ē-bā́-tis
3rd pl.	audi-ḗ-ba-nt	capi-ḗ-ba-nt

Notes

1 Imperfect ind. act. is formed by taking the present stem (+ key vowel *-ē-* in 3rd, 4th and 3rd/4th conjugations) and adding *-bam, -bās, -bat, -bāmus, -bātis, -bant*.

2 Note the regular personal endings: *-m, -s, -t, -mus, -tis, -nt*.

3 The imperfect conjugation, being based on the stem of the present tense, is the tense of vivid, eyewitness descriptions for past events ('I *was* in the process of —ing', cf. present 'I *am* in the process of —ing'). The action, which is uncompleted (*imperfectus* 'uncompleted', cf. *perfectus* 'completed'), is depicted as continuing, or being repeated, or beginning or being attempted. Thus the most common translations for the imperfect are:

> 'I was —ing' }
> 'I used to —' } (continuing, repeated)
>
> 'I began to —' ('inceptive' imperfect, cf. *incipiō inceptus* 'begin')
> 'I tried to —' ('conative' imperfect, cf. *cōnor cōnātus* 'try')

Since English does not always distinguish between completed and uncompleted actions, it will often be possible to translate the imperfect as a simple past tense, e.g. *uidēbātur* 'it seemed'.

4 Learn the following irregulars:

sum→	*1st s.*	ér-a-m 'I was' *etc.*		eō→	*1st s.*	í-ba-m 'I went' *etc.*
	2nd s.	ér-ā-s			*2nd s.*	í-bā-s
	3rd s.	ér-a-t			*3rd s.*	í-ba-t
	1st pl.	er-ā́-mus			*1st pl.*	ī-bā́-mus
	2nd pl.	er-ā́-tis			*2nd pl.*	ī-bā́-tis
	3rd pl.	ér-a-nt			*3rd pl.*	í-ba-nt

possum→	*1st s.*	pót-eram 'I was able', 'I could' *etc.*
	2nd s.	pót-erās
	3rd s.	pót-erat
	1st pl.	pot-erā́mus
	2nd pl.	pot-erā́tis
	3rd pl.	pót-erant

5 *uolō* (*uolēbam*), *nōlō* (*nōlēbam*) and *mālō* (*mālēbam*) are all regular.

6 Semi-deponents (see **76**) take the active form of the imperfect, i.e. *audē-bam* 'I was daring', *fīē-bam* 'I was being made'. In summary, semi-deponents have ACTIVE forms in the present, future and imperfect (*audeō, audēbō, audēbam*) and DEPONENT forms in the perfect (*ausus sum*).

90 **Imperfect indicative deponent**

	1	**2**	**3**
	'*I was threatening*'	'*I was promising*'	'*I was speaking*'
1st s.	minā́-ba-r	pollicé-ba-r	loqu-é-ba-r
2nd s.	minā-bā́-ris (-re)	pollicē-bā́-ris (-re)	loqu-ē-bā́-ris (-re)
3rd s.	minā-bā́-tur	pollicē-bā́-tur	loqu-ē-bā́-tur
1st pl.	minā-bā́-mur	pollicē-bā́-mur	loqu-ē-bā́-mur
2nd pl.	minā-bā́-minī	pollicē-bā́-minī	loqu-ē-bā́-minī
3rd pl.	minā-bá-ntur	pollicē-bá-ntur	loqu-ē-bá-ntur

	4	**3/4**
	'*I was lying*'	'*I was advancing*'
1st s.	menti-é-ba-r	prōgredi-é-ba-r
2nd s.	menti-ē-bā́-ris (-re)	prōgredi-ē-bā́-ris (-re)
3rd s.	menti-ē-bā́-tur	prōgredi-ē-bā́-tur

1st pl.	menti-ē-bá-mur	prōgredi-ē-bá-mur
2nd pl.	menti-ē-bá-minī	prōgredi-ē-bá-minī
3rd pl.	menti-ē-bá-ntur	prōgredi-ē-bá-ntur

Notes

1 The imperfect ind. dep. is formed by taking the present stem (+ key vowel -ē- in 3rd, 4th and 3rd/4th conjugations) and adding -bar -bāris (or -bāre) -bātur -bāmur -bāminī -bantur.

2 Note the regular personal endings for the deponent: -r -ris (or -re) -tur -mur -minī -ntur.

3 For meaning, see **89³**.

Exercises

Morphology

1 *Form and conjugate the imperfect, giving the meaning of 1st person singular imperfect, of*: uideor, expugnō, fīō, perueniō, sum, cōnor, iubeō, redūcō, īrāscor, faciō, (*optional*: legō, eō, affirmō, soleō, moror, proficīscor, adgredior, ferō, nōlō, sentiō).

2 *Translate each verb, then change s. to pl. and vice versa*: tenēbās, loquēbantur, praeerat, minābāminī, imperābam, ueniēbātis, audēbant; oblīuīscēbāris; audiēbat; patiēbāmur; auferēbāmus; sequēbar, (*optional*: negābam, pollicēbāris, pōnēbat, adipīscēbantur, tollēbātis, īrāscēbātur, faciēbās, mentiēbar, putābāmus, cōnspicābāminī, uetābant, arbitrābāmur).

3 *Give the Latin for*: I used to think; he was abandoning; they were throwing; we used to follow; you (*s.*) were reporting; she was going out; they were accustomed; you (*pl.*) were; we were stating strongly; (*optional*: he used to find; they were daring; you (*s.*) were speaking; they used to lie; I was encouraging; you (*pl.*) were setting out; we were removing; I was asserting).

4 *Give 3rd s. and pl. of the following verbs in present, future, imperfect and perfect*: sentiō, minor, uetō, tollō, eō, sum, audeō, adipīscor, uideor, teneō, adgredior, mentior, accūsō, colō, (*optional*: loquor, negō, soleō, taceō, reperiō, proficīscor, perueniō, dēferō, sequor, faciō).

5 *Locate and translate the imperfects in this list, stating the tense of each of the other verbs*: loquar, sentiēbat, amābit, negābat, solēbunt, audēbant,

pōnam, tollēbātis, relīquit, habēbit, tacēbant, opīnāberis, arbitrābāris, expugnant, repellēbās, iūdicābātis, coniēcistis, (*optional*: dormiēbātis, iubēbitis, sequēbātur, hortābimur, uolēbās, sciētis, prōmittis, habuistis, inueniēbāmus, inībimus, coquēbat, āmittis, crēdēbant, recordābitur).

1 *iste a ud* 'that (of yours)'

iste declines as follows:

	s.			pl.		
	m.	*f.*	*n.*	*m.*	*f.*	*n.*
nom.	íst-e	íst-a	íst-ud	íst-ī	íst-ae	íst-a
acc.	íst-um	íst-am	íst-ud	íst-ōs	íst-ās	íst-a
gen.	←——— ist-íus ———→			ist-ṓrum	ist-ā́rum	ist-ṓrum
dat.	←——— íst-ī ———→			←——— íst-īs ———→		
abl.	íst-ō	íst-ā	íst-ō	←——— íst-īs ———→		

Notes

1 *iste* declines exactly like *ille* **64**. Cf. *is* **70**. *iste* also has a neuter s. in -*d*, a gen. s. in -*īus* and dat. s. in -*ī*.

2 *iste* is frequently used contemptuously of an opponent in a lawsuit and is so used of Verres by Cicero throughout his Verrine speeches.

Exercises

1 *Say with which of the nouns in each line the given form of* iste *agrees:*

istīus: seruī, fēminae, templī, manūs, reī, custōdis, impetūs
istā: lēge, uirginem, seruī, sacerdōte, negōtiō
istī: seruī, uirtūtī, manuī, negōtiō, mīlitēs
ista: fēmina, clāmor, rēs, simulācra, puellā

2 *Make* iste *agree with these nouns:* seruī (*2 possibilities*), negōtiō (*2 possibilities*), uirtūtī, custōdibus, manūs (*3 possibilities*).

92 *quīdam, quaedam, quoddam* 'a', 'a certain'

s.

	m.	*f.*	*n.*	
nom.	quī-dam	quaé-dam	quód-dam	(quid-dam)
acc.	quén-dam	quán-dam	quód-dam	(quid-dam)
gen.		←cuiús-dam→		
dat.		←cuí-dam→		
abl.	quó-dam	quá-dam	quó-dam	

pl.

	m.	*f.*	*n.*
nom.	quī-dam	quaé-dam	quaé-dam
acc.	quós-dam	quás-dam	quaé-dam
gen.	quōrún-dam	quārún-dam	quōrún-dam
dat.	←——— quibús-dam ———→		
abl.	←——— quibús-dam ———→		

Notes

1 The forms correspond with those of *quī* 'who?' **29** + *-dam*.

2 *quīdam* is the nearest classical Latin ever got to an indefinite article, 'a', 'a certain'.

Exercises

1 *Translate and identify the case of*: seruōrum quōrundam; custōdī cuidam; signa quaedam; clāmōrēs quōsdam; dolō quōdam; iūdicibus quibusdam.

2 *Say with which of the nouns in each line the given form of* quīdam *agrees*:

> cuiusdam: seruā, templī, sacerdōtis, custōdum, manūs, impetū
> quaedam: fēmina, rēs, negōtia, mīlitēs, lēgēs, loca
> quīdam: custōs, nūntius, puerī, mīlitēs, magistrātūs, iūdicēs

93 *num* 'surely . . . not'

You have already met *nōnne*, which means 'doesn't?' 'surely?' ('it *is* the case, isn't it?') (**85**), e.g. *nōnne seruī templum intrāuērunt?* 'the slaves *have* entered the temple, haven't they?'

num puts the opposite emphasis, i.e. 'surely something is *not* the case?', 'it *isn't* the case, is it?', e.g.

> *num peiōra audīuistis?* 'surely you have *not* heard worse things?', 'you *haven't* heard worse things, have you?'
> *num seruī effūgērunt?* 'surely the slaves haven't run away?', 'the slaves *haven't* run away, have they?'

nōnne ('surely x *is* the case?') is used to ask a question in such a way that the speaker is trying to get the listener to answer 'yes'.

num ('surely x *isn't* the case?') is used to ask a question in such a way that the speaker is trying to get the listener to say 'no'.

94 Forming the infinitive in Latin

You have already met present infinitives (cf. **41, 58**), but here is a revision table:

	1	2	3	4	3/4
Active	-āre	-ēre	-ere	-īre	-ere
Deponent	-ārī	-ērī	-ī	-īrī	-ī

Here are the other infinitive (active and deponent) tables:

95 Perfect infinitive active 'to have —ed'

1	2	3
'to have loved'	'to have had'	'to have said'
amāu-isse (*or* amásse)	habu-isse	dīx-isse

4	3/4
'to have heard'	'to have captured'
audīu-isse (*or* audiísse *or* audísse)	cēp-isse

Notes

1 Perfect infins. act. are formed by taking the stem of the 3rd p. p. and adding *-isse*.
2 Note how *-ui-* can be dropped, giving e.g. *amāsse* (*amāuisse*) 'to have loved', *dēlēsse* (*dēlēuisse*) 'to have destroyed', *nōsse* (*nōuisse*) 'to have got to know', 'to know' (from *nōscō* 3 *nōuī*).

96 Perfect infinitive deponent 'to have —ed'

1	*2*
'to have threatened'	*'to have promised'*
minát-us a um ésse	pollícit-us a um ésse

3	*4*	*3/4*
'to have said'	*'to have lied'*	*'to have advanced'*
locútus a um ésse	mentít-us a um ésse	prōgréss-us a um ésse

Notes

1 The perfect infin. dep is formed by combining the perfect participle with the infin. of the verb 'to be', *esse*.

2 The perfect participle acts as an adjective and must agree with the person doing the action, e.g.

> 'he seems to have lied' *uidētur mentītus esse*
> 'the girls seem to have spoken' *puellae uidentur locūtae esse*

97 Future infinitives active and deponent 'to be about to—'

	1	*2*	*3*
Active	*'to be about to love'*	*'to be about to have'*	*'to be about to say'*
	amātúr-us a um ésse	habitúr-us a um ésse	dictúr-us a um ésse
Deponent	*'to be about to threaten'*	*'to be about to promise'*	*'to be about to speak'*
	minātúr-us a um ésse	pollicitúr-us a um ésse	locūtúr-us a um ésse

	4	*3/4*
Active	*'to be about to hear'*	*'to be about to capture'*
	audītúr-us a um ésse	captúr-us a um ésse
Deponent	*'to be about to lie'*	*'to be about to advance'*
	mentītúr-us a um ésse	prōgressúr-us a um ésse

Notes

1 The future infinitives active and deponent are formed in exactly the same way, i.e. combining the future participle with *esse* (cf. perfect deponent infinitives **96**).

2 The future participle acts as an adjective and will agree with the person 'about to—', e.g.

> 'he seems to be about to speak' *uidētur dictūrus esse*
> 'she seemed to be about to listen' *uidēbātur audītūra esse*

3 The future infinitive of 'to be' is either (regular) *futūrus esse* or the fixed form *fore*.

4 Verbs which have no future participle have no future infinitive. Among these are: *uolō, mālō, nōlō, possum*. Note that *uīsūrus esse* means 'to be about to see' (never 'seem'), *factūrus esse* means 'to be about to make/do' (never 'become').

Exercises

1 *Form the present, perfect and future infinitives of:* sum, accūsō, expugnō, cōnfirmō, iubeō, redūcō, tollō, coniciō, ēgredior, mentior, ueniō, eō, (*optional:* sentiō, audeō, ferō, nōlō (*no future infinitive*), adipīscor, cōnor, faciō, patior, dō, colō).

2 *State the tense of these infinitives and say which verbs they come from:* passūrus esse, loquī, amāuisse, sentīre, habitūrus esse, sustulisse, minātus esse, uelle, itūrus esse, expugnāre, secūtus esse, poscere, posuisse, adeptus esse, iūdicāsse, repertūrus esse, dēferre.

3 *Give the Latin for:* to seem; to have forbidden; to be about to think; to report; to have found; to be about to remove; to follow; to have remembered; to be about to lie; to promise; to have spoken; to be about to forget; (*optional:* to have driven back; to be about to worship; to throw; to be about to confirm).

4 *Pick out the infinitives and say what tense each is, stating also what part of the verb the others are:* solitus es, dētulistis, cōnfirmāuēre, affirmāre, sequere, coluisse, putā, hortātus esse, reperīre, mentīre, accūsātūrus esse, ausus est, repellere, loquere, expugnāuisse, audītūrus esse, dēferēbat, iudicātūrus esse.

98 **Indirect (or reported) statements: the accusative and infinitive**

Observe the following utterances:

(a) *dīcit Verrem uenīre* 'he says Verres to be coming' i.e. 'that Verres is coming'.

(b) *nūntiant seruōs peruēnisse* 'they announce the slaves to have arrived' i.e. 'that the slaves arrived'.

(c) *nōn putō Verrem abitūrum esse* 'I do not consider Verres to be about to go' i.e. 'that Verres will go'.

In all these cases, where English uses a 'that' clause, Latin (i) dispenses with the equivalent of 'that', (ii) puts the subject of the clause in the accusative and (iii) puts the verb in the infinitive.

This is Latin's way of reporting a statement (the *direct* statement of (a) above being 'Verres is coming', of (b) 'the slaves have arrived' etc.).

So be on the lookout for verbs of *saying, thinking, knowing, reporting, announcing* followed by the *accusative and infinitive*. Translate such sentences literally first, and then adjust to the English 'that' form.

Notes

1   English has a parallel construction, e.g. 'he knows *me to be* wise', or 'he knows that I am wise'.

2   Latin uses the reflexive (*sē, suus*) to refer in the 'that' clause to the *subject of the main verb*, e.g.

> *Caesar dīxit sē peruēnisse* 'Caesar said that he (= Caesar) had arrived'
> *Caesar dīxit eum peruēnisse* 'Caesar said that he (= someone else) had arrived'

3   Observe the correct English form when the main verb is past, e.g.

> *Caesar dīxit Rōmam sē uentūrum esse* 'Caesar said himself to be about to come to Rome', i.e. 'Caesar said that he would come to Rome'
> *Caesar dīxit Rōmam sē uēnisse* 'Caesar said himself to have come to Rome', i.e. 'Caesar said that he had come to Rome'
> *Caesar dīxit Rōmam sē uenīre* 'Caesar said himself to be coming to Rome' i.e. 'Caesar said that he was coming to Rome'

4   Note that the normal position for *sē* is second word in its sentence or clause (see examples in n. 3 above). If it comes first word in its clause, or first word after a natural break in the sense, it is usually emphatic, e.g. *Caesar mihi heri dīxit sē Rōmam uentūrum esse* 'Caesar said to me yesterday | that as for himself *he* would come to Rome'. This rule applies to all pronouns.

5   The accusative and infinitive construction is so common in Latin that Latin will sometimes use it *with an introductory noun (implying speech)* e.g. *nūntium accēpī seruōs templum intrāuisse* 'I received a message (saying) that the slaves had entered the temple'. Very often, several indirect statements (sometimes a whole speech) follow one another with no repetition of the introductory word(s). So remember always

to start your final translation of a Latin accusative and infinitive with the English word THAT, e.g.

> *dīxit seruōs templum intrāuisse; custōdēs effūgisse; seruōs simulācrum commouēre* 'he said THAT the slaves had entered the temple; THAT the guards had fled; THAT the slaves were shifting the statue'

99 *negō* **'I say (that) . . . not', 'I deny'**

Latin generally does not use *dīcō* + negative to express the idea 'I say that . . . not', but prefers *negō*, e.g.

> *negat seruōs templum intrāuisse* 'he says that the slaves did not enter the temple' (lit. 'he denies the slaves to have entered the temple')

Exercises

1 *Translate these sentences*:

(a) Cicerō affirmat Agrigentīnōs Herculis simulācrum habēre.
(b) Agrigentīnī Verrem praetōrem bonum fuisse negābant.
(c) fāma erat seruōs istīus in templum ingressōs esse et signum sustulisse.
(d) nūntium quendam haec omnia nūntiāuisse Agrigentīnīs Cicerō dīxit.
(e) ego putō istum semper uōbīs mentītūrum esse.
(f) opīnābatur Cicerō nēminem umquam scelera peiōra quam istum factūrum esse.
(g) Verrēs seruōs in templa mittēbat, cīuibus aurum uī auferēbat, amīcīs etiam contrā (= *against*) lēgem fauēbat, scelera omnia amplexābātur.
(h) Verrem seruī cuiusdam nōmen dēlātūrum esse audiō.
(i) Verres, quod nōlēbat in crīmine esse, amīcum quendam mentīrī iussit.
(j) Verrem sciō innocentīs accūsāre solitum esse.
(k) num facinora scelestiōra umquam audīuistis, iūdicēs?
(l) nōnne Verrēs homo est scelestissimus?
(m) Agrigentīnōs in Verris seruōs impetum fēcisse audīuī.

2 *Translate these sentences*:

(a) ratiō docet esse deōs. (*Cicero*)
(b) ēuentus docuit fortīs fortūnam iuuāre. (*Livy*)
(c) homo sum: hūmānī nīl ā mē aliēnum putō. (*Terence*)
(d) Dēmocritum aiunt numquam sine rīsū in pūblicō fuisse. (*Seneca*)
(e) spērat adulēscēns diū sē uīctūrum (*sc.* esse). (*Cicero*)
(f) glōria uarium et uolūbile quiddam est. (*Seneca*)
(g) nūper mē cuiusdam amīcī languor admonuit, optimōs esse nōs dum īnfirmī sumus. quem enim īnfirmum aut auāritia aut libīdō sollicitat? (*Pliny*)
(h) hīc, ubi nunc Rōma est, incaedua silua uirēbat, tantaque rēs paucīs pāscua būbus erat. (*Ovid*)

---

ratiō ratiōn-is 3f. reason
doceō 2 I teach, inform
ēuent-us ūs 4m. outcome; event
fortūn-a ae 1f. fortune
iuuō 1 I help
hūmānī nīl nothing (of) human
aliēn-us a um of no concern to (x: *ā* + abl.)
Dēmocrit-us ī 2m. Democritus (Greek philosopher)
aiō I say
rīs-us ūs 4m. laughter, laughing
in pūblicō in public
spērō 1 I hope

adulēscēns adulēscent-is 3m. youth
diū for a long time
uīuō 3 *uīxī uīctūrus* I live
glōri-a ae 1f. fame, renown
uari-us a um fickle, inconstant
uolūbil-is e unstable, liable change
nūper recently
languor languōr-is 3m. illness
admoneō 2 I remind
īnfirm-us a um weak, feeble

auāriti-a ae 1f. avarice, greed
libīdō libīdin-is 3f. lust
Rōm-a ae 1f. Rome
incaedu-us a um uncut, unfelled
silu-a ae 1f. wood
uireō 2 I am green (with foliage)
pauc-ī ae a a few
pāscu-a ōrum 2n. pl. pasture
bōs bou-is 3m. or f. ox, cow; (pl.) cattle: dat. and abl. *būbus*

Reading exercises

1 *In each of these accusative and infinitive phrases, state who is doing the action, the tense of the action (i.e. when it would have occurred in direct speech) and, if applicable, the object or complement of the infinitive: then translate, remembering to begin with 'that'. See* **98⁴** *for normal position of* sē *etc. Note that in some cases (e.g. (d)) there is ambiguity. E.g.:*

eum fīliam amāre (*a*) eum: '*that he*' *or* '*that him*' (*i.e. someone other than the subject of the introductory verb*)

(b) fīliam: 'the daughter' *(subject or object of* amāre)

(c) amāre: *(present)* 'loves'

i.e. 'that he loves the daughter' or 'that the daughter loves him'

(a)   seruōs templum expugnātūrōs esse.
(b)   Verrem seruōs ad templum mīsisse.
(c)   Assōrīnōs Chrȳsam colere.
(d)   Verrem mē accūsātūrum esse.
(e)   simulācra sē amāre.
(f)   Scīpiōnem hominem summā hūmānitāte fuisse.
(g)   omnia sē cōnspicātās esse.
(h)   istum nocte ex urbe ēgressūrum esse.
(i)   clāmōrem magnum factum esse.
(j)   eum domum īre.

2 *In the following passage, as you read, underline the acc. + inf. phrase with a single line and the introductory verb with a double line (be careful, as the introductory verb may appear before, in the middle, or at the end of the phrase). As you meet each acc. + inf. phrase, repeat the process outlined for Exercise 1 above. Next, translate the passage and finally read it aloud in Latin, taking care to phrase correctly.*

Cicerō templum esse apud Agrigentīnōs dīxit. id affirmāuit nōn longē ā forō esse. in hoc templum intrāuisse dīxit Verris seruōs. eōs Verrem mīsisse Cicerō opīnātus est. Verrēs autem sē hoc fēcisse negābat. fāma percrēbrēscēbat Verris seruōs in templum ingressōs esse et custōdēs templum dēfendere cōnātōs esse. magnum clāmōrem custōdēs fēcisse putāuit Cicerō; Agrigentīnōs igitur ex urbe prōgressōs esse et ad templum uēnisse. fūgisse tum seruōs Verris affirmāuit. Cicerō negābat umquam sē scelera peiōra audītūrum esse.   5

3 *Before translating, say whether each sentence contains an acc. + inf. phrase (reported statement) or merely a prolative infinitive (i.e. after verbs like* uolō *etc.).*

(a)   negārunt fierī id posse.
(b)   id uōs facere nōluit.
(c)   tē Chrȳsae simulācrum tollere iubeō.
(d)   seruōs sē necāre cōnātōs esse affirmābat.
(e)   Verrem simulācrum sustulisse fāma erat.
(f)   mē Verrem accūsāre, iūdicēs, uolēbant omnēs Agrigentīnī.

4 *Using the introductory verbs given, change the bracketed sentences from direct to indirect statements (acc. + inf.), then translate the passage*:

Cicerō dīcit (templum apud Agrigentīnōs est nōn longē ā forō). affirmat (ibi est simulācrum Herculis pulcherrimum). negat (pulchrius simulācrum quam illud numquam cōnspicātus sum[1]). fāma est (ad hoc templum Verrēs repente nocte seruōs quōsdam armātōs mīsit). dīcit (hī concurrērunt et templum expugnāuērunt). affirmat (custōdēs templī clāmāuēre et seruīs obsistere templumque dēfendere cōnātī sunt). dīcit (mox et peiōra et scelestiōra audiētis[2]).

[1] Use *sē* to introduce this; change *numquam* to *umquam*.
[2] Use *eōs* to introduce this.

Reading exercise / Test exercise

audiō apud Catinēnsīs esse Cereris sacrārium. in sacrārium illud uirīs intrāre nōn licēre omnēs sciunt. fāma est mulierēs et uirginēs ibi sacra cōnficere solēre. in eō sacrāriō fuisse signum Cereris perantīquum multī affirmant. hoc signum seruōs Verris Cicerō dīxit nocte ex illō locō sustulisse; omnibus rem atrōcissimam uīsam esse. Verrem deinde iussisse   5 amīcum quendam aliquem reperīre et accūsāre Cicerō dīxit. nam eum in crīmine esse nōlle. Cicerō amīcum affirmāuit seruī cuiusdam nōmen dētulisse, seruum accūsāuisse, in eum fictōs dedisse testīs. senātum autem Catinēnsium sacerdōtēs uocāuisse et dē omnibus rēbus rogāuisse. sacerdōtēs dīxit Cicerō omnia omnīs cōnspicātās esse, senātum seruum   10 innocentem esse dīxisse. iūdicēs numquam peiōra audīuisse scelera arbitrābātur Cicerō, mox autem peiōra audītūrōs esse.

English–Latin

1 *Translate into Latin*:

(a) I think that Verres did this.
(b) Cicero said that the slaves entered the temple.
(c) Many citizens used to come to the city, do business, then return home.
(d) Verres' friend reported the name of a certain slave.
(e) We all know that the defendant is a scoundrel.
(f) Surely you don't think that the slaves took away the statue?

(g)   Cicero was an excellent man, used gladly to defend his friends, and¹ never forgot the crimes of our enemies.

(h)   Cicero thinks the judges will never hear of a worse crime.

¹ No need to translate.

2 *Read the text of* **4A(iv)** *again, then translate this passage:*

The Syracusans have a law concerning the priesthood of Jupiter. Cicero says that this law enjoins the Syracusans to elect three men; that the Syracusans must then cast lots; that one of the three men becomes priest. He states that Verres wanted to give the priesthood to a friend, called Theomnastus, that the Syracusans refused, but¹ that Verres by a trick achieved his object.

¹ No need for an equivalent in Latin (just use a comma).

Deliciae Latinae

Word-building

Prefixes

per-, rather like *prae-*, often intensifies the meaning of the word to which it is added, e.g. *antīquus* 'old', *perantīquus* 'very old'.

Note the way the following prefixes may change in response to the consonant to which they are attached (this is called assimilation):

> *ad + capiō = accipiō*¹ 'I receive'
> *ad + firmō = affirmō*² 'I assert'
> *ad + loquor = alloquor* 'I address'
> *ad + propinquō = appropinquō* 'I draw near'
> *ad + tulī = attulī* 'I have brought (to)'
> *ad + rapiō = arripiō* 'I seize'
> *inter + legō = intellegō* 'I understand'
> *sub + capiō = suscipiō* 'I undertake'
> *sub + cēdō = succēdō* 'I go under'
> *sub + gerō = suggerō* 'I supply'
> *sub + rapiō = surripiō* 'I steal'
> *sub + tulī = sustulī* 'I filched'

¹ Observe how a short *a* (*capiō*) becomes *i* (*accipiō*) when a prefix is added. Cf. *rapiō→arripiō* etc.
² It is common for the prefixes *ad-* and *con-* to be printed without assimilation. e.g. *adloquor, conlocō*.

con + locō = collocō 'I place'
con + pellō (3 'I drive') = compellō 'I compel'
con + rapiō = corripiō 'I snatch up'
con + moueō = commoueō 'I move'

Suffixes: revision

-c(u)lum, -crum added to a verb stem give neuter nouns, e.g. simulō 'I copy', 'I pretend' + -crum = simulācrum 'image', 'statue'; pō-tus 'drink' + culum = pōculum 'drink', 'cup'; uehō 'carry' + -culum = uehiculum 'carriage'. Such words are usually instruments for carrying out the action.

-iō, -iōnis 3f. added to the stem of the perfect participle gives an abstract noun, e.g. legō lēct-us 'I read' →lēctiō 'reading'; audiō audītus 'I hear' →audītiō 'hearing' etc. Cf. sessiō, mōtiō, accūsātiō etc. Such words show an action, or its result.

Word exercises

Give the meaning and connection with Latin of: clamour, custodial, temple, repulsion, renunciation (*NB.* nūntiō *becomes* nūnciō *in Medieval Latin*), total, pugnacious, convention, sign, cult, relic, sensibility, sacerdotal, conjecture, putative, veto, legal, amicable, defamation, impetuous, judicial, triumvirate.

Real Latin

Catullus[1]
nūllī sē dīcit mulier mea nūbere mālle
    quam mihi, nōn sī sē Iuppiter ipse petat.
dīcit: sed mulier cupidō⌐ quod dīcit ⌐amantī
    in uentō et rapidā scrībere oportet aquā. (*Catullus 70*)

nūbō 3 (+ dat.) I marry (said of women only)	quod what (postponed – in English it would	amāns amant-is 3m. lover uent-us ī 2m. wind
ipse himself (nom. s. m.)	come after sed)	rapid-us a um fast-flowing
petat 'were to seek'	cupid-us a um passionate	oportet 'one ought'

[1] C. 84–54. Famous for his love poems addressed to his woman, Lesbia. See section **6A**.

Martial

omnia prōmittis, cum tōtā nocte bibistī.
    māne nihil praestās. Pōllio, māne bibe. (*12.12*)

cum when	*māne* in the morning	*Pōllio* O Pollio
bibō 3 *bib-ī* I drink	*praestō* 1 I provide	

numquam sē cēnāsse domī Philo iūrat, et hoc est.
nōn cēnat, quotiēns nēmo uocāuit eum. (*5.47*)

cēnō 1 I dine	*iūrō* 1 I swear	*quotiēns* as often as,
Philo Philōn-is 3m. Philo	*est* 'is the case'	whenever

Aulus Gellius[1]

cum (*when*) mentior et mē mentīrī dīcō, mentior, an (*or*) uērum dīcō?

[1] C. 123–165 A.D. His *Noctēs Atticae* in twenty books is a compendium of scholarly discussions of diverse topics.

An epitaph

sum quod eris, fuī quod es.

quod what

Section 4B

Running vocabulary for 4B(i)

Asi-a ae 1f. Asia Minor
calamitās calamitāt-is 3f.
  disaster, calamity
cēter-ī ae a the rest; the
  others
cēterīs 'than the others'
cīuitās cīuitāt-is 3f. state
clār-us a um famous, well-
  known
collocō 1 I lodge
comes comit-is 3m.
  companion, friend;
  (pl.) retinue
cupiō 3/4 I desire, yearn
  for, want desperately
excitō 1 I raise, arouse
fruor 3 dep. (+abl.) I
  enjoy

Graec-us -ī 2m. Greek
Hellēspont-um ī 2n.
  Hellespont
hospes hospit-is 3m. host
Iānitor Iānitōr-is 3m.
  Ianitor
ipse a um (him-, her-, it-)
  self, (them-) selves
Lampsacēnus-ī 2m. person
  from Lampsacum (or
  Lampsacus)
Lampsac-um ī 2n.
  Lampsacum (or
  Lampsacus)
nōbil-is e renowned,
  distinguished
ōlim once

omnibus aliīs 'than all the
  others'
omnibus aliīs hominibus
  'than all other men'
perniciēs perniciē-ī 5f.
  destruction
prope almost
quiēt-us a um peaceful,
  law-abiding
tumult-us ūs 4m. riot,
  outcry, disorder
turp-is e disgusting, filthy,
  outrageous
ūllus a um any
ūtor 3 dep. (+abl.) I use,
  make use of

Learning vocabulary for 4B(i)

Nouns

Asi-a ae 1f. Asia Minor
calamitās calamitāt-is 3f. disaster, calamity
comes comit-is 3m.

companion, friend; (pl.) retinue
hospes hospit-is 3m. host; friend; guest;

connection
Lampsacēnus-ī 2m. person from Lampsacum

Adjectives

cēterī ae a the rest; the others
clār-us a um famous, well-known
Graec-us a um Greek

nōbil-is e renowned, distinguished; well-born, noble
turp-is e disgusting, filthy, outrageous; ugly

ūllus a um any (gen. *ūllīus* dat. *ūllī* – cf. *nūllus* 62)

Verbs

cupiō 3/4 *cupīuī cupītus* I desire, yearn for, want desperately

fruor 3 dep. *frūctus* (+ abl.) I enjoy

ūtor 3 dep. *ūsus* (+ abl.) I use, make use of; adopt

Others

prope (adv.) almost; (prep., + acc.) near

Running vocabulary for 4B(ii)

artifici-um ī 2n. skill, ingenuity
coep-ī (perf.) I began
cōnsul cōnsul-is 3m. consul
cupiditās cupiditāt-is 3f. lust, desire
dīcam 'should I say'
exārdeō 2 *exārsī* I burn, am on fire
eximi-us a um outstanding
exīstimātiō exīstimātiōn-is 3f. reputation
factus ad made for
Iānitor Iānitōr-is 3m. Ianitor
integritās integritāt-is 3f. integrity

inuestīgō 1 I look into, search out
libīdō libīdin-is 3f. lust, passion
migrō 1 I move
mīr-us a um wonderful, amazing
modesti-a ae 1f. discretion
mūnus mūner-is 3n. job, duty
neglegō 3 *neglēxī* I ignore
offendō 3 *offendī* I offend
omnibus aliīs Lampsacēnīs 'than all other men of Lampsacum'
Philodām-us ī 2m. Philodamus

postulāt-um ī 2n. demand
praetor praetōr-is 3m. praetor (state official)
pudīciti-a ae 1f. chastity
pulchritūdō pulchritūdin-is 3f. beauty
quī 'who' (nom. s. m.)
recipiō 3 *recēpī receptus* I welcome, receive, take in
retineō 2 I hold back
Rubri-us ī 2m. Rubrius
summā celeritāte 'with the utmost speed'
suspicor 1 dep. I suspect

Learning vocabulary for 4B(ii)

Nouns

cōnsul cōnsul-is 3m. consul

cupiditās cupiditāt-is 3f. lust, greed, desire

Verbs

coep-ī (perf. in form) I began

neglegō 3 *neglēxī neglēctus* I ignore, overlook, neglect

recipiō 3/4 *recēpī receptus* I welcome, receive, take in

retineō 2 *retinuī retentus* I hold back, detain, restrain; maintain

---

Running vocabulary for 4B(iii)

accumbō 3 I lie down, recline

aliīs prōuinciālibus 'than the other provincials'

alius ex aliā parte 'different people from different parts'

bibō 3 *bibī* I drink

caleō 2 I am warm/hot

celebrō 1 I fill x (acc.) with y (abl.)

claudō 3 I close

comparō 1 I prepare, get ready

concitō 1 I stir up

conueniō 4 *conuēnī (ad)* I meet (at)

conuīui-um ī 2n. party

discumbō 3 *discubuī* I lie down, spread myself about

effugiō 3 I escape

feruēns feruent-is boiling

festīnō 1 I hurry

forās out

grauitās grauitāt-is 3f. seriousness, solemnity

hospitāl-is e welcoming

iānu-a ae 1f. door

intellegō 3 *intellēxī* I perceive, understand

inter (+acc.) among

inuītō 1 I invite

inuīt-us a um unwilling

ips-e a um (him- her- it-) self

laetiti-a ae 1f. merriment, festivity, joy

libīdo libīdin-is 3f. lust

maiōribus pōculīs 'with larger cups'

multō (by) much

nūntiārunt = nūntiāuērunt

oportēre 'ought'

perfundō 3 *perfūdī* I drench, soak

Philodām-us ī 2m. Philodamus

postquam after

propinqu-us ī 2m. relative

quaesō 'I say', 'please'

Rubri-us ī 2m. Rubrius

sermō sermōn-is 3m. conversation, discussion

simul at the same time

simul ut as soon as

sōlum only

summā celeritāte 'with the utmost speed'

tant-us a um so great, so much

tumult-us ūs 4m. riot, outcry

uehementer strongly

Note

ll. 110–13. Roman custom allowed free citizen women at *conuīuia*, but Greek custom did not. The only women at Greek parties were slaves or *hetairai* ('courtesans').

Learning vocabulary for 4B(iii)

Nouns

conuīui-um ī 2n. party

grauitās grauitāt-is 3f. seriousness, solemnity; importance, authority

iānu-a ae 1f. door

laetiti-a ae 1f. merriment, festivity, joy

sermō sermōn-is 3m. conversation, discussion

Adjectives

ali-us a ud other (see **102**)

sōl-us a um alone (gen. s. *sōlīus*, dat. s. *sōlī*)

tant-us a um so much; so great; so important

Verbs

bibō 3 *bibī* I drink

comparō 1 I prepare, provide, get ready; get

conueniō 4 *conuēnī conuentum (ad)* I meet (at)

effugiō 3 *effūgī* I escape

festīnō 1 I hurry

intellegō 3 *intellēxī intellēctus* I perceive, understand, comprehend, grasp

inuītō 1 I invite

oportet 2 *oportuit* x (acc.) ought (to + inf.); it is right, fitting for x (acc.) to y (inf.)

Others

inter (+ acc.) among, between

simul at the same time

sōlum (adv. of *sōlus*) only

Running vocabulary for 4B(iv)

---

assentiō 4 *assēnsī* I agree

caedō 3 I cut (down); beat (down)

circumdō 1 I surround

concurrō 3 *concurrī* I run together

eōdem sēnsū et dolōre 'with the same sentiment and anguish'

ferr-um ī 2n. iron (implement), sword

hōc modō 'in this way'·

Lampsacī 'at Lampsacum'

multō (by) much, far

negōtior 1 dep. I do business

omnibus aliīs 'than all others'

ōrō 1 I beg, pray

parcō 3 (+ dat.) I spare

peccāt-um ī 2n. crime, error

potius quam rather than

praetor praetōr-is 3m. praetor (Roman state official)

quī 'who' (nom. pl. m.)

Rōmān-us a um Roman

sax-um ī 2n. stone, rock

scelerāt-us a um wicked

summa celeritāte 'with the utmost speed'

Learning vocabulary for 4B(iv)

Nouns

celeritās celeritāt-is 3f.
speed

praetor praetōr-is 3m.
praetor (Roman state
official)

Adjectives

Rōmān-us a um Roman

Verbs

caedō 3 *cecīdī caesus* I cut
(down); flog, beat; kill

concurrō 3 *concurrī*
concursum I run
together

ōrō 1 beg, pray

parcō 3 *pepercī parsūrus*
(+ dat.) I spare

Others

multō (by) much, (by) far

Grammar and exercises for 4B

100A The ablative case: summary of forms and usages to date

Here is a summary of the forms of the ablative:

	1st/2nd decl.			*3rd decl.*	*4th decl.*	*5th decl.*
	m.	*f.*	*n.*	*m./f./n.*		
s.	-ō	-ā	-ō	-e/ī	-ū	-ē
pl.	-īs	-īs	-īs	-ibus	-ibus	-ēbus

Notes

1 If you pay attention to the length of the vowels in the ending, you will cut out some of the possible confusions, e.g. *-is* = nom. s. (e.g. *cīu-is*) or gen. s. (e.g. *urb-is*) of 3rd decl., while the dat./abl. pl. of the 1st/2nd decl. is *-īs* (e.g. *seru-īs*). Confusion may result, however, from the acc. pl. form of 3rd decl. *-i-* stems, which is *-īs* (e.g. *cīu-īs*).

2 Watch out for the long *-ā* of 1st decl. abl. s. (e.g. *seru-ā*) and do not confuse it with the short *-a* of the 1st decl. nom. s. f. (e.g. *seru-a*) and the 2nd/3rd decl. n. plurals (e.g. *cōnsilia, scelera, ingentia*).

3 The *-ō* of the 2nd decl. can be dat. *or* abl. (e.g. *seru-ō*).

4 The *-e* of the 3rd decl. (e.g. *urb-e*) should not be confused with the *-e* of the nom. acc. s. n. of adjectives (e.g. *trīst-e*).

213

5 The *-ī* of the 3rd decl. adjectives (e.g. *trīst-ī*) and one noun-type (*mare*, which you will meet in **125**) should not be confused with 2nd decl. *-ī* in the gen. s. (*seru-ī*) and nom. pl. (*seru-ī*).

None of these problems will arise if you make sure you know to which declension nouns and adjectives which you learn belong.

The ablative: survey of uses

Four usages of the ablative have been met so far: with prepositions meaning in, at and from (**10.23**) (e.g. *in templō, ē fānō*); in descriptions (**49**) (e.g. *homo summā uirtūte*); in time phrases (**67**) (e.g. *illō tempore, decem annīs*); and the 'ablative of means (or instrument)' (**84**) (e.g. *pugnīs mē uerberat*).

It is now time to bring these usages together and add some more. Basically, the ablative has three functions:

(a) the 'true' ablative (*ablātus* from *auferō* – 'I take away'), the point *from which* the action, literally or figuratively, moves, e.g. *ē templō, ā fānō*.

(b) the 'locative' ablative, i.e. the point in *time or space where or when* something takes place, e.g. *in templō, illō tempore, decem annīs*.

(c) the 'instrumental-accompanying' ablative, i.e. the means/in-strument *by which* the action is carried out, or the people, qualities or circumstances *which accompany* the action (in English, often 'by' or 'with'), e.g. *uir summā uirtūte* (qualities which accompany the action) and *pugnīs mē uerberat* (means/instrument by which the action takes place).

The ablative often seems a difficult case because it appears to have so many uses, but if you remember these three basic functions you will see how (what appear to be) separate uses slip into place.

100B Further uses of the ablative

1 Under 'true' ablative: the ablative of comparison (the standard *from which* comparisons can be made), e.g.

'this town is more famous than all others' *hoc oppidum clārius est omnibus aliīs* ('all the others' are the starting-point *from which* comparisons are made)

Observe that there is no equivalent of 'than' in this construction. Cf. the construction using *quam* which you have met at **72⁴**, where the two things compared are put in the same case, e.g. *hoc oppidum clārius est quam omnia alia.*

2 Under 'instrumental-accompanying' ablative: the ablative of attendant circumstances, 'together with', e.g. *peruēnit cum magnā calamitāte cīuitātis* 'he came with great disaster for the state', 'he came and the circumstances in which he came led to great disaster'. *cum* + abl. is frequent, but sometimes *cum* is omitted and the plain ablative used.

3 Under 'instrumental-accompanying' ablative: the ablative of manner, which shows *how* something is done. This can again be constructed with *cum* or not, e.g.

> *summā celeritāte peruēnit* ⎫
> *summā cum celeritāte peruēnit* ⎬ he arrived with great speed'
> ⎭

4 Under 'instrumental-accompanying' ablative, the ablative after *ūtor* 3 dep. *ūsus* 'I use', and *fruor* 3 dep. *frūctus* 'I enjoy', e.g. *hīs uerbīs ūsī* 'using these words'.

5 Under 'instrumental-accompanying' ablative: the ablative expressing measure of difference. E.g.

> *Verrēs multō turpior est quam comitēs suī* 'Verres is much (i.e. by a great amount) viler than his companions'
> *sōl multīs partibus maior est quam terra* 'The sun is many times (lit. 'by many parts') larger than the earth' (Cicero)

101 Genitive of description

The genitive case is often used for description (cf. the ablative at **49**), e.g.

> *eum fīliam habēre <u>eximiae pulchritūdinis</u>* 'that he had a daughter <u>of outstanding beauty</u>'

Cf. English idiom. Note that an *adjective* always accompanies the noun in this usage.

Exercises

1 *Revision of ablative forms*

(a)   *Give the ablative s. and pl. of these noun + adj. phrases*: comes clārus; calamitās magna; conuīuium Graecum; amīcus nōbilis; magistrātus innocēns; fōrma turpis; rēs Rōmāna.

(b)   *Pick out the ablatives in this list*: praetōrī, comitibus, Asiā, cōnsulis, conuīuiīs, laetitia, sermōne, cupiditātem, uī, amīcō, diēbus, homine turpī, uirō nōbilī, manū celerī.

(c)   *In each list, with which nouns will the adjective go?*

ingentī: nūntius, puella, templō, uirgine, cūrā
audācibus: uirum, fēminīs, sacerdōtibus, amīcus
solā: uirō, agrō, fēmina, uirtūte
magnīs: puerīs, comitis, manibus, cōnsilia
tantō: cupiditāte, proeliō, sceleribus, praetōre
longiōre: noctī, perīculō, sermōnis, clāmor, uiā

2 *Translate these sentences*:

(a)   uir multō melior omnibus aliīs erat.
(b)   negāuit sē summā uī hominem cecīdisse.
(c)   iste saxīs iānuam cecīdit.
(d)   Cicerō Agrigentīnōs affirmāuit uirōs esse magnae uirtūtis.
(e)   praetōrēs, uirī summā grauitāte, conuīuiīs nōn fruuntur.
(f)   Lampsacēnī mōre Graecō rēs suās gerēbant.
(g)   mālunt Graecī ōtiō et pāce uītam dēgere (= *to pass*) quam bellō et calamitātibus.
(h)   Cicerō Verrem cēterīs praetōribus peiōrem esse putābat.
(i)   Verris seruōs fāma erat summā uī ūsōs esse.
(j)   eō tempore Iānitor ad Verrem summā celeritāte uēnit et eum multīs uerbīs retinēre cōnābātur.

102   Pronoun/adjectives: *alius* 'other' and *aliquis* 'some'

alius alia aliud *'other' 'another' 'different'*

	s.			*pl.*		
	m.	*f.*	*n.*	*m.*	*f.*	*n.*
nom.	áli-us	áli-a	áli-ud	áli-ī	áli-ae	áli-a
acc.	áli-um	áli-am	áli-ud	áli-ōs	áli-ās	áli-a

gen.	←——— alíus ———→			ali-ṓrum	ali-ā́rum	ali-ṓrum
dat.	←——— áli-ī ———→			←——— áli-īs ———→		
abl.	áli-ō	áli-ā	áli-ō	←——— áli-īs ———→		

Notes

1 Observe the idiom *alius ex aliā parte* '<u>different</u> men from <u>different</u> places'. This idiom can appear with the parts of *alius* in any case, e.g. *alius aliud laudat* or *aliī alia laudant* 'different people praise different things' or with other indefinite words e.g. *alius alibī* 'different people in different places'.

2 Note also *aliī . . . aliī* 'some . . . others' (sometimes *aliī . . . pars* or *pars . . . pars*).

3 Note *aliās* 'at another time', *alibī* 'in another place' and *aliēn-us a um* 'belonging to another' (and the English 'alias', 'alibi' and 'alien').

aliquis aliqua aliquid *'someone'* **and aliquī aliqua aliquod** *'some'*

	aliquis 'someone'			*aliquī 'some' (adj.)*		
	m.	*f.*	*n.*	*m.*	*f.*	*n.*
nom.	áli-quis	áli-qua	áli-quid	áli-quī(s)	áli-qua	áli-quod
acc.	áli-quem	áli-quam	áli-quid	áli-quem	áli-quam	áli-quod
gen.	←——— ali-cúius ———→			←——— ali-cúius ———→		
dat.	←——— áli-cui ———→			←——— áli-cui ———→		
abl.	áli-quō	áli-quā	áli-quō	áli-quō	áli-quā	áli-quō

Notes

1 Note other *ali-* indefinites: *aliquandō* 'at some time', *alicubī* 'somewhere', *aliquantō* 'to some extent', *aliquot* 'some', 'several'.

2 The pl. is the same as for *ali* + *quī* (see **29**), except that the n. pl. is *aliqua*.

3 Note *aliquid* + gen. = 'some', e.g. *aliquid artificī* 'some (of) skill'. Cf. **31** *satis, nimis*.

Exercises

1 *With which nouns do the adjectives go?*

alíus: hospitis, comes, cōnsulī, calamitātis, praetōrēs
aliī: Lampsacēnō, sermōnēs, Rōmānōs, conuīuī, iānuae
alia: calamitāte, conuīuia, cōnsule, uirgō, cupiditātibus

aliā: iānua, conuīuiō, sermōnī, cōnsul, calamitāte
aliqua: sermō, iānuae, mulier, uerba, amīcōs
aliquā: cōnsule, fēmina, rē, conuīuia, seruā

2 *Translate*:

(a) alius aliud dīcit.
(b) aliī Lampsacēnī, aliī Agrigentīnī erant.
(c) aliī alibī in oppidum impetum faciunt.
(d) aliī ex agrīs, pars ex oppidō concurrērunt.
(e) dīcet aliquis aliquid.
(f) at quis appellat? magistrātus aliquī? nēmō. (*Cicero*)
(g) Catilīna, dubitās . . . abīre in aliquās terrās? (*Cicero*)
(h) Verrēs cum aliquō comite domō exiit.

appellō 1 I call
dubitō 1 I hesitate

103   *ipse ipsa ipsum* 'very', 'actual', 'self'

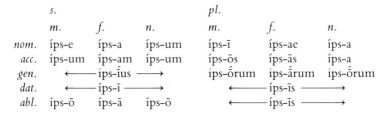

	s.			*pl.*		
	m.	*f.*	*n.*	*m.*	*f.*	*n.*
nom.	íps-e	íps-a	íps-um	íps-ī	íps-ae	íps-a
acc.	íps-um	íps-am	íps-um	íps-ōs	íps-ās	íps-a
gen.	⟵———— ips-íus ————⟶			ips-órum	ips-árum	ips-órum
dat.	⟵———— íps-ī ————⟶			⟵———— íps-īs ————⟶		
abl.	íps-ō	íps-ā	íps-ō	⟵———— íps-īs ————⟶		

Notes

1 Gen./dat. s. are normal for pronouns, cf. *huius, illīus, istīus, eius, cuius*
   (also *nūllīus, ūllīus, ūnīus, tōtīus, sōlīus*) *illī, istī, eī, cui* (also *nūllī, ūllī, ūnī,*
   tōtī, sōlī). For nom. s. m. cf. *ille* and *iste*; other forms are like *mult-us a*
   um.
2 *ipse* is an emphatic and intensive adjective often used to resolve
   ambiguities as to subject or object, e.g.

> *retinēte uōs ipsōs* 'restrain you/yourselves', 'restrain your*selves*'
> *ipse hoc faciō* 'It is actually I *myself* who am doing this'

Compare the phrase *ipsō factō* 'by the actual/very act'. *ipse* can be
translated 'self', 'very', 'actual', e.g. *id ipsum mihi placet* 'that's the *very*
thing I like'. It can stand on its own as a noun, e.g. *ipsī* 'the men
themselves'.

218

Exercises

1 *With which nouns do the parts of* ipse *agree?*

ipsī: calamitātī, cōnsulēs, conuīuiō, templī, nūntiī
ipsa: grauitās, cupiditāte, signa, fāmā, simulācra
ipsā: laetitia, sermōne, grauitāte, conuīuia, celeritās

2 *Translate:* ipsī uoluēre; signum ipsum; ipsae clāmārunt; cōnsiliō ipsō; ipsī hominī pepercērunt (*two possibilities; after translating, read aloud, distinguishing by your phrasing which is which*); ipsa laetitia; obsecrārunt ipsī ōrāruntque; nolī ipsam retinēre.

3 *Translate these sentences:*

(a) tranquillō animō esse potest nēmo. (*Cicero*)
(b) sapiēns uincit uirtūte fortūnam. (*Seneca*)
(c)   heu, Fortūna, quis est crūdēlior in nōs
tē deus? (*Horace*)
(d) is maximē dīuitiīs fruitur quī minimē dīuitiīs indiget. (*Seneca*)
(e) heu, quam difficile est crīmen nōn prōdere uultū. (*Ovid*)
(f) uīlius argentum est aurō, uirtūtibus aurum. (*Horace*)
(g) honesta mors turpī uītā potior. (*Tacitus*)
(h) ex Africā semper aliquid nouī. (*Pliny*)
(i) hominis tōta uīta nihil aliud quam ad mortem iter est. (*Seneca*)
(j) aliud aliī nātūra iter ostendit. (*Sallust*)

tranquill-us a um calm	*indigeō* 2 (+ abl.) I want,	*argent-um ī* 2n. silver
sapiēns sapient-is wise	need	*honest-us a um* honourable
fortūn-a ae 1f. fortune	*heu* alas!	*potior* preferable, better
(*Fortūna* = the goddess	*crīmen crīmin-is* 3n.	*Āfric-a ae* 1f. Africa
Fortune)	offence, crime	*nou-us a um* new
crūdēl-is e cruel	*prōdō* 3 I betray, reveal	*iter itiner-is* 3n. journey;
dīuiti-ae ārum 1f. pl. riches	*uult-us ūs* 4m. face,	route
quī (nom. s. m.) who	expression	*nātūr-a ae* 1f. nature
	uīl-is e cheap	

Reading

Pick out the ablative phrases in Exercise 2 p. 216 above. Write your translation next to each. Then say what each phrase adds to the sentence (you may use the formal categories, but it is more important that you try to define their function in your own way first). E.g.

mōre Graecō bibērunt: '*they drank in the Greek way*'
mōre Graecō: *this tells us the* way *they drank; ablative of manner.*

Do not be surprised if occasionally you find it difficult to be precise or if a phrase may fit more than one category.

Reading exercise / Test exercise

in Hellēspontō oppidum esse scītis, iūdicēs, cēterīs oppidīs Asiae clārius et nōbilius, nōmine Lampsacum. Lampsacēnōs ipsōs affirmō hominēs esse quiētōs. illī mōre Graecō uītam dēgunt (= *spend*). mālunt enim ōtiō ūtī et pāce quam bellō et calamitātibus uītam dēgere. iste Lampsacum tempore quōdam peruēnit. ad Iānitōrem, uirum summae grauitātis, Lampsacēnī   5
eum dēdūxērunt. iste autem mox sē ad Philodāmum quendam migrātūrum esse dīcēbat; Philodāmus enim domī habēbat fīliam pulcherrimam. Verrem scītis, iūdicēs, fēminās pulchrās semper omnibus modīs et omnibus temporibus uehementer sequī. Iānitor sē Verrem offendisse aliquō modō opīnatus est atque istum summā retinēre uī   10
coepit. Verrēs igitur Rubrium ad Philodāmum mīsit, cōnsiliō ūsus pessimō, quod Philodāmus uir erat magnae apud Lampsacēnōs exīstimātiōnis et praetōrēs cōnsulēsque recipere solēbat, nōn amīcōs eōrum. sed Verrēs Philodāmum per uim Rubrium dēdūcere iussit. Philodāmus autem, quod inuītus uidērī nōluit, conuīuium parāuit,   15
Rubrium comitēs inuītāre omnīs iussit. illī summā celeritāte uēnērunt; discubuēre; prīmō Graecō bibērunt mōre, mox pōculīs maiōribus. conuīuium sermōnibus celebrābant hōc tempore et laetitiā. mox autem Rubrius, 'Philodāme,' inquit, 'fīliam uocā tuam'. sed ille, uir grauitāte summā, īrāscēbātur. mulierēs in conuīuiō cum uirīs accumbere oportēre   20
negāuit. clāmor factus est maximus per aedīs. Lampsacēnī ubi tumultum audiuēre, nocte celeritāte summā ad Philodāmī aedīs conueniēbant.

postrīdiē (= *next day*) autem ad Verris hospitium[1] profectī sunt. ferrō iānuam et saxīs caedere coepērunt, eōdem tempore ignī circumdare. Verrī autem Lampsacēnī pepercērunt, quod cīuēs quīdam Rōmānī eīs   25
hoc melius fore dīxērunt quam praetōrem necāre Rōmānum.

[1] *hospiti-um* ī 2n. lodging.

English–Latin

1 *Translate into Latin*:
   (a)   Verres was more wicked than Rubrius.
   (b)   The people of Lampsacum used to enjoy peace and leisure.

(c) Philodamus was a man of great seriousness,[1] Verres a man of great lust.[1]
(d) The cooks were getting the party ready amid conversation and merriment.
(e) Verres and his friends were drinking in the Greek way.
(f) The people of Lampsacum were beating the door with their fists and at the same time shouting at the top of their voices[2].

[1] Translate each phrase in two different ways.
[2] Use abl. s. of *summa uōx*.

2 *Reread the text of* **4B(iii)**, *then translate this passage into Latin*: Philodamus was a man of great seriousness, but[1] nevertheless always much more hospitable than others. He invited Rubrius and his friends to a party. They all came very quickly. They were drinking amid conversations and merriment. But suddenly Rubrius ordered Philodamus to call his daughter. Philodamus said that he would not call her. Then there was a scene.

[1] Leave this out; just translate 'nevertheless'.

Deliciae Latinae

Word-building: revision

Suffixes
Abstract nouns are formed with the suffixes *-i-um -ī* 2n. and *-i-ēs -ēī* 5f., e.g.

> *artifici-um ī* 2n. trick
> *cōnsili-um ī* 2n. plan
> *conuīui-um ī* 2n. feast
> *perniciēs perniciē-ī* 5f. destruction

Word exercise

Give the meaning and Latin connections of: calamity, hospitable, clarity, turpitude, cupidity, use, vim, negligence, reception, gravity, sermon, convenient, intellect, oration, retention, bibulous, celerity, usufruct, concurrent.

Everyday Latin

(a) *Some ablative usages*

A.D. = *annō Dominī* 'in the year (abl. of time) of our Lord'
bonā fidē 'in good faith'
in tōtō 'in the whole', 'entirely'
s.p. (attached to an epitaph) = *suā pecūniā* '(buried) at his own expense'
mōre suō 'after his own manner' '(he did it) his way'
prīmā faciē 'at first sight', 'apparently'

(b) *Uses of* ipse

ipsō factō 'by the very fact itself'
ipsissima uerba 'the very words themselves' (note the superlative of *ipse*)
An *ipse dīxit* lit. 'he himself said it' i.e. an authoritarian assertion, dogmatic statement

(c) *Uses of* inter

inter alia 'among other things'
inter aliōs 'among other persons'
inter sē 'among/between themselves'
inter vīvōs lit. 'between living people' i.e. 'from one living person to another'
inter nōs 'between ourselves'
inter pōcula lit. 'between cups', i.e. 'over a glass'

Real Latin

Horace[1]

damnōsa quid nōn imminuit diēs?
aetās parentum, peior auīs, tulit
　　nōs nēquiōrēs, mox datūrōs
　　　　prōgeniem uitiōsiōrem. (*Odes 3.6.45ff.*)

---

[1] Quīntus Horātius Flaccus 65–8 B.C.

An illustration 1 auī
                         ↓   ⎫
                    2 aetās parentum ⎬ *past*
                         ↓   ⎭

                    3 nōs ⎫   *present*
                         ↓ ⎭

                    4 prōgeniēs ⎫   *future*

damnōs-us a um
  detrimental, causing
  loss [Hold until solved,
  by *diēs*]
immineō 2 I diminish

aetās aetāt-is 3f. age
parēns parent-is parent 3m.
  or f.
au-us ī 2m. grandfather

nēquior nēquiōr-is worse
prōgeniēs progeniē-ī 5f.
  offspring
uitiōs-us a um corrupt

Real Latin howlers

Not everyone could handle Latin as Cicero did. It is comforting to know that ordinary Romans and later ordinary clerics made all sorts of mistakes in speech and in writing. Here are a few examples.

In Petronius' *Satyricon* (1st century A.D.) an ex-slave uses the forms *loquis* (active for *loqueris* deponent) and *uīnus* (m. for *uīnum* n.).

Suetonius (first century A.D.) reports that the emperor Augustus dismissed a scribe for spelling *ipsī* as *ixī*.

Graffiti written on the walls of Pompeii buried by the eruption of Vesuvius (24 August 79 A.D.) are full of spelling errors, e.g.

> *Felix ad ursōs pugnābet* (= *pugnābit*) 'Felix will fight against bears'
> *futuī fōrmōsa fōrmā puella* (= *fōrmōsam . . . puellam*) 'I laid a beautiful girl'
> *Paris isse* (= *ipse*) 'Paris himself'

The Appendix Probi (third or fourth century A.D.) lists correct pronunciations and spellings alongside common incorrect versions, e.g.

> *frīgida nōn fricda*
> *aqua nōn acqua* (cf. Italian: *acqua*)
> *auris* (= 'ear') *nōn oricla* (cf. Italian: *orecchio*)

Later things got even worse. This inscription on a gravestone in Pannonia (3rd century A.D.?) shows not just spelling errors, but the accusative being used as the subject!

> *hīc quēscunt duās mātrēs* (= *hīc quiēscunt duae mātrēs*) 'here lie two mothers'

Boniface (c. 700 A.D.) heard a priest carrying out a baptism:

> *in nōmine patriā et fīliā et spīritūs sānctī* (= *in nōmine patris et fīliī et spīritūs sānctī*)

One MS. of Petronius' *Satyricon*, written in the mediaeval period, writes *abbās sēcrēuit* 'the abbot hid' instead of *ab asse crēuit* 'he grew from nothing' (lit. 'from a penny').

A fuller account of the development of Latin from the first century A.D. to the twelfth appears in *Reading Medieval Latin.*[1]

The Roman general Crassus left for Parthia in 55 never to return. He died at Carrhae in 53. After the event, Cicero said he should have listened to the fig-seller on the quayside as he boarded ship. He was crying *cauneās* ('figs'). But what he was really saying, said Cicero, was *cauē nē eās* 'beware lest you go'! This joke has been used as evidence for the pronunciation of Latin.

[1] Keith Sidwell, Cambridge 1995. For a brief survey, see Appendix p. 548.

Section 4C

Running vocabulary for 4C(i)

absum abesse I am away from, I am absent

argent-um ī 2n. silver; silver-plate

artifici-um ī 2n. skill

ausus erat 'he had dared' (plupf. of *audeō*)

cognōuerant '(they) had become acquainted with', '(they) knew' (plupf. of *cognōscō*)

collēgerat 'he had collected' (plupf. of *colligō* 3 *collēgī*)

cōnstituerat '(he) had decided' (plupf. of *cōnstituō* 3 *cōnstituī*)

dēdūxerat 'he had brought (down)' (plupf. of *dēdūcō*)

Diodōr-us ī 2m. Diodorus

fēcerant '(they) had made' (plupf. of *faciō*)

fēcerat '(he) had made' (plupf. of *faciō*)

genus gener-is 3n. family, stock

grātiōs-us a um popular

habitābat: tr. 'had been living'

īnflammāt-us a um inflamed, on fire

Lilybaeī (locative) at Lilybaeum

Lilybaeō (abl.) from Lilybaeum

Lilybaeum (acc.) to Lilybaeum

Lilybītān-us ī 2m. person from Lilybaeum

Melitae (locative) in Malta

Melitam (acc.) to Malta

Melitēnsis Melitēns-is 3m. person from Malta, Maltese

mentiō mentiōn-is 3f. mention

mentiōnem facere to make mention (of x: gen.)

Mentōr Mentōr-is 3m. Mentor

nāt-us a um (+ abl.) born
of, from
pauc-ī ae a few
paulisper for a while
perlegō 3 *perlēgī* I read
through, peruse
pōcul-um ī 2n. cup
potius quam rather than
propinqu-us ī 2m. relative
quae (acc. pl. n.) which;
(and) these

quam (acc. s. f.) which
quās (acc. pl. f.) which;
(and) this (sc. letter)
quem (acc. s. m.) whom
quī (nom. s. m.) who
quibus (abl. pl. f.) which;
(and) this
quod (acc. s. n.) which;
(and) this
quōrum (gen. pl. n.) of
which

quōs (acc. pl. m.) whom
seruō 1 I keep safe,
preserve
splendid-us a um fine,
excellent
Verre praetōre 'with
Verres (as) praetor'
(abl.)

Learning vocabulary for 4C(i)

Nouns

argent-um ī 2n. silver;
silver-plate; money

genus gener-is 3n. family,
stock; tribe

pōcul-um ī 2n. cup

Adjectives

īnflammāt-us a um
inflamed, on fire

nāt-us a um (+ abl.) born
of, from

Verbs

absum abesse āfuī āfutūrus I
am away from, I am
absent
cōnstituō 3 *cōnstituī*

cōnstitūtus I decide
perlegō 3 *perlēgī perlēctus* I
read through, peruse

seruō 1 I keep safe,
preserve

Others

potius quam rather than

Running vocabulary for 4C(ii)

absēns absent-is absent,
away
careō 2 (+ abl.) I do
without, lack, stay
away from
caueō 2 I am wary, am on
guard, take care
circum (+ acc.) around
circumeō circumīre I go
round

cognōuerat 'he had got to
know' 'he knew'
(plupf. of *cognōscō*)
collēgerat 'he had
collected' (plupf. of
colligō 3 *collēgī*)
commōuerat '(he) had
moved' (plupf. of
commoueō 2 *commōuī*)
castra commōuerat '(he)

had moved camp'
(metaphor used
ironically)
concupīuerat '(he) had
desired' (plupf. of
concupīscō 3)
condemnō 1 I find guilty,
condemn
conquīrō 3 I look for,
search out

225

cōnseruō 1 I save, keep
safe
crīmen crīmin-is 3n.
charge, accusation
dīcam 'should I say'
Diodōr-us ī 2m. Diodorus
excōgitō 1 I think up,
devise
fict-us a um trumped-up
furor furōr-is 3m. passion,
anger, rage
gerere: sē gerere lit. 'to
conduct himself', i.e.
'to behave'
hōc ūnō crīmine 'as a result
of this single
accusation' (abl.)
īnsāni-a ae 1f. madness,
lunacy
īnsāniō 4 I am mad
inuidiōs-us a um unpopular
lacrimor 1 dep. I burst
into tears, cry
mediocr-is e moderate,
ordinary

metū 'from fear' (abl.)
mod-us ī 2m. way,
fashion, manner
palam openly, publicly
patrōn-us ī 2m. patron (see
Text p. 87)
pereō perīre periī peritum I
perish, am done for
perspicu-us a um clear,
obvious
postrēmō finally
potuerat 'he had been able'
(plupf. of possum)
prīm-us a um first
prōuinci-a ae 1f. province
pudōre 'from shame' (abl.)
quae (acc. pl. n.) which;
(and) these (sc. things)
quās (acc. pl. f.) which;
(and) this (sc. letter)
quem (acc. s. m.) whom
quī (nom. s. m.) who
quōs (acc. pl. m.) whom
ratiō ratiōn-is 3f. plan,
reason

reprimō 3 repressī I
restrain, keep a grip on
reuocō 1 I call back
Rōmae (locative) at Rome
sordidāt-us a um poorly
dressed (a sign of
mourning or of being
on a charge)
stultē stupidly
timōre 'from
apprehension' (abl.)
tōtā prōuinciā 'over the
whole province' (abl.)
tōtā Rōmā 'all over Rome'
(abl.)
tōtā Siciliā 'all over Sicily'
(abl.)
trienni-um -ī 2n. a period
of three years
uehemēns uehement-is
strongly worded
Verre praetōre 'with
Verres (as) praetor'
(abl.)

Learning vocabulary for 4C(ii)

Nouns

mod-us ī 2m. way,
fashion, manner
prōuinci-a ae 1f. province

ratiō ratiōn-is 3f. plan,
method; reason; count,
list; calculation

Rōm-a ae 1f. Rome
Sicili-a ae 1f. Sicily

Adjectives

absēns absent-is absent,
away

prīm-us a um first

Verbs

circumeō circumīre circumiī
circumitum I go around
colligō 3 collēgī collēctus I
collect, gather; gain,
acquire

commoueō 2 commōuī
commōtus I move;
remove; excite, disturb
excōgitō 1 I think up,
devise

reuocō 1 I call back

Others

circum (+ acc.) around

postrēmō finally

stultē stupidly

226

Grammar and exercises for 4C

4 **Pluperfect indicative active 'I had —ed'**

	1	2	3
	'I had loved'	*'I had had'*	*'I had said'*
1st s.	amáu-era-m (*or* amáram *etc.*)	habú-era-m	díx-era-m
2nd s.	amáu-erā-s	habú-erā-s	díx-erā-s
3rd s.	amáu-era-t	habú-era-t	díx-era-t
1st pl.	amáu-erā-mus	habu-erā-mus	díx-erā-mus
2nd pl.	amáu-erā-tis	habu-erā-tis	díx-erā-tis
3rd pl.	amáu-era-nt	habú-era-nt	díx-era-nt

	4	3/4
	'I had heard'	*'I had captured'*
1st s.	audíu-era-m (*or* audíeram *etc.*)	cép-era-m
2nd s.	audíu-erā-s	cép-erā-s
3rd s.	audíu-era-t	cép-era-t
1st pl.	audíu-erā-mus	cép-erā-mus
2nd pl.	audíu-erā-tis	cép-erā-tis
3rd pl.	audíu-era-nt	cép-era-nt

Notes

1 The pluperfect (*plūs quam perfectum* 'more than finished') means 'had —ed', and pushes the merely 'finished' (*perfectum*) perfect even further back into the past. In other words, the action of the pluperfect occurs before that of the perfect.

2 It is formed by taking the stem of the 3rd p. p. and adding:

> *-eram*
> *-erās*
> *-erat*
> *-erāmus*
> *-erātis*
> *-erant*

Note that the normal active personal endings are used (*-m, -s, -t, -mus, -tis, -nt*).

3 As we have observed elsewhere (**65**), the *ue* and *u* can be dropped, giving e.g. *amā-ram amā-rās* etc. and *audi-eram audi-erās* etc.

4 Whereas in Latin *ubi* 'when' and *postquam* 'after' are generally followed by the perfect tense, English usually translates with the pluperfect, e.g.

ubi Verrēs haec fēcit, domum rediit 'when Verres had done this, he went home'.

105 Pluperfect indicative deponent 'I had —ed'

	1	2	3
	'I had threatened'	*'I had promised'*	*'I had spoken'*
1st s.	mināt-us a um éram	pollícit-us a um éram	locút-us a um éram
2nd s.	mināt-us a um érās	pollícit-us a um érās	locút-us a um érās
3rd s.	mināt-us a um érat	pollícit-us a um érat	locút-us a um érat
1st pl.	mināt-ī ae a erámus	pollícit-ī ae a erámus	locút-ī ae a erámus
2nd pl.	mināt-ī ae a erátis	pollícit-ī ae a erátis	locút-ī ae a erátis
3rd pl.	mināt-ī ae a érant	pollícit-ī ae a érant	locút-ī ae a érant

	4	3/4
	'I had lied'	*'I had advanced'*
1st s.	mentít-us a um éram	prōgréss-us a um éram
2nd s.	mentít-us a um érās	prōgréss-us a um érās
3rd s.	mentít-us a um érat	prōgréss-us a um érat
1st pl.	mentít-ī ae a erámus	prōgréss-ī ae a erámus
2nd pl.	mentít-ī ae a erátis	prōgréss-ī ae a erátis
3rd pl.	mentít-ī ae a érant	prōgréss-ī ae a érant

NB. The deponent pluperfect is formed by taking the perfect participle in *-us -a -um* as appropriate, and adding the imperfect of *sum, eram erās* etc. The perfect participle acts as an adjective and will agree with the subject of the verb (see on perfect deponents **75**).

Exercises

1 *Form and conjugate the pluperfect indicative of these verbs (give the meaning of 1st s. pluperfect):* cōnor, excōgitō, uideor, moneō, ūtor, faciō, absum, colligō, commoueō, (*optional:* cōnstituō, reuocō, nōlō, ferō, fruor, cupiō, recipiō, proficīscor, coepī).
2 *Translate each verb, then change s. to pl. and vice versa:* ōrāuerātis, cōnspicātus erās, commōuerat, hortātae erant, peperceram, recordāta

erat, recēperāmus, amplexus eram, cecīderās, oblītī erāmus, neglēxerant, prōgressī erātis, (*optional*: āfuerant, cōnātus eram, circumierās, suspicāta erat, reuocāuerātis, passī erant, excōgitāuerat, ausa erās, cōnstituerāmus, precātae erātis, cognōueram, uīsī erāmus).

3 *Give the Latin for*: I had decided; you (*s. m.*) had suffered; they had called back; they had remembered; he had become acquainted with; she had obtained; we had devised; you (*pl. m.*) had embraced; we had collected; you (*s.*) had disturbed (*optional*: he had cut; you (*s. m.*) had spoken; we had besought; they (*f.*) had set out; you (*pl.*) had run together; she had gone out; they had understood; we had forgotten).

4 *Give 3rd s. and pl. of the following verbs in present, future, imperfect, perfect and pluperfect indicative*: reuocō, teneō, arbitror, uideor, neglegō, sentiō, ūtor, patior, fīō, nōlō, sum, colligō, cōnstituō, (*optional*: circumeō, commoueō, cognōscō, adgredior, faciō, precor, mentior, fruor, cupiō, absum, polliceor).

5 *Locate and translate the pluperfects in this list, stating the tense of each of the other verbs*: excōgitābam, reuocāuerat, passus est, collēgerās, circumībit, commouet, perlēgerant, cognōscet, cōnātus erās, āfuērunt, fuerātis, recēpit, ēgressī erant, ingressa est, pōnit, ūtētur, cecīderāmus, (*optional*: obsecrāuērunt, ōrāuerās, suspicātus sum, amplectar, hortātus erat, dēdūcēbātis, cupīueram, precābimur, pollicita es, oblītus eram, fruēmur, secūtī erant, audēbis, audiēbam, ausus erās).

6 The relative pronoun *quī quae quod* 'who', 'which'

	s.			*pl.*		
	m.	*f.*	*n.*	*m.*	*f.*	*n.*
nom.	quī	quae	quod	quī	quae	quae
acc.	quem	quam	quod	quōs	quās	quae
gen.	←—— cúius ——→			quōrum	quārum	quōrum
dat.	←—— cui ——→			←—— quíbus (quīs) ——→		
abl.	quō	quā	quō	←—— quíbus (quīs) ——→		

Notes

1 The forms of *quī* relative are identical with those of the interrogative adjective *quī* 'who?', 'what?' (**29**).

Punctuation will normally tell you whether you are dealing with a form of the interrogative.

2 The function of a relative is *adjectival*: it is to identify or describe a noun. It does this by means of a complete subordinate clause, i.e. a clause with a finite verb of its own, e.g.

(a) 'I see the cat <u>which is sitting on the mat</u>': 'which . . . mat' is the relative clause, describing 'cat'.

(b) 'the barge <u>(which) she sat in</u>, like a burnished throne, burned in the water': relative clause '(which) she sat in' describing barge. Note how English can omit the relative. Latin *never* does.

(c)   '. . . the oars were silver,
<u>Which to the tune of flutes kept stroke</u>, and made
The water <u>which they beat</u> to follow faster'

'which . . . stroke': relative clause describing 'oars'; 'which . . . beat': relative clause describing 'water'.

(*Anthony and Cleopatra* II.ii, describing Cleopatra's barge)

3 'Antecedent' (*antecēdō* 'I go before') is the technical term for the word which the relative refers back to, e.g. 'I dropped the books which I was carrying' ('books' = antecedent); 'the cups which belonged to Diodorus went to Verres' ('cups' = antecedent).

4 The relative takes its gender (m. f. or n.) and its number (s. or pl.) from the antecedent. When you come across a relative in Latin, you must check that it is the same *gender* and *number* as the word you think is its antecedent. The *case* of the antecedent is irrelevant.

5 The relative takes its case *not* from the antecedent, but from its function inside the relative clause. Consider the following sentences:

(a) 'Verres hated Diodorus, who wanted to keep his own property'

'who' is m. and s., because the antecedent is Diodorus. But while Diodorus is object of 'hated' (in Latin *Diodōrum*), 'who' is subject of 'wanted' (since Diodorus, the person meant by 'who', 'wanted to keep his own property'). The relative form will therefore be m., s. and nom., i.e. *quī*.

Verrēs ōderat Diodōrum, quī sua seruāre uolēbat.

(b) 'Diodorus, whom Verres hated, was afraid'

'whom' will be m. and s., since it refers back to Diodorus, but will be accusative in case, since it is the object of 'Verres hated' ('Verres hated <u>Diodorus</u>', the person represented by 'whom').

Diodōrus, quem Verrēs ōderat, timēbat.

   (c)   Now determine the case of the relative for the examples in n. 3 above.

▶7   The connecting relative

A relative at the start of the sentence, referring *back* to something or somebody in the *previous* sentence, is best translated by English 'this', 'he', 'she', 'it'; e.g.

> *hominēs audīuī. quōs ubi audīuī, . . .* 'I heard the men. Which (men) when I heard, . . .' i.e. 'when I heard these men / them'.

Note in particular the *order of words*. The relative comes first, to emphasise that it is picking something up from the previous sentence, even though it may belong to an *ubi* 'when' or *postquam* 'after' clause. Cf.

> *ad amīcum litterās mīsit. quās ubi ille perlēgit, . . .* 'he sent a letter to a friend. When that man had read it . . .' (Latin word-order 'which when that man had read . . .').

Exercises

1   *Translate these sentences and locate the antecedent of* quī *in each*:

   (a)   Diodōrus parua pōcula, quae Mentōr fēcerat, habēbat.
   (b)   litterae, quās scrīpserat, mox in Siciliam peruēnērunt.
   (c)   uirōs, quī sē Rōmae esse affirmāuerant, reuocābat.
   (d)   rēs scelesta est quam excōgitāuistī.
   (e)   Diodōrus, quem Verrēs pōcula quaedam pulcherrima habēre sciēbat, abierat.
   (f)   Diodōrus genere nōbilī nātus erat, quod clārum numquam factum erat.

2   *In these sentences, the antecedent is underlined, but the correct part of* quī *is omitted and replaced by the English. Insert the correct part of* quī *and translate the sentences*:

   (a)   <u>uir</u> erat (whom) omnēs fēminae amābant.
   (b)   <u>fēmina</u> erat (to whom) omnis uir placēbat.
   (c)   <u>uirgō</u>, (whom) Verres amāre uoluerat, nōbilis erat.
   (d)   multī <u>hominēs</u>, (who) Verris comitēs factī erant, fīliī nōbilium erant.

(e) pōcula parua, (which) Verris comitēs cōnspicātī erant, Mentōr fēcerat.

(f) multī hominēs, (whose) cupiditātem cīuēs bonī maximam esse arbitrātī erant, ad Verrem ībant.

(g) Verris comitēs simulācrum, (which) ille cupīre ausus erat, ē templō sustulērunt.

(h) comitēs, (whom) Verrēs Lilybaeum sēcum dēdūxerat, Diodōrī pōcula cōnspicātī erant.

3 *Say which noun is the antecedent of the given relative:*

quae: poculīs, annum, praetōrēs, templum
quem: fēminam, mulieris, uirōs, seruus
cuius: litterās, hominum, genus, prōuinciās
quī: fīliō, ratiōne, cupiditātī, lēgēs
quibus: senātū, fāna, uirtūtis, amīcum

4 *Translate these* ubi *clauses (see* **104⁴**), *which all begin with a connecting relative* (**107**). *E.g.* quem ubi uīdit . . . *'and when he had seen him . . .'*

(a) quod ubi audīuit . . .
(b) quae ubi nārrāuit . . .
(c) quās ubi reuocāuērunt . . .
(d) quōs ubi cōnspicātī sunt . . .
(e) cui ubi minātus est . . .

108 More uses of the ablative

1 Under 'true' ablative: 'ablative of origin, or source' ('from'):

nātus genere nōbilī 'born from a good family'

2 Under 'instrumental-accompanying' ablative: 'ablative of cause', showing why an action was carried out ('out of', 'because of', 'from'):

timōre hoc fēcit 'he did this from fear' (i.e. because of his fear).
Verrēs hominem argentī cupiditāte accūsāuit 'Verres accused the man out of desire for silver'.

109 The ablative absolute

If you come across a noun *in the ablative* in agreement with another noun or adjective (especially a participle) *in the ablative*, regard it as an ablative of 'attendant circumstances' and translate 'with' or 'in the circumstances of', e.g.

> *Verre praetōre* 'with Verres (as) praetor', 'in the circumstances of Verres (as) praetor'
>
> *tē praetōre* 'with you (as) praetor', 'in the circumstances of you (as) praetor'
>
> *mē amīcō* 'with me (as) friend', 'in the circumstances of me (as) friend'

You can then retranslate to make a better English phrase or clause which points up the circumstances more clearly, e.g.

> *Metellō et Afrāniō cōnsulibus* 'with Metellus and Afranius as consuls' → 'in the consulship of Metellus and Afranius', 'when Metellus and Afranius were consuls'.

(This expression is used to date events: the year indicated here is 60, where Horace dated the origin of the civil wars.)

10 The locative

Names of towns and one-town islands (e.g. *Melita* = 'the town of Malta') do *not* use a preposition to express 'in(to)', 'towards', 'at' and 'from'. In this way they follow the example of *domus*, which you have already met, for which *domum* = to home, *domī* = at home, *domō* = from home.

Such words use the *accusative* to express 'to', e.g. *Rōmam* 'to Rome'; *Carthāginem* 'to Carthage'.

They use the *ablative* to express 'from', e.g. *Rōmā* 'from Rome'; *Carthāgine* 'from Carthage'.

They use the *locative* to express 'at'. Here are the locative endings:

1st decl. s. -*ae*	} = gen. s.	pl. -*īs*	} = abl. pl.	
2nd decl. s. -*ī*		pl. -*īs*		
3rd decl. s. -*ī*	= dat.s.	pl. -*ibus*		

Some examples:

> 'at Rome' *Rōmae*
> 'at/from Athens' (pl.) *Athēnīs*
> 'at Carthage' *Carthāginī*

Note

1 With certain sorts of word (denoting place or district) the ablative *without* a preposition is used to express 'at' or 'in', e.g. *eō locō* 'in that place'. Note the common phrase *terrā marīque* 'on land and sea'.

2 'To/from the *vicinity of*' a town is expressed by *ad/ab*, e.g. *ad Rōmam* 'to the vicinity of Rome'; *ā Rōmā* 'from the vicinity of Rome'.

3 There are a very few locatives of common nouns (cf. *domī*). Note *rūrī* (from *rūs* 3n.) 'in the country'; *humī* (*humus* 2f.) 'on the ground'; *bellī* (*bellum* 2n.) 'in war'; *mīlitiae* (*mīlitia* 1f.) 'in war', 'on military service'; *animī* (*animus* 2m.) 'in the mind'.

Exercises

1 *Translate these phrases and sentences*:

(a) uirgō fāmae optimae.
(b) Cicerōne et Antōniō cōnsulibus (*the year 63*).
(c) mē duce.
(d) uirginēs nātae genere nōbilī.
(e) audāciā et cupiditāte aurum sustulit.
(f) Rōmā.
(g) domī.
(h) Lilybaeō.
(i) tōtā prōuinciā.
(j) praetōribus absentibus.

2 *Give the Latin for*: (*NB. the previous exercise will help*)

(a) A man of great courage (*2 ways*).
(b) In Verres' praetorship.
(c) Under your (*s.*) leadership.
(d) A boy born of a noble family.
(e) He acted thus from lust.
(f) At Rome.
(g) From home.
(h) To Lilybaeum.
(i) In the whole of Sicily.
(j) In the absence of the rest.

3 *Translate these sentences*:

(a) quī multum habet, plūs cupit. (*Seneca*)
(b) nōn quī parum habet, sed quī plūs cupit pauper est. (*Seneca*)
(c) dīmidium factī quī coepit habet. (*Horace*)
(d) nihil ēripit fortūna nisi quod dedit. (*Seneca*)
(e) quae fuit dūrum patī, meminisse dulce est. (*Seneca*)
(f) nūper erat medicus, nunc est uespillo Diaulus:
    quod uespillo facit, fēcerat et medicus. (*Martial*)

quī = he who	*quod* and *quae* = what	*nūper* recently
parum too little	*dūr-us a um* hard	*medic-us ī* 2m. doctor
dīmidi-um ī 2n. half	*meminī* (perf.)	*Diaul-us ī* 2m. Diaulus
fact-um ī 2n. deed	I remember	*uespillo uespillōn-is* 3m.
ēripiō 3/4 I snatch away	*dulc-is e* sweet, pleasant	undertaker
fortūn-a ae 1f. fortune		

Reading exercise / Test exercise

Diodōrum Melitēnsem, quī multō ante Melitā ēgressus erat et illō tempore Lilybaeī habitābat, iste cupiditāte suā ā prōuinciā reppulit. ille apud Lilybītānōs, quī eum summā uirtūte uirum esse cognōuerant, uir multī honōris fuerat. sed Verre praetōre, domō caruit prope triennium propter pōcula quaedam pulchra, quae habēbat. istī enim comitēs, quōs   5
sēcum, ubi ad prōuinciam peruēnit, dūxerat, Diodōrum haec pōcula habēre nūntiāuerant; quod ubi cognōuit, cupiditāte īnflammātus iste ad sē Diodōrum uocāuerat et pōcula poposcerat. Diodōrus autem, quī pōcula āmittere nōlēbat, ea Melitae esse apud propinquum quendam affirmāuerat. sed ubi Verrēs ad propinquum illum litterās, in quibus   10
pōcula rogābat, scrīpsit, ille ea paucīs illīs diēbus Lilybaeum mīsisse dīxerat. intereā Diodōrus Lilybaeō abierat.

English–Latin

1 *Translate into Latin*:

(a) Diodorus, who possessed many beautiful cups, had gone away from Lilybaeum to Rome.
(b) In Verres' praetorship, in the whole province men were able to devise wicked crimes.
(c) Verres, who was born of a noble family, always acted from lust, rather than from courage.

(d)   The friends, whom Verres had brought with him to the province, were scoundrels.

2   *Reread the text of 4C(ii), then translate this passage into Latin:*
When Verres heard this[1], from madness he decided to accuse Diodorus in his absence[2]. In the whole province the matter was well known. The story was that Verres through greed for silver had accused an innocent man in his absence[2]. Diodorus, who was at this time in Rome, told his patrons everything which he had heard. When Verres' father learned this[1], he sent a letter to him. In this[1] letter[3] he said that everyone throughout the city knew that Verres was a scoundrel. When Verres had read this[1], he held back his lust, from fear, rather than from shame.

[1] Use a part of *quī* at the beginning of the sentence.
[2] Use *absēns, absentis* agreeing with 'Diodorus', 'man'.
[3] Place *in* after part of *quī* and before 'letter'.

Deliciae Latinae

Word-building

Suffixes
-ēnsis frequently makes an adjective out of a place-name, e.g. *Melita* (Malta)→*Melitēnsis*; *Londinium*→*Londiniēnsis*; *Cantabrigia* (Cambridge) →*Cantabrigiēnsis* etc.
   -ānus can also serve this function, e.g. *Rōma*→*Rōmānus* 'Roman', but has a wider range too, e.g. *mōns mont-is* 'mountain'→*montānus* 'from the mountains'.

Revision
-i-a ae 1f. forms an abstract noun, e.g. *insānus* 'mad'→*insānia* 'madness'; *miser* 'wretched'→*miseria* 'wretchedness'.
   -or (or *-ōs*) *-ōr-is* 3m. forms abstract nouns of condition, e.g. *furor* 'madness', *amor* 'love', *timor* 'fear', *honor* (or *honōs*) 'respect', etc.

Word exercises

Give the meaning and Latin connections of: generation, literal (*note change of spelling in mediaeval Latin from* litterae *to* literae), ante-natal, mode,

236

rational, primary, constitution, revoke, circuit, circumlocution, conservation, commotion, collection.

Everyday Latin

(a) *Relative usages*

> *quī facit per alium facit per sē* 'he who acts through another is himself responsible' (lit. 'acts through himself')
>
> *quī tacet cōnsentit* 'he who keeps silence consents'
>
> *q.v.* = *quod vidē* 'which see', 'see this'
>
> *q.e.d.* = *quod erat dēmōnstrandum* 'which was to-be-proved' (and now has been)
>
> *quod ubīque, quod semper, quod ab omnibus* 'that which everywhere, that which always, that which by all (sc. has been believed)' – definition of orthodoxy by St Vincent of Lérins
>
> *sine quā nōn* 'without which not', i.e. an absolute essential
>
> *status quō* (*ante*) 'the position in which (things were before)'

(b) *Ablative absolute usages*

> *cēterīs paribus* '(with) other things (being) equal'
>
> *vīvā vōce* 'with living voice'
>
> *mē iūdice* 'with me being judge', 'in my opinion'

(c) *Others*

> *etc.* = *et cētera* 'and the rest'
>
> The Classical degree at Oxford is called *lit. hum.* = *literae hūmāniōrēs* 'humane letters' (lit. 'more human literature' as opposed to theology, originally)

Mottoes

In all of these, the relative comes first, and means 'he who, she who, the thing(s) which' etc. Here are some examples, with translation.

quae habet, manus tenēbit (*'What things* (or *the things which*) *it has, my hand will hold': Templeman*)

quod sors fert, ferimus (*'What/that which fate brings, we bear': Clayton*)

quī patitur, vincit (*'(He) who endures, wins': Kinnaird*)

Note the verb 'to be' is often omitted, e.g. quae rēcta, sequor (*'The things which (are) right, I follow': Campbell*)

quae moderāta, firma (*Ogilvie*)
quae sērāta, sēcūra (*Douglas*)
quae sursum, volō (*Macqueen, Quin*)
quae vult, valdē vult (*Wilmot*)
quī invidet, minor est (*Cadogan, Leigh, Pugh*)
quī mē tangit, poenitēbit (*Gillespie, Macpherson*)
quī plānē, sānē vādit (*Taylor*)
quī stat, caveat (*Domville*)
quod Deus vult, fīet (*Dimsdale*)
quod Deus vult, volō (*Mountford*)
quod dīxī, dīxī (*Dixie, Dixon*)
quod faciō, valdē faciō (*Holmes*)
quod honestum, ūtile (*Lawson*)
quod iūstum, nōn quod ūtile (*Philips*)
quod potuī, perfēcī (*Dundas, Turner*)
quod tibi vīs fierī, fac alterī (*Ram*)
quod tuum, tenē (*Cheetham*)
quod vērum, tūtum (*Courtenay, Sim*)
quod volō, erit (*Wright*)

moderāt-us a um moderate
firm-us a um permanent
sērāt-us a um locked
sēcūr-us a um safe
sursum above, in Heaven
ualdē strongly

inuideō 2 I am envious
tangō 3 I touch
poenitet 2 he regrets (it)
plānē plainly
sānē safely
uādō 3 I go

caueat 'let him beware'
honest-us a um honourable
ūtil-is e profitable
iūst-us a um just
tūt-us a um safe

Real Latin

ō fortūnātam nātam mē cōnsule Rōmam. (*Cicero*)
fortūnāt-us a um lucky

nīl dēspērandum Teucrō duce et auspice Teucrō. (*Horace, Odes I.7.27*)

dēspērandum 'should be despaired of'
auspex auspic-is 3m. augur, interpreter of omens

Teucer Teucr-ī 2m. Teucer (brother of Ajax; he is comforting his men as they face another leg of their journey into exile from Salamis)

quī uitia ōdit, et hominēs ōdit. (*Pliny*)

uiti-um ī 2n. vice   *ōd-ī* (perf.) I hate

nūllum quod tetigit nōn ōrnāvit (*Dr Johnson's epitaph on Goldsmith*)

tangō 3 *tetigī* I touch   *ōrnō* 1 I enhance

Unreal Latin

Revise all the cases with the following horrendous 'poem' about the Motor Bus by A. D. Godley. Note that he envisages *Mōtor* as a 3rd. decl. m. noun, *Bus* as 2m.; and observe what the poem tells you about one school of Latin pronunciation in the early 20th c. Would *your* pronunciation give these rhymes?

Motor Bus

What is this that roareth thus?
Can it be a Mōtor Bus?
Yes, the smell and hideous hum
Indicat Mōtōrem Bum!
Implet[1] in the Corn and High[2]   5
Terror mē Mōtōris Bī:
Bō Mōtōrī clāmitābō
Nē Mōtōre caedar[3] ā Bō –
Dative be or Ablative
So thou only let us live: 10
Whither shall thy victims flee?
Spare us, spare us, Mōtor Be!
Thus I sang; and still anigh
Came in hordes Mōtōrēs Bī,
Et complēbat[4] omne forum   15
Cōpia Mōtōrum Bōrum.
How shall wretches live like us
Cīnctī[5] Bīs Mōtōribus?
Domine, dēfende nōs
Contrā[6] hōs Mōtōrēs Bōs!   20

[1] *implet* 'there fills'.
[2] two streets in Oxford (Cornmarket and High Street).
[3] 'so that I may not be killed by . . .'
[4] *complēbat* 'there filled'.
[5] *cīncti* 'surrounded'.
[6] *contrā* (+ acc.) against.

Section 4D

Running vocabulary for 4D(i)

ā/ab (+ abl.) by (after
  passive verbs)
abdūcō 2 *abdūxī abductus* I
  appropriate, withdraw,
  remove
abducta est '(it) was
  appropriated' (perf.
  passive of *abdūcō*)
abductī (*sunt*) '(they) were
  removed' (perf. passive
  of *abdūcō*)
act-a ae 1f. shore
appellitur lit. '(it) is
  brought to shore' (pres.
  passive of *appellō* 3)
  [Translate as *past* tense]
archipīrāt-a ae 1m. pirate
  chief
artifex artific-is 3m.
  craftsman
Caesēti-us ī 2m. Caesetius
capta est '(it) was
  captured' (perf. passive
  of *capiō*)
classis class-is 3f. fleet
cohors cohort-is 3f.
  governor's retinue
datam esse 'to have been
  given' '(that) (it) had
  been given' (perf.
  passive infin. of *dō*)
datī sunt '(they) were
  given' (perf. passive of
  dō)
dēfōrm-is e misshapen,
  ugly

distribūtī sunt '(they) were
  divided up among'
  (+ dat.) (perf. passive
  of *distribuō* 3 *distribuī
  distribūtus*)
ēbri-us a um drunk
ērigō 3 *ērēxī* I draw up,
  lift up
exhibērī 'to be put on
  display' (pres. infin.
  passive of *exhibeō* 2)
exspectātur lit. '(it) is
  awaited' (pres. passive
  of *exspectō* 1) [Translate
  as *past* tense]
fōrmōs-us a um handsome
habitī sunt '(they) were
  held, regarded' (perf.
  passive of *habeō*)
iaceō 2 I lie
inuenta est '(it) was found'
  (perf. passive of
  inueniō)
līberātum esse 'to have
  been freed' '(that) (he)
  had been freed' (perf.
  passive infin. of *līberō*
  1)
missī sunt '(they) were
  sent' (perf. passive of
  mittō 3 *mīsī missus*)
muliercul-a ae 1f. woman
  (with sneering tone)
naut-a ae 1m. sailor

nūntiātum est 'it was
  announced' (perf.
  passive of *nūntiō*)
P. = *Pūbliō* (*Pūbli-us ī*
  2m.) Publius
percussī sunt '(they) were
  struck' (perf. passive of
  percutiō 3/4 *percussī
  percussus*)
pīrāt-a ae 1m. pirate
port-us ūs 4m. harbour
praedō praedōn-is 3m.
  pirate
praefect-us ī 2m. captain,
  prefect
secūris secūr-is 3f. axe (abl.
  s. *secūrī*)
sēmiplēn-us a um half-full;
  undermanned
supplici-um ī 2n.
  punishment; death
  penalty
symphōniac-us ī 2m.
  musician
Syrācūs-ae ārum 1f.
  Syracuse
Tadi-us ī 2m. Tadius
uestis uest-is 3f. clothes
uidēbantur '(they) seemed'
  (imperf. passive of
  uideō: lit. 'they were
  seen' (sc. 'as'))
uīsus est '(he) was seen'
  (perf. passive of *uideō*)

Learning vocabulary for 4D(i)

Nouns

classis class-is 3f. fleet
cohors cohort-is 3f.
  governor's retinue;
  cohort
naut-a ae 1m. sailor

pīrāt-a ae 1m. pirate
port-us ūs 4m. harbour
praedō praedōn-is 3m.
  pirate; robber

praefect-us ī 2m. captain,
  prefect; (adj.) in charge
  of (+ dat.)

Adjectives

ēbri-us a um drunk

Verbs

exspectō 1 I await, wait
  for

iaceō 2 I lie

līberō 1 I free, release

Others

ā/ab by (usually a person,
  after passive verbs);
  (away from)

Running vocabulary for 4D(ii)

abductī erant '(they) had
  been removed' (plupf.
  pass. of *abdūcō*)
abductī (sc. *sunt*) '(they)
  were) removed' (perf.
  passive of *abdūcō*)
ablāt-a/um (sc. *est*) '(it
  was) taken away' (perf.
  passive of *auferō*)
anteā formerly, previously
arguō 3 I claim, charge
artifex artific-is 3m.
  craftsman
artifici-um ī 2n. skill: the
  gen. *artificī* depends on
  aliquid, 'some skill' –
  cf. *satis, nimis* with gen.
  (**31** and **102**)
āuersum (sc. *est*) '(it was)
  stolen' (perf. passive of
  āuertō 3 *āuertī āuersus*)

aut . . . aut either . . . or
capta est '(it) was
  captured' (perf. passive
  of *capiō*)
captī erant '(they) had
  been captured' (plupf.
  passive of *capiō*)
carcer carcer-is 3m. prison
cognōscēbantur 'they were
  recognised' (imperf.
  passive of *cognōscō*)
coniūnctōs esse 'to have
  been linked' '(that
  they) were linked'
  (perf. passive infin. of
  coniungō 3 *coniūnxī
  coniūnctus*)
cotīdiē daily
dēfendēbantur '(they) were
  defended' (imperf.
  passive of *dēfendō*)

dēsum dēesse I am missing,
  lacking
feriēbantur '(they) were
  being struck' (imperf.
  passive of *feriō* 4)
fōrmae [Gen. follows
  aliquid: cf. *artificium* and
  the note on it]
fōrmōs-us a um handsome,
  graceful, shapely
gesta (*est*) '(it) was
  achieved' (perf. passive
  of *gerō*)
habita erat '(it) had been
  had' (plupf. passive of
  habeō) tr. 'had been
  made'
hūmān-us a um
  considerate, civilised
līberātus (sc. est) '(he) was
  freed' (perf. passive of
  līberō)

241

missī (sc. *sunt*) '(they
  were) sent' (perf.
  passive of *mittō*)
nefāri-us a um wicked,
  vile, criminal
numer-us ī 2m. number
percussī (*sunt*) '(they were)
  executed' (perf. passive
  of *percutiō* 3/4 *percussī
  percussus*)
perīt-us a um
  knowledgeable, skilful

praeclār-us a um very
  famous, outstanding,
  brilliant
popul-us ī 2m. the people
remōtī (*erant*) '(they) had
  been got out of the
  way' (plupf. pass. of
  remoueō 2 *remōuī
  remōtus*)
rēm-us ī 2m. oar
secūris secūr-is 3f. axe

Sertōriān-us a um of
  Sertorius (Roman who
  led a revolt against the
  Roman dictator Sulla
  from Spain in 83 and
  gained some support.
  See Text 4F(ii))
substituō 3 I substitute
symphōniac-us ī 2m.
  musician
uestis uest-is 3f. clothing
uoluntās uoluntāt-is 3f.
  will, wish

Learning vocabulary for 4D(ii)

Nouns

numer-us ī 2m. number

secūris secūr-is 3f. axe

uestis uest-is 3f. clothes,
  clothing, dress

Adjectives

fōrmōs-us a um handsome,
  graceful, shapely

nefāri-us a um wicked,
  vile, criminal

praeclār-us a um very
  famous, outstanding,
  brilliant

Verbs

desum dēesse dēfuī dēfutūrus
  I am missing, lacking;
  fail; abandon (+ dat.)

feriō 4 I strike, beat; kill
  (no 3rd or 4th
  principal parts – these
  tenses are supplied by
  percussī, percussus, from
  percutiō 3/4 I strike,
  beat; kill)

Others

aut . . . aut either . . . or
cotīdiē daily

Grammar and exercises for 4D

11 The passive

The active 'voice' (as it is called) usually indicates that the subject is doing something e.g. 'Tom hits the ball'. The passive voice is used to say exactly the same thing, only another way round, this time with the subject *having something done to it* (cf. *passus* 'having undergone, suffered' from *patior*) e.g. 'The ball *is hit* by Tom'. The subject 'ball' here is not doing anything – it is having something done to it *by Tom* (who is called (when he functions like this in a sentence) 'the agent', lit. 'the doer', 'person doing' (from *agō*)).

Here are the forms of the passive, with meanings, of all four conjugations, in present, future, imperfect, perfect and pluperfect indicative, the present, perfect and future infinitive, and the present imperative. It should not be too long before you recognise that the *forms* of the passive and the *forms* of the deponent are ABSOLUTELY IDENTICAL. Consequently, THERE IS VIRTUALLY NOTHING NEW TO LEARN HERE.

12 Present indicative passive (all conjugations): 'I am being —ed'

	1	*2*	*3*
	'*I am (being) loved*'	'*I am (being) held*'	'*I am (being) said*'
1st s.	ám-o-r	hábe-o-r	díc-o-r
2nd s.	amá-ris (-re)	habé-ris (-re)	díc-e-ris (-re)
3rd s.	amá-tur	habé-tur	díc-i-tur
1st pl.	amá-mur	habé-mur	díc-i-mur
2nd pl.	amá-minī	habé-minī	dīc-í-minī
3rd pl.	amá-ntur	habé-ntur	dīc-úntur

	4	*3/4*
	'*I am (being) heard*'	'*I am (being) captured*'
1st s.	aúdi-or	cápi-o-r
2nd s.	audí-ris (-re)	cáp-e-ris (-re)
3rd s.	audí-tur	cápi-tur
1st pl.	audí-mur	cápi-mur
2nd pl.	audí-minī	capí-minī
3rd pl.	audi-úntur	capi-úntur

NB. Latin sometimes uses the 'vivid' present tense, where in English we would naturally use a past tense. Consequently, do not hesitate to translate a Latin present tense into the past in English if it suits the passage better. E.g. *nāuis pīrātārum Syrācūsās . . . appellitur* in **4D(i)** means 'a pirate-ship *was brought to shore at* Syracuse'.

113 Future indicative passive (all conjugations): 'I shall be —ed'

	1	2	3
	'I shall be loved'	*'I shall be held'*	*'I shall be said'*
1st s.	amā́-bo-r	habḗ-bo-r	dī́c-a-r
2nd s.	amā́-be-ris (-re)	habḗ-be-ris (-re)	dīc-ḗ-ris (-re)
3rd s.	amā́-bi-tur	habḗ-bi-tur	dīc-ḗ-tur
1st pl.	amā́-bi-mur	habḗ-bi-mur	dīc-ḗ-mur
2nd pl.	amā-bí-minī	habē-bí-minī	dīc-ḗ-minī
3rd pl.	amā-bú-ntur	habē-bú-ntur	dīc-é-ntur

	4	3/4
	'I shall be heard'	*'I shall be captured'*
1st s.	aúdi-a-r	cápi-a-r
2nd s.	audi-ḗ-ris (-re)	capi-ḗ-ris (-re)
3rd s.	audi-ḗ-tur	capi-ḗ-tur
1st pl.	audi-ḗ-mur	capi-ḗ-mur
2nd pl.	audi-ḗ-minī	capi-ḗ-minī
3rd pl.	audi-é-ntur	capi-é-ntur

114 Imperfect indicative passive (all conjugations): 'I was being —ed'

	1	2	3
	'I was being loved'	*'I was being held'*	*'I was being said'*
1st s.	amā́-ba-r	habḗ-ba-r	dīc-ḗ-ba-r
2nd s.	amā-bā́-ris (-re)	habē-bā́-ris (-re)	dīc-ē-bā́-ris (-re)
3rd s.	amā-bā́-tur	habē-bā́-tur	dīc-ē-bā́-tur
1st pl.	amā-bā́-mur	habē-bā́-mur	dīc-ē-bā́-mur
2nd pl.	amā-bā́-minī	habē-bā́-minī	dīc-ē-bā́-minī
3rd pl.	amā-bá-ntur	habē-bá-ntur	dīc-ē-bá-ntur

	4	3/4
	'I was being heard'	*'I was being captured'*
1st s.	audi-é-ba-r	capi-é-ba-r
2nd s.	audi-ē-bá-ris (-re)	capi-ē-bá-ris (-re)
3rd s.	audi-ē-bá-tur	capi-ē-bá-tur
1st pl.	audi-ē-bá-mur	capi-ē-bá-mur
2nd pl.	audi-ē-bá-minī	capi-ē-bá-minī
3rd pl.	audi-ē-bá-ntur	capi-ē-bá-ntur

115 **Perfect indicative passive (all conjugations): 'I was —ed', 'I have been —ed'**

	1	2	3
	'I was loved',	*'I was held',*	*'I was said',*
	'I have been loved'	*'I have been held'*	*'I have been said'*
1st s.	amát-us a um sum	hábit-us a um sum	díct-us a um sum
2nd s.	amát-us a um es	hábit-us a um es	díct-us a um es
3rd s.	amát-us a um est	hábit-us a um est	díct-us a um est
1st pl.	amát-ī ae a súmus	hábit-ī ae a súmus	díct-ī ae a súmus
2nd pl.	amát-ī ae a éstis	hábit-ī ae a éstis	díct-ī ae a éstis
3rd pl.	amát-ī ae a sunt	hábit-ī ae a sunt	díct-ī ae a sunt

	4	3/4
	'I was heard',	*'I was captured',*
	'I have been heard'	*'I have been captured'*
1st s.	audít-us a um sum	cápt-us a um sum
2nd s.	audít-us a um es	cápt-us a um es
3rd s.	audít-us a um est	cápt-us a um est
1st pl.	audít-ī ae a súmus	cápt-ī ae a súmus
2nd pl.	audít-ī ae a éstis	cápt-ī ae a éstis
3rd pl.	audít-ī ae a sunt	cápt-ī ae a sunt

NB.   As with deponent verbs, the perfect participle acts as an *adjective* and will agree with the subject in gender, number and case.

116 **Pluperfect indicative passive (all conjugations): 'I had been —ed'**

	1	2	3
	'I had been loved'	*'I had been held'*	*'I had been said'*
1st s.	amát-us éram	hábit-us éram	díct-us éram
2nd s.	amát-us érās	hábit-us érās	díct-us érās
3rd s.	amát-us érat	hábit-us érat	díct-us érat

245

1st pl.	amāt-ī erāmus	hábit-ī erāmus	díct-ī erāmus
2nd pl.	amāt-ī erātis	hábit-ī erātis	díct-ī erātis
3rd pl.	amāt-ī érant	hábit-ī érant	díct-ī érant

	4	3/4
	'I had been heard'	*'I had been captured'*
1st s.	audīt-us éram	cápt-us éram
2nd s.	audīt-us érās	cápt-us érās
3rd s.	audīt-us érat	cápt-us érat
1st pl.	audīt-ī erāmus	cápt-ī erāmus
2nd pl.	audīt-ī erātis	cápt-ī erātis
3rd pl.	audīt-ī érant	cápt-ī érant

NB. See perfect passive (**115**) for agreement of perfect participle with the subject.

117 Passive imperative (all conjugations): 'be —ed'

	1	2	3	4	3/4
	'be loved!'	*'be held!'*	*'be said!'*	*'be heard!'*	*'be captured!'*
s.	amā-re	habē-re	dīc-e-re	audī-re	cáp-e-re
pl.	amā-minī	habē-minī	dīc-í-minī	audī-minī	capí-minī

118 Passive infinitive (all conjugations)

Present 'to be —ed'

1	2	3	4	3/4
'to be loved'	*'to be held'*	*'to be said'*	*'to be heard'*	*'to be captured'*
amā-rī	habē-rī	dīc-ī	audī-rī	cáp-ī

Perfect 'to have been —ed'

1	2	3
'to have been loved'	*'to have been held'*	*'to have been said'*
amāt-us a um ésse	hábit-us a um ésse	díct-us a um ésse

4	3/4
'to have been heard'	*'to have been captured'*
audīt-us a um ésse	cápt-us a um ésse

Form traditionally described as 'future infinitive passive': used only in indirect statement (acc. + inf.)

1	2
'that there is a movement to love'	'that there is a movement to have'
amātum īrī	hábitum īrī

3	4
'that there is a movement to say'	'that there is a movement to hear'
díctum īrī	audītum īrī

3/4
'that there is a movement to capture'
cáptum īrī

Notes

1 *īrī* is the impersonal passive infinitive of *eō* 'I go', i.e. 'to be gone'. In the context of an acc. + inf. clause, this means 'that there is a movement'.
2 The forms *amātum, habitum* etc. are called 'supine'. Basically, the supine expresses purpose, e.g. *amātum* 'to love', *audītum* 'to hear' etc. Cf. *cubitum it* 'he goes *to lie down*', *sessum it* 'he goes *to sit*', *Vārus mē uīsum dūxerat* 'Varus had brought me *to see*' (Catullus).
3 Consequently, the literal meaning of the so-called 'future infinitive passive' is 'that there is a movement to . . .', e.g.

> *putant sē audītum īrī* 'they think that there is a movement to hear them' i.e. 'that they will be heard'
> *fēmina negat sē amātum īrī* 'the woman denies that there is a movement towards loving her', i.e. 'that she will be loved'

4 The supine has a *fixed form* (ending -*um*). Its stem is the same as that of the 4th p.p. See **A7**.

Exercises

1 *Form and translate the 'future infinitive passive' of*: capiō, līberō, iubeō, auferō, reperiō.
2 *Translate these sentences*:

   (a) Verrēs praedōnēs captum īrī dīxit.
   (b) Verrēs cīuīs Rōmānōs negābat līberātum īrī.

(c) Verrēs Diodōrī pōcula ablātum īrī affirmat.
(d) Diodōrus pōcula ā Verre repertum īrī negat.
(e) Verrēs amīcōs dīxit pōcula reperīre iussum īrī.
(f) ībō uīsum sī domī est. (*Terence*)
(g) lūsum it Maecēnās, dormītum ego Vergiliusque. (*Horace*)

lūdō 3 supine *lūsum* I play   *Maecēnās* (nom.)   *Vergilius* Virgil
                                   Maecenas

119 Irregular *ferō*, transitive compounds of *eō*

Present

1st s.	fér-o-r 'I am (being) carried'
2nd s.	fér-ris
3rd s.	fér-tur
1st pl.	fér-i-mur
2nd pl.	fer-í-minī
3rd pl.	fer-ú-ntur

Present infinitive
fér-rī 'to be carried'

Imperative

s.	fér-re
pl.	fer-í-minī

}'be carried!'

NB. *ferō* is regular in the formation of all its other tenses. Its principal parts are *ferō ferre tulī lātus.*

Present

1st s.	ád-eo-r 'I am (being) approached'
2nd s.	ad-í-ris (-re)
3rd s.	ad-í-tur
1st pl.	ad-í-mur
2nd pl.	ad-í-minī
3rd pl.	ad-eú-ntur

Future

ad-í-bo-r *etc.* 'I will be approached'

Imperfect

ad-í-ba-r *etc.* 'I was being approached'

Perfect

    ád-it-us sum *etc.* 'I was / have been approached'

Notes

1 The *forms* of the passive are identical with those of deponents. But while deponent verbs only have an active *meaning* (e.g. *sequor* 'I follow' (you cannot say 'I am being followed' using *sequor*)), active verbs will have an active meaning when they use active forms, and a passive meaning when they use passive forms, e.g. *amō* 'I love', *amor* 'I am loved'.

2 'By' a *person* in Latin is expressed by *ā/ab* + abl.; 'by'/'with' a *thing* is expressed by the plain ablative (ablative of instrument – see **100A(c)**). E.g.

    'The boat was captured <u>by Tadius</u>' *nāuis ā Tadiō capta est*
    'They were being hit <u>by/with an axe</u> (i.e. executed)' *feriēbantur*
    <u>*secūrī*</u>

If a person is seen as a tool, or is unwillingly involved, *ā/ab* can be dropped, e.g.

    uxōre paene cōnstrictus 'almost strangled by his wife'

ab uxōre would mean she meant it.

3 *uideor* 'I seem' is actually the *passive* of *uideō* and not a real deponent verb. It can also, therefore, mean 'I am seen'. *uīsūrus* is fut. participle of *uideō*, and means 'about to see' (never 'about to seem').

4 *fīō fierī factus sum* is the passive of *faciō*, meaning 'I am made' (as well as 'I become', 'I happen').

Exercises

1 *Form the passive parts of these verbs as specified in the bracket. Conjugate imperatives and indicatives. Translate imperatives, infinitives and 1st s. of indicatives:* līberō (*pres.*), adiuuō (*impf.*), iubeō (*fut.*), uideō (*pres.*), ferō (*plupf.*), caedō (*perf.*), reuocō (*pres. inf.*), cōnfirmō (*perf. inf.*), recipiō (*pres.*), dīcō (*fut.*), (*optional:* commoueō (*imperative*), colligō (*pres.*), uideō (*perf. inf.*), recipiō (*pres. inf.*), sentiō (*pres.*), dēdūcō (*imperative*), accūsō (*plupf.*), relinquō (*impf.*), auferō (*perf.*), pōnō (*fut.*)).

2 *These verbs include both deponents and passives. Say which each is and translate*: secūta est, accūsātur, ablāta sunt, relictus est, portātur, loquitur, mentītus est, cōnspicābātur, arbitrābitur, cōnābitur, nārrābitur, nūntiātum est, uīsum est, ausum est, (*optional*: fertur, adipīscitur, dīcitur, fruētur, colligētur, ōrābātur, opīnābātur, passus erat, iussus erat, amplexus est, caesus est, relinquī, sequī, dīcere, ūtere).

3 *Give the Latin for*: he will be captured; to be freed; they were being struck; it had been taken away; to have been called back; it has been read through.

4 *Transform these English sentences from* active *to* passive, *e.g.*

> The pirate found the ship (*active*)
> The ship was found by the pirate (*passive*)

(a) Our fleet did not capture the ship.
(b) A messenger announced the news to Verres.
(c) The sailors brought the ship to Syracuse.
(d) Verres took away the craftsmen.
(e) The Romans executed the pirates with an axe.

5 *Translate these sentences*:

(a) nihil ā Verre dictum erat.
(b) nāuis ā praedōne capta est.
(c) iuuenēs ā Verre Rōmam mittuntur.
(d) nāuis praedōnum ā nostrīs abdūcēbātur.
(e) amīcīs thēsaurus meus dabitur.
(f) Verrī nūntiātum est nāuem captam esse et praedōnēs secūrī necārī.

6 *Transform these sentences from* active *to* passive, *e.g.* praedō nāuem inuēnit '*the pirate found the ship*'; nāuis ā praedōne inuenta est '*the ship was found by the pirate*':

(a) Rōmānī hominēs dēfendēbant.
(b) tū numerum praedōnum cognōuistī.
(c) Verrēs pecūniam dedit.
(d) Verrēs cīuīs Rōmānōs secūrī ferit.
(e) ille nautās līberābit.
(f) Diodōrus pōcula abstulerat.

Reading exercise / Test exercise

P. Caesētiō et P. Tadiō praefectīs nāuem pīrātārum quandam captam esse Verrī nūntiātum est; plēnam esse eam nāuem iuuenum fōrmōsissi- mōrum, argentī, uestium. Verrēs nāuem Syrācūsās ā nautīs appellī iussit. tum exspectābātur ab omnibus supplicium. sed quamquam senēs statim necātī sunt, iuuenēs tamen fōrmōsī ab eō abductī et amīcīs datī sunt. 5 nēmo praedōnēs līberātum īrī arbitrātus erat. hoc tamen ā Verre factum est.

sed posteā facinus multō scelestius ab istō factum est. nam in locum praedōnum, quī līberātī erant, Verrēs cīuīs Rōmānōs substituere coepit, quī in carcerem anteā coniectī erant. quamquam illī ā multīs cognitī 10 erant, secūrī tamen feriēbantur.

English–Latin

1 *Translate these sentences into Latin*:

(a) The ship was found by Romans.
(b) Money was being given to Verres by the pirates.
(c) Young men are being sent to Rome.
(d) It had been announced that the ship had been captured and was being brought[1] to Syracuse.
(e) No one had realised that the pirates would be captured.
(f) Verres will be accused at Rome.

[1] Use *appellō* 3.

2 *Reread the text of* **4D(ii)**, *then translate this passage into Latin*:
The Syracusans had an account of the pirates who had been executed. This[1] account had been made[2] from the number of oars which had been taken. A large number of pirates was missing, because many had been set free by Verres. However, in the pirates' place Roman citizens were substituted. Verres claimed that they had been soldiers of Sertorius. Although they were known[3] by many Syracusans, they were killed with the axe.

[1] Use connecting relative (*quī, quae, quod*).
[2] Use *habeō*.
[3] Use pluperfect of *cognōscō*.

The achievements of Augustus

From now on till the end of the Verres texts, each grammar section will contain a passage from the *rēs gestae* (lit. 'things done', i.e. 'achievements') of the first Roman emperor Augustus, written by himself to commemorate himself. He ordered them to be inscribed on bronze tablets and set up in front of his mausoleum.

The period of Roman history in which the Verres story is set was one of increasing turmoil. The Roman republic was passing more and more into the domination of army-backed factions, led by men like Sulla, Pompey, and later Julius Caesar, whose power brought them the leading positions in the state. In 49, civil war broke out between Caesar and Pompey, and Caesar emerged as victor. But on the Ides of March 44, Julius Caesar was murdered by a group of pro-republican activists (led by Brutus) who felt that Rome was becoming a one-man state. In the ensuing civil war, two factions emerged: that of Gaius Octavius, known as Octavian, the adopted son of Julius Caesar, and that of Marcus Antonius (Mark Antony), who looked to the East and the wealth of the Egyptian queen Cleopatra to support his bid for power. At the battle of Actium in 31, Octavian emerged triumphant, but he faced problems as serious as those faced by Julius Caesar, i.e. how to reconcile the Roman aristocracy, with their implacable hatred of any idea of 'monarchy', to the fact that the old-style 'Republic' was dead, and that the rule of one man was Rome's only hope of survival. Granted the additional name 'Augustus' by a grateful Roman people and senate in 27, he succeeded by making himself the embodiment of Roman standards, ideals and above all, stability, and by presenting the new order, which was in fact the foundation of an imperial dynasty, to make it look like the old republic restored, though he was in fact in control of it. As we shall see, he restored ancient rituals and customs and temples, and engaged writers (like Virgil and Horace) to play their part in propagating his image and ideals, but the most authentic 'statement' about what he stood for is his own – the *rēs gestae dīuī Augustī* ('the achievements of the divine Augustus'), which he wrote himself.

These extracts are adapted only by the excision of the more difficult passages, so you are reading here Augustus' actual words.

Rēs gestae dīuī Augustī

rēs gestae dīuī Augustī, quibus orbem terrārum imperiō populī Rōmānī
subiēcit, et impēnsae quās in rem pūblicam populumque Rōmānum
fēcit.

annōs ūndēuīgintī nātus exercitum prīuātō cōnsiliō et prīuātā impēnsā
comparāuī, per quem rem pūblicam⌐ ā dominātiōne fac-   5
tiōnis ⌐oppressam in lībertātem uindicāuī. senātus in ōrdinem suum mē
adlēgit, C. Pānsā et A. Hirtiō cōnsulibus, et imperium mihi dedit.
populus eōdem annō mē cōnsulem et triumuirum creāuit.

cūriam templumque Apollinis, aedem dīuī Iūlī, Lupercal, porticum ad
circum Flāminium, aedēs in Capitōliō Iouis Feretrī et Iouis Tonantis, 10
aedem Quirīnī, aedēs Mineruae et Iūnōnis Rēgīnae et Iouis Lībertātis in
Auentīnō, aedem Larum in summā sacrā uiā, aedem deum Penātium in
Veliā, aedem Iuuentātis, aedem Mātris Magnae in Palātiō fēcī.

Capitōlium et Pompēium theātrum refēcī sine ūllā īnscrīptiōne
nōminis meī. rīuōs aquārum complūribus locīs uetustāte lābentīs refēcī. 15
forum Iūlium et basilicam, quae fuit inter aedem Castoris et aedem
Sāturnī, perfēcī.

ter mūnus gladiātōrium dedī, quibus mūneribus dēpugnāuērunt
hominum circiter decem mīllia.

uēnātiōnēs bēstiārum Āfricānārum in circō aut in forō aut in 20
amphitheātrīs populō dedī sexiēns et uīciens, quibus cōnfecta sunt
bēstiārum circiter tria mīllia et quīngentae. (Rēs gestae *1–4, 19–23*)

NB.   The glossaries for these passages contain both vocabulary and
hints on how to read each sentence as it comes. The instruction 'hold'
suggests that the meaning of the word cannot be finally decided at that
point in the sentence; you are asked to keep information about the word
in mind until it is 'solved' by later developments.

rēs gestae rērum gestārum 5f. pl. + 1/2
   adj. (lit.) things done; achievements
dīu-us a um divine
August-us ī 2m. Augustus
quibus [Pl., so what must it pick up?
   Dat or abl., but why? Hold]
orbis orb-is 3m. circle
   (+ *terrārum* = 'circle of the lands', i.e.
   world) [Acc., but why? Hold]
imperi-um ī 2n. command, rule,
   authority. [Dat. or abl., but why?
   Hold]

popul-us ī 2m. people
subiciō 3/4 subiēcī subject x (acc.) to y
   (dat.) [This should solve *imperiō* and
   quibus (abl. of means)]
impēns-a ae 1f. money, expense
quās [f. pl., so what must it pick up?
   Acc., but why? Hold]
rēs pūblica rēī pūblicae 5f. + 1/2 adj.
   republic
fēcit [Explains *quās* in the acc.]
ūndēuīgintī nineteen
nāt-us a um born, aged [Nom., m., but
   who does it refer to? Hold]

253

priuāt-us a um his own [*priuātō* is dat.
  or abl., but why? Hold]
5 *comparō* 1 I put together, gather, raise
  [Person (tells you who *nātus* is)?
  Explains why *exercitum* in acc.
  Solves *priuātō . . . impēnsā*]
per quem ['through whom' (i.e.
  through me) or 'through which'
  (referring to the army)? Wait]
dominātiō dominātiōn-is 3f. tyranny
factiō factiōn-is 3f. political clique
oppress-us a um crushed, ground under
in lībertātem uindicō 1 I free (lit. 'I claim
  into freedom') [Person? Shows that
  quem must = army, solves case of *rem
  pūblicam*]
adlegō 3 *adlēgī* I enrol
C. *Pānsā et A. Hirtiō cōnsulibus* i.e. 43
triumuir triumuir-ī 2m. triumvir,
  member of commission of three
creō 1 I elect
cūri-a ae 1f. senate house [Acc., but
  why? You will not solve this
  sentence till you come to the very
  last word! So this is an important
  exercise in holding on]
templ-um ī 2n. temple [Since it is
  linked by *-que* to *cūriam*, one
  assumes it also is acc. But what is
  the function of the accusatives? This
  question will not be asked again –
  but you must ask it]
Apollō Apollin-is 3m. Apollo
dīu-us a um divine
Iūli-us ī 2m. Julius (Caesar)
Lupercal 3n. the Lupercal
portic-us ūs 4f. portico
10 *circ-us ī* 2m. circus
Flāmini-us a um of Flaminius
Capitōli-um ī 2n. the Capitol (hill)
Feretri-us a um Feretrian
Tonāns Tonant-is thunderer
Quirīn-us ī 2m. Quirinus (= Romulus
  deified)
Mineru-a ae 1f. Minerva (Athena)
Iūnō Iūnōn-is 3f. Juno (Hera), wife of
  Jupiter
Rēgīn-a ae 1f. queen
254

Lībertās Lībertāt-is 3f. freedom
Auentīn-um ī 2n. the Aventine (hill)
Larēs Lar-um 3m. pl. the Lares
  (household gods)
deum [Gen. pl., not acc. s.]
Penātēs Penāt-ium 3m. pl. the Penates
  (household gods)
Veli-a ae 1f. The Velian ridge,
  connecting two hills in Rome
Iuuentās Iuuentāt-is 3f. youth
Māter Magna Mātr-is Magn-ae Cybele
Palāti-um ī 2n. the Palatine (hill)
fēcī [At last! Solves all the accusatives]
Capitōli-um ī 2n. the Capitol (hill)
Pompēi-us a um of Pompey
theātr-um ī 2n. theatre [Nom., or acc.?
  Hold . . . but not for long]
reficiō 3/4 *refēcī* I rebuild, restore
īnscrīptiō īnscrīptiōn-is 3f. inscription
15 *rīu-us ī* 2m. *aquārum* aqueduct [Why
  acc.? Hold]
complūr-ēs ium very many, several
uetustās uetustāt-is 3f. age [Why abl.?
  Hold]
lābēns lābent-is collapsing (explains
  uetustāte)
Iūli-us a um of Julius (Caesar) [Nom.
  or acc.?]
basilic-a ae 1f. courtyard (used for
  business and law–courts) [Its case
  shows that *forum Iūlium* must also be
  acc.]
inter (+ acc.) in between
Castor Castor-is 3m. Castor (god,
  brother of Pollux)
Sāturn-us ī 2m. Saturn (ancient Roman
  god, = Greek Kronos)
ter three times
mūnus mūner-is 3n. public show
  [Neuter, so hold whether nom. or
  acc.]
gladiātōri-us a um involving gladiators
dedī [Solves *mūnus*]
quibus mūneribus [Connecting relative.
  But why dat. or abl.? Hold]
dēpugnō 1 I fight [Plural: will there
  follow a subject which tells us who
  fought? *hominum* 'of men' – it looks
  like it]

circiter about
decem 10
mīllia (usually *mīlia*) thousands [So we
  have '*quibus mūneribus* about 10,000
  men fought'. Now translate *quibus
  mūneribus*]
20 *uēnātiō uēnātiōn-is* 3f. hunt [Nom. or
  acc.? Hold]
bēsti-a ae 1f. wild animal
Āfricān-us a um from Africa
circ-us ī 2m. circus
amphitheātr-um ī 2n. amphitheatre
sexiēns et uīciēns six and twenty times

quibus [Pl., so it must pick up –
  uēnātiōnēs? bēstiārum? amphitheātrīs?
  Wait]
cōnficiō 3/4 *cōnfēcī cōnfect-us* I destroy
  [Passive, so something 'was
  destroyed'; *sunt* shows pl., but why
  cōnfect-a neuter? Wait for subject]
tria mīllia (neuter!) three thousands
quīngent-ī ae a 500 [But why *-ae*
  feminine? So we have '*quibus* 3,500
  (of) animals were destroyed'. Now
  tr. *quibus*]

Deliciae Latinae

Word-building

Suffixes
-cul-us a um and *-ol/ul-us a um* often indicate diminutives, which can be
endearing or condemnatory, e.g.

> *mulier* 'woman' – *muliercula* 'silly woman'
> *homo* 'man' – *homunculus* 'little jerk'
> *Vērānius* – *Vērāniolus* 'dear Veranius'

Word exercises

Give the meaning and Latin connections of: class, decimate, juvenile, prefect,
inebriated, adjacent, liberate, vest, nefarious, quotidian.

Everyday Latin

> *contrāria contrāriīs cūrantur* 'opposites are cured by opposites'
> *data et accepta* 'expenditures and receipts' (lit. 'things given and
>   received')
> *Graecum est: nōn legitur* 'it is Greek: it is not read' (found beside
>   Greek words in medieval MSS – when knowledge of the
>   language was rare)
> *negātur* 'it is denied'
> *probātum est* 'it has been proved'

255

Real Latin

Lucretius[1]
(*On the nature of the gods*)

sēmōta ab nostrīs rēbus sēiūnctaque longē;
nam prīuāta dolōre omnī, prīuāta perīclīs,
ipsa suīs pollēns opibus, nīl indiga nostrī,
nec bene prōmeritīs capitur neque tangitur īrā.

(*Dē rērum nātūrā 2.648ff.*)

sēmōta removed [It is f., referring to *dīuum nātūra* 'the nature of the gods' a few lines earlier]	*dolor dolōr-is* 3m. pain; grief	*indig-us a um* in need of (+ gen.)
sēiūncta separated	*perīclīs = perīculīs*	*bene prōmerit-a (ōrum* 2n. pl.) good deeds
prīuātus a um (+ abl.) relieved of	*pollēns pollent-is* powerful	*capiō* (here) I win over
	suīs . . . opibus 'in (respect of) their own resources'	*tangō* 3 I touch, move, affect
	nīl 'in no way'	*īr-a ae* 1f. anger

[1] C. 95–c. 50. Philosopher poet, author of *Dē rērum nātūrā* 'On the nature of matter', 'On the nature of the universe'.

Publilius Syrus[1]

(a) amāns īrātus multa mentītur sibi.
(b) auārus ipse causa miseriae suae.
(c) amāre iuuenī frūctus est, crīmen senī.
(d) amāre et sapere uix deō concēditur.
(e) amōris uulnus īdem sānat quī facit.
(f) amōrī finem tempus, nōn animus, facit.

[1] First writer of stage 'mimes', full of wit and satire and memorable quotes, c. 44.

amāns amant-is 3m. lover	*sapere* 'to be wise'	*sānō* 1 I heal
auār-us ī 2m. miser	*uix* scarcely	*īdem* is antecedent of *quī*)
frūct-us ūs 4m. enjoyment	*concēdō* 3 I yield, grant	*finis fin-is* 3m. end
crīmen crīmin-is 3n. reproach	*uulnus uulner-is* 3n. wound	

Martial

septima⌐ iam, Philerōs, tibi conditur ⌐uxor in agrō.
plūs nūllī, Philerōs, quam tibi reddit ager. (*10.43*)

septim-us a um seventh	*tibi* 'by you' (dative of agent)	*condō* 3 I bury
Philerōs (voc.) Phileros ('friend of Eros')		*reddō* 3 I yield, return

256

Part of the Creed

(*Christ*) quī propter nōs hominēs et propter nostram salūtem dēscendit dē caelīs.

Et incarnātus est dē spīritū sānctō ex Mariā uirgine; et homo factus est. Crucifīxus etiam prō nōbīs, sub Pontiō Pilātō passus et sepultus est. Et resurrēxit tertiā diē secundum scrīptūrās.

salūs salūt-is 3f. salvation
dēscendō 3 *dēscendī* I descend
dē (+abl.) from
cael-a ōrum 2n. pl. heaven(s)
incarnātus est 'he was made flesh'

crucifīxus (sc. *est*) 'he was crucified'
sub (+abl.) under
passus (sc. *est*) 'he suffered'
sepultus est 'he was buried'

resurgō 3 *resurrēxī* I rise again
terti-us a um third
secundum (+acc.) according to
scrīptūr-a ae 1f. scripture

Section 4E

Running vocabulary for 4E(i)

---

adeuntīs (acc. pl. m.) '(as they were) approaching' (pres. part. of *adeō*)
adpulsa esset 'had landed' (plup. subj. of *adpellor*)
aduolāuisset '(it) had flown' (plup. subj. of *aduolō* 1)
aggredior 3/4 I attack (lit. 'I go up to')
agrest-is e wild
amāns (nom. s. m.) 'making love' (pres. part. of *amō*)
ancor-a ae 1f. anchor-cable
Anthrōpin-us ī 2m. Anthropinus
Apollōniēns-is e from Apollonia (a town in Sicily)

capta esset '(it) had been captured' (plup. subj. pass. of *capiō*)
cib-us ī 2m. food
Cleomenēs Cleomen-is 3m. Cleomenes
cuius (gen. s.) 'whose', 'of which'
cum when (ll. 204, 210 and 217); although (l. 212)
dēnique finally
egentēs (nom. pl. m.) 'lacking', 'needing' (pres. part. of *egeō* 2 (+abl.) I need, lack)
egentibus (abl. pl. m.) '(as they were) lacking, needing' (pres. part. of *egeō* 2 (+abl.) I need, lack)

ēgredientem (acc. s. m.) '(as he was) leaving' (pres. part. of *ēgredior*)
ērigō 3 I erect
fugiēns (nom. s. f.) 'fleeing' (pres. part. of *fugiō*)
fugientēs (nom. pl. m./f.) 'fleeing', 'as they were fleeing' (pres. part. of *fugiō*)
Haluntīn-us ī 2m. person from Haluntium (a town in N. Sicily)
Helōr-us ī 2f. Helorus (city on east coast of Sicily)
imperātor imperātōr-is 3m. leader, general, commander

257

incrēdibil-is e amazing,
unbelievable
lītus lītor-is 3n. shore
māl-us ī 2m. mast
muliercul-a ae 1f. woman
(sneering tone)
nāuigō 1 I sail
nītor 3 dep. *nīxus* (+ abl.)
I lean on
occīdō 3 *occīdī occīsus* I kill
Odyssē-a ae 1f. Odyssea (a
promontory on the
southern extremity of
Sicily)
Pachȳn-us ī 2m./f.
Pachynus (the south-
eastern promontory of
Sicily)

palli-um ī 2n. Greek cloak
palm-a ae 1f. palm-tree
paulō slightly, rather
Phȳlarch-us ī 2m.
Phylarchus
popul-us ī 2m. people
postrēm-us a um last
pōtāns (nom. s. m.)
'drinking' (pres. part.
of *pōtō* 1)
pōtante (abl. s. m.)
'drinking' (pres. part.
of *pōtō* 1)
praecīdō 3 I cut
prīnceps prīncip-is 3m.
leader; (adj.) first
purpure-us a um purple;
crimson

quīnt-us a um fifth
rādīx rādīc-is 3f. root
sēmiplēn-us a um half-full;
under-manned
sequentēs (nom. pl. m.)
'following' (pres. part.
of *sequor* 3 dep.)
sequentīs (acc. pl. f.)
'following', 'as they
were following' (pres.
part. of *sequor* 3 dep.)
soleāt-us a um be-
slippered, in slippers
tard-us a um slow
uīdisset 'he had seen'
(plup. subj. of *uideō*)

Learning vocabulary for 4E(i)

Nouns

cib-us ī 2m. food
Cleomenēs Cleomen-is 3m.
Cleomenes

imperātor imperātōr-is 3m.
leader, general,
commander
lītus lītor-is 3n. shore

popul-us ī 2m. people
prīnceps prīncip-is 3m.
leader, chieftain; (adj.)
first

Adjectives

postrēm-us a um last
quīnt-us a um fifth

Verbs

aggredior 3/4 dep. *aggressus*
I attack (go up to)
egeō 2 *eguī* (+abl. or
gen.) I lack, need, am
in want of

nāuigō 1 I sail
nītor 3 dep. *nīsus* or *nīxus*
(+abl.) I lean on; I
strive, exert myself

occīdō 3 *occīdī occīsus* I kill

Others

dēnique finally; in a word
paulō slightly (cf. *multō*
(by) much: both
ablatives expressing
'amount of difference')

Running vocabulary for 4E(ii)

accipiō 3/4 *accēpī acceptus* I
sustain, meet with
admittō 3 I let in
amor amōr-is 3m. love,
passion
ante earlier, before (adv.)
ausus esset 'he had dared'
(plup. subj. of *audeō*)
calamitōs-us a um
disastrous
cant-us ūs 4m. song,
singing
concursō 1 I rush together
cōnflagrantem (acc. s. m./
f.) '(as he/it was)
burning' (pres. part. of
cōnflagrō 1)
cōnflagrantīs (acc. pl. f.)
'burning', (pres. part.
of *cōnflagrō* 1)
cuius (gen. s.) 'whose', 'of
which'
cum when (l. 220); since
(ll. 222 and 226)
disciplīn-a ae 1f. order,
control
dormientem (acc. s. m.)
'(while he was)
sleeping' (pres. part. of
dormiō)

ēiciō 3/4 *ēiēcī* I throw out;
mē ēiciō I throw myself
out
excitō 1 I rouse
exeuntem (acc. s. m.)
'departing' (pres. part.
of *exeō*)
fluctuantem (acc. s. f.)
'tossing about' (pres.
part. of *fluctuō* 1)
grau-is e serious,
important, weighty
Helōr-us ī 2f. Helorus
(city on east coast of
Sicily)
Hēracleō Hēracleōn-is 3m.
Heracleo
incendi-um ī 2n. fire
incendō 3 *incendī incēnsus* I
burn
inclūdō 3 *inclūsī* I shut up
īnflammō 1 I set on fire
manente (abl. s. m.)
'remaining' (pres. part.
of *maneō*)
mare mar-is 3n. sea (abl. s.
marī)
marī (abl. s.) on the sea
multitūdō multitūdin-is 3f.
crowd, number

nēquiti-a ae 1f. wickedness
ō oh! (exclamation:
followed by acc.)
peruēnisset 'he had
reached' (plup. subj. of
peruēniō)
praetōri-um ī 2n.
governor's residence
pūblic-um ī 2n. public
place
quārum (gen. pl. f.) 'of
which', '(and) of these'
quō to where
quōrum (gen. pl. m.)
'whose'
reliqu-us a um remaining,
left
seuēr-us a um strict
symphōni-a ae 1f. band
tard-us a um slow
uīdissent 'they had seen'
(plup. subj. of *uideō*)

Learning vocabulary for 4E(ii)

Nouns
incendi-um ī 2n. fire
mare mar-is 3n. sea (*marī*
(abl. s.) 'on the sea')

multitūdō multitūdin-is 3f.
mob, crowd, number

nēquiti-a ae 1f. wickedness

Adjectives
grau-is e serious,
important, weighty

reliqu-us a um remaining,
left

tard-us a um slow

Verbs

accipiō 3/4 *accēpī acceptus* I
sustain, meet with;
(receive, welcome;
learn; obtain)

cōnflagrō 1 I burn
(intrans.)

incendō 3 *incendī incēnsus* I
set fire to, burn (trans.)

Others

ante (adv.) earlier, before;
((+ acc.) before, in
front of)

quō to where, whither (in
direct q. = whither? to
where?)

Running vocabulary for 4E(iii)

---

accēdō 3 *accessī* I approach,
reach
acerb-us a um bitter
Carthāginiēns-is e
Carthaginian, Punic
commorātī essent 'they had
waited' (plup. subj. of
commoror 1 dep.)
cōnflagrantīs (acc. pl. f.)
'burning' (pres. part. of
conflagrō)
cum when (l. 241)
fact-um ī 2n. achievement
glōri-a ae 1f. glory,
renown, fame
Helōrī (locative) at
Helorus

immortāl-is e everlasting,
immortal
lūdibriō esse to be a
laughing-stock/joke (to
x: dat.) [*lūdibriō* is
predicative dative from
lūdibri-um ī 2n.]
mentiō mentiōn-is 3f.
mention
met-us ūs 4m. fear
moenia moen-ium 3n. pl.
walls
ō oh! (exclamation
followed by acc.)
penetrō 1 I penetrate,
reach into
peruagor 1 dep. I rove
freely about

pīrātic-us a um (of a)
pirate
plūrimum possum I am
very powerful
prō! in the name of!
Pūnic-us a um Punic,
Carthaginian
quōrum (gen. pl. n.) 'of
which'
saepe often
Siciliēns-is e Sicilian
spectācul-um ī 2n. sight
statuō 3 *statuī* I decide,
determine
tot so many (indecl.)
uidēlicet presumably
usque right up as far as

Learning vocabulary for 4E(iii)

Nouns

glōri-a ae 1f. glory,
renown, fame

mentiō mentiōn-is 3f.
mention
met-us ūs 4m. fear, terror

moenia moen-ium 3n. pl.
walls, fortifications

Adjectives

tot so many (indecl.)

Verbs

accedō 3 *accessī accessum* I
approach, reach

commoror 1 dep. I delay,
wait

possum posse potuī
(+ adv.) I am
powerful, have power;
(am able, can)

Others

cum (+ subj.) when; since;
although; (+ abl. with)

saepe often

Grammar and exercises for 4E

20 **Present participles '—ing', 'while —ing'**

Present participles of both active and deponent verbs are formed in the
same way – with -*ns* added to the stem (+ key vowel-*e*- in 3rd, 4th and
3rd/4th conjugations). They are declined like *ingēns* (*ingent-*), e.g.

	s.		pl.	
	m./f.	*n.*	*m./f.*	*n.*
nom.	ámā-ns	ámā-ns	amánt-ēs	amánt-ia
acc.	amánt-em	ámā-ns	amánt-īs (-ēs)	amánt-ia
gen.	←amánt-is→		←amánt-ium (-um)→	
dat.	←amánt-ī→		←amánt-ibus→	
abl.	←amánt-e (-ī)→		←amánt-ibus→	

So in conspectus we get:

Active

1	2	3	4	3/4
'loving'	*'having'*	*'saying'*	*'hearing'*	*'capturing'*
ámāns	hábēns	dícēns	aúdiēns	cápiēns
amánt-	habént-	dīcént-	audiént-	capiént-

Deponent

1	2	3	4	3/4
'threatening'	*'promising'*	*'speaking'*	*'lying'*	*'advancing'*
mínāns	póllicēns	lóquēns	méntiēns	prōgrédiēns
minánt-	pollicént-	loquént-	mentiént-	prōgrediént-

Notes

1 Observe that the very word 'present' is itself a participle form (*praesēns praesentis*) from *praesum* 'I preside'; so the word 'present' is in itself a clue to the form and meaning of present participles. (Cf. 'future', which gave the clue to the *-ūr-us* ending of future participles, **81**).

2 Present participles mean '——ing', and indicate that the action of the participle is going on at the same time as the verb of the clause.

3 As with future participles and deponent past participles, present participles act like adjectives in agreeing with the person 'doing' in gender, number and case. But they are most often used predicatively. See **77**.

4 The ablative s. usually ends in *-e*, and the gen. pl. in *-ium*. The ablative s. ends in *-ī* when the verb is being used *adjectivally*. (Cf. English 'a charming man came here', 'I saw a man charming snakes': the first participle is being used adjectivally, the second with verbal force – predicatively. See **77**).

5 Note the irregular *iēns*, *eunt-is* 'going' (from *eō*).

6 Note the common use of a noun in the ablative with a present participle (in s. always ending in *-e*), to mean 'while x is/was ——ing', e.g. *Cleomenē pōtante* 'while Cleomenes was drinking'. Cf. the ablative absolute with nouns/adjectives, **109**.

Exercises

Morphology

1 *Form the present participle of each of these verbs. Give also gen. s. and translate:* reuocō, incendō, accipiō, sentiō, iubeō, adipīscor, ēgredior, fruor, recordor, exeō, (*optional:* loquor, intellegō, commoror, cōnflagrō, egeō, nītor, nāuigō, mentior, oblīuīscor, cōnor).

2 *Say with which noun(s) in each line the given present participle agrees:*

> īnspicientī: seruae, muliere, mīlitis, uirō
> accēdentem: imperātōrum, prīncipem, multitūdine, incendium
> nītente: Verrī, mulieris, seruā, imperātōrēs
> commorantum: populum, mulierum, manum
> cōnflagrantibus: moenibus, cibus, nāuis, cēterīs
> circumiēns: Iouis, Cicerō, mulier, imperātōrēs

3 *Translate these sentences*:

    (a) Verrēs muliere nītēns in lītore stābat.
    (b) illīs rogantibus praedō respondit sē nāuīs fugientīs uīdisse.
    (c) nautīs cibō egentibus, Cleomenēs nihil fēcit.
    (d) Verre mulierem amante, nūntiātum est nāuem captam esse.
    (e) nāuem incendiō cōnflagrantem uidēre potes.
    (f) reliquōs paulō tardius sequentīs cōnspicātī sunt.
    (g) Syrācūsīs commorantēs praedōnēs moenia urbis uīdērunt.
    (h) Verrēs negāuit nāuīs sē ad portum accēdentīs uīdisse.
    (i) nūllus agentī[1] diēs longus est. (*Seneca*)
    (j) nīl difficile amantī. (*Cicero*)

[1] *agō* 3 I am busy.

4 *Translate into Latin (using ablative absolute with present participle). E.g. as the leader delayed* prīncipe commorante.

in Verres' absence; while the sailors were following; with the people watching; as the ships were burning; with Cleomenes delaying; although the crowd was encouraging the leader.

21 Pluperfect subjunctive active ('had —ed')

	1	2	3
1st s.	amāu-ísse-m (*or* amássem etc.)	habu-ísse-m	dīx-ísse-m
2nd s.	amāu-íssē-s	habu-íssē-s	dīx-íssē-s
3rd s.	amāu-ísse-t	habu-ísse-t	dīx-ísse-t
1st pl.	amāu-issé-mus	habu-issé-mus	dīx-issé-mus
2nd pl.	amāu-issé-tis	habu-issé-tis	dīx-issé-tis
3rd pl.	amāu-ísse-nt	habu-ísse-nt	dīx-ísse-nt

	4	3/4
1st s.	audīu-ísse-m (*or* audíssem *etc.*)	cēp-ísse-m
2nd s.	audīu-íssē-s	cēp-íssē-s
3rd s.	audīu-ísse-t	cēp-ísse-t
1st pl.	audīu-issé-mus	cēp-issé-mus
2nd pl.	audīu-issé-tis	cēp-issé-tis
3rd pl.	audīu-ísse-nt	cēp-ísse-nt

Notes
1 Remember pluperfect subjunctive active as formed from the perfect infinitive active plus the normal personal endings (*-m, -s, -t, -mus, -tis, -nt*).

2 Observe how the *-ui-* can drop out (cf. 65, 104³), e.g. *amā-ssem, dēlē-ssem (dēlēuissem)* etc.

122 Pluperfect subjunctive deponent ('had —ed')

	1	2	3
1st s.	mināt-us a um éssem	pollícit-us a um éssem	locút-us a um éssem
2nd s.	mināt-us a um éssēs	pollícit-us a um éssēs	locút-us a um éssēs
3rd s.	mināt-us a um ésset	pollícit-us a um ésset	locút-us a um ésset
1st pl.	mināt-ī ae a essḗmus	pollícit-ī ae a essḗmus	locút-ī ae a essḗmus
2nd pl.	mināt-ī ae a essḗtis	pollícit-ī ae a essḗtis	locút-ī ae a essḗtis
3rd pl.	mināt-ī ae a éssent	pollícit-ī ae a éssent	locút-ī ae a éssent

	4	3/4
1st s.	mentít-us a um éssem	prōgréss-us a um éssem
2nd s.	mentít-us a um éssēs	prōgréss-us a um éssēs
3rd s.	mentít-us a um ésset	prōgréss-us a um ésset
1st pl.	mentít-ī ae a essḗmus	prōgréss-ī ae a essḗmus
2nd pl.	mentít-ī ae a essḗtis	prōgréss-ī ae a essḗtis
3rd pl.	mentít-ī ae a éssent	prōgréss-ī ae a éssent

NB. The pluperfect subjunctive deponent is formed from the perfect participle in *-us -a -um* (agreeing with the subject) and the auxiliary verb *essem essēs esset* etc. (imperfect subjunctive of *sum*).

123 Pluperfect subjunctive passive ('had been —ed')

	1	2	3
1st s.	amāt-us éssem	hábit-us éssem	díct-us éssem
2nd s.	amāt-us éssēs	hábit-us éssēs	díct-us éssēs
3rd s.	amāt-us ésset	hábit-us ésset	díct-us ésset
1st pl.	amāt-ī essḗmus	hábit-ī essḗmus	díct-ī essḗmus
2nd pl.	amāt-ī essḗtis	hábit-ī essḗtis	díct-ī essḗtis
3rd pl.	amāt-ī éssent	hábit-ī éssent	díct-ī éssent

	4	3/4
1st s.	audít-us éssem	cápt-us éssem
2nd s.	audít-us éssēs	cápt-us éssēs
3rd s.	audít-us ésset	cápt-us ésset
1st pl.	audít-ī essḗmus	cápt-ī essḗmus
2nd pl.	audít-ī essḗtis	cápt-ī essḗtis
3rd pl.	audít-ī éssent	cápt-ī éssent

NB. For formation of the pluperfect subjunctive passive, see note on plupf. deponent above, **122**.

24 *cum* + subjunctive 'when', 'since', 'although'

cum followed by the pluperfect subjunctive means 'when' or 'since x had —ed' (it can sometimes mean 'although').

Here are two examples of *cum* + pluperfect subjunctive:

> *cum abiissent, laetus eram* 'when/since they had gone, I was delighted'
>
> *cum haec locūtī essent, abiērunt* 'when/since they had said this, they left'

Notes

1 Distinguish *cum* = 'with' (followed closely by an ablative) from *cum* = 'since', 'when', 'although'.

2 Remember *mēcum* 'with me', *tēcum* 'with you' *nōbīscum* 'with us' etc., and *quōcum, quibuscum* 'with whom'.

3 *cum* 'although' is often signposted by e.g. *tamen* or *nihilōminus* in the main clause, e.g. *cum sapiēns esset, stultē tamen sē gessit* 'though he was wise, all the same he acted foolishly'.

4 It is common for conjunctions like *cum, sī* 'if', *ubi* 'when' etc. to drift towards the verb, i.e. away from the start of the sentence, e.g. *ad templum cum peruēnisset*, 'when he had reached the temple'. Be prepared for this when you translate.

Exercises

1 *Form and conjugate the pluperfect subjunctive of these verbs (form passive only where asked)*: egeō, cōnflagrō, commoror, sequor, accipiō (*passive*), incendō (*passive*), nītor, occīdō, sentiō, līberō (*passive*), accēdō, (*optional:* dēsum, circumeō, nōlō, ferō (*passive*), recordor, audeō, cōnspicor, iaceō, cōnstituō (*passive*), excōgitō, nāuigō).

2 *Translate these sentences (taking care over the meaning of* cum = 'when, since, although'):

   (a)   cum Cleomenēs fūgisset, cēterī secūtī sunt.

   (b)   cum praedōnēs celerrimē prōgressī essent, nāuēs Rōmānōrum postrēmae in perīculō prīncipēs erant.

(c) cum imperātor ad lītus celeriter accessisset, cēterī tamen tardius nāuigābant.

(d) Cleomenēs ad lītus cum nāue cum peruēnisset, sē domī cēlāuit.

(e) cēterī quoque, cum marī nūllō modō praedōnēs effugere potuissent, nāuīs relīquērunt.

(f) praedōnum dux nāuīs, cum captae essent, incendī iussit.

3 *Translate into Latin (using* cum + *pluperfect subjunctive):*

(a) When the commander had sailed to the shore . . .

(b) Since the ships had been burned . . .

(c) Although the pirates had delayed at Syracuse . . .

(d) When the walls had been examined . . .

(e) Although the crowd had caught sight of the fire . . .

(f) Since the sailors had lacked food . . .

4 *Say which of these verbs are subjunctive, which indicative*: eguit, cōnflagrāsset, tulerat, recordātus essēs, cōnstituisse, excōgitāuerās, accēpissent, captus esse, occīsī essent, cōnspicātī sunt, (*optional*: iacuistī, commorātī sunt, secūta esset, fuisse, fūgissent, cēlāuerant, nāuigāssent, nōluistis, potuissēs, incēnsus esse).

125 3rd decl. neuter -*i*- stem nouns in -*al*, -*ar*, -*re* and -*le*, e.g. *mare mar-is* 3n. 'sea'

All these nouns decline in the same way, like *mare*:

	s.	*pl.*
nom.	máre	már-ia
acc.	máre	már-ia
gen.	már-is	már-ium (mar-um *is found*)
dat.	már-ī	már-ibus
abl.	már-ī (máre *is found*)	már-ibus

Cf. *animal* 'animal', *calcar* 'spur' and *cubīle* 'couch'.

NB.   Abl. s. in -*ī*, nom. acc. pl. in -*ia*, gen. pl. in -*ium* – exactly like other neuter *i*-stems (see **44**). Cf. **12** and contrast **26**.

126 Relative pronoun in the genitive

cuius and *quōrum quārum quōrum* nearly always mean 'whose', 'of which' or 'of whom', e.g.

nāuis cuius imperātor erat Phȳlarchus 'the ship the captain of which was Phylarchus'

hominēs quōrum argentum Verrēs cupīuit 'the men whose silver Verres desired'

Reading exercise / Test exercise

Here is a slightly cut (but otherwise unadapted) passage from the original text of **4E(ii)**. *Read the passage, analysing explicitly your procedure as you go. End, after translation, with a reading aloud of the Latin.*

ita prīma Haluntīnōrum nāuis capitur, cui praeerat Haluntīnus homo
nōbilis, Phȳlarchus, quem ab illīs praedōnibus Locrēnsēs[1] posteā pūblicē
redēmērunt[2] . . . deinde Apollōniēnsis nāuis capitur, et eius praefectus
Anthrōpinus occīditur. haec dum aguntur, intereā Cleomenēs iam ad
Helōrī lītus peruēnerat; iam sēsē in terram ē nāuī ēiēcerat,   5
quadrirēmemque[3] fluctuantem in salō (= marī) relīquerat. reliquī
praefectī nāuium, cum in terram imperātor exiisset, Cleomenem
persecūtī[4] sunt. (*From* Cicero, In Verrem *II 5, 34.90–35.91*)

[1] *Locrēnsis Locrēns-is* 3m. person from Locri.
[2] *redimō 3 redēmī* I ransom, buy back (thus English 'redeem').
[3] *quadrirēmis quadrirēm-is* 3f. ship – with 4 banks of oars.
[4] *per-* intensifies the simple verb *sequor*.

English–Latin

1 *Translate these sentences into Latin:*

   (a) The crowd caught sight of the ships as they were burning.
   (b) When Cleomenes had disembarked, the rest of the ships' captains followed him.
   (c) Cleomenes, whose wife was on the shore with Verres, left harbour with the ships following.
   (d) Since they had not been able to escape the pirates by sea, the captains followed their leader and disembarked.

2 *Read the text of* **4E(iii)** *again, then translate this passage:*

When the ships had been set on fire, the pirates decided to go to Syracuse. They had heard that the harbour of the Syracusans was very beautiful and knew that they would never see it except in Verres' praetorship. When they had decided this,[1] they sailed to Syracuse. A pirate ship, in Verres' praetorship, while our ships were burning, came up to the actual harbour of the Syracusans. Ye gods! What a vile deed!

[1] Use connecting relative (quī quae quod).

Rēs gestae dīuī Augustī

mare pācāuī ā praedōnibus. iūrāuit in mea uerba tōta Italia sponte suā, et mē bellī quō uīcī ad Actium ducem dēpoposcit; iūrāuērunt in eadem uerba prōuinciae Galliae, Hispāniae, Āfrica, Sicilia, Sardinia. omnium prōuinciārum populī Rōmānī quibus fīnitimae fuērunt gentēs quae nōn pārērent imperiō nostrō fīnīs auxī. Galliās et Hispāniās prōuinciās, item   5
Germāniam pācāuī. Alpēs ā regiōne eā quae proxima est Hadriānō marī ad Tuscum pācificāuī. classis mea per Ōceanum ab ostiō Rhēnī ad sōlis orientis regiōnem usque ad fīnīs Cimbrōrum nāuigāuit. Aegȳptum imperiō populī Rōmānī adiēcī. plūrimae aliae gentēs expertae sunt p. R. fidem, mē prīncipe, quibus anteā cum populō Rōmānō nūllum exstiterat   10
lēgātiōnum et amīcitiae commercium. (Rēs gestae 25–7)

pācō I bring peace to x (acc.) from (ā + abl.) y
praedō praedōn-is 3m. pirate
iūrō 1 *in uerba* I take the oath of allegiance [Await subject, if there is one quoted]
sponte suā of its own accord, willingly
mē bellī [Wait to solve both these]
quō . . . Actium [Relative clause. *quō* picks up *bellī*]
Acti-um ī 2n. (battle of) Actium, 31, when Octavian–Augustus defeated Mark Antony and Cleopatra and became sole ruler of Roman world
ducem [Acc. – with *mē*? Yes: *mē ducem bellī* solves *bellī*]
dēposcō 3 *dēpoposcī* I demand [Solves case of *mē ducem*. Who 'demanded'? Ans.: *tōta Italia* from the previous clause]
iūrāuērunt [Pl., so 'they' – but who? Await subject(s)]
prōuinci-a ae 1f. province [Ah – here come(s) the subject(s)]
Galli-ae ārum 1f. pl. the provinces of Gaul

Hispāni-ae ārum 1f. pl. the provinces of Spain
omnium . . . populī Rōmānī [A long phrase in the genitive. Probably 'of all . . .', but hold till a suitable noun which it can qualify emerges]
quibus . . . nostrō [Two sub-clauses here – first *quibus . . . gentēs*, then *quae . . . nostrō*. Hold tight]
fīnitim-us a um close to (+ dat.) [Solves *quibus* – 'to which were close . . .']
gēns gent-is 3f. tribe, people
quae [By position probably picks up 'tribes'. Nom., so 'the tribes which . . .']
5 *pārērent* '(they) obeyed' (+ dative)
fīnēs fīn-ium 3f. pl. boundaries [Nom. or acc.?]
augeō 3 *auxī* I increase, enlarge [Solves *fīnīs*. But whose *fīnīs*? Ans.: *omnium . . .*; so we only solve *omnium . . . populī* at the end of the sentence]
item similarly
Germāni-a ae 1f. Germany
Alpēs Alp-ium 3f. pl. the Alps [Nom. or acc.? Hold]

regiō region-is 3f. area
proxim-us a um closest (to + dat.)
Hadriān-us a um Adriatic
Tusc-us a um Tuscan (sc. *mare*)
pācificō 1 I pacify, bring peace to
Ōcean-us ī 2m. Ocean, i.e. the North
  Sea
osti-um ī 2n. mouth
Rhēn-us ī 2m. Rhine
sōl oriēns sōl-is orient-is rising sun, East
usque ad (+ acc.) right up to
Cimbr-ī ōrum 2m. pl. the Cimbri, a
  German tribe (modern Denmark)
Aegȳpt-us ī 2f. Egypt [Case? Hold;
  hold also *imperiō*]
adiciō 3/4 *adiēcī* I add x (acc.) to y
  (dat.)
experior 4 dep. *expert-us* I experience
p. R. = populī Rōmānī

10 *fidēs fidē-ī* 5f. protection,
  trustworthiness
quibus [Pl., so who must it refer to?
  Case = dat. or abl. Hold]
anteā previously
nūllum [But no what? Wait]
exsistō 1 *exstitī* exist [What had
  existed? Since 'exist' cannot have a
  direct object, one assumes *nūllum*
  must be a subject, so '*quibus*
  previously no something had
  existed']
lēgātiō lēgātiōn-is 3f. embassy, i.e.
  international relations
amīciti-a ae 1f. friendship
commerci-um ī 2n. [Ah! *nūllum*]
  exchange [So '*quibus* previously no
  exchange of . . .' Translate *quibus*]

Deliciae Latinae

Word-building

Suffixes: revision

-bil-is e is the suffix often used to form adjectives with passive force, e.g.
amābilis 'lovable', *crēdibilis* 'credible', 'which can be believed'. Cf. English
'-ble'.

Exercise

Give the meaning of: stabilis, mōbilis, laudābilis, dūrābilis, nāuigābilis.

Present participles

Many English words are based on the present participle stem in *-ent* and
-ant, and these frequently tell you what conj. the verb is. If *-ant*, the verbs
are 1st conj., if *-ent*, 2nd/3rd conj., if *-ient*, 4th or 3rd/4th conj.

Discuss the origins of: gradient, intelligent, permanent, Vincent,
inhabitant, tangent.

Some words, however, come through French, whose present participle always ends in *-ant*. So: descendant, defendant, tenant, attendant.

But we sometimes use the French form as a noun e.g. 'a depend*ant*', the Latin as an adjective, 'depend*ent*' (*dēpendeō* 2 I hang from).

Word exercises

1 *The following words all use the stem of a Latin noun you should know. Say what is the nom. s. of the noun in each case:* legal, pacify, military, ducal, capital, custodian, pedal.

2 *Give an English word derived from the stem of:* tempus, uōx, nōmen, opus, lītus[1], prīnceps, multitūdō.

  [1] Clue: double the -*t*-.

Everyday Latin

Ablative absolutes and present participles

> *D.V.* = *Deō uolente* '(with) God willing'
>
> *nem. con.* = *nēmine contrādīcente* '(with) no-one contradicting', 'unanimously'
>
> A *locum* in medical parlance means someone who takes the place of a doctor who is away for whatever reason. Its origin is *locum tenēns* '(one) taking the place' (cf. French '*lieu-tenant*', identical in formation)
>
> *et seq.* = *et sequēns* 'and (the one) following', *et seqq.* = *et sequentēs* 'and (the ones) following'. Note how a double letter indicates the plural. Cf. *ex.* = example; *exx.* = examples.
>
> *timeō Danaōs, et dōna ferentīs* 'I fear the Greeks even (though they are) bearing gifts' (Virgil, *Aeneid* 2, 49).
>
> *volentī nōn fit iniūria* 'to one willing, injury does not happen' (i.e. no wrong is done to one who consents). An important legal principle at the heart of many cases involving e.g. rape.

Adapted mediaeval Latin: St Columba subdues the Loch Ness Monster[1]

ōlim sānctus Columba in prōuinciā Pictōrum per aliquot diēs manēbat et necesse habuit transīre fluuium Nēsam. ubi ad ripam aduēnit, aliquōs ex incolīs huius regiōnis aspicit humantēs miserum homunculum quem, ut ipsī incolae dīcēbant, natantem paulō ante in fluuiō aquātilis bēstia dentibus magnīs momorderat. uir sānctus haec audiēns iussit ūnum ex   5 comitibus suīs natāre ad alteram rīpam et nāuigium, quod ibi stābat, ad sē

redūcere. comes ille, nōmine Lugneus Mocumin, sine morā uestīmenta
exuit et, tunicam sōlam gerēns, immittit sē in aquās.

sed bēstia quae in profundō flūminis latuerat, sentiēns aquam super sē
turbātam, subitō ēmergēns ad hominem in mediō flūmine natantem cum 10
ingentī fremitū, apertō ōre, properāuit. inter Lugneum et bēstiam nōn
amplius erat quam longitūdō ūnīus contī. tum uir beātus haec uidēns,
dum barbarī et frātrēs timōre pauent, sānctam manum ēleuāns, signum
crucis in āëre facit dīcēns bēstiae: 'nōlī ultrā prōcēdere; nōlī hominem
tangere sed celeriter abī.' tum uērō bēstia iussū sānctī uirī retrō uēlōciter 15
fūgit tremefacta. frātrēs cum ingentī admīrātiōne glōrificāuērunt Deum
in beātō uirō, et barbarī, propter mīraculum quod ipsī uīderant, Deum
magnificāuērunt Christiānōrum.

ōlim one day	*flūmen flūmin-is* 3n. loch (lit. river)
sānct-us a um holy, Saint	*lateō* 2 I lie hidden
Columb-a ae 1m. Columba	10 *turbāt-us a um* disturbed
Pict-ī ōrum 2m. pl. Picts	*ēmergō* 3 I emerge
aliquot several	*fremit-us ūs* 4m. roar
necesse habeō I find it necessary	*apert-us a um* opened
trānseō trānsīre I cross	*ōs ōr-is* 3n. mouth
rīp-a ae 1f. bank	*properō* 1 I hurry
fluui-us ī 2m. loch (lit. river)	*amplius* more
incol-a ae 1m. inhabitant	*longitūdō longitūdin-is* 3f. length
regiō regiōn-is 3f. region	*cont-us ī* 2m. pole
aspiciō 3/4 I spot	*beāt-us a um* blessed
humō 1 I bury	*barbar-ī ōrum* 2m. pl. locals
natō 1 I swim	*timor timōr-is* 3m. fear
aquātil-is bēsti-a ae 1f. monster, water	*paueō* 2 I shake, tremble
beast	*ēleuō* 1 I raise
5 *dēns dent-is* 3m. tooth	*crux cruc-is* 3f. cross
mordeō 2 *momordī* I bite	*āër āër-is* 3m. air
nāuigi-um ī 2n. boat	*ultrā* any further
Lugne-us ī 2m. Lugneus	*prōcēdō* 3 I advance
(*Mocumin* = indecl.)	15 *iussū* 'at the command'
mor-a ae 1f. delay	*retrō* back
uestīment-um ī 2n. clothes	*tremefact-us a um* terrified
exuō 3 I take off	*admīrātiō admīrātiōn-is* 3f. wonder
tunic-a ae 1f. tunic	*glōrificō* 1 I glorify
gerō 3 I wear	*mīrācul-um ī* 2n. miracle
immittō 3 I hurl into	*magnificō* 1 I magnify
profund-um ī 2n. depths	*Christiān-us ī* 2m. a Christian
medi-us a um middle of	

[1] Adapted by Sidney Morris (*Fōns perennis*) from Adomnan's Life of St Columba, the Irish saint, who
was the founder of the monastery of Iona. St Columba lived from about 545 to 615. The original of
this passage can be read in Keith Sidwell, *Reading Medieval Latin* (Cambridge 1995), pp. 89–90.

Section 4F

Running vocabulary for 4F(i)

---

abiciō abicere abiēcī abiectus
I throw down
abūtor 3 dep. (+abl.) I
misuse
accidit ut (+subj.) it
happened that
ad (+acc.) for the
purpose of, to fulfil (l.
280)
adesset (impf. subj. of
adsum adesse) '(he) was
present'
adfluō 3 I flow, drip
adīret (impf. subj. of *adeō
adīre*) '(to) come (sc. to
him)' '(that) he should
come (sc. to him)'
agō causam I plead a case,
conduct a case before
(+dat.)
argente-us a um (of) silver
argūment-um ī 2n. proof
bon-a ōrum 2n. pl. goods
C. = Gāiō: Gāi-us ī 2m.
Gaius
caederent (impf. subj. of
caedō caedere) '(to) beat',
'(that) they should
beat'
caus-a ae 1f. case; reason
circumsisterent (impf. subj.
of *circumsistō
circumsistere*) '(to)
stand round' '(that)
they should stand
round'
clāmitantī 'to the
disadvantage of him, as
he kept shouting': tr.
'as he shouted'

compleō 2 *complēuī
complētus* I fill
concidō 3 *concidī* I fall
down, collapse
cui 'to whom', 'whose'
Cupīdō Cupīdin-is 3m.
(statue of) Cupid
dē (+abl.) from
dētis (pres. subj. of *dō*)
'(to) give' '(that) you
(pl.) should give'
dīligēns dīligent-is careful
exspectētis (pres. subj. of
exspectō) '(not to)
await', '(and that) you
(pl.) should (not)
await'
fortūn-a ae 1f. fortune
iacentī 'to the
disadvantage of him as
he lay': tr. 'as he lay'
immortāl-is e immortal
latus later-is 3n. side
lepōs lepōr-is 3m. charm
līctor līctōr-is 3m.
magistrate's attendant,
lictor
Lilybae-um ī 2n.
Lilybaeum (locative
Lilybaeī)
loquerētur (impf. subj. of
loquor 3 dep.) '(he)
talked'
morior 3/4 dep. *mortuus* I
die
nēue 'and (that x should)
not . . .'
nihilōminus nevertheless
nocturn-us a um night-
time, nocturnal

persuādeō 2 *persuāsī* I
persuade x (dat.) (to:
ut+subj.; not to
nē+subj.)
pertineō (ad) 2 I am
relevant (to)
proxim-us a um nearest
quā in causā
and in this case
quibus 'to whom', 'before
whom'
quibus modīs '(and) by
these means'
respondēret (impf. subj. of
respondeō respondēre)
'(to) reply', '(that) he
should reply'
salūs salūt-is 3f. safety
sanguis sanguin-is 3m.
blood
sēmimortu-us a um half-
dead
Seruīli-us ī 2m. Servilius
Sexti-us ī 2m. Sextius
sit (pres. subj. of *sum*)
'(to) be' '(that) it
should be'
soci-us ī 2m. ally
tacēret (impf. subj. of *taceō
tacēre*) '(and not to) be
silent' '(and that) he
should (not) be silent'
testis test-is 3m. witness
tunderet (impf. subj. of
tundō tundere) '(to) beat'
'(that) he should beat'
tundō 3 I beat
uehementer strongly
Venere-us a um devoted to
Venus

Venus Vener-is 3f. Venus
ueníret (impf. subj. of
uenió ueníre) '(to) come'
'(that) he should come'
uenustás uenustát-is 3f.
elegance, desirability

uerber uerber-is 3n. blow
uirg-a ae 1f. rod (symbol
of a lictor's authority
when bound in a
bundle (also called
fascés))

uót-um í 2n. vow
ut (+subj.) 'to . . .', 'that
. . . should'

Learning vocabulary for 4F(i)

Nouns

caus-a ae 1f. case; reason
líctor líctór-is 3m.
magistrate's attendant,
lictor

salús salút-is 3f. safety
sanguis sanguin-is 3m.
blood

testis test-is 3m. witness
uerber uerber-is 3n. blow;
whip

Adjectives

proxim-us a um nearest;
next

Verbs

abició abicere abiécí abiectus
I throw down/away
accidit 3 *accidit* (*ut/ut
nón* +subj.) it happens
(that/that not)

concidó 3 *concidí* I fall,
collapse; am killed
morior 3/4 dep. *mortuus* I
die, am dying

persuádeó 2 *persuásí
persuásum* I persuade x
(dat.) (*ut/né* +subj.
'that/that . . . not' 'to
. . ./not to')

Others

ad (+acc.) for the pur-
pose of (towards; at)
dé (+abl.) from; down
from, (about,
concerning)

néue 'and (that x should)
not . . .' 'and not to'
uehementer strongly

ut (+subj.) 'to . . .' 'that
. . . should' (negative
né 'not to . . .' 'that
. . . should not')

Running vocabulary for 4F(ii)

á quó by whom
agó 3 I drive
ardeó 2 I blaze
atróciter appallingly
audíretur (impf. subj. pass.
of *audió audíre*) '(it) was
heard'

caedant (pres. subj. of
caedó 3) '(to) beat'
'(that) they should
beat'
caedátur (pres. subj. pass.
of *caedó* 3) 'should be
beaten'

caederet (impf. subj. of
caedó caedere) '(not to)
beat' '(that) he should
(not) beat'
caederétur (impf. subj.
pass. of *caedó caedere*)
'(he) was beaten'

273

clāmāret (impf. subj. of clāmō clāmāre) '(he) was shouting'

cognitor cognitōr-is 3m. one who would know him, a referee

comparārētur (impf. subj. pass. of comparō comparāre) '(it) was obtained/prepared'

Cōnsān-us a um from Consa [See map in Text]

crūdēlitās crūdēlitāt-is 3f. cruelty

crux cruc-is 3f. cross

deferrētur (impf. subj. pass. of dēferō dēferre) '(it) should be reported'

dēlātūrum sc. esse

dēligent (pres. subj. of dēligō 1) '(that) they should bind' '(to) bind'

dēligētur (pres. subj. pass. of dēligō 1) '(that) he should be bound'

ēmineō 2 I project, stand out

eques equit-is 3m. 'knight' (Roman business class)

furor furōr-is 3m. rage, fury

Gaui-us ī 2m. Gavius

itūrum sc. esse

lautumi-ae ārum 1f. pl. stone quarries

Lūci-us Raeci-us ī 2m. Lucius Raecius (a Roman eques)

medi-us a um middle (of)

Messān-a ae 1f. Messana (city on E. coast of Sicily)

minitor 1 dep. I threaten (+ dat.)

modo only

nōmināret (impf. subj. of nōminō nōmināre) '(he) was naming'

nūdent (pres. subj. of nūdō nūdāre) '(to) strip' '(that) they should strip'

nūdētur (pres. subj. pass. of nūdō nūdāre) '(that) he should be stripped'

ōs ōr-is 3n. face

parceret (impf. subj. of parcō parcere) '(to) spare' '(that) he should spare'

perficiō 3/4 perfēcī ut + subj. I bring it about that

profugeret (impf. subj. of profugiō profugere) 'he escaped'

peruenīret (impf. subj. of perueniō peruenīre) 'arrived'

queror 3 dep. questus I complain

quibus uerbīs 'and these words' (object of ūsus)

quō (ll. 283, 287) 'to which place' tr. '(and) there'

quō in locō 'in which (= this) place'

retrahō 3 retrāxī retractus I drag back

Sertōri-us ī 2m. Sertorius (opponent of Sulla (the former dictator) who led resistance to the regime from Spain and attracted Romans and local Spaniards to his cause)

uenīret (impf. subj. of ueniō uenīre) '(he) came'

uinc(u)l-um ī 2n. chain, bond

uirg-a ae 1f. rod

Learning vocabulary for 4F(ii)

Nouns

furor furōr-is 3m. rage, fury; madness

ōs ōr-is 3n. face; mouth

uinc(u)l-um ī 2n. chain, bond

Adjectives

medi-us a um middle (of)

Verbs

agō 3 *ēgī āctus* I drive, lead, direct (do, act)
nūdō 1 I strip

perficiō 3/4 *perfēcī perfectus* *ut/ut nōn* + subj. I bring it about that/that not; (finish, complete, carry out)

profugiō 3/4 *profūgī* I escape, flee away

Others

modo only
nōn modo . . . sed etiam

not only . . . but also (also *nōn sōlum . . . sed etiam*)

Grammar and exercises for 4F

27   Present subjunctive active

	1	2	3	4	3/4
1st s.	ám-e-m	hábe-a-m	díc-a-m	aúdi-a-m	cápi-a-m
2nd s.	ám-ē-s	hábe-ā-s	díc-ā-s	aúdi-ā-s	cápi-ā-s
3rd s.	ám-e-t	hábe-a-t	díc-a-t	aúdi-a-t	cápi-a-t
1st pl.	am-é-mus	habe-á-mus	dīc-á-mus	audi-á-mus	capi-á-mus
2nd pl.	am-é-tis	habe-á-tis	dīc-á-tis	audi-á-tis	capi-á-tis
3rd pl.	ám-e-nt	hábe-a-nt	díc-a-nt	aúdi-a-nt	cápi-a-nt

Notes

1 Observe the regular personal endings *-m -s -t -mus -tis -nt*.
2 The key vowel in conjs. 2–3/4 is *A* while in 1st conj. it is *E* (to distinguish it from the indicative). One could summarise the present subjunctive with the following chart:

     1   2   3   4   3/4
     E   EA   A   IA   IA

3 There is no way of distinguishing between *dīcam* meaning 'I shall say' (future) and *dīcam* as the subjunctive except by context. The same goes for *audiam* and *capiam*.
4 Particular attention should be paid to the learning of which conjugation each verb belongs to, since the *subjunctive endings of 1st conj.* are almost identical to the *present indicative endings of 2nd conj.* (cf. *amem amēs amet* with *habeō habēs habet* etc.), whilst the *subjunctive endings of the 3rd conj.* are almost the same as those of the *indicative endings of the 1st conj.* (cf. *dīcam dīcās dīcat* with *amō amās amat* etc.).

128   Present subjunctive deponent

	1	2	3
1st s.	mín-e-r	pollíce-a-r	lóqu-a-r
2nd s.	min-ḗ-ris (-re)	pollice-ā́-ris (-re)	loqu-ā́-ris (-re)
3rd s.	min-ḗ-tur	pollice-ā́-tur	loqu-ā́-tur
1st pl.	min-ḗ-mur	pollice-ā́-mur	loqu-ā́-mur
2nd pl.	min-ḗ-minī	pollice-ā́-minī	loqu-ā́-minī
3rd pl.	min-é-ntur	pollice-á-ntur	loqu-á-ntur

	4	3/4
1st s.	ménti-a-r	prōgrédi-a-r
2nd s.	menti-ā́-ris (-re)	prōgredi-ā́-ris (-re)
3rd s.	menti-ā́-tur	prōgredi-ā́-tur
1st pl.	menti-ā́-mur	prōgredi-ā́-mur
2nd pl.	menti-ā́-minī	prōgredi-ā́-minī
3rd pl.	menti-á-ntur	prōgredi-á-ntur

Notes

1 Observe the regular personal endings *-r -ris (-re) -tur -mur -minī -ntur*
2 For notes on regularities and ambiguities, see notes 2–4 of the active above.

129   Present subjunctive passive

	1	2	3
1st s.	ám-e-r	hábe-a-r	dī́c-a-r
2nd s.	am-ḗ-ris (-re)	habe-ā́-ris (-re)	dīc-ā́-ris (-re)
3rd s.	am-ḗ-tur	habe-ā́-tur	dīc-ā́-tur
1st pl.	am-ḗ-mur	habe-ā́-mur	dīc-ā́-mur
2nd pl.	am-ḗ-minī	habe-ā́-minī	dīc-ā́-minī
3rd pl.	am-é-ntur	habe-á-ntur	dīc-á-ntur

	4	3/4
1st s.	aúdi-a-r	cápi-a-r
2nd s.	audi-ā́-ris (-re)	capi-ā́-ris (-re)
3rd s.	audi-ā́-tur	capi-ā́-tur
1st pl.	audi-ā́-mur	capi-ā́-mur
2nd pl.	audi-ā́-minī	capi-ā́-minī
3rd pl.	audi-á-ntur	capi-á-ntur

Notes

1 See under deponent (above) for notes.

2 Learn these irregular subjunctives:

	sum	*possum*	*uolō*	*nōlō*	*mālō*
1st s.	s-i-m	pós-sim	uél-i-m	nôl-i-m	mâl-i-m
2nd s.	s-î-s	pós-sîs	uél-î-s	nôl-î-s	mâl-î-s
3rd s.	s-i-t	pós-sit	uél-i-t	nôl-i-t	mâl-i-t
1st pl.	s-î-mus	pos-sîmus	uel-í-mus	nōl-í-mus	māl-í-mus
2nd pl.	s-î-tis	pos-sîtis	uel-í-tis	nōl-í-tis	māl-í-tis
3rd pl.	s-i-nt	pós-sint	uél-i-nt	nôl-i-nt	mâl-i-nt

3 The subjunctive of *eō* is regular: *e-a-m, e-ā-s* etc.

130 Imperfect subjunctive active

	1	*2*	*3*	*4*	*3/4*
1st s.	amâre-m	habére-m	dícere-m	audíre-m	cápere-m
2nd s.	amârē-s	habérē-s	dícerē-s	audírē-s	cáperē-s
3rd s.	amâre-t	habére-t	dícere-t	audíre-t	cápere-t
1st pl.	amārê-mus	habērê-mus	dīcerê-mus	audīrê-mus	caperê-mus
2nd pl.	amārê-tis	habērê-tis	dīcerê-tis	audīrê-tis	caperê-tis
3rd pl.	amâre-nt	habére-nt	dícere-nt	audíre-nt	cápere-nt

Notes

1 Remember the imperfect subjunctive as formed from the present infinitive plus the personal endings. Thus *amāre-m amārē-s* etc. Even irregulars follow this rule, e.g. *sum→esse→essem; eō→īre→īrem; ferō→ferre→ferrem*; cf. *uellem, nōllem, māllem, possem.* Cf. pluperfect subjunctive active, **121**[1].

2 Note the alternative impf. subjunctive of *sum: fore-m, forē-s, fore-t* etc. (formed from the future inf. *fore*: see **97**[3]).

131 Imperfect subjunctive deponent

	1	*2*	*3*
1st s.	minâre-r	pollicére-r	lóquere-r
2nd s.	minārê-ris (-re)	pollicērê-ris (-re)	loquerê-ris (-re)
3rd s.	minārê-tur	pollicērê-tur	loquerê-tur
1st pl.	minārê-mur	pollicērê-mur	loquerê-mur
2nd pl.	minārê-minī	pollicērê-minī	loquerê-minī
3rd pl.	mināré-ntur	pollicēré-ntur	loquerê-ntur

	4	*3/4*
1st s.	mentíre-r	prōgrédere-r
2nd s.	mentīrḗ-ris (-re)	prōgrederḗ-ris (-re)
3rd s.	mentīrḗ-tur	prōgrederḗ-tur
1st pl.	mentīrḗ-mur	prōgrederḗ-mur
2nd pl.	mentīrḗ-minī	prōgrederḗ-minī
3rd pl.	mentīré-ntur	prōgrederé-ntur

NB. The imperfect deponent subjunctive may be regarded as formed by taking a hypothetical ACTIVE infinitive, and adding the deponent personal endings, e.g. not *minārī* but *mināre* giving *mināre-r -ris -tur* etc. Likewise with *pollicērī→pollicēre-r, loquī→loquere-r, mentīrī→mentīre-r, prōgredī→prōgredere-r.*

132 Imperfect subjunctive passive

	1	*2*	*3*
1st s.	amā́re-r	habḗre-r	dī́cere-r
2nd s.	amārḗ-ris (-re)	habērḗ-ris (-re)	dīcerḗ-ris (-re)
3rd s.	amārḗ-tur	habērḗ-tur	dīcerḗ-tur
1st pl.	amārḗ-mur	habērḗ-mur	dīcerḗ-mur
2nd pl.	amārḗ-minī	habērḗ-minī	dīcerḗ-minī
3rd pl.	amāré-ntur	habēré-ntur	dīceré-ntur

	4	*3/4*
1st s.	audī́re-r	cápere-r
2nd s.	audīrḗ-ris (-re)	caperḗ-ris (-re)
3rd s.	audīrḗ-tur	caperḗ-tur
1st pl.	audīrḗ-mur	caperḗ-mur
2nd pl.	audīrḗ-minī	caperḗ-minī
3rd pl.	audīré-ntur	caperé-ntur

For notes, see deponent (above).

133 Summary of subjunctive forms

Present subjunctive

Present stem + key vowel + personal endings. Key vowels: 1st conj. *-e-*, 2nd, 3rd, 4th, 3rd/4th *-a-*. Personal endings, active: *-m -s -t* etc.; deponent/ passive: *-r -ris (-re) -tur* etc. Irregular: *sim, uēlim, nōlim, mālim, possim.*

Imperfect subjunctive

Active infinitive + personal endings (active: *-m -s -t* etc.; deponent/ passive: *-r/-ris* (*-re*) *-tur* etc.)

Deponent verbs are constructed on a hypothetical active infinitive, e.g.

1st conj. *mināri* becomes *mināre-*
2nd conj. *pollicēri* becomes *pollicēre-*
3rd conj. *loqui* becomes *loquere-*
4th conj. *mentiri* becomes *mentire-*
3rd/4th conj. *prōgredi* becomes *prōgredere-*

Exercises

Morphology

1 *Form and conjugate the present and imperfect subjunctive of these verbs (where '(passive)' is written, give active* and *passive; for other active verbs give only active tenses):* concidō, hortor, morior, sum, timeō, auferō (*passive*), reuocō (*passive*), nāuigō, (*optional:* abiciō (*passive*), cōnor, egeō, uolō, dēsum, perlegō (*passive*), excōgitō, ūtor).

2 *Say which of these verbs is subjunctive, which indicative or infinitive (state tense of all verbs):* clāmet, amat, dormīret, auferret, cōnspicātus esse, cōnāti essent, dat, dīcētur, excōgitat, cūret, nescīrem, cupīuisse, loquitur, abstulisset, moneāris, accidat, aget, persuādet, perficiās, (*optional:* commorātur, moriātur, placēret, redībat, rogāssent, conciderēmus, accūsētis, parcēmus, profūgisse, nītātur, proficīscitur, oppugnantur, uocant, uincant, uincientur, uocāuissētis).

3 *Form 3rd s. of present, imperfect and pluperfect indicative and subjunctive of these verbs (where '(passive)' is written, give active* and *passive; for other active verbs give only active tenses):* agō (*passive*), perficiō, commoror, līberō (*passive*), iaceō, sequor, nōlō, accidit, (*optional:* īnspiciō (*passive*), circumeō, mālō, ōrō, persuādeō, recordor, patior, caedō (*passive*)).

134 Indirect (reported) commands *ut/nē* + subjunctive

Observe the following sentences:

(a) *Caesar imperat mīlitibus ut prōgrediantur* 'Caesar gives orders to the soldiers that they should advance' or 'to advance'.

(b)   *eōs hortātus sum nē hoc facerent* 'I urged them that they should not do this' or 'not to do this'.

(c)   *mihi persuādēbit ut sēcum ambulem* 'he will persuade me that I should walk with him' or 'to walk with him'.

To express these *reported* commands (the original command of (a) was 'Soldiers, advance!', of (b) 'Do not do this' etc.), Latin commonly adopts the form 'that x should' (*ut* + subjunctive) or 'that-not x should' (*nē* + subjunctive).

English does use this construction with verbs like e.g. ordain (e.g. 'he ordained that I should go'), though English more commonly uses the straight 'to / not to' form: e.g. (a) above is most easily translated 'Caesar gives orders to the soldiers to advance'.

Translate literally to start with, then convert to normal English.

Which verbs take ut/nē?

hortor + *ut*/*nē* 'I urge x (acc.) that he should / should not'

ōrō + *ut*/*nē* 'I beg x (acc.) that he should / should not'

imperō + *ut*/*nē* 'I give orders to x (dat.) that he should / should not'

persuādeō + *ut*/*nē* 'I persuade x (dat.) that he should / should not'

petō + *ut*/*nē* 'I beg *ā*/*ab* x (abl.) that he should / should not'

postulō + *ut*/*nē* 'I demand *ā*/*ab* x (abl.) that he should / should not'

rogō + *ut*/*nē* 'I ask x (acc.) that he should / should not'

moneō 'I advise', *obsecrō* 'I beseech', *precor* 'I pray' also take *ut*/*nē*.

Exceptions

iubeō 'I order' and *uetō* 'I forbid', 'tell x *not* to' both, like English, usually take a plain present infinitive. Compare:

iubeō tē abīre
imperō tibi ut abeās } 'I order you to go'

uetō uōs manēre
imperō uōbis nē maneātis } 'I tell you not to stay'

Notes

1 The subjunctive will be *present* when the main verb is 'primary', *imperfect* when it is 'secondary/historic' (see **A–G Intro. (a)**).

2 Any reference, inside the *ut*/*nē* clause, to subject of main verb will be *reflexive*, e.g.

> *Caesar imperat nōbīs ut sibi pāreāmus* 'Caesar gives orders to us to obey him (= Caesar)'

3 Note that 'that no-one' = *nē quis*, 'that nothing' = *nē quid*, e.g.

> *imperat nē quis exeat* 'he orders that no-one should go out'

For the forms of *quis* (indefinite) see **I4**. Cf. 'that never' = *nē umquam*; 'that none', 'not any' = *nē ūllus*; 'that nowhere' = *nē usquam*.

Exercises

1 *Translate these sentences (remember* ut + *indicative means 'as' or 'when' and that* ut *may be used without a verb to mean 'as'):*

(a) Verrēs Seruīliō persuāsit ut Lilybaeum adīret.
(b) Seruīlius, ut Lilybaeum peruēnit, ā līctōribus caesus est.
(c) Verrēs līctōribus imperāuerat ut uirum caederent.
(d) Seruīlius, ut cīuis Rōmānus, Verrem ōrat nē sē caedat nēue necet.
(e) ut Verrēs cīuīs Rōmānōs caedit, ita ipsum affirmō ā cīuibus Rōmānīs caesum īrī.
(f) Verrēs seruōs quōsdam hortātur nē Seruīliō parcant nēue ōrantī auxilium dent.

2 *Translate the underlined words into Latin (using* ut/nē + *subjunctive); take care to get the correct sequence (see* **134**[1]):

(a) Verres orders Servilius <u>to come to Lilybaeum</u>.
(b) I beg you (*pl.*) <u>not to go away</u>.
(c) Verres ordered <u>the lictors to beat Servilius</u>.
(d) In the end Verres persuaded Servilius <u>not to keep quiet</u>.
(e) How can I persuade you <u>to believe me?</u>
(f) I ordain[1] <u>that no one shall escape and that you (*pl.*) shall not go away.</u>

[1] *dēcernō 3.*

35 *accidit, perficiō ut* + **subjunctive**

accidit ut (*nōn*) 'it happens that (not)', and *perficiō ut* (*nōn*) (and *nē*) 'I bring it about that (not)' are followed by the subjunctive, e.g.

accidit ut perfugeret 'it happened that he escaped' (= so-called 'result' clause – see **144**)

perficiam ut effugiam 'I shall bring it about that I escape' (= so-called 'purpose' clause – see **145**).

In primary sequence the subjunctive is *present*; in secondary, *perfect* (still to be met) or *imperfect*.

Exercises

1 *Translate these sentences (take care to check the tense of subjunctive in clauses introduced by* accidit, *since* accidit *may be present or perfect)*:

(a)　accidit ut Seruīlius dē Verris nēquitiā paulō līberius loquātur.
(b)　Verrēs perfēcit ut Seruīlius Lilybaeum adīret.
(c)　accidit ut Seruīlius, cum Lilybaeum peruēnisset, ā līctōribus caederētur.
(d)　Gauius, cum in uinclīs Syrācūsīs esset, dīxit sē perfectūrum ut profugeret Messānamque peruenīret.
(e)　Verrēs perficiet ut cīuēs Rōmānī necentur.

2 *Prefix each of these statements with* perficiam ut (*following rules for primary sequence*) *and* accidit ut (*following rules for secondary sequence*). *You will thus need to change the verbs to present subjunctive (for* perficiam ut) *and imperfect (for* accidit ut). *Translate the new sentences*:

(a)　Verrēs Lilybaeum adit.
(b)　uir ā līctōribus caeditur.
(c)　seruī eum ad terram abiciunt.
(d)　uerberibus moritur.
(e)　sociī Rōmam profugiunt.

136　Present participle

When a participle is used on its own, and in agreement with no other word, there are two ways in which it may be being used:

(a)　As a noun 'a/the person —ing', e.g.

> *iacet corpus <u>dormientis ut mortuī</u>* 'The body <u>of a person sleeping</u> lies like (that) <u>of a dead person</u>' (Cicero)

Cf. *moritūrī tē salūtant* 'men about to die salute you'

(b) Agreeing with a noun or pronoun which has been left out, referring to a person already mentioned, e.g.

haec dīcentis latus hastā trānsfixit 'He pierced with a spear the side of (the man) as he was saying this' (Curtius). Note that 'the man' must be known to us already (he has just spoken *haec*).

37 Relative pronoun (dat. and abl.)

1 *cui* and *quibus* (dat.) normally mean 'to whom, for whom', e.g.

puer cui pecūniam dedī 'the boy to whom I gave the money'

But since the verb in the relative clause may control a dative, or require a dative of disadvantage etc, it will usually be necessary to 'hold' the relative pronoun until it is 'solved' by the construction, e.g.

nāuis cui praeerat Phӯlarchus 'the ship of which Phylarchus was in charge' (because *praesum* 'I am in charge of' takes a dat.)
uir cui Verrēs pōcula abstulerat 'the man from whom Verres had taken the cups' (because *auferō* has its meaning completed by a dative of disadvantage)

2 *quō/quā* and *quibus* (abl.) bear a very wide range of meanings, but 'by', 'with', 'in/at' and 'from' should all be kept in mind. It will often be necessary to 'hold' the abl. relative pronoun until 'solved' by the construction (as with the dative). E.g.

incendium quō urbs incēnsa est 'the fire by which the city was burned'
genus quō nātus erat 'the family from which he was born'
celeritās quā nāuem cēpit 'the speed with which he took the ship'

Bear in mind again that some verbs put *objects* in the ablative, e.g.

cōnsilium quō ūsus sum 'the plan which I used' ('which' is object of *ūtor*; *ūtor* takes the abl.)

3 *quō* very often means '(to) where'; *quā* can mean 'where'.

Reading exercise / Test exercise

Gauius hic, quem dīcō, Cōnsānus, cum in illō numerō cīuium Rōmānōrum ab istō in uincla coniectus esset et nesciō quā ratiōne clam ē

lautumiīs profūgisset Messānamque uēnisset, quī tam prope iam Italiam
et moenia Rēgīnōrum, cīuium Rōmānōrum, uidēret, et ex illō metū
mortis ac tenebrīs quasi lūce lībertātis et odōre aliquō lēgum recreātus   5
reuīxisset, loquī Messānae et querī coepit sē cīuem Rōmānum in uincla
coniectum, sibi rēctā iter esse Rōmam, Verrī sē praestō aduenientī
futūrum. (*Cicero, in Verrem II 5, 61.160 (original of* **F(ii)**))

Cōnsān-us a um from Consa
nesciō quis (lit. 'I do not know who')
  some (or other)
quī + subj. = 'since he'
Itali-a ae 1f. Italy
Rēgīn-ī ōrum 2m. pl. inhabitants of
  Rhegium (on the toe of Italy)
5 *tenebr-ae ārum* 1f. pl. darkness, shadows
quasi as if
lūx lūc-is 3f. light
lībertās lībertāt-is 3f. liberty
odor odōr-is 3m. smell, scent

recreāt-us a um renewed
reuīuō 3 reuīxī I revive, come back to
  life
Messānae: locative of *Messān-a ae* 1f.
  Messana
queror 3 dep. I complain
coniectum: understand *esse*
rēctā directly
iter itiner-is 3n. way, route
praestō 'to face' (+ dat. + part of *esse*)
adueniō 4 I arrive
futūrum: understand *esse*

English–Latin

Read the text of **4F(ii)** *again and translate this passage into Latin*:

Verres had thrown into chains a man whose name was Gavius[1]. This[2]
Gavius had managed to escape and arrive at Messana[3]. He declared that
he would accuse Verres at Rome. Verres, however, when he had heard
this, ordered his slaves to capture the man. They[4] dragged him back as he
was embarking[5] and took him to the magistrate. When Verres had
arrived at Messana[3], he gave orders that Gavius be stripped in the middle
of the forum and beaten. The lictors did not spare the man[5] although he
was begging and kept asserting[5] that he was a Roman citizen. In this way
it happened that a Roman citizen was murdered by Verres.

[1] Use dative with *sum*. Remember that the idiom is to put the name into dative also.
[2] 'This': use connecting relative.
[3] 'at Messana': use accusative, since movement towards is indicated, although English idiom is
different.
[4] 'They': change of subject; use part of *ille*.
[5] 'him as he was embarking': use present participle on its own; 'the man although he was begging and
kept asserting': use present participles and join 'begging' to 'kept asserting' with *et* or *-que*.

Rēs gestae dīuī Augustī

quī parentem meum trucīdāuērunt, eōs in exsilium expulī iūdiciīs
lēgitimīs ultus eōrum facinus, et posteā bellum īnferentīs rēī pūblicae uīcī
bis aciē.

    bella terrā et marī cīuīlia externaque tōtō in orbe terrārum saepe gessī,
uictorque omnibus ueniam petentibus cīuibus pepercī. externās gentīs,   5
quibus tūtō ignōscī potuit, cōnseruāre quam excīdere māluī. in triumphīs
meīs ductī sunt ante currum meum rēgēs aut rēgum līberī nouem.

    cum ex Hispāniā Galliāque, rēbus in iīs prōuinciīs prosperē gestīs,
Rōmam rediī, Ti. Nerōne P. Quīntiliō cōnsulibus, āram Pācis Augustae
senātus prō reditū meō cōnsacrandam cēnsuit ad campum Mārtium, in   10
quā magistrātūs et sacerdōtēs uirginēsque Vestālēs anniuersārium
sacrificium facere iussit.

    Iānum Quirīnum, quem claussum esse maiōrēs nostrī uoluērunt cum
per tōtum imperium populī Rōmānī terrā marīque esset parta uictōriīs
pāx, cum, priusquam nāscerer, ā conditā urbe bis omnīnō clausum fuisse   15
prodātur memoriae, ter mē prīncipe senātus claudendum esse cēnsuit.

    lēgibus nouīs mē auctōre lātīs, multa exempla maiōrum exolēscentia
iam ex nostrō saeculō redūxī et ipse multārum rērum exempla imitanda
posterīs trādidī. (Rēs gestae *2–4, 12–13, 8*)

---

quī [To be picked up by *eōs*]
parentem [I.e. Julius Caesar (by adoption)]
trucīdō 1 I slaughter
exsili-um ī 2n. exile
expellō 3 *expulī* I drive out
iūdici-um ī 2n. tribunal [But why dat./abl.? Hold]
lēgitim-us a um legal
ulcīscor 3 *ultus* I punish [Explains *iūdiciīs* – the means by which he acted]
posteā afterwards
bellum [Nom. or acc.? Wait]
īnferō 3 I bring, wage x (acc.) against y (dat.) [Participle, so possibly 'waging war'. Case is acc. pl. (*-īs*). Does it agree with anyone? Yes, with *eōs* 'them', which is not repeated. So it must mean 'them waging war' – in the acc.]
rēī pūblicae [Must surely be dat. after *bellum īnferō*]

uīcī [Subject and verb, explaining why *īnferentīs* is acc.]
bis twice
aciēs aciē-ī 5f. battle-line [Why abl.?]
bella [Nom. or acc. pl.? Wait]
cīuīl-is e civil
extern-us a um foreign
orbis orb-is 3m. (*terrārum*) the world
5 *uictor uictōr-is* 3m. victor
omnibus [Dat. or abl. pl.? And who are these 'all'?]
ueni-a ae 1f. pardon
petentibus [What are the 'all' doing?]
cīuibus [Ah. Who the 'all' are]
parcō 3 *pepercī* I spare (+ dat.) [Explains *omnibus . . . cīuibus*]
gēns gent-is 3f. nation [*externās* confirms it must be acc., so wait]
quibus . . . potuit lit. 'to whom it could safely be pardoned' i.e. 'whom one could pardon safely'
cōnseruō 1 I protect, preserve

quam than [Await verb taking
  infinitive + *quam*]
excīdō 3 I exterminate
triumph-us ī 2m. triumph
ductī sunt ['some masculine plurals
  were led': wait to find out who]
curr-us ūs 4m. chariot
līber-ī ōrum 2m. pl. children
nouem nine
cum [Followed by ablative? No. So
  'when', 'since', 'although']
Hispāni-a ae 1f. Spain
Galli-a ae 1f. Gaul
rēbus . . . gestīs [Looks suspiciously like
  an abl. abs., and so it is]
prosperē successfully
Nerō Nerōn-is 3m. Nero
Quīntili-us ī 2m. Quintilius [i.e. the
  year 13]
ār-a ae 1f. *Pācis* altar of peace [Why
  acc.? Wait]
August-us a um of Augustus
10 *redit-us ūs* 4m. return
cōnsacrandam (esse) 'should be
  consecrated' [Acc. and (inf.) after
  cēnsuit. Since *cōnsacrand-am* is acc. s.
  f., it must agree with *āram*]
cēnseō 2 I vote
camp-us Mārti-us camp-ī Mārt-ī 2m. the
  Campus Martius (of Mars), in Rome
  [*in quā* (f.), so refers back to what?]
magistrāt-us ūs 4m. magistrate [But
  nom. or acc. pl.? Do any of the
  following nouns (to *Vestālēs*) tell
  you definitely?]
sacerdōs sacerdōt-is 3m. or f. priest(ess)
uirgō Vestālis uirgin-is Vestāl-is 3f. + 3
  adj. Vestal Virgin [Still problem
  whether these nom. or acc., so
  continue to hold]
anniuersāri-us a um yearly
sacrifici-um ī 2n. sacrifice [Also nom. or
  acc., so hold!]
iussit [Singular. So *magistrātūs . . .
  uestālēs* cannot be the subject. A
  'yearly sacrifice' cannot 'order'. So
  'senate' must be the understood
  subject from the previous clause.]

Hence 'on which the senate
  ordered . . .']
Iān-us ī Quirīn-us ī 2m. the archway
  (or arched passage) of Janus
  Quirinus in the forum, with doors
  at both ends, forming the god's
  shrine [Why acc.? Hold, till the end
  of the sentence]
claudō 3 *clausī claus(s)us* I close
maiōrēs maiōr-um 3m. pl. ancestors
pariō 3/4 *peperī partus* I win, gain
  [Hold *parta*]
uictoriīs [Abl. of means after *parta*]
15 *pāx* [Solves *parta*]
cum although
priusquam [+ subj.) before
nāscor 3 dep. I am born
condita urbs the founded city i.e. the
  foundation of the city
bis twice
omnīnō in all
prōdō 3 I transmit x (acc.) to y (dat.)
  [The dative is given by *memoriae* 'to
  history/memory': but what is the
  subject of *cum prodātur*? No subject
  is quoted, so try 'it', i.e. 'although it
  is transmitted to memory/history',
  when *clausum fuisse* becomes acc.
  and inf., i.e. 'that (it) had been
  closed']
ter thrice
claudendum esse 'that it should be
  closed' [What is 'it'? Back to the
  start of the sentence − *Iānum
  Quirīnum*]
nou-us a um new
auctor auctōr-is 3m. initiator
exempl-um ī 2n. example
maiōrēs maiōr-um 3m. pl. ancestors
exolēscō 3 I go out of fashion
saecul-um ī 2n. age
redūcō 3 *redūxī* I bring back
imitanda 'to be copied' [Refers to
  exempla. But still hold case]
poster-ī ōrum 2m. pl. future generations
trādō 3 *trādidī* I hand down x (acc.) to
  y (dat.)

Deliciae Latinae

(Word-building, word exercises and everyday Latin sections are no longer supplied. From now on there will be further reading in real Latin in the *Dēliciae Latīnae* sections.)

Martial

ut recitem tibi nostra rogās epigrammata. nōlō.
 nōn audīre, Celer, sed recitāre cupīs. (*1.63*)

recitō 1 I read out loud,   *epigramma epigrammat-is*
 recite my own poetry   3n. epigram

Elio Giulio Crotti *c.* 1564

NARCISSUS

(*who fell in love with himself, looking at his reflection in a pool*)

hicne amor est? hicne est furor? aut īnsānia mentis?
 nōlo, uolō, atque iterum nōlō, iterumque uolō.
hicne gelū est? hicne est ignis? nam spīritus aequē
 mī ignēscit, gelidō⌐ et torpet in ⌐ōre anima.
uērum nōn amor aut furor est, ignisue gelūue: 5
 ipse ego sum, quī mē mī ēripuī ac rapuī.

amor amōr-is 3m. love
īnsāni-a ae 1f. madness
mēns ment-is 3f. mind
gelū n. ice
spīrit-us ūs 4m. spirit
aequē equally
mī = mihi (dat. of advantage/
 disadvantage)

ignēscō 3 I catch fire
gelid-us a um cold
torpeō 2 I am numb
anim-a ae 1f. breath
5 *-ue* or
ēripiō 3/4 *ēripuī* I tear x (acc.) away
 from Y (dat.)
rapiō 3/4 *rapuī* I seize, snatch

Notes
1 Crotti uses much elision (cutting off a final vowel before a following vowel). In l. 1 *hicn(e) est*; l. 2 *atqu(e) iterum*, *nōl(ō) iterumque*; l. 3 *gel(ū) est*, *hicn(e) est*; l. 4 *m(ī) ignēscit*, *gelid(ō) et* . . . *ōr(e) anima*; l. 6 *ips(e) ego* . . . *m(ī) ēripu(ī) ac* . . .
2 He also shortens a long vowel in l. 2: *nŏlo* for *nōlō*.
3 See p. 318 for rules of Latin metre and **185** for the elegiac couplet (the metre Crotti uses here).

Section 4G

Running vocabulary for 4G(i)

āctum [Understand *esse*: perf. inf. pass.]
adesset '(he) were present' (impf. subj. of *adsum*)
anteā before (adv.)
archipīrāt-a ae 1m. chief pirate
assecūtūrum [Understand *esse*: fut. inf.]
assequor 3 *assecūtus* I achieve, gain
at enim 'but, one may object'
audīret 'he were hearing' (impf. subj. of *audiō*)
captam [Understand *esse*: perf. inf. pass.]
cīuitās cīuitāt-is 3f. state
clāmēs 'would you shout' (pres. subj. of *clāmō*)
clāmitō 1 I keep on shouting
cōnfiteor 2 dep. I confess, acknowledge
cōnstituās 'you (s.) were to decide' (pres. subj. of *cōnstituō*)
content-us a um happy, satisfied
crux cruc-is 3f. cross
dīcās 'you (s.) were to say' (pres. subj. of *dīcō*)
dīceret 'would he be saying' (impf. subj. of *dīcō*)

dūcāris '(you) (s.) were to be led' (pres. subj. pass. of *dūcō*)
dulc-is e sweet
effugi-um ī 2n. escape
eximi-us a um excellent
extrēm-us a um farthest
futūram [Understand *esse*: fut. inf.]
Gaui-us ī 2m. Gavius
haereō 2 I stick
ignōscō 3 (+ dat.) I forgive
immortāl-is e immortal
incēnsam [Understand *esse*: perf. inf. pass.]
Indi-a ae 1f. India
iūdicāret 'he were judging' (impf. subj. of *iūdicō*)
iūs iūr-is 3n. law, justice
līberātum [Understand *esse*; perf. inf. pass.]
lībertās lībertāt-is 3f. freedom
mor-a ae 1f. delay
neglegenti-a ae 1f. carelessness
ō oh! [Exclamation]
obscūr-us a um undistinguished, mean
omittō 3 I pass over
ops op-is 3f. help
orbis (*orb-is* 3m.) *terrārum* the world
per (+ acc.) in the name of

percussōs [Understand *esse*: perf. inf. pass.]
Pers-ae ārum 1m. pl. the Persians
petō 3 I seek
possēs? 'would you (s.) be able?' (impf. subj. of *possum*)
posset? 'would he be able?' (impf. subj. of *possum*)
praeclūdās 'you (s.) would shut off' (pres. subj. of *praeclūdō* 3)
praesidi-um ī 2n. protection, defence [*praesidiō* predicative dat., lit. 'for a protection']
putēs 'you (s.) would think' (pres. subj. of *putō*)
quaerō 3 I seek, look for
rēgn-um ī 2n. kingdom
speculātor speculātōr-is 3m. spy
supplici-um ī 2n. punishment
tenu-is e small, humble
tollās 'you (s.) were to remove' (pres. subj. of *tollō*)
ueni-a ae 1f. pardon
uirg-a ae 1f. lictor's rod

Learning vocabulary for 4G(i)

Nouns

lībertās lībertāt-is 3f.
 freedom, liberty

mor-a ae 1f. delay
neglegenti-a ae 1f.
 carelessness

praesidi-um ī 2n.
 protection, defence,
 guard

Adjectives

immortāl-is e immortal

tūt-us a um safe

Verbs

clāmitō 1 I keep on
 shouting (= *clāmō* + *it-*)
cōnfiteor 2 dep. *cōnfessus* I
 confess, acknowledge

ignōscō 3 (+ dat.) *ignōuī*
 ignōtum I forgive
petō 3 *petīuī petītus* I seek

quaerō 3 *quaesīuī quaesītus*
 I seek, look for; ask

Others

anteā before (adv.: cf.
 ante)

per (+ acc.) in the name
 of (through, by)

Running vocabulary for 4G(ii)

---

appellō 1 I call
bēsti-a ae 1f. beast
caus-a ae 1f. cause
cīuitās cīuitāt-is 3f. state
cognitor cognitōr-is 3m. one
 who would support
 (him), referee
cognōsceret '(he) had
 recognised' (impf. subj.
 of *cognōscō*)
commouērentur '(they)
 would be moved'
 (impf. subj. of
 commoueō)
commūn-is e common
conqueror 3 dep. I
 complain of
cōnstituerēs 'you would
 have established' (impf.
 subj. of *cōnstituō*)
crux cruc-is 3f. cross
dēplōrō 1 I denounce

dīcam 'should I say' (pres.
 subj. of *dīcō*)
dign-us a um worthy
eques equit-is 3m. 'knight'
 (member of Roman
 business class)
Gaui-us ī 2m. Gavius
ignōrāret 'he had not
 known', 'he had been
 unacquainted with'
 (impf. subj. of *ignōrō* 1)
inanim-us a um inanimate
īnfest-us a um hateful,
 hostile
inimīc-us a um hostile,
 enemy
iūs iūr-is 3n. law, justice
Lūci-us ī 2m. Lucius
mūt-us a um mute, dumb
nōminō 1 I name
nou-us a um new

parricīdi-um ī 2n.
 parricide; treason
quamuīs (+ subj.)
 although
Raeci-us ī 2m. Raecius
remitterēs 'you would
 have remitted' (x (acc.)
 from y (*dē* + abl.))
 (impf. subj. of *remittō*)
supplici-um ī 2n.
 punishment; *summum*
 supplicium the death
 penalty
tollerēs 'you would have
 lifted' (impf. subj. of
 tollō)
uellem 'I were wishing'
 (impf. subj. of *uolō*)
uidērētur 'it had seemed
 right' (impf. subj. pass.
 of *uideō*)

Note

1. 334 *sed quid ego plūra dē Gauiō?* sc. *dīcam* (pres. subj.); tr. 'But why should I say more . . .'

Learning vocabulary for 4G(ii)

Nouns

caus-a ae 1f. cause; (case; reason)	*eques equit-is* 3m. 'knight'; (member of Roman business class) (horseman; pl. cavalry)	*iūs iūr-is* 3n. law, justice
cīuitās cīuitāt-is 3f. state		*supplici-um ī* 2n. punishment; *summum supplicium* the death penalty

Adjectives

inimīc-us a um hostile, enemy

nou-us a um new

Grammar and exercises for 4G

---

138 The subjunctive: special usages

Subjunctive means 'subordinated' (*subiungō subiūnctus* 'I join under'), and came to be used in clauses just because they were subordinate (e.g. *cum* + subjunctive **124**, which always took the indicative in early Latin, and does occasionally in classical). But it does have a specific meaning of its own: to simplify, it indicates that the speaker wants an action to take place (because he thinks it should or because it is his desire that it should) or that the speaker thinks it possible that under certain conditions it *could* take place. (Sometimes, but rarely, it indicates that the speaker expects the action to take place, but this function is normally carried out by the future indicative.)

Observe how the subjunctives met so far fit into these categories: indirect commands ('he ordered him to go': *ut/nē* + subjunctive) use the subjunctive to express the speaker's *will* that something should happen; 'it happens that' (*accidit ut (nōn)* + subjunctive) uses the subjunctive to indicate that *conditions make it possible* for x to happen; 'I bring it about that' (*perficiō ut/nē* + subjunctive) often expresses the speaker's *intentions* that something should happen.

9 Conditionals with subjunctive verbs ('if x were . . . y would')

Given the above functions of the subjunctive, it is not surprising that Latin uses the subjunctive in conditional sentences where the conditions stated are *unreal* or *unfulfilled*, i.e. they contain the words 'would' or 'should' in English. E.g.

> 'If I were rich, I would not (now) be working' (referring to present time)
> 'If I were to become rich, I would give all my money to the poor' (referring to future time)

Consider the Latin translations:

> *sī dīues essem, nōn labōrārem*
> *sī dīues fīam, omnem pecūniam pauperibus dem*

Observe that the imperfect subjunctive is used *in both clauses* where reference is to the present time, and the present subjunctive *in both clauses* where the reference is to the future time. Study the following examples and check this rule:

> *sī pater adesset, quid dīceret?* 'if father were (now) here, what would he (now) be saying?'
> *sī Verrī ignōscātis, nēmo uōbīs ignōscat* 'if you were to pardon Verres (some time in the future), no-one would pardon you'
> *sī fugiant, sequāmur* 'if they were to flee, we would follow'
> *sī mentīrēris, tē caederem* 'if you were (now) lying, I would (now) be beating you'

So the basic rules are:

> *sī* + subjunctive (followed by a main clause with subjunctive verb) indicates conditions with 'would' or 'should'
> *sī* + imperfect subjunctive (main clause verb in imperfect subjunctive): 'if x were (now) the case, y would (now) be the case'
> *sī* + present subjunctive (main clause verb in present subjunctive) 'if x were to be (in the future) the case, y would be the case'

We say 'basic' rules, because Latin is flexible and can mix subjunctive and indicative in these clauses.

Notes

1 *sī quis* = 'if anyone', e.g. *sī quis exeat, puniātur* 'if anyone were to go out, he would be punished' (cf. on *nē quis* **134³** and **145²**; forms **I4**).
2 *nisi* 'if not', 'unless' follows the same rules, e.g. *nisi pulcher essēs, tē nōn amārem* 'if you were not (now) so handsome, I would not (now) be in love with you'. *nisi quis* = 'unless anyone', see n.1 above.
3 In some instances, the imperfect subjunctives refer to the *past*, e.g. *sī Raecius cognōsceret hominem, aliquid . . . remitterēs* 'if Raecius had recognised the fellow, you would have remitted something'.
4 Quite often, a statement includes only the main clause of a condition omitting the *sī* clause, e.g. *uidērēs* 'you would have seen', *uelim* 'I would like'.

Exercises

Morphology/syntax

1 *Translate these sentences*:

(a) sī Verris pater adesset, fīlium suum cīuitātī nostrae hostem esse iūdicāret (*2 possibilities*).
(b) sī Verrī ignōscāmus, stultī sīmus.
(c) sī Verrēs mea pōcula postulet, ego sine morā ad eum litterās mittam.
(d) etiam animālia, sī haec audīrent, commouērentur (*2 possibilities*).
(e) nisi tē cīuem Rōmānum esse clāmitēs, necēris.
(f) sī hoc praesidium habērēs, etiam hostēs tibi parcerent (*2 possibilities*).
(g) sī esset prōuidentia, nūlla essent mala. (*Gellius*)
(h) uīna parant animum Venerī, nisi plūrima sūmās. (*Ovid*)

prōuidenti-a ae 1f.   *Venus Vener-is* 3f. Venus;   *sūmō* 3 I take
  foresight, providence   love-making
uīn-um ī 2n. wine

2 *Give the Latin for the following* (*remember reference to future 'were to' = present subjunctive, and 'would' also = present; 'were ——ing', 'were (now)' = imperfect subjunctive; 'would have' also = imperfect subjunctive*):

(a) If I were (*now*) a Roman citizen . . .
(b) If he were to demand protection . . .

(c) If there were not (*now*) a delay . . .
(d) If our friends were to be moved . . .
(e) If we were asking for protection . . .
(f) If I were to keep shouting . . .
(g) I would like to say . . .
(h) I would have liked to ask . . .
(i) I would have demanded . . .
(j) I would be moved . . .

0 Subjunctive in relative clauses

The subjunctive can be used in relative clauses as well, sometimes with virtually no change in meaning at all, but note the following specific usages:

1 Consecutive (so-called 'generic'): establishing conditions for possible action, especially common after (a) *est quī* / *sunt quī* 'there exists/exist the sort of person/people who', (b) *is quī* 'the sort of person who', e.g.

  (a) *sunt quī sciant* 'there are (those of the sort) who know'
  (b) *ea nōn est quae hoc faciat* 'she is not the one who does this' = 'not the sort of person who . . .'

2 Causal, i.e. the relative clause shows the *reason why* something is happening, e.g.

  sānus tū nōn es quī mē fūrem uocēs (Plautus) 'you are not sane who call me a thief' = 'because you call me a thief'

This usage is sometimes strongly 'signposted' by the addition of the fixed form *quippe* 'in as much as', e.g.

  sōlis candor inlūstrior est quam ūllīus ignis, quippe quī inmēnsō mundō tam longē lātēque conlūceat (Cicero) 'The brightness of the sun is more brilliant than that of any fire, inasmuch as it shines so far and wide in an immeasurable universe'

41 *cum, quamuīs* + subjunctive

1 We have already met *cum* + pluperfect subjunctive meaning 'when', 'since', 'although' 'x had —ed' (**124**). *cum* is also used with the imperfect subjunctive, to mean 'when', 'since', 'although' 'x was — ing', and with the present subjunctive, to mean 'since', 'although' 'x is —ing'. (NB. NOT 'when'.)

2 *quamuīs* means 'although' (really 'however') and takes the subjunctive, e.g. *quamuīs fortis esset ab hostibus fūgit* 'although he was courageous, he fled from the enemy' (really 'however brave he might have been, he still fled from the enemy'. Contrast *quamquam* 'although', which takes the indicative.)

142 Subjunctive in reported speech

In reported speech subordinate clauses have their verb in the subjunctive. Since this is simply a way of showing that the clause belongs in the indirect quotation, the meaning is the same as the indicative, e.g.

Direct: 'because I am handsome, everyone loves me' *quod pulcher sum, omnēs mē amant*
Indirect (past): 'he said that, because (as he said) he was handsome, everyone loved him' *dīxit omnīs sē, quod pulcher esset, amāre*
Indirect (present): 'he says that, because he is handsome, all love him' *dīcit omnīs sē, quod pulcher sit, amāre*
Cf. *Gauium . . . dīcis . . . clāmitāsse sē cīuem Rōmānum esse quod moram mortī quaereret* 'you say that Gavius shouted continually that he was a Roman citizen because he was seeking a delay to his death'

Note
Generally speaking, it will be obvious from context what tense in the original statement is represented by the subjunctive. Here is a summary of the main rules determining the tense of the subjunctive:

	Subjunctive used in 'reported' speech	
	Primary sequence	*Secondary sequence*
If the 'unreported' verb was originally present indicative	Present	Imperfect
If the 'unreported' verb was originally future indicative	-*ūrus* (i.e. fut. part.) + *sim* (sometimes present)	-*ūrus essem* (sometimes imperfect)
If the 'unreported' verb was originally past indicative	Perfect	Pluperfect

3 Infinitives without *esse* in reported speech

In accusative and infinitive constructions, *esse* is often dropped, e.g.

> *dīxit sē moritūrum (esse)* 'he said that he would die'
> *dīxērunt urbem captam (esse)* 'they said that the city had been captured'
> *negat sē secūtūram (esse)* 'she says that she will not follow' (how do you know it is 'she'?)

Here are two examples from *Text*, **4G(i)**:

> *sī audīret ā tē cīuīs Rōmānōs secūrī percussōs* 'if he heard that Roman citizens had been executed by you'
> *arbitrātī . . . hanc rem sibi praesidiō futūram* 'thinking that this would be a protection for them'

Reading exercise / Test exercise

*Here is part of the original of section **4F(ii)**. Gavius has just been arrested at Messana. Remember that Latin literature was composed to be read aloud. The final product of your study of each passage should be a well-phrased* recitātiō *('reading aloud').*

itaque ad magistrātum Māmertīnum statim dēdūcitur Gauius, eōque
ipsō diē cāsū Messānam Verrēs uēnit. rēs ad eum defertur, esse cīuem
Rōmānum quī sē Syrācūsīs in lautumiīs fuisse quererētur; quem iam
ingredientem in nāuem et Verrī nimis atrōciter minitantem ab sē
retractum esse et adseruātum . . . agit hominibus grātiās et eōrum   5
beneuolentiam ergā sē dīligentiamque conlaudat, ipse īnflammātus
scelere et furōre in forum uēnit; ārdēbant oculī, tōtō ex ōre crūdēlitās
ēminēbat . . . repente hominem prōripī atque in forō mediō nūdarī ac
dēligārī et uirgās expedīrī iubet. clāmābat ille miser sē cīuem esse
Rōmānum mūnicipem Cōnsānum; meruisse cum L. Raeciō,   10
splendidissimō equite Rōmānō, quī Panhormī negōtiārētur, ex quō haec
Verrēs scīre posset. tum iste, sē comperīsse eum in Siciliam ā ducibus
fugitīuōrum esse missum . . . deinde iubet undique hominem
uehementissimē uerberārī. caedēbātur uirgīs in mediō forō Messānae
cīuis Rōmānus, iūdicēs, cum intereā nūllus gemitus, nūlla uōx alia illīus   15
miserī inter dolōrem crepitumque plāgārum audiēbātur nisi haec 'cīuis
Rōmānus sum'. hāc sē commemorātiōne cīuitātis omnia uerbera
depulsūrum cruciātumque ā corpore dēiectūrum arbitrābātur; is nōn
modo hoc nōn perfēcit, ut uirgārum uim dēprecārētur, sed cum

implōrāret saepius ūsūrpāretque nōmen cīuitātis, crux – crux, inquam –   2(
īnfēlīcī et aerumnōsō, quī numquam istam pestem uīderat,
comparābātur. (*Cicero, In Verrem II 5, 62.160–2*)

Māmertīn-us a um of Messana
cāsū 'by chance'
esse cīuem . . . [Acc. + inf. after *dēfertur*]
sē [Hold – expect reflexive verb or
  acc. + inf.]
lautumi-ae ārum 1f. pl. stone-quarries
queror 3 dep. I complain
quem [Connecting relative – who is the
  antecedent?]
Verrī [Hold: it will be governed by
  minitantem]
minitor 1 dep. I threaten continually
  [*minor* + *-it-*]
sē [I.e. the people reporting to Verres]
5 *retrahō* 3 *retrāxī retractus* I drag back
  [Subject of *agit* is *Verres*]
beneuolenti-a ae 1f. good will
ergā (+ acc.) towards
dīligenti-a ae 1f. care
conlaud-ō 1 I praise
ārdeō 2 I burn (intrans.)
crūdēlitās crūdēlitāt-is 3f. cruelty
ēmineō 2 I stand out
prōripiō 3/4 I drag forward
dēligō 1 I bind
uirg-a ae 1f. rod
expediō 4 I get ready
ille miser [I.e. Gavius]
10 *mūniceps mūnicip-is* 3m. citizen of a
  mūnicipium (= free town)
Cōnsān-us a um of Consa
meruisse [Acc. + inf. construction
  continues with *sē* still as subject]
mereō 2 I serve (in the army)
splendid-us a um distinguished
Panhorm-us ī 2f. Palermo [Cf. *Lilybaeī*
  for case]
negōtior 1 dep. I do business
haec [Hold]

iste [Change of subject to Verres. The
  introductory verb for the acc. + inf.
  sē comperīsse is omitted –supply
  dīxit]
comperiō 4 *comperī* I find out, learn
eum [I.e. Gavius]
fugitīu-us ī 2m. deserter
undique from all sides
15 *gemit-us ūs* 4m. groan
  [Note lack of *et* between *nūllus gemitus*,
  nūlla uōx (though they are to be taken
  together): this is called *asyndeton*: see
  p. 314(c)]
dolor dolōr-is 3m. pain
crepit-us ūs 4m. noise
plāg-a ae 1f. blow
sē [Hold: it is part of an acc. + inf.
  phrase (in unemphatic position: see
  98⁴)]
commemorātiō commemorātiōn-is 3f.
  mention
cīuitās cīuitāt-is 3f. (here) citizenship
dēpulsūrum [Understand *esse*]
dēpellō 3 *dēpulī dēpulsus* I turn away,
  prevent
cruciāt-us ūs 4m. torture [Cf. *crux cruc-is*]
corpus corpor-is 3n. body
dēiectūrum [Understand *esse*]
dēiciō 3/4 *dēiēcī dēiectus* I drive away
hoc [Refers forward to the *ut* clause]
dēprecor 1 dep. I ward off (by earnest
  prayer)
20 *implōrō* 1 I implore, beseech
ūsūrpō 1 I use
crux cruc-is 3f. cross
īnfēlīx īnfēlīc-is unfortunate [Used as
  noun here]
aerumnōs-us a um miserable [Used as
  noun here]
pestis pest-is 3f. curse, bane [Refers to
  crux]

English–Latin

Reread the text of 4G(ii) and then translate this passage into Latin:

Although[1] Gavius had named Raecius as his guarantor, you did not send a letter to him. I would like[2] you to tell me, Verres, this. Why did you delay? Why did you not send him a letter at once? Did not Gavius say[3], 'If you were to[4] send a letter to Raecius, he would[4] say that I am a Roman citizen. If he were[5] present, here, he would[5] declare that I, whom you are accusing[6], am innocent.' But you, Verres, with the utmost disregard for Gavius, got a cross ready. If I were telling[5] this story[7] to wild beasts, even they would[5] be moved.

[1] *quamquam* + indicative: *quamuīs* or *cum* + subjunctive.
[2] Potential – use present subjunctive. See **139⁴**.
[3] 'say': open inverted commas and start the next part before inserting *inquit*.
[4] 'were to . . . would': present subjunctives.
[5] 'were . . ., . . .would': use imperfect subjunctives.
[6] Subordinate clause in indirect speech: use present subjunctive verb.
[7] 'story': use n. s. or pl. of *hic*, or use *rēs*.

Rēs gestae dīuī Augustī

in cōnsulātū sextō et septimō, postquam bella cīuīlia exstīnxeram, per cōnsēnsum ūniuersōrum potītus rērum omnium, rem pūblicam ex meā potestāte in senātūs populīque Rōmānī arbitrium trānstulī. quō prō meritō meō, senātūs cōnsultō, Augustus appellātus sum et laureīs postēs aedium meārum uestītī pūblicē corōnaque cīuica super iānuam meam 5
fīxa est et clupeus aureus in cūriā Iūliā positus, quem mihi senātum populumque Rōmānum dare uirtūtis clēmentiaeque et iūstitiae et pietātis caussā testātum est per eius clupeī īnscrīptiōnem. post id tempus, auctōritāte omnibus praestitī, potestātis autem nihilō amplius habuī quam cēterī quī mihi quōque in magistrātū conlēgae fuērunt. 10
  tertium decimum cōnsulātum cum gerēbam, senātus et equester ōrdō populusque Rōmānus ūniuersus appellāuit mē patrem patriae, idque in uestibulō aedium meārum īnscrībendum et in cūriā Iūliā et in forō Aug. sub quadrīgīs quae mihi ex s.c. positae sunt cēnsuit. cum scrīpsī haec, annum agēbam septuagēnsumum sextum. (Rēs gestae *34–5*) 15

cōnsulāt-us ūs 4m.
consulship   ⎫
sext-us a um sixth   ⎬ [i.e. 28 and
septim-us a um seventh ⎭ 27]
postquam after
cīuīl-is e civil
exstinguō 3 exstīnxī I put out
cōnsēns-us ūs 4m. agreement
ūniuers-ī ōrum 2m. pl. everyone
potior 4 dep. (+gen.) I gain control of
potestās potestāt-is 3f. power
arbitri-um ī 2n. judgement, arbitration
trānsferō 3 trānstulī I transfer
quō [Connecting relative, governed by *prō*]
merit-um ī 2n. good deeds
cōnsult-um ī 2n. decree
appellō 1 I call
laure-a ae 1f. laurel-wreath [Dat. or abl.? Hold]
postis post-is 3m. doorpost
5 *uestiō 4* I clothe [Solves *laureīs*]
pūblicē publicly
cīuic-us a um civic
super (+acc.) above
fīgō 3 4th p.p. *fīx-us* I place, fix
clupe-us ī 2m. shield [see frontispiece]
cūri-a ae 1f. senate-house
Iūli-us a um Julian
quem . . . dare lit. 'which (that) the senate and the Roman people gave to me'
clēmenti-a ae 1f. mercy
iūstiti-a ae 1f. justice
pietās pietāt-is 3f. respect for gods, family and homeland

caus(s)ā (+gen.) for the sake of [Follows the noun(s) it qualifies]
testātum est 'it was witnessed'
īnscrīptiō īnscrīptiōn-is 3f. inscription
post (+acc.) after
auctōritās auctōritāt-is 3f. authority, prestige
praestō 1 praestitī I excel x (dat.) in y (abl.)
nihilō amplius nothing more, no more [Governs *potestātis*]
10 *magistrāt-us ūs* 4m. office
conlēg-a ae 1m. colleague
terti-us decim-us a um thirteenth
cōnsulāt-us ūs 4m. consulship [i.e. 2]
equester equestr-is e of knights
ōrdō ōrdin-is 3m. order
patri-a ae 1f. fatherland
ūniuers-us a um whole
uestibul-um ī 2n. forecourt
īnscrībendum to be inscribed [Wait to solve *īnscrībendum* and *id*, which agree, till end of sentence]
Aug. = Augustō, from *August-us a um* of Augustus
quadrīg-ae ārum 1f. pl. four-horse chariot
s.c. = senātūs cōnsultō (*cōnsult-um ī* 2n. decree)
cēnseō 2 I vote [Solves *id . . . īnscrībendum*. Subject of *cēnsuit*?]
15 *agō 3* I pass, live
septuagēnsum-us sext-us a um seventy-sixth

SECTION FIVE

Section 5A

Notes
1 From now on you will find notes on new grammar at the end of each running vocabulary. Consult these as you read the chapter.
2 Names are given only on their first occurrence in this section. Consult the list on *Text* pp. 89–92 if you forget them.

Running vocabulary for 5A(i)

adeō to such an extent
agitō 1 I stir up, discuss [See note]
Antōni-us ī 2m. Gaius Antonius
C. = Gāi-us ī 2m. Gaius
Catilīn-a ae 1m. Catiline
cēnsor cēnsōr-is 3m. censor (official appointed every 5 years to vet senate)
Cicerō Cicerōn-is 3m. Cicero
comiti-a ōrum 1 n. pl. elections
concutiō 3/4 concussī concussus I shake, alarm
coniūrātiō coniūrātiōn-is 3f. conspiracy
coniūrātor coniūrātōr-is 3m. conspirator
cōnsuētūdō cōnsuētūdin-is 3f. amorous association (+ gen. 'involving')

cōnsulāt-us ūs 4m. consulship
Curi-us ī 2m. Quintus Curius
dēclārō 1 I declare
dēdit-us a um devoted to (+ dat.)
efficiō 3/4 effēcī effectus I bring (it) about (that: *ut* + subj.)
ēgregi-us a um outstanding
fact-um ī 2n. deed, happening
Faesul-ae ārum 1f. pl. Faesulae (Fiesole)
ferōx ferōc-is savage, wild
Fului-a ae 1f. Fulvia
glōrior 1 dep. I boast
grāt-us a um pleasing (to x: dat.)
in diēs day by day
in prīmīs especially
īnsolēns īnsolent-is arrogant
īnsolenti-a ae 1f. arrogance

īnsum inesse īnfuī (+ dat.) I am in
interdum sometimes
inuidi-a ae 1f. envy, hatred
inuid-us a um envious
Itali-a ae 1f. Italy
libīdō libīdin-is 3f. lust
mandō 1 I entrust (x acc. to y dat.)
M. = Mārc-us ī 2m. Marcus
Mānli-us ī 2m. Manlius
minuō 3 I diminish, weaken
mōns mont-is 3m. mountain
moueō 2 I remove (x acc. from y abl.)
namque for, in fact
nārrātae 'told' (nom. pl. f.)
nārrō 1 I tell, relate
nōbilitās nōbilitāt-is 3f. nobility

obnoxi-us a um servile (to
   x: dat.) [see note on
   l. 9]
obscūr-us a um ignoble (lit.
   'dark')
opportūn-us a um strategic
parō 1 I get ready [See
   note]
perīculōs-us a um
   dangerous
plērusque plēraque
   plērumque the majority
   of
polluō 3 I pollute
portāre [See note]
post '(put) behind (them)'

Q. = Quīnt-us ī 2m.
   Quintus
quaecumque whatever
   (things) (acc. pl. n.)
quamuīs however [See
   note]
rēs pūblic-a rē-ī pūblic-ae
   (5f. + 1/2 adj.) state
reticeō 2 I keep quiet
   (about)
stupr-um ī 2n. sexual
   intercourse [Outside
   marriage, and frowned
   upon because of
   Fulvia's status]

superbi-a ae 1f. pride,
   arrogance
Tulli-us ī 2m. Tullius
uānitās uānitāt-is 3f.
   vanity, boasting
uetus ueter-is old, long-
   established (like *dīues.*
   See **47**)
ut (+ subj. preceded by
   adeō, tantus, tam:
   indicating result) that

Notes

1. 2 *adeō* points forward to *ut* (= 'that': result).
ll. 3, 4 *tanta* points forward to *ut* (= 'that': result).
1. 6 *tam* points forward to *ut* (= 'that': result).
1. 7 *adeō* points forward to *ut* (= 'that': result).
1. 8 *tam* points forward to *ut* (= 'that': result).
1. 9 *nisi . . . esset* reports his conditional statement 'if you don't lick my
   boots, I'll . . .' Translate 'if she *were* not . . .'
1. 10 *causā cognitā* 'with the reason having been found out' (ablative
   absolute). *tam* points forward to *ut* (= 'that': result).
1. 13 *tam* points forward to *ut* (= 'that': result).
1. 14 *nouus homo* i.e. a man whose family had not previously held a
   consulship. *nōllent* is pl. because *plēraque nōbilitās* = 'most of the *nobles*'.
1. 15 *quamuīs* qualifies *ēgregius*: 'a *homo nouus* however *ēgregius*'.
ll. 16–17 *comitiīs habitīs* 'with the elections having been held' (ablative
   absolute).
1. 19 *agitāre*: infinitive, but used as main verb: translate 'he stirred up'.
1. 20 *parāre*: infinitive but used as main verb: translate 'he got ready'.
1. 21 *portāre*: infinitive but used as main verb: translate 'he conveyed'.

Learning vocabulary for 5A(i)

Nouns

arm-a ōrum 2n. pl. arms;
   armed men
coniūrātiō coniūrātiōn-is 3f.
   conspiracy

coniūrātor coniūrātōr-is 3m.
   conspirator
cōnsulāt-us ūs 4m.
   consulship

mōns mont-is 3m.
   mountain
rēs pūblic-a rē-ī pūblic-ae
   (5f. + 1/2 adj.) state,
   republic

Adjectives

grāt-us a um pleasing (to x: dat.)

uetus ueter-is (like *dīues*, 47) old; long-established

Verbs

agitō 1 I stir up, incite (*agō* + *-it-*)

efficiō 3/4 *effēcī effectus* I bring about (often followed by *ut* + subj.); cause, make; complete

īnsum inesse īnfuī I am in (x: dat.)

mandō 1 I entrust (x acc. to y dat.)

moueō 2 *mōuī mōtus* I remove; move; cause, begin

nārrō 1 I tell, relate (x acc. to y dat.)

parō 1 I prepare, get ready; provide; obtain

Others

adeō to such an extent

in diēs day by day

in prīmīs especially

quamuīs however, ever such a (qualifying an adj.; cf. *quamuīs* + subj. – 'although')

Running vocabulary for 5A(ii)

---

absurd-us a um foolish, silly

accēns-us a um on fire, aroused

adiungō 3 *adiūnxī adiūnctus* I join (x acc. to y dat.)

aes aliēn-um aer-is aliēn-ī (3n. + 1/2 adj.) debt (lit. 'someone else's bronze')

aetās aetāt-is 3f. age

aliquot several

cant-us ūs 4m. singing

cār-us a um dear

committō 3 *commīsī* I commit

decus decor-is 3n. honour

doct-us a um skilled (in x: abl.)

facēti-ae ārum 1f. pl. wit

fortūnāt-us a um fortunate

(in x: abl.)

incidō 3 *incidī* I fall into (*in* + acc.)

ingeni-um ī 2n. intellect

interficiō 3/4 *interfēcī interfectus* I kill

ioc-us ī 2m. joke (*iocum mouēre* = 'to crack a joke')

Latīn-us a um Latin

lepōs lepōr-is 3m. charm

līber-ī ōrum 2m. pl. children

libīdō libīdin-is 3f. lust

litter-ae ārum 1f. pl. literature

mātrōn-a ae 1f. lady, wife and mother

modest-us a um chaste

moll-is e gentle

petō 3 I proposition, court

procāx procāc-is bold, forward

prōrsus in a word

pudīciti-a ae 1f. chastity

quaest-us ūs 4m. living

saltātiō saltātiōn-is 3f. dancing

Semprōni-a ae 1f. Sempronia

sollicitō 1 I stir up

stupr-um ī 2n. prostitution

tolerō 1 I sustain

uel . . .uel . . .uel either . . . or . . . or

uers-us ūs 4m. verse; (pl.) poetry

uirīl-is e of a man

urbān-us a um of the city

ut (+ subj.) in order that / to [See notes ll. 25–6]

ut (+ subj.) that [Result: see note on l. 33]

301

Notes

ll. 25–6 *ut* + subjunctive = 'in order to' (purpose).

ll. 30–1 *genere atque fōrmā,* . . . *uirō atque līberīs*: ablatives (of respect) – await *fortūnāta* to solve them.

ll. 31–2 *litterīs Graecīs et Latīnīs* and then *cantū et saltātiōne*: ablatives of respect – await *docta* to solve them.

l. 33 *sīc* 'so' points forward to *ut* ('that': result). Supply *erat* with *accēnsa*.

l. 34 *uērum* . . . *absurdum*: no verb, so supply *erat* or *fuit*.

l. 35 *posse*: infinitive, but used as main verb, so translate 'she could'.

l. 36 *inerat* is governed by both *facētiae* and *lepōs*, but it is singular by attraction to the last-mentioned nominative noun. A common phenomenon.

Learning vocabulary for 5A(ii)

Nouns

aes aliēn-um aer-is aliēn-ī 3n. + 1/2 adj. debt (lit. 'someone else's bronze')

aetās aetāt-is 3f. age; lifetime; generation

līber-ī ōrum 2m. pl. children

libīdō libīdin-is 3f. lust

litter-ae ārum 1f. pl. literature; (letter)

mātrōn-a ae 1f. wife, mother; lady

uers-us ūs 4m. verse; (pl.) poetry

Adjectives

doct-us a um skilled (in x: abl.), learned

fortūnāt-us a um fortunate, lucky (in x: abl.)

Latīn-us a um Latin

modest-us a um chaste, modest, discreet

Verbs

adiungō 3 adiūnxī adiūnctus I join (x acc. to y dat.)

interficiō 3/4 interfēcī interfectus I kill

petō 3 petiuī petītus I proposition, court; (beg; seek); attack, make for

Others

aliquot several

uel . . . *uel* either . . . or

Running vocabulary for 5A(iii)

agere [See note on l. 44]
armāt-us a um armed
C. = Gāi-us ī 2m. Gaius
collocō 1 I place [For
collocāre see note on l.
44]
comiti-a ōrum 2n. pl.
elections
conuocō 1 I call together,
summon
Cornēli-us ī 2m. Gaius
Cornelius
dē imprōuīsō: see *imprōuīsō*
dīuers-us a um different
ēnūntiō 1 I declare,
announce (x acc. to y
dat.)
esse [See note on l. 45]
ēuītō 1 I avoid
Faesul-ae ārum 1f. pl.
Faesulae (Fiesole)
fatīgō 1 I tire [For *fatīgārī*
see note on l. 47]
festīnāre [See note on l.
46]
frūstrā in vain
hortārī [See note on l. 46]
impediō 4 I impede,
hinder
impendeō 2 I hang over,
threaten (x: dat.)
imprōuīsō: dē imprōuīsō
unexpectedly

initi-um ī 2n. beginning
īnsidi-ae ārum 1f. pl.
ambush, trap
īnsomni-a ae 1f.
sleeplessness (pl. = bouts
of sleeplessness)
intent-us a um vigilant
intro-eō (-īre) I go in
Itali-a ae 1f. Italy
itaque and so, therefore
item likewise
L. = Lūci-us ī 2m. Lucius
labor labōr-is 3m. toil,
hard work
nē (+ subj.) in order that
. . . not [See notes on
ll. 51, 57]
nihilōminus nevertheless
obsideō 2 I besiege [See
note on l. 45 for
obsidēre]
oper-a ae 1f. service
opportūn-us a um strategic
parāre [See note on l. 44]
parāt-us a um prepared
pars part-is 3f. part
perterrit-us a um terrified
petō 3 I stand for
postquam after
praemittō 3 *praemīsī* I send
in advance

prius first
prōcēdō 3 *prōcessī* I go
forward, succeed
prōdō 3 I betray, reveal
prohibeō 2 *prohibuī*
prohibitus I keep x
(acc.) away from y
(abl.)
properē hastily
quiēt-us a um quiet
repuls-a ae 1f. defeat
repulsam ferre to be
defeated
senātor senātōr-is 3m.
senator
soci-us ī 2m. ally
suscipiō 3/4 *suscēpī* I
undertake
tēl-um ī 2n. weapon
Varguntēi-us ī 2m. Lucius
Vargunteius
uigilō 1 I stay awake [For
uigilāre see note on l.
47]
uīuō 3 I am alive, live
ut (+ subj.) in order to
[See notes on ll. 39, 42,
55]

Notes

l. 37 *hīs rēbus comparātīs* 'with these things having been prepared' (ablative
absolute).

l. 39 *ut . . . (ēuītāret)* 'in order to . . .' (purpose).

l. 42 *ut . . . (habēret)* 'in order to . . .' (purpose).

l. 44 *agere*: infinitive but used as main verb: translate 'he did'. Similarly
collocāre 'he placed', *parāre* 'he prepared'.

l. 45 *obsidēre* 'he besieged'. *esse* 'he was' (i.e. 'went around').

l. 46 *hortārī* 'he urged'. *festīnāre* 'he hurried'.

l. 47 *uigilāre* 'he stayed awake'. *fatīgārī* 'he was made weary'.

ll. 49–50 *quī . . . faciant* 'to make' (purpose: *quī* + subjunctive).

l. 51 *nē . . . (impediat)* 'in order that . . . not' (negative purpose).

l. 52 *perterritīs cēterīs coniūrātōribus* 'with the rest of the conspirators terrified' (ablative absolute).

l. 55 *ut . . . interficerent* 'in order to . . .' (purpose).

l. 57 *nē . . . interficerētur* 'in order that . . . not' (negative purpose).

Learning vocabulary for 5A(iii)

Nouns

īnsidi-ae ārum 1f. pl. trap, ambush

Itali-a ae 1f. Italy

oper-a ae 1f. service (attention)

pars part-is 3f. part

soci-us ī 2m. ally, friend

tēl-um ī 2n weapon

Adjectives

armāt-us a um armed

dīuers-us a um different

opportūn-us a um strategic, suitable, favourable

Verbs

collocō 1 I place, station

conuocō 1 I summon, call together

impediō 4 I prevent, impede, hinder

petō 3 *petīuī petītus* I stand for (public office); (beg; seek; proposition, court; make for, attack)

prohibeō 2 I prevent, hinder, keep x (acc.) away from y (abl. or *ā* (*ab*) + abl.)

Other

frūstrā in vain

itaque and so, therefore

postquam after (+ indicative – usually perfect: translate 'after . . . had —ed')

prius before, previously, first

Grammar and exercises for 5A

---

144   **Result (or 'consecutive') clauses: 'so . . . that'**

Result clauses are expressed in Latin by an introductory word such as *tam*, *adeō*, *sīc*, *ita* (all 'so'), *tot* 'so many', *tantus* 'so big' picked up by *ut* 'that' (negative *ut nōn/numquam/nēmo/nūllus* etc.) The verb in the *ut* clause is in the subjunctive (present or perfect (to be met) in primary sequence, perfect or imperfect in secondary sequence).

Diagrammatically:

'*so*' *word*	*that (not)*
tam 'so'	
adeō 'to such an extent'	
sīc ⎫ 'in such a way'	
ita ⎭	*ut (nōn)* + verb in subjunctive
tantus 'so great'	
tot 'so many'	
tālis 'of such a kind'	

E.g.

> *tam ferōx est ut omnēs eum timeant* 'he is so fierce that everyone fears him'
>
> *tam pauper erat ut fēminīs grātus nōn esset* 'he was so poor that he was not attractive to women'
>
> *sīc . . . Deus dīlēxit mundum, ut . . . daret* 'God so loved the world that he gave . . .' (John 3.16)

Cf. this example from *Text* **5A(i)**:

> *huic hominī tanta uānitās inerat ut nōn posset reticēre quae audierat* 'There was so much vanity in this man that he could not keep quiet what he had heard'

Notes

1 These are often called 'consecutive' clauses – from *cōnsequor cōnsecūtus* 'I follow closely' – because the result follows closely on, is the consequence or result of, the action.

2 Compare this construction with *accidit ut* (**135**). Both establish the *conditions* that make the result *possible*, and so fall within the range of specific usages of the subjunctive (**138**). Compare *est/sunt quī* and *is quī* **140.1** and *perficiō ut* **135**.

3 Similar constructions are:

> *longē abest ut* + subjunctive 'he is far from —ing', e.g. *longē abest ut timeat* 'he is far from being afraid'
>
> *fierī potest ut* + subjunctive 'it can come about that', e.g. *fierī potest ut rem perficiat* 'it can happen that he will achieve his ends'

Exercises

1 *Translate into English*:
(a) Catilīnae tantus furor inerat ut in diēs plūra agitāret.
(b) tantum perīculum est ut Fuluia omnia cōnsulī nārrāre uelit.
(c) Semprōnia litterīs Latīnīs tam docta erat ut uersūs faceret.
(d) coniūrātiō tanta facta est ut hominī nōbilī cōnsulātus nōn mandārētur.
(e) Catilīna furōre adeō incenditur, ut cōnsulibus īnsidiās collocet, sociōs saepe hortētur, ipse cum tēlō sit, numquam dormiat.

2 *Translate into Latin the underlined words*:
(a) So great (*s. f.*) was the senate's anxiety, that the consulship was entrusted to a new man.
(b) Sempronia is so clever that she writes poetry.
(c) Catiline was inflamed to such an extent by his eagerness for revolution, that he placed armed men in strategic spots throughout Italy.
(d) Curius was so vile, that he was removed from the Senate.
(e) The conspirators are undertaking such an important crime, that no-one can sleep.

145 Purpose (or 'final') clauses: 'in order that/to', 'to'

Purpose (or 'final': *fīnis* 'end') clauses in Latin are expressed by *ut* ('in order that, in order to, to') or its negative *nē* ('lest', 'in order that . . . not', 'in order not to', 'not to'), followed by the subjunctive: present subjunctive in primary sequence, imperfect subjunctive in secondary sequence. E.g.

> *hoc facit ut grātus sit* 'he is doing this (in order) to be popular', '(in order) that he may be popular'
> *hoc fēcit nē inuidiōsus esset* 'he did this (in order) not to be unpopular', 'lest he be unpopular', '(in order) that he might not be unpopular'

(Observe how English favours 'may' in primary sequence, and 'might' in secondary.)
Cf. this example from *Text* **5A(ii)**:

> *igitur sē Catilīnae adiūnxērunt ut sē aere aliēnō līberārent* 'They joined Catiline in order to free themselves from debt'

The construction falls within the scope of specific usages of the subjunctive. It shows the speaker's *intention* that something should happen. Cf. *perficiō ut* (**135**).

Notes

1 Any references to the subject of the main verb inside the *ut*/*nē* clause will be reflexive, e.g.

> 'Cicero said this in order that Catiline should fear him (= Cicero)' *Cicerō haec dīxit ut Catilīna sē timēret*

2 The Latin for 'in order that no-one' is *nē quis* (lit. 'lest anyone'); 'in order that nothing' is *nē quid* (lit. 'lest anything') etc. E.g.:

> 'Euclio hides the gold in order that no-one may see it' *Eucliō aurum cēlat nē quis id uideat*

See **134**³ for *nē quis* in Indirect Command, and **I4** for forms.

3 *quī quae quod* + subjunctive can express purpose, especially after a main verb of motion, e.g.

> <u>nūntiōs mīsit quī nūntiārent</u> . . . 'he sent messengers <u>who would announce</u>' '. . . <u>to announce</u>'
> <u>cōnsilium patefēcit quō effugerent</u> 'he revealed the plan <u>by which they might escape</u>', '<u>for them to escape by</u>'
> <u>locum petit unde</u> (= *ex quō*) *hostem inuādat* 'he is looking for a position <u>from which to attack the enemy</u>'

Cf. this example from *Text* **5A(iii)**:

> *praemīsī . . . aliōs . . .* <u>*quī initium bellī faciant*</u> 'I have sent ahead others <u>to begin</u> the war'

Exercises

1 *Translate into English*:

(a) mulierēs aliquot sē Catilīnae adiūnxēre ut sē aere aliēnō līberārent.

(b) Catilīna Mānlium ad exercitum mīsit, quī bellum parāret.

(c) Cornēlius et Varguntēius ad Cicerōnem eunt ut eum interficiant.

(d) custōdēs Cicerōnis domūs Cornēlium et Varguntēium ianuā prohibuērunt, nē cōnsul necārētur.

(e) Fuluia omnia quae audierat cōnsulī nārrāuit, ut ille magnum perīculum effugeret.

(f) scrībēbat Aelius ōrātiōnēs[1] quās aliī dīcerent. (*Cicero*)

(g) nihil tam absurdē[2] dīcī potest quod nōn dīcātur ab aliquō philosophōrum[3] (*Cicero*).

[1] *ōrātiō ōrātiōn-is* 3f. speech.
[2] *absurdē* stupidly. See **140.1** for the construction in this sentence.
[3] *philosoph-us ī* 2m. philosopher.

2 *Translate the underlined words into Latin (take care to get the right sequence of tenses — see* **145**):

(a) Curius went to Fulvia <u>to ask for money</u>.
(b) Catiline sent two comrades <u>to[1] kill Cicero</u>.
(c) Curius told Fulvia everything, <u>so that she would believe him[2]</u>.
(d) Fulvia relates the story to the consul, <u>so that he will not be killed</u>.
(e) <u>In order not to be attacked by the conspirators</u>, Cicero orders the guards <u>to lock the door</u>.

[1] Use *quī* + subjunctive.
[2] 'him': use part of *sē*.

146 The historic infinitive

In places where the narrative is drawn in rapid, broad strokes, especially where one action follows swiftly upon another, Latin can use the *infinitive* where we would expect an indicative (usually perfect or imperfect). The infinitive tells us what the verbal action is; subject is nominative, tense has to be gathered from the broad context. E.g.

> *intereā Catilīna Rōmae multa simul <u>agere</u>; īnsidiās <u>collocāre</u>, <u>parāre</u> incendia, loca <u>obsidēre</u>, ipse cum tēlō <u>esse</u>.*
> 'Meanwhile, Catiline <u>put</u> many schemes into operation simultaneously in Rome: he <u>set up</u> ambushes, <u>prepared</u> fires, <u>laid siege</u> to places, <u>went around</u> himself under arms'.

Note the atmosphere of busy activity, in which historic infinitives most commonly occur.

Exercise

Translate these sentences and say whether the infinitive is prolative (i.e. completes the meaning of a verb, e.g. uolō, possum *etc.), reporting speech (accusative and infinitive), or historic:*

(a) nōbilēs Catilīnae cōnsulātum mandāre nōluērunt.
(b) Fuluia multīs Catilīnam coniūrātiōnem parāre dīxerat.
(c) Catilīna in diēs plūra agitāre, arma collocāre, pecūniam ad Mānlium mittere.
(d) coniūrātiōnem sē facere negat Catilīna.
(e) Semprōnia uersūs facere, sermōne ūtī modestō.
(f) Cicerō Cornēlium et Varguntēium in aedīs suās intrāre uetuit.

47 Ablative of respect: 'in point of'

A common use of the ablative, especially in poetry, is to specify the *respect in which* something is the case. E.g.

> *numquam uictus est uirtūte* 'he was never conquered in point of / in respect of courage'
> *litterīs Latīnīs docta* 'learned in point of / in respect of Latin literature'
> *genere fortūnāta* 'lucky in point of / in respect of her birth'

Exercise

Translate these sentences; pick out ablatives, distinguishing ablatives of respect from other usages:

(a) Semprōnia, genere nōbilī nāta, litterīs Latīnīs docta erat.
(b) uir quīdam, Curius nōmine, eō tempōre Fuluiam amābat.
(c) nōn tōtā rē, sed temporibus errāstī.[1] (*Cicero*)
(d) eā nocte Cornēlius et Varguntēius Cicerōnis iānuā prohibitī sunt.
(e) Catilīna, quamuīs genere atque fōrmā fortūnātus esset, uir tamen minimā sapientiā fuit.

[1] *errō* 1 I am wrong.

Reading: *ut*

You have now met *ut* as a conjunction in several different senses.

ut + *indicative*

   (a)   'how!'
   (b)   'as', 'when'.

ut + *subjunctive*

   (a)   Indirect command (after e.g. *imperō, persuādeō* etc.) 'to . . .'
   (b)   Result (after e.g. *tam, tantus, adeō* etc.) 'so . . . that'.
   (c)   Purpose 'in order that/to'.
   (d)   After *perficiō* 'I bring it about that', *accidit* 'it happens that'.

To solve *ut*, watch out for: (i) indicative or subjunctive? (ii) if subjunctive, a verb of commanding will suggest (a), a 'flag' such as *tam, tantus* will suggest (b), and a negative *ut nōn* will suggest (b) or (d), while the negative *nē* will suggest (a) or (c). E.g.

> *Cicerō custōdibus imperat ut . . .* 'Cicero to the guards gives orders that . . .'

solves itself very quickly. But

> *Cicerō ut custōdibus . . .* leaves doubts about *ut* and *custōdibus*, so hold these words till solved.

NB.   *ut* is also found in the meaning 'as', qualifying a noun. e.g. *canem et fēlem ut deōs colunt* 'They worship the dog and the cat *as gods*'.

Exercise

Read these sentences, making explicit your steps in understanding, especially when you reach ut *(or equivalent). State the moment when you can solve* ut:

   (a)   eōs ut armātī essent hortābātur.
   (b)   Semprōnia tam docta est ut uersūs facillimē faciat.
   (c)   ut ego iubēbō, ita tū faciēs.
   (d)   hōrum contumēliās[1] sapiēns[2] ut iocōs accipit. (*Seneca*)
   (e)   Cicerō effēcit ut nōn interficerētur.

---

[1] *contumēli-a ae* 1f. 'insult'.
[2] *sapiēns* nom. s. m. 'wise man'.

(f)   nē cōnsulem Catilīnae sociī necārent, rem tōtam Fuluia amīcīs
      suīs nārrāuit.
(g)   ut fortūnāta Semprōnia est!

Reading: *quī*

quī too has different meanings, as follows.

quī + *indicative*
This is the descriptive relative 'who', 'which', 'what', 'that'.

quī + *subjunctive*

(a)   Purpose (with verbs of motion).
(b)   Consecutive (*est quī*, *is quī*) 'the sort of person who'.
(c)   Causal, 'since'.
(d)   Indirect speech, where it may = ordinary relative, unless context
      demands otherwise.
(e)   Concessive 'although' e.g. *uir quī fortis esset tamen effūgit* 'the
      man, who was brave, nevertheless fled' i.e. 'the man, although
      he was brave, fled'.

Exercise

Read these sentences, using the information just outlined. State the moment when
quī *is solved:*

(a)   Catilīna Rōmam sociōs mittit, quī urbem incendant.
(b)   Semprōnia, quae uirōs semper petēbat, mātrōna Rōmāna erat.
(c)   Clūsīnī[1] lēgātōs Rōmam, quī auxilium ā senātū peterent, mīsēre.
      (*Livy*)
(d)   multī arbitrābantur coniūrātiōnem uiam esse, quā aere aliēnō sē
      līberāre possent.
(e)   fēminae etiam aliquot sē coniūrātiōnī adiūnxērunt, quae in aes
      aliēnum maximum conciderant.
(f)   quī reī pūblicae sit hostis, fēlīx[2] esse nēmo potest. (*Cicero*)
(g)   tē amō quī sīs tam fortis.

---
[1] *Clūsīnī* 2m. pl. 'the people of Clusium'.
[2] *fēlīx fēlīc-is* 'fortunate'.

Reading exercise / Test exercise

Catiline has just made a speech to his fellow conspirators, rousing them to action. Sallust describes their demand for a clear-cut goal and Catiline's promises of various rewards.

postquam accēpēre ea hominēs, quibus mala abundē omnia erant, sed neque rēs neque spēs bona ūlla, tametsī illīs quiēta mouēre magna mercēs uidēbatur, tamen postulāuēre plērīque ut prōpōneret condiciōnēs bellī et praemia. tum Catilīna pollicērī tabulās nouās, prōscrīptiōnem locuplētium, magistrātūs, sacerdōtia, rapīnās, alia omnia, quae bellum 5 atque libīdō uictōrum fert. (*Sallust,* Catiline *21, slightly adapted*)

ea [Refers back to Catiline's speech]
abundē plentifully
spēs spē-ī 5f. hope
tametsī although
quiēt-us a um quiet, peaceful
mercēs mercēd-is 3f. reward
plērīque plēraeque plēraque the majority
prōpōnō 3 I state
condiciō condiciōn-is 3f. term
praemi-um ī 2n. reward
Catilīna pollicērī [Note (1) case of *Catilīna* (2) What part of the verb *pollicērī* is: refer, if necessary, to **146**]

tabul-ae ārum 1f. pl. accounts [*tabulae nouae* implies the cancellation of existing debts]
prōscrīptiō prōscrīptiōn-is 3f. proscription (i.e. notice proclaiming someone an outlaw, and confiscation of his goods)
5 *locuplēs locuplēt-is* rich
sacerdōti-um ī 2n. priesthood
rapīn-a ae 1f. plunder, forcible seizure of property
uictor uictōr-is 3m. victor

English–Latin

Re-read the text of **5A(iii)***, then translate this passage:*

Although Catiline[1] had got ready the conspiracy, he nevertheless stood for the consulship again. Meanwhile, he kept attempting to persuade his allies to attack Cicero. Cicero, however, had made plans in order to escape the danger. Through Fulvia and Curius he had managed to hear of Catiline's plans.

Again the nobles were so afraid that they did not entrust the consulship to Catiline. He then decided to wage war. He stationed his supporters in various parts of Italy. Meanwhile at Rome he set a trap[2] for the consul, went around[2] with a weapon, and[3] encouraged[2] his supporters to be brave.

[1] Catiline is subject of both clauses, so place him before the conjunction.
[2] Use historic infinitives.
[3] Omit – use asyndeton (no connections: see p. 314(c)).

Roman poetry

Introduction

Consider the following lines from Pope's *Epistle to a Lady* (1735):

> Pleasures the Sex, as Children Birds, pursue,
> Still out of Reach, but never out of View

Put bluntly, it means 'The (female) sex pursues pleasures as children pursue birds; the pleasures remain out of reach, but never out of view.' The utterance is different from prose in a number of important ways:

(a)   It is in metre.

(b)   The word-order is different from prose.

(c)   It is very compressed ('pursue' serves for both limbs of the first line).

(d)   It is cleverly balanced (e.g. the balance of 'Pleasures [object] the Sex [subject] as Children [subject] Birds [object]').

(e)   The image is striking: women pursuing pleasure as children pursue birds.

Until one gets used to it, reading this sort of poetry, even in English, is quite hard work. Balance, compression, striking word-order and powerful imagery are all features of Latin poetry too, and since Latin is an inflected language, the dislocation of expected symmetry by means of calculated asymmetry (= *uariātiō*) can be that much more violent. But no less important to a Roman poet is balance. Consider the following haunting lines from Virgil:

> *tum pinguēs agnī, et tum mollissima uīna,*
> *tum somnī dulcēs, dēnsaeque in montibus umbrae*

> 'then fat the lambs, and then most sweet the wine,
> then sleep (is) sweet, and deep on the mountains (are) the shadows'

Observe the compression (no verbs), and the balance with variety. Of the four *cōla* (limbs), three start with *tum*, but not the fourth; the first line runs adjective–noun, adjective–noun; the second runs noun–adjective, adjective (prepositional phrase) noun. The metre adds to the effect by being slow and heavy, and allowing, unusually, two adjacent vowels (*agnī et*) their full value. (Note that in l. 2 *dēnsaeque in* the -*e* of -*que* is, as normally, lost before the following *i*-.)

313

The word-order of the above example is not, however, difficult. Generally, Roman poets do not go in for extremes of word-order (or hyperbaton, 'leap-frog', as the technical term is). Here is an example of an extreme word-order from that most arch and sophisticated of poets, Ovid:

sī quis quī quid agam forte requīrat erit

'If there will perhaps be anyone who asks what I am doing.' (Natural order would be *sī quis forte erit quī requīrat quid agam*.) One can compare the strained balance of the Ovid with e.g. Sidney's

Vertue, beautie and speeche did strike, wound, charme
My heart, eyes, ears, with wonder, love, delight.

In both English and Latin there is a limit to how much one can take of this sort of thing.

(See further L.P. Wilkinson, *Golden Latin Artistry* C.U.P. 1963, Chapter 8. Bristol Classical Press reprint 1985.)

Rhetorical features of Latin prose and poetry

Here are the technical terms, with examples, for some of the most important figures of Latin writing:

(a) Ellipse (sometimes called by its Greek term *apo koinou*): a figure in which a word or words needed to complete the sense are understood from another part of the sentence, e.g.

Player King (*Hamlet* III.ii):
thirty years have passed,
Since love our hearts and Hymen did our hands
Unite

i.e. 'since love (united) our hearts'.

(b) Antithesis: a figure in which ideas are sharply contrasted by the use of words of opposite or very different meaning, e.g.:

Pope (*Epistle to Dr Arbuthnot*) on the danger of flatterers:
Of all mad Creatures, if the Learn'd are right,
It is the Slaver kills, and not the Bite

'Slaver' and 'Bite' are in antithesis.

(c) Asyndeton: a figure in which conjunctions are missed out, to give an effect of speed and economy, e.g.:

Rochester (*The Imperfect Enjoyment*):
    With arms, legs, lips close clinging to embrace

(d) Chiasmus: a figure in which corresponding parts of a sentence
    are placed criss-cross (a b b a) e.g.

Shakespeare, *Sonnet* 154:
    Love's fire heats water, water cools not love
    a   *b*   *b*   *a*

Pope (*On Women*)
    A Fop their Passion, but their Prize, a Sot.
    a   *b*   *b*   *a*

(e) The golden line: term applied to a line in Latin poetry which
    consists of two adjectives and two nouns with a verb in between,
    in the pattern a b (verb) A B, e.g.

impiaque aeternam timuērunt saecula noctem
    a   b   (verb)   A   B
    'and the unholy ages feared the everlasting night'

A 'silver' line takes the order a b (verb) B A.

(f) Tricolon: a group consisting of three equivalent units, e.g. 'I
    came, I saw, I conquered', 'with arms, legs, lips'. Frequently,
    these units increase in length ('ascending tricolon') e.g. 'Friends,
    Romans, countrymen'. (Cf. tetracolon – four units.)

(g) Anaphora: a figure in which a word (or words) is repeated in
    successive clauses or phrases (usually at the start of the clause or
    phrase), e.g.

Shakespeare, *Richard II* II.ii:
    With mine own tears I wash away my balm,
    With mine own hands I give away my crown
    With mine own tongue deny my sacred state

(h) Assonance: similarity of vowel sounds of words near each other,
    e.g.

Thomas Gray:
Along the heath and near his favourite tree

(i) Alliteration: any repetition of the same sounds or syllables
    (especially the beginnings of words) of two or more words close
    to each other, e.g.

'Low lies the level lake'   315

(j)   Hyperbaton: a figure in which the natural word-order is upset, e.g.

Milton (translating Horace's *rīdentem dīcere uērum quid uetat?*): 'Laughing to teach the truth, what hinders?'

i.e. 'What hinders one-who-is-laughing from teaching the truth?' The Latin word-order, however, is normal.

Poetic word-order

Adjectives and nouns
One of the most frequent word-orders in poetry is adjective, then something else, then the noun with which the adjective agrees, e.g.

Lāuīnaque uēnit lītora 'and he came to the Lavinian shores'
altae moenia Rōmae 'the walls of high Rome'
Trōiānō ā sanguine 'from Trojan blood'
Rōmānam condere gentem 'to found the Roman race'
quem dās fīnem? 'what end do you give?'
noua pectore uersat cōnsilia 'she turned over new plans in her heart'

Here is a double example:

saeuae memorem Iūnōnis ob īram 'on account of the unforgetting anger of savage Juno'

The best tactic to adopt is to register the adjective and *move on*: concentrate your attention on nouns and verbs first and foremost, and try to solve them as you come to them. This will lay clear the bare bones of the sentence. You can then reread, concentrating on the adjectives and seeing where they fit. Thus a first reading should concentrate on the underlined words:

ingentia cernēs
moenia surgentemque nouae Karthāginis arcem.

'(something about 'large') you will see the walls and (something about 'rising' and 'new') the citadel of Carthage'.
Then reread, concentrating on *ingentia, surgentem* and *nouae*, seeing where they agree:

'you will see the *huge* walls and *arising* the citadel of *new* Carthage'

NB. When adjectives precede and are separated from their nouns in prose, the effect is to emphasise strongly one element or the other (usually the first).

Exercise

Translate the following (adjectives underlined):

(a) Tyriam quī aduēneris urbem.
(b) templum Iūnōnī ingēns.
(c) uidet Īliacās ex ōrdine pugnās.
(d) bellaque iam fāmā tōtam uulgāta per urbem.
(e) feret haec aliquam tibi fāma salūtem.
(f) animum pictūrā pāscit inānī.
(g) ardentīsque āuertit equōs.
(h)   iuuat īre et Dōrica castra
       dēsertōsque uidēre locōs.
(i) summā dēcurrit ab arce.
(j) tacitae per amīca silentia lūnae.

Tyri-us a um Carthaginian	*fām-a ae* 1f. reputation	*summ-us a um* top (of)
quī aduēneris 'since you	*pictūr-a ae* 1f. scene	*dēcurrō* 3 I run down
have come to'	*pāscō* 3 I feed	*arx arc-is* 3f. citadel
Iūnō Iūnōn-is 3f. the	*inān-is e* illusory	*tacit-us a um* quiet
goddess Juno	*ardēns ardent-is* fiery	*amīc-us a um* friendly
Īliac-us a um of Troy,	*āuertō* 3 I turn aside	*silenti-a ōrum* 2n. pl.
Trojan	*equ-us ī* 2m. horse	silences
fām-a ae 1f. rumour	*iuuat* it gives pleasure	*lūn-a ae* 1f. moon
uulgāt-us a um spread	*Dōric-us a um* Greek	
aliquam (acc. s. f.) some	*dēsert-us a um* abandoned	

Verbs

It is extremely common for verbs to come early in the sentence, sometimes well before the quoted subject. So you must hang on to the person of the verb and wait for a subject to appear, e.g.:

> *obstipuit prīmō aspectū Sīdōnia Dīdō* 'he/she/it fell silent at the first look' – ah, that is 'Carthaginian Dido fell silent . . .'
> *conticuēre omnēs* 'they fell silent' – ah, 'everyone fell silent'

NB. Verb–subject is also a common order in prose.

Word groups

We have 'phrased' together words that can usefully be taken in groups together, e.g.

tālibus ōrantem dictīs ārāsque tenentem
audiit Omnipotēns

'the one begging (*acc.*) with such words and holding (*acc.*) the altars the All-powerful (*i.e. Jupiter*) heard'

Delayed introductory word

Conjunctions like *cum, dum, ubi, sī, sed, et* are often held back in the sentence, (as in prose: see **124**[4]) e.g.

namque sub ingentī lūstrat dum singula templō 'for while he surveys individual items under the great temple'
magnum rēginae sed enim miserātus amōrem 'but pitying the queen's great love'

Latin metre

Latin metre is more complex than English because in Latin metre *every syllable counts* (cf. English, where metre depends largely on stress).

For the purpose of metre, every syllable in Latin counted as either *heavy* (–) or *light* (∪). Heavy syllables may be compared to longer notes in music, light to shorter.

Heavy and light syllables

Here are some basic rules:

(a)   A syllable is *heavy* if its vowel is pronounced *long* e.g. *pōnō, īrātō*

(b)   A syllable is *heavy* if the vowel is followed by two consonants or a double consonant (*x, z*) e.g. *ingentēs*.

  Word division makes no difference, e.g. *et* is 'light', but *et fugit* would make *et* heavy, because the *t* is followed by an *f*, making two consonants.

(c)   A syllable is *heavy* if it contains a diphthong, e.g. *aedēs*. (cf.1 above).

(d)   A syllable is *light* if it contains a short vowel followed by only one consonant (or none), e.g. *et omnibus*. Contrast *ēt vĕniō*.

Elision

If a word ends in a vowel or in -*m*, and the next word begins with a vowel
(or *h*), the final vowel or -*m* syllable is 'elided' ('crushed out of existence')
and does not count for the purposes of the metre, e.g.:

> eg[o] et tū
> uirtūt[em] et
> c[um] habeās

Notes

1 The 'heaviness' or 'lightness' of a vowel *has no effect on its natural
pronunciation*. Thus the *et* of *et fugit* may count as heavy for the
purposes of scansion, but it would not be pronounced *ēt* as a
consequence. To help you to see the difference between *vowel length*
and *syllable quantity* we have continued to mark long vowels
(immediately above the letter), as well as setting out the metrical
pattern (above the line), e.g. *corrì pŭḗre* indicates that the first vowel
(-*o*-) is pronounced *short*, but belongs in a *heavy* syllable (because
followed by two consonants -*rr*-); the fourth vowel, however (-*ē*-), is
pronounced *long* (the syllable will therefore be *heavy*).

2 Verse was read with the *normal* word stress (see p. xv). Do not allow
the rhythmic stress of the metre to distort the natural stress of the
words.

The hexameter: Virgil's metre

The hexameter has six feet, consisting of a mixture of dactyls (– ∪ ∪) and
spondees (– –), on the following pattern:

$$
\begin{array}{c|c|c|c|c|c}
1 & 2 & 3 & 4 & 5 & 6 \\
-\,\cup\,\cup & -\,\cup\,\cup & -\,\cup\,\cup & -\,\cup\,\cup & -\,\cup\,\cup & -\,\cup \\
-\ - & -\ - & -\ - & -\ - & (-\ -) &
\end{array}
$$

Here are the first three lines of the first Virgil passage scanned for you:

> corrĭpuḗre uĭ[am] intereā, quā sēmĭta mōnstrat
>
> iamqu[e] ascendēbant collem, quī plūrĭmŭs urbī
>
> immĭnet aduersāsqu[e] aspectat dēsŭper arcēs.

Notes
1 Foot 5 is usually a dactyl, very occasionally a spondee.
2 The line usually has a word-division (*caesūra*, lit. 'cutting') in the middle of the third foot or the fourth. E.g. the *caesura* in the above examples is after *intereā* (4th foot), *ascendēbant*, *aduersāsqu(e)* (3rd foot).

Exercise

Scan the next ten lines (p. 321), adding the correct word stress (see rule, p. xv). Mark foot divisions with |, caesuras with ⟩. Then read aloud, thinking through the meaning as you read.

Virgil reading exercises: introduction

Pūblius Vergilius Marō (Virgil) was born in 70 near Mantua. He early on established powerful connections, notably with the governor of Cisalpine Gaul, C. Asinius Pōlliō, himself a scholar and poet. It was Pōlliō who introduced him to Octavian. In the early 30s Virgil became a member of the circle of Maecēnās, the great literary patron and powerful political ally of Octavian.

Virgil was the author of three major works. The first two were the *Bucolics* (or *Eclogues*), and *Georgics*, whose apparently rural themes have political overtones, e.g. at the end of *Georgics* I, there is an appeal to the native gods of Italy to allow Octavian to come to the aid of the civil-war-stricken land. His final work, begun around 30 and still undergoing final revision at his death in 19, was the *Aeneid*, an epic in twelve books, relating how Aeneas, mythical founder of the Roman race, escaped from the burning city of Troy and finally established a foothold in Italy, after defeating the Rutulian King Turnus in single combat. The ancients saw the purpose of Virgil in this work as twofold: to rival Homer (on whose *Iliad* and *Odyssey* the poem draws heavily) and to glorify Augustus. The latter he achieved in three ways. First he accepted and stressed the family connection between Aeneas and the *gēns Iūlia* (family of Julius Caesar and Augustus), so that the early history of the Roman race is also the family history of Augustus. Secondly, he introduced mentions of Augustus into the poem in prophecies (by Jupiter in Book I and Anchises in Book VI) and on the shield of Aeneas (Book VIII). Thirdly, he reflected the old Roman values which Augustus propagated and supported even by legislation, in the characters of his epic, especially that of Aeneas, a man distinguished by his *pietās* (respect for gods, family, home and country).

Virgil's *Aeneid*

Aeneas, storm-tossed from Troy, arrives after many adventures off the North African coast, and is led by his divine mother, Venus, to Carthage. Here he sees the city of Carthage being built.[1]

corripuēre uiam intereā, quā sēmita mōnstrat,
iamque ascendēbant collem, quī plūrimus urbī
imminet aduersāsque aspectat dēsuper arcēs.
mīrātur mōlem Aenēās, māgālia quondam,
mīrātur portās strepitumque et strāta uiārum.   5
īnstant ārdentēs Tyriī: pars dūcere mūrōs
mōlīrīque arcem et manibus subuoluere saxa.
pars optāre locum tectō et conclūdere sulcō;
iūra magistrātūsque legunt sānctumque senātum.
hīc portūs aliī effodiunt; hīc alta theātrīs   10
fundāmenta locant aliī, immānīsque columnās
rūpibus excīdunt, scaenīs decora apta futūrīs;

quālis apēs aestāte nouā per flōrea rūra exercet sub sōle labor, cum gentis adultōs ēdūcunt fētūs, aut cum līquentia mella 15 stīpant et dulcī distendunt nectare cellās, aut onera accipiunt uenientum, aut agmine factō ignāuum fūcōs pecus ā praesēpibus arcent;	They were like bees at the beginning of summer, busy in the sunshine in the flowery meadows, bringing out the young of the race just come of age or treading the oozing honey and swelling the cells with sweet nectar, or taking the loads as they came in or mounting guard to keep the herds of idle drones out of their farmstead.

feruet opus redolentque thymō fraglantia mella.
'ō fortūnātī, quōrum iam moenia surgunt!'   20
Aenēās ait et fastīgia suspicit urbis. (*Aeneid 1.418–37*)

[1] In all the Virgil extracts, phrases which you should take as a whole are marked with
‗‗‗‗‗‗‗‗‗.

corripiō 3/4 *corripuī* I seize, devour, hasten along
quā where
sēmit-a ae 1f. path
mōnstrō 1 I show
ascendō 3 I climb
collis coll-is 3m. hill
quī plūrimus 'which in its great bulk' [Register nom., so subject]
urbī [Why dat? Wait]
immineō 2 (+ dat.) I overlook, loom over [Solves *urbī*]
aduers-us a um facing [The -*que* suggests another clause or phrase, so 'and the facing . . .', but *aduersās* is acc. pl. f., so we are waiting for a noun which can be described as 'facing', and then (presumably) a verb which explains the acc. case]
aspectō 1 I look at, observe [So probably 'and looks at the facing . . .']
dēsuper from above
arx arc-is 3f. citadel, stronghold [Solves *aduersās*]
mīror 1 dep. I marvel at
mīrātur [Subject? Wait]
mōlēs mōl-is 3f. mass, bulk, size (of the city)
Aenē-ās ae 1m. [Greek declension, see **H6**] Aeneas [Subject]
māgālia māgāl-ium 3n. pl. huts
quondam once upon a time
5 *port-a ae* 1f. gate
strepit-us ūs 4m. hustle and bustle
strāt-um ī 2n. (lit. 'laid flat') paving
īnstō 1 I press on [Subject? Wait]
ārdēns ārdent-is enthusiastic, eager
Tyri-us ī 2m. Carthaginian [Subject]
pars part-is 3f. some [So we may be waiting for 'others']
dūcō 3 (here) build [Infinitive: so why? Wait]
mūr-us ī 2m. wall
mōlior 4 dep. I work at [Note infinitive]
manibus [Dat. or abl. pl., but since the men are working, probably abl.]

subuoluō 3 I roll uphill [Note infinitive]
sax-um ī 2n. stone [Solved infinitive yet?]
pars [Must mean 'others']
optō 1 I decide on [Note: still infinitive]
tect-um ī 2n. building, house
conclūdō 3 I contain, mark out enclose [Infinitive]
sulc-us ī 2m. furrow, trench [But why these infinitives? There appears to be no controlling verb. So they must be – what sort of infinitives?]
iūs iūr-is 3n. law [Subj. or obj? No clue. Wait]
magistrātūs [Subj. or obj? No clue. Wait]
legō 3 I select [Do 'laws and magistrates' select?]
sānct-us a um holy, revered [Case? What does this suggest about *iūra* etc?]
10 *port-us ūs* 4m. harbour [Case? So wait]
aliī [Looks like another string of the *pars* sort above. Await another *aliī*]
effodiō 3/4 I dig
hīc [So here is another place where they are working: we can surely expect another *aliī* soon]
alt-us a um deep [Case? Many possibilities. Wait]
theātr-um ī 2n. theatre [Cannot agree with *alta*, so register dat. or abl. pl. and wait. So far 'here, something about deep things, something about theatres']
fundāment-um ī 2n. foundation [Solves *alta*: 'here, something about deep foundations'. So what case is *theātrīs*, with what meaning, probably?]
locō 1 I place [And *aliī* follows, solving the whole thing]
immān-is e gigantic [Register case, pl.]
column-a ae 1f. column [Immediate agreement, happily]
rūpes rūp-is 3f. rock [Dat. or abl. pl. Something about 'rocks']

excīdō 3 I cut out, quarry [All solved (note force of *ex-*)]
scaenīs [Register cases, wait]
decus decor-is 3n. ornament, decoration
apt-us a um fit for (+ dat.) [That solves *scaenīs*]

ferueō 2 I seethe
redoleō 2 I give off a smell (of x: abl.) [Plural, so await subject. 'They give off a smell']
thym-um ī 2n. thyme (plant noted for its nectar) [Case? Construe with *redolent*? Or wait?]

fraglāns fraglant-is sweet [Make *thymum* depend on *fraglantia*?]
mel mell-is 3n. honey [Pl. for s. A common poetic device]
20 *fortūnāt-us ī* 2m. lucky man, person
moenia moeni-um 3n. walls
surgō 3 I rise
ait said
fastīgi-um ī 2n. roof, height
suspiciō 3/4 I look up to [Aeneas has by now descended the hill]

SECTION 5B

Running vocabulary for 5B(i)

addūcō 3 *addūxī adductus* I lead to, draw to
adductī (nom. m. pl.) (having been) drawn into
Allobrogēs Allobrog-um 3m. pl. Allobroges [Gallic tribe, see name list, *Text* p. 91 and map]
ampl-us a um large, great
aperiō 4 I reveal
arcessō 3 I summon
auāriti-a ae 1f. avarice, greed
auctōritās auctōritāt-is 3f. weight, authority
bellicōs-us a um warlike
cās-us ūs 4m. fortune
cōnspiciō 3/4 *cōnspexī* I catch sight of

dīmittō 3 I send away
exīstimō 1 I think, consider
fore ut (+ subj.) 'that it would happen that . . .'
Gabīni-us ī 2m. P. Gabinius Capito
Galli-a ae 1f. Gaul
Gallic-us a um Gallic
gēns gent-is 3f. race
idōne-us a um qualified (for), suitable (for) (+ dat.)
impellō 3 I urge, persuade
innoxi-us a um innocent
Lentul-us ī 2m. P. Cornelius Lentulus Sura
misereor 2 dep. I take pity on (+ gen.)

miseri-a ae 1f. misery, distress
nātūr-a ae 1f. nature
negōtior 1 dep. I do business
nōminō 1 I name
nōscō 3 *nōuī nōtus* I get to know (*nōuī*=I know)
nōt-us a um known (to x: dat.)
nouae rēs nouārum rērum (1/2 adj. + 5f. noun) revolution (lit. 'new things')
P. = *Pūbliō: Pūbli-us ī* 2m. Publius
pauc-ī ae a a few
perdūcō 3 I bring to
plērīque plēraeque plēraque the majority of

praecipiō 3/4 *praecēpī* I
instruct, order
praesēns praesent-is present
prīuātim individually
propinqu-us a um near (to
x: dat.)
pūblicē publicly, as a state
queror 3 dep. I complain
quīcumque quaecumque
quodcumque whoever,
whatever (declines like
quī quae quod)

quō + comparative +
subjunctive 'in order
that . . . more' [See
notes on ll. 75–76, 77–
8]
remedi-um ī 2n. cure
requīrō 3 I seek out
sīcutī (+ indicative) just as
societās societāt-is 3f.
alliance, partnership
(+ gen. expressing

sphere of alliance; tr.
'in x')
sollicitō 1 I rouse up,
incite to revolt
spēs spē-ī 5f. hope
stat-us ūs 4m. state
ubi prīmum as soon as
Vmbrēn-us ī 2m. Publius
Umbrenus

Notes

l. 62 *bellī* governed by *societās* and completing the idea of partnership by expressing what the partners will share in.

l. 63 *oppressōs*: sc. *esse* (see **143** for the suppression of *esse* in reported speech).

l. 69 *quod . . . esset*: subjunctive within reported speech (see **142**)

l. 71 *quā . . . effugiātis*: note the mood of the verb. See **145**[3].

l. 72 *ōrāre*: historic infinitive.

l. 73 *quod . . . factūrī essent*: subjunctive within reported speech (see **142**). There is strong emphasis on the future, hence the composite future subjunctive (= fut. participle + subj. of *sum*)

ll. 75–6, 77–8 *quō maior . . . inesset* ⎫ All express purpose, with a com-
quō facilius . . . ⎬ parative idea: 'in order the more
persuādēret ⎪ —ly to —' (adv.); 'in order that
quō . . . amplior esset ⎭ more —' (adj.)'

Learning vocabulary for 5B(i)

Nouns

auctōritās auctōritāt-is 3f.
weight, authority

gēns gent-is 3f. tribe; race;
family; people
nātūr-a ae 1f. nature

spēs spē-ī 5f. hope(s);
expectation

Adjectives

ampl-us a um large, great
idōne-us a um suitable
(for), qualified (for)
(+ dat.)

nōt-us a um known, well-
known
pauc-ī ae a (pl.) a few, a
small number of

plērīque plēraeque plēraque
the majority of

Verbs

aperiō 4 *aperuī apertus* I
open; reveal
dīmittō 3 *dīmīsī dīmissus* I
send away (*dis-*
+ mittō)
exīstimō 1 I think,
consider (*ex + aestimō*
= I value)

nōscō 3 *nōuī nōtus* I get to
know (perfect tenses = I
know etc.)
queror 3 dep. *questus* I
complain

requīrō 3 *requīsīuī requīsītus*
I seek out; ask for (*re-*
+ quaerō)
sollicitō 1 I stir up, arouse;
incite to revolt

Others

ubi prīmum as soon as
(with perfect
indicative)

Running vocabulary for 5B(ii)

cert-us a um sure, certain
cōnsīderō 1 I ponder,
consider
diū for a long time
Fabi-us ī 2m. Fabius
[Quintus Fabius Sanga]
fortūn-a ae 1f. fortune
incert-us a um uncertain
manifest-us a um in the
open, caught in the act,
plainly guilty

mercēs mercēd-is 3f. profit,
reward
nōndum not yet
opēs op-um 3f. pl.
resources
patrōn-us ī 2m. patron
praecipiō 3 I give
instructions to (x dat.:
to do y: *ut* + subj.)
praemi-um ī 2n. reward,
prize
prō (+ abl.) instead of

Q. = Quīntō: Quīnt-us ī
2m. Quintus
quam maximē as much as
possible
Sang-a ae 1m. Q. Fabius
Sanga
simulō 1 I feign
studi-um ī 2n. enthusiasm
(for) (+ gen.)
tūt-us a um safe
uoluō 3 I turn over,
reflect on
utī = ut

Notes

l. 82 *at in alterā*: supply *parte* and *erant*.

l. 86 *cōnsiliō cognitō*: 'with the plan having been discovered' (abl. abs.).

l. 87–8 *simulent . . . adeant . . . polliceantur dentque*: all verbs in the *ut* clause
introduced by *praecipit* (l. 86).

l. 87 *bene polliceantur*: tr. 'make fine promises'.

Learning vocabulary for 5B(ii)

Nouns

fortūn-a ae 1f. fortune,
luck; (pl.) wealth

opēs op-um 3f. pl.
resources; wealth (s. *ops*
op-is help, aid)

praemi-um ī 2n. prize,
reward
. *studi-um ī* 2n. enthusiasm,
zeal

Adjectives

cert-us a um sure, certain	*manifest-us a um* in the open; obvious, clear; caught in the act

Verbs

cōnsīderō 1 I consider, ponder

praecipiō 3/4 *praecēpī praeceptus* I instruct, give orders to (x dat. to do Y: *ut* + subj.) (*prae* + *capiō*)

simulō 1 I feign

Others

diū for a long time (comp. *diūtius*, sup. *diūtissimē*)

nōndum not yet
prō (+ abl.) instead of (for, in return for; on behalf of; in front of)

quam + superlative adv. as . . . as possible
utī = *ut*

Running vocabulary for 5B(iii)

āctiō āctiōn-is 3f. public action
adit-us ūs 4m. approach
Bēsti-a ae 1m. Lucius Bestia
caedēs caed-is 3f. carnage, slaughter
Cethēg-us ī 2m. C. Cornelius Cethegus
contiō contiōn-is 3f. public meeting; *contiōnem habēre* to hold a public meeting

dīuidō 3 I divide
duodecim twelve
ērumpō 3 I break out, rush out
exsequor 3 dep. *exsecūtus* I carry out
frangō 3 *frēgī frāctus* I break (down)
L. = Lūci-us ī 2m. Lucius
nōbilitās nōbilitāt-is 3f. nobility

obsideō 2 I besiege
parēns parent-is 3m. parent
percellō 3 *perculī perculsus* I scare, unnerve
propius nearer (comp. of *prope*)
quō + comp. + subj. 'in order that . . . more' [See note on ll. 95–6]
Statili-us ī 2m. L. Statilius

Notes

l. 90 *parātīs* . . . *magnīs cōpiīs*: 'with great forces having been got ready' (ablative absolute).

ll. 91, 92 (*eā*) *contiōne habitā*: 'with a (this) public meeting having been held' (ablative absolute).

ll. 95–6 *quō facilior* . . . *fieret*: 'in order that there might be . . . an easier . . .' (purpose with comparative idea).

l. 97 *iānuā frāctā*: 'with the door having been broken (down)' (ablative absolute). *fīliī familiārum* i.e. sons subject to *patria potestās*. The power of a father over his children was absolute: he could even kill them with impunity.

l. 98 *urbe incēnsā*: 'with the city having been burned' (ablative absolute).

l. 99 *Cicerōne necātō*: 'with Cicero having been killed' (ablative absolute). *perculsīs omnibus*: 'with everyone unnerved (by . . .)' (ablative absolute).

Learning vocabulary for 5B(iii)

Nouns

caedēs caed-is 3f. slaughter, carnage

parēns parent-is 3m. father, parent; f. mother

Adjectives

duodecim twelve

Verbs

frangō 3 *frēgī frāctus* I break

obsideō 2 *obsēdī obsessus* I besiege (*ob* + *sedeō*)

Grammar and exercises for 5B

48 **Purpose clauses: *quō* + comparative + subjunctive 'in order that . . . more'**

When a purpose clause contains a comparative (adverb or adjective), it is introduced NOT by *ut* but by *quō*, e.g.

> *hoc fēcit quō celerius peruenīret* 'he did this (in order) to arrive more quickly'

Cf.

> *quō facilior aditus ad cōnsulem fieret* 'in order that there might be an easier approach to the consul'

The verb in the *quō* clauses follows the normal rule, and will be either present or imperfect subjunctive. This construction is not difficult to spot, since it has three markers in a sentence: (i) *quō* (ii) a comparative (iii) verb in the subjunctive. Remember, when these clues are given, to translate *quō* by 'in order that/to'.

149   *fore ut* + subjunctive 'that it will/would come about that. . .'

Latin often 'talks its way round' (the technical term for this is 'periphrasis') the so-called future infinitive passive (see **118**) by using *fore ut* + subjunctive, e.g.

> *dīxit sē captum īrī* 'he said that he would be seized' (lit. 'he said that there was a movement towards seizing him')

could also be expressed thus:

> *dīxit fore ut* (fixed form) *caperētur* lit. 'he said that it would come about that he would be seized'

Thus both *dīcit eōs remissum īrī* and *dīcit fore ut remittantur* mean 'he says that they will be sent back'.

So in reported speech, watch out for *fore ut* (*nōn*) + subjunctive, and translate literally 'that it will/would (not) come about that', then retranslate for smoother final effect.

Exercise

Translate these sentences:

(a)   Catilīna sociīs suīs nūntiāuit fore ut incendium et caedēs in urbe fierent.

(b)   Vmbrēnus Gabīnium uocāuit, quō facilius Allobrogibus uerbīs suīs persuādēret.

(c)   Allobrogēs, quippe quī praemia bellī magna fore arbitrārentur, rem diū cōnsīderābant.

(d)   sed lēgātī tandem sēnsērunt fore ut opibus cīuitātis Rōmānae facillimē uincerentur.

(e)   igitur Allobrogum lēgātī Cicerōnī omnia nārrāuērunt, quō maius auxilium cīuitātī suae ferrent.

50   Ablative absolute

You have already seen (**109, 120⁶**) how Latin likes to put a noun with
another noun, adjective or present participle in the ablative as a separate
phrase in a sentence, e.g. *Verre praetōre* 'with Verres as praetor', *Cleomenē
ēbriō* 'with Cleomenes drunk', *Cleomenē pōtante* 'with Cleomenes
drinking'.

The most common usage, however, is to put the noun with a *past
participle*, e.g.

> *nāuibus captīs* '(with) the ships having been captured'
> *hominibus interfectīs* '(with) the men having been killed'

51   Past (perfect) participle passive

The past (or perfect) participle of deponent verbs is *active* in meaning, e.g.
morātus 'having delayed', *locūtus* 'having spoken' etc. (Cf. *locūtus sum* 'I
have spoken'.)

The past (or perfect) participle of all other verbs is *passive* in meaning,
e.g. *amātus* 'having been loved', *audītus* 'having been heard', *factus*
'having been made', *captus* 'having been captured' etc. (Cf. *captus sum* 'I
have been captured'.) Like deponents, they act as 1/2 adjectives (*amāt-us a
um*) in agreeing with the person or thing 'having been —ed' and in
describing action prior to the main verb. But they are most frequently
used predicatively (see **77**). E.g.

> *mulieris amātae* 'of the woman having-been-loved', 'of the
> woman when she had been loved'
> *lēgātī audītī* 'the ambassadors having-been-heard', 'the ambassa-
> dors after they had been heard'
> *nāuis capta* 'the ship having-been captured', 'the ship after it had
> been captured'

Watch out for this usage in the ablative absolute construction, e.g.

> *nāue captā* '(with) the ship having been captured'
> *uirō necātō* '(with) the man having been killed'
> *signō uīsō* '(with) the signal having been seen'

This style of ablative absolute construction is very common indeed in
Latin. Since it is not very common in English, it is best not to settle for a
wholly literal translation. Try the following suggestions:

signō uīsō, coniūrātōrēs fūgērunt (lit.) 'with the signal having been
seen, the conspirators fled'

This can be translated as:

'Because/when/after they saw the signal, the conspirators fled'
'The conspirators saw the signal and fled'
'The signal was seen and the conspirators fled'
'After/when/because the signal was seen, the conspirators fled'

Notes

1 Sometimes 'although' will be the best translation for an abl. abs., e.g.
mīlitibus captīs, Catilīna tamen pugnābat 'though the soldiers were taken,
Catiline fought on'. As with *cum* = 'although' and *quī* = 'although',
some word for 'nevertheless' (*tamen, nihilōminus* etc.) will often be
found. Cf. *exiguā parte aestātis reliquā Caesar tamen in Britanniam
proficīscī contendit* 'though only a small part of the summer remained,
Caesar hastened to set out for Britain' (Caesar).
2 The construction is called 'absolute' (*absoluō absolūtus* 'having been
released': note the passive past participle!) because the phrase does not
appear to be integral to its clause, since it qualifies neither subject nor
object – it seems to stand all alone, 'released' from its surroundings.
3 Cf. *uice uersā* '(with) the position turned/changed'; *pollice uersō* '(with)
the thumb turned' (*up* to indicate death, the evidence suggests).

Exercises

1 *Form the perfect participle passive of these verbs and translate them*: dīmittō,
requīrō, opprimō, aperiō, simulō, cōnsīderō, frangō, obsideō,
exīstimō, sollicitō, (*optional*: quaerō, petō, tollō, agitō, mandō, parō,
nārrō, efficiō, moueō, interficiō).
2 *Say which of these perfect participles are deponent and which passive
(translating each example)*: adiūnctus, questus, profectus, impedītus,
adeptus, locūtus, nīxus, conuocātus, prohibitus, collocātus, adlocūtus,
mortuus, abiectus, āctus, perfectus, (*optional*: repulsus, secūtus, positus,
cultus, solitus, relictus, ausus, uetitus, mentītus, occīsus, exspectātus,
uīsus, īrātus, passus, acceptus).
3 *Translate these ablative absolute phrases (at first use the pattern 'with* x
having been —*ed')*:

(a) coniūrātiōne parātā.
(b) hīs rēbus nārrātīs.
(c) conuocātīs mīlitibus.
(d) exercitū collocātō.
(e) datō signō.
(f) simulātō studiō.
(g) hostibus oppressīs.
(h) praemiīs cōnsīderātīs.
(i) interfectīs parentibus.
(j) paucīs dīmissīs.

4 *Translate these sentences. Say whether the ablative absolute is better regarded as temporal ('when — had been —ed'), causal ('because — had been —ed'), or concessive ('although — had been —ed'):*

(a) Catilīnā ex urbe ēgressō Lentulus nouōs sociōs petēbat.
(b) lēgātīs Allobrogum Rōmae manentibus Vmbrēnus ā sociō quōdam uocātus est.
(c) Vmbrēnus, Gabīniō uocātō quō maior auctōritās sermōnī inesset, cōnsilium aperuit.
(d) cōnsiliō apertō, nōminātīs sociīs, Vmbrēnus tamen Allobrogibus persuādēre nōn poterat ut coniūrātōrēs fierent.
(e) Cicerō cōnsiliō cognitō coniūrātōrēs quam maximē manifestōs habēre uolēbat.
(f) bene facta male locūta[1] male facta arbitror. (*Ennius*)
(g) nihil est simul inuentum et perfectum. (*Cicero*)

[1] *locūta* 'spoken of', 'described'. (For passive usage of deponent past participle see Reference Grammar **C4 Note 2.**)

English–Latin

1 *Translate these clauses into Latin, using ablative absolute with past participle:*

(a) When all hope had been taken away . . .
(b) Although the soldiers had been sent away . . .
(c) Because allies had been sought out . . .
(d) Once things had been pondered . . .
(e) Although a reward had been given . . .
(f) If the city had been besieged . . .

2 *Reread the text of **5B(i)–(ii)**, then translate this passage:*

Umbrenus led the ambassadors of the Allobroges out of the forum into a certain person's house. Next he called Gabinius, a man of great

331

weight, so as to persuade them more quickly. When Gabinius had been[1] called, Umbrenus persuaded the ambassadors to promise their aid. But they had not yet decided to join the conspiracy, inasmuch as they thought that they would be defeated[2] by the resources of the Roman state. Finally, they revealed the whole matter to Sanga. When Cicero had found out the plan[1] via Sanga, he instructed the Allobroges to feign enthusiasm, so that he might more easily capture the conspirators.

[1] Use ablative absolute.
[2] Use *fore ut* + subjunctive ('that it would turn out that . . .').

Virgil's *Aeneid*

Aeneas, welcomed warmly into Carthage by the queen Dido (who is slowly falling in love with him) is encouraged to tell the story of the destruction of his homeland Troy. Here Aeneas describes how the wooden horse was brought into the city – and laments the blindness of the Trojans.

dīuidimus mūrōs et moenia pandimus urbis.

accingunt omnēs operī pedibusque rotārum

subiciunt lāpsūs, et stuppea uincula collō

intendunt; scandit fātālis māchina mūrōs

fēta armīs. puerī circum innūptaeque puellae   5

sacra canunt fūnemque manū contingere gaudent;

illa subit mediaeque mināns inlābitur urbī.

ō patria, ō dīuum domus Īlium et incluta bellō

moenia Dardanidum! quater ipsō in līmine portae

substitit atque uterō sonitum quater arma dedēre;   10

īnstāmus tamen immemorēs caecīque furōre

et mōnstrum īnfēlīx sacrātā sistimus arce.

tunc etiam fātīs aperit Cassandra futūrīs	Even at this last moment Cassandra opened
ōra deī iussū nōn umquam crēdita Teucrīs.	her lips to prophesy the future, but the gods
nōs dēlūbra deum miserī, quibus ultimus 15	had ordained that those lips were never
esset	believed by Trojans. This was the last day for
ille diēs, festā uēlāmus fronde per urbem.	a doomed people, and we spent it adorning
	the shrines of the gods throughout the city
	with festal garlands.

(*Aeneid 2.234–49*)

dīuidō 3 I open up
mūr-us ī 2m. wall
moenia moeni-um 3n. pl. buildings
[Nom. or acc.? Wait]
pandō 3 I reveal, disclose
urbis [Gen., so must qualify *moenia*]
accingō 3 I get ready for (+ dat.)
pedibusque [-*que* shows another clause/
phrase, so hold 'and something to
do with feet in the dat./abl.']
rot-a ae 1f. wheel [Can this be 'feet of
the wheels'? Seems unlikely]
subiciō 3/4 I place x (acc.) under y
(dat.) [Are *pedibus* y?]
lāps-us ūs 4m. slipping [So: 'they place
slippings under the feet'. Can
rotārum construe with 'slippings', i.e.
'they place slippings of wheels under
the feet'? But under whose feet?
Ans.: the feet of whatever is coming
into Troy. In other words . . .
What might 'slippings of wheels'
mean?]
stuppe-us a um made of tow [Hold case
possibilities]
uincul-um ī 2n. halter, rope [Solves
stuppea: n. pl., nom. or acc. Which?
Wait. 'And something about tow
halters']
coll-um ī 2n. neck [Must be 'on the
neck' (dat.)]
intendō 3 I stretch, draw tight x (acc.)
on(to) y (dat.) [Solves it]
scandō 3 I climb [What climbs? Wait]
fātāl-is e deadly
māchin-a ae 1f. device, siege-engine
[Subject]
5 *fēt-us a um* pregnant with (+ abl.)
[Agreeing with what?]
puerī [Probably subject, but hold]
circum around about
innūpt-us a um unwed
sacra [Cannot agree with 'boys and
girls', whatever else it agrees with]
canō 3 I sing [So 'boys and girls
sing . . .' – perhaps *sacra*. What
gender and case is *sacra*?]

fūnis fūn-is 3m. rope ['And something
to do with a rope in the acc.']
contingō 3 I touch [Infinitive. Why?]
gaudeō 2 I rejoice, delight (to) [Solves
the infinitive]
illa [Change of subject. *illa* is f. – so
what does it refer to?]
subeō I come up
mediaeque ['and something about the
middle'; numerous case possibilities.
Wait for agreement]
mināns [Something in the nom.
'threatening'. Presumably *illa* is
threatening. *minor* takes a dat. – is
there one about? Not yet . . .]
inlābor 3 dep. I slide in, slip into
(+ dat.)
urbī [Ah! Dat., and f., so what agrees
with it?]
patri-a ae 1f. fatherland
dīuum = *dīuōrum* 'of the gods'
Īli-um ī 2n. Troy
inclut-us a um famous [But famous
what? Wait]
bellō [Perhaps shows you in what
whatever-it-is is famous, i.e. 'famous
in war']
moenia moeni-um 3n. pl. walls, town
[Solves it]
Dardanid-ae 1m. pl. (gen. *Dardanidum*)
Trojans
quater four times
līmen līmin-is 3n. threshold
port-a ae 1f. gate(way)
10 *subsistō* 3 *substitī* I stop, halt. [What
must the subject be?]
uter-us ī 2m. belly, womb [Case?
Hold]
sonit-us ūs 4m. sound [Register case]
arma [Subject? Object? Probably
subject, since *sonitum* must be obj.
So the weapons do something to a
sound. H'm]
dedēre = *dedērunt* [Of course, that's what
they do to the sound! This should
now solve *uterō*]
īnstō 1 I press on

immemor immemor-is mindless(ly),
  forgetful
caec-us a um blind
furor furōr-is 3m. madness [Dependent
  on *caecī*?]
mōnstr-um ī 2n. monster [Subject or
  object? Hold]

īnfēlīx (n.s.) catastrophic, ill-boding
sacrāt-us a um sacred [Register case.
  Can you solve it yet? No]
sistō 3 I bring to a halt [Solves
  mōnstrum īnfēlīx]
arce [Solves *sacrātā*]

Section 5C

Running vocabulary for 5C(i)

ad hoc in addition
aliter otherwise
breuī (sc. *tempore*) shortly,
  soon
Cassi-us ī 2m. L. Cassius
  Longinus
cūnctor 1 dep. I delay,
  hesitate (+ inf.)
eō to that place (i.e. to
  the Allobroges'
  territory)
exempl-um ī 2n. copy

impellō 3 I drive to,
  persuade
īnfim-us a um lowest
īnfrā below
item likewise
iūs iūrandum iūr-is iūrand-ī
  (3n. + 1/2 adj.) oath
mandāt-um ī 2n. order
nē + subj. don't
perferō perferre I carry to
praecept-um ī 2n.
  instruction

prius quam before
  (+ subj.)
propius nearer
repudiō 1 I reject
signāt-us a um sealed (*signō*
  1)
societās societāt-is 3f.
  alliance
T. = Titō: Tit-us ī 2m.
  Titus
Volturci-us ī 2m. Titus
  Volturcius

Notes

l. 103 *quod . . . perferant*: note mood of verb (*quī* + subj. expressing purpose).

l. 104 *fore ut*: assume a verb of saying before this, 'they said'.

l. 105 *uentūrum*: *esse* has been suppressed.

l. 111 *intellegās*: subjunctive 'you should understand', 'understand'.

l. 112 *cōnsīderēs*: subjunctive 'you should consider', 'consider'. *petās*: subjunctive 'you should seek', 'seek'.

l. 115 *accipiās*: subjunctive 'you should take on', 'take on'. *proficīscāris*: subjunctive 'you should set out', 'set out'.

Learning vocabulary for 5C(i)

Nouns

exempl-um ī 2n. copy;
example

iūs iūrandum iūr-is iūrand-ī
(3n. + 1/2 adj.) oath

Verbs

cūnctor 1 dep. I delay,
hesitate (+ inf.)

Others

breuī shortly, soon (sc.
tempore)

eō to that place
item likewise

propius nearer

Running vocabulary for 5C(ii)

citō quickly
cohortor 1 dep. I
encourage
comitāt-us ūs 4m. retinue
cūnct-us a um the whole
(of)
dēprehendō 3 I capture,
arrest
dēserō 3 *dēseruī dēsertus* I
desert

diffīdō 3 I distrust, despair
of (+ dat.)
ēdoct-us a um having been
informed (of x: acc.)
exorior 4 dep. *exortus* I
arise
Gall-ī ōrum 2m. pl. the
Gauls
gladi-ī ī 2m. sword
itum est 'they went' (pf.
pass. of *eō*) [see note]

mīlitār-is e military
Mului-us a um Mulvian
occultē secretly, in hiding
pōns pont-is 3m. bridge
sēsē = sē
sīcutī just as
timid-us a um frightened
trādō 3 I hand over
tumult-us ūs 4m. noise
uelut as, just as

Notes

l. 117 *quā proficīscerentur*: note mood of verb (*quī* + subj. indicating
purpose.)

l. 118 *cūncta ēdoctus*: verbs which take two accusatives in the active (like
doceō 'I teach x y') often retain one of them in the passive: here it
expresses the thing taught.

l. 120 *itum est*: lit. 'it was gone'; tr. 'they went', 'there was a general
movement to the bridge'.

l. 121 *praeceptum erat*: note the gender of the part.

l. 122 *ad id locī*: 'to that place' (cf. *quid cōnsilī*).

Learning vocabulary for 5C(ii)

Nouns
gladi-us ī 2m. sword
pōns pont-is 3m. bridge

Pronouns
sēsē = sē

Adjectives
mīlitār-is e military
timid-us a um frightened,
  fearful

Verbs
cohortor 1 dep. I
  encourage, exhort (*con-*
  + hortor)

exorior 4 dep. *exortus* I
  arise (*ex + orior*)

trādō 3 *trādidī trāditus* I
  hand over; hand down,
  relate (*trāns + dō*)

Others
sīcutī or *sīcut* (just) as
uelut as, just as

Running vocabulary for 5C(iii)

aduocō 1 I summon
afferre = adferre
anxi-us a um worried,
  anxious
committō 3 *commīsī* I
  commit
Concordi-a ae 1f. Concord
cōnficiō 3/4 *cōnfēcī cōnfectus*
  I finish
cōnstāns cōnstant-is
  resolute, steady
cōnstanti-a ae 1f.
  resolution, steadiness
decet it is fitting (for x
  acc. to do to y inf.)
dēclārō 1 I declare, report
dēdecorī est it is a disgrace
  (to x dat.)

dederō 'I shall have given'
  [Tr. 'I give'] (fut. pf.
  of *dō*)
dēprehendō 3 *dēprehendī*
  dēprehēnsus I catch,
  detect
eōdem to the same place
ēripiō 3/4 *ēripuī ēreptus* I
  rescue x (acc.) from y
  (dat.)
Flacc-us ī 2m. L. Valerius
  Flaccus
interfectī erunt '(they) will
  have been killed' [Tr.
  '(they) are killed'] (fut.
  pf. pass. *of interficiō*)
intrōdūcō 3 I bring in, lead
  in

iussū by the order (of x:
  gen.)
laetor 1 dep. I rejoice, am
  happy
nihilōminus nevertheless
noceō 2 I harm (+ dat.)
occupō 1 I seize
onerī est it is a burden (to
  x dat.)
paenitet 2: *mē paenitet* I
  regret (x gen.)
patefaciō 3/4 *patefēcī*
  patefactus I reveal,
  expose
perdūcō 3 I lead
poen-a ae 1f. penalty
porrō furthermore, besides

336

postulāuerō 'I shall have demanded' [Tr. 'I demand'] (fut. perf. of *postulō*)

praebeō 2 I show (*mē*: myself [to be] y acc.)

praepōnō 3 I put x (acc.) before y (dat.)

properē hastily

pūniō 4 I punish

pūnītī erunt 'they will have been punished' [Tr. 'they are punished'] (fut. pf. pass. *of pūniō*)

quod sī but if

saltem at least

sententi-a ae 1f. opinion

seruāuerō 'I shall have saved' (fut. pf. *of seruō*)

uocāuerimus 'we shall have called' [Tr. 'we call'] (fut. pf. *of uocō*)

Notes

ll. 134–5 *sī eīs ā nōbīs parcātur, magnō sit reī pūblicae dēdecorī*: remember the rule for *sī* + pres. subj. (if x were to happen, y would happen). *eīs ā nōbīs parcātur*: *parcō* takes dative in active forms; in passive 'it' is the subject; *eīs* the people to be spared, *ā nōbīs* the agent (the people sparing). *dēdecorī* is further defined by *magnō*.

l. 136 *noceātur*: passive of a verb which takes dative object in active. 'It' is subject (cf. *parcātur*), *reī pūblicae* the thing to be harmed.

l. 141–2 *ut huius cōnstantiae mē umquam paeniteat*: *mē paenitet* = I regret, taking a genitive of what is regretted.

Learning vocabulary for 5C(iii)

Nouns

poen-a ae 1f. penalty

sententi-a ae 1f. opinion; judgement; sentence; maxim

Verbs

committō 3 *commīsī commissus* I commit

cōnficiō 3/4 *cōnfēcī cōnfectus* I finish

ēripiō 3/4 *ēripuī ēreptus* I snatch away, rescue (x acc. from y dat.)

noceō 2 I harm (+ dat.)

occupō 1 I seize

patefaciō 3/4 *patefēcī patefactus* I reveal, expose, throw open

praebeō 2 I show, display (myself to be x: *mē* + acc. adj. or noun)

pūniō 4 I punish

Others

iussū by the order (of x: gen.)

nihilōminus nevertheless

porrō besides, moreover

Predicative dative phrases

dēdecorī est it is a disgrace   *onerī est* it is a burden (to
    (for x: dat.)   x: dat.)

Grammar and exercises for 5C

---

152 Jussive subjunctives

Jussive subjunctives (*iubeō iussus* 'ordered') are so called because the
subjunctive in these cases acts as an imperative (cf. on specific usages of
the subjunctive **138**). A subjunctive in this sense stands on its own as the
main verb of a sentence (it is thus an 'independent' use), e.g.

> (1st pl.) *audiāmus* 'let us listen'; *interficiāmus* 'let us kill'; *eāmus*
> 'let's go'
> (2nd s./pl.) *accipiās* 'please welcome', 'welcome!', 'see that you
> welcome' (often used in poetry)
> (3rd s./pl.) *fīat* 'let there become' 'may there be' (cf. *fīat lūx* 'let
> there be light' (Genesis))

Cf. phrases very often used in English: *habeās corpus* 'you may have the
body'; *caueat ēmptor* 'let the buyer beware'; *stet* 'let it stand'.

Notes

1 When a jussive subjunctive occurs in a question, it is known as
'deliberative' (from *dēlīberō* 1 'I weigh carefully', 'consider'), e.g.

> *quid scrībam?* 'What am I to write?' (Plautus)
> *utrum Karthāgō dīruātur . . . ?* 'Should Carthage be destroyed
>   . . . ?' (Cicero)
> *quid ego faciam? maneam aut abeam?* 'What should (shall) I do?
>   Should (shall) I stay, or leave?' (Plautus)

In these circumstances, the negative is *nōn*. The imperfect subjunctive
indicates past time here, e.g.

> *'nōn ego illī argentum redderem?' 'nōn redderēs.'* 'Shouldn't I have
>   paid the money to him?' 'You shouldn't have paid it.'
>   (Plautus)

2 The negative for jussives is *nē*, e.g. *nē ueniant* 'let them not come'.

Exercises

1 *Translate*:

(a) abeās.
(b) commorēmur.
(c) maneāmus.
(d) nē querātur.
(e) nē praemium requīrant.
(f) nē frūstrā moriāmur.

(g) ueniat.
(h) abeāmus.
(i) quid dīcerem?
(j) quid dīcam?
(k) quid faceret?

2 *Translate these sentences*:

(a) moriāmur et in media arma ruāmus. (*Virgil*)
(b) uiuāmus, mea Lesbia, atque amēmus. (*Catullus*)
(c) nē difficilia optēmus. (*Cicero*)
(d) cautus sīs, mī Tīrō. (*Cicero*)
(e) faciāmus hominem ad imāginem et similitūdinem nostram et praesit piscibus maris . . . (*Genesis*)
(f) et dīxit Deus: 'fīat lūx!' et lūx facta est. (*Genesis*)
(g) dīxit quoque Deus: 'fīat firmāmentum in mediō aquārum et dīuidat aquās ab aquīs.' (*Genesis*)
(h)   sapiās, uīna liquēs, et spatiō breuī
    spem longam resecēs. (*Horace*)
(i) quid faciat?[1] pugnet? uincētur fēmina pugnāns.
        clāmet? at in dextrā quī uetet, ēnsis erat. (*Ovid*)
(j) haec cum uidērem, quid agerem, iūdicēs? (*Cicero*)

[1] The subject of the verbs *faciat, pugnet, clāmet* is 'she'.

ruō 3 I rush	*piscis pisc-is* 3m. fish	*spati-um ī* 2n. space,
optō 1 I wish for	*firmāment-um ī* 2n. prop,	distance
caut-us a um careful (perf.	firmament	*resecō* 1 I cut back, prune
participle of *caueō*)	*dīuidō* 3 I divide	*dextr-a ae* 1f. right hand
imāgō imāgin-is 3f. image	*sapiō* 3/4 I am sensible	*quī* + subj. expressing
similitūdō similitūdin-is 3f.	*uīn-um ī* 2n. wine	purpose
likeness	*liquō* 1 I strain	*ēnsis ēns-is* 3m. sword

153 Subjunctives expressing wishes and possibility

There are two other independent uses of the subjunctive.

1 Expressing wishes

This usage is often marked by *utinam* (negative *utinam nē*). The tenses are used as for conditions (see **S2(c)**).

Present is used to express a wish for the FUTURE, e.g.

> *ualeant cīuēs meī!* 'May my fellow-citizens fare well!' (Cicero)

Imperfect is used to express a wish for the PRESENT (see also Note), e.g.

> *illud utinam nē uērē scrīberem* 'Would that I were not writing this in all truth' (Cicero)

Pluperfect is used to express a regret about what happened (or did not happen) in the PAST, e.g.

> *utinam susceptus nōn essem* 'I wish I'd never been reared!' (Cicero)

NB. Imperfect subjunctive, as with conditionals and jussives, sometimes refers to the past. See **139³**, **152¹**

2 *Expressing possibility – the 'potential' subjunctive (cf. 138)*

The range of expressions covers much of what is expressed in English by 'may/might', 'can/could', 'should' and 'would'. In 1st s. we have:

> *uelim* 'I would like'
> *nōlim* 'I would not like'
> *mālim* 'I would prefer'

These are commonly followed by another subjunctive, e.g.

> *uelim adsīs* 'I should like you to be here'

Other 1st s. expressions are

> *ausim* 'I would dare' (from *audeō*; normal subjunctive *audeam*)
> *possim* 'I would be able'

(Note the imperfect *uellem* 'I would have wished' etc.)

2nd s. is used in 'generalising' statements, e.g.

> (present) *haud inueniās* 'you (= one) may scarcely find'
> (imperfect) *crēderēs* 'you (= one) would have believed'

3rd s. expressions include, e.g.

> (present) *dīcat aliquis* 'someone may say' (Livy) (see **171**)
> (imperfect) *quis arbitrārētur* 'who would have thought . . .?' (Cicero)

Exercise

Translate:

(a) uellem mē ad cēnam inuitāssēs[1]. (*Cicero*)
(b) putārēsne umquam accidere posse ut mihi uerba dēessent? (*Cicero*)
(c) utinam populus Rōmānus ūnam ceruīcem[2] habēret. (*Caligula*)

[1] *inuītō 1* I invite.
[2] *ceruīx ceruīc-is* 3f. neck

54 Impersonal verbs: active

These impersonal verbs appear *only in the 3rd person singular active*, but in any tense (present, future, imperfect, perfect etc.) in indicative or subjunctive. They also possess an infinitive form, so that they can appear in accusative and infinitive constructions.

You have already met (**88.5**) *licet licēre licuit* (or *licitum est*) 'it is permitted to x (dat.) to y (inf.)', e.g.

> *illīs licuit exīre* 'it was permitted to them to leave', 'they were allowed to leave'

and *placet placēre placuit* (or *placitum est*) 'it is pleasing to x (dat.) to y (inf.)', e.g.

> *mihi placēbit sequī* 'it will be pleasing for me to follow', 'I shall vote to follow'
> *negat sibi placuisse hoc dīcere* 'he denies that it was pleasing (lit. 'it to have been pleasing') to him to say this', 'he denies that he voted to say this'

and (**4B(iii)**) *oportet oportēre oportuit* 'it is right/proper for x (acc.) to y (inf.)' 'x should/ought', e.g.

> *mē oportuit abīre* 'it was right for me to leave', 'I ought to have left'

Now learn the following, some of which take a slightly different construction:

> *decet decēre decuit* 'it is fitting for x (acc.) to y (inf.)'
> *dēdecet dēdecēre dēdecuit* 'it is unseemly for x (acc.) to y (inf.)'

paenitet paenitēre paenituit 'it repents x (acc.) of y (gen.)' *or* 'it
   repents x (acc.) to y (inf.)' (i.e. 'x regrets / is dissatisfied with
   y')
miseret miserēre miseruit 'it moves x (acc.) to pity at/for y (gen.)'
pudet pudēre puduit 'it moves x (acc.) to shame for y (gen.)' (i.e. 'x
   is ashamed at/for y')
libet libēre libuit (or *libitum est*) 'it is pleasing/agreeable for x (dat.)
   to y (inf.)' 'x chooses to'

Examples of these are:

uōs decēbit nihil dīcere 'it will be fitting for you to say nothing'
tē dēdecet audīre 'it is unseemly for you to hear'
eōs paenituit illīus uerbī 'it repented them of that word', 'they
   regretted that word'
tē paenitēbit hoc facere 'it will repent you to do this', 'you will
   repent/regret doing this'
hominēs miseruit poenae 'it moved the men to pity at the
   punishment', 'the men were moved to pity / felt sorry at the
   punishment'
mē eius miseret 'it moves me to pity for him', 'I feel sorry for him'
miseret tē aliōrum, tuī tē nec miseret nec pudet 'you feel sorry for
   others, but for yourself you have neither pity nor shame'
   (Plautus)
libet mihi tē accusāre 'it is pleasing to me to accuse you', 'I want to
   accuse you', 'I choose to accuse you'

NB.   Differentiate *licet* 'it is permitted' (cf. licence) from *libet* 'it is
agreeable' (cf. libidinous; *ad lib.* = *ad libitum* 'to the point that pleases').

Exercises

1 *Translate into English*:

   (a)   mē decet hanc sententiam dīcere.
   (b)   abīre tē oportēbat.
   (c)   lēgātīs placuit studium coniūrātiōnis simulāre.
   (d)   Lentulum illīus iūris iūrandī paenitēbit.
   (e)   omnibus licet spem habēre.
   (f)   nōn omnibus eadem placent. (*Pliny*)

2 *Translate into Latin:*

   (a) I regret my enthusiasm for the conspiracy.
   (b) Catiline decided to leave Rome.
   (c) You may complain.
   (d) You (*pl.*) ought to hand yourselves over to the consul.
   (e) It is fitting for a man to die in battle.

155 Impersonal verbs: passive

Verbs which control any other case than the plain accusative (such as e.g. *parcō* (+ dat.) 'I spare') only occur in the passive *in the 3rd person singular*, e.g.

> *mihi parcēbātur* lit. 'it was being spared to me', i.e. 'I was being spared', 'clemency was being extended to me'
> *eīs nocētur* lit. 'it is being harmed to them', i.e. 'they are being harmed', 'harm is being done to them'
> *eī nōn crēdētur* lit. 'it will not be trusted to him', i.e. 'he will not be trusted', 'there will be no trust extended to him'

Hint: when a verb controlling the dative appears in the *passive*, LOOK FOR THE DATIVE TO BE THE SUBJECT.

Notes

1 Note the common impersonal passive idiom with verbs of 'going' and 'coming' to denote general movement, e.g.

> *ītur* lit. 'it is being gone', i.e. 'people are going'
> *itum est* lit. 'it was gone', i.e. 'people went'
> *uentum est* lit. 'it has been come', i.e. 'there has been an arrival'

2 There is a passive impersonal *infinitive*, for use in accusative and infinitive constructions, e.g.

> *dīxit mīlitibus imperārī* lit. 'he said it to be being ordered to the soldiers', i.e. 'he said that orders were being given to the soldiers', 'he said that the soldiers were being given their orders'
> *nescit fēminae fautum esse* lit. 'he does not know it to have been favoured to the woman', i.e. 'he does not know that the woman was favoured / given support'

See **149** for futures, where *fore ut* is always used.

3 The *agent* (person by whom the action of the passive verb is done) is expressed, as usual, by *ā/ab* + abl. e.g.

ā mīlitibus mihi crēditum est 'I was believed <u>by the soldiers</u>'

Exercises

1 *Translate into English*:

(a) concurritur. (*Horace*)
(b) diū pugnātum est.
(c) ad forum uentum est.
(d) ītur ad arma.
(e) tibi nōn crēditum est.
(f) ā nōbīs nōn parcētur labōrī.[1] (*Cicero*)
(g) ā coniūrātōribus cīuitātī nocēbitur.
(h) nōbīs imperātum est, ut in proelium inīrēmus.
(i) cibus, somnus,[2] libīdō – per hunc circulum[3] curritur.[4] (*Seneca*)

[1] *labor labōr-is* 3m. work, toil.
[2] *somn-us ī* 2m. sleep.
[3] *circul-us ī* 2m. unending cycle.
[4] *currō* 3 I run, continue, go on.

2 *Translate into Latin*:

(a) Fighting is going on.
(b) There was a rush.
(c) You (*s.*) will not be spared.
(d) Catiline was not believed by Cicero.
(e) An instruction had been given to Lentulus.

156 Future perfect indicative active 'I shall have —ed'

	1 'I shall have loved'	*2* 'I shall have had'	*3* 'I shall have said'
1st s.	amáu-er-ō (amárō *etc.*)	habú-er-ō	díx-er-ō
2nd s.	amáu-eri-s	habú-eri-s	díx-eri-s
3rd s.	amáu-eri-t	habú-eri-t	díx-eri-t
1st pl.	amāu-éri-mus	habu-éri-mus	dīx-éri-mus
2nd pl.	amāu-éri-tis	habu-éri-tis	dīx-éri-tis
3nd pl.	amáu-eri-nt	habú-eri-nt	díx-eri-nt

	4 '*I shall have heard*'	3/4 '*I shall have captured*'
1st s.	audīu-er-ō (audíerō *etc.*)	cḗper-ō
2nd s.	audīu-eri-s	cḗp-eri-s
3rd s.	audīu-eri-t	cḗperi-t
1st pl.	audīu-éri-mus	cēp-éri-mus
2nd pl.	audīu-éri-tis	cēp-éri-tis
3rd pl.	audīu-eri-nt	cḗp-eri-nt

Notes

1 The fut. perf. means 'I shall have —ed'. It is often best translated into English either as the plain present or as the plain perfect ('I have —ed'), because English does not express the strict temporal relationship between two future events, one of which is prior to the other, as Latin usually does, e.g.

> *ubi cōnsulēs uocāuerō, sententiam dīcam* 'When I (shall) have called the consuls, I shall speak my mind'
> *nisi pūnītī erunt, reī pūblicae nocēbō* 'unless they are (= shall have been) punished, I shall be hurting the republic'

2 The future perfect active is formed by taking the stem of the 3rd p.p. and adding: *-erō -eris -erit -erimus -eritis -erint*. Note that the normal active personal endings (*-ō, -s, -t, -mus, -tis, -nt*) are used.

3 Note the alternative forms of 1st and 4th conjugation *amārō* and *audierō*, where *-u-* has been dropped. This also occurs with some other verbs, e.g. *dēlērō = dēlēuerō*.

157 Future perfect indicative deponent 'I shall have —ed'

	1 '*I shall have threatened*'	2 '*I shall have promised*'	3 '*I shall have spoken*'
1st s.	mināt-us a um érō	pollícit-us a um érō	locút-us a um érō
2nd s.	mināt-us a um éris	pollícit-us a um éris	locút-us a um éris
3rd s.	mināt-us a um érit	pollícit-us a um érit	locút-us a um érit
1st pl.	mināt-ī ae a érimus	pollícit-ī ae a érimus	locút-ī ae a érimus
2nd pl.	mināt-ī ae éritis	pollícit-ī ae éritis	locút-ī ae éritis
3rd pl.	mināt-ī ae a érunt	pollícit-ī ae a érunt	locút-ī ae a érunt

	4 '*I shall have lied*'	3/4 '*I shall have advanced*'
1st s.	mentít-us a um érō	prōgréss-us a um érō
2nd s.	mentít-us a um éris	prōgréss-us a um éris
3rd s.	mentít-us a um érit	prōgréss-us a um érit

1st pl.	mentĩt-ī ae a érimus	prōgréss-ī ae a érimus
2nd pl.	mentĩt-ī ae a éritis	prōgréss-ī ae e éritis
3rd pl.	mentĩt-ī ae a érunt	prōgréss-ī ae a érunt

NB.   The future perfect deponent is formed by taking the stem of the perfect participle, adding the appropriate endings *-us -a -um* etc. to agree with the subject, and adding *erō eris erit erimus eritis erunt*, the future of *sum*.

158   **Future perfect indicative passive 'I shall have been —ed'**

	1	*2*	*3*
	'*I shall have been loved*'	'*I shall have been held*'	'*I shall have been said*'
1st s.	amãt-us érō	hábit-us érō	díct-us érō
2nd s.	amãt-us éris	hábit-us éris	díct-us éris
3rd s.	amãt-us érit	hábit-us érit	díct-us érit
1st pl.	amãt-ī érimus	hábit-ī érimus	díct-ī érimus
2nd pl.	amãt-ī éritis	hábit-ī éritis	díct-ī éritis
3rd pl.	amãt-ī érunt	hábit-ī érunt	díct-ī érunt

	4	*3/4*
	'*I shall have been heard*'	'*I shall have been captured*'
1st s.	audĩt-us érō	cápt-us érō
2nd s.	audĩt-us éris	cápt-us éris
3rd s.	audĩt-us érit	cápt-us érit
1st pl.	audĩt-ī érimus	cápt-ī érimus
2nd pl.	audĩt-ī éritis	cápt-ī éritis
3rd pl.	audĩt-ī érunt	cápt-ī érunt

NB.   For formation of the future perfect indicative passive, see note on future perfect deponent (above) **157**.

Exercises

1   *Form and conjugate these verbs in the future perfect tense (where 'passive' is written, give active* and *passive – give deponent and passive in m. form).* cūnctor, trādō, occupō (*passive*), ēripiō, praebeō, committō (*passive*), exorior, sum, (*optional:* cohortor, pūniō (*passive*), nōlō, adeō, patefaciō (*passive*), ūtor, patior, noceō).

2   *Translate these future perfects, then change s. to pl. or vice versa:* mõuerit, ĩnfueritis, parãta erit, conuocãtī erunt, putãuerint, cōnãtus eris,

impedīuerimus, uīxerō, exorta erunt, potuerint, (*optional*: adiūnxerit, mandāuerimus, agitātus erit, petīuerint, nārrāta erunt, recordātus eris, prohibuerō, simulātum erit, profectī eritis, questa erit).

3 *Give the Latin for*: I shall have lived; he will have attacked; they will have thought; she will have been sought out; it will have seemed; you (*pl.*) will have handed over; they will have been seized; you (*s.*) will have punished; (*optional*: it will have arisen; they will have hesitated; I shall have rescued; it will have been revealed; she will have committed; we will have finished; you (*pl.*) will have besieged; they (*n.*) will have been broken).

4 *Locate and translate the future perfects in this list (say which tense the others are)*: cupīueram, cohortātī erunt, parāuerās, pūnīta eris, seruāuissent, ērepta erit, imperāuistī, exortī eritis, trādidistis, uocāuerātis, nocuerō, cōnsīderāuerit, līberāuimus, cūnctāta esset, praebuerit, questus erō, aperuistis, nārrāuērunt, simulāuerint, requīsīuit, adierimus, aggressus esset, ēffēcerit, uīsum erat.

5 *Translate these sentences*:

(a) nisi cōnsulibus Rōmānōs in perīculō esse nūntiāuerimus, coniūrātōrēs rem pūblicam occupābunt.

(b) cōnsul ubi cīuīs malōs pūnīuerit, omnibus nūntiābit rem pūblicam saluam esse.

(c) sī coniūrātōrēs in templum Concordiae īre iusserō, illī nōn cūnctābuntur.

(d) paucīs diēbus illī interfectī erunt.

(e) ubi coniūrātōrēs occīsī erunt, Cicerōnī poena eōrum onerī erit.

(f) nisi cōnstituerit cōnsul fore ut coniūrātōrēs necentur, cīuitās in magnō perīculō erit.

(g) sapientī[1] nōn nocētur ā paupertāte,[2] nōn ā dolōre.[3] (*Seneca*)

[1] *sapiēns sapient-is* 3m. wise man.
[2] *paupertās paupertāt-is* 3f. poverty.
[3] *dolor dolōr-is* 3m. pain.

159 Numerals: cardinal 11–90 and ordinal 1st–10th

Cardinal

11	XI	úndecim
12	XII	duódecim
13	XIII	trédecim
14	XIV	quattuórdecim
15	XV	quíndecim

16	XVI	sēdecim
17	XVII	septéndecim
18	XVIII	duodēuigíntī
19	XIX	ūndēuigíntī
20	XX	uigíntī
30	XXX	trīgíntā
40	XL	quādrāgíntā
50	L	quīnquāgíntā
60	LX	sexāgíntā
70	LXX	septuāgíntā
80	LXXX	octōgíntā
90	XC	nōnāgíntā

Ordinal

1st	prímus (príor)
2nd	secúndus (álter)
3rd	tértius
4th	quártus
5th	quíntus
6th	séxtus
7th	séptimus
8th	octáuus
9th	nónus
10th	décimus etc.

Notes

1 Ordinals decline like *mult-us a um*.

2 See **54** for cardinals 1–10, 100–1,000.

English–Latin

Reread the text of **5C(iii)***, then translate this passage into Latin:*

Cicero was seized by great anxiety[1]. He therefore spoke to himself as follows: 'You should realise[2] that you have saved the state from danger. Do not hesitate to demand the death-penalty from the conspirators. If they are spared[3,4] by you, the state will be harmed[3]. If Roman citizens are killed[4] on the say-so of a consul, this death-penalty will be a burden on you. Nevertheless, you ought to be bold. I think that you won't regret[5] this boldness. For you will have saved the state.'

[1] Turn the sentence into the active, with 'anxiety' as subject, 'Cicero' as object.

[2] Use jussive subjunctive.

[3] Remember that *noceō/parcō* take dative, so you must use impersonal passives here ('they' and 'the state' will be dative; 'by you' *ā* + abl.).

[4] Use future perfect tense.

[5] Use *fore ut* + subjunctive.

Virgil's *Aeneid*

Aeneas, still telling the story of the fall of Troy, recounts how Achilles' son Pyrrhus (also called Neoptolemus) caught up with Troy's aged king Priam and slaughtered him at the very altar where he and his family had been taking refuge. His headless corpse now lies on the beach.

sic fātus senior tēlumque imbelle sine ictū
coniēcit, raucō quod prōtinus aere repulsum
et summō clipeī nequīquam umbōne pependit.
cūī Pyrrhus: 'referēs ergō haec et nūntius ībis
Pēlīdae genitōrī. illī mea trīstia facta   5
dēgeneremque Neoptolemum nārrāre mementō.
nunc morere.'

With these words the old man hurled his spear, but it did no damage. There was no strength in it. It rattled on the bronze of Pyrrhus' shield without penetrating, and hung there useless, sticking in the central boss on the surface of the shield. Pyrrhus then made his reply. 'In that case you will take this message from me and go with it to my dead father Achilles. Describe my cruelty to him and remember to tell him that Neoptolemus [= *Pyrrhus*] is a disgrace to his father. Now, die.'

hoc dīcēns altāria ad ipsa trementem

trāxit et in multō lāpsantem sanguine nātī,

implicuitque comam laeuā, dextrāque coruscum   10

extulit ac laterī capulō tenus abdidit ēnsem.

haec fīnis Priamī fātōrum, hic exitus illum

sorte tulit Trōiam incēnsam et prōlāpsa uidentem

Pergama, tot quondam populīs terrīsque superbum

rēgnātōrem Asiae. iacet ingēns lītore truncus,   15

āuulsumque umerīs caput et sine nōmine corpus.

(*Aeneid 2.544–58*)

hoc dīcēns [Take together to solve *hoc* (n.) at once]
altāri-um ī 2n. altar
tremō 3 I tremble [With *age* not fear, here. Present participle in acc., so something or someone is 'trembling'. If no noun, 'the person trembling'. Await subject and verb]
trahō 3 *trāxī* I drag [Solves *trementem*: and who is it who is 'trembling'?]
in multō [But *multō* what? Wait]

lāpsō 1 I slip [Surely the same person as *trementem*]
sanguine [Solves *multō*]
nāt-us ī 2m. son [Priam's son Polites had just been killed by Neoptolemus]
10 *implicō implicuī* 1 I wrap x (acc.) in y (abl.)
com-a ae 1f. hair
laeu-a ae 1f. left hand
dextr-a ae 1f. right hand

corusc-us a um gleaming [But what? 'something gleaming, nom. or acc.']
extulit [Probably what he does to whatever it is that is gleaming]
ecferō 3 extulī I take out
latus later-is 3n. side [Register dative, wait]
capul-us ī 2m. hilt [Dat. or abl. Wait]
tenus (+abl.) as far as, right up to [Solves *capulō*]
abdō 3 abdidī I bury
ēnsis ēns-is 3m. sword [So 'he buried the sword right up to the hilt *laterī*': whose *laterī*? Can you now solve *coruscum*?]
fīnis fīn-is 3f. end [Sc. *fuit*]
fāt-a ōrum 2n. pl. fate, destiny
exit-us ūs 4m. death
illum [Presumably Priam, in acc.. Wait]
sors sort-is 3f. allocation, lot, fate [Hold]
tulit [So 'this death took him off *sorte*'. Meaning of *sorte*?]
Trōiam incēnsam [What is this acc. doing? The meaning appeared to be complete, but we now have an unaccountable acc.. Be patient. 'Something about "burned Troy" in the acc.']
prōlābor 3 prōlapsus I collapse, fall [Probably acc. pl. n., to complement *Trōiam* in the acc. So 'and something fallen']
uidentem [Acc. s. m. At last! Who must this agree with? What does it solve?]

Pergam-a ōrum 2n. pl. the citadel of Troy [Solves *prōlāpsa*]
tot [Here we go again, when we thought the sense complete]
quondam once upon a time
populīs terrīsque [Probably with *tot*. Hold dat. or abl.]
superb-us a um proud, splendid [Could this be acc. s. m. referring to Priam, who has just seen Troy burnt (etc.)? Wait]
15 *rēgnātor rēgnātōr-is* 3m. ruler [Acc. s. m., so *superbum rēgnātōrem* looks very much as if it does refer to Priam]
Asiae [Confirms the above]
iaceō 2 I lie [Who? Probably Priam . . . but wait. *ingēns* 'mighty Priam'? Wait]
lītus lītor-is 3n. shore
trunc-us ī 2m. torso [Ah. 'He lies, a mighty torso, *lītore*.' How did it get *lītore*? One tradition held Priam was killed at Achilles' tomb on the shore, so Virgil has moved from palace to shore to accommodate it. There may be another reason: Pompey was beheaded on a beach in Egypt (see **6C(iii)**). Virgil may be reminding his readers of that]
āuellō 3 āuulsī āuuls-us I rip ['Something ripped']
umer-us ī 2m. shoulder [Abl., perhaps 'ripped from']

Deliciae Latinae

From the 'Life of Aurelian'

A ditty composed by fellow-soldiers of Aurelian (Emperor A.D. 270) on the basis of his exploits against the Sarmatians (before his principate). He was reported to have slain over 950 in the course of just a few days.

mīlle mīlle mīlle dēcollāuimus.
ūnus homo! mīlle dēcollāuimus.
mīlle bibat quī mīlle occīdit.
tantum uīnī habet nēmo, quantum fūdit sanguinis.

mīlle 'a thousand men'
    (acc.)
dēcollō 1 I behead,
    decapitate

tantum . . . *quantum* as
    much . . . as [cf. *satis/*
    nimis + gen. **31**]
uīn-um ī 2n. wine

fundō 3 *fūdī* I spill, shed
    (the subject is Aurelian,
    who is also the *ūnus*
    homo of l. 2)

The Vulgate: *creātiō caelī et terrae*

in prīncipiō creāuit Deus caelum et terram. terra autem erat inānis et
uacua, et tenebrae erant super faciem abyssī, et Spīritus Deī ferēbātur
super aquās. dīxitque Deus, 'fīat lūx', et facta est lūx. et uīdit Deus lūcem
quod esset bona: et dīuīsit lūcem ā tenebrīs. appellāuitque lūcem Diem, et
tenebrās Noctem: factumque est uespere et māne, diēs ūnus.   5
    dīxit quoque Deus, 'fīat firmāmentum in mediō aquārum: et dīuidat
aquās ab aquīs.' et fēcit Deus firmāmentum, dīuīsitque aquās, quae erant
sub firmāmentō, ab hīs, quae erant super firmāmentum. et factum est ita.
uocāuitque Deus firmāmentum Caelum: et factum est uespere et māne,
diēs secundus.   10
    dīxit uērō Deus, 'congregentur aquae, quae sub caelō sunt, in locum
ūnum, et appāreat ārida.' et factum est ita. et uocāuit Deus āridam
Terram, congregātiōnēsque aquārum appellāuit Maria. et uīdit Deus
quod esset bonum. et ait, 'germinet terra herbam uirentem et facientem
sēmen, et lignum pōmiferum faciēns frūctum iuxtā genus suum, cuius   15
sēmen in sēmetipsō sit super terram.' et factum est ita. et prōtulit terra
herbam uirentem, et facientem sēmen iuxtā genus suum, lignumque
faciēns frūctum, et habēns ūnumquodque sēmentem secundum speciem
suam. et uīdit Deus quod esset bonum. et factum est uespere et māne, diēs
tertius.   20
    dīxit autem Deus, 'fīant lūmināria in firmāmentō caelī, et dīuidant
diem ac noctem, et sint in signa et tempora, et diēs et annōs; ut lūceant in
firmāmentō caelī, et illūminent terram.' et factum est ita. fēcitque Deus
duo lūmināria magna: lūmināre maius ut praeesset diēī: et lūmināre
minus ut praeesset noctī: et stellās. et posuit eās in firmāmentō caelī, ut   25
lūcērent super terram et praeessent diēī ac noctī, et dīuiderent lūcem ac
tenebrās. et uīdit Deus quod esset bonum. et factum est uespere et māne,
diēs quārtus.
    dīxit etiam Deus, 'prōdūcant aquae rēptile animae uīuentis et uolātile

351

super terram sub firmāmentō caelī.' creāuitque Deus cētē grandia, et   30
omnem animam uīuentem atque mōtābilem, quam prōdūxerant aquae
in speciēs suās, et omne uolātile secundum genus suum. et uīdit Deus
quod esset bonum. benedīxitque eīs, dīcēns, 'crēscite, et multiplicāminī,
et replēte aquās maris: auēsque multiplicentur super terram.' et factum
est uespere et māne, diēs quīntus.   35

dīxit quoque Deus, 'prōdūcat terra animam uīuentem in genere suō,
iūmenta, et rēptilia, et bēstiās terrae secundum speciēs suās.' factumque
est ita. et fēcit Deus bēstiās terrae iuxtā speciēs suās, et iūmenta, et omne
rēptile terrae in genere suō. et uīdit Deus quod esset bonum. et ait,
'faciāmus hominem ad imāginem et similitūdinem nostram, et praesit   40
piscibus maris, et uolātilibus caelī, et bēstiīs, ūniuersaeque terrae,
omnīque rēptilī, quod mouētur in terrā.' et creāuit Deus hominem ad
imāginem suam: ad imāginem Deī creāuit illum, masculum et fēminam
creāuit eōs. benedīxitque illīs Deus, et ait, 'crēscite et multiplicāminī, et
replēte terram, et subicite eam, et domināminī piscibus maris, et   45
uolātilibus caelī, et ūniuersīs animantibus, quae mouentur super terram.'
dīxitque Deus, 'ecce dedī uōbīs omnem herbam afferentem sēmen super
terram, et ūniuersa ligna quae habent in sēmetipsīs sēmentem generis suī,
ut sint uōbīs in ēscam: et cūnctīs animantibus terrae, omnīque uolucrī
caelī, et ūniuersīs quae mouentur in terrā, et in quibus est anima uīuēns, ut   50
habeant ad uēscendum.' et factum est ita. uīditque Deus cūncta quae
fēcerat, et erant ualdē bona. et factum est uespere et māne, diēs sextus.

igitur perfectī sunt caelī et terra, et omnis ōrnātus eōrum.
complēuitque Deus diē septimō opus suum quod fēcerat: et requiēuit diē
septimō ab ūniuersō opere quod patrārat. et benedīxit diēī septimō et   55
sānctificāuit illum, quia in ipsō cessāuerat ab omnī opere suō quod creāuit
Deus ut faceret. (*Genesis 1.1–2.3*)

---

creātiō creātiōn-is 3f. creation
cael-um ī 2n. heaven, sky; *pl. cael-ī ōrum*
 2m.
prīncipi-um ī 2n. beginning
creō 1 I create
inān-is e empty
uacu-us a um void
tenebr-ae ārum 1f. pl. shadows, darkness
faci-ēs faciē-ī 5f. face
abyss-us ī 2f. depths of the sea
super (+ acc.) over, above
spīrit-us ūs 4m. spirit; breath
lūx lūc-is 3f. light

quod that (+ subj.) [*Also in* ll. 14, 19,
 27, 33, 39]
dīuidō 3 *dīuīsī* I divide
appellō 1 I call
5 *uespere* n. evening
māne n. morning
ūnus = prīmus
firmāment-um ī 2n. prop; stay; sky
 above the earth
sub (+ abl.) underneath
11 *congregō* 1 I gather
appāreō 2 I appear
ārid-a ae 1f. dry land

congregātiō congregātiōn-is 3f. gathering
ait 'he said'
germinō 1 I produce
herb-a ae 1f. grass
uirēns uirent-is green
15 *sēmen sēmin-is* 3n. seed
lign-um ī 2n. wood, tree
pōmifer pōmifer-a um fruit-bearing
frūct-us ūs 4m. fruit
iuxtā (+ acc.) in accordance with
genus gener-is 3n. kind, type
sēmetipsō 'itself' [*Pl.* l. 48: *sēmetipsīs* 'themselves']
prōferō prōferre prōtulī I produce
ūnumquodque each one
sēmentis sēment-is 3f. sowing
secundum (+ acc.) in accordance with
speciēs speciē-ī 5f. species
20 *lūmināre lūminār-is* 3n. light
in (+ acc.) for the purpose of [*Also* l. 49]
lūceō 2 I shine
illūminō 1 I light up
25 *stell-a ae* 1f. star
prōdūcō 3 *prōdūxī* I produce, bring forth
rēptile rēptil-is 3n. crawling creature
anim-a ae 1f. soul, animal
uolātile uolātil-is 3n. flying creature
30 *cētē* n. pl. sea-beasts, monsters

grand-is e huge, vast
mōtābil-is e moving
in (+ acc.) in accordance with
benedīcō 3 *benedīxī* I bless (+ dat.)
crēscō 3 I increase
multiplicor 1 dep. I multiply
34 *repleō* 2 I fill
auis au-is 3f. bird
iūment-um ī 2n. beast
bēsti-a ae 1f. wild beast
imāgō imāgin-is 3f. image
40 *similitūdō similitūdin-is* 3f. likeness
piscis pisc-is 3m. fish
ūniuers-us a um whole, all
mascul-us ī 2m. male
subiciō 3/4 I subdue
45 *dominor* 1 dep. I rule (+ dat.)
animāns animant-is 3m./f. animal
in ēscam 'for food'
uolucris uolucr-is 3f. bird
51 *ad uēscendum* 'for eating'
cūnct-us a um every, all
ualdē very
ōrnāt-us ūs 4m. decoration, trimmings
compleō 2 *complēuī* I finish
requiēscō 3 *requiēuī* I rest
patrō 1 I effect
sānctificō 1 I sanctify
cessō 1 I stop, cease

Section 5D

Running vocabulary for 5D(i)

acerb-us a um bitter
an: see *utrum*
arcessō 3 I summon
arx arc-is 3f. citadel
aspect-us ūs 4m. appearance

atrōcitās atrōcitāt-is 3f. harshness
attribuō 3 I assign, give x (acc.) to Y (dat.) (as his share)

bacchor 1 dep. I rave, revel, act like a Bacchant
clēmēns clēment-is merciful
concitō 1 I incite
coniūnx coniug-is 3f. wife

contrā (+acc.) against
crūdēl-is e cruel
dīripiend-us a um to be torn apart (*dīripiō* 3/4)
dolor dolōr-is 3m. pain, anguish
domicili-um ī 2n. dwelling
dūcend-us a um to be led
etenim for in fact, and indeed
ēuertend-us a um to be overturned (*ēuertō* 3)
ferre-us a um made of iron, unfeeling
fug-a ae 1f. flight
fundāment-um ī 2n. foundation
Gall-ī ōrum 2m. pl. Gauls
hūmānitās hūmānitāt-is 3f. humanity, kindness
idcircō for this reason, therefore
importūn-us a um cruel, savage
incendend-us a um to be burned
inhūmān-us a um cruel, savage
interficiend-us a um to be killed

lāmentātiō lāmentātiōn-is 3f. lamentation
lēniō 4 I soothe
lūx lūc-is 3f. light
māter familiās mātr-is familiās 3f. mother (of the household)
miserand-us a um to be pitied
misericordi-a ae 1f. pity
misericors misericord-is compassionate
mīt-is e gentle, mild
necand-us a um to be killed
neglegend-us a um to be ignored
orbis terrārum orb-is terrārum 3m. the world (lit. the circle of lands)
pater familiās patr-is familiās 3m. father (head of the household)
perhorrēscō 3 I shudder greatly at, have a great fear of
prōpōnō 3 I imagine (*mihi prōpōnō* = I set before my mind's eye)

rēgnō 1 I rule (as king)
remiss-us a um mild, slack
seuēr-us a um strict, stern
sīn but if
singulār-is e unparalleled, extraordinary
singul-ī ae a individual
sūmō 3 I take
supplicium sūmere to exact the penalty (from x: *dē* + abl.)
timend-us a um to be feared
trucīdō 1 I butcher
uāstand-us a um to be laid waste (*uāstō* 1)
uehemēns uehement-is violent
uersor 1 dep. I stay
Vestāl-is e Vestal (belonging to the goddess Vesta)
uexātiō uexātiōn-is 3f. ill-treatment
ūniuers-us a um whole, entire
utrum . . . an = double question, i.e. A or B?

Notes

l. 153 *in uestrā caede* 'in your slaughter' = 'in slaughter of you'. Possessive adjectives are often used in this way.

ll. 159–62 *sī . . . sūmat, . . . uideātur*: note mood of verbs, and remember *sī* + pres. subj., pres. subj. = 'if x were to happen, y would happen.'

l. 160 *quam acerbissimum* 'as bitter as possible'. See *learning vocabulary* **5B(iii)**.

ll. 163–4 *uideātur . . . nisi . . . lēniat*: see note on ll. 159–62. *nocentis* 'of the person who harmed him': pres. part. used as a noun.

ll. 170–1 *ad ēuertenda fundāmenta*: tr. 'to overturn the foundations'.

l. 171 *ad incendendam urbem*: tr. 'to set the city on fire'.

l. 172 *ad dūcendum . . . exercitum*: tr. 'to lead an army'.

Learning vocabulary for 5D(i)

Nouns

arx arc-is 3f. citadel

dolor dolōr-is 3m. pain,
anguish

fug-a ae 1f. flight
lūx lūc-is 3f. light

Adjectives

crūdēl-is e cruel
miserand-us a um to be
pitied

misericors misericord-is
compassionate
seuēr-us a um strict, stern
uehemēns uehement-is
impetuous, violent

Vestāl-is e Vestal
(belonging to the
goddess Vesta)

Verbs

arcessō 3 arcessiuī arcessītus
I summon
attribuō 3 attribuī attribūtus
I assign, give
(ad + tribuō)

prōpōnō 3 prōposuī
prōpositus I set before;
imagine; offer
(prō + pōnō)

sūmō 3 sūmpsī sūmptus I
take; put on; eat;
supplicium sūmere dē
(+ abl.) to exact the
penalty from x

Others

contrā (+ acc.) against
idcircō for this/that reason,
therefore

utrum . . . an = double
question, i.e. A or B?
(negative: annōn, i.e. A
or not?)

Running vocabulary for 5D(ii)

acerb-us a um bitter
adit-us ūs 4m. entrance
commūn-is e shared, in
common
cōnscrīpt-us a um chosen,
elected
cōnseruand-us a um to be
preserved (cōnseruō 1)
cum . . . tum both . . . and
dīligenti-a ae 1f. diligence
genus gener-is 3n. kind,
type
imperi-um ī 2n. power,
authority, dominion

nē (+ subj.) that, lest
nefand-us a um impious,
execrable
ōrdō ōrdin-is 3m. rank
patrēs cōnscrīptī =
senātōrēs senators
patri-a ae 1f. fatherland
prōuideō 2 prōuīdī prōuīsus
I take care of
remissiō remissiōn-is 3f.
remission, relaxation
retinend-us a um to be
retained (retineō 2)

timend-us a um to be
feared (timeō 2)
trānsigend-us a um to be
accomplished (trānsigō
3)
uerend-us a um to be
feared (uereor 2 dep.)
uereor 2 dep. I fear, am
afraid ('that': nē +
subj.; 'that not': ut +
subj.)
uoluntās uoluntat-is 3f.
will, wish
ut (+ subj.) (after uereor)
'that . . . not'

355

Notes

ll. 174, 175, 177 *nē*: following *timeō* or *uereor* – '(I am afraid) that x will happen'.

l. 175 *seuēriōrēs*: remember that comparatives may mean 'rather' and 'too' as well as 'more'.

ll. 178–9 *uererī . . . ut*: 'be afraid that x will *not* happen'.

l. 179 *ad cōnsilia . . . trānsigenda*: tr. 'to accomplish your plans'.

l. 180–1 *cum . . . tum*: 'both . . . and' – a favourite construction in Cicero.

l. 181–2 *ad summum . . . retinendum*: tr. 'to retain the sovereign power'.

l. 182 *ad commūnīs . . . cōnseruandās*: tr. 'to preserve the fortunes we share'.

Learning vocabulary for 5D(ii)

Nouns

genus gener-is 3n. type, kind (family; stock; tribe)

imperi-um ī 2n. power, authority, dominion (order, command)

ōrdō ōrdin-is 3m. rank (i.e. section of society or line of soldiers)

patrēs cōnscrīptī = *senātōrēs* senators

patri-a ae 1f. fatherland

uoluntās uoluntāt-is 3f. will, wish

Adjectives

acerb-us a um bitter

commūn-is e shared in, common, universal

Verbs

cōnseruō 1 I keep safe, preserve (*con* + *seruō*)

prōuideō 2 *prōuīdī prōuīsus* I take care (often followed by *nē* + subj.) (*prō* + *uideō*)

uereor 2 dep. *ueritus* I fear, am afraid (usually followed by *nē*/*ut* + subj.)

Others

cum . . . tum both . . . and (especially common in Cicero)

Running vocabulary for 5D(iii)

aspect-us ūs 4m. appearance
cār-us a um dear, valued
concordi-a ae 1f. harmony
coniungō 3 I bring x (acc.) to support y (*ad* + acc.)
cōnsentiō 4 I agree
cōnseruand-us a um to be preserved (*cōseruō* 1)

dēfendend-us a um to be defended (*dēfendō* 3)
dignitās dignitāt-is 3f. position
dīligenti-a ae 1f. care, diligence
dulc-is e sweet
iūcund-us a um pleasant
par par-is equal

parāt-us a um prepared (to: *ad* + acc.–*parō* 1)
perhorrēscō 3 I shudder greatly at
possessiō possessiōn-is 3f. possession
quantum as much as
tribūn-us ī aerārius 2m. citizen of the class below *equitēs*

Notes

l. 186 *in quā . . . sentiant*: the subjunctive is generic (see **140.1**).

ll. 187–8 *ad salūtem . . . dēfendendam dignitātemque cōnseruandam*: tr. 'to defend the safety . . . and preserve the position'.

ll. 186–8 *quī nōn . . . cōnsentiat*: the subjunctive is generic (see **140.1**).

ll. 188, 189 *quis eques: quis tribūnus aerārius: quis* is used here as an adjective (cf. **102³**).

ll. 188–9 *quem . . . nōn . . . coniungat*: the subjunctive is generic (see **140.1**).

l. 190 *dēfendendae rēī pūblicae*: tr. 'of defending the state'.

ll. 189–90 *quī nōn . . . conueniat*: the subjunctive is generic (see **140.1**).

ll. 190–1 *cui nōn . . . sit*: the subjunctive is generic (see **140.1**).

l. 192 *nēmō*: here used as an adjective (= *nūllus*).

ll. 192–4 *quī nōn . . . perhorrēscat, quī nōn . . . cupiat, quī nōn . . . sit*: generic statements, using the subjunctive (see **140.1**).

ll. 193–4 *ad salūtem . . . dēfendendam*: tr. 'to defend . . . the safety . . .'

Learning vocabulary for 5D(iii)

Nouns

concordi-a ae 1f. harmony

dignitās dignitāt-is 3f. distinction, position; honour; rank, high office

dīligenti-a ae 1f. care, diligence

Adjectives

dulc-is e sweet
iūcund-us a um pleasant

Others

quantum as much as

Running vocabulary for 5D(iv)

anim-a ae 1f. soul, life
ār-a ae 1f. altar
auct-us a um increased
 (*augeō* 2)
benignitās benignitāt-is 3f.
 kindness
commendō 1 I entrust x
 (acc.) to y (dat.)
coniūnx coniug-is 3f. wife
cōnsentiō 4 I agree
cōnseruand-us a um to be
 preserved (*cōnseruō* 1)
cūrand-us a um to be taken
 care of (*cūrō* 1)
dēfendend-us a um to be
 defended (*dēfendō* 3)
fax fac-is 3f. torch,
 firebrand
fundāt-us a um established
 (*fundō* 1)

immō uērō nay rather
impi-us a um with no
 respect for gods,
 parents or fatherland
iūdicand-us a um to be
 judged (*iūdicō* 1)
labor labōr-is 3m. toil,
 hard work, trouble
lībertās lībertāt-is 3f.
 freedom
memor memor-is mindful
 of (x: gen.)
mēns ment-is 3f. mind
nē (+ subj.) after *prōuideō*
 'in case', 'lest'
oblīuīscor 3 dep. *oblītus* I
 forget (+ gen. of
 person)
obsess-us a um besieged
 (*obsideō* 2)

paene almost
parāt-us a um prepared
 (to: *ad* + acc. – *parō* 1)
Penātēs Penāt-ium 3m. pl.
 gods of the household
posthāc after this time,
 hereafter, in future
prōuidend-us a um to be
 taken care about
 (*prōuideō* 2)
sempitern-us a um eternal
stabilīt-us a um made firm
 (*stabiliō* 4)
supplex supplic-is suppliant
tendō 3 I stretch forth
uel even
ūniuers-us a um whole
Vest-a ae 1f. Vesta
 (goddess of the hearth)

Notes

l. 196 *prōuidendum est nē*: lit. 'it is to be taken care about lest . . .'.

l. 197 *ad uītam suam dēfendendam*: 'to defend his own life'.

ll. 197–8 *ad uestram salūtem cūrandam*: 'to take care of your safety'.

ll. 198–9 *ad cōnseruandam rem pūblicam*: 'to keep the state safe'.

ll. 200–1 *uōbīs sē . . .*: not solved until *commendat* in l. 8. Tr. 'to you herself
(obj.) . . .' etc.

l. 204 *uōbīs iūdicandum est*: tr. 'you ought to judge' (lit. 'it is to-be-judged
as-far-as-you-are-concerned').

ll. 209–10 *nē . . .*: 'that', 'lest', picked up by *prōuidendum est*, lit. 'it is to be
taken care about'.

l. 210 *uōbis prōuidendum est nē . . .*: tr. 'you must take care, lest . . .' (lit. 'it
is to-be-taken–care-about as-far-as-you-are-concerned').

Learning vocabulary for 5D(iv)

Nouns

ār-a ae 1f. altar
labor labōr-is 3m. toil,
 hard work; trouble

Adjectives

impi-us a um with no respect for gods, parents or fatherland

memor memor-is remembering (x: gen.), mindful of (x: gen.)

supplex supplic-is suppliant (also a noun)

Verbs

augeō 2 auxī auctus I increase (trans.)

oblīuīscor 3 dep. oblītus I forget (+ gen. of person)

tendō 3 tetendī tēnsus or *tentus* I stretch (out); offer; direct; travel

Others

paene almost
uel even (either . . . or)

Grammar and exercises for 5D

60 **Gerundives: *-ndus -nda -ndum* 'to be —ed'**

The gerundive is an adjective based on a verb and declining like *mult-us a um*. Its meaning is passive, 'to be —ed'. Here is the formation:

1	*2*	*3*
amá-nd-us a um	habé-nd-us a um	dīc-é-nd-us a um
'to be loved'	'to be had'	'to be said'
miná-nd-us a um[1]	pollicé-nd-us a um	loqu-é-nd-us a um
'to be threatened'	'to be promised'	'to be said'

4	*3/4*
audi-é-nd-us a um	capi-é-nd-us a um
'to be heard'	'to be captured'
menti-é-nd-us a um[1]	prōgredi-é-nd-us a um[1]
'to be lied'	'to be advanced'

[1] These verbs, being intransitive, would normally be found only in the neuter. See **161**[1].

61 **Uses of the gerundive**

1 As an adjective meaning 'to be —ed', e.g.

trādidit nōs necandōs 'he handed us over to be killed'

A number of other verbs take this construction e.g. *dō, petō, cūrō* etc., e.g.

> *Caesar pontem in Arare faciendum cūrat* 'Caesar saw to the making of a bridge over the Arar.' (Caesar)

2 With any tense of *sum*, carrying the idea of obligation, duty, necessity (i) personally, e.g.

> *mīlitēs erant reuocandī* 'the soldiers were to be called back', 'had to be recalled', 'needed to be recalled'

(ii) impersonally, in the neuter singular, e.g.

> *prōuidendum est* 'it is to be taken care about', 'care needs to be taken'
> *eundum est* 'it is to be gone', 'one must go'

3 With nouns, especially *ad* + acc. to denote purpose, e.g.:

> *ad ēuertenda fundāmenta* 'for the foundations to be overturned', i.e. 'for overturning the foundations' / 'with a view to overturning foundations'.

The ablatives *causā/grātiā* 'for the sake of' (which *follow* the phrase which they govern), are commonly used with a gerundive construction to express purpose, e.g.

> *templī uidendī causā* 'for the sake of the temple-to-be-seen', 'for the sake of seeing the temple', 'to see the temple'.

(Cf. *honōris causā* (or *grātiā*) 'for honour's sake', 'as an honour'; e.g. = *exemplī grātiā* 'for (the sake of) an example'.)

NB. Where awkwardness results from literal translation of the gerundive, turn the phrase into an *active* form in English, e.g. *ad mīlitēs necandōs* lit. 'with a view to the soldiers to be killed' → 'with a view to killing the soldiers'.

Notes

1 The impersonal construction is very common with verbs which do not take a direct object in the accusative. These cannot be used personally in the passive, so appear in the passive impersonally with a number of adjustments (cf. **155**), e.g.

> *parcendum est fēminae* 'it is to be spared to the woman', 'the woman must be spared'

Deponents also are used thus, e.g.

> *ūtendum est sapientiā* 'one should use wisdom'

2 'By' a person is normally expressed by a *plain dative* with gerundives, e.g. *omnia sunt paranda Caesarī* 'everything is to be prepared by Caesar'. But where the verb in gerundive form normally takes the dative, *ā/ ab* + abl. is used instead, e.g. *parcendum est fēminae ā mē* 'the woman must be spared by me', 'I must spare the woman'.

Exercises

1 *Form the gerundive of the following verbs and translate (using n.s. for intransitive verbs, 'it must be —ed')*: arcessō, dēleō, augeō, prōpōnō, necō, dormiō, commoror, uereor, prōgredior, (*optional*: attribuō, sūmō, cōnseruō, tendō, praebeō, ūtor, pūniō, cohortor).

2 *Translate*:

   (a) mihi prōuidendum est.
   (b) ad urbem dēlendam.
   (c) labōris agendī causā.
   (d) dux mīlitibus supplicem interficiendum trādidit.
   (e) ad arcem dēfendendam.
   (f) nōbīs prōgrediendum erat.
   (g) Cicerō cīuīs cōnseruandōs cūrat.
   (h) ad manūs tendendās.
   (i) ducis necandī grātiā.
   (j) tibi eundum erit.
   (k) Cicerō custōdibus coniūrātōrēs cūrandōs trādet.
   (l) ad ārās dēlendās.
  (m) Catilīnae arcessendī causā.
   (n) ad uoluntātem cōnseruandam.
   (o) Lentulus omnia Catilīnae dēlenda attribuit.
   (p) dēlenda est Karthāgō.
   (q) arx capienda erat.
   (r) dolor augendus nōn est.
   (s) supplicium sūmendum erit.
   (t) supplicēs trādendī nōn sunt.
   (u) ā tē cīuibus parcendum est.
   (v) cīuibus ā mē nocendum nōn erat.

   (w)   moriendum est omnibus. (*Cicero*)
   (x)   nīl sine ratiōne faciendum est. (*Seneca*)
   (y)   ōrandum est ut sit mēns[1] sāna[2] in corpore sānō. (*Juvenal*)
   (z)   nūllī enim nisi audītūrō dīcendum est. (*Seneca*)

[1] *mēns ment-is* 3f. mind.
[2] *sān-us a um* healthy.

3 *Give the Latin for*:

   (a)   I must go away.
   (b)   Cicero will have to take care.
   (c)   To preserve harmony. (*Use ad + acc.*)
   (d)   For the sake of exacting the penalty. (*Use* causā *or* grātiā + *gen. after the phrase*)
   (e)   To summon the citizens. (*Use* ad + *acc.*)
   (f)   We had to go forward.
   (g)   Our fatherland must be preserved.
   (h)   The conspirators must be punished.
   (i)   We must not harm our fatherland.
   (j)   Cicero should spare no conspirator.

162 *timeō, metuō, uereor* 'I am afraid to/that/lest'

These 'verbs of fearing' can take an infinitive or subjunctive construction.

They take an *infinitive* construction when English does, e.g.

> *timeō īre* 'I am afraid to go'
> *ueritī sunt dīcere* 'they were afraid to say'

They take a *subjunctive* construction with *nē* (negative *ut* or *nē nōn*) when the meaning is 'fear that/lest'. One would expect a subjunctive here: the certainties about the usual conditions and nature of events have disappeared (cf. **138**). E.g.

> *uereor nē Caesar mox redeat* 'I am afraid that/lest Caesar will soon return'
> *timent ut ad patriam ueniant* 'they are afraid that they will not reach their fatherland'
> *metuimus nē Cicerō satis praesidī nōn habeat* 'we fear that Cicero does not have enough of a guard'

Observe that

> fearing + *nē* = 'fear that/lest' (i.e. what you want *not* to happen may happen)
>
> fearing + *ut/nē nōn* = 'fear that . . . NOT' (i.e. what you want to happen may *not*)

Notes

1 The subjunctive is controlled by rules of sequence (see **A–G Intro.(a)**).

2 Any verb of effort or precaution (i.e. which expresses the idea of apprehension, worry, danger or anxiety) can use this construction, e.g.

> *prōuidendum est nē populō Rōmānō dēsīs* 'care must be taken lest you fail the Roman people'

3 As with purpose clauses, any reference to the subject of the main verb inside the clause will be reflexive; cf. **145**[1].

Exercises

1 *Translate*:

(a) uereor nē urbs incendātur.
(b) prōuidendum est nē hostēs in urbem ingrediantur.
(c) perīculum est nē supplex captus interficiātur.
(d) Cicerō metuēbat ut satis seuērus esse uidērētur.
(e) omnēs ōrdinēs ueritī sunt nē hostēs impiī urbem caperent.
(f) cūra erat nē uirginēs Vestālēs agitārentur.
(g) tibi haec omnia dīcere uereor.
(h) multī cīuēs timēbant nē cōnsul satis īrātus nōn esset.
(i) ante senectūtem[1] cūrāuī ut[2] bene uīuerem, in senectūte[1] ut[2] bene moriar. bene autem morī est libenter[3] morī (*Seneca*)

[1] *senectūs senectūt-is* 3f. old age.
[2] *ut*. Is the construction 'fearing'?
[3] *libenter* willingly.

2 *Give the Latin for*:

(a) I am afraid that I will see the flight of our citizens.
(b) Everyone was afraid to speak.

(c) Cicero feared that the senate would not be strict enough.
(d) A suppliant does not fear his enemies.
(e) There is anxiety in case children are killed.
(f) There was a danger of the city being destroyed.

Reading exercise / Test exercise

Caesar, advancing against the Gallic tribe the Nervii, has pitched camp on the other side of a river-valley from them. As the work of building proceeds, the Nervii launch an unexpected attack.

Caesarī omnia ūnō tempore erant agenda: uexillum prōpōnendum, quod erat īnsigne cum ad arma concurrī oportēret; signum tubā dandum; ab opere reuocandī mīlitēs; quī paulō longius aggeris petendī causā prōcesserant arcessendī; aciēs īnstruenda; mīlitēs cohortandī; signum dandum. quārum rērum magnam partem temporis breuitās et successus 5 hostium impediēbat . . . Caesar, necessāriīs rēbus imperātīs, ad cohortandōs mīlitēs quam in partem fors obtulit dēcucurrit et ad legiōnem decimam dēuēnit. (*Caesar, Dē Bellō Gallicō 2.20.1–2 and 2.21.1*)

Caesarī [Hold until solved by *agenda*]
uexill-um ī 2n. flag
prōpōnendum [Supply *erat* – watch out for suppression of *esse* throughout this passage with gerundives]
īnsigne īnsign-is 3n. mark
concurrī [See **155²**]
tub-a ae 1f. trumpet
opus oper-is 3n. the work of building a camp
agger agger-is 3m. material for an earthwork

prōcēdō 3 *prōcessī* I advance
aciēs aciē-ī 5f. battle-line
īnstruō 3 I draw up
5 *breuitās breuitāt-is* 3f. shortness
success-us ūs 4m. coming up close, approach
necessāri-us a um necessary
fors fort-is 3f. fortune, luck
offerō offerre obtulī I bring
dēcurrō 3 *dēcucurrī* I run down
dēueniō 4 *dēuēnī* I come down

English–Latin

1 *Translate into Latin (refer back to **140.1** for the grammar of consecutive* quī *clauses):*

(a) The suppliant stretches forth his hands towards the sort of people who are compassionate.
(b) Lentulus is the sort of man everyone fears.
(c) He is the sort who performs wicked acts.

(d) There is no one who doesn't desire the harmony of all the sections of society.

(e) I fear the sort of man who is always complaining.

2 *Reread the text of* **5D(iv)**, *then translate this passage into Latin*:

Conscript fathers, you must take care[1], lest you fail the Roman people. I, the consul, am prepared to[2] defend the safety of the state. All ranks are in agreement. There is not a slave who[3] is not prepared to[2] defend the state. Our land herself stretches forth to you suppliant hands. You must protect[4] our land. All are afraid that other conspirators may destroy our freedom. You must[1] take care that this cannot happen ever again.

[1] Use impersonal gerundive (n.) + dat. of 'you'.
[2] *parātus ad* + gerundive construction.
[3] Use subjunctive.
[4] Use gerundive in nom. with 'land', dat. of 'you'.

Virgil's *Aeneid*

Dido, for all her prayers and entreaties, has fallen irrevocably in love with Aeneas. She lives in his company all day, and when he is absent, clutches Aeneas' son Ascanius to her bosom. All work on the city stops.

heu, uātum ignārae mentēs! quid uōta furentem,

quid dēlūbra iuuant? ēst mollīs flamma medullās

intereā et tacitum uīuit sub pectore uulnus.

ūritur īnfēlīx Dīdō totāque uagātur

urbe furēns,

5   quālis coniectā cerua sagittā,
quam procul incautam nemora inter Crēsia fīxit
pāstor agēns tēlīs liquitque uolātile ferrum
nescius: illa fugā siluās saltūsque peragrat
Dictaeōs; haeret laterī lētālis harundō.

like a wounded deer on the wooded hills of Crete. The shepherd who has been hunting her has shot his iron-tipped arrow from long range and caught her by surprise. As she takes to flight and runs over the hills and woods of Crete, the huntsman does not know it but the arrow that will bring her to her death is sticking in her side.

10 nunc media Aenēān sēcum per moenia dūcit

Sīdoniāsque ostentat opēs urbemque parātam,

incipit effārī mediāque in uōce resistit;

nunc eadem lābente diē conuīuia quaerit,
Iliacōsque iterum dēmēns audīre labōrēs
15 exposcit pendetque iterum nārrantis ab ōre.

post ubi dīgressī, lūmenque obscūra uicissim
lūna premit suādentque cadentia sīdera somnōs,
sōla domō maeret uacuā strātīsque relictīs
incubat.

After they had parted, when the fading moon was now beginning to quench its light and the setting stars seemed to speak of sleep, she was alone in her empty house, lying in despair on the couch where Aeneas had lain to banquet.

illum absēns absentem auditque uidetque,
20 aut gremiō Ascanium genitōris imāgine capta
dētinet, īnfandum sī fallere possit amōrem.
nōn coeptae adsurgunt turrēs, nōn arma iuuentūs
exercet portūsue aut prōpugnācula bellō
tūta parant: pendent opera interrupta minaeque
25 mūrōrum ingentēs aequātaque māchina caelō.

(*Virgil*, Aeneid *4.65–89*)

Dido, yielding to her passion, gets her sister Anna to act as the go-between with Aeneas. But he will not be moved by their pleas.

tālibus ōrābat, tālīsque miserrima flētūs
fertque refertque soror. sed nūllīs ille mouētur
flētibus aut uōcēs ūllās tractābilis audit;
fāta obstant placidāsque uirī deus obstruit aurīs.

30 ac uelut annōsō ualidam cum rōbore quercum
Alpīnī Boreae nunc hinc nunc flātibus illinc
ēruere inter sē certant; it strīdor, et altae
cōnsternunt terram concussō stīpite frondēs;
ipsa haeret scopulīs et quantum uertice ad aurās
35 aetheriās, tantum rādīce in Tartara tendit;

As the North winds off the Alps vie with each other to uproot a mighty oak whose timber has strengthened over long years of life; they blow upon it from this side and from that and whistle through it; the foliage from its head covers the ground and the trunk of it feels the shock, but it holds on to the rocks with roots plunging as deep into the world below as its crown soars towards the winds of heaven.

haud secus adsiduīs hinc atque hinc uōcibus hērōs
tunditur, et magnō persentit pectore cūrās;
mēns immōta manet, lacrimae uoluuntur inānēs.
tum uērō īnfēlīx fātīs exterrita Dīdō
40 mortem ōrat.

(*Virgil*, Aeneid *4.437–51*)

heu alas!
uātēs uāt-is 3m. seer
ignār-us a um ignorant, blind
mēns ment-is 3f. intellect, mind
quid 'in what respect?'
uōt-um ī 2n. prayer [Subject or object?]
furō 3 I am mad [Since the participle is acc., one assumes *uōta* is subject. So 'in what respect do prayers something the one-who-is-mad?']
dēlūbr-um ī 2n. shrine [Looks like a repeat, i.e. 'in what respect do prayers, in what respect shrines something one-who-is-mad?']
iuuō I help
iuuant [Solves it]
ēst: 3rd s. pres. of *edō*, I eat, consume [Await subject]
moll-is e gentle, soft [NB. case. So hold]
flamm-a ae 1f. flame (of love)
medull-a ae 1f. marrow, inmost being
tacitum [New phrase/clause, so hold till solved]
pectus pector-is 3n. breast
uulnus uulner-is 3n. wound (caused by love)
4 *ūror* 3 I burn
īnfēlīx (nom. s.f.) unhappy
Dīdō Dīdōn-is 3f. Dido
uagor 1 (dep.) I range, wander
urbe [Solves *totāque*]
10 *Aenēān* [Acc. of *Aenēās*]
Sīdoni-us a um Carthaginian [Case? Hold]

ostentō 1 I show off, display
opēs op-um 3f. pl. wealth
incipiō 3/4 I begin
effor 1 (dep) I speak out
resistō 3 I stop
eadem [Nom. s.f. (i.e. Dido)? But why call her 'the same woman'? What other form might it be? Hold]
lābor 3 (dep.) I slip by
Īliac-us a um Trojan [Acc. pl. m., so hold]
dēmēns mad [Nom., so whom does it refer to?]
audīre [Why inf.? Hold]
labōrēs [Solves *Īliacōs*]
15 *exposcō* I demand to (+ inf.) [Solves *audīre*]
pendeō 2 I hang on (*ab* + abl.)
nārrantis [Genitive present participle. No noun to agree with it, so 'of the one narrating']
20 *illum . . . absentem* [Take together; *absēns* 'she, absent' (i.e. not in Aeneas' presence: subject).]
gremi-um ī 2n. breast, lap [Hold]
Ascani-us ī 2m. Ascanius, son of Aeneas [Acc., wait for verb]
genitor genitōr-is 3m. father
imāgō imāgin-is 3f. likeness to (+ gen.)
capta: 'Dido, captivated'
dētineō 2 I hold. [So, 'she holds Ascanius *gremiō*' – must be 'in her lap']
īnfand-us a um unspeakable, appalling [Neuter nom.? Masc. acc.? Hold]

sī sc. 'to see'
fallō 3 I elude, beguile, solace
amōrem [Solves *īnfandum*]
nōn . . . adsurgunt: adsurgō 3 I rise
coept-us a um begun
turris turr-is 3f. tower [Solves *coeptae*]
arma [Nom. or acc. pl.? Wait]
iuuent-ūs iuuentūt-is 3f. young men
  [Subject, so *arma* must be acc. So
  'the young men do not — their
  arms']
exerceō 2 I practise with
-ue or
port-ūs [Case possibilities?]
prōpugnācul-um ī 2n. ramparts (of the
  city). [Has this solved case
  problem?]
25 *tūt-us a um* safe [Solves *bellō*: 'in time
  of war']
parant [Who must the subject be, even
  though that noun is s.? So what case
  are *portūs, prōpugnācula*?]
pendeō 2 I hang idle, stand in idle
  suspension [Pl., three subjects
  follow]
interruptus a um broken off
min-ae ārum 2f. pl. (lit.) menaces,
  threats [But these 'threats' are
  'threats' *mūrōrum*, i.e. 'threats
  (consisting) of walls', i.e.
  'threatening walls']

aequāt-us a um raised up to, equal (to
  x: dat.)
māchin-a ae 1f. crane
cael-um ī 2n. sky
26 *tālibus*: abl. 'with such (words, prayers,
  pleas)'
tālīsque [Await agreeing acc. pl.]
miserrima 'wretched' [Nom. s. f.?
  Hold]
flēt-us ūs 4m. tears
referō 3 *rettulī* I bring back
soror [*miserrima*, of course]
tractābil-is e amenable
29 *fāt-um ī* 2n. fate
placid-us a um gracious, kindly, ready
  to yield [Case? Hold]
obstruō 3 I block up
auris aur-is 3f. ear [Solves *placidās*]
36 *secus* differently
adsidu-us a um persistent
hinc atque hinc from this side and that
hērōs (nom) hero
tundō 3 I pound, assault
persentiō 4 I feel, am aware of
immōt-us a um unmoved
lacrim-a ae 1f. tear
uoluō 3 I roll down
inān-is e useless(ly), (in) vain
39 *īnfēlīx* (nom. s.f.) unhappy
fāt-um ī 2n. fate
exterrit-us a um terrified

Rēs gestae dīuī Augustī

*In this passage we read how Augustus was offered oversight of public morals.
One wonders how he might have responded to Virgil's picture of Aeneas'
entanglement with Dido.*

cōnsulibus M. Viniciō et Q. Lucrētiō, et posteā P. Lentulō et Cn.
Lentulō, et tertium Paullō Fabiō Maximō et Q. Tuberōne, senātū
populōque Rōmānō cōnsentientibus, ut cūrātor lēgum et mōrum
summā potestāte sōlus creārer, nūllum magistrātum contrā mōrem
maiōrum dēlātum recēpī. (Rēs gestae 6.)   5

posteā afterwards
tertium for a third time [The dates are
19, 18 and 11]
cōnsentiō 4 I agree (*ut* + subj. 'agree
that' x should happen)
cūrātor cūrātōr-is 3m. guardian

creō 1 I make
5 *maiōrēs maiōr-um* 3m. f. pl. ancestors
dēferō 3 *dētulī dēlāt-us* I hand down
recipiō 3/4 *recēpī* I accept, take up

Section 5E

Running vocabulary for 5E(i)

appellāt-us a um called
(*appellō* 1)
capitāl-is e involving a
capital charge,
punishable by death
carcer carcer-is 3m. prison
Catō Catōn-is 3m. M.
Porcius Cato
circiter about
cōnsulār-is e consular
Cornēli-ī ōrum 2m. pl. the
Cornelii
dēduct-us a um led down
(*dēdūcō* 3)
dēmiss-us a um sent down
(*dēmittō* 3)
dēpress-us a um sunk
(*dēprimō* 3)
dign-us a um worthy of
(x: abl.)

discēdō 3 *discessī* I depart;
discēdō in sententiam (x:
gen.) I go over to x's
view
dispōnō 3 *disposuī dispositus*
I place, station
dum (+ indicative) while;
(+ subjunctive) until
faciēs faciē-ī 5f. appearance
fact-um ī 2n. deed
foedāt-us a um made foul
(*foedō* 1)
gul-a ae 1f. throat (tr.
'neck')
humī in the ground
incult-us ūs 4m. neglect
iuss-us a um ordered (*iubeō*
2)
laque-us ī 2m. garotte

nouō 1 I make changes
odor odōr-is 3m. smell,
stench
patrici-us ī 2m. patrician
(member of a select
group of families)
tenebr-ae ārum 1f. pl.
darkness
terribil-is e frightful,
dreadful
triumuir-ī ōrum 2m. pl.
triumvirs (a
commission responsible
for prisons and
executions)
Tulliān-um ī 2n.
Tullianum
uindex uindic-is 3m.
punisher

Notes

ll. 212–13 *nē quid . . . nouārētur: quid* is accusative of respect. Tr. 'in any
respect'. *nouārētur* impersonal passive 'changes might be made' (with
the overtone of 'revolution', the expression for which was *rēs nouae*).
ll. 219–20 *dum . . . frangerent*: 'until . . . they should break', 'for . . . to
break'. *uindicēs rērum capitālium*: i.e. the executioners.
l. 222 *cōnsulāre*: he had been consul in 71.

Learning vocabulary for 5E(i)

Nouns

carcer carcer-is 3m. prison; barrier

faciēs faciē-ī 5f. appearance; face
fact-um ī 2n. deed

hum-us ī 2f. ground (NB. *humum* (acc.) to the ground; *humī* (locative) on or in the ground)

Adjectives

dign-us a um worthy; worthy of (x: abl.)

terribil-is e dreadful, frightening

Verbs

discēdō 3 *discessī discessum* I depart; (with *in sententiam* + gen.) I go over to x's view (*dis- + cēdō*)

dispōnō 3 *disposuī dispositus* I set, place (in different places) (*dis- + pōnō*)

Running vocabulary for 5E(ii)

---

abdūcō 3 I lead away
absum abesse I am distant
addūcō 3 *addūxī* I bring
aduentō 1 I approach, advance
aduers-us a um unfavourable
aequ-us a um level
agmen agmin-is 3n. column
antequam (+ subj.) before
asper asper-a um rough
Celer Celer-is 3m. (Q. Metellus) Celer
circiter about
claudō 3 *clausī clausus* I shut in
commūnicō 1 I share (x (acc.) with y (*cum* + abl.))
cōnflīgō 3 I fight (with x: *cum* + abl.)
coniungō 3 *coniūnxī* I join (I join x: *mē coniungō* + dat.)

cōnsīdō 3 *cōnsēdī* I take up position, encamp
cōpi-a ae 1f. multitude, crowd
dēscēns-us ūs 4m. descent
difficultās difficultāt-is 3f. difficulty
dīlābor 3 dep. I slip away
dum (+ ind.) while; (+ subj.) until (see note on l. 241); (+ subj.) provided that (l. 232)
fugitīu-us a um runaway
Galli-a ae 1f. Gaul
īnstituō 3 *īnstituī* I draw up
īnstrūct-us a um (l. 227) equipped; (l. 237) drawn up
interclūdō 3 I cut off
iter itiner-is 3n. journey; route; *magnum iter* = a forced march
lance-a ae 1f. lance, spear

Metell-us ī 2m. Q. Metellus Celer
miss-us a um sent (*mittō* 3)
modo . . . modo at one time . . . at another
occāsiō occāsiōn-is 3f. opportunity (for x: gen.)
occultē secretly
perfug-a ae 1m. deserter
perfugiō 3/4 I flee for refuge
perturbāt-us a um worried, disturbed (*perturbō* 1)
Pīcēn-us a um of Picenum
Pistōriēns-is e of Pistoria
praeacūt-us a um sharpened to a point (*praeacuō* 3)
procul far off
properē hastily
properō 1 I hurry
pugn-a ae 1f. battle
Q. = Quīnt-us ī 2m. Quintus

quā where [See **137.3**]
quam prīmum as soon as
  possible
rādīx rādīc-is 3f. foot (lit.
  'root')
rapīn-a ae 1f. plunder

repudiō 1 I reject
spar-us ī 2m. hunting-
  spear
spērō 1 I hope, expect
sub (+abl.) beneath
sudis sud-is 3f. stake

temptō 1 I test, try
Trānsalpīn-us a um across
  the Alps, Transalpine
utpote (*quī*) (+subj.)
  inasmuch as, since (he)

Notes

l. 227 *pars quārta* i.e. ¼.

ll. 230–1 *facere . . . mouēre . . . dare*: see **146**.

l. 232 *habitūrum: esse* suppressed.

ll. 234ff. *nūntius*: remember that a noun may generate an indirect statement quite as easily as a verb, i.e. 'a messenger (with a message to the effect that . . .)'.

l. 236 *sūmptum: esse* suppressed

ll. 236–7 *quī sē . . . coniūnxissent*: causal clause, see **140.2**.

l. 241 *dum . . . mouēret*: 'until . . .' 'for . . . to . . .' (purpose).

ll. 245–6 Note *properantī* agreeing with *Catilīnae*, dat. of advantage or possession.

l. 248 *in urbe* i.e. in Rome (often known simply as *urbs*).

Learning vocabulary for 5E(ii)

Nouns

agmen agmin-is 3n.
  column

iter itiner-is 3n. journey;
  route

occāsiō occāsiōn-is 3f.
  opportunity
pugn-a ae 1f. battle, fight

Adjectives

aequ-us a um level (fair,
  balanced, equal)
asper asper-a um rough

Verbs

absum abesse āfuī I am
  distant (am absent,
  away)
cōnsīdō 3 *cōnsēdī cōnsessum*
  I settle down; encamp

īnstruō 3 *īnstrūxī īnstrūctus*
  I draw up; prepare,
  equip
properō 1 I hurry, make
  haste

spērō 1 I hope, expect
temptō 1 I try, test,
  attempt; attack

Others

circiter about (adv.)

modo . . . modo at one
  time . . . at another

quam prīmum as soon as
  possible

Grammar and exercises for 5E

163 **Passive perfect participles**

You have already met passive perfect participles being used in ablative absolute construction (**151**). They can, of course, be used in agreement with any noun in any case, though they are less often used as adjectives (*nāuis capta* = 'the captured ship') than predicatively (*nāuis capta* = 'the ship, having been captured' . . .). See **77**.

> *mīlitēs captī in carcerem dēductī sunt* 'the soldiers, having been captured, were taken off to prison'. (Here *captī* is nom. pl. m. to agree with 'soldiers', the subject of the sentence.)
>
> *custōdēs uīsōs secūtī sunt* 'they followed the guards after they had been seen', 'they saw the guards and followed them'. (Here *uīsōs* is acc. pl. m. to agree with 'the guards', the object of the sentence.)
>
> *mihi captō auxilium dedit* 'he gave help to me having-been-captured', 'though I had been captured, he gave me help'. (*captō* is dat. s. m. to agree with *mihi*.)

NB.   Another common meaning of *nāuis capta* is 'the capture of the ship', e.g.

> *ab urbe conditā* 'from the foundation of the city'
> *Hannibal uictus Rōmānōs metū līberāuit* 'the defeat of Hannibal freed the Romans from fear'

164 **Summary of participles**

(a) Present participles, '—ing': 1 *-āns* (*-ant-*), 2 *-ēns* (*-ent-*), 3 *-ēns* (*-ent-*), 4 and 3/4 *-iēns* (*-ient-*); cf. **120**

(b) Future participles, 'about to —': stem of perfect participle + *-ūrus -ūra -ūrum*; cf. **81–3**

(c) Perfect participles, (deponent) 'having —ed': stem of perfect participle + *-us -a -um*; (others) 'having been —ed'; cf. **77**, **151**

All are adjectives, and agree with the person or thing they describe.

NB.   Only active verbs which take an object in the *accusative* have a passive participle used as an adjective. For example, *uentus* and *parsus* are impossible in that form because both come from verbs which are intransitive: *ueniō* takes *ad* + acc., and *imperō* takes a dative. These forms exist only in the impersonal perfect passive, e.g. *uentum est* lit. 'it has been come', i.e. 'people have come'; *imperātum est* lit. 'it has been ordered' i.e. 'orders have been given'. You will have noticed that the 4th p.p. of intransitive verbs is always given in the *-um* form.

Exercises

1 *Translate the participles in this list. Say whether they are deponent or passive*: commorātus, coctus, mortuus, ūsus, datus, adiūtus, agitātus, lātus, gestus, cognitus, cōnātus, secūtus, intellēctus, locūtus, exortus, prōmissus, sūmptus, frāctus, mōtus, (*optional*: portātus, pollicitus, inuentus, hortātus, nūntiātus, minātus, necātus, reductus, perfectus, uocātus, amplexus, arbitrātus, seruātus, īnstructus, dispositus, ueritus, tēnsus, obsessus, questus).

2 *Translate these sentences*:

(a) Lentulus tenebrās cōnspicātus nihilōminus negāuit sē mortem timēre.
(b) cēterī custōdēs ā cōnsulibus dispositōs sequēbantur.
(c) cōnsul sēcum multa locūtus supplicium sūmere cōnstituerat.
(d) Celer ā senātū missus in agrō Pīcēnō erat.
(e) agmen ā cōnsule īnstructum Catilīna uīdit.
(f) Catilīnae montibus et cōpiīs hostium clausō[1] fuga erat nūlla.

[1] *claudō* 3 *clausī clausus* I shut in, cut off.

3 *Translate into Latin using perfect participles passive to translate 'when' and 'as' clauses. NB. None of these sentences calls for the ablative absolute.*

(a) When they had captured the soldier, the guards killed him.
(b) After the column had been seen, Catiline hurried towards it.
(c) When the guards had been set Cicero gave them instructions.
(d) The appearance of the column as it had been drawn up was not worthy of the commander.
(e) Catiline's soldiers advanced, using weapons previously[1] captured.

[1] Leave out 'previously'.

165 *dum, antequam/priusquam*

1 dum + *indicative* 'while'

dum takes the *present* indicative where 'while' means 'at one point during', e.g.

> *dum Cicerō haec loquitur, Catilīna abiit* '(At one point) while Cicero was speaking, Catiline left'

But *imperfect* indicative is used where the 'while' clause covers the whole period described by the main verb, e.g.

> *dum Cicerō sequēbatur, Catilīna fugiēbat* 'while Cicero was following, Catiline was fleeing'

2 dum 'until'

dum + indicative indicates the idea of time only, e.g.

> *manē dum redierō* 'wait until I get back'

dum + subjunctive indicates anticipation or intention, e.g.

> *manē dum redeam* 'wait for me to come back'
> Cf. *manēbat dum Catilīna castra mouēret* (subjunctive) 'he was waiting for Catiline to move camp'
> *mānsit dum Catilīna castra mōuit* (indicative) 'he waited until Catiline (actually) moved camp'

3 antequam/priusquam 'before'

antequam and *priusquam* work rather like *dum*: indicative expresses purely time, subjunctive anticipation or intention, e.g.

> with indicative: *antequam abiit, epistolam scrīpsit* 'before he left, he wrote a letter'
> with subjunctive: *Catilīna abiit antequam legiōnēs Rōmānae peruenīrent* 'Catiline left before the Roman legions should arrive'

NB. *ante-* and *prius-* are often split from *quam*, e.g. *ante uenī quam uir* 'I arrived before the man' (Ovid).

4 dum (dummodo, modo) + *subjunctive*

A specialised meaning of *dum* is 'provided that', 'on condition that', e.g.

> *omnia faciam dum amīcus fīās* 'I will do anything provided you become my friend'

66 *utpote quī (quae quod)* + **subjunctive**

utpote reinforces the causal sense of *quī* i.e. 'as is natural for one who'. The verb is subjunctive. Cf. *quippe quī* **140.2**. E.g.

> *miser sum, utpote quem Cynthia amet* 'I am wretched, as is natural for one whom Cynthia loves'

NB.   *ut quī* is also used in this way.

Exercises

1   *Translate into English*:

   (a)   dum senātus rem cōnsīderābat, Catilīna legiōnēs suās īnstruēbat.
   (b)   Catilīna exspectābat, dum sociī cōnsilia Rōmae perficerent.
   (c)   Catilīna, antequam in Galliam īret, nouās cōpiās ex urbe exspectābat.
   (d)   dum Catilīna prope Pistōriam manet, Rōmae Cicerōnī sē coniūrātōrēs trādidērunt.
   (e)   cōnsul laetus est, dum salua sit rēs pūblica.
   (f)   tē omnēs amant mulierēs, quī sīs tam pulcher. (*Plautus*)

2   *Translate into Latin*:

   (a)   While this was happening at Rome, Catiline spoke to his soldiers.
   (b)   He said, 'I shall wait until our friends arrive.'
   (c)   'Provided they are safe, our plans can be completed.'
   (d)   'I must relate certain matters to Lentulus, before I depart for Gaul.'
   (e)   But all the time Catiline was speaking, the consul was preparing war.

Reading exercise / Test exercise

Note especially in reading this passage (i) the use of the participle in Latin, where a clause or other formulation would be needed in English; (ii) that accusative future and perfect participles may actually be infinitives without esse *and form part of an indirect statement.*

L. Tarquinius, another captured Catilinarian, gives information to the senate, similar to that of Volturcius.

post eum diem quīdam L. Tarquinius ad senātum adductus erat, quem ad Catilīnam proficīscentem ex itinere retractum aiēbant. is cum sē dīceret indicātūrum dē coniūrātiōne, sī fidēs pūblica data esset, iussus ā cōnsule quae scīret ēdīcere, eadem ferē quae Volturcius dē parātīs incendiīs, dē caede bonōrum, dē itinere hostium senātum docet; praetereā sē missum   5 quī Catilīnae nūntiāret nē eum Lentulus et Cethēgus aliīque ex coniūrātiōne dēprehēnsī terrērent, eōque magis properāret ad urbem adcēdere, quō et cēterōrum animōs reficeret et illī facilius ē perīculō ēriperentur. (*Sallust*, Catiline *48.3–4*)

post (+ acc.) after	*dē parātīs incendiīs* [See **163** Note]
addūcō 3 *addūxī adductus* I bring (to)	5 *doceō* 2 I inform (x acc. of y acc.)
retrahō 3 *retrāxī retractus* I drag back	*quī . . . nūntiāret* [Expresses purpose]
aiō 3 I say	*dēprehendō* 3 *dēprehendī dēprehēnsus* I
indicō 1 I make a declaration, give	capture [Tr. *aliī . . . dēprehēnsī* 'the
information	capture of the others . . .' – what
fidēs pūblica (5f. + 1/2 adj.) public	does it mean literally?]
pledge (of impunity or protection)	*terreō* 2 I frighten
ēdīcō 3 I declare	*eō magis* 'by that much the more'
eadem . . . quae 'the same . . . as'	*adcēdere = accēdere*
ferē almost	*reficiō* 3/4 I revive, restore

English–Latin

Reread the text of **5E(ii)**, *then translate this passage into Latin.*

While at Rome this punishment was being exacted[1] from Lentulus, Catiline drew up his forces. He was waiting until[2] troops should be sent from his allies. But after it was reported that Lentulus was dead and the conspiracy revealed, he started to make[3] his way through the mountains. The consul Antonius, sent by the senate with the purpose of[4] defeating him in battle, pursued him. Metellus also moved his camp from Picenum, to obstruct Catiline as he hurried towards Transalpine Gaul. After Catiline saw that he was shut in by mountains and enemy troops, he decided to join battle as soon as possible with Antonius, in order to give more[5] hope to his soldiers.

[1] Use *dum* + present indicative.
[2] Use *dum* + imperfect subjunctive.
[3] Use historic infinitive.
[4] Either *eō cōnsiliō ut* or *quī* + subjunctive.
[5] *quō* + comparative adjective + subjunctive.

Virgil's *Aeneid*

At the command of the gods, Aeneas abandons Dido (who commits suicide) and continues on his journey. Eventually he arrives in Italy, befriends the local King Latinus, and is offered the hand of his daughter Lavinia in marriage. This causes civil war to break out between Aeneas and Turnus, to whom Lavinia had previously been betrothed. In preparation for this epic contest, Venus has Vulcan make Aeneas a special shield, on which the whole of Roman history to come is foreshadowed. Aeneas gazes in wonder at it: the final scene his eyes rest on is that of Augustus triumphant over his enemies.

at Caesar, triplicī inuectus Rōmāna triumphō

moenia, dīs Italīs uōtum immortāle sacrābat,

maxima ter centum tōtam dēlūbra per urbem.

laetitiā lūdīsque uiae plausūque fremēbant;

5 omnibus in templīs mātrum chorus, omnibus ārae;

ante ārās terram caesī strāuēre iuuencī.

ipse sedēns niueō candentis līmine Phoebī

dōna recognōscit populōrum aptatque superbīs

postibus; incēdunt uictae longō ōrdine gentēs,

10 quam uariae linguīs, habitū tam uestis et armīs.

hīc Nomadum genus et discīnctōs Mulciber Āfrōs,	Here Vulcan had moulded the No-
hīc Lelegās Cārāsque sagittiferōsque Gelōnōs	mads and the Africans with their
fīnxerat; Euphrātēs ībat iam mollior undīs,	streaming robes; here were the
extrēmīque hominum Morinī, Rhēnusque bicornis,	Lelegians and Carians of Asia and the
15 indomitīque Dahae, et pontem indignātus Araxēs.	Gelonians from Scythia carrying their
tālia per clipeum Volcānī, dōna parentis,	quivers; there was the Euphrates mov-
mīrātur rērumque ignārus imāgine gaudet	ing now with a chastened current;
attollēns umerō fāmamque et fāta nepōtum.	here were the Morini from the ends of

the earth in Gaul, the two-horned Rhine, the Scythians from beyond the Caspian, never conquered before, and the River Araxes chafing at his bridge. Such was the shield that Vulcan made, and Venus gave her son. Aeneas marvelled at it, and rejoicing at the things pictured on it without knowing what they were, he lifted onto his shoulder the fame and fates of his descendants.

(*Virgil*, Aeneid *8.714–31*)

Caesar: i.e. Augustus
triplex triplic-is threefold [*triplicī* and
Rōmāna are both adjectives awaiting
solution]
inuehor 3 dep. *inuectus* I am carried
into, ride into (+acc.)
triumph-us ī 2m. triumph [Solves —?]
moenia moen-ium 3n. pl. city walls
[Solves —?]
dīs from *deus* 16 [Cases? Hold]
Ital-us a um of Italy
uōt-um ī 2n. offering
immortāl-is e immortal, everlasting
sacrō 1 I consecrate x (acc.) to y (dat.)
ter centum 300 [*maxima* and *tōtam* both
await solution]
dēlūbr-um ī 2n. shrine
laetiti-a ae 1f. joy
lūd-us ī 2m. game, revel
uiae ['games of/for the road'? Or is this
nom. pl.? Answer coming up in
verb]
plaus-us ūs 4m. applause, cheers [Note
case and -*que*, linking it with which
previous nouns?]
fremō 3 I resound, echo [With x: abl. –
solves it]
5 *chor-us ī* 2m. chorus, choir [Sc. *est*]

ār-a ae 1f. altar
caedō 3 *cecīdī caesus* I kill, slaughter
sternō 3 *strāuī* I lie over (+acc.)
iuuenc-us ī 2m. bullock
ipse [I.e. Augustus]
sedeō 2 I sit
niueō candentis [Both adjectives. Hold
for their soution]
niue-us a um white
candeō 2 I shine
līmen līmin-is 3n. threshold
Phoeb-us ī 2m. Phoebus (Apollo)
dōn-um ī 2n. gift
recognōscō 3 I review
aptō 1 I fit x (acc.) to y (dat.) [What is
the (understood) x?]
superb-us a um fine, proud
postis post-is 3m. door-post, portal
incēdō 3 I march past
10 *quam . . . tam* as . . . as
uari-us a um different
lingu-ae ārum 2f. pl. tongues, languages
[Abl. of respect]
habit-us ūs 4m. look, fashion [Abl. of
respect]
uestis uest-is 3f. clothes

Deliciae Latinae

Martial

quem recitās meus⌐ est, ō Fīdentīne, ⌐libellus.
sed male cum recitās, incipit esse tuus. (*1.38*)

recitō 1 I read out, recite
Fīdentīn-us ī 2m.
  Fidentinus

libell-us ī 2m. book [This
  is the antecedent of
  quem]

incipiō 3/4 I begin

nīl recitās et uīs, Māmerce, poēta uidērī?
quidquid uīs estō, dummodo nīl recitēs. (*2.88*)

Māmerc-us ī 2m.
  Mamercus

poēt-a ae 1m. poet
quidquid whatever

estō be! (=*es*, 2nd. s.
  imperative of *sum*)

The Vulgate: *nātīuitās Christī*

factum est autem in diēbus illīs, exiit ēdictum ā Caesare Augustō ut
dēscrīberētur ūniuersus orbis. haec dēscrīptiō prīma facta est ā praeside
Syriae Cyrīnō; et ībant omnēs ut profitērentur singulī in suam cīuitātem.
ascendit autem et Iōsēph ā Galilaeā dē cīuitāte Nazareth in Iūdaeam in
cīuitātem Dauid, quae uocātur Bēthlehem, eō quod esset dē domō et   5
familiā Dauid, ut profitērētur cum Mariā dēspōnsātā sibi uxōre
praegnante. factum est autem, cum essent ibi, implētī sunt diēs ut pareret.
et peperit fīlium suum prīmōgenitum et pannīs eum inuoluit et reclīnāuit
eum in praesēpiō, quia nōn erat eīs locus in dīuersōriō.

et pāstōrēs erant in regiōne eādem uigilantēs et custōdientēs uigiliās   10
noctis super gregem suum. et ecce angelus Dominī stetit iuxtā illōs, et
clāritās Deī circumfulsit illōs, et timuērunt timōre magnō, et dīxit illīs
angelus: 'nōlīte timēre; ecce enim euangelizō uōbīs gaudium magnum,
quod erit omnī populō; quia nātus est uōbīs hodiē Saluātor quī est
Christus Dominus, in ciuitāte Dauid. et hoc uōbīs signum: inueniētis   15
īnfantem pannīs inuolūtum et positum in praesēpiō. et subitō facta est
cum angelō multitūdō mīlitiae caelestis laudantium Deum et dīcentium:

Glōria in altissimīs Deō,
et in terrā pāx hominibus bonae uoluntātis. (*Luke 2:1–14*)

ēdict-um ī 2n. edict
dēscrībor 3 (pass.) I am subject of a
   census
ūniuers-us a um all, whole
orbis orb-is 3m. world
dēscrīptiō dēscrīptiōn-is 3f. census
praeses praesid-is 3m. governor
Syri-a ae 1f. Syria
Cyrīn-us ī 2m. Quirinius
profiteor 2 dep. I make a census return
singul-ī ae a (as) individuals
ascendō 3 I go up
Iōsēph nom. Joseph
Galilae-a ae 1f. Galilee
Nazareth [Abl. with *cīuitāte*]
Iūdae-a ae 1f. Judaea
5 *Dauid* (gen.) of David
Bēthlehem (nom.) Bethlehem
eō quod + subj. 'for this reason, that'
Mari-a ae 1f. Mary
dēspōnsāt-us a um betrothed

praegnāns praegnant-is being pregnant
impleō 2 *implēuī implētus* I complete
pariō 3/4 *peperī* I give birth (to)
prīmōgenit-us a um first-born
pann-ī ōrum 2m. pl. rags, pieces of
   cloth, swaddling clothes
inuoluō 3 *inuoluī inuolūtus* I wrap
praesēpi-um ī 2n. enclosure, pen, fold;
   manger
dīuersōri-um ī 2n. hostel, inn
10 *pāstor pāstōr-is* 3m. shepherd
regiō regiōn-is 3f. area
uigilō 1 I am on watch, keep awake
custōdiō 4 I guard, keep
uigili-ae ārum 1f. pl. watches
grex greg-is 3m. flock
angel-us ī 2m. messenger
iuxtā (+ acc.) beside
clāritās clāritāt-is 3f. clearness, brightness
circumfulgeō 2 *circumfulsī* I shine around
timor timōr-is 3m. fear

euangelizō I announce, tell good news
gaudi-um ī 2n. joy
saluātor saluātōr-is 3m. saviour
15 *Christ-us ī* 2m. Christ

īnfāns īnfant-is 3m. child, infant
caelest-is e celestial, heavenly
laudō 1 I praise
alt-us a um high

Section 5F

Running vocabulary for 5F(i)

ā/ab (+abl.) from (the direction of)
addō 3 I add, increase
aduers-us a um hostile
aduocō 1 I summon
attulerit '(it) has brought' (perf. subj. of *adferō*)
cēdō 3 *cessī* I yield
certō 1 I contend, fight
contiō contiōn-is 3f. meeting, assembly
conuocāuerim 'I have called together' (perf. subj. of *conuocō* 1)
decus decor-is 3n. honour
dextr-a ae 1f. right hand
dīuiti-ae ārum 1f. pl. riches
dubi-us a um doubtful
egestās egestāt-is 3f. lack
equidem at any rate
ex [Here = instead of]

ferr-um ī 2n. sword
frūment-um ī 2n. corn
fuerit '(he) has been' (pf. subj. of *sum*)
Galli-a ae 1f. Gaul
huiuscemodī of this kind
ignāui-a ae 1f. laziness; cowardice
ignāu-us a um idle; cowardly
impendeō 2 I threaten, overhang (+dat.)
iūst-us a um just
meminī I remember (perfect in form)
meminerītis '(you) remember' (subj. of *meminī* 'I remember' – perfect in *form*)
necessitūdō necessitūdin-is 3f. necessity

ōrātiō ōrātiōn-is 3f. speech; *ōrātiōnem habeō* I make a speech
persecūtī sint '(they) have pursued' (perf. subj. of *persequor*)
posuerītis 'you (pl.) have placed' (perf. subj. of *pōnō* 3)
potenti-a ae 1f. power
prīstin-us a um former
quant-us a um how much, how big
quīn (+subj.) (ll. 261, 266 after *nōn dubium est*) that; (l. 269) 'who . . . not' [See **140.1**]
quō (+subj.) (l. 254) in order to
quōcumque wherever
quōminus (+subj.) from (—ing)
quot how many

Notes

l. 254 *quō pauca monērem*: 'in order to give advice on a few points' lit. 'advise a few things'.

l. 257 *quantum perīculī*: see **31**.

Learning vocabulary for 5F(i)

Nouns

contiō contiōn-is 3f.
  meeting, assembly
decus decor-is 3n. honour;
  beauty
dextr-a ae 1f. right hand

dīuiti-ae ārum 1f. pl. riches
ferr-um ī 2n. sword; iron
frūment-um ī 2n. corn
ignāui-a ae 1f. laziness;
  cowardice

ōrātiō ōrātiōn-is 3f. speech
potenti-a ae 1f. power

Adjectives

aduers-us a um hostile;
  opposite; unfavourable

ignāu-us a um lazy;
  cowardly

quant-us a um how much,
  how great

Verbs

addō 3 *addidī additus* I add;
  increase
aduocō 1 I summon
cēdō 3 *cessī cessum* I yield;
  go

certō 1 I struggle, fight;
  vie
meminī meminisse
  (defective: perfect form
  only) I remember

persequor 3 dep. *persecūtus*
  I pursue, follow after

Others

ōrātiōnem habēre to make a
  speech

quōcumque (to) wherever

quot how many

Running vocabulary for 5F(ii)

---

agō 3 *ēgī* I spend, pass
anim-a ae 1f. life
bon-a ōrum 2n. pl. goods
cauēte (+ subj. or
  nē + subj.) beware of
  —ing
cōgō 3 *coēgī* I compel (x
  acc. to ʏ inf.)
cōnsilium capere to make a
  plan
conuocāuerim 'I have
  summoned' (pf. subj.
  of *conuocō* 1)
cruent-us a um bloody
dēmenti-a ae 1f. madness
dēspērō 1 I lose hope
exsili-um ī 2n. exile
foed-us a um disgraceful

intolerand-us a um
  unbearable
inuideō 2 *inuīdī* I
  begrudge, envy
  (+ dat.)
inult-us a um unavenged
locūtus sim 'I have spoken'
  (pf. subj. of *loquor*)
lūctuōs-us a um grief-
  stricken, mournful
mōre in the manner of (x:
  gen.)
necessitūdō necessitūdin-is
  3f. necessity
necne or not (following
  utrum 'whether')
neu = nēue and that . . .
  not

opus est there is need of
  (x: abl.)
particeps particip-is sharer
  in (+ gen.)
pecus pecor-is 3n. sheep;
  cattle
quīn (+ subj.) from
  (—ing)
quod sī but if
quōminus (+ subj.) from
  (—ing)
rem bene gerere to succeed
trucīdō 1 butcher
turpitūdō turpitūdin-is 3f.
  disgrace, dishonour
utrum . . . necne whether
  . . . or not

Notes

ll. 272–3 *nisi. . .factī fuissētis. . .ēgissētis:* 'if. . .had not. . .,. . .would
have'. There are several other examples of this construction. *sī/
nisi* + pluperfect subjunctive, pluperfect subjunctive. The basic formula is 'if x had / had not happened, Y would not have happened'.
Other examples are in lines 274–5, 275–6, 278–9, 281–2. See **173**, cf.
139³.

Learning vocabulary for 5F(ii)

Nouns

bon-a ōrum 2n. pl. goods   *exsili-um ī* 2n. exile   *necessitūdō necessitūdin-is* 3f. necessity

Verbs

agō 3 *ēgī āctus* I spend,
  pass (do, act; drive,
  lead, direct)
cōgō 3 *coēgī coāctus* I force,
  compel; gather

inuideō 2 *inuīdī inuīsum* I
  envy, begrudge
  (+ dat.)

trucīdō 1 I butcher,
  slaughter

Others

mōre in the manner of,
  like (x: gen.)
opus est there is need of
  (x: abl.)

Grammar and exercises for 5F

---

167 **Perfect subjunctive active**

	1	2	3
1st s.	amā́u-eri-m (amā́rim *etc.*)	habú-eri-m	díx-eri-m
2nd s.	amā́u-erī-s	habú-erī-s	díx-erī-s
3rd s.	amā́u-eri-t	habú-eri-t	díx-eri-t
1st pl.	amā́u-erí-mus	habu-erí-mus	díx-erí-mus
2nd pl.	amā́u-erí-tis	habu-erí-tis	díx-erí-tis
3rd pl.	amā́u-eri-nt	habú-eri-nt	díx-eri-nt

	4	3/4
1st s.	audíu-eri-m (audíerim *etc.*)	cép-eri-m
2nd s.	audíu-erī-s	cép-erī-s
3rd s.	audíu-eri-t	cép-eri-t
1st pl.	audíu-erī-mus	cép-erī-mus
2nd pl.	audíu-erī-tis	cép-erī-tis
3rd pl.	audíu-eri-nt	cép-eri-nt

Notes

1 The perfect subjunctive active is formed by taking the stem of the 3rd p.p. and adding *-erim -erīs -erit -erīmus -erītis -erint*. Observe that, in this respect, it is *almost identical* in form to the future perfect (see **156**). (The only difference is that the future perfect has the 1st s. in *-erō* and usually a short *i* at *-eris, -erimus, -eritis*.) Note the normal active personal endings (*-m, -s, -t, -mus, -tis, -nt*).

2 Note that in 1st and 4th conjugations the forms *amā-rim* etc. and *audi-erim* are common. Cf. *dēlēu-erim* and *dēlē-rim*.

168 Perfect subjunctive deponent

	1	2	3
1st s.	minát-us a um sim	pollícit-us a um sim	locút-us a um sim
2nd s.	minát-us a um sīs	pollícit-us a um sīs	locút-us a um sīs
3rd s.	minát-us a um sit	pollícit-us a um sit	locút-us a um sit
1st pl.	minát-ī ae a símus	pollícit-ī ae a símus	locút-ī ae a símus
2nd pl.	minát-ī ae a sítis	pollícit-ī ae a sítis	locút-ī ae a sítis
3rd pl.	minát-ī ae a sint	pollícit-ī ae a sint	locút-ī ae a sint

	4	3/4
1st s.	mentít-us a um sim	prōgréss-us a um sim
2nd s.	mentít-us a um sīs	prōgréss-us a um sīs
3rd s.	mentít-us a um sit	prōgréss-us a um sit
1st pl.	mentít-ī ae a símus	prōgréss-ī ae a símus
2nd pl.	mentít-ī ae a sítis	prōgréss-ī ae a sítis
3rd pl.	mentít-ī ae a sint	prōgréss-ī ae a sint

NB. The perfect subjunctive deponent is formed by taking the stem of the perfect participle, adding the appropriate endings *-us -a -um* etc. to agree with the subject, and adding *sim sīs sit sīmus sītis sint*, the present subjunctive of *sum*.

169 Perfect subjunctive passive

	1	2	3	4	3/4
1st s.	amāt-us sim	hábit-us sim	díct-us sim	audít-us sim	cápt-us sim
2nd s.	amāt-us sīs	hábit-us sīs	díct-us sīs	audít-us sīs	cápt-us sīs
3rd s.	amāt-us sit	hábit-us sit	díct-us sit	audít-us sit	cápt-us sit
1st pl.	amāt-ī sīmus	hábit-ī sīmus	díct-ī sīmus	audít-ī sīmus	cápt-ī sīmus
2nd pl.	amāt-ī sītis	hábit-ī sītis	díct-ī sītis	audít-ī sītis	cápt-ī sītis
3rd pl.	amāt-ī sint	hábit-ī sint	díct-ī sint	audít-ī sint	cápt-ī sint

NB. For formation of perfect subjunctive passive, see note on deponent (above) **168**.

Summary

Perfect active subjunctive: 3rd p.p. in *-erim -erīs -erit -erīmus -erītis -erint.*

Perfect deponent/passive subjunctive: perfect participle + *sim sīs sit sīmus sītis sint.*

Exercises

1 *Form and conjugate the perfect subjunctive of these verbs* (*form passive only when requested*): dispōnō (*passive*), cohortor, perueniō, occupō, pūniō (*passive*), moueō, ūtor, cōnficiō, uereor, sūmō (*passive*), (*optional*: portō, oblīuīscor, eō, possum, ferō (*passive*), audeō, cōnsīdō, īnstruō (*passive*), persequor, aduocō (*passive*)).

2 *Pick out the perfect subjunctives in this list, detailing tense and mood* (*i.e. indicative or subjunctive*) *of the others*: frēgistī, curāuerīs, mōueris, āfueram, ēgisset, īnstrūxerō, sūmpserim, properāuit, adlocūtus sit, ūsus esset, praebuerit, rogāuerint, arbitrātus erit, iussī sītis, nōluimus, mīseritis, dūxerīmus, conuocāta sit, interfectus erit, petīta sīs, (*optional*: uīceram, uīnxerīs, secūtae sīmus, passa est, prohibitus sit, conuocāuerītis, temptāuerimus, impedīuissem, cōnsiderāuimus, exorta essem, uīsum sit, collocāuerim, questus erō, oppresserīmus).

170 Use of perfect subjunctive

It is used in certain constructions already met, e.g.

(a) Subordinate clauses in indirect speech (**142**)
(b) Result clauses, *tam* (etc) . . . *ut* + subj. '(so) . . . that', **144**, e.g.

> *potest fierī ut īrātus dīxerit* 'it may be that he spoke in anger'
> (Cicero).

(c) *cum* + subj. 'since', 'although' **124, 141** (but not usually 'when').
(d) *quī* + subj. in generic or causal sense, **140**.
(e) Fearing clauses (*timeō* (etc.) *nē*), **162**.

In these cases it should be translated as a plain past ('I —ed') or perfect ('I have —ed'), whichever fits better.

71 Perfect subjunctive: independent usages

The use of the present subjunctive in an imperative or potential sense has already been met (**152** and **153**). The perfect subjunctive is also used in these senses, e.g.

(a) Jussive: *nē petīuerīs* 'do not seek' (= *nōlī petere*).
(b) Potential: *dīxerit aliquis* 'someone may say'
     errāuerim fortasse 'I may/could perhaps have been wrong'.

Exercises

1 *Translate*:

(a) tū nē quaesierīs . . . (*Horace*)
(b) nūllam aciem, nūllum proelium timuerīs. (*Livy*)
(c) nē hostibus cesserīs.
(d) nūllī inuīderīs.
(e) nē restiterīs.
(f) quis tibi hoc dīxerit?

2 *Translate into Latin (using* nē + *perfect subjunctive for prohibitions)*:

(a) Do not be daring.
(b) Do not reveal this plan.
(c) Do not give yourself up.
(d) Do not harm the state.
(e) Do not kill the consul.
(f) Someone may assert.

172 **Indirect (reported) questions**

You have already met indirect statements ('I say *that*': **98–9, 143**) and indirect commands ('I tell/urge/persuade etc. someone *to*': **134**). Consider the following examples:

(a)   *rogō quid faciās* 'I ask what you are doing'.
(b)   *nescīuit cūr uēnisset* 'he did not know why he had come'.
(c)   *quaerō quō itūrus sīs* 'I am enquiring to where you are about to go'.

All these report direct questions: (a) 'What are you doing?' (b) 'Why have you come?' etc. Quite simply, Latin reports these questions in exactly the same way that English does, except that the verb is in the *subjunctive*. All you have to do is to translate the subjunctive *as if it were the identical tense of the indicative*.

Notes

1   *num* (or *an*) in indirect questions mean 'if', 'whether'; *num quis* means 'if anyone' (cf. *nē quis, sī quis* **134[3], 145[2], 139[1]**; forms **I4**).
2   *necne* in indirect questions means 'or not'.
3   As with indirect statements and commands, references to the subject of the main verb are reflexive, e.g.

> *Caesar mīlitēs rogāuit utrum sē audīre possent necne* 'Caesar asked the soldiers whether they could hear him (= Caesar) or not'

4   Where Latin uses future participle + *sim/essem* to express the future, you should translate this into a simpler future in English, e.g.

> *Strobīlus nescīuit ubi aulam cēlātūrus esset* 'Strobilus did not know where he was about to hide the pot' i.e. 'would hide the pot'

Exercises

1   *Translate these sentences*:

(a)   omnēs rogant num seruōs accēperit Catilīna.
(b)   nescit cōnsul utrum ad urbem an ad Galliam Catilīna itūrus sit.
(c)   Metellus sciēbat quō Catilīna prōgressūrus esset.
(d)   nēmo scit quot mīlitēs habuerit Mānlius.
(e)   nesciō quantam praedam Catilīna adeptus sit.

(f) cīuēs rogant num cōnsul coniūrātōrēs pūnīre cōnstituerit.
(g) quis rogāuit utrum ignāuus esset Lentulus necne?
(h) Sallustius nārrat quālis Tulliānī faciēs fuerit.
(i) omnēs scīmus quot legiōnēs Catilīna īnstrūxerit.
(j) cōnsulēs rogāuērunt num cōpiae Catilīnae magnae futūrae essent.
(k) scīre uelim utrum Catilīna an cōnsul uictūrus sit.
(l) rogāuī utrum Catilīna ipse suōs mīlitēs in proelium dūxisset necne.

2 *Translate these sentences*:

(a) scrībis tē uelle scīre quī sit status[1] rēī pūblicae. (*Cicero*)
(b) quid faciendum sit, ā faciente discendum[2] est. (*Seneca*)
(c) cōnsīderābimus quid fēcerit, quid faciat, quid factūrus sit. (*Cicero*)
(d) uīuam an[3] moriar, nūlla est in mē metus[4]. (*Ennius*)
(e) nihil est difficilius quam quid deceat uidēre. (*Cicero*)

[1] *stat-us ūs* 4m. situation
[2] *discō* 3 I learn.
[3] *an* or: note that there is no preceding *utrum*.
[4] *metus* (unusually) is f. here.

3 *Translate into Latin* (See **R3 Note 4** *for strict rules*):

(a) I would like to tell you why you have been called together.
(b) You all know how idle Lentulus has been.
(c) Do not tell me how many enemies are pursuing us.
(d) I urge you to remember how much hope you have placed in this battle.
(e) Someone may ask why we are fighting.

73 Conditional clauses: 'if x had happened, y would have happened'

Where a *sī* ('if') clause uses the pluperfect subjunctive and the main clause uses a pluperfect subjunctive, the meaning is 'if x had happened, y would have happened' (cf. **139**), e.g.

> *sī Catilīnam uīdissem, fūgissem* 'if I had seen Catiline, I would have fled'
> *sī effūgissent, Rōma dēlēta esset* 'if they had escaped, Rome would have been destroyed'

Notes

1 This meaning is sometimes expressed by imperfect subjunctives (see **139**³).

2 Mixtures of the set formulae are also possible, e.g. *sī hoc fēcissem, laetus essem* 'If I had done this, I would (now) be happy'.

Exercises

1 *Translate into English:*

(a) nisi Lentulus ignāuus fuisset, rēs pūblica magnō in perīculō fuisset.

(b) sī coniūrātōrēs dīuitiās habuissent, Catilīnae sē numquam adiūnxissent.

(c) Catilīnae mīlitēs, nisi eōs necessitūdō pugnāre coēgisset, effugere cōnātī essent.

(d) uīcisset Catilīna, nisi Fortūna eī inuīdisset.

(e) sī Catilīnae satis frūmentī fuisset, in montibus manēre cōnstituisset.

2 *Translate into Latin:*

(a) You would all have lived your life in exile, if I had not made this plan.

(b) If Lentulus had been brave, our danger would not now be so great.¹

(c) If you had possessed wealth, you would now be fighting against me.²

(d) Catiline would have gone into exile, if he had foreseen the idleness of Lentulus.

(e) If Catiline had not made a speech, his soldiers would not have realised how much danger there was.

¹ Use *sī* + plup. subj., impf. subj.
² Use *sī* + plup. subj., impf. subj.

174 *quōminus, quīn* + **subjunctive**

1 *quōminus* (= *quō minus*, 'so that . . . not') is used after verbs of preventing, hindering, restraining, obstructing, and is an extension of the purpose or result clause constructions already met (**144**, **148**). The best translation in these circumstances is usually 'from', e.g.

mē impedit quōminus eam 'he hinders me so that I cannot go / from going'

eīs obstitit quōminus īrent 'he stood in their way so that they could not go', 'he opposed their departure'

nāuēs uentō tenēbantur quōminus in portum uenīre possent 'The ships were prevented by the wind from coming (= 'so that they could not come') into the harbour'

NB.   See further Reference Grammar **S2(f)**.

2 *quīn* (*quī ne* 'how not?') is generally found in a negative context and has a number of usages of deliberative, consecutive and indirect force using the subjunctive:

(a)   After negative expressions of preventing e.g. *nīl tē impedit quīn eās* 'nothing prevents you from going / so that you cannot go'.

(b)   Meaning 'but that', 'without', 'that not' in negative contexts, e.g. *numquam eum uideō quīn rīdeam* 'I never see him but that I laugh / without laughing', *numquam ēgressus sum quīn uidērer* 'I never went out but that I was seen / without being seen'; *nēmo tam sapiēns est quīn erret* 'no-one is so wise but that he makes a mistake / that he does not make a mistake'.

Note also the expressions *facere nōn possum quīn* 'I cannot do (a thing) but that' 'I cannot help —ing'; *fieri nōn potest quīn* 'it cannot come about but that . . .', 'it is impossible that . . . not'; *nōn multum abest quīn* 'it is not far from being the case that . . .'

(c)   In certain negative expressions of doubting meaning '(but) that', e.g. *dubium nōn est quīn* 'there is no doubt (but) that . . .'; *nōn dubitō quīn* 'I do not doubt (but) that . . .'; *dubitārī nōn potest quīn* 'it cannot be doubted (but) that'.

Examine the following examples:

nōn dubium erat quīn Catilīna uincerētur 'there was no doubt that Catiline was being defeated'

nēmo dubitābit quīn Lentulus ignāuus fuerit 'no-one will doubt that Lentulus was a coward'

nēmo est quīn sciat 'everyone knows'

fierī nōn potest quīn rēs pūblica salua sit 'it is impossible that the state will not be safe'

Catilīna facere nōn poterat quīn frūstrā loquerētur 'Catiline could not help speaking to no purpose'

NB.   See further Reference Grammar **Q2(a), S2(a) 3(i)–(iv), S2(e)**.

Exercises

1 *Translate into English*:

(a) impedior quōminus tibi nārrem quid Catilīna dīxerit.
(b) nec aetās impedit quōminus et cēterārum rērum et in prīmīs agrī
colendī studia teneāmus. (*Cicero*)
(c) nōn dubium est quīn Catilīna coniūrātor fuerit.
(d) quīn loquar, numquam mē potes dēterrēre.[1] (*Plautus*)
(e) dubitārī nōn potest quīn Fortūna Catilīnae inuīderit.
(f) quis dubitet quīn in uirtūte dīuitiae sint? (*Cicero*)
(g) nēmo est tam senex quī sē annum nōn putet posse uīuere (*Cicero*)
(h) nōn potest iūcundē[2] uīuī nisi cum uirtūte uīuātur. (*Cicero*)

[1] *dēterreō* 2 I frighten off, prevent.
[2] *iūcundē* happily.

2 *Translate into Latin* (*see Note on* **174** *for references to Reference Grammar
discussions*):

(a) Nothing stops you from speaking.[1]
(b) There is no doubt that[2] this is true.
(c) Catiline was prevented from[3] leaving the mountains.
(d) I am being held back by necessity from following the rest of the
army.[4]
(e) There was no doubt that Catiline was forced to fight.

[1] *quōminus* or *quīn*.
[2] *quīn*.
[3] *nē* or *quōminus*.
[4] 'I hold back' = *teneō* 2; *nē* or *quōminus*.

Reading exercise / Test exercise

*In indirect speech there are three basic constructions: (i) statements are expressed
by acc. + inf.; (ii) commands by* ut/nē + *subjunctive; (iii) indirect questions by a
question word + subjunctive. As you know, subordinate clauses within it also
have subjunctive verbs. You need also to know that in extended passages, indirect
commands are often represented by subjunctive alone. In reading, the most
important thing is to be aware when such an extended passage begins: once the
fact of indirect speech is spotted, the next thing is to remember that the tense of the
introductory verb will affect the tense of all subjunctives.*

*58: Caesar has just won a battle at the river Arar against one canton (pāg-us ī
2m.) of the migrating Helvetii. They send him an embassy, headed by Divico.*

is ita cum Caesare ēgit: sī pācem populus Rōmānus cum Heluetiīs faceret,
in eam partem itūrōs atque ibi futūrōs ubi eōs Caesar cōnstituisset atque
esse uoluisset; sīn bellō persequī perseuērāret, reminīscerētur et ueteris
incommodī et prīstinae uirtūtis Heluetiǫrum. quod imprōuīsō ūnum
pāgum adortus esset, cum eī quī flūmen trānsīssent suīs auxilium ferre   5
nōn possent, nē ob eam rem aut suae magnopere uirtūtī tribueret aut
ipsōs dēspiceret. sē ita ā patribus maiōribusque suīs didicisse, ut magis
uirtūte quam dolō contenderent aut īnsidiīs nīterentur. quārē nē
committeret ut is locus ubi cōnstitissent ex calamitāte populī Rōmānī et
interneciōne exercitūs nōmen caperet aut memoriam prōderet.   10

(Caesar, Dē Bellō Gallicō 1, 13, 3–7)

is = Diuicō
agō 3 *ēgī* I deal, do business [Indirect
Speech begins after the colon]
faceret [Indirect: it represents either
faciat ('were to make') or *faciet* ('is
going to make')]
itūrōs, futūrōs sc. *esse*: 'they would go
. . . and stay' [Both refer to the
Helvetii]
cōnstituō 3 *cōnstituī* I place, put
sīn but if
perseuērāret [Indirect: represents either
perseuēret ('were to continue') or
perseuērābit ('is going to continue')]
perseuērō 1 I continue
reminīscerētur [Indirect command]
reminīscor 3 dep. I remember (+ gen.)
incommod-um ī 2n. misfortune [Inflicted
by the Helvetii upon L. Cassius in
107.]
prīstin-us a um former
quod 'as for the fact that' [The reported
speech continues]
imprōuīsō unexpectedly

5 *adorior* 4 dep. *adortus* I attack
flūmen flūmin-is 3n. river
trānseō trānsīre trānsiī I cross
nē [introduces an indirect command,
negative]
suae [Hold until solved]
tribuō 3 I attribute [I.e. 'it', 'the fact
that' – the *quod* clause is the object
of this verb]
ipsōs [I.e. the Helvetii]
dēspiciō 3/4 I look down on
sē [I.e. the Helvetii]
discō 3 *didicī* I learn
contendō 3 I struggle, fight
quārē therefore
nē [Introduces another negative
indirect command]
committeret [Tr. 'act in such a way']
cōnsistō 3 *cōnstitī* I stop
10 *interneciō interneciōn-is* 3f. killing,
slaughter
memori-a ae 1f. remembrance, record
prōdō 3 I hand down, transmit;
produce

NB.   For rules governing *conditions* in indirect speech, see Reference
Grammar **R4(b)**.

English–Latin

Reread the text of **5F(i)**, *then translate this passage into Latin*:

'You can see, soldiers, in what danger our affairs are. Two armies prevent
us from leaving these mountains without a battle. If we had not relied

upon Lentulus, we would have already escaped. Now, however, we must fight, for our fatherland, for our liberty and for our lives. Do not be[1] cowards. If we win[2] there is no doubt that[3] safety is ours. If we yield[2] through fear, nothing will stop us from[4] being butchered.'

[1] *nē* + perfect subjunctive. [3] *quīn* + subjunctive.
[2] Use future perfect. [4] *quōminus* + subjunctive or *quīn* + subjunctive.

Virgil's *Aeneid*

Eventually, Aeneas and his rival Turnus come face to face. Aeneas is about to kill him, but Turnus pleads for his life. In this passage, Aeneas is about to yield to Turnus' entreaty, when he sees Pallas' sword-belt glittering on him (see note). Aeneas kills him, and the Aeneid ends.

stetit ācer in armīs

Aenēās uoluēns oculōs dextramque repressit;
et iam iamque magis cūnctantem flectere sermō
coeperat, īnfēlīx umerō cum appāruit altō
balteus et nōtīs fulsērunt cingula bullīs   5
Pallantis puerī, uictum quem uulnere Turnus
strāuerat atque umerīs inimīcum īnsigne gerēbat.
ille, oculīs postquam saeuī monimenta dolōris
exuuiāsque hausit, furiīs accēnsus et īrā
terribilis: 'tūne hinc spoliīs indūte meōrum   10
ēripiāre mihī? Pallās tē hōc uulnere, Pallās
immolat et poenam scelerātō ex sanguine sūmit.'
hoc dīcēns, ferrum aduersō sub pectore condit
feruidus; ast illī soluuntur frīgore membra
uītaque cum gemitū fugit indignāta sub umbrās.   15

(Virgil, Aeneid 12.935–52)

stetit [Subject? Wait]
uoluō 3 I roll, shift
reprimō 3 *repressī* I check, restrain
iam iamque magis 'now more and more'
cūnctantem [Refers to Aeneas. Register case and hold]
flectō 3 I bend, persuade
sermō [I.e. the words (of Turnus)]

īnfēlīx īnfēlīc-is ill-starred, disastrous
  [Wait for noun for *īnfēlīx* and introduction word to this new clause]
umer-us ī 2m. shoulder [Dat. or abl.? Hold]
cum [Introduces the clause]

appāreō 2 I appear, come into view
[Where? *umerō*]
alt-us a um on the top of
5 *balte-us ī* 2m. sword-belt
nōt-us a um well-known
fulgeō 2 *fulsī* I shine, glitter
cingul-a ōrum 2n. pl. baldric
bull-a ae 1f. stud [Solves *nōtīs*. But
what case?]
Pallās Pallant-is 3m. Pallas, the young
man entrusted to Aeneas' charge by
his father Evander. Turnus killed
Pallas in battle (*Aeneid* 10.439ff.)
uictum quem [*quem* introduces the
clause, object of *strāuerat*]
uulnus uulner-is 3n. wound
sternō 3 *strāuī* I lay low
inimīc-us a um hostile, of his enemy
īnsigne īnsign-is 3n. insignia, a sign
gerō 3 I wear [What? Where? Solves
umerīs]
ille [I.e. Aeneas]
postquam [Introduces clause]
moniment-um ī 2n. memorial (to + gen.)
exuui-ae ārum 2f. pl. spoils
hauriō 4 *hausī* I drink in

furi-ae ārum 1f. pl. the spirits of
vengeance
accendō 3 *accendī accēnsus* I burn up,
consume
īr-a ae 1f. anger
10 *spoli-a ōrum* 2n. pl. spoils
indūt-us a um dressed in (+ abl.)
meōrum 'of mine' [I.e. 'of my people']
ēripiō 3/4 I snatch away [Deliberative
subj. 'are you to be . . .?']
immolō 1 I sacrifice
poenam sūmō 3 I take revenge
scelerāt-us a um villainous
aduers-us a um facing
pectus pector-is 3n. chest
condō 3 I hide, bury
feruid-us a um hot, in passion
ast = at
illī (dat.) [I.e. Turnus]
frīgus frīgor-is 3n. cold, chill (of death)
membr-um ī 2n. limb
15 *gemit-us ūs* 4m. groan
indignāt-us a um complaining
sub (+ acc.) down to
umbr-a ae 1f. shade

Deliciae Latinae

Martial

quārē nōn habeat, Fabulle, quaeris,
uxōrem Themisōn? habet sorōrem. (*12.20*)

Themisōn Themisōn-is 3m.
Themison [Subject of
habeat and *habet*]

aestīuō seruēs ubi piscem tempore, quaeris?
in thermīs seruā, Caeciliāne, tuīs. (*2.78*)

aestīu-us a um hot,
summer [Hold *aestīuō*
until solved by *tempore*]
seruēs deliberative
subjunctive [See **152¹**]

piscis pisc-is 3m. fish
therm-ae ārum 1f. pl. baths
(which were *supposed*
to be hot)

Caeciliān-us ī 2m.
Caecilianus (a bath-
keeper)

393

Section 5G

Running vocabulary for 5G(i)

---

accendō 3 I fire
aciēs aciē-ī 5f. battle-line
aeger aegr-a aegr-um ill
amplius more than
appellō 1 I address
canō 3 I sound (lit. 'sing')
centuriō centuriōn-is 3m.
    centurion (commander
    of a century – actually
    less than 100 men)
circumeundō by going
    round (abl. gerund of
    circumeō)
corn-ū ūs 4n. wing (dat. s.
    cornū)
cuiusque (gen. s. m.) of
    each (man)
dexter dextr-a um right
exaequō 1 I make equal
Faesulān-us ī 2m. man
    from Faesulae
foc-us ī 2m. hearth
frōns front-is 3f. front
inerm-is e unarmed

interficiendum killing (acc.
    gerund of *interficiō*)
latrō latrōn-is 3m. bandit
lēgāt-us ī 2m. commander
locō 1 I place
M. = Mārcō: Mārc-us ī
    2m. Marcus
moriendum dying (acc.
    gerund of *morior*)
nārrandō by relating (abl.
    gerund of *nārrō*)
nōminandō by naming
    (abl. gerund of *nōminō*)
nōminō 1 I name
parāt-us a um prepared
    (to: *ad* + gerund)
pedes pedit-is 3m. foot-
    soldier
permittō 3 I entrust x
    (acc.) to y (dat.)
Petrēi-us ī 2m. M.
    Petreius

post (+ acc.) after; ((adv.)
    afterwards, later)
praeficiō 3/4 *praefēcī*
    praefectus I put x (acc.)
    in charge of y (dat.)
prō (+ abl.) in accordance
    with
pugnandum fighting (acc.
    gerund of *pugnō*)
quemque (acc. s. m.)
    (l. 301) each; (l. 293)
    optimum quemque = all
    the best men; (ll. 298,
    302) *ūnum*
    quemque = each
    individual
remoueō 2 *remōuī remōtus* I
    remove
sign-um ī 2n. (l. 288)
    trumpet-call; (l. 292)
    standard
sinister sinistr-a um left
subsidi-um ī 2n. (or pl.)
    reserve
ueterān-us a um veteran

Notes

l. 290 *qūo . . . esset* see **148.**
l. 292 *reliquārum*: sc. '(of the) cohorts'.

Learning vocabulary for 5G(i)

Nouns

aciēs aciē-ī 5f. battle-line;
    sharp edge, point;
    keenness (of sight)
centuriō centuriōn-is 3m.
    centurion
corn-ū ūs 4n. wing (of
    army); horn

latrō latrōn-is 3m. robber,
    bandit
lēgāt-us ī 2m. commander
    (pl. ambassadors)

sign-um ī 2n. standard,
    trumpet-call (seal;
    signal, sign; statue)
subsidi-um ī 2n. reserve;
    help

394

Adjectives

aeger aegr-a um ill

dexter dextr-a um right, favourable

sinister sinistr-a um left; unfavourable

Verbs

appellō 1 I name, call; address

cūrō 1 I am in command (look after, care for)
nōminō 1 I name

praeficiō 3/4 *praefēcī praefectus* I put x (acc.) in charge of y (dat.)

Others

amplius more than (from *ampl-us a um* great)

post (+ acc.) behind; after (adv. afterwards, later; behind)

prō (+ abl.) in accordance with (for, in return for; on behalf of; in front of; instead of)

Running vocabulary for 5G(ii)

ācriter fiercely, spiritedly
alibī (with *aliōs*) in different places [See **102¹**]
cadō 3 I fall, die
comminus to close quarters
committō [See *proelium committere*]
cōnfert-us a um close-packed
cōnfodiō 3/4 I stab
contrā ac (+ indic.) contrary to what
expedīt-us ī 2m. light-armed soldier
explōrō 1 I investigate, reconnoitre
exsequor 3 dep. I carry out, perform
ferentāri-us ī 2m. light-armed soldier (armed only with missiles)
fundō 3 *fūdī fūsus* I rout
incēdō 3 I advance

incurrō 1 I run into
indūcō 3 I lead (x: acc. into y: *in* + acc.)
īnfest-us a um hostile; *cum īnfestīs signīs* = 'with standards set for attack'
īnstō 1 I press on, approach
integer integr-a um fresh, not wounded
labōrō 1 I am in difficulties
latus later-is 3n. flank
omittō 3 I leave out, leave aside; let fall
paulātim little by little, gradually
perturbō 1 I disturb, confuse
pīl-um ī 2n. heavy javelin (normally thrown by soldiers before hand-to-hand fighting began)

praetōri-us a um praetorian (i.e. the best fighters)
prīstin-us a um former
proelium committere to join battle
reor 2 dep. *ratus* I think, believe, suppose
resistō 3 I resist
sauci-us a um wounded
strēnu-us a um energetic
succurrō 3 I run to help (+ dat.)
tendō 3 I struggle, fight
tub-a ae 1f. trumpet
uersor 1 dep. I am occupied
ueterān-us ī 2m. veteran
unde from where
uterque (nom. s. m.) each (of two) [Note the pl. verb]
utrōque (abl. s. n.) each (of the two)

Notes

l. 307 *eō*: 'to that place . . .' picked up by *unde* 'from where'.
l. 308 *uentum est* ⎱
l. 311 *certātur* ⎰ impersonal passives (see **155**).
l. 311 *īnstāre*   ⎫
l. 312 *uersārī, succurrere*   ⎪
l. 313 *arcessere, prōuidēre, pugnāre,* ⎬ historic infinitives.
l. 314 *ferīre*   ⎪
ll. 319 *fūsās . . . relictum*: sc. *esse*. ⎭

Learning vocabulary for 5G(ii)

Nouns
latus later-is 3n. side; flank
pīl-um ī 2n. heavy javelin

Adjectives

integer integr-a um whole, untouched

prīstin-us a um former; original

sauci-us a um wounded

Verbs

cadō 3 *cecidī cāsum* I fall, die
īnstō 1 *institī* I press upon; urge; pursue; am at hand, approach; strive after (*in + stō*)
omittō 3 *omīsī omissus* I give up; let fall; omit, leave aside (*ob + mittō*)

reor 2 dep. *ratus* I think, believe, suppose
resistō 3 *restitī* (+ dat.) I resist; stand back, halt; pause (*re + sistō*)
succurrō 3 *succurrī succursum* I run to help, assist (+ dat.) (*sub + currō*)

tendō 3 *tetendī tēnsus* or *tentus* I strive, fight; (stretch (out); offer; direct; (intrans.) travel)
uersor 1 dep. I am occupied; stay, dwell; am in a certain condition

Others

alibī somewhere else

paulātim little by little, gradually

unde from where, whence

Running vocabulary for 5G(iii)

aduers-us a um in front
anim-a ae 1f. soul, life
cadāuer cadāuer-is 3n. corpse

cernō 3 I see
cognāt-us ī 2m. kinsman, blood-relative
corpus corpor-is 3n. body

ferē almost
gaudi-um ī 2n. joy
hostīl-is e of the enemy
incruent-us a um bloodless

ingenu-us a um free-born
lūct-us ūs 4m. mourning
maeror maerōr-is 3m. grief
occidō 3 *occidī* I die, fall
paululum a very little
prōcēdō 3 *prōcessī* I
 advance, proceed,
 come forth
pugnandō by fighting (abl.
 gerund of *pugnō*)
quisquam (nom. s. m.)
 (l. 325) anyone
 (pronoun); (l. 328) any
 (adj.)

quisque (nom. s. m.)
 (l. 323) each person;
 (l.331) *strēnuissimus*
 quisque all the most
 energetic men
spīrō 1 I breathe
spoliandī of stripping
 (corpses) (gen. gerund
 of *spoliō* 1)
strēnu-us a um energetic
tegō 3 I cover
uariē in different ways

uīsendī of visiting/viewing
 (gen. gerund of *uīsō* 3)
uīu-us a um living, alive
uoluō 3 I turn (over)
 (trans.)
uulnerō 1 I wound
uulnus uulner-is 3n.
 wound
uult-us ūs 4m. face,
 expression

Notes

l. 322 *cernerēs*: referring to the past (see **153.2**).
l. 323 *quem* with *locum*: *locum* picked up by *eum*.
l. 334 *aliī . . . pars*: 'some . . . others'. A variant of *aliī . . . aliī*.

Learning vocabulary for 5G(iii)

Nouns

anim-a ae 1f. soul, life,
 breath
corpus corpor-is 3n. body
gaudi-um ī 2n. joy

lūct-us ūs 4m. grief,
 mourning

uulnus uulner-is 3n.
 wound
uult-us ūs 4m. face,
 expression

Adjectives

aduers-us a um in front
 (i.e. facing the enemy)
 (hostile; opposite;
 unfavourable)

uīu-us a um alive, living

Verbs

occidō 3 *occidī occāsum* I
 fall, die (*ob + cadō*)
tegō 3 *tēxī tēctus* I cover

uoluō 3 *uoluī uolūtus* I roll,
 turn (over) (trans.)

uulnerō 1 I wound

Grammar and exercises for 5G

175 Gerunds: -nd- forms, '—ing'

We have already seen that verbs can form adjectives (i.e. participles and gerundives), when they act like adjectives in agreeing with nouns or pronouns, e.g.

> *nāue captā nautae effūgērunt* 'with the ship captured, the sailors fled'
>
> *hic homo monendus est* 'this man is to be / must be warned'.

Verbs can also form nouns. As such, verbs take the form of the *infinitive*, or the *gerund*, which has exactly the same forms as the neuters of the *gerundive* (see **160**). The declension is as follows (acc. to abl. as for 2n. nouns):

	1 'loving'	*2* 'having'	*3* 'speaking'
nom.	amā́-re	habḗ-re	dī́c-e-re
acc.	amá-nd-um amā́-re	habé-nd-um habḗ-re	dīc-é-nd-um dī́c-e-re
gen.	amá-nd-ī	habé-nd-ī	dīc-é-nd-ī
dat.	amá-nd-ō	habé-nd-ō	dīc-é-nd-ō
abl.	amá-nd-ō	habé-nd-ō	dīc-é-nd-ō

	4 'hearing'	*3/4* 'capturing'
nom.	audī́-re	cáp-e-re
acc.	audi-é-nd-um audī́-re	capi-é-nd-um cáp-e-re
gen.	audi-é-nd-ī	capi-é-nd-ī
dat.	audi-é-nd-ō	capi-é-nd-ō
abl.	audi-é-nd-ō	capi-é-nd-ō

Deponents have exactly the same forms and *active* meaning, i.e. *mina-nd-um* 'threatening', *pollice-nd-um* 'promising', *loqu-e-nd-um* 'speaking', *menti-e-nd-um* 'lying', *prōgredi-e-nd-um* 'advancing'.

Usages

1 The infinitive is used as a noun-gerund in e.g. *dulce est amāre* 'it is sweet to make love' 'love-making is pleasant'. Here *amāre* is noun-subject. Cf. *cupiō ambulāre* 'I desire to walk' 'I like walking'. Here the infinitive is a noun-object. With prepositions, the *-nd-* form is used, e.g. *ad amandum* 'with a view to loving'.

2 *ad* + acc. 'for the purpose of', e.g. *ad dīcendum* 'for the purpose of speaking', 'with a view to speaking'. The gerund may take an object, e.g. *ad nāuem capiendum* 'to capture the ship'. Cf. **161**.3 (gerundives).

3 *causā/grātiā* + gen. 'for the sake of', 'for the purpose of', e.g. *dīcendī causā* 'for the sake of speaking' (note word-order), *habendī grātiā* 'for the sake of having', 'in order to have'. Cf. **161**.3 (gerundives).

4 In the abl., e.g. *dīcendō* 'by speaking', *ambulandō* 'by walking' (cf. *innuendō* 'by hinting'), e.g. *ūnus homō nōbīs cūnctandō restituit rem* 'one man (i.e. Q. Fabius Maximus Cunctator) restored our fortunes by delaying' (Ennius).

N.B.   Remember the irregular gerunds *eund-um* 'going' (*eō*), *oriund-um* 'rising' (*orior*). *faciundum* 'making', 'doing', *gerundum* 'doing' etc. are also found, for *faciendum gerendum*. The key vowel was originally *-u-*.

Exercises

1 *Form, translate and decline the gerunds of the following verbs*: exorior, dormiō, petō, nōscō, fugiō, commoror, teneō, eō, (*optional*: uoluō, uulnerō, occidō, uersor, reperiō, agō, gerō, taceō).

2 *Translate*:

  (a) ad ūtendum.
  (b) eundī causā.
  (c) discēdendō.
  (d) resistendī grātiā.
  (e) ad uulnerandum.
  (f) uidendō.
  (g) uoluendī causā.

3 *Give the Latin for (using gerunds)*:

  (a) To wound.
  (b) For the purpose of delaying.

(c)   By holding.
(d)   For the sake of arising.
(e)   To assist.
(f)   Of seeking.
(g)   In doing.

4 *Translate these sentences or phrases saying whether gerund or gerundive is being used:*

(a)   ad mīlitēs uulnerandōs.
(b)   mihi eundum est.
(c)   prōgrediendī causā.
(d)   mīlitibus nōminandīs.
(e)   fortiter resistendō.
(f)   ad corpora uoluenda.
(g)   sauciīs ab integrīs succurrendum erat.
(h)   coniūrātōrēs cōnsul praetōribus pūniendōs trādidit.
(i)   discēdendī grātiā.
(j)   ad exercitum īnstruendum.
(k)   hominis mēns[1] discendō[2] alitur[3] et cōgitandō. (*Cicero*)
(l)   nihil tam difficile est quīn quaerendō inuestīgārī possit. (*Terence*)

[1] *mēns ment-is* 3f. mind.
[2] *discō* 3 I learn.
[3] *alitur* 'is fed', 'grows'.
[4] *inuestīgō* 1 I trace out.

176 *quisque* and *quisquam*

quisque means 'each and every', 'everyone'. It is often used with the superlative, e.g. *optimus quisque* 'each and every best (male)', 'all the best men'; *pessima quaeque* 'each and every most wicked woman', 'all the most wicked women'.

quisquam means 'anyone', 'any' and is normally found in negative contexts, e.g. *nec quisquam* 'and not anyone', 'and no-one'.

quisque and *quisquam* decline like *quis* (**29**) + *que/quam*. Note the neuter of *quisquam* is *quicquam* and the neuter of *quisque* is *quidque* or *quodque*.

77 *uterque*

uterque means 'both', 'each (of two)' and declines as follows:

s.

	m.	*f.*	*n.*
nom.	utér-que	útr-a-que	utr-úm-que
acc.	utr-úm-que	utr-ám-que	utr-úm-que
gen.	←——— utr-ī́us-que———→		
dat.	←——— utr-ī́us-que———→		
abl.	utr-ṓ-que	utr-ā́-que	utr-ṓ-que

pl.

	m.	*f.*	*n.*
nom.	utr-ī́-que	utr-aé-que	útr-a-que
acc.	utr-ṓs-que	utr-ā́s-que	útr-a-que
gen.	utr-ōrúm-que	utr-ārúm-que	utr-ōrúm-que
dat.	←——— utr-ī́s-que———→		
abl.	←——— utr-ī́s-que———→		

Cf. *alter, nūllus, tōtus, ūnus, sōlus* etc. which also decline exactly like *mult-us a um* except for the gen. s. in *-īus* and the dat. s. in *-ī*.

78 **4th declension neuter *corn-ū ūs* 'horn', 'wing of army'**

	s.	*pl.*
nom.	córnū	córnu-a
acc.	córnū	córnu-a
gen.	córnū-s	córnu-um
dat.	córnū	córn-ibus
abl.	córnū	córn-ibus

NB. The only other noun of this type you are likely to meet is *genū* 'knee' (cf. 'genuflect', to bend the knee).

Exercises

1 *Translate these sentences:*

(a) pessimus quisque coniūrātiōnī fauet.
(b) stultissimus quisque haec intellegere potest.

(c) nec quisquam hoc dīcere ausus est.
(d) interdīcitque[1] omnibus nē quemquam interficiant. (*Caesar*)
(e) in omnī arte[2] optimum quidque rārissimum[3] est. (*Cicero*)
(f) remedia utrīusque fortūnae. (*Title of a book by fourteenth-century Italian Petrarch*)
(g) tū mihi uidēris utrumque factūrus. (*Cicero*)
(h) aut enim nēmo aut, sī quisquam, ille sapiēns fuit. (*Cicero*)
(i) prō sē quisque ad populum loquēbātur. (*Cicero*)
(j) . . . nec quisquam ex agmine tantō audet adīre uirum. (*Virgil*)

[1] *interdīcō* 3 (+dat.) I forbid.
[2] *ars art-is* 3f. art.
[3] *rār-us a um* rare.
[4] *sapiēns sapient-is* wise.

2 *Give the Latin for*:

(a) All the best men resist their enemies.
(b) Nor did the commander send anyone wounded into battle.
(c) The commander of each of the two armies encouraged his soldiers.
(d) It is not possible to say anything good[1].
(e) Petreius encouraged each individual.
(f) By relating each man's deeds he encouraged the soldiers.

[1] Genitive; cf. *quid negōtī*.

179 Further comparative clauses

1 atque/ac

atque/ac is used after adjectives or adverbs which express 'likeness' or 'unlikeness', such as *īdem* 'the same', *alius* 'different', 'other', *aliter* 'differently', *contrā* 'opposite', 'contrary', *par* 'equal', *pariter* 'equally', *perinde* 'in like manner', *similis* 'like', 'similar'. E.g.

> *iussērunt simulācrum Iouis, contrā atque anteā fuerat, ad orientem conuertere* 'they ordered (them) to turn the statue of Jupiter towards the East, contrary to what it had been before'
> *perinde ēgit ac dīxit* 'he acted just as he said'

2 Correlatives

You have already met *ut* meaning 'as', which acts as a correlative to *sīc* or *ita* 'thus', e.g. *ut tū imperās, sīc/ita ego faciō* 'as you order, so I do'. In the same way, *tam* 'so' is answered by *quam* 'as', e.g.

> *tam beātus erat ille quam miser ego* 'he was as (lit. so) happy as I unhappy'

tot 'so many' is answered by *quot* 'as many', e.g.

> *tot uirī sunt quot fēminae* 'so many men there are, as many (as) (there are) women', 'there are as many men as women'

Cf. *tantus* ('so great') . . . *quantus* ('as great', 'as'); *tālis* ('of such a sort') . . . *quālis* ('of which sort', 'as'), e.g.

> *tanta sapientia eī inest quanta uīs* 'there is so great wisdom in him as great (as there is) force', 'he is as much brain as brawn'
> *tālem uirtūtem praebēbat quālem Horātius* 'he showed bravery of such a sort as the sort (which) Horatius (showed)'

3 Unreal comparisons

quasi, uelut, tamquam mean 'as if', 'as though' and (with or without *sī* added) take a *subjunctive* where the comparison is unreal or hypothetical. Constructions under **179.1** add *sī*. e.g.

> *ita sē gerit quasi stultus sit* 'he is behaving as though he were a fool' (but he is not)
> *perinde agit ac sī hostis sit* 'he acts just as though he were an enemy' (but is not)

Exercises

1 Translate into English:

(a) Catilīna aliter ac Petrēius ratus erat agēbat.
(b) tam ignāuus erat Gabīnius quam Lentulus.
(c) perinde atque eī imperātum erat, sīc Mānlius ēgit.
(d) rēs gestae sunt contrā atque exspectāuerat Petrēius.
(e) loquitur quasi stultus sit.

2　*Translate these sentences:*

(a)　nihil est hominī tam timendum quam inuidia. (*Cicero*)
(b)　nihil est tam fallāx quam uīta hūmāna, nihil tam īnsidiōsum.
　　　(*Seneca*)
(c)　quot hominēs, tot sententiae. (*Terence*)
(d)　plērīque habēre amīcum tālem uolunt, quālēs ipsī esse nōn
　　　possunt. (*Cicero*)
(e)　paruī sīc iacent, tamquam omnīnō sine animō sint. (*Cicero*)

inuidi-a ae 1f. envy,	*hūmān-us a um* human	*omnīnō* altogether,
hatred	*īnsidiōs-us a um* dangerous	completely
fallāx fallāc-is deceitful	*paruī* = babies	

3　*Give the Latin for (using comparative clauses):*

(a)　This man is as good as that man.
(b)　My son is acting against my wishes.
(c)　You are the sort of person that your father was.
(d)　He is acting differently from the way he was told to.
(e)　I will act in accordance with your commands.
(f)　He was walking as though he had been wounded.

Reading exercises / Test exercises

1　*The speaker is Cato the Censor (234–149). He is talking about old age with
Gaius Laelius (b. 186) and Publius Scipio Africanus (Minor) (c 185–129),
who are pictured as young men at the time of the conversation. His particular
theme here is what can be done to overcome what are normally seen as the
peculiar drawbacks of old age.*

resistendum, Laelī et Scīpiō, senectūtī est eiusque uitia dīligentiā
compēnsanda sunt, pugnandum tamquam contrā morbum sīc contrā
senectūtem, habenda ratiō ualētūdinis, ūtendum exercitātiōnibus
modicīs, tantum cibī et pōtiōnis adhibendum, ut reficiantur uīrēs, nōn
opprimantur. nec uērō corporī sōlum subueniendum est, sed mentī　　5
atque animō multō magis; nam haec quoque, nisi tamquam lūminī
oleum īnstillēs, exstinguuntur senectūte. et corpora quidem exerci-
tātiōnum dēfatīgātiōne ingrauēscunt, animī autem sē exercendō
leuantur. nam quōs ait Caecilius 'cōmicōs stultōs senēs', hōs significat
crēdulōs oblīuiōsōs dissolūtōs, quae uitia sunt nōn senectūtis, sed　　10
inertis ignāuae somniculōsae senectūtis. ut petulantia, ut libīdō magis

est adulēscentium quam senum, nec tamen omnium adulēscentium,
sed nōn probōrum, sīc ista senīlis stultitia, quae dēlīrātiō appellārī solet,
senum leuium est, nōn omnium. (*Cicero*, Dē senectūte (Catō Maior)
35–6)   15

senectūs senectūt-is 3f. old age
uiti-um ī 2n. fault, shortcoming
compēnsō 1 I balance
pugnandum sc. *est* [Note the ellipse of
   est, which is understood from the
   previous part of the sentence
   resistendum . . . est (also in l. 3:
   habenda, ūtendum; l.4: *adhibendum*)]
tamquam just as, as though
morb-us ī 2m. disease
ratiō ratiōn-is 3f. method, regimen
ualētūdō ualētūdin-is 3f. health
exercitātiō exercitātiōn-is 3f. exercise
modic-us a um moderate
pōtiō pōtiōn-is 3f. drink
adhibeō 2 I use
reficiō 3/4 I refresh
5 *corporī* [Hold until solved, reading as a
   phrase with *sōlum*]
subueniō 4 (+ dat.) I help
mēns ment-is 3f. mind
lūmen lūmin-is 3n. light
ole-um ī 2n. oil
īnstillō 1 I drop x (acc.) into y (dat.)
   [Note mood of *īnstillēs*: subjunctive
   expressing generalised 2nd s. (see
   153.2)]
exstinguō 3 I quench, put out

quidem indeed [Emphasising *corpora*]
dēfatīgātiō dēfatīgātiōn-is 3f. exhaustion,
   weariness
ingrauēscō 3 I grow heavier (i.e. stiffer)
exerceō 2 I train, exercise
leuō 1 I relieve [The prevalent
   metaphor centres on the stems *grau-*
   'heavy', *leu-* 'light']
ait '(he) calls'
Caecilius = C. Statius, an early Roman
   comic poet
cōmic-us a um comic
significō 1 I mean
10 *crēdul-us a um* credulous
oblīuiōs-us a um forgetful
dissolūt-us a um slack
iners inert-is idle
somniculōs-us a um drowsy
ut [Hold until solved]
petulanti-a ae 1f. impudence,
   waywardness
adulēscēns adulēscent-is 3m. youth
prob-us a um honest, upright
senīl-is e of old men
stultiti-a ae 1f. foolishness
dēlīrātiō dēlīrātiōn-is 3f. dementia,
   dotage, madness
leu-is e frivolous, weak

2 *The rape of Ceres' daughter Proserpina. She is picking flowers with her girl-
friends. Her uncle, the god of the Underworld, Pluto, sees her, falls in love
with her and snatches her off to Hades. Suspension of adjective in the first half
of the line is particularly noticeable in this piece.* (See **185** for the metre)

fīlia, cōnsuētīs ut erat comitāta puellīs,
   errābat nūdō per sua prāta pede.
ualle sub umbrōsā locus est aspergine multā
   ūuidus ex altō dēsilientis aquae.
tot fuerant illīc, quot habet nātūra, colōrēs,   5
   pictaque dissimilī flōre nitēbat humus.
quam simul aspexit, 'comitēs, accēdite', dīxit

'et mēcum plēnōs flōre referte sinūs!'
praeda puellārīs animōs prōlectat inānis,
et nōn sentītur sēdulitāte labor.   10

Proserpina wanders off, by chance not followed by any of her friends.

hanc uidet et uīsam patruus uēlōciter aufert,
rēgnaque caeruleīs in sua portat equīs.
illa quidem clāmābat, 'iō, cārissima māter,
auferor!' ipsa suōs abscideratque sinūs:
panditur intereā Dītī uia, namque diurnum   15
lūmen inassuētī uix patiuntur equī.
at chorus aequālis, cumulātae flōre ministrae,
'Persephonē', clāmant 'ad tua dōna uenī!'
ut clāmāta silet, montīs ululātibus implent,
et feriunt maestā pectora nūda manū.   20
                              (Ovid, *Fastī 4.425–34 and 445–54*)

cōnsuētīs [Hold until solved]
cōnsuēt-us a um usual
comitō 1 I accompany
errō 1 I wander
nūdō [Hold until solved]
nūd-us a um naked
prāt-a ōrum 2n. pl. meadows
uallis uall-is 3f. valley
umbrōs-us a um shady
aspergō aspergin-is 3f. spray
ūuid-us a um wet [Read *aspergine multā*
   ūuidus as one phrase]
alt-um ī 2n. high place
dēsiliō 4 I leap down [Read *ex altō*
   dēsilientis aquae as one phrase,
   dependent on *aspergine*]
5 *tot . . . quot* as many . . . as
color colōr-is 3m. colour
picta [Hold until solved]
pingō 3 *pīnxī pictus* I paint
dissimil-is e diverse
flōs flōr-is 3m. flower
niteō 2 I shine
humus [Remember this is f.]
simul as soon as
aspiciō 3/4 *aspexī* I spot
plēnōs [Hold until solved: *plēnus* takes
   gen. or abl. when it means 'full of']

referō referre I bring back
sin-us ūs 4m. fold of garment, bosom
puellār-is e girlish
prōlectō 1 I entice away
inān-is e vain, empty
10 *sentītur* [Passive: await subject]
sēdulitās sēdulitāt-is 3f. earnest
   application, concentration
uīsam [Refers to Proserpina]
patru-us 2m. uncle
uēlōciter swiftly
rēgna [Hold until solved]
rēgn-um ī 2n. kingdom, realm
caeruleīs [Hold until solved]
caerule-us a um dark
portat sc. 'her'
quidem indeed
iō help!
cār-us a um dear
suōs [Hold until solved]
abscindō 3 *abscidī* I tear apart
-que = even
15 *panditur* [Passive: await subject]
pandō 3 I open
Dīs Dīt-is 3m. Hades, Pluto
   [*Dītī* = dative of agent, 'by']
namque for in fact

diurn-us a um of the day [Don't stop reading at the line-end]
lūmen lūmin-is 3n. light
inassuētī [Hold until solved]
inassuēt-us a um unaccustomed
uix with difficulty
chor-us ī 2m. group
aequāl-is e of the same age
cumulō 1 I load
ministr-a ae 1f. attendant

cumulātae . . . ministrae [In apposition to *chorus aequālis*]
Persephonē [Vocative]
dōn-um ī 2n. gift
sileō 2 I am silent
ululāt-us ūs 4m. cry, wail
impleō 2 I fill (x acc. with y abl.)
20 *maestā* [Hold until solved]
maest-us a um sad
pectus pector-is 3n. breast

English–Latin

Reread the text of **5G(iii)** *and then translate this passage into Latin:*

When the fighting[1] was finished, you would have seen many corpses in the place. It was also possible to see[2] how much daring[1] there had been in Catiline and in his army. Each man had fallen in the place which he had seized by fighting. Nor had anyone run away. Catiline, who had run into the middle of the enemy for the purpose of dying quickly, was found far from his own men. He still retained the ferocity of expression[3] he had had[3] when[4] alive. But the victory was not a joyful event for the Romans. All the best men had died or been wounded seriously. Those who had come out for the purpose of stripping corpses found not only enemies, but also friends and relatives as they turned over the cadavers. There were both joy and sorrow in the camp that night.

[1] Do not use a gerund here, but a noun.
[2] Use *uidērī poterat* (lit. 'it could be seen').
[3] Do not forget to insert a *quī* clause here, though English neglects it.
[4] Not needed: use adj. alone, agreeing with subject.

Deliciae Latinae

Martial

cūr nōn mitto meōs⌐ tibi, Pontiliāne, ⌐libellōs?
nē mihi tū mittās, Pontiliāne, tuōs. (7.3)

libell-us ī 2m. book   *Pontiliān-us ī* 2m. Pontilianus

crās tē uīctūrum, crās dīcis, Postume, semper.
dīc mihi, crās istud, Postume, quando uenit?
quam longē est crās istud? ubi est? aut unde petendum?
numquid apud Parthōs Armeniōsque latet?
iam crās istud habet Priamī uel Nestoris annōs.   5
crās istud quantī, dīc mihi, possit emī?
crās uīuēs: hodiē iam uīuere, Postume, sērum est.
ille sapit, quisquis, Postume, uīxit heri. (5.58)

crās tomorrow
numquid 'can it be that it . . .?'
Parth-ī ōrum 2m. pl. Parthians
Armeni-ī ōrum 2m. pl. Armenians
lateō 2 I lie hidden
5 Priam-us ī 2m. Priam
   (king of Troy)
Nestōr Nestor-is 3m.

Nestor (Greek
warrior-king)
[both renowned
for their longevity!]
quantī (gen.) 'at what price'
emō 3 I buy
sērum too late
sapiō 3/4 I am wise
quisquis who
heri yesterday

īnscrīpsit tumulīs septem ⌐ scelerāta ⌐uirōrum
'sē fēcisse' Chloē. quid pote simplicius? (9.15)

īnscrībō 3 īnscrīpsī I write
   upon (+ dat.)
tumul-us ī 2m. tomb

scelerāt-us a um infamous
Chloē Chloe (Greek f.
   nom.)

pote (sc. est) 'can be'
simplex simplic-is
   straightforward, frank

The Vulgate: *sapiēns iūdicium Salamōnis*

tunc uēnērunt duae mulierēs meretrīcēs ad rēgem, stetēruntque cōram
eō. quārum ūna ait, 'obsecrō, mī domine; ego et mulier haec
habitābāmus in domō ūnā, et peperī apud eam in cubiculō. tertiā autem
diē postquam ego peperī, peperit et haec; et erāmus simul, nūllusque alius
nōbīscum in domō, exceptīs nōbīs duābus. mortuus est autem fīlius   5
mulieris huius nocte, dormiēns quippe oppressit eum. et cōnsurgēns
intempestae noctis silentiō, tulit fīlium meum dē latere meō ancillae tuae
dormientis, et collocāuit in sinū suō: suum autem fīlium, quī erat
mortuus, posuit in sinū meō. cumque surrēxissem māne ut darem lac fīliō
meō, appāruit mortuus; quem dīligentius intuēns clārā lūce, dēprehendī 10
nōn esse meum quod genueram.'
   respōnditque altera mulier, 'nōn est ita ut dīcis, sed fīlius tuus mortuus
est, meus autem uīuit.' ē contrāriō illa dīcēbat, 'mentīris: fīlius quippe

meus uīuit, et fīlius tuus mortuus est.' atque in hunc modum
contendēbant cōram rēge.   15
   tunc rēx ait, 'afferte mihi gladium.' cumque attulissent gladium cōram
rēge, 'dīuidite', inquit, 'īnfantem uīuum in duās partīs, et date dīmidiam
partem ūnī, et dīmidiam partem alterī.'
   dīxit autem mulier, cuius fīlius erat uīuus, ad rēgem (commōta sunt
quippe uīscera eius super fīliō suō), 'obsecrō, domine, date illī īnfantem   20
uīuum, et nōlīte interficere eum.' ē contrāriō illa dīcēbat, 'nec mihi, nec
tibi sit: sed dīuidātur.' respondit rēx et ait, 'date huic īnfantem uīuum, et
nōn occīdātur: haec est enim māter eius.' audīuit itaque omnis Israel
iūdicium quod iūdicāsset rēx et timuērunt rēgem, uidentēs sapientiam
Deī esse in eō ad faciendum iūdicium. (*I Kings 3.16ff.* (*Vulgate: III Kings
3.16ff*), *slightly abridged*)

cōram (+ abl.) in the presence of
ait 'said'
pariō 3/4 *peperī* I give birth
cubicul-um ī 2n. bedroom
simul = together
5 *excipiō* 3/4 *excēpī exceptus* I except
quippe since [Tends to come late in the
   clause it controls]
cōnsurgō 3 I rise, get up
intempest-us a um middle of, 'dead of'
silenti-um ī 2n. silence
ancillae 'that is (of me), your
   maidservant'
sin-us ūs 4m. breast, bosom
surgō 3 *surrēxī* I get up
māne in the morning

lac lact-is 3n. milk
10 *appāreō* 2 I appear
dīligēns dīligent-is close, careful
intueor 2 dep. I examine
lūx lūc-is 3f. light
dēprehendō 3 *dēprehendī* I realise
gignō 3 *genuī* I bear, produce
ē contrāriō in reply, contradicting
15 *contendō* 3 I squabble
īnfāns īnfant-is 3m. baby
dīmidi-us a um half
uīscer-a um 3n. pl. heart, deepest
   feelings
super (+ abl.) for, over
Israel (nom.) Israel
iūdici-um ī 2n. judgement
sapienti-a ae 1f. wisdom

SECTION SIX

Section 6A

Running vocabulary for 6A(i)

amor amōr-is 3m. love
[See note for meaning
of pl.]
arāne-a ae 1f. cobweb
cachinn-us ī 2m. laugh
candid-us a um beautiful
Catull-us ī 2m. Catullus
cēnō 1 I have dinner, dine
contrā in return
Cupīdō Cupīdin-is 3m.
Cupid (god of desire)

dōnō 1 I give;
dōnārunt = dōnāuērunt
[See Ref. Gr. **A4**]
ēlegāns ēlegant-is elegant
Fabull-us ī 2m. Fabullus
mer-us a um unmixed,
pure
mī vocative of *meus*
nās-us ī 2m. nose
noster = mī (vocative)
olfaciō 3/4 I smell

saccul-us ī 2m. little purse
sal sal-is 3m. salt; wit
seu or if [See note]
suāu-is e sweet
-ue or
Venus Vener-is 3f. Venus
(goddess of love)
uenust-us a um charming,
smart [Used as a noun
here]
uīn-um ī 2n. wine
unguent-um ī 2n. perfume

Notes

l. 2 Hold *paucīs* (which is solved by *diēbus*).

l. 8 *plēnus*: placed early to set up a surprise: remember it takes gen.
sacculus: diminutive. See p. 255.

l. 9 The pl. *amōrēs* in Catullus usually means 'girl-friend': but it can mean
'sexual intercourse' or 'passion'; 'the gods of love' or 'an object
arousing love' are other suggestions you may like to consider.

l. 10 *seu quid*: after *sī, nē* and *num, quis* = anyone/anything (see **139**[1]).
seu = sīue. Tr. 'or something that . . .'

l. 11 *meae puellae*: dative, solved by *dōnārunt*.

l. 14 *tōtum*: with *tē*: the joke is held back until the last word.

Learning vocabulary for 6A(i)

Nouns

amor amōr-is love; (pl.)
 girl-friend; sexual
 intercourse
uīn-um ī 2n. wine

Adjectives

mer-us a um unmixed,
 pure

Verbs

dōnō 1 I give

Running vocabulary for 6A(ii)

---

aestimātiō aestimātiōn-is 3f.
 value
Asini-us ī 2m. Asinius
 [See note]
bellē nicely, properly
differt-us a um crammed
 with (+ gen.)
Fabull-us ī 2m. Fabullus
facētī-ae ārum 1f. pl. wit
fūrt-um ī 2n. theft
hendecasyllab-us ī 2m.
 hendecasyllable [the
 Greek metre used for
 poems of personal
 abuse: the metre also of
 this poem: see **180**]
Hibēr-ī ōrum 2m. pl.
 Spaniards
inept-us a um stupid

inuenust-us a um not
 smart, charmless
ioc-us ī 2m. joke, joking,
 fun
lepōs lepōr-is 3m. charm
linte-um ī 2n. table-napkin
Marrūcīn-us ī 2m.
 Marrucinus [See note]
mnēmosyn-um ī 2m.
 keepsake (a Greek
 word Latinised)
mūnus mūner-is 3n. gift
 [*mūnerī* 'as a gift':
 predicative dative, see
 L(e)2]
mūtō 1 I change
neglegēns neglegent-is
 careless [Note the
 comparative form]

Pōlliō Pōlliōn-is 3m. (C.
 Asinius) Pollio
quamuīs ever such a
quārē therefore
remittō 3 I send back
Saetab-us a um from
 Saetabis (a Spanish
 town famous for its
 linen goods)
sals-us a um witty, smart
sodālis sodāl-is 3m. friend
sordid-us a um cheap, low,
 dirty
sūdāri-um ī 2n.
 handkerchief, napkin
talent-um ī 2n. talent [A
 huge sum, see note]
Vērāniol-us ī 2m. dear
 Veranius
Vērāni-us ī 2m. Veranius

Notes

1. 1 Marrūcīnus may be this man's *cognōmen*, normally the last of three –
praenōmen (e.g. Gāius), *nōmen* (e.g. Valērius, the family name),
cognōmen (e.g. Āfrīcānus, sometimes from some exploit or ancestor's

exploit). Asinius will be the *nōmen*. *manū sinistrā*: the abl. is solved in l. 2 by *ūteris*.

l. 2 *in iocō atque uīnō* i.e. *in conuīuiō*.

l. 3 *neglegentiōrum*: comp. adj. used as a noun. Tr. 'rather . . .' (not 'more').

l. 4 *fugit tē*: lit: 'it escapes you'. Tr. 'you're wrong'.

l. 7 *talentō*: abl. of the price Pollio would be willing to pay. Tr. 'for a talent'. Reference Grammar **L(f)4(v)**.

l. 8 *uelit*: 'he would like': potential subjunctive, see **153.2**.

ll. 8–9 *lepōrum*: hold: it is solved by *differtus* (which also governs *facētiārum*).

ll. 16–17 *haec amem necesse est*: *ut* has been left out before the clause *haec amem*. This is common: see **6A(iii)**, ll. 18,19. Tr. 'that I should . . .' The *ut* in l. 17 means 'as' sc. 'I love'.

l. 17 *Vērāniolum*: diminutive. See p. 255.

Learning vocabulary for 6A(ii)

Nouns

facēti-ae ārum 1f. pl. wit

ioc-us ī 2m. joke, joking, fun

lepōs lepōr-is 3m. charm

mūnus mūner-is 3n. gift; duty

sodālis sodāl-is 3m. friend

Verbs

mūtō 1 I change, alter, exchange (trans.)

Others

quārē therefore (lit. (abl.) 'from which thing' = wherefore; as question = why?)

Running vocabulary for 6A(iii)

caue + subjunctive beware of —ing [See note]

cauētō beware of (+ infin.) [See note]

conuenit 4 *conuēnit* it is agreed

dēfess-us a um tired out

dēlicāt-us a um sophisticated, decadent, gay

dēspuō 3 I spit out, reject completely

hestern-us a um yester- (with *diē*)

indomit-us a um uncontrollable

iuuat 1 (it) pleases

laedō 3 I harm, do down

lectul-us ī 2m. bed
[Diminutive of *lectus*:
see p. 255]
Licini-us ī 2m. Licinius
[See note]
lūdō 3 *lūsī* I play, have a
good time, make jokes
membr-um ī 2n. limb
mūtu-us a um in return,
reciprocal [Sc. 'verses']
Nemesis f. (Greek word)
Nemesis, goddess of
revenge
numer-us ī 2m. metre

ocell-us ī 2m. (l. 10) eye;
(l. 19) apple of my eye
ōtiōs-us a um at leisure,
enjoying oneself
perspiciō 3/4 I see clearly,
understand fully [See
note]
poēma n. (Greek word)
poem (from the Greek
equivalent of *faciō*)
precēs prec-um 3f. pl.
prayers
quiēs quiēt-is 3f. sleep, rest

reposcō 3 I exact (in
return)
sēmimortu-us a um half-
dead
simul together (sc. with
you)
somn-us ī 2m. sleep
uēmēns = uehemēns
uersicul-us ī 2m. scrap of
verse, epigram
[Diminutive of *uersus*:
see p. 255]
uersor 1 (passive) I toss
and turn

Notes

l. 1 *Licinī*: C. Licinius Calvus Macer, orator and poet.

l. 5 *illōc*: = *illō*. Cf. *hōc* – in earlier Latin both words had the suffix *-ce*.

l. 6 *per iocum atque uīnum*: cf. *in iocō atque uīno* in **6A(ii)** l. 2.

l. 9 *ut*: 'with the result that'.

l. 11 *tōtō*: hold – it is solved by *lectō*, not *furōre*, which is abl. of cause after *indomitus*.

l. 16 *iūcunde*: the adjective is used in the vocative as a noun; cf. *uenuste noster* in **6A(i)**.

l. 17 *ex quō perspicerēs*: purpose clause introduced by relative pronoun (see **145.3**).

ll. 18, 19 *caue sīs* and *caue dēspuās*: 'beware of —ing'. Here you would normally expect *nē* (see **S2(d)** 'verbs of fearing'), but as with *haec amem necesse est* in **6A(ii)** l. 16, the conjunction has been omitted. This is a common idiom with certain words.

l. 21 *cauētō*: future imperative, i.e. 'beware (in future)'. Reference Grammar **A2** Note 1.

Learning vocabulary for 6A(iii)

Nouns

membr-um ī 2n. limb   *quiēs quiēt-is* 3f. sleep, rest   *somn-us ī* 2m. sleep

Adjectives

ōtiōs-us a um at leisure

Verbs

iuuat 1 *iūuit* it pleases   *laedō* 3 *laesī laesus* I harm   *lūdō* 3 *lūsī lūsum* I play

Running vocabulary for 6A(iv)

aestimō 1 I value [See note]

as ass-is 3m. as (a coin of small value) [Tr. 'penny', 'dime'; see note]

bāsi-um ī 2n. kiss

conturbō 1 I confuse; wreck the account of

dein = deinde

Lesbi-a ae 1f. Lesbia [See Intro. to **6A**]

mī = mihi

occidō 3 *occidī* I set (other meanings: I fall, die)

perpetu-us a um unending

rūmor rūmōr-is 3m. (piece of) gossip, unfavourable report

semel once; *cum semel =* as soon as

sōlēs (pl. of *sōl*) = 'light of the sun' 'the sun each day'

usque continually, without a break

Notes

1. 2 *rūmōrēs*: acc. – hold until solved (by *aestimēmus*). *seuēriōrum*: cf. *neglegentiōrum* in **6A(ii)** 1. 3. Tr. 'rather . . .' (not 'more').

1. 3 *ūnius . . . assis*: genitive of price or value after *aestimēmus*. Tr. 'at one penny/dime'.

1. 5 *nōbīs*: hold until solved (by *dormienda*).

1. 10 *fēcerīmus*: future perfect (not perf. subj.), despite the long -*i* of -*īmus*.

1. 13 *tantum . . . bāsiōrum*: cf. *satis/nimis* + gen.(**31**). Tr. 'so many . . .' (lit. 'such and such an amount of . . .').

Learning vocabulary for 6A(iv)

Nouns

rūmor rūmōr-is 3m. rumour, (piece of) gossip, unfavourable report

Verbs

aestimō 1 I value; estimate

occidō 3 *occidī occāsum* I set (intrans.); (I fall; die)

Others

dein = deinde then, next

mī = mihi [NB. *mī* is also vocative of *meus*]

semel once (*cum semel =* as soon as)

usque continually, without a break (often used with *ad =* right up to)

Running vocabulary for 6A(v)

aestuōs-us a um sweltering, hot

bāsiātiō bāsiātiōn-is 3f. kiss [See note]

bāsiō 1 I kiss

bāsi-um ī 2n. kiss

Batt-us ī 2m. Battus (first king of Cyrene)

cūriōs-us a um inquisitive, prying

Cyrēn-ae ārum 1f. pl. Cyrene (city in N.W. Libya, or the territory of Cyrene)

fascinō 1 I bewitch, cast a spell on

fūrtīu-us a um stolen

harēn-a ae 1f. sand

lāsarpīcifer lāsarpīcifer-a um silphium-bearing

Libyss-a ae f. adj. African

lingu-a ae 1f. tongue [See note]

ōrācl-um ī 2n. oracle

pernumerō 1 I tally up

sepulcr-um ī 2n. tomb

sīdus sīder-is 3n. star

super more than enough (adv.)

uēsān-us a um crazed, maddened

Notes

l. 1 *bāsiātiō*: a sort of abstract noun (!) formed from the usual word *bāsium*.

l. 3 *quam magnus*: lit. 'how great . . .', picked up eventually by *tam . . . multa* (l. 9) 'so many'.

l. 5 *inter*: the preposition governs *ōrāclum*: notice the word pattern in ll. 5–6.

l. 7 *quam . . . multa*: lit. 'how many', picked up by *tam . . . multa* (l. 9) 'so many'. Cf. *quam magnus* (l. 3).

l. 8 *fūrtīuōs*: hold until solved (by *amōrēs*).

l. 9 *bāsia bāsiāre*: cf. *pugnam pugnāre* 'to fight a fight'. Note that here *tē* is the object, *bāsia* is an internal or cognate accusative. Eng. 'to give you . . . kisses'.

l. 10 *uēsānō*: hold until solved (by *Catullō*).

l. 11 *possint*: potential subjunctive (see **153.2**).

l. 12 *mala lingua*: another subject of *possint*.

Learning vocabulary for 6A(v)

Nouns

harēn-a ae 1f. sand

lingu-a ae 1f. tongue; language

ōrāc(u)l-um ī 2n. oracle

sepulc(h)r-um ī 2n. tomb

sīdus sīder-is 3n. star

Others

super (adv.) more than enough; above, over; (prep. + acc./abl.) over, above; (+ abl.) about

Running vocabulary for 6A(vi)

bell-us a um beautiful
candid-us a um bright
dēsinō 3 I cease (from x: infin.) [See note]
dēstināt-us a um stubborn, obstinate
doleō 2 I grieve, feel anguish
dūcō 3 (l. 2) I consider, think [See note]
fulgeō 2 *fulsī* I shine
ineptiō 4 I play the fool, am silly
inpotēns inpotent-is powerless (sc. 'as you are')

inuīt-us a um unwilling [See note]
iocōs-us a um full of fun
labell-um ī 2n. lip
mēns ment-is 3f. mind
mordeō 2 I bite
nōbīs tr. 'by me' [See note]
nūlla (l. 5) 'no woman'; (l. 14) 'not at all'
obdūrō 1 I am firm, hold out
obstināt-us a um resolute, stubborn
perdō 3 *perdidī perditus* I lose, destroy

pereō perīre periī I pass away, die
perferō perferre I endure (to the end)
quondam once
sector 1 dep. I keep pursuing (= *sequor* + *-it-*)
sōlēs (pl. of *sōl*) 'light of the sun'
uae (+ acc.) alas for
uentitō 1 I keep coming (= *ueniō* + *-it-*)
uērē truly
uolt = *uult*

Notes

l. 1 *dēsinās*: jussive subjunctive (see **152**).

l. 2 *quod*: tr. 'that which', picked up by *perditum*. *dūcās*: jussive subjunctive, cf. *dēsinās* (see **152**).

l. 5 *nōbīs*: pl. for s. is very common in poetry, especially with personal pronouns. The dative expresses the agent (usually expressed by *ā/ ab* + abl.).

l. 6 *illa*: n. pl. 'those things (sc. I am reflecting on)'. Note *cum* is postponed, though it introduces the clause. *iocōsa* is used as a noun.

l. 10 *quae fugit*: the clause is introduced by the next word *sectāre*: sc. *eam* to make sense of it.

l. 13 *inuītam*: agrees with *tē*: sc. 'since you are . . .'

l. 18 *cuī*: sympathetic dative (!); see **88.2**.

Learning vocabulary for 6A(vi)

Adjectives

candid-us a um white; bright, beautiful

inuīt-us a um unwilling

Verbs

doleō 2 I suffer pain, grieve

dūcō 3 *dūxī ductus* I think, consider (lead)

fulgeō 2 *fulsī* I shine

obdūrō 1 I am firm, hold out, persist

pereō perīre periī peritum I perish, die; (*periī* I am lost)

perferō perferre pertulī perlātus I endure (to the end); complete; carry to; announce

---

Running vocabulary for 6A(vii)

aequor aequor-is 3n. l. 8 plain; l. 11 sea

Alpēs Alp-ium 3f. pl. Alps

alt-us a um high

Arabs Arab-is 3m. Arab (Greek acc. pl. *Arabas*)

arātr-um ī 2n. plough

Aurēli-us ī 2m. Aurelius

Britann-ī ōrum 2m. pl. Britons

caelitēs caelit-um 3m. pl. gods (lit. 'dwellers in heaven')

Caesar Caesar-is 3m. (C. Julius) Caesar [See note]

colōrō 1 I dye, stain [See note]

complector 3 dep. *complexus* I embrace

culp-a ae 1f. fault (often used of sexual misconduct)

dict-um ī 2n. word

Eō-us a um Eastern, oriental

extrēm-us a um furthest

flōs flōr-is 3m. flower

Fūri-us ī 2m. Furius

Gallic-us a um Gallic, of Gaul

gradior 3/4 dep. I go

horribil-is e terrible, dreadful [See note]

Hyrcān-ī ōrum 2m. pl. the Hyrcani (a people dwelling to the S.E. of the Caspian sea)

identidem again and again

īlia īl-ium 3n. pl. groin, private parts

Ind-ī ōrum 2m. pl. the Indians

moech-us ī 2m. adulterer

moll-is e soft, luxurious, effeminate

moniment-um ī 2n. testimonial

Nīl-us ī 2m. the River Nile

Parth-ī ōrum 2m. pl. the Parthians (a people on Rome's eastern boundaries)

penetrō 1 I make my way, penetrate as far as

praetereō praeterīre I pass by [See note]

prāt-um ī 2n. meadow, field

quīcumque quaecumque quodcumque whoever, whatever

resonō 1 I re-echo

respectō 1 I look for, count on

Rhēn-us ī 2m. the River Rhine [See note]

rumpō 3 I burst

Sag-ae ārum 1m. pl. the Sacae (a Scythian people: dwelling to the N.E. of Rome's borders)

sagittifer sagittifer-a um arrow-bearing

septemgemin-us a um sevenfold (i.e. with seven mouths)

seu or (if) [= *sīue*: see note on structure]

simul together

sīue . . . sīue (*seu*) whether . . . or [See note on structure]

trāns (+ acc.) across

tundō 3 I beat, pound

ualeō 2 lit. 'I am well' [See note]

-ue (added to the end of a word) or

uērē truly

uīsō 3 I go and look at, view, visit

ultim-us a um (ll. 11–12) furthest; (l. 23) the edge of

und-a ae 1f. water, wave

ut (l. 3, + indic.) where

Notes

Structure: in l. 1, Furius and Aurelius are addressed as friends of Catullus, and in ll. 2–12, their friendship is shown by the number of places they are prepared to go to with Catullus – whether (*sīue*) Catullus will go to x or (*sīue/seu*) y or (*sīue*) z. Ll. 13–14 summarise the past 12 lines, describing Furius and Aurelius as *parātī* (ready) to do all this (*omnia haec* (13)). At 15, we find out what they should in fact do: *nūntiāte* 'give a message' to Lesbia. Ll. 17–24 describe the content of the message, in subjunctives (*uīuat . . . ualeat . . . respectet*) – 'let her . . .'

l. 2 *extrēmōs*: hold until solved (by *Indōs*).

ll. 3–4 *lītus*: subject of the *ut* clause. Take *longē* closely with *resonante* and hold *longē resonante Eōā* until solved (by *undā*: the function of the abl. phrase is revealed by the passive form of *tunditur*). NB. Here *ut* means 'where'.

ll. 7–8 *quae*: n. pl. – hold until solved (by *aequora*: 'the plains which . . .' obj. of *colōrat*). *colōrat*: possibly refers to the silt left by the Nile after its annual flood.

l. 9 *altās*: hold until solved (by *Alpēs*).

ll. 10–12 Caesar was engaged in the conquest of Gaul from 58–49. In 55 he crossed the Rhine and made an expedition into Germany. In the same year came the first of his two forays across the Channel to Britain. The words in l. 11–12 are in apposition to *monimenta*. The *horribile aequor* may refer to the English Channel (which caused Caesar many problems). But it is a scholar's correction, not the version preserved by the MSS.

l. 17 *cum suīs*: hold until solved (by *moechīs*). *ualeat*: a 3rd. person form of *uale* 'farewell' (but see also the basic meaning of the verb).

l. 18 *trecentōs*: agreeing with *quōs* – '300 of them' (!) – held back for effect.

l. 21 *meum*: hold until solved (by *amōrem*)

ll. 23–4 The word-order is complex: hold *praetereunte* until solved by *arātrō* – the abl. is not absolute, but instrumental after the passive verb *tāctus . . . est*. As often, *postquam*, which introduces the clause, is postponed. The subject is *flōs*.

Learning vocabulary for 6A(vii)

Nouns

aequor aequor-is 3n. plain; sea

culp-a ae 1f. fault; blame (often of sexual misconduct)

Adjectives

alt-us a um high; deep
extrēm-us a um furthest

*quīcumque quaecumque
quodcumque* whoever,
whatever [Declines like
quī **106** + *cumque*]

ultim-us a um furthest;
last; greatest

Verbs

gradior 3/4 dep. *gressus* I
step, walk, go (cf.
compounds in *–gredior*)

*praetereō praeterīre praeteriī
praeteritus* I pass by;
neglect, omit

ualeō 2 I am strong; am
well; am powerful; am
able (cf. *ualē*
'Farewell!')

Others

simul together (at the
same time)

sīue (seu) . . . *sīue (seu)*
whether . . . or
trāns (+ acc.) across

-ue (added on to the end
of a word: cf. *-ne* and
-que) or

30 *Hendecasyllables* (= 'eleven syllables')

The first five poems of Catullus which you have read make use of the
following new metrical elements:

$$\cup = anceps\ (\text{'doubtful', 'two-edged'})$$
$$- \cup \cup -\cup - = choriambocretic\quad (choriamb\quad - \cup \cup -\quad \text{blended}$$
$$\text{together with } cretic\ - \cup -)$$
$$\cup \_\ \cup = bacchiac$$

The poems scan as follows:

$$\cup \cup \big| - \cup \cup - \cup - \big| \cup - \cup$$

i.e. two *anceps*, *choriambocretic*, *bacchiac*, e.g.

cēnābis bene mī Fabull[e] apud mē

Exercise

Using the above scheme, scan any one of the five poems in this metre,
adding the correct word-stress (see rule, p. xv). Then read it aloud,
thinking through the meaning as you read.

NB. Remember to check for elision.

181 *Scazon* ('limping iambics')

Poem **6A(vi)** makes use of the following metrical elements:

$$\underset{\smile}{} = anceps \text{ (doubtful syllable)}$$
$$- \cup - = cretic$$

(The combination *anceps* + *cretic* is known as an iambic 'measure'.) The poem scans as follows:

$$\underset{\smile}{} - \cup - \mid \underset{\smile}{} - \cup - \mid \cup - - \underset{\smile}{}$$

i.e. two iambic measures + $\cup - - \underset{\smile}{}$, e.g.

miser Catulle dēsinās ineptīre

The metre is called 'limping iambics' because it seems to limp to a close. The sprightly iambics of the first two measures are rounded off not by a third, but by the 'limping' $\cup - - \underset{\smile}{}$.

Exercise

Using the above scheme, scan **6A(vi)**, adding the correct word stress (see rule, p. xv). Then read it aloud, thinking through the meaning as you read.

NB. Remember to check for elision.

182 Sapphics

Poem **6A(vii)** is made up of stanzas in *Sapphic* metre, so named after the seventh-century Greek poetess from Lesbos, Sappho, who specialised in them. *Sapphics* use the following metrical elements, all of which you have already met:

$$- \cup - = cretic$$
$$\underset{\smile}{} = anceps \text{ (doubtful syllable)}$$
$$- \cup \cup - \cup - = choriambocretic \text{ (see 180)}$$
$$- \cup \cup - = choriamb$$

Sapphics scan as follows:

First three lines: $- \cup - \mid \underset{\smile}{} \mid - \cup \cup - \cup - \mid \underset{\smile}{}$
Last line: $- \cup \cup - \mid \underset{\smile}{}$

I.e. *cretic, anceps, choriambocretic, anceps* (× 3), *choriamb, anceps.* E.g.

$$\acute{F}\bar{u}r[\bar{i}]\ \breve{e}t\ \bar{A}\bar{u}r\bar{e}l\bar{i}\ c\acute{o}m\bar{i}t\bar{e}s\ \acute{C}\bar{a}t\bar{u}ll\bar{i}\ .\ .\ .$$

$$t\acute{u}nd\breve{i}t\breve{u}r\ \acute{u}nd\bar{a}$$

Exercise

Using the above scheme, scan poem **6A(vii)**, adding the correct word-stress (see rule, p. xv). Then read it aloud, thinking through the meaning as you read.

NB.   Remember to check for elision.

Section 6B

Running vocabulary for 6B(i)

A.V.C. = *ab urbe condita* 'from the city having been founded', 'from the city's foundation'

adroganti-a ae 1f. conceit, presumption

animaduertō 3 I observe, take note of

argūt-us a um verbose, wordy

certior fīō I am informed (lit. 'I am made more certain')

certiōrem faciō I inform x (acc.) (lit. 'make x more certain')

commod-us a um satisfactory, convenient

condemnō 1 I condemn x (acc.) for Y (gen.)

cūriōs-us a um curious

dēlectō 1 I please

dēlectārit = *dēlectāuerit*

dēlēgō 1 I entrust

dēprecor 1 dep. I pray earnestly

dīligēns dīligent-is careful

ēdict-um ī 2n. edict

excūsō 1 I excuse

exhibeō 2 I cause

exīstimātiō exīstimātiōn-is 3f. view

exspectātiō exspectātiōn-is 3f. expectation

fābul-a ae 1f. story

forte by chance, perchance

impēns-a ae 1f. expense

memori-a ae 1f. remembering, memory

molesti-a ae 1f. annoyance

nimium = *nimis*

omnīnō altogether, completely

operāri-us ī 2m. hireling

peregrīnō 1 I am abroad, travel

perscrībō 3 *perscrīpsī perscrīptus* I write in detail

quem ad modum how

quīn 'that . . . not'

S. = *salūtem dīcit* 'greets' (+ dat.)

sēdulitās sēdulitāt-is 3f. zeal, earnestness

senātūs cōnsult-um ī 2n. decree of the senate

suāu-is e delightful, sweet, pleasant

tametsī however, though

uolūmen uolūmin-is 3n. volume (i.e. papyrus roll)

urbān-us a um of the city, city

Notes

l. 1 *discēdēns*: Caelius had gone with Cicero as far as Pompeii, it seems.

l. 3 *sciō tū*: *tū* belongs with *sīs*, within the *quam* clause. *quam*: solved by *grātum* (cf. *quam . . . cūriōsūs* l. 3). Now await an infinitive phrase to complete *quam . . . grātum sit* (*fierī certiōrēs* l. 5).

ll. 8–9 *nesciō cuius ōtī esset*: 'I don't know of what leisure it would be (sc. the job)' i.e. 'I don't know what amount of spare time it would take . . .' The subjunctive is potential (see **153.2**).

l. 11 *nē*: purpose clause (explained by *fac mē certiōrem*).

l. 12 *sī quid . . . maius*: i.e. 'if anything more important'.

l. 13 *quod . . . possint*: the subjunctive is potential (see **153.2**).

l. 14–15 *secūta*: sc. *sit*.

Learning vocabulary for 6B(i)

Nouns
fābul-a ae 1f. story; play
memori-a ae 1f.
    remembering,
    memory, recollection;
    record

Adjectives
commod-us a um   *dīligēns dīligent-is* careful,   *suāu-is e* sweet, pleasant,
    satisfactory, convenient   diligent   delightful

Verbs
animaduertō 3 *animaduertī*   *condemnō* 1 I condemn (x   *perscrībō* 3 *perscrīpsī*
animaduersus I observe,   acc. for y gen.)   *perscrīptus* I write in
    take note of   *excūsō* 1 I excuse   detail

Phrases
certiōrem faciō I inform x   *salūtem dicit* 'he greets'
    (acc.)   (+ dat.) (at the head of
certior fīō I am informed   letters, abbreviated to
                                    S. or S.D.)

Others
forte by chance, perchance   *quem ad modum* (often
omnīnō altogether,   written as one word)
    completely   how

Running vocabulary for 6B(ii)

adhūc up to now
Bellouac-ī ōrum 2m. pl.
  Bellovaci (a tribe living
  in N.W. Gaul)
bell-us a um pretty
circumsedeō 2 I besiege,
  blockade
crēber crēbr-a um frequent
dumtaxat only, merely

fingō 3 *fīnxī fictus* I make
  up, fabricate
iactō 1 I discuss
incert-us a um uncertain
interclūdō 3 *interclūdī*
  interclūsus I cut off
nōstī = nōuistī
offendō 3 *offendī* I meet
palam openly

perdō 3 *perdidī* I lose
Pompēi-us ī Cn. Pompeius
  Magnus
sēcrētō secretly
susurrātor susurrātōr-is 3m.
  whisperer, tale-bearer
uāpulō 1 I am beaten
  (*uāpulāsse = uāpulāuisse*)
uulgō generally

Notes

l. 17 *fac* + subjunctive: 'make sure you . . .' (cf. *caue* + subj. in **6A(iii)** 18, 19).

ll. 17–18 *quī . . . sit*: 'how he seemed to be' (old abl. of *quī*: see **I4 Note 3**) i.e. 'what you thought of him'.

l. 19 *aliud sentīre et loquī*: 'to think one thing and say another'. *quod ad Caesarem*: 'as (lit. 'as to that which') regards Caesar'. The verb *attinet* = 'concerns' is omitted.

l. 20 *rūmōrēs*: sc. *sunt*.

l. 21 *alius*: sc. *dīcit. ipsum*: i.e. Caesar.

ll. 23–4 *certī quicquam*: 'anything (of) certain' cf. *satis* + gen. 'enough (of)' **31**.

Learning vocabulary for 6B(ii)

Adjectives

bell-us a um beautiful,
  pretty

crēber crēbr-a um frequent;
  thick, close

incert-us a um uncertain

Verbs

circumsedeō 2 *circumsēdī*
  circumsessus I besiege,
  blockade

fingō 3 *fīnxī fictus* I make
  up, fabricate
iactō 1 I discuss; throw;
  boast; toss about

offendō 3 *offendī offēnsus* I
  meet with; offend
perdō 3 *perdidī perditus* I
  lose; destroy

Others

adhūc up to now
palam openly

Running vocabulary for 6B(iii)

abs = ab
aedifici-um ī 2n. building
complector 1 dep. I
  embrace
complūr-ēs a several
compositiō compositiōn-is 3f.
  pairing, match
cūrō 1 I want [See note]
differō differe distulī dīlātus
  I put off, postpone
ēgregi-us a um
  outstanding, excellent

gladiātor gladiātōr-is 3m.
  gladiator
habētō 'be sure' [See note]
M. = Mārcus (Mārcō with
  Caeliō)
mandō 1 I order (x dat.)
  to (*ut* + subj.)
nē . . . quidem not even
  (emphasising the word
  enclosed)
pertineō 2 I affect, relate
  to (*ad* + acc.)
poster-um ī 2n. future

praesēns praesent-is present
praeteritus a um past (perf.
  part. pass. of *praetereō*)
PRŌCŌS. = prōcōnsul
  prōcōnsul-is 3m.
  proconsul (i.e.
  governor of a
  province)
prōspiciō 3/4 I look
  forward, see ahead
quāl-is e what sort of
tantum (just) so much
uadimōni-um ī 2n. court
  appearance (lit. 'bail')

Notes

ll. 27–8 *ea quae . . . audeat*: generic subjunctive (see **140.1**).

l. 28 (*cūrō*) . . . *scrībās*: 'you to write' – cf. *caue* + subj. in **6A(iii)** 18, 19 and *fac* + subj. in **6B(ii)** 17. *illa* is the object of *scrībās*.

l. 32 *ut*: purpose, solved (eventually) by *scīre possim*.

l. 37 *habētō*: future imperative, cf. *cauētō* in **6A(iii)**. The force may not be strongly future, since this is a common form with *habeō*. See Reference Grammar **A2 Note 1**.

ll. 39–40 *īdem . . . quī*: 'the same people . . . as'.

Learning vocabulary for 6B(iii)

Adjectives

complūr-ēs a several

ēgregi-us a um
  outstanding, excellent

praesēns praesent-is present
quāl-is e what sort of

Verbs

complector 3 dep.
  complexus I embrace

mandō 1 I order (x (dat.)
  to Y (*ut* + subj.));
  (entrust x (acc.) to Y
  (dat.))

Others

nē . . . quidem not even
  (emphasising the word
  enclosed)

Running vocabulary for 6B(iv)

Āfricān-us a um African
aiō irr. I say
alō 3 I tend, feed
Cibyrāt-a ae from Cibyra
  [See map]
collēg-a ae 1m. colleague
Cūriō Cūriōn-is 3m. C.
  Scribonius Curio:
  tribune in 50, friend
  and correspondent of
  Cicero

dēportō 1 I transport
ferē almost
istō to the place where
  you are
labōrō 1 I am concerned
  with
Pamphȳli-a ae 1f.
  Pamphylia [See map]
panthēr-a ae 1f. panther

Patisc-us ī 2m. Patiscus, a
  Roman businessman in
  Asia
seorsus apart
simulatque as soon as

Notes

l. 42 *multīs partibus*: 'by many parts' i.e. 'many times' (abl. of measure of difference, **100B.5**).

l. 44 *Cibyrātās*: understand *panthērās*.

l. 46 *collēgā*: M. Octavius was the other curule aedile with Curio.

l. 47 *paranda*: understand *esse*. *amābō tē*: 'please' (lit. 'I shall love you'). *imperā tibi hoc*: *hoc* is direct object (in the place usually taken by *ut* + subj.). *nūlla tua*: hold until solved (by *cūra*).

l. 49 *habēs eōs*: Caelius had sent some men to deal with a financial transaction in the vicinity. *quī alant . . . dēportent*: subjunctive, to indicate purpose (see **145³**).

l. 50 *missūrum*: sc. *esse*.

Learning vocabulary for 6B(iv)

Nouns

collēg-a ae 1m. colleague

Verbs

aiō irr. I say
alō 3 *aluī altus* or *alitus* I
  feed, nourish, rear;
  support; strengthen

Others

ferē almost
simulatque as soon as (also
  simulac or *simul*)

425

Running vocabulary for 6B(v)

aedīl-is aedīl-is 3m. aedile
[See explanation in
Text **6B(iii)**]
agitur impersonal 'it is
being done' (i.e. 'things
are being done')
Cāri-a ae 1f. Caria [See
map]
cognōrō = cognōuerō
curūl-is e curule

dēcēdō 3 I leave
fit: impersonal 'it is being
done' (i.e. 'things are
being done')
mandāt-us ūs 4m. order
mīr-us a um amazing
panthēr-a ae 1f. panther
Patisc-us ī 2m. Patiscus
(see previous letter)

paucitās paucitāt-is 3f.
paucity, lack
quisquis quicquid whoever,
whatever
sēdulō assiduously
stat-us ūs 4m. position
ualdē very much, strongly
uēnor 1 dep. I hunt

Notes

l. 52 *ualdē*: hold – it qualifies *querī*.

l. 53 *nihil cuiquam īnsidiārum*: tr. 'no (of) ambushes for anyone'.

l. 56 *esset*: lit. 'was going to be'. Cicero writes as if the time of the letter were when Caelius was actually reading it. Hence *nesciēbāmus* and *esset*. Tr. 'we (=I) don't know, what it is (going to be)'.

ll. 57–8 *tū uelim . . . perscrībās*: 'I would like you to write'; *uelim* is potential subjunctive (see **153.2**). For *perscrībās*, subjunctive without a conjunction, cf. *caue* + subj. **6B(ii)** ll. 18 and 19, *fac* + subj. **6B(ii)** l. 17 and *cūrō* + subj. **6B(iii)** l. 28.

Learning vocabulary for 6B(v)

Adjectives

mīr-us a um amazing,
wonderful

quisquis quicquid whoever,
whatever (declines like
quis + quis, but it is not
found in all forms)

Others

ualdē very much, strongly

Running vocabulary for 6B(vi)

aliter for a second time
alter uter one or the other
appāreō 2 I appear
C. = Gāium: Gāi-us ī 2m.
Gaius
clār-us a um clear
condiciō condiciōn-is 3f.
condition, term
condiciōnem ferre to
propose a condition
cōnferō cōnferre I compare
coniūnctiō coniūnctiōn-is 3f.
union
contentiō contentiōn-is 3f.
struggle
dēlīberātiō dēlīberātiōn-is 3f.
question
dīmicō 1 I fight

discordi-a ae 1f. strife,
quarrel
dubitō 1 I doubt
ēligō 3 I choose
eō [See note on l. 60]
ērumpō 3 I break out
(with *sē*)
Gn. (l. 62) = *Gnaeus ī* 2m.
Gnaeus; (l.
69) = *Gnaeum*
impendeō 2 I impend,
threaten, am at hand
inuidiōs-us a um odious
obtrectātiō obtrectātiōn-is 3f.
backbiting
occult-us a um secret,
covert

pars part-is 3f. side (part)
Parthic-us a um Parthian
perturbō 1 I disturb
potior 4 dep. I control
(+ gen.)
prōposit-um ī 2n. question
quō (l. 60) [See note]
recēdō 3 *recessī* I leave
(*ab* + abl.)
recidō 3 I come to, issue in
(*ad* + acc.)
spati-um ī 2n. time
spectācul-um ī 2n. show
summ-a ae 1f. total; *ad*
summam to sum up
timor timōr-is 3m. fear
uter see *alter*

Notes

l. 59 *summā*: i.e. 'high politics'. *in annum*: 'in a year's time'.

l. 60 *quō* (+ comp.) . . . *eō* (+ comp.): 'the . . . —er, the . . . —er' (lit. 'by how much the more . . . by so much the more'). (Watch for comparative adverbs in *-ius*.)

l. 64 *Caesarī persuāsum est*: impersonal passive: lit. 'it has been persuaded to Caesar' i.e. 'Caesar has been persuaded' (see **155**).

l. 65 *fert*: subject is Caesar.

l. 66 *occultam*: hold until solved (by *obtrectātiōnem*).

l. 67 *capiam*: the subjunctive is deliberative (indirect); see **152¹**.

l. 69 *quīque*: 'and those who' (i.e. senators and men of equestrian rank – rich and respectable).

l. 70 *habitūrum*: understand *esse*. *accessūrōs*: understand *esse*.

ll. 70–1 *quī . . . uīuant*: subjunctive in indirect speech, but probably generic. *exercitum . . . esse*: still in indirect statement after *uideō*.

ll. 74–5 *sī . . . nōn eat*: note mood of verb – the main clause, unusually, has an indicative verb, *uideō*.

ll. 75–6 *sī . . . posset*: see note on ll. 74–5. The main verb is *parābat* – see next note for its tense.

l. 77 *parābat*: Caelius writes as if the time of the letter were when Cicero was actually reading it. See previous letter; tr. 'is preparing'. This usage is known as 'epistolary tense'.

Learning vocabulary for 6B(vi)

Nouns

condiciō condiciōn-is 3f.
condition, term;
condiciōnem ferre to
make terms

discordi-a ae 1f. strife,
quarrel

pars part-is 3f. side; (part)
spati-um ī 2n. space; time
timor timōr-is 3m. fear

Adjectives

clār-us a um clear (famous,
well-known)

Verbs

dīmicō 1 I fight

dubitō 1 I doubt; hesitate
(+ infin.)

potior 4 dep. I control
(+ gen.)

Others

quō + comparative . . .
eō + comparative
'the more . . . the
more . . .'

Running vocabulary for 6B(vii)

aduent-us ūs 4m. arrival
aduersāri-us ī 2m. enemy
amīciti-a ae 1f. friendship
atrōx atrōc-is fierce,
unyielding
cēnseō 2 I propose; think
[See note]
cognōrim = *cognōuerim*
cōnsulō 3 I take measures
contendō 3 *contendī* I strive
for
dēcernō 3 I decide
dēmittō 3 I let fall, cast
down
dēprecātiō dēprecātiōn-is 3f.
asking for pardon
dēspērāt-us a um hopeless
ēligō 3 I choose
errō 1 I am wrong

etiam atque etiam again
and again
ēuertō 3 I upset, overturn
exanimāt-us a um upset
exit-us ūs 4m. way out
expōnō 3 *exposuī* I relate
funditus utterly
hauē greetings, hello
Hispāni-a ae 1f. Spain
(there were two
provinces)
iactātiō iactātiōn-is 3f.
vanity
īlicō at once
incitō 1 I rouse
incolumitās incolumitāt-is
3f. safety
īnsolenti-a ae 1f. insolence

intercessiō intercessiōn-is 3f.
veto
medius fidius I call heaven
to witness; so help me
God
mehercūlēs by Hercules
nōn nūll-ī ae a some
optimātēs optimāt-ium 3m.
pl. optimates
pariō 3/4 *peperī partus* I
obtain
percurrō 3 *percurrī* I run
along
praedīcō 3 *praedīxī* I
foretell, tell in advance
prūdēns prūdent-is
foreseeing
quod sī but if
remaneō 2 I remain

saltem at least	*significō* 1 I make clear to	*tōtum* (adv.) completely
sapienter wisely	*temere* casually,	*uacu-us a um* free (from)
scītur: impersonal passive	thoughtlessly	(*ā* + abl.)
'it is known'	*testificor* 1 dep. I call to	*ubicumque* wherever
	witness	

Notes

l. 79 *scrīpsī*: epistolary perfect 'I am writing'.

l. 81 *grauius*: tr. 'too serious'.

ll. 83–4 *conuēnerim . . . cognōrim*: subjunctives in a subordinate clause in indirect speech.

l. 87 *hīs intercessiōnibus*: vetoes moved by the tribune L. Metellus to obstruct Caesar.

ll. 89–90 *quid . . . agāmus*: i.e. whether we win there or not.

l. 90 *istī*: i.e. Pompey's supporters ('those people of yours').

l. 101 *eō . . . unde*: 'to that point . . . from where'.

l. 102 *optimātium*: the supporters of the Senate.

l. 103 *ēligās cēnseō*: 'I propose that you should . . .' For subjunctive without conjunction, cf. **6A(iii)** ll. 18, 19, (*caue*), **6B(ii)** l. 17 (*fac*), **6B(iii)** l. 28 (*cūrō*) and **6B(v)** ll. 57–8 (*uelim*).

Learning vocabulary for 6B(vii)

Nouns

amīciti-a ae 1f. friendship

Adjectives

atrōx atrōc-is fierce, unyielding	*nōn nūll-ī ae a* some (lit. 'not none' – often written as one word)	*uacu-us a um* empty; free (from) (+ abl. or *ā* + abl.)

Verbs

errō 1 I am wrong; wander	*pariō* 3/4 *peperī partus* I bring forth, bear, produce; obtain, acquire

Others

etiam atque etiam again and again	*quod sī* but if	*ubicumque* wherever
	saltem at least	

Running vocabulary for 6B(viii)

acerbitās acerbitāt-is 3f.
anguish, affliction,
bitterness
adulēscēns adulēscent-is 3m.
youth
aliquandō at some time
astūtē craftily, cunningly
cās-us ūs 4m. outcome
cīuīl-is e civil [See note]
cōnstanti-a ae 1f.
constancy, steadfastness
dēspērātiō dēspērātiōn-is 3f.
hopelessness, despair
dēspērō 1 I lose hope of
domestic-us a um domestic,
personal
etenim for; and indeed
exit-us ūs 4m. outcome
extrēm-us a um final, last
(i.e. word)
familiāris familiār-is 3m.
friend
fidēs fidē-ī 5f. loyalty,
honour
fīd-us a um faithful, loyal
fortasse perhaps
glōrior 1 dep. I boast

Hispāniēns-is e Spanish, in
Spain
Hortēnsi-us ī 2m. Q
Hortensius Hortalus,
consul in 69; Rome's
leading forensic orator
before Cicero; they
were not always on the
best of terms
imitor 1 dep. I imitate
impendeō 2 I threaten
(+ dat.)
incommod-um ī 2n.
inconvenience,
misfortune
intersum interesse interfuī I
take part in (+ dat.)
[See note]
laus laud-is 3f. praise
libentissimē very gladly
miseri-a ae 1f. misery
orbis terr-ārum orb-is terr-
ārum 3m. the world
(lit. 'the circle of the
lands')
perturbātiō perturbātiōn-is
3f. disturbance

prīuat-us a um private
profectō undoubtedly,
assuredly
Q. = Quīntum: Quīnt-us ī
2m. Quintus
quandō at any time
quidem indeed
redimō 3 *redēmī* I buy off
x (acc.) from y
(*ā* + abl.)
sīn but if
solitūdō solitūdin-is 3f.
deserted place
temere rashly,
thoughtlessly
terreō 2 I make afraid,
frighten
tribuō 3 I put down [See
note]
tueor 2 dep. I look after,
stand by
turbulenter violently,
seditiously
uāticinor 1 dep. I
prophesy; rave, talk
wildly
uiti-um ī 2n. defect, fault

Notes

l. 107 *uelim* + subj: 'I would like (you to ...)'. See l. 125 (and cf. **6A(iii)** ll. 18, 19 (*caue*), **6B(ii)** l. 17 (*fac*), **6B(iii)** l. 28 (*cūrō*), **6B(v)** ll. 57–8 (*uelim*), **6B(vii)** l. 103 (*cēnseō*).

l. 109 *tam . . . quam*: 'so much . . . as' (see **179.2**). *arma cīuīlia = bellum cīuīle* (ll. 111–12). *huius mē cōnstantiae: huius . . . cōnstantiae* gen. and *mē* acc. with *paeniteat* '(of) this . . . I . . . regret'.

l. 112 *interfuisset*: subjunctive in a subordinate clause in indirect speech (see **142**). *hōc . . . quod*: 'in this respect . . . that'. *illī*: 'in his case'. *tribuēbātur*: impersonal – the subject is 'Hortensius' refusal to take part in the Civil War'.

l. 114 *ad timōrem*: i.e. 'to make me afraid'.

ll. 115–16 *omnibus*: dat. – hold until solved (by *impendēre*).

430

l. 116 *hāc . . . perturbātiōne*: locative–temporal abl. *uideātur*: generic subjunctive (see **140.1**). *quam*: i.e. *acerbitātem*.

l. 117 *meīs prīuātīs et domesticīs incommodīs*: . . . 'at the cost of . . .' abl. of price. Cf. *talentō*, **6A(ii)** l. 7.

l. 125 *uelim* + subj: 'I would like (it to)'. See l. 107 and note.

l. 127 *quibuscumque*: hold until solved (by *in terrīs*).

Learning vocabulary for 6B(viii)

Nouns

adulēscēns adulēscent-is 3m. youth

cās-us ūs 4m. outcome; event, occurrence; disaster, death; *cāsū* by accident, by chance

fidēs fidē-ī 5f. loyalty, honour; trust, faith; promise; protection

Adjectives

fīd-us a um faithful, loyal

Verbs

imitor 1 dep. I imitate

terreō 2 I frighten

tueor 2 dep. I look after, protect; look at

Others

aliquandō at some time
fortasse perhaps

quidem indeed (places emphasis on the preceding word)

sīn but if

Section 6C

Running vocabulary for 6C(i)

---

abūtor 3 I misuse (+ abl.)
alteruter alterutr-a um one or the other (declines like *alter*)
ārdeō 2 I burn (intrans.)
commemorō 1 I mention, recall
Crāstin-us ī 2m. Crastinus

ēuocāt-us ī 2m. recalled veteran
exposcō 3 I entreat
faciō ut (+ subj.) I bring it about that
prīuō 1 I deprive (x acc. of y abl.)
prōcurrō 3 *prōcucurrī* I run forward, advance

reciperō 1 I regain, recover
respiciō 3/4 I turn my gaze upon, look round at
singulār-is e outstanding, remarkable
supersum superesse I am left, remain
tub-a ae 1f. trumpet

Notes

l. 1 Caesar is subject throughout the 1st paragraph.

l. 2 *testibus*: 'as witnesses' (predicative with *mīlitibus*).

ll. 8–9 *quam . . .*: hold until picked up (by *operam*).

ll. 11–12 *uīuō mihi aut mortuō*: solved by *grātiās agās*.

Learning vocabulary for 6C(i)

Verbs

ārdeō 2 ārsī ārsūrus I burn; am in love
faciō ut + subj. I bring it about that . . . (cf. *efficiō/perficiō ut*)

prōcurrō 3 prōcucurrī prōcursum I run forward, advance

respiciō 3/4 respexī respectus I look round (back) at, turn my gaze upon; reflect upon; care for

---

Running vocabulary for 6C(ii)

adorior 4 dep. adortus I attack
alacritās alacritāt-is 3f. enthusiasm, liveliness
animum aduertō = animaduertō
appropinquō 1 I approach
concurs-us ūs 4m. attack, engagement
cōnficiō 3/4 cōnfēcī cōnfectus I weaken
cōnsistō 3 cōnstitī I stop, stand my ground
cōnsūmō 3 cōnsūmpsī cōnsūmptus I use up
conuertor 3 dep. conuersus I turn round
curs-us ūs 4m. distance to run; running
dēstituō 3 dēstituī dēstitūtus I leave, abandon
distendō 3 I stretch out
distrahō 3 I pull apart
duplicō 1 I double
equitāt-us ūs 4m. cavalry

exanimō 1 I deprive of breath, exhaust
excēdō 3 I depart, leave (+ abl. of separation 'from')
excipiō 3/4 excēpī I sustain, receive
excurs-us ūs 4m. attack
exercitō 1 I train
explicō 1 I unfold; *mē explicō* I deploy
funditor funditōr-is 3m. slinger
incitō 1 I set in motion; (passive) I rush
incitātiō incitātiōn-is 3f. energy
inerm-is e unarmed
īnfest-us a um hostile [With *pīlum* = 'at the ready'; with *signa* = 'indicating attack']
īnfringō 3 I break
innāt-us a um innate (in x: dat.)

intermittō 3 intermīsī intermissus I leave, let pass
lassitūdō lassitūdin-is 3f. weariness
mittō 3 mīsī missus I throw
nātūrāliter by nature naturally
perīt-us a um skilled
Pompēiān-ī ōrum 2m. pl. the followers of Pompey
praedīcō 3 praedīxī I tell x (dat.) beforehand
profundō 3 profūdī I pour out; *sē profundere* to pour forth
prōtinus at once
renouō 1 I renew, start again
reprimō 3 repressī I hold back, check
rūrsus again

sagittāri-us ī 2m. archer	*summoueō* 2 *summōuī*	*turmātim* in squadrons
sponte of one's own	*summōtus* I dislodge	*uertō* 3 *uertī* I turn (trans.)
accord; *suā sponte* of	*superior superiōr-is* earlier	*ūniuers-us a um* all
their own accord	*sustineō* 2 I withstand	together
stringō 3 *strīnxī* I draw	*terg-um ī* 2n. back	*ūs-us ūs* 4m. experience

Notes

l. 14 *tantum* governs *spatī*.

l. 24 *cum*: 'when' (not governing *īnfestīs pīlīs*).

l. 25 *nōn concurrī ā*: impersonal passive (indirect speech) – 'that it was not being rushed together by . . .' i.e. 'that . . . were not making a charge' (see **155²**).

l. 30 *neque . . . dēfuērunt*: i.e. they were equal to the situation.

l. 36 *hōc*: 'at this', 'because of this' (abl.).

l. 37 *ā latere apertō*: i.e. from the left (the sword was in the right hand).

Learning vocabulary for 6C(ii)

Nouns

curs-us ūs 4m. running; course; direction; voyage	*equitāt-us ūs* 4m. cavalry
	terg-um ī 2n. back

Adjectives

inerm-is e unarmed	*īnfest-us a um* hostile; at the ready; indicating attack	*ūniuers-us a um* all together, whole, entire

Verbs

adorior 4 dep. *adortus* I attack, rise up against	*excēdō* 3 *excessī excessum* I depart, go out; surpass	*reprimō* 3 *repressī repressus* I hold back, check
animum aduertō = *animaduertō*	*excipiō* 3/4 *excēpī exceptus* I sustain, receive; welcome; catch; make an exception	*sustineō* 2 *sustinuī sustentus* I withstand; support
appropinquō 1 I approach (+ dat.)		*uertō* 3 *uertī uersus* I turn (trans.)
cōnsistō 3 *cōnstitī* I stop, stand my ground	*mittō* 3 *mīsī missus* I throw; (send)	

Running vocabulary for 6C(iii)

agō 3 (*dē* + abl.) I discuss
aquor 1 dep. I fetch water
circummūniō 4 I fortify, enclose (by a wall)
cōnficiō 3/4 *cōnfēcī cōnfectus* I weaken
coniungō 3 *coniūnxī* I join (trans.); *mē coniungō* (+ dat.) I join x
contendō 3 *contendī* I demand (of x: *ā* + abl.; that Y: *ut* + subj.)
continēns continent-is continual
dēditiō dēditiōn-is 3f. surrender
diffīdō 3 semi-dep. *diffīsus* I distrust (+ dat.)
dīuidō 3 *dīuīsī* I divide
etsī although, even though

facultās facultāt-is 3f. opportunity
flūmen flūmin-is 3n. river
impetrō 1 I obtain by request
īnstituō 3 *īnstituī* I begin
iug-um ī 2n. ridge
Lārīs-a ae 1f. Larisa
mūnitiō mūnitiōn-is 3f. fortification
noctū by night
occupāt-us a um busy (with x: *in* + abl.)
occurrō 3 I intercept (+ dat.)
opus oper-is 3n. earthwork, fortification
pass-us ūs 4m. pace, step; *mīlle passūs* = 1 Roman mile (pl. *mīlia passuum*)

Pompēiān-ī ōrum 2m. pl. the followers of Pompey
potior 4 dep. I gain control of (+ abl.)
recipiō 3/4: *mē recipiō* I retreat
remaneō 2 I remain
remittō 3 *remīsī* I send back
sēclūdō 3 *sēclūsī* I cut off (x acc. from Y *ā* + abl.)
senatōri-us a um senatorial
subsum subesse I am close at hand
subluō 3 I flow at the foot of
uersus (placed after an acc.) in the direction of

Notes
l. 51 *iugīs*: 'on . . .', 'by means of . . .'

Learning vocabulary for 6C(iii)

Nouns
flūmen flūmin-is 3n. river
opus oper-is 3n. fortification; (job, work, task)

Verbs
agō 3 *ēgī āctus* I discuss; (do, act; drive, lead; spend, pass; direct)
cōnficiō 3/4 *cōnfēcī cōnfectus* I weaken; (finish)
diffīdō 3 semi-dep. *diffīsus* I distrust (+ dat.)

impetrō 1 I obtain by request
īnstituō 3 *īnstituī īnstitūtus* I begin; construct; resolve
potior 4 dep. I gain control of (+ abl.); (control (+ gen.))

recipiō 3/4: *mē recipiō* I retreat; (welcome, receive, take in)
remaneō 2 *remānsī remānsum* I remain
remittō 3 *remīsī remissus* I send back; remit

Others

etsī although, even
though, even if

noctū by night

Running vocabulary for 6C(iv)

adhibeō 2 I show, use
commendō 1 I charge (x:
  dat., that y should not
  happen: nē + subj.)
cōnsōlor 1 dep. I reassure
cōnsurgō 3 I get up
dēscendō 3 I descend
dēsīderō 1 I lose, find
  missing
fleō 2 I weep
inuicem in turn

Lārīs-a ae 1f. Larisa
lēnitās lēnitāt-is 3f.
  clemency
neu = nēue ('and that . . .
  not')
occurrō 3 I come to meet
  (+ dat.)
palm-a ae 1f. palm, hand
pandō 3 pandī passus I
  spread out (trans.)

plānitiēs plānitiē-ī 5f. plain
prōiciō 3/4 prōiēcī prōiectus
  I throw down
recūsātiō recūsātiōn-is 3f.
  objection, refusal
requiēscō 3 I rest
reuertor 3 dep. I return
superior superiōr-is higher
uiolō 1 I maltreat

Notes

l. 63 *prīmā lūce*: i.e. at dawn.

l. 66 *cōnsōlātus*: the subject is Caesar.

l. 67 *quō minōre essent timōre*: purpose clause (see **148**). For the abl., cf. *bonō animō esse*.

l. 68 *nē quī*: 'that none . . .'

l. 69 *quid suī*: 'anything of his own (possession)'.

ll. 70–1 The infinitives are solved by *iussit*.

Learning vocabulary for 6C(iv)

Adjectives

superior super-ius (gen.
  superiōr-is) higher;
  earlier

Verbs

dēscendō 3 dēscendī
  dēscēnsum I descend
fleō 2 flēuī flētum I weep

occurrō 3 occurrī occursum I
  run to meet, meet;
  attack (+ dat.)

prōiciō 3/4 prōiēcī prōiectus
  I throw down
reuertor 3 dep. reuersus I
  return

Others

neu = nēue and that . . .
  not

Section 6D

Running vocabulary for 6D(i)

---

adiungō 3 *adiūnxī* I join,
    add
cael-um ī 2n. heaven, sky
cernō 3 I discern, perceive,
    see
dēlūbr-um ī 2n. temple,
    shrine
dīu-us ī 2m. god
faciō 3/4 I suppose,
    imagine (l. 5)
fax fac-is 3f. torch
flamm-a ae 1f. flame
flectō 3 I steer, guide,
    control
fremit-us ūs 4m. roar
fulmen fulmin-is 3n.
    lighting, thunderbolt
gemit-us ūs 4m. groan
grandō grandin-is 3f. hail
hūmān-us a um human
imber imbr-is 3m. rain,
    storm
īnfēlīx īnfēlīc-is unhappy
īr-a ae 1f. anger
lacrim-a ae 1f. tear
lapis lapid-is 3m. stone
locārunt = locāuērunt

locō 1 I place
mage = magis
mēns ment-is 3f. mind
min-ae ārum 1f. pl. threats
minōrēs minōr-um 3m. pl.
    descendants
murmur murmur-is 3n.
    murmur
nectō 3 I link, string
    together (x acc. to y
    dat.)
nix niu-is 3f. snow
noctiuag-us a um
    wandering in the night
nūbil-a ōrum 2n. pl. clouds
nūt-us ūs 4m. nod,
    command
ōrdō ōrdin-is 3m. order
palm-a ae 1f. palm, hand
pandō 3 I spread out,
    extend
perfugi-um ī 2n. refuge
pietās pietāt-is 3f. respect
    for the gods
plācāt-us a um calm,
    tranquil
prōcumbō 3 I bow down

prōstrāt-us a um prostrate
quadrupēs quadruped-is 3m.
    (four-footed) beast
rapid-us a um rapid, swift
ratiōnēs 'workings'
sēdēs sēd-is 3f. abode
spargō 3 I sprinkle
templ-um ī 2n. region
    (inhabited by particular
    beings), quarter
tempor-a um 3n. pl.
    seasons
tribuō 3 I assign
uari-us a um diverse,
    various
uēlāt-us a um veiled, with
    covered head [See
    note]
uent-us ī 2m. wind
uertier: passive infinitive
    (present) of *uertō* 3
    (passive means 'I turn'
    intrans.)
uertor 3 passive = *reuertor*
    (l. 2)
uolō 1 I fly
uōt-um ī 2n. vow, prayer

Notes

For the metre see p. 318 and **183**.

l. 1 *praetereā*: Lucretius has noted that men have an inborn knowledge of
the gods' existence, but misinterpret the evidence of their senses so as
to think the gods responsible for phenomena in the world. *caelī
ratiōnēs*: part of an indirect statement introduced by *cernēbant* (verb
uertī).

l. 2 *uaria*: acc. pl. n. Hold until solved (by *tempora*) – second subject of
uertī.

l. 3 *quibus*: abl. pl. f. – solved by *causīs*; normal order would be: *nec poterant cognōscere quibus causīs id fieret.*

l. 5 *trādere et . . . facere*: these two infinitives are in apposition to *perfugium*, i.e. 'handing over . . . supposing . . .'. *omnia flectī*: indirect statement depending on *facere* (*illōrum nūtū* also belongs to this indirect statement).

l. 6 *-que*: postponed – it joins this line to the previous one. *deum*: gen. pl. (see **16**).

l. 7 *quia*: postponed (it introduces the clause which begins *per caelum uoluī*).

l. 8 *noctis signa seuēra*: i.e. the stars.

l. 9 *noctiuagae . . . facēs, flammae . . . uolantēs*: i.e. shooting-stars or meteors.

l. 11 The two phenomena referred to in this line are probably both the same: thunder. *minārum*: i.e. the threats of the gods (as men imagine these noises signify).

l. 13 *cum*: postponed – it introduces the clause beginning *tālia dīuīs*.

ll. 14–15 This sentence is arranged as a *tricolon* with *anaphora* (see p. 315). The verb (*peperēre*) is held back until the third limb. The subject is *ipsī* (i.e. early men), the exclamatory words (*quantōs . . . quanta . . . quās*) are all acc., agreeing with the objects. The verb constructs with acc. and dative to mean 'I produce x for y'. *minōribu'* = *minōribus* (the *s* is cut off to make the syllable light).

l. 16 *ūllast* = *ūlla est. ūelātum*: sc. 'for a person (to . . .)'. It was the Roman custom to pray with the head veiled.

l. 17 *uertier ad lapidem*: Romans approached statues of the gods from the right, then, after praying, turned right to face them, and prostrated themselves (see l. 18). Apart from stone statues, though, there were boundary-stones (*terminī*) and other sacred rocks which were venerated by the placing of garlands on them, or the pouring of oil. *omnīs*: acc. pl. f. Hold until solved (by *ad ārās*).

l. 18 *pandere palmās*: i.e. to stretch out the arms with the hands palm-uppermost.

l. 19 *deum*: gen. pl. (see above l. 6).

l. 21 *plācātā*: abl. s. f. Hold until solved (by *mente*).

Learning vocabulary for 6D(i)

Nouns

cael-um ī 2n. sky, heaven
dīu-us ī 2m. god
flamm-a ae 1f. flame
mēns ment-is 3f. mind

nix niu-is 3f. snow
ōrdō ōrdin-is 3m. order
　(rank)

pietās pietāt-is 3f. respect
　for the gods (also for
　one's family, home and
　native land)
uent-us ī 2m. wind
uōt-um ī 2n. vow, prayer

Adjectives

uari-us a um diverse,
　various

Verbs

pandō 3 *pandī passus* I
　spread out, extend;
　throw open, disclose

Running vocabulary for 6D(ii)

Acherōn Acheront-is 3m.
　Acheron (one of the
　rivers of the
　Underworld)
aes aer-is 3n. bronze statue
aestuō 1 I boil, seethe
amict-us ūs 4m. cloak
ann-us ī 2m. season
aprīc-us a um sunny
arceō 2 I keep away (x
　acc. from y abl.)
ars art-is 3f. skill, art,
　accomplishment
ast = at
āter ātr-a um black
auis au-is 3f. bird
autumn-us ī 2m. autumn,
　fall
caen-um ī 2n. mud
cānitiēs cānitiē-ī 5f. white
　hair
Charōn Charont-is 3m.
　Charon (the ferryman
　of the dead)

Cōcȳt-us ī 2m. Cocytus
　('the wailing river')
　[See note]
color colōr-is 3m. colour
condō 3 *condidī* I hide
cont-us ī 2m. pole
crūd-us a um (lit. 'unripe')
　youthful, vigorous
cumb-a ae 1f. boat
dēbellō 1 I subdue,
　conquer
dēfungor 3 dep. *dēfūnctus* I
　have done with, finish
　(+ abl.)
dēpendeō 2 I hang down
dēscrībō 3 I delineate
Dīs Dīt-is 3m. Dis
　(= Pluto, god of the
　Underworld)
effūs-us a um hurrying,
　rushing (lit. 'poured
　out')
equidem indeed; for my
　part

ēructō 1 I belch forth,
　spout up
excūdō 3 I beat out,
　fashion
ferrūgine-us a um dark (lit.
　'rust-coloured')
ferō ferre I lead (intrans.)
foli-um ī 2n. leaf
frīgid-us a um cold
frīgus frīgor-is 3n. cold
fugō 1 I put to flight
glomerō 1 (passive) I
　gather, assemble
gurges gurgit-is 3m.
　torrent, flood, sea,
　river
hērōs hērō-is 3m. hero
　(human being of divine
　parentage)
horrend-us a um dreadful,
　terrible (lit. 'to be
　shuddered at')
immittō 3 I send (x acc. to
　y dat.)

impōnō 3 *imposuī impositus*
(l. 41) I put on (to x:
dat.); (l. 55) I add (x
acc. to Y dat.)

inān-is e empty,
insubstantial

incult-us a um neglected,
disordered

innūpt-us a um unmarried

lābor 3 dep. *lāpsus* I fall

lūmin-a um 3n. pl. eyes

magnanim-us a um great-
hearted [*magnanimum* is
gen. pl. Cf. *deum* in
6D(i) l. 6]

malign-us a um niggardly,
grudging

marmor marmor-is 3n.
marble

meāt-us ūs 4m. motion,
revolution

mementō remember, be
sure (to: + infin.)
(imperative of *meminī*)

ment-um ī 2n. chin

ministrō 1 I attend to
(+ dat.)

moll-is e soft, pliant,
flexible

mōs mōr-is 3m. civilisation

nāuit-a ae 1m. sailor
(= *nauta*)

nōd-us ī 2m. knot

obscūr-us a um dark (tr. 'in
darkness')

pont-us ī 2m. sea

portitor portitōr-is 3m.
harbour-officer, excise-
man

quāle just as [See note]

radi-us ī 2m. rod

ratis rat-is 3f. boat

regō 3 I govern, direct

rēgn-um ī 2n. kingdom,
realm

rīp-a ae 1f. bank

rog-us ī 2m. funeral pyre

ruō 3 I rush

senectūs senectūt-is 3f. old
age

senior seniōr-is very old
(comparative of *senex*)

seruō 1 I guard

silu-a ae 1f. wood

sōl-us a um lonely

sordid-us a um dirty, filthy

spīrō 1 I breathe

squālor squālōr-is 3m. filth,
squalor (lit. 'stiffness')

subiect-ī ōrum 2m. pl. the
conquered

subigō 3 I push on, thrust
forward

subuectō 1 I convey,
transport

summoueō 2 *summōuī*
summōtus I drive away,
remove

superb-us a um proud,
arrogant

surgō 1 I rise

Tartare-us a um of
Tartarus, Tartarean

trānsmittō (*cursum*) 3 I
make a crossing [See
note]

turbid-us a um thick,
murky (with: + abl.)

uāst-us a um huge, vast

uēl-um ī 2n. sail

uirid-is e green

ulterior ulteriōr-is further

umbr-a ae 1f. shadow,
darkness

umer-us ī 2m. shoulder

und-a ae 1f. water

uorāgō uorāgin-is 3f. abyss,
gulf

Notes

l. 1 For the metre, see p. 319. *ībant*: the subjects are Aeneas and the Sibyl.
sōlā: with *sub nocte*. The adjectives are, in a sense, both with the wrong
noun (a figure called *hypallage*) – *obscūrus* would describe *nox* well, and
sōlus the travellers.

l. 2 *inānia rēgna*: also governed by *per*.

l. 3 *quāle . . . iter*: lit. 'what sort of journey (there is)'. Understand 'they
were going on' from l. 1. and tr. 'the sort of journey one makes . . .'

l. 4 *caelum*: object – hold until solved (by *condidit . . . Iuppiter*).

l. 5 *Iuppiter*: Jupiter controls the weather (along with much else). *rēbus*:
dat. of disadvantage (solved by *abstulit*). Tr. 'the world'.

l. 28 *hinc uia*: sc. *est. Tartareī*: gen. s. m. Hold (until solved by *Acherontis*).
It belongs in the clause introduced by *quae*.

l. 29 *turbidus*: with abl. of respect *caenō*. Used predicatively with *gurges* (i.e. 'a torrent, murky . . .' not 'a murky torrent'). *uāstā* . . . *uorāgine*: abl. of description (qualifying *gurges*). The prose order of this line would be: *hīc gurges, turbidus caenō, uāstāque uorāgine, aestuat* . . .

l. 30 *omnem*: acc. s. f. Hold (solved by *harēnam*). *Cōcȳtō*: = *in Cōcȳtum*.

l. 31 *portitor*: in apposition to the subject *Charōn*. Tr. 'as harbour-officer' (since he, like similar people in the Roman world, collects tolls and controls access to the harbour where his boat stands). *hās*: acc. pl. f. Hold until solved (by *aquās*); the phrase is the object of *seruat*.

l. 32 *terribilī squālōre*: abl. of description. *cūi* . . . *mentō*: lit: 'for whom on the chin'. Tr. 'on whose chin'. Dative is commonly used in poetry for genitive in such expressions. *plūrima*: nom. s. f. Hold until solved (by *cānitiēs*).

l. 33 *stant flammā*: lit. 'stand with flame' i.e. 'are staring and ablaze'.

l. 34 *sordidus*: nom. s. m. Hold until solved (by *amictus*). *nōdō*: abl. of means 'by –'. Charon is wearing a cloak knotted (not fastened with a pin) over his left shoulder, leaving his right arm and shoulder bared for his work.

l. 36 *ferrūgineā*: abl. s. f. Hold until solved (by *cumbā*: the abl. expresses place). *corpora*: i.e. the dead.

l. 37 *sed crūda deō uiridisque senectūs*: sc. *est. deō* 'the god's'.

ll. 39–41 All these people make up the *turba* of l. 38; the nominatives (*mātrēs, uirī, corpora, puerī, puellae* and *iuuenēs*) are in apposition to *turba*.

l. 39 *dēfūncta*: nom. pl. n. governs *uītā*, and is used predicatively with *corpora* (i.e. 'bodies finished with . . .' not 'finished-with bodies'. Cf. *turbidus* in l. 29).

l. 40 *magnanimum hērōum*: depends on *corpora*.

l. 41 *impositī*: nom. pl. m. – cf. *dēfuncta* . . . *corpora* (l. 39). Used predicatively with *iuuenēs*, i.e. 'youths placed . . .' not 'placed youths . . .'

ll. 42, 44 *quam multa . . . quam multae*: 'as many as (the . . . which)'.

l. 42 *autumnī frīgore prīmō*: *autumnī* depends on *frīgore*. The abl. phrase expresses time.

l. 43 *cadunt*: here tr. 'die' (or *lāpsa* as 'having slipped' (sc. 'off the tree') and *cadunt* as 'fall' (sc: 'to the ground')). *aut ad terram gurgite ab altō*: this belongs in the new simile, introduced by *quam multae* in l. 44.

l. 45 *fugat*: sc. *eās* (= 'the birds').

l. 46 *trānsmittere*: infinitive of indirect command (poetic use of a Greek construction instead of the normal *ut* + subj.; see **134**). *prīmī* belongs with *trānsmittere cursum*.

l. 47 *amōre*: abl. of cause 'from desire (for)'.

l. 48 *sed*: postponed (normally first word in a clause). *nunc hōs*: sc. *accipit*.

l. 49 *harēnā*: = *rīpīs* (where the boat is standing and where access is gained to it). This line is the cue for Aeneas to ask the Sibyl why some people are allowed to sail, while others are kept on the shore. The answer is that only the buried may cross; the unburied, quite apart from the religious taboo on their crossing, have no coin with which to pay for their passage. Among the unburied, Aeneas meets his steersman Palinurus, who was lost overboard before the Trojans arrived in Italy.

l. 50 *aliī* i.e. the Greeks (also for the other things mentioned in ll. 50–3).

ll. 50–2 *mollius . . . melius*: the comparison is with the Romans, sc. 'than you Romans'. *mollius*: qualifies *spīrantia*. Tr. 'in more flowing (i.e. lifelike) lines'.

l. 51 *uīuōs*: acc. pl. m. Hold until solved (by *uultūs*: possibly the adjective is used predicatively (cf. lines 39 and 41 above), i.e. 'faces which live', not 'living faces'). *dūcent*: in the sense 'bring forth'.

l. 52 *caelī*: i.e. 'of the heavenly bodies'. The phrase *caelī meātūs* is object of *dēscrībent*.

l. 54 *surgentia sīdera*: i.e. 'the risings of the stars'. Cf. **163** *Note*.

Learning vocabulary for 6D(ii)

Nouns

ars art-is 3f. skill, art, accomplishment

autumn-us ī 2m. autumn, fall

frīgus frīgor-is 3n. cold; pl. cold spells

lūmen lūmin-is 3n. light; (pl.) eyes

rīp-a ae 1f. bank

silu-a ae 1f. wood

umbr-a ae 1f. shadow, darkness; shade, ghost

umer-us ī 2m. shoulder

und-a ae 1f. water, wave

Adjectives

obscūr-us a um dark; obscure; mean, ignoble

sōl-us a um lonely (alone)

superb-us a um proud, haughty, arrogant

Verbs

fugō 1 I put to flight

impōnō 3 *imposuī impositus* I put x (acc.) on Y (dat.)

lābor 3 dep. *lāpsus* I slip, glide, fall down; make a mistake

surgō 3 *surrēxī surrēctum* I rise, arise, get up

Running vocabulary for 6D(iii)

abrumpō 3 I break
adiciō 3/4 I add
Aenēās (Greek nom.)
  Aeneas (Trojan hero,
  mythical founder of
  Roman race)
aestās aestāt-is 3f. summer
alm-us a um bountiful,
  nourishing [See note]
amīc-us a um friendly [See
  note]
an whether
Anc-us ī 2m. Ancus (third
  king of Rome)
arbitri-um ī 2n. judgement
arbor arbor-is 3f. tree
auid-us a um greedy
brūm-a ae 1f. winter
caelest-is e in the heavens
camp-us ī 2m. field, plain
cār-us a um dear
chor-us ī 2m. dance
com-a ae 1f. foliage
crāstin-us a um
  tomorrow's
cūnct-us a um all, the
  whole of
damn-um ī 2n. loss
dēcidō 3 I go (lit. 'fall')
  down
dēcrēscō 3 I decrease

Diān-a ae 1f. Diana [See
  note]
diffugiō 3/4 *diffūgī* I
  disperse, scatter
  (intrans.)
effundō 3 *effūdī* I pour out
fācundi-a ae 1f. eloquence
frūgēs frūg-um 3f. pl.
  produce, fruits
gemin-us a um twin
grāmen grāmin-is 3n. grass
Grāti-a ae 1f. Grace (one
  of the three Graces)
hērēs hērēd-is 3m. heir
Hippolyt-us ī 2m.
  Hippolytus [See note]
hodiern-us a um today's
iners inert-is sluggish,
  motionless
infern-us a um of the
  Underworld
*intereō interīre interiī
  interitum* I die
Lēthae-us a um of Lethe
  [See note]
Mīnōs Mīnō-is 3m. Minos
  (one of the judges in
  the Underworld)
mītēscō 3 I grow mild
nūd-us a um naked
Nymph-a ae 1f. Nymph

Pēritho-us ī 2m. Perithous
  [See note]
pōmifer pōmifer-a um
  apple-bearing
prōterō 3 I trample on
pudīc-us a um chaste
puluis puluer-is 3m. dust
rapiō 3/4 I snatch (away)
recurrō 3 I run back,
  return
reparō 1 I make good
restituō 3 I bring back,
  revive
simul = simulatque
splendid-us a um splendid,
  brilliant
summ-a ae 1f. total
super-ī ōrum 2m. pl. the
  gods above
tenebr-ae ārum 1f. pl.
  shadows, darkness
Thēseus (Greek nom.)
  Theseus [See note]
Torquāt-us ī 2m.
  Torquatus
Tull-us ī 2m. Tullus
  (second king of Rome)
uēr uēr-is 3n. spring
uic-ēs 3f. pl. successive
  forms/conditions
Zephyr-us ī 2m. West
  Wind

Notes

For the metre, see **184**.

l. 3 *dēcrēscentia*: nom. pl. n. – solved by *flūmina praetereunt*: i.e. flow
  between.

l. 7 *immortālia*: 'immortality'. *almum*: acc. m. s. – hold (solved by *diem*).
  hōra and *annus* are both subjects of *monet*. The prose order would be:
  hōra quae diem almum rapit.

l. 9 *Zephyrīs*: abl. of cause.

l. 13 *celerēs . . . lūnae*: i.e. months passing quickly.

l. 15 *quō*: '(to) where': understand *decidērunt* with *Aenēās*, *Tullus* and
  Ancus as subject.

ll. 17–18 *hodiernae*: dat. s. f. – solved by *summae*. *crāstina*: acc. pl. n. solved by *tempora*: the subject of *adiciant* is *dī superī*.

l. 19–20 *amīcō . . . animō*: dat. 'to your friendly heart' (imitating a Greek expression meaning 'to your dear heart'). The clause means 'whatever you have gratified your dear heart with'.

l. 21 *occiderīs*: future perfect, despite the long vowel in *-īs*. *splendida*: acc. pl. n. – hold until solved (by *arbitria*).

ll. 23–4 *genus*, *fācundia* and *pietās* are all subjects of *restituet*. Note the anaphora (*nōn . . . nōn tē . . . nōn tē*): see p. 315.

l. 25 *īnfernīs . . . tenebrīs*: abl. of separation 'from'. *pudīcum*: acc. s. m. – hold until solved (by *Hippolytum*).

ll. 25–6 Diana, goddess of the hunt and of chastity, could not save her dearest devotee Hippolytus (whose death was devised by Aphrodite, whom he had spurned).

l. 27 *Lēthaea*: acc. pl. n. – hold until solved (by *uincula*). Lethe was the River of Forgetfulness.

ll. 27–8 *cārō . . . Pērithoō*: abl. of separation 'from'. See Reference Grammar **L(f)1**. Theseus had gone down to Hades with his friend Perithous, to bring back Persephone, with whom Perithous was in love, and who had been abducted by Pluto. Both had been enchained, but Theseus had been rescued by Heracles, and returned to the world above. Now dead, and back in Hades for ever, he is unable to rescue his friend.

Learning vocabulary for 6D(iii)

Nouns

arbor arbor-is 3f. tree
camp-us ī 2m. field, plain
com-a ae 1f. hair; foliage

tenebr-ae ārum 1f. pl. shadows, darkness

Adjectives

caelest-is e in the heavens

cūnct-us a um all, the whole of

nūd-us a um naked

Verbs

rapiō 3/4 *rapuī raptus* I snatch, seize, carry off, plunder

Others

an whether (in indirect questions, + subj.: = *num*); = *ne*(= ?) (in direct question)

443

Running vocabulary for 6D(iv)

adapert-us a um open
adpōnō 3 *adposuī* I lay
aegrē with difficulty
aest-us ūs 4m. (lit. 'heat')
hot part of the day
apt-us a um fit
castīgāt-us a um well-
formed (lit. 'well-
disciplined')
claus-us a um closed
coll-um ī 2n. neck [Pl.
used for s.]
Corinn-a ae 1f. Corinna
crepuscul-um ī 2n. twilight
[Pl. used for s.]
dēripiō 3/4 *dēripuī* I tear
off
dīuidu-us a um parted
exigō 3 *exēgī* I complete
femur femor-is 3n. thigh
fenestr-a ae 1f. window
iuuenāl-is e youthful
lacert-us ī 2m. arm
Lāis Lāid-is 3f. Lais (a
famous Corinthian
courtesan)
lass-us a um weary, tired
out

latebr-ae ārum 1f. pl.
hiding-place
laudābil-is e worthy of
praise
leuō 1 I relieve, rest
mend-a ae 1f. blemish
nusquam nowhere
orior 4 dep. *ortus* I arise
papill-a ae 1f. breast [See
note]
Phoeb-us ī 2m. (lit.
Phoebus, god of the
sun) the sun
plān-us a um flat
pōnō 3 *posuī positus* I lay
aside
praebeō 2 I provide, offer
premō 3 *pressī* I press
prōditiō prōditiōn-is 3f.
betrayal
prōueniō 4 I turn out, am
successful
pudor pudōr-is 3m.
modesty, sense of
shame
quālia/quāle [See note]

quāliter just as, just the
way in which
rār-us a um thin [See note]
recingō 3 *recīnxī recīnctus* I
unfasten, unbelt
referō referre I relate [See
note]
requiēscō 3 *requiēuī* I take a
rest, relax
Semīramis Semīramid-is 3f.
Semiramis (legendary
queen of Assyria)
singul-ī ae a individual,
one by one
sublūceō 2 I glow faintly
thalam-us ī 2m. bedroom
[Pl. used for s.]
tor-us ī 2m. bed, couch
[See note]
tunic-a ae 1f. tunic
uēlāmen uēlāmin-is 3n.
clothing
uēlō 1 I clothe
uenter uentr-is 3m.
stomach
uerēcund-us a um shy,
modest

Notes

For the metre, see **185**.

l. 1 *mediam*: acc. s. f. – hold until solved (by *hōram*).

l. 2 *mediō*: dat. s. m. – hold until solved (by *torō*). *torō*: dat. of motion towards. Tr. 'on . . .' Cf. **6D(ii)** l. 30 *omnem Cōcȳtō ēructat harēnam* 'belches forth all its sand into Cocytus.'

l. 3 *pars . . . pars altera*: the window had two shutters. *clausa*: sc. *fuit*.

l. 4 *quāle . . . lūmen*: lit: 'what sort of light'. Tr. 'the sort of light which . . .'

l. 5 *quālia . . . crepuscula*: lit. 'what sort of twilight . . .' Tr. 'the sort of twilight which . . .' *fugiente*: abl. s. m. Hold until solved (by *Phoebō* – abl. abs.).

l. 6 *orta*: sc. *est*.

l. 7 *illa*: nom. s. f. – *lūx* is the complement. Tr. 'that is the (sort of) light . . .' *uerēcundīs*: dat. pl. f. Hold until solved (by *puellīs*). (The dat. means 'to'.)

l. 8 *timidus*: nom. s. m. Hold until solved (by *pudor*). *spēret*: generic subjunctive (see tr. for *illa*, l. 7). (See **140.1**.)

l. 10 *candida*: acc. pl. n. Hold (solved by *colla* – but await a verb still). *dīuiduā*: abl. s. f. Hold until solved (by *comā*) – *tegente* is also abl. s. f., and provides the verb governing *candida . . . colla*. The phrase is abl. abs.

l. 12 *multīs*: dat. pl. m. Hold until solved (by *uirīs*). The dative expresses agent 'by', after the passive participle *amāta*. Cf. **6A(vi)** l. 5 *amāta nōbīs* 'loved by me'. See Reference Grammar **L(e)(iv)**. *Lāis*: second subject (with *Semīramis*) of *dīcitur*. Carry over also *in thalamōs . . . īsse*.

l. 13 *multum . . . nocēbat*: adverbial acc. (or internal). Tr. 'did it do much harm'. *rāra*: i.e. *tunica*. Tr. 'being thin'.

l. 14 *tunicā*: abl. of instrument 'with', 'by'. Solved by *tegī*. *sed tamen*: postponed – normally one would expect these words at the beginning of a clause.

l. 15 *ita . . . tamquam quae . . . nōllet*: 'just like one who did not want . . .' Generic subjunctive (see above, l.8).

l. 17 *ut* = 'when'.

l. 18 *in tōtō*: await a solving noun (*corpore*).

ll. 19–22 *quōs . . . quālis . . . quam . . . quam . . . quantum . . . quāle . . . quam*: all exclamatory. Cf. **6D(i)** ll. 14–15.

l. 19 *quōs umerōs, quālis . . . lacertōs*: obj. of *uīdī tetigīque*. Hold *quālīs* as obj. until solved by *lacertōs*.

l. 20 *fōrma papillārum*: = *papillae fōrmōsae*. The subject of the exclamation here precedes the introductory words *quam . . . apta*. *premī*: explanatory (epexegetic) infin. after *apta*. Tr. *premō* here as 'caress'.

l. 21 *quam*: qualifies *plānus*. *castīgātō*: abl. s. n. Hold until solved (by *sub pectore*).

l. 23 *referam*: deliberative subj.: see **152¹**. Cf. *quid plūra dīcam?* 'Why should I say more?'

l. 24 *nūdam*: acc. s. f., adj. used as a noun. It refers to Corinna. *corpus ad usque meum*: normal order would be *usque ad corpus meum*.

l. 26 *prōueniant*: subjunctive expressing a wish for the future. See Reference Grammar **L–V Intro. (a)4.** *mediī*: nom. pl. m. Hold until solved (by *diēs*).

Learning vocabulary

Nouns

coll-um ī 2n. neck
lacert-us ī 2m. arm, upper
  arm
latebr-ae ārum 1f. pl.
  hiding-place, lair

pudor pudōr-is 3m.
  modesty, sense of
  shame
thalam-us ī 2m. chamber,
  bedchamber

tor-us ī 2m. couch; bed
tunic-a ae 1f. tunic

Adjectives

plān-us a um level, flat;
  plain, distinct

singul-ī ae a individual,
  one by one

Verbs

orior 4 dep. *ortus* I rise;
  spring from, originate

pōnō 3 *posuī positus* I lay
  aside (= *dēpōnō*); (place,
  position, put)

praebeō 2 I provide, offer;
  (show, display)
premō 3 *pressī pressus* I
  press; oppress

Others

aegrē with difficulty

Grammar and exercises for 6D

See pp. 318–20 for the principles of Latin metre, and the scheme for hexameter.

183 The hexameter in Lucretius

The metre is used by both Lucretius and Virgil, but Lucretius is in some ways less strict. Lucretius for instance allows elision of *-s* to produce a light syllable, e.g.

minlōribu' nlostrīs (for *minlōribus nlostrīs*)

Here are the first three lines of the Lucretius passage scanned for you:

praetereļā caeļlī ratilōnēs | ōrdineļcertō

et uariļ[a] annōrļum cernļēbant |temporaļuertī

nec poterļant quibusļ id fierļet cognļōscere clausīs.

NB. The caesura (see above p. 320, note 2) comes after *caelī, annōrum, id* (3rd foot).

84 Archilochean

The metre Horace uses in Odes 4.7 is called Archilochean, after the seventh-century BC poet Archilochus of Paros. The scheme is a couplet, made up as follows:

(a) Hexameter (see above p. 000).
(b) Half-hexameter, with dactyls (–∪∪) only: –∪∪ | –∪∪ | ∪̲ .

E.g.

dīffūglēre nĭŭlēs, rĕdĕlŭnt ĭăm glrāmĭnă clāmpīs
      ărbŏrĭblŭsquĕ cŏmlae

85 Elegiac couplet

The metre used by Martial (e.g. pp. 208–9), Crotti (p. 287) and Ovid in *Fastī* (p. 405) and *Amōrēs* I.5 is the elegiac couplet. It consists of a *hexameter* (see above p. 319), followed by a *pentameter*, the scheme of which is:

–∪∪ | –∪∪ | – ‖ –∪∪ | –∪∪ | ∪̲

E.g.

adpŏsŭlī mĕdĭlō ‖ mēmbră lĕŭlāndă tŏrlō

There is always a caesura (see p. 320, note 2) in the place marked by ‖ in the example and the scheme.

Exercise

Scan the lines which you have translated in each section, taking care to watch for elisions. Mark foot divisions with | . Mark caesuras in hexameters with { , in pentameters with ‖ . Add the correct word stress (see rule, p. xv). Read each piece aloud, thinking through the meaning as you read.

REFERENCE GRAMMAR

The Reference Grammar pulls together the Running Grammar sections, and adds to them features of the language which did not seem appropriate for a beginner dealing with basics. For the fuller philological picture we recommend:

> L. R. Palmer, *The Latin Language*, London 1954
> E. C. Woodcock, *A New Latin Syntax*, London 1959 (Bristol Classical Press reprint 1985)

A–G Verbs

Introduction

(a) Sequence

When the main verb of a sentence is PRESENT, FUTURE, FUTURE PERFECT, or PERFECT (meaning 'have —ed'), the sequence is 'primary', and subordinate subjunctives can only be present, perfect, or future participle + *sim*. When the main verb of a sentence is IMPERFECT, PERFECT ('I —ed'), or PLUPERFECT, the sequence is 'secondary' or 'historic', and subordinate subjunctives can only be imperfect, pluperfect, or future participle + *éssem* (or *fórem*). (For an exception, see **144**.)

(b) Transitive/intransitive

A verb is said to be 'transitive' (*tránseō tránsitus* 'I cross over') when it controls a direct object in the accusative, e.g. *pórtō* 'I carry' is transitive (in *aúlam pórtō* 'I carry a pot' *aulam* = object, accusative), but *páreō* 'I obey' is not (in *éī páreō* 'I obey him' *éī* = object, but dative), nor is *uéniō* 'I come' (in *ad pórtam uéniō* 'I come to the gate', *pórtam* is controlled by *ad*).

(c) Meaning

témpus tríbus pártibus cṓnstat ('consists of' + abl.): *praetéritō, praesénte, futū́rō* (Seneca).

448

Present tense (durative)

This is a durative form, and means 'I am —ing', but also serves to mean 'I —', 'I do —'. It can also mean 'I begin to —', 'I can —', 'I try to —' and 'I have —ed and still am —ing', e.g. *sexāgíntā ánnōs uíuō* 'I have been living for sixty years (and still am)'.

The present tense can also be used where one would naturally expect a past tense. It makes the action more vivid. This usage is called the 'historic' present.

Future tense (durative)

This is again durative, and means 'I shall be —ing', but is used also for 'I shall —'.

Imperfect tense (durative)

This means 'I was —ing', 'used to —', 'kept on —ing', 'tried to —', 'began to —'. But it can also be translated 'I —ed', since English does not always pay as close attention to the durative aspect of the verb as Latin.

Perfect tense (completed)

This means 'I have —ed', 'I did —', 'I —ed', 'I have done with —ing'.

Pluperfect tense (completed)

This means 'I had —ed', 'I had been —ing', 'I finished —ing'.

Future perfect tense (completed)

This means 'I shall have —ed'. Frequently it is best translated 'I shall —' or 'I have —ed' in English, e.g. *póstquam líbrum légerō* 'after I have read the book'.

(d) Principal parts

Active verbs generally have four principal parts, deponents have three (see the list at **G**). The principal parts give the key to all the forms of the verb, as follows.

Active verbs

> *hábe-ō*: stem of *active/passive* forms of the present, future and imperfect indicative, subjunctive, imperative, gerund(ive) and present participle. (Note that 1st conj. verb stems end in

449

-a-, e.g. *ámō*, stem *ama-*; contrast *hábe-ō*, stem *habe-*; *díc-ō*, stem *dīc-*; *aúdi-ō*, stem *audi-*; *cápi-ō*, stem *capi-*)

habē-re: key to correct conjugation (so the correct endings of present, future and imperfect forms). Stem of imperfect subjunctive (*habēre-m* etc.)

hábu-ī: key to all the perfect *active* forms

hábit-us: key to all the perfect *passive* forms, and the future participle/infinitive active

Deponent verbs

pollíce-or: stem of all present, future and imperfect forms. (See note on 1st conj. stems above, under *hábeō*)

pollicē-rī: key to conjugation

pollícit-us: key to all perfect forms, and future participle/ infinitive

NB. We give the fourth principal part of all deponent and transitive verbs in the form of the perfect participle (ending in *-us*), e.g. *amātus* (*ámō*). Intransitive verbs have the 4th p.p. printed in the n.s. (*-um*), e.g. *cúrsum* (*cúrrō*). Where no perfect participle exists, we have printed the 4th p.p. in the form of the future participle (ending in *-ūrus*), e.g. *fugitūrus* (*fúgiō*). Where neither future part. nor past part. is known, we print — in the 4th p.p. position. All dictionaries give as the 4th p.p. the 'supine' (see **A7** for form and function).

A1 Present active: personal endings: *-ō -s -t -mus -tis -nt*

Present indicative active 'I —', 'I am —ing', 'I do —'

Key: A E I Ī I

	1st conjugation 'I love'	2nd conjugation 'I have'	3rd conjugation 'I say'
1st s.	ámō	hábeō	dícō
2nd s.	ámās	hábēs	dícis
3rd s.	ámat	hábet	dícit
1st pl.	amāmus	habēmus	dícimus
2nd pl.	amātis	habētis	dícitis
3rd pl.	ámant	hábent	dícunt

	4th conjugation	3rd/4th conjugation
	'I hear'	*'I capture'*
1st s.	aúdiō	cápiō
2nd s.	aúdīs	cápis
3rd s.	aúdit	cápit
1st pl.	audímus	cápimus
2nd pl.	audítis	cápitis
3rd pl.	aúdiunt	cápiunt

Present participle active '—ing'

Key: -NT-

1	2	3
'loving'	*'having'*	*'saying'*
ámāns (amánt-)	hábēns (habént-)	dícēns (dīcént-)

4	3/4
'hearing'	*'capturing'*
aúdiēns (audiént-)	cápiēns (capiént-)

Pattern of declension

	s.		*pl.*	
	m./f.	*n.*	*m./f.*	*n.*
nom.	ámāns	ámāns	amántēs	amántia
acc.	amántem	ámāns	amántīs (amántēs)	amántia
gen.	←amántis→		←amántium (amántum)→	
dat.	←amántī→		←amántibus→	
abl.	←amánte (amántī)→		←amántibus→	

Present infinitive active 'to —'

Key: -ĀRE -ĒRE -ERE -ĪRE -ERE

1	2	3	4	3/4
'to love'	*'to have'*	*'to say'*	*to hear'*	*'to capture'*
amā́re	habḗre	dícere	audī́re	cápere

Gerund (a noun, cf. present participles) '(the act of) —ing'

Key: -ND-

1	2	3
'*(the act of) loving*'	'*(the act of) having*'	'*(the act of) saying*'
amáre, amánd-um ī 2n.	habére, habénd-um ī 2n.	dícere, dīcénd-um ī 2n.

4	3/4
'*(the act of) hearing*'	'*(the act of) capturing*'
audíre, audiénd-um ī 2n.	cápere, capiénd-um ī 2n.

Notes

1 The only gerund forms which verbs have are as above, based on the present stem.
2 The infinitive form often acts as a nominative noun, e.g. *erráre hūmánum est* 'to err (i.e. the act of erring) is human'. The gerund itself has no nominative.

Present imperative active '—!'

Key: Ā Ē E/I Ī E/I

	1	2	3
	'*love!*'	'*have!*'	'*demand!*'
2nd s.	ámā	hábē	pósce[1]
2nd pl.	amáte	habéte	póscite

	4	3/4
	'*hear!*'	'*capture!*'
2nd s.	aúdī	cápe
2nd pl.	audíte	cápite

[1] We use *poscō* here because *dīcō* has an irregular s. imperative.

Present subjunctive active 'I —', 'I may —', 'I would —'

Key: E A

	1	2	3	4	3/4
1st s.	ámem	hábeam	dícam	aúdiam	cápiam
2nd s.	ámēs	hábeās	dícās	aúdiās	cápiās
3rd s.	ámet	hábeat	dícat	aúdiat	cápiat

1st pl.	amḗmus	habeā́mus	dīcā́mus	audiā́mus	capiā́mus
2nd pl.	amḗtis	habeā́tis	dīcā́tis	audiā́tis	capiā́tis
3rd pl.	ā́ment	hábeant	dī́cant	aū́diant	cápiant

A2   Future active

Future indicative active 'I shall/will —', 'I shall/will be —ing'

Key: ĀBI ĒBI E IE IE

	1	*2*	*3*	*4*	*3/4*
	'I shall love'	*'I shall have'*	*'I shall say'*	*'I shall hear'*	*'I shall capture'*
1st s.	amā́bō	habḗbō	dī́cam	aū́diam	cápiam
2nd s.	amā́bis	habḗbis	dī́cēs	aū́diēs	cápiēs
3rd s.	amā́bit	habḗbit	dī́cet	aū́diet	cápiet
1st pl.	amā́bimus	habḗbimus	dīcḗmus	audiḗmus	capiḗmus
2nd pl.	amā́bitis	habḗbitis	dīcḗtis	audiḗtis	capiḗtis
3rd pl.	amā́bunt	habḗbunt	dī́cent	aū́dient	cápient

Future participle active 'about to —' 'on the point of —ing', 'with a view to —ing'

Key: perfect participle stem + ŪR-US A UM

1	*2*	*3*
'about to love'	*'about to have'*	*'about to say'*
amātū́r-us a um	habitū́r-us a um	dictū́r-us a um

4	*3/4*
'about to hear'	*'about to capture'*
audītū́r-us a um	captū́r-us a um

NB.   *-ū́r-us a um* declines like *lóngus*, **J1(a)**.

Future infinitive active 'to be about to —'

Key: perfect participle stem + ŪR-US A UM + ESSE

1	*2*	*3*
'to be about to love'	*'to be about to have'*	*'to be about to say'*
amātū́r-us a um ésse	habitū́r-us a um ésse	dictū́r-us a um ésse

4	3/4
'to be about to hear'	*'to be about to capture'*
audītŭr-us a um ésse	captŭr-us a um ésse

NB. *-ŭr-us a um* declines like *lóngus*, **J1(a)**.

Notes

1 The future (or 'second') imperative is formed by adding *-tō* (s.), *-tóte* (pl.) to the present stem (e.g. *amátō, habétō, póscitō, audítō, cápitō*). It expresses an order which is not to be obeyed immediately. E.g. *laédere hanc cauétō* 'Take care (in future) not to rub her up the wrong way' (Catullus).

2 'Future' subjunctive active is formed by future participle + *sim sīs sit*, e.g. *amatŭr-us sim* etc. or future participle + *éssem éssēs ésset* (sometimes *fórem fórēs fóret*), e.g. *amātŭrus essem* (*amātŭrus fórem*). Sequence (see **A–G Intro.(a)**) determines whether *sim* or *éssem/fórem* is used.

A3 Imperfect active

Imperfect indicative active 'I was —ing', 'I used to —', 'I began —ing'

Key: ĀBA ĒBA

	1	2	3
	'I was loving'	*'I was having'*	*'I was saying'*
1st s.	amábam	habébam	dīcébam
2nd s.	amábās	habébās	dīcébās
3rd s.	amábat	habébat	dīcébat
1st pl.	amābámus	habēbámus	dicēbámus
2nd pl.	amābátis	habēbátis	dīcēbátis
3rd pl.	amábant	habébant	dīcébant

	4	3/4
	'I was hearing'	*'I was capturing'*
1st s.	audiébam[1]	capiébam
2nd s.	audiébās	capiébās
3rd s.	audiébat	capiébat

[1] Sometimes *audíbam audíbās* etc.

1st pl.	audiēbāmus	capiēbāmus
2nd pl.	audiēbātis	capiēbātis
3rd pl.	audiēbant	capiēbant

Imperfect subjunctive active 'I was —ing', 'I might —', 'I would —'

Key: infinitive + endings

	1	2	3	4	3/4
1st s.	amārem	habērem	dīcerem	audīrem	cáperem
2nd s.	amārēs	habērēs	dīcerēs	audīrēs	cáperēs
3rd s.	amāret	habēret	dīceret	audīret	cáperet
1st pl.	amārēmus	habērēmus	dīcerēmus	audīrēmus	caperēmus
2nd pl.	amārētis	habērētis	dīcerētis	audīrētis	caperētis
3rd pl.	amārent	habērent	dīcerent	audīrent	cáperent

NB.   No imperfect participles, imperatives or infinitives exist.

A4 Perfect active

Perfect indicative active 'I —ed', 'I have —ed'

Key: perf. stem + Ī ISTĪ *etc.*

	1	2	3
	'I loved', 'I have loved'	*'I had', 'I have had'*	*'I said', 'I have said'*
1st s.	amā́uī	hábuī	dī́xī
2nd s.	amāuístī (amā́stī)	habuístī	dīxístī (dī́xtī)
3rd s.	amā́uit	hábuit	dī́xit
1st pl.	amā́uimus	habúimus	dī́ximus
2nd pl.	amāuístis (amā́stis)	habuístis	dīxístis
3rd pl.	amāuḗrunt (amāuḗre/amā́runt)	habuḗrunt (habuḗre)	dīxḗrunt (dīxḗre)

	4	3/4
	'I heard', 'I have heard'	*'I captured', 'I have captured'*
1st s.	audī́uī	cḗpī
2nd s.	audīuístī (audiístī/audī́stī)	cēpístī
3rd s.	audī́uit	cḗpit
1st pl.	audī́uimus	cḗpimus
2nd pl.	audīuístis (audī́stis)	cēpístis
3rd pl.	audīuḗrunt (audīuḗre/audiḗrunt/audiḗre)	cēpḗrunt (cēpḗre)

Perfect infinitive active 'to have —ed'

Key: perf. stem + -ISSE

1	2	3
'to have loved'	'to have had'	'to have said'
amāuísse (*or* amásse)	habuísse	dīxísse

4	3/4
'to have heard'	'to have captured'
audīuísse (*or* audísse)	cēpísse

NB. No perfect participle active; perfect imperative only found for *meminī* (see **F1(a)**).

Perfect subjunctive active 'I —ed', 'I have —ed'

Key: perf. stem + -ERIM -ERĪS *etc.*

	1	2	3
1st s.	amāuerim (amárim *etc.*)	habúerim	dīxerim
2nd s.	amāuerīs	habúerīs	dīxerīs
3rd s.	amāuerīt	habúerit	dīxerit
1st pl.	amāuerímus	habuerímus	dīxerímus
2nd pl.	amāuerítis	habuerítis	dīxerítis
3rd pl.	amauerint	habúerint	dīxerint

	4	3/4
1st s.	audīuerim (audíerim *etc.*)	cēperim
2nd s.	audíuerīs	cēperīs
3rd s.	audíuerit	cēperit
1st pl.	audīuerímus	cēperímus
2nd pl.	audíuerítis	cēperítis
3rd pl.	audíuerint	cēperint

A5 Pluperfect active

Pluperfect indicative active 'I had —ed'

Key: perf. stem + -ERAM -ERĀS *etc.*

456

	1	2	3
	'*I had loved*'	'*I had had*'	'*I had said*'
1st s.	amāueram (amāram *etc.*)	habúeram	dīxeram
2nd s.	amāuerās	habúerās	dīxerās
3rd s.	amāuerat	habúerat	dīxerat
1st pl.	amāuerāmus	habuerāmus	dīxerāmus
2nd pl.	amāuerātis	habuerātis	dīxerātis
3rd pl.	amāuerant	habúerant	dīxerant

	4	3/4
	'*I had heard*'	'*I had captured*'
1st s.	audīueram (audíeram *etc.*)	cēperam
2nd s.	audīuerās	cēperās
3rd s.	audīuerat	cēperat
1st pl.	audīuerāmus	cēperāmus
2nd pl.	audīuerātis	cēperātis
3rd pl.	audīuerant	cēperant

NB.   No pluperfect participles, infinitives or imperatives.

Pluperfect subjunctive active 'I had —ed', 'I would have —ed'

Key: perf. stem + -ISSEM -ISSĒS *etc.*

	1	2	3
1st s.	amāuíssem (amāssem *etc.*)	habuíssem	dīxíssem
2nd s.	amāuíssēs	habuíssēs	dīxíssēs
3rd s.	amāuísset	habuísset	dīxísset
1st pl.	amāuissēmus	habuissēmus	dīxissēmus
2nd pl.	amāuissētis	habuissētis	dīxissētis
3rd pl.	amāuíssent	habuíssent	dīxíssent

	4	3/4
1st s.	audīuíssem (audíssem *etc.*)	cēpíssem
2nd s.	audīuíssēs	cēpíssēs
3rd s.	audīuísset	cēpísset
1st pl.	audīuissēmus	cēpissēmus
2nd pl.	audīuissētis	cēpissētis
3rd pl.	audīuíssent	cēpíssent

A6 Future perfect active

Future perfect indicative active 'I shall have —ed'

Key: perf. stem + -ERŌ -ERIS *etc.*

	1 '*I shall have loved*'	*2* '*I shall have had*'	*3* '*I shall have said*'
1st s.	amáuerō (amárō *etc.*)	habúerō	díxerō
2nd s.	amáueris	habúeris	díxeris
3rd s.	amáuerit	habúerit	díxerit
1st pl.	amāuérimus	habuérimus	dīxérimus
2nd pl.	amāuéritis	habuéritis	dīxéritis
3rd pl.	amáuerint	habúerint	díxerint

	4 '*I shall have heard*'	*3/4* '*I shall have captured*'
1st s.	audíuerō (audíerō *etc.*)	céperō
2nd s.	audíueris	céperis
3rd s.	audíuerit	céperit
1st pl.	audīuérimus	cēpérimus
2nd pl.	audīuéritis	cēpéritis
3rd pl.	audíuerint	céperint

NB. No future perfect participles, imperatives, infinitives or subjunctives.

A7 Supine

1 '*to love*'	*2* '*to have*'	*3* '*to say*'	*4* '*to hear*'	*3/4* '*to capture*'
amátum	hábitum	díctum	audítum	cáptum

Notes

1 The stem is identical with that of the perfect participle. The form is identical with acc. s. of 4th declension nouns. It is used in the acc. (-*um*) and abl. (-*ū*).

2 The main uses are:

(i)   To express purpose, after verbs of motion, e.g. *lēgātōs ad Caésarem míttunt rogátum auxílium* 'They send ambassadors to Caesar *to ask for* help' (Caesar).

(ii) To form the 'future infinitive passive'. See below **B2, 118²⁻³**.

(iii) In the ablative with a few adjectives, e.g. *mīrábile díctū* 'wonderful *to relate*'.

B1   Present passive: personal endings *-r -ris -tur -mur -minī -ntur*

Present indicative passive 'I am (being) —ed'

Key: A E I I I

	1 'I am (being) loved'	2 'I am (being) held'	3 'I am (being) said'
1st s.	ámor	hábeor	dícor
2nd s.	amáris (amáre)	habéris (habére)	díceris (dícere)
3rd s.	amátur	habétur	dícitur
1st pl.	amámur	habémur	dícimur
2nd pl.	amáminī	habéminī	dīcíminī
3rd pl.	amántur	habéntur	dīcúntur

	4 'I am (being) heard'	3/4 'I am (being) captured'
1st s.	aúdior	cápior
2nd s.	audíris (audíre)	cáperis (cápere)
3rd s.	audítur	cápitur
1st pl.	audímur	cápimur
2nd pl.	audíminī	capíminī
3rd pl.	audiúntur	capiúntur

Present infinitive passive 'to be —ed'

Key: -ĀRĪ -ĒRĪ -Ī -ĪRĪ -Ī

1 'to be loved'	2 'to be held'	3 'to be said'	4 'to be heard'	3/4 'to be captured'
amárī	habérī	dícī	audírī	cápī

Present imperative passive 'be —ed!'

Key: -RE -MINĪ

	1	2	3	4	3/4
	'be loved!'	'be held!'	'be said!'	'be heard!'	'be captured!'
2nd s.	amā́re	habḗre	dī́cere	audī́re	cápere
2nd pl.	amā́minī	habḗminī	dīcíminī	audī́minī	capíminī

Gerundive 'to be —ed', 'requiring, needing to be —ed', 'must be —ed'

Key: -ND-

1	2	3
'to be loved'	'to be held'	'to be said'
amánd-us a um	habénd-us a um	dīcénd-us a um

4	3/4
'to be heard'	'to be captured'
audiénd-us a um	capiénd-us a um

Pattern of declension
See *lóng-us a um* (**J1(a)**).

Notes
1 The only gerundive forms which verbs have are as above, based on the present stem.
2 Many verbs retain the old form in -*únd*-, e.g. *eúndum*, *oriúndum*, *gerúndus*.

Present subjunctive passive 'I am —ed', 'I may be —ed', 'I would be —ed'

Key: E A

	1	2	3
1st s.	ámer	hábear	dī́car
2nd s.	amḗris (amḗre)	habeā́ris (habeā́re)	dīcā́ris (dīcā́re)
3rd s.	amḗtur	habeā́tur	dīcā́tur
1st pl.	amḗmur	habeā́mur	dīcā́mur
2nd pl.	amḗminī	habeā́minī	dīcā́minī
3rd pl.	améntur	habeántur	dīcántur

	4	3/4
1st s.	aúdiar	cápiar
2nd s.	audiáris (audiáre)	capiáris (capiáre)
3rd s.	audiátur	capiátur
1st pl.	audiámur	capiámur
2nd pl.	audiáminī	capiáminī
3rd pl.	audiántur	capiántur

B2 Future passive

Future indicative passive 'I shall be —ed'

ĀBI ĒBI E IE IE

	1	2	3
	'I shall be loved'	*'I shall be held'*	*'I shall be said'*
1st s.	amábor	habébor	dícar
2nd s.	amáberis (amábere)	habéberis (habébere)	dícéris (dícére)
3rd s.	amábitur	habébitur	dícétur
1st pl.	amábimur	habébimur	dícémur
2nd pl.	amābíminī	habēbíminī	dícéminī
3rd pl.	amābúntur	habēbúntur	dícéntur

	4	3/4
	'I shall be heard'	*'I shall be captured'*
1st s.	aúdiar	cápiar
2nd s.	audiéris (audiére)	capiéris (capiére)
3rd s.	audiétur	capiétur
1st pl.	audiémur	capiémur
2nd pl.	audiéminī	capiéminī
3rd pl.	audiéntur	capiéntur

NB. The future (or 'second') imperative s. is formed as for the active (see above **A2 Note 1**), but with *-r* added at the end, e.g. *amátor* 'be loved'. There is no 2nd person pl. form.

Form traditionally described as 'future infinitive passive': used only in indirect statement (acc. + inf.)

Key: -UM -ĪRĪ

1	2	3
'that there is a movement to love'	'that there is a movement to have'	'that there is a movement to say'
amătum[1] īrī	hábitum[1] īrī	díctum[1] īrī

4	3/4
'that there is a movement to hear'	'that there is a movement to capture'
audĭtum[1] īrī	cáptum[1] īrī

[1] These are fixed forms: see above **A7**.

NB. There are no future passive participles, or future passive subjunctives.

B3 Imperfect passive

Imperfect indicative passive 'I was (being) —ed'

Key: ĀBA ĒBA

	1	2	3
	'I was (being) loved'	'I was (being) held'	'I was (being) said'
1st s.	amăbar	habébar	dīcébar
2nd s.	amābáris (amābáre)	habēbáris (habēbáre)	dīcēbáris (dīcēbáre)
3rd s.	amābátur	habēbátur	dīcēbátur
1st pl.	amābámur	habēbámur	dīcēbámur
2nd pl.	amābáminī	habēbáminī	dīcēbáminī
3rd pl.	amābántur	habēbántur	dīcēbántur

	4	3/4
	'I was (being) heard'	'I was (being) captured'
1st s.	audiébar	capiébar
2nd s.	audiēbáris (audiēbáre)	capiēbáris (capiēbáre)
3rd s.	audiēbátur	capiēbátur
1st pl.	audiēbámur	capiēbámur
2nd pl.	audiēbáminī	capiēbáminī
3rd pl.	audiēbántur	capiēbántur

NB. There are no imperfect passive participles, imperatives or infinitives.

Imperfect subjunctive passive 'I was being —ed', 'I might be —ed', 'I would be —ed'

Key: active infinitive + endings

	1	2	3
1st s.	amā́rer	habḗrer	dī́cerer
2nd s.	amārḗris (amārḗre)	habērḗris (habērḗre)	dīcerḗris (dīcerḗre)
3rd s.	amārḗtur	habērḗtur	dīcerḗtur
1st pl.	amārḗmur	habērḗmur	dīcerḗmur
2nd pl.	amārḗminī	habērḗminī	dīcerḗminī
3rd pl.	amārḗntur	habērḗntur	dīcerḗntur

	4	3/4
1st s.	audī́rer	cáperer
2nd s.	audīrḗris (audīrḗre)	caperḗris (caperḗre)
3rd s.	audīrḗtur	caperḗtur
1st pl.	audīrḗmur	caperḗmur
2nd pl.	audīrḗminī	caperḗminī
3rd pl.	audīrḗntur	caperḗntur

B4 Perfect passive

Perfect indicative passive 'I was —ed', 'I have been —ed'

Key: perfect participle + SUM

	1	2	3
	'I was loved',	*'I was held',*	*'I was said',*
	'I have been loved'	*'I have been held'*	*'I have been said'*
1st s.	amā́t-us a um sum	hábit-us a um sum	díct-us a um sum
2nd s.	amā́t-us a um es	hábit-us a um es	díct-us a um es
3rd s.	amā́t-us a um est	hábit-us a um est	díct-us a um est
1st pl.	amā́t-ī ae a súmus	hábit-ī ae a súmus	díct-ī ae a súmus
2nd pl.	amā́t-ī ae a éstis	hábit-ī ae a éstis	díct-ī ae a éstis
3rd pl.	amā́t-ī ae a sunt	hábit-ī ae a sunt	díct-ī ae a sunt

	4 *'I was heard'*, *'I have been heard'*	3/4 *'I was captured'*, *'I have been captured'*
1st s.	audĭt-us a um sum	cápt-us a um sum
2nd s.	audĭt-us a um es	cápt-us a um es
3rd s.	audĭt-us a um est	cápt-us a um est
1st pl.	audĭt-ī ae a súmus	cápt-ī ae a súmus
2nd pl.	audĭt-ī ae a éstis	cápt-ī ae a éstis
3rd pl.	audĭt-ī ae a sunt	cápt-ī ae a sunt

Perfect participle passive 'having been —ed'

Key: perfect participle ending in -US -A -UM

1 *'having been loved'* amāt-us a um	2 *'having been held'* hábit-us a um	3 *'having been said'* díct-us a um

4 *'having been heard'* audĭt-us a um	3/4 *'having been captured'* cápt-us a um

Pattern of declension
See *lóng-us a um*, **J1(a)**.

Perfect infinitive passive 'to have been —ed'

Key: perfect participle ending in -US -A -UM + ESSE

1 *'to have been loved'* amāt-us a um ésse	2 *'to have been held'* hábit-us a um ésse	3 *'to have been said'* díct-us a um ésse

4 *'to have been heard'* audĭt-us a um ésse	3/4 *'to have been captured'* cápt-us a um ésse

Perfect subjunctive passive 'I was —ed', 'I have been —ed'

Key: perfect participle + SIM

	1	2	3
	1	*2*	*3*
1st s.	amātus sim	hábitus sim	díctus sim
2nd s.	amātus sīs	hábitus sīs	díctus sīs
3rd s.	amātus sit	hábitus sit	díctus sit
1st pl.	amātī símus	hábitī símus	díctī símus
2nd pl.	amātī sítis	hábitī sítis	díctī sítis
3rd pl.	amātī sint	hábitī sint	díctī sint

	4	3/4
	4	*3/4*
1st s.	audítus sim	cáptus sim
2nd s.	audítus sīs	cáptus sīs
3rd s.	audítus sit	cáptus sit
1st pl.	audítī símus	cáptī símus
2nd pl.	audítī sítis	cáptī sítis
3rd pl.	audítī sint	cáptī sint

B5 Pluperfect passive

Pluperfect indicative passive 'I had been —ed'

Key: perfect participle + ERAM

	1	2	3
	1	*2*	*3*
	'I had been loved'	*'I had been held'*	*'I had been said'*
1st s.	amātus éram	hábitus éram	díctus éram
2nd s.	amātus érās	hábitus érās	díctus érās
3rd s.	amātus érat	hábitus érat	díctus érat
1st pl.	amātī erámus	hábitī erámus	díctī erámus
2nd pl.	amātī erátis	hábitī erátis	díctī erátis
3rd pl.	amātī érant	hábitī érant	díctī érant

	4	3/4
	4	*3/4*
	'I had been heard'	*'I had been captured'*
1st s.	audítus éram	cáptus éram
2nd s.	audítus érās	cáptus érās
3rd s.	audítus érat	cáptus érat

465

1st pl.	audítī erámus	cáptī erámus
2nd pl.	audítī erátis	cáptī erátis
3rd pl.	audítī érant	cáptī érant

Pluperfect subjunctive passive 'I had been —ed', 'I would have been —ed'

Key: perfect participle + ESSEM

	1	*2*	*3*
1st s.	amátus éssem	hábitus éssem	díctus éssem
2nd s.	amátus éssēs	hábitus éssēs	díctus éssēs
3rd s.	amátus ésset	hábitus ésset	díctus ésset
1st pl.	amátī essémus	hábitī essémus	díctī essémus
2nd pl.	amátī essétis	hábitī essétis	díctī essétis
3rd pl.	amátī éssent	hábitī éssent	díctī éssent

	4	*3/4*
1st s.	audítus éssem	cáptus éssem
2nd s.	audítus éssēs	cáptus éssēs
3rd s.	audítus ésset	cáptus ésset
1st pl.	audítī essémus	cáptī essémus
2nd pl.	audítī essétis	cáptī essétis
3rd pl.	audítī éssent	cáptī éssent

B6 Future perfect passive

Future perfect indicative passive 'I shall have been —ed'

Key: perfect participle + ERŌ

	1	*2*	*3*
	'I shall have been loved'	*'I shall have been held'*	*'I shall have been said'*
1st s.	amátus érō	hábitus érō	díctus érō
2nd s.	amátus éris	hábitus éris	díctus éris
3rd s.	amátus érit	hábitus érit	díctus érit
1st pl.	amátī érimus	hábitī érimus	díctī érimus
2nd pl.	amátī éritis	hábitī éritis	díctī éritis
3rd pl.	amátī érunt	hábitī érunt	díctī érunt

	4	3/4
	'I shall have been heard'	*'I shall have been captured'*
1st s.	audítus érō	cáptus érō
2nd s.	audítus éris	cáptus éris
3rd s.	audítus érit	cáptus érit
1st pl.	audítī érimus	cáptī érimus
2nd pl.	audítī éritis	cáptī éritis
3rd pl.	audítī érunt	cáptī érunt

C1   Present deponent

Present indicative deponent 'I —', 'I am —ing', 'I do —'

Key: as for passive

	1	2	3
	'I threaten'	*'I promise'*	*'I speak'*
1st s.	mínor	pollíceor	lóquor
2nd s.	minā́ris (minā́re)	pollicḗris (pollicḗre)	lóqueris (lóquere)
3rd s.	minā́tur	pollicḗtur	lóquitur
1st pl.	minā́mur	pollicḗmur	lóquimur
2nd pl.	minā́minī	pollicḗminī	loquíminī
3rd pl.	minántur	pollicéntur	loquúntur

	4	3/4
	'I lie'	*'I advance'*
1st s.	méntior	prōgrédior
2nd s.	mentíris (mentíre)	prōgréderis (prōgrédere)
3rd s.	mentítur	prōgréditur
1st pl.	mentímur	prōgrédimur
2nd pl.	mentíminī	prōgredíminī
3rd pl.	mentiúntur	prōgrediúntur

Present participle deponent '—ing'

1	2	3
'threatening'	*'promising'*	*'speaking'*
mínāns (minánt-)	póllicēns (pollicént-)	lóquēns (loquént-)

4   3/4
'*lying*'   '*advancing*'
méntiēns (mentiént-)   prōgrédiēns (prōgrediént-)

NB. For declension, see **A1**.

Present infinitive deponent 'to —'

1	2	3	4	3/4
'*to threaten*'	'*to promise*'	'*to speak*'	'*to lie*'	'*to advance*'
minā́rī	pollicḗrī	lóquī	mentī́rī	prṓgredī

Present imperative deponent '—!'

	1	2	3	4	3/4
	'*threaten!*'	'*promise!*'	'*speak!*'	'*lie!*'	'*advance!*'
2nd s.	minā́re	pollicḗre	lóquere	mentī́re	prōgrédere
2nd pl.	minā́minī	pollicḗminī	loquíminī	mentī́minī	prōgredíminī

Gerundive 'to be —ed', 'requiring, needing to be —ed', 'must be —ed' (see 160 footnote)

1	2	3
'*to be threatened*'	'*to be promised*'	'*to be spoken*'
minánd-us a um	pollicénd-us a um	loquénd-us a um

4   3/4
'*to be lied*'   '*to be advanced*'
mentiénd-us a um   prōgrediénd-us a um

Notes
1 For declension, see *lóng-us* (**J1(a)**).
2 *órior* 'rise' retains the old gerundive form *oriúndum*.

Gerund '(the act of) —ing'

1	2	3
'*(the act of) threatening*'	'*(the act of) promising*'	'*(the act of) speaking*'
minā́rī, minánd-um ī 2n.	pollicḗrī, pollicénd-um ī 2n.	lóquī, loquénd-um ī 2n.

4	3/4
'(the act of) lying'	*'(the act of) advancing'*
mentírī, mentiénd-um ī 2n.	prógredī, prōgrediénd-um ī 2n.

NB. The infinitive form often acts as a nominative noun; the gerund itself has no nominative.

Present subjunctive deponent 'I —', 'I may —', 'I would —'

	1	*2*	*3*
1st s.	míner	pollícear	lóquar
2nd s.	minéris (minére)	polliceáris (polliceáre)	loquáris (loquáre)
3rd s.	minétur	polliceátur	loquátur
1st pl.	minémur	polliceámur	loquámur
2nd pl.	minéminī	polliceáminī	loquáminī
3rd pl.	minéntur	polliceántur	loquántur

	4	*3/4*
1st s.	méntiar	prōgrédiar
2nd s.	mentiáris (mentiáre)	prōgrediáris (prōgrediáre)
3rd s.	mentiátur	prōgrediátur
1st pl.	mentiámur	prōgrediámur
2nd pl.	mentiáminī	prōgrediáminī
3rd pl.	mentiántur	prōgrediántur

C2   Future deponent

Future indicative deponent 'I shall —', 'I shall be —ing'

	1	*2*	*3*
	'I shall threaten'	*'I shall promise'*	*'I shall speak'*
1st s.	minábor	pollicébor	lóquar
2nd s.	mináberis (minábere)	pollicéberis (pollicébere)	loquéris (loquére)
3rd s.	minábitur	pollicébitur	loquétur
1st pl.	minábimur	pollicébimur	loquémur
2nd pl.	minābíminī	pollicēbíminī	loquéminī
3rd pl.	minābúntur	pollicēbúntur	loquéntur

	4	3/4
	'*I shall lie*'	'*I shall advance*'
1st s.	méntiar (*rarely* mentíbor)	prōgrédiar
2nd s.	mentiéris (mentiére)	prōgrediéris (progrediére)
3rd s.	mentiétur	prōgrediétur
1st pl.	mentiémur	prōgrediémur
2nd pl.	mentiéminī	prōgrediéminī
3rd pl.	mentiéntur	prōgrediéntur

Future participle deponent 'about to —', 'on the point of —ing', 'with a view to —ing'

Key: perfect participle stem + ŪR-US -A -UM

1	2	3
'*about to threaten*'	'*about to promise*'	'*about to speak*'
minātúr-us a um	pollicitúr-us a um	locūtúr-us a um

4	3/4
'*about to lie*'	'*about to advance*'
mentītúr-us a um	prōgressúr-us a um

Future infinitive deponent 'to be about to'

Key: future participle + ESSE

1	2	3
'*to be about to threaten*'	'*to be about to promise*'	'*to be about to speak*'
minātúr-us a um ésse	pollicitúr-us a um ésse	locūtúr-us a um ésse

4	3/4
'*to be about to lie*'	'*to be about to advance*'
mentītúr-us a um ésse	prōgressúr-us a um ésse

Notes

1 For future (or 'second') imperative, see **A2 Note 1**.
2 For 'future' subjunctive, see **A2 Note 2**.

C3 Imperfect deponent

Imperfect indicative deponent 'I was —ing', 'I used to —', 'I began —ing'

	1 *'I was threatening'*	*2* *'I was promising'*	*3* *'I was speaking'*
1st s.	minábar	pollicébar	loquébar
2nd s.	minābáris (minābáre)	pollicēbáris (pollicēbáre)	loquēbáris (loquēbáre)
3rd s.	minābátur	pollicēbátur	loquēbátur
1st pl.	minābámur	pollicēbámur	loquēbámur
2nd pl.	minābáminī	pollicēbáminī	loquēbáminī
3rd pl.	minābántur	pollicēbántur	loquēbántur

	4 *'I was lying'*	*3/4* *'I was advancing'*
1st s.	mentiébar	prōgrediébar
2nd s.	mentiēbáris (mentiēbáre)	prōgrediēbáris (prōgrediēbáre)
3rd s.	mentiēbátur	prōgrediēbátur
1st pl.	mentiēbámur	prōgrediēbámur
2nd pl.	mentiēbáminī	prōgrediēbáminī
3rd pl.	mentiēbántur	prōgrediēbántur

NB. No participles, infinitives or imperatives.

Imperfect subjunctive deponent 'I was —ing', 'I might —', 'I would —'

	1	*2*	*3*
1st s.	minárer	pollicérer	lóquerer
2nd s.	mināréris (minārére)	pollicēréris (pollicērére)	loqueréris (loquerére)
3rd s.	minārétur	pollicērétur	loquerétur
1st pl.	minārémur	pollicērémur	loquerémur
2nd pl.	mināréminī	pollicēréminī	loqueréminī
3rd pl.	mināréntur	pollicēréntur	loqueréntur

	4	*3/4*
1st s.	mentírer	prōgréderer
2nd s.	mentīréris (mentīrére)	prōgrederéris (prōgrederére)
3rd s.	mentīrétur	prōgrederétur
1st pl.	mentīrémur	prōgrederémur
2nd pl.	mentīréminī	prōgrederéminī
3rd pl.	mentīréntur	prōgrederéntur

C4 Perfect deponent

Perfect indicative deponent: 'I —ed', 'I have —ed'

	1 '*I threatened*', '*I have threatened*'	*2* '*I promised*', '*I have promised*'	*3* '*I spoke*', '*I have spoken*'
1st s.	mināt-us a um sum	pollícit-us a um sum	locūt-us a um sum
2nd s.	mināt-us a um es	pollícit-us a um es	locūt-us a um es
3rd s.	mināt-us a um est	pollícit-us a um est	locūt-us a um est
1st pl.	mināt-ī ae a súmus	pollícit-ī ae a súmus	locūt-ī ae a súmus
2nd pl.	mināt-ī ae a éstis	pollícit-ī ae a éstis	locūt-ī ae a éstis
3rd pl.	mināt-ī ae a sunt	pollícit-ī ae a sunt	locūt-ī ae a sunt

	4 '*I lied*', '*I have lied*'	*3/4* '*I advanced*', '*I have advanced*'
1st s.	mentīt-us a um sum	prōgréss-us a um sum
2nd s.	mentīt-us a um es	prōgréss-us a um es
3rd s.	mentīt-us a um est	prōgréss-us a um est
1st pl.	mentīt-ī ae a súmus	prōgréss-ī ae a súmus
2nd pl.	mentīt-ī ae a éstis	prōgréss-ī ae a éstis
3rd pl.	mentīt-ī ae a sunt	prōgréss-ī ae a sunt

Perfect participle deponent 'having —ed'

Key: perfect participle stem + -US -A -UM

1 '*having threatened*' mināt-us a um	*2* '*having promised*' pollícit-us a um	*3* '*having spoken*' locūt-us a um

4 '*having lied*' mentīt-us a um	*3/4* '*having advanced*' prōgréss-us a um

Notes

1 The perfect participle of many deponents is used to mean '—ing' (i.e. as a present participle): e.g. *rátus* 'thinking', *uéritus* 'fearing', *arbitrātus* 'thinking' etc.

472

2 Many deponents have a *passive* as well as an active meaning in the perfect participle: e.g. *pollícitus* 'having promised' or 'having *been* promised'.

Perfect infinitive deponent 'to have —ed'

Key: perfect participle + ESSE

1	2	3
'to have threatened'	*'to have promised'*	*'to have spoken'*
minãt-us a um ésse	pollícit-us a um ésse	locũt-us a um ésse

4	3/4
'to have lied'	*'to have advanced'*
mentĩt-us a um ésse	prōgréss-us a um ésse

NB.   There is no perfect imperative.

Perfect subjunctive deponent 'I —ed', 'I have —ed'

	1	2	3
1st s.	minãtus sim	pollícitus sim	locũtus sim
2nd s.	minãtus sĩs	pollícitus sĩs	locũtus sĩs
3rd s.	minãtus sit	pollícitus sit	locũtus sit
1st pl.	minãtī sĩmus	pollícitī sĩmus	locũtī sĩmus
2nd pl.	minãtī sĩtis	pollícitī sĩtis	locũtī sĩtis
3rd pl.	minãtī sint	pollícitī sint	locũtī sint

	4	3/4
1st s.	mentĩtus sim	prōgréssus sim
2nd s.	mentĩtus sĩs	prōgréssus sĩs
3rd s.	mentĩtus sit	prōgréssus sit
1st pl.	mentĩtī sĩmus	prōgréssī sĩmus
2nd pl.	mentĩtī sĩtis	prōgréssī sĩtis
3rd pl.	mentĩtī sint	prōgréssī sint

C5 Pluperfect deponent

Pluperfect indicative deponent 'I had —ed'

	1	2	3
1st s.	minātus éram	pollícitus éram	locūtus éram
2nd s.	minātus érās	pollícitus érās	locūtus érās
3rd s.	minātus érat	pollícitus érat	locūtus érat
1st pl.	minātī erāmus	pollícitī erāmus	locūtī erāmus
2nd pl.	minātī erātis	pollícitī erātis	locūtī erātis
3rd pl.	minātī érant	pollícitī érant	locūtī érant

	4	3/4
	'*I had lied*'	'*I had advanced*'
1st s.	mentītus éram	prōgréssus éram
2nd s.	mentītus érās	prōgréssus érās
3rd s.	mentītus érat	prōgréssus érat
1st pl.	mentītī erāmus	prōgréssī erāmus
2nd pl.	mentītī erātis	prōgréssī erātis
3rd pl.	mentītī érant	prōgréssī érant

NB.   There is no pluperfect participle, infinitive or imperative.

Pluperfect subjunctive deponent 'I had —ed', 'I would have —ed'

	1	2	3
1st s.	minātus éssem	pollícitus éssem	locūtus éssem
2nd s.	minātus éssēs	pollícitus éssēs	locūtus éssēs
3rd s.	minātus ésset	pollícitus ésset	locūtus ésset
1st pl.	minātī essēmus	pollícitī essēmus	locūtī essēmus
2nd pl.	minātī essētis	pollícitī essētis	locūtī essētis
3rd pl.	minātī éssent	pollícitī éssent	locūtī éssent

	4	3/4
1st s.	mentītus éssem	prōgréssus éssem
2nd s.	mentītus éssēs	prōgréssus éssēs
3rd s.	mentītus ésset	prōgréssus ésset
1st pl.	mentītī essēmus	prōgréssī essēmus
2nd pl.	mentītī essētis	prōgréssī essētis
3rd pl.	mentītī éssent	prōgréssī éssent

C6 Future perfect deponent

Future perfect indicative deponent 'I shall have —ed'

	1 '*I shall have threatened*'	*2* '*I shall have promised*'	*3* '*I shall have spoken*'
1st s.	minātus érō	pollícitus érō	locū́tus érō
2nd s.	minātus éris	pollícitus éris	locū́tus éris
3rd s.	minātus érit	pollícitus érit	locū́tus érit
1st pl.	minā́tī érimus	pollícitī érimus	locū́tī érimus
2nd pl.	minā́tī éritis	pollícitī éritis	locū́tī éritis
3rd pl.	minā́tī érunt	pollícitī érunt	locū́tī érunt

	4 '*I shall have lied*'	*3/4* '*I shall have advanced*'
1st s.	mentī́tus érō	prōgréssus érō
2nd s.	mentī́tus éris	prōgréssus éris
3rd s.	mentī́tus érit	prōgréssus érit
1st pl.	mentī́tī érimus	prōgréssī érimus
2nd pl.	mentī́tī éritis	prōgréssī éritis
3rd pl.	mentī́tī érunt	prōgréssī érunt

Notes

1 There is no future perfect participle, infinitive, imperative or subjunctive.
2 For supine forms and meanings see above, **A7**.

D   Semi-deponents

Some verbs in Latin have present, future and imperfect tenses in ACTIVE forms, but perfect, pluperfect and future perfect tenses in DEPONENT forms. Meaning is NOT affected by this change. E.g.

aúdeō 2 aús-us '*I dare*'		*fíō fíerī fáctus* '*I become*', '*I am made*', '*I am done*'	
aúdeō	'I dare'	fíō	'I become'
audḗbō	'I shall dare'	fíam	'I shall become'
audḗbam	'I was daring'	fíēbam	'I was becoming'
aúsus sum	'I have dared'	fáctus sum	'I became'
aúsus éram	'I had dared'	fáctus éram	'I had become'
aúsus érō	'I shall have dared'	fáctus érō	'I shall have become'

Note the irregular conjugation of *fíō*:

1st s.   fíō
2nd s.   fís
3rd s.   fit
1st pl.   —[1]
2nd pl.   —[1]
3rd pl.   fíunt

[1] *fímus* and *fítis* are not found.

Notes

1 Semi-deponents have past participles just like full deponents, e.g. *aúsus* 'having dared', *fáctus* 'having been made', 'having become'.

2 Similar verbs are *gaúdeō* 2 *gāuísus* 'I rejoice', *sóleō* 2 *sólitus* 'I am accustomed; *fídō* 3 *físus* 'I trust'.

3 *aúdeō* has a regular subjunctive *aúdeam -ās* etc. and a form *aúsim* used only as a potential, meaning 'I would dare'. Cf. *uélim* 'I would like'. See **153.2**.

E1   Irregular verbs: *sum*

---

sum ésse futúr-us 'I am'

	Present	Future	Imperfect
	Indicative 'I am'	Indicative 'I shall be'	Indicative 'I was'
1st s.	sum	érō	éram
2nd s.	es	éris	érās
3rd s.	est	érit	érat
1st pl.	súmus	érimus	erámus
2nd pl.	éstis	éritis	erátis
3rd pl.	sunt	érunt	érant

	Infinitive 'to be'	Infinitive 'to be about to be'
	ésse	futúr-us a um esse *or* fóre

Participle 'about to be'
futúr-us a um

Imperative 'be!'	Imperative	
2nd s. es	*2nd/3rd s.*	éstō 'be!'
2nd pl. éste		'let him be!'
	2nd pl.	estóte 'be!'
	3rd pl.	súntō 'let them be!'

	Subjunctive		Subjunctive
1st s.	sim		éssem (*sometimes* fórem fórēs *etc.*)
2nd s.	sīs		éssēs
3rd s.	sit		ésset
1st pl.	sîmus		essêmus
2nd pl.	sîtis		essêtis
3rd pl.	sint		éssent

NB.   All perfect forms regularly derived from *fú-ī*.

E2   Irregular verbs: *ferō*

Active

férō férre túlī lātus 'I bear', 'I carry', 'I endure', 'I lead'

	Present	Future	Imperfect
	Indicative 'I carry'	Indicative 'I shall carry'	Indicative 'I was carrying'
1st s.	férō	féram	ferêbam
2nd s.	fers	férēs	ferêbās
3rd s.	fert	féret	ferêbat
1st pl.	férimus	ferêmus	ferēbâmus
2nd pl.	fértis	ferētis	ferēbâtis
3rd pl.	férunt	férent	ferêbant

Infinitive 'to carry'
férre

Imperative 'carry!'
2nd s. fer
2nd pl. férte

Participle 'carrying'
férēns (ferént-)

	Subjunctive		Subjunctive
1st s.	féram		férrem
2nd s.	férās		férrēs
3rd s.	férat		férret
1st pl.	ferâmus		ferrêmus
2nd pl.	ferâtis		ferrētis
3rd pl.	férant		férrent

Passive

	Present Indicative 'I am being carried'	Future Indicative 'I shall be carried'	Imperfect Indicative 'I was (being) carried'
1st s.	féror	férar	ferḗbar
2nd s.	férris	ferḗris (ferḗre)	ferēbā́ris (ferēbā́re)
3rd s.	fértur	ferḗtur	ferēbā́tur
1st pl.	férimur	ferḗmur	ferēbā́mur
2nd pl.	feríminī	ferḗminī	ferēbā́minī
3rd pl.	ferúntur	feréntur	ferēbántur

Infinitive
'to be carried'
férrī

Imperative
'be carried!'
2nd s. férre
2nd pl. feríminī

	Subjunctive	Subjunctive
1st s.	férar	férrer
2nd s.	ferā́ris (ferā́re)	ferrḗris (ferrḗre)
3rd s.	ferā́tur	ferrḗtur
1st pl.	ferā́mur	ferrḗmur
2nd pl.	ferā́minī	ferrḗminī
3rd pl.	ferántur	ferréntur

NB. All perfect forms are regularly derived from *túl-ī lā́t-us*.

E3 Irregular verbs: *possum*

Póssum pósse pótuī 'I can', 'I am able'

	Present Indicative 'I can'	Future Indicative 'I shall be able'	Imperfect Indicative 'I was able'
1st s.	póssum	póterō	póteram
2nd s.	pótes	póteris	póterās
3rd s.	pótest	póterit	póterat
1st pl.	póssumus	potérimus	poterā́mus
2nd pl.	potéstis	potéritis	poterā́tis
3rd pl.	póssunt	póterunt	póterant

478

Infinitive 'to be able'

pósse

	Subjunctive		Subjunctive
1st s.	póssim		póssem
2nd s.	póssīs		póssēs
3rd s.	póssit		pósset
1st pl.	possímus		possḗmus
2nd pl.	possítis		possḗtis
3rd pl.	póssint		póssent

NB.   All perfects regularly derived from *pótu-ī*.

E4   Irregular verbs: *eō*

Active

	Present	Future	Imperfect
	Indicative 'I go'	Indicative 'I shall go'	Indicative 'I was going'
1st s.	éō	íbō	íbam
2nd s.	īs	íbis	íbās
3rd s.	it	íbit	íbat
1st pl.	ímus	íbimus	ībámus
2nd pl.	ítis	íbitis	ībátis
3rd pl.	éunt	íbunt	íbant

Infinitive 'to go'   *Infinitive 'to be about to go'*

íre   itúr-us a um ésse

Imperative 'go!'

2nd s. ī
2nd pl. íte

Participle 'going'   *Participle 'about to go'*

íēns (eúnt-is)   itúr-us a um

Gerund 'to go'
'(the act of) going'

íre, eúnd-um ī 2n.

	Subjunctive		Subjunctive
1st s.	éam		írem
2nd s.	éās		írēs
3rd s.	éat		íret
1st pl.	eámus		īrémus
2nd pl.	eátis		īrétis
3rd pl.	éant		írent

Passive (used in compounds)

	Present
	Indicative 'I am approached'
1st s.	ádeor
2nd s.	adíris (adíre)
3rd s.	adítur
1st pl.	adímur
2nd pl.	adíminī
3rd pl.	adeúntur

NB. All other parts are regularly formed from *íu-ī*/*í-ī ít-us*.

E5 Irregular verbs: *uolō, nōlō, mālō*

uólō uélle uóluī 'I wish'
nōlō nōlle nōluī 'I am unwilling', 'I refuse'
mālō mālle māluī 'I prefer'

These are formed regularly as third conjugation verbs except in the following forms.

	Present	Present	Present
	Indicative 'I wish'	Indicative 'I refuse'	Indicative 'I prefer'
1st s.	uólō	nōlō	mālō
2nd s.	uīs	nōn uīs	māuīs
3rd s.	uult	nōn uult	māuult
1st pl.	uólumus	nōlumus	mālumus
2nd pl.	uúltis	nōn uúltis	māuúltis
3rd pl.	uólunt	nōlunt	mālunt
	Infinitive 'to wish'	Infinitive 'to refuse'	Infinitive 'to prefer'
	uélle	nōlle	mālle

480

Imperative '*do not (wish)!*'
2nd s. nōlī
2nd pl. nōlīte

	Present subjunctive	Present subjunctive	Present subjunctive
1st s.	uélim	nōlim	mālim
2nd s.	uélīs	nōlīs	mālīs
3rd s.	uélit	nōlit	mālit
1st pl.	uelīmus	nōlīmus	mālīmus
2nd pl.	uelītis	nōlītis	mālītis
3rd pl.	uélint	nōlint	mālint

	Imperfect subjunctive	Imperfect subjunctive	Imperfect subjunctive
1st s.	uéllem	nōllem	māllem
2nd s.	uéllēs *etc.*	nōllēs *etc.*	māllēs *etc.*

Notes

1 *-se* was the original infinitive ending (cf. *és-se*). Since *s* becomes *r* in between vowels (cf. *ónus*, **H3(d)Note**), *amāse* becomes *amāre*. When attached to a consonant stem, *s* becomes assimilated to it, e.g. *uel-se→uélle*; *nōl-se→nōlle*.

2 *uólō* and *mālō* have no imperative. But the original imperative of *uólō*, *uel*, became the conjunction meaning 'or'.

F1   Defective verbs

These verbs lack certain forms.

(a) *coepī, meminī, ōdī*

cóepī 'I have begun' (generally), *méminī* 'I remember' and *ōdī* 'I hate' (always) have only perfect-stem *forms*. Note that *meminī* and *ōdī* are present in meaning.

	Indicative	
Perfect	cóepī 'I began'	méminī 'I remember'
Future perfect	cóeperō 'I shall have begun'	memínerō 'I shall remember'
Pluperfect	cóeperam 'I had begun'	memíneram 'I remembered'

481

Perfect	ṓdī 'I hate'	
Future perfect	ṓderō 'I shall hate'	
Pluperfect	ṓderam 'I hated'	

	Infinitive, imperative, participles	
Perfect infinitive	coepísse 'to have begun'	meminísse 'to remember'
Future infinitive	coeptúr-us a um esse 'to be about to begin'	*none*
Imperative	*none*	2nd s. meméntō ⎫ 'remember!' 2nd pl. mementṓte ⎭
Perfect participle	coépt-us a um 'having begun', 'having been begun'	*none*
Future participle	coeptúr-us a um 'about to begin'	*none*

Perfect infinitive	ōdísse 'to hate'
Future infinitive	ōsúr-us a um esse 'to be about to hate'
Imperative	*none*
Perfect participle	ṓs-us a um 'hating'
Future participle	ōsúr-us a um 'about to hate'

	Subjunctive		
Perfect	coéperim	memínerim	ṓderim
Pluperfect	coepíssem	meminíssem	ōdíssem

NB. *nṓscō* 'I get to know' has a perfect form *nōuī*, meaning 'I have got to know' i.e. 'I know'. Thus *nōuerō* (often *nṓrō*) 'I shall know', *nōueram* (often *nṓram*) 'I knew', *nōuísse* (often *nṓsse*) 'to know'.

(b) aiṓ

	Present indicative 'I say'	Imperfect indicative 'I said', 'I was saying'
1st s.	áiō	aiḗbam
2nd s.	áis	aiḗbās *etc.*
3rd s.	áit	
1st pl.	—	
2nd pl.	—	
3rd pl.	áiunt	

(c) *inquam* 'I say'

	Present indicative 'I say'	Future indicative 'I will say'	Imperfect indicative 'I was saying', 'I said'
1st s.	ínquam	—	—
2nd s.	ínquis	ínquiēs	—
3rd s.	ínquit	ínquiet	inquiēbat
1st pl.	ínquimus	—	—
2nd pl.	ínquitis	—	—
3rd pl.	ínquiunt	—	—

NB.   *ínquam* is used only to introduce direct speech.

F2   Impersonal verbs

These verbs have only the third person singular in each tense, an infinitive and a gerund:

>   *opórtet* 'it is right for (the *accusative*) to (*infinitive*)'
>   *décet* 'it is fitting for (the *accusative*) to (*infinitive*)'
>   *dédecet* 'it is unseemly for (the *accusative*) to (*infinitive*)'
>   *míseret* 'it moves (the *accusative*) to pity for/at (the *genitive*)', 'x (acc.) is sorry for y (gen.)'
>   *paénitet* 'it repents (the *accusative*) of (the *genitive*)', 'x (acc.) regrets y (gen.)'
>   *píget* 'it vexes (the *accusative*) at (the *genitive*)', 'x (acc.) is sick of y (gen.)'
>   *púdet* 'it moves (the *accusative*) to shame at (the *genitive*)', 'x (acc.) feels shame at y (gen.)'
>   *taédet* 'it wearies (the *accusative*) at (the *genitive*)', 'x (acc.) is tired of y (gen.)'
>   *líbet* 'it is agreeable to (the *dative*) to (*infinitive*)', 'x (dat.) chooses to y (infin.)'
>   *lícet* 'it is permitted to (the *dative*) to (*infinitive*)' (also with *ut* + subj.)
>   *plácet* 'it is pleasing to (the *dative*) to (*infinitive*)', 'x (dat.) decides to y (infin.)'

Note the principal parts: they are all regular 2nd conjugation, e.g. *opórtet oportēre opórtuit. líbet, lícet* and *plácet* are also commonly used in the passive perfect, *líbitum est* 'it pleased', *lícitum est* 'it was allowed', *plácitum est* 'it was decided'.

The following impersonal verbs are followed by *ut* + subjunctive or accusative and infinitive constructions:

> *áccidit* 'it happens (that)' (*ut* + subj.)
> *appáret* 'it is evident (that)' (*ut* + subj. or acc. + inf.)
> *cōnstat* 'it is agreed (that)' (acc. + inf.)
> *rēfert*
> *interest* } 'it is important (that)' (acc. + inf. or *ut* + subj.)

NB. 'It is of importance to me, you etc.' *méā, túā, súā, nóstrā, uéstrā rēfert* or *interest*. Both *rēfert* and *interest* take a genitive, e.g. *interest ómnium* 'it is in the interests of all' (Cicero).

Verbs which do not control an object in the accusative cannot be turned into the passive directly, and have to adopt an impersonal third person singular form, e.g.

> *ítur* lit. 'it is being gone', i.e. 'people are going'
> *uéntum est* lit. 'it has been come', i.e. 'there has been an arrival', 'people came'
> *míhi nōn crēditur* lit. 'it is not being believed to me', i.e. 'credence is not being given to me'
> *éīs parcēbátur* lit. 'it was being spared to them', i.e. 'they were being spared', 'clemency was being extended to them'

G Principal parts of irregular verbs

This list contains the principal parts of all irregular verbs met in the course together with a few important additions. Verbs are listed without their prefixes (e.g. for *inuéniō* see under *uéniō*). There are two exceptions:

(a) Where a verb is normally found only with a prefix, e.g. *cōnflígō*.

(b) Where a verb has been met in the course only with a prefix.

The Total Learning Vocabulary (p. 557) contains the principal parts of all compound irregular verbs learned. Note that where a verb has no perfect participle, the future participle appears where that exists.

> *abíciō* see *iáciō*
> *accúmbō* 3 *accúbuī accúbitum* I lie at table
> *adipíscor* 3 dep. *adéptus* I get, gain, acquire

adiúngō see *iúngō*
ádiuuō see *iúuō*
ágō 3 *égī áctus* (compounds *-igō* 3 *-égī -áctus*) I do, act; drive, lead,
   direct; spend, pass; discuss
áiō (no inf., perf. or perf. part.) I say
álō 3 *áluī áltus* I feed, nourish, rear; support, strengthen
apériō 4 *apéruī apértus* I open; reveal
arcéssō 3 *arcessíuī arcessítus* I summon
árdeō 2 *ársī ársúrus* I burn; am in love
árguō 3 *árguī argútus* I charge; make clear, prove
aúdeō 2 semi-dep. *aúsus* I dare
aúferō auférre ábstulī ablátus I take away
aúgeō 2 *aúxī aúctus* I increase
bíbō 3 *bíbī* — (*pótus* used as perf. part; *pótúrus* as fut. part.) I drink
cádō 3 *cécidī cásum* (compounds *-cidō* 3 *-cidī -cásus*) I fall; die
caédō 3 *cecídī caésus* (compounds *-cídō* 3 *-cídī -císus*) I cut (down);
   flog, beat; kill
cánō 3 *cécinī* — (compounds *-cinō*) I sing; play
cápiō 3/4 *cépī cáptus* (compounds *-cípiō* 3/4 *-cépī -céptus*) I take,
   capture
cárpō 3 *cárpsī cárptus* (compounds *-cérpō* 3 *-cérpsī -cérptus*) I pluck
cáueō 2 *cáuī caútus* I am wary
cédō 3 *céssī céssum* I yield; go
cérnō 3 *créuī crétus* I decide; see
cíngō 3 *cínxī cínctus* I gird; surround
circumsédeō see *sédeō*
claúdō 3 *claúsī claúsus* (compounds *-clúdō* 3 *-clúsī -clúsus*) I shut
cólō 3 *cóluī cúltus* I worship; cultivate, till; inhabit
coépī coepísse coéptus I have begun
compléctor 3 dep. *compléxus* I embrace
cómpleō 2 *compléuī complétus* I fill up; accomplish
comprehéndō see *prehéndō*
concútiō 3/4 *concússī concússus* (see *quátiō*) I shake violently;
   disturb, alarm
cōnfíteor see *fáteor*
cōnflígō 3 *cōnflíxī cōnflíctus* I fight
cōnfódiō see *fódiō*
coníciō see *iáciō*
coniúngō see *iúngō*
cōnsídō 3 *cōnsédī* — I settle down; encamp
cōnsístō 3 *cónstitī* — (see *sistō*) I stop, stand my ground

cōnspíciō 3/4 *cōnspéxī cōnspéctus* I catch sight of; observe, gaze on
cōnsulō 3 *cōnsúluī cōnsúltus* I consult
cóquō 3 *cóxī cóctus* I cook
crēdō 3 *crēdidī crēditum* I believe (in); entrust
crépō 1 *crépuī crépitus* I rattle
crēscō 3 *crēuī crētum* (= sprung from) I grow (intrans.)
cúbō 3 *cúbuī cúbitum* I lie; sleep; recline at table
cúpiō 3/4 *cupíuī cupítus* I desire, yearn for; want desperately
cúrrō 3 *cucúrrī cúrsum* (compounds often have perf. *-cúrrī*) I run
dēféndō 3 *dēféndī dēfēnsus* I defend
dēfúngor see *fúngor*
dēleō 2 *dēlēuī dēlētus* I destroy
dēprehéndō see *prehéndō*
dēscéndō see *scándō*
dēserō see *sérō*
dēspuō see *spúō*
dícō 3 *díxī díctus* I speak, say
diffídō see *fídō*
díscō 3 *dídicī* — I learn
díuidō 3 *díuīsī díuīsus* I divide
dō 1 *dédī dátus* (compounds *-dō* 3 *-didī -ditus*) I give
dóceō 2 *dócuī dóctus* I teach
dúcō 3 *dúxī dúctus* I lead; think, consider
édō *ésse édī ésus* (3rd s. pres. *ēst*) I eat
ēíciō see *iáciō*
émō 3 *émī émptus* (compounds *-imō* 3 *-émī -émptus*) I buy
éō íre íī ítum I go/come
expéllō see *péllō*
exstínguō 3 *exstínxī exstínctus* I extinguish
fáciō 3/4 *fēcī fáctus* (most compounds *-fíciō* 3/4 *-fēcī -féctus*) I make; do
fállō 3 *feféllī fálsus* I deceive
fáteor 2 dep. *fássus* (compounds *-fíteor* 2 dep. *-féssus*) I acknowledge
fáueō 2 *fáuī faútum* I am favourable to
fériō 4 (*percússī percússus*) I strike; beat; kill
férō férre túlī lātus I bear; lead
férueō 2 *féruī* (or *férbuī*) — I boil
fídō 3 semi-dep. *físus* I trust
fígō 3 *fíxī fíxus* I fix

fīō fierī fáctus (semi-dep.) I become; am done, am made
fíndō 3 *fídī físsus* I cleave, split
fíngō 3 *fínxī fíctus* I make up, fabricate
fléctō 3 *fléxi fléxus* I bend
fléō 2 *fléuī flétum* I weep
flúō 3 *flúxī* — I flow
fódiō 3/4 *fódī fóssus* I dig
frángō 3 *frḗgī fráctus* (compounds *-fríngō* 3 *-frḗgī -fráctus*) I break
frúor 3 dep. *frúctus* I enjoy
fúgiō 3/4 *fúgī fugitū́rus* I escape, run off, flee
fúlgeō 2 *fúlsī* — I shine
fúndō 3 *fū́dī fū́sus* I pour; rout
fúngor 3 dep. *fúnctus* I perform, discharge
gaúdeō 2 semi-dep. *gauī́sus* I am glad, rejoice
gérō 3 *géssī géstus* I do, conduct
gígnō 3 *génuī génitus* I beget, produce
grádior 3/4 dep. *gréssus* (compounds *-grédior* 3/4 *-gréssus*) I step, walk, go
haéreō 2 *haésī haésum* I stick
haúriō 4 *haúsī haústus* I drain, draw
iáciō 3/4 *iḗcī iáctus* (compounds *-íciō* 3/4 *-iḗcī -iéctus*) I throw
incéndō 3 *incéndī incénsus* I set fire to; burn
indúlgeō 2 *indúlsī* — I yield, give myself up to
índuō 3 *índuī indū́tus* I put on
ínquam no inf. *ínquiī* — I say
īnstituō see *státuō*
īnstruō see *strúō*
inuádō see *uádō*
īráscor 3 dep. *īrā́tus* I grow angry
irrídeō see *rídeō*
iúbeō 2 *iússī iússus* I order, command
iúngō 3 *iúnxī iúnctus* I yoke; join
iúuō 1 *iū́uī iū́tus* I help; delight, please
lā́bor 3 dep. *lā́psus* I slip, glide, fall down; make a mistake
lacéssō 3 *lacessíuī lacessī́tus* I provoke
laédō 3 *laésī laésus* (compounds *-lī́dō* 3 *-lī́sī -lī́sus*) I harm
láuō 1 *lā́uī lauā́tus/laútus/lótus* I wash
légō 3 *lḗgī léctus* (compounds *-ligō* 3 *-lḗgī -léctus*) I read; choose
líbet 2 *líbuit* or *líbitum est* it pleases
lícet 3 *lícuit* or *lícitum est* it is permitted

lóquor 3 dep. *locū́tus* I speak, say
lū́dō 3 *lū́sī lū́sum* I play
mā́lō mā́lle mā́luī — I prefer
mā́neō 2 *mā́nsī mā́nsum* I remain, wait
mémini meminísse (perfect form) I remember
métuō 3 *métuī metū́tus* I fear
mínuō 3 *mínuī minū́tus* I lessen
mísceō 2 *míscuī míxtus* or *místus* I mix
míttō 3 *mī́sī míssus* I send; throw
mórdeō 2 *momórdī mórsus* I bite
mórior 3/4 dep. *mórtuus* I die, am dying
móueō 2 *mó̆uī mó̆tus* I move; remove; cause, begin
nancī́scor 3 dep. *náctus/nánctus* I gain
nā́scor 3 dep. *nā́tus* I am born
néctō 3 *néxī néxus* I link together
néqueō see *quéō*
nī́tor 3 dep. *nī́xus/nī́sus* I lean on; strive, exert myself
nṓlō nṓlle nṓluī — I refuse, am unwilling
nṓscō 3 *nṓuī nṓtus* (compounds: some have perf. part. *-nitus*, e.g.
  cógnitus from *cognṓscō*) I get to know (*perfect tenses* = I know
  etc.)
nū́bō 3 *nū́psī nū́ptus* I marry (of a bride; + dat. of man)
oblīuī́scor 3 dep. *oblī́tus* I forget
ṓdī ōdísse ṓsus (perfect participle = 'hating') I hate
offéndō 3 *offéndī offḗnsus* I meet with; offend
órior 4 dep. *órtus* (note pres. *órĕris*, *órĭtur*, *órĭmur*; fut. part.
  oritū́rus; gerundive *oriúndum*; compound *adórior* has 4th
  conjugation present) I rise; spring from, originate
pacī́scor 3 dep. *páctus* I make an agreement
pándō 3 *pándī pássus* I spread out, extend; throw open, disclose
párcō 3 *pepércī* (or *pársī*) *parsū́rus* (compounds *-pércō* 3 *-pérsī*) I
  spare
páriō 3/4 *péperī pártus* (fut. part. *paritū́rus*; compounds *-périō* 4
  -perī -pértus) I bring forth, bear, produce; obtain, acquire
pátior 3/4 dep. *pássus* (compounds *-pétior* 3/4 dep. *-péssus*) I
  endure, suffer; allow
péllo 3 *pépulī púlsus* (compounds *-péllō* 3 *-pulī -púlsus*) I push,
  drive back
péndeō 2 *pepéndī* — (compounds: perf. *-péndī*) I hang (intrans.)
percellō 3 *pérculī percúlsus* I strike down; unnerve, scare

pérgō 3 *perréxī perréctum* (see *régō*) I go on, go ahead, continue
pétō 3 *petíuī petītus* I beg; seek; proposition, court; attack, make for; stand for (public office)
píget 2 *píguit* or *pígitum est* it vexes
píngō 3 *pīnxī píctus* I paint
plaúdō 3 *plaúsī plaúsus* (compounds sometimes *-plódō* 3 *-plósī -plósus*) I clap
pónō 3 *pósuī pósitus* I place, position, put; lay aside
póscō 3 *popóscī* — I demand
possídeō see *sédeō*
póssum pósse pótuī —I am able, can; am powerful, have power
pótō 1 *pōtáuī pótus* ('having drunk' – see *bíbō*) I drink
prehéndō 3 *prehéndī prehénsus* I lay hold of
prémō 3 *préssī préssus* (compounds *-primō* 3 *-préssī -préssus*) I press; oppress
procúmbō 3 *procúbuī procúbitum* I collapse
proficíscor 3 dep. *proféctus* I set out
prōspíciō 3/4 *prōspéxī prōspéctus* I look out (on); foresee
púdet 2 *púduit* or *púditum est* it shames
quaérō 3 *quaesíuī quaesítus* (compounds *-quírō* 3 *-quīsíuī -quīsítus*) I seek, look for; ask
quátiō 3/4 — *quássus* (compounds *-cútiō* 3/4 *-cússī -cússus*) I shake (trans.)
quéō quíre quíuī quítus I am able
quéror 3 dep. *quéstus* I complain
quiéscō 3 *quiéuī quiétus* I rest
rádō 3 *rásī rásus* I scrape, shave
rápiō 3/4 *rápuī ráptus* (compounds *-rípiō* 3/4 *-rípuī -réptus*) I snatch, seize, carry away, plunder
rédimō see *émō*
régō 3 *réxī réctus* (compounds *-rigō* 3 *-réxī -réctus*: except *pérgō*, *súrgō*, q.v.) I keep straight, rule
relínquō 3 *relíquī relíctus* I leave, abandon
réor 2 dep. *rátus* I think, believe, suppose
répō 3 *répsī* — I creep
repéllō see *péllō*
requiéscō see *quiéscō*
resístō 3 *réstitī* — (see *sístō*) I resist
respíciō 3/4 *respéxī respéctus* I look round (back) at, turn my gaze upon; reflect upon; care for

respóndeō 2 *respóndī respōnsum* I reply
rétrahō see *tráhō*
rídeō 2 *rīsī rīsus* I smile, laugh
rúmpō 3 *rūpī rúptus* I break
rúō 3 *rúī rūtus* (fut. part. *ruitūrus*: compounds have perf. part.
   -rŭtus) I rush; fall
scándō 3 (compounds *-scéndō* 3 *-scéndī -scēnsus*) I climb
   climb
scíndō 3 *scídī scíssus* I tear, cut
scrībō 3 *scrípsī scríptus* I write
sécō 1 *sécuī séctus* I cut
sédeō 2 *sēdī séssum* (some compounds *-sídeō* 2 *-sēdī -séssus*) I sit
séntiō 4 *sēnsī sēnsus* I feel; understand; perceive, realise
sepéliō 4 *sepelíuī sepúltus* I bury
séquor 3 dep. *secūtus* I follow
sérō 3 —— —— (compounds *-serō* 3 *-séruī -sértus*) I put in rows
sídō 3 *sídī* —— (compounds have perf. and perf. part. of *sédeō*: *-sēdī*
   -séssus) I settle (intrans.)
sínō 3 *síuī sítus* (compounds drop *-u-* in perf., e.g. *dēsinō* 3 *désiī*) I
   allow
sístō 3 *stítī* (or *stétī*) *státus* (compounds all intransitive, with no
   perf. part.: cf. *cōnsístō, resístō*) I set, stay
sóleō 2 semi-dep. *sólitus* I am accustomed, am used
sóluō 3 *sóluī solūtus* I release, undo; pay
spárgō 3 *spársī spársus* (compounds *-spérgō* 3 *-spérsī -spérsus*) I
   scatter, sprinkle
spérnō 3 *sprēuī sprētus* I reject, despise
spúō 3 *spúī spútum* I spit
státuō 3 *státuī statūtus* (compounds *-stítuō* 3 *-stítuī -stitūtus*) I set up,
   settle
stérnō 3 *strāuī strātus* I throw on the ground, strew
stō 1 *stétī státum* (most compounds *-stō* 3 *-stitī* with fut. part.
   -statūrus, but no perf. part.) I stand
stríngō 3 *strínxī stríctus* I draw; strip; graze
strúō 3 *strūxī strúctus* I heap up, build
suádeō 2 *suāsī suāsum* I recommend
suēscō 3 *suēuī suētus* I accustom myself
sum ésse fúī futūrus I am
sūmō 3 *sūmpsī sūmptus* I take; consume
súrgō 3 *surrēxī surréctum* (see *régō*) I rise, arise, get up

taédet 2 *taésum est* it wearies

tángō 3 *tétigī táctus* (compounds *-tíngō* 3 *-tigī -táctus*) I touch, lay hands on

tégō 3 *téxī téctus* I cover

témnō 3 *-témpsi -témptus* (perf. and perf. part. in compounds only) I despise

téndō 3 *teténdī téntus* (or *ténsus*) (compounds *-téndo* 3 *-téndī -téntus*) I stretch (out); offer; direct; travel; strive, fight

téneō 2 *ténuī téntus* (compounds *-tíneō* 2 *tínuī -téntus*) I hold

térō 3 *trīuī trītus* I rub

tóllō 3 *sústulī sublátus* I lift, remove, take away

tóndeō 2 *totóndī tónsus* I shear

tráhō 3 *tráxī tráctus* I drag

tríbuō 3 *tríbuī tribútus* I assign, grant

túeor 2 dep. *túitus* (or *tútus*) I look after, protect; look at

túndō 3 *tútudī túsus* (or *túnsus*) (compounds *-túndō* 3 *-tudī -túsus/-túnsus*) I beat, strike, pound

uádō 3 —— (compounds *-uádō* 3 *-uásī -uásus*) I go

uéhō 3 *uéxī uéctus* I carry

uéllō 3 *uéllī* (or *uúlsī*) *uúlsus* I pull, pluck

uéniō 4 *uénī uéntum* I come, arrive

uértō 3 *uértī uérsus* I turn (trans.)

uétō 1 *uétuī uétitus* I forbid

uídeo 2 *uídī uísus* I see (passive: I seem)

uínciō 4 *uínxī uínctus* I bind

uíncō 3 *uícī uíctus* I conquer

uísō 3 *uísī* —— I visit

uíuō 3 *uíxī uíctum* I am alive, live

ulcíscor 3 dep. *últus* I avenge myself on, avenge

uólō uélle uóluī —— I wish, want

uóluō 3 *uóluī uolútus* I roll, turn over (trans.)

úrō 3 *ússī ústus* I burn

ūtor 3 dep. *ūsus* I use, make use of; adopt

H–I Nouns, pronominal nouns/adjectives

H1 Nouns: first declension

séru-a ae 1f. 'slave-woman'

	s.	*pl.*
nom.	sérua	séruae
acc.	séruam	séruās
gen.	séruae (seruāī)	seruārum
dat.	séruae	séruīs
abl.	séruā	séruīs

Notes

1 1st decl. nouns are feminine except for e.g. *agrícola* 'farmer', *naúta* 'sailor' and other males.

2 *fília* 'daughter' and *déa* 'goddess' have dat./abl. pl. in *-ābus*, i.e. *fíliābus*, *deábus* (to avoid confusion with *fílius* and *déus*).

H2 Nouns: second declension

(a) *séru-us ī* 2m. 'male slave'

	s.	*pl.*
nom.	séruus	séruī
acc.	séruum	séruōs
gen.	séruī	seruōrum
dat.	séruō	séruīs
abl.	séruō	séruīs

Notes

1 Virtually all 2nd decl. nouns are masculine. An exception is *húm-us ī* f. 'ground'.

2 Originally, this noun declined *séru-os séru-om* – forms often found in inscriptions and early Latin. The gen. pl. sometimes ends in plain *-um* rather than *-ōrum* (cf. **H2(e)** *deus*).

(b) *púer púer-ī* 2m. 'boy'

	s.	pl.
nom.	púer	púerī
acc.	púerum	púerōs
gen.	púerī	puerórum
dat.	púerō	púerīs
abl.	púerō	púerīs

(c) *cúlter cúltr-ī* 2m. 'knife'

	s.	pl.
nom.	cúlter	cúltrī
acc.	cúltrum	cúltrōs
gen.	cúltrī	cultrórum
dat.	cúltrō	cúltrīs
abl.	cúltrō	cúltrīs

(d) *uir uír-ī* 2m. 'man'

	s.	pl.
nom.	uir	uírī
acc.	uírum	uírōs
gen.	uírī	uírórum (uírum – *cf.* déus)
dat.	uírō	uírīs
abl.	uírō	uírīs

(e) *dé-us ī* 2m. 'god'

	s.	pl.
nom.	déus	dī (déī, díī)
acc.	déum	déōs
gen.	déī	deórum (déum)
dat.	déō	dīs
abl.	déō	dīs

(f) (Neuter) *sómni-um ī* 2n. 'dream'

	s.	pl.
nom.	sómnium	sómnia
acc.	sómnium	sómnia
gen.	sómnī (*or* sómniī)	somniórum
dat.	sómniō	sómniīs
abl.	sómniō	sómniīs

H3 Nouns: third declension

(a) (Consonant stem): *fūr fūr-is* 3m. 'thief'

	s.	*pl.*
nom.	fūr	fúrēs
acc.	fúrem	fúrēs
gen.	fúris	fúrum
dat.	fúrī	fúribus
abl.	fúre	fúribus

NB. Monosyllables with *two* consonants at the end of the stem have genitive plural in *-ium*, e.g. *mōns mónt-is* 'mountain', gen. pl. *móntium*. Such nouns are in fact *i*-stem.

(b) (*i*-stem): *aedis aed-is* 3f. 'temple'; pl. 'temples' or 'house'

	s.	*pl.*
nom.	aédis	aédēs
acc.	aédem	aédīs (aédēs)
gen.	aédis	aédium
dat.	aédī	aédibus
abl.	aéde (aédī)	aédibus

NB. Historically, the *-i-* was wholly dominant, cf. the declension of *túrris* 'tower': *túrris túrrim túrris túrrī túrrī*.

(c) (Neuter consonant stem) *nōmen nōmin-is* 3n. 'name'

	s.	*pl.*
nom.	nōmen	nōmina
acc.	nōmen	nōmina
gen.	nōminis	nōminum
dat.	nōminī	nōmínibus
abl.	nōmine	nōmínibus

(d) (Neuter consonant stem) *ónus óner-is* 3n. 'load, burden'

	s.	*pl.*
nom.	ónus	ónera
acc.	ónus	ónera
gen.	óneris	ónerum
dat.	ónerī	onéribus
abl.	ónere	onéribus

NB. The original stem was *onos-* alternating with *ones-*. The final *-o-* became *-u-* in nom. s. (*onus*), and the *-s-* became *-r-* between vowels, i.e. *onesis→óneris* (a common feature of Latin).

(e) (Neuter *i*-stem) nouns in *-al -ar -re* and *-le: máre mar-is* 3n. 'sea'

	s.	*pl.*
nom.	máre	mária
acc.	máre	mária
gen.	máris	márium (márum *is found*)
dat.	márī	máribus
abl.	márī (máre *is found*)	máribus

Cf. *ánimal* 'animal', *cálcar* 'spur' and *cubíle* 'couch'.

(f) Four irregular 3rd declension nouns: *Iuppiter, bōs, uīs, nēmo*

Iúppiter Ióu-is 3m. *'Jupiter'*

nom.	Iúppiter
acc.	Ióuem
gen.	Ióuis
dat.	Ióuī
abl.	Ióue

bōs bóu-is 3m. *'ox', 3f. 'cow'.*

	s.	*pl.*
nom.	bos	bóuēs
acc.	bóuem	bóuēs
gen.	bóuis	bóum
dat.	bóuī	bóbus (búbus)
abl.	bóue	bóbus (búbus)

uīs 3f. (s.) 'force', (pl.) 'strength'

	s.	pl.
nom.	uīs	uírēs
acc.	uim	uírēs
gen.	—	uírium
dat.	—	uíribus
abl.	uī	uíribus

némo 3 m.f. 'no-one', 'none', 'no'ʾ (pronoun)

	s.
nom.	némo
acc.	néminem
gen.	nūllíus
dat.	néminī
abl.	núllō

Notes

1 Consonant- and *i*-stem nouns can be masculine, feminine or neuter. The following clues can help:

> *Masculine*: nouns ending in *-ōs, -ō, -or, -er* (main exceptions: *dōs* 'dowry', f.; *ōs ōris* 'mouth', n.; *arbor* 'tree', f.)
>
> *Feminine*: nouns ending in *-x, -ās, -dō, -gō, -iō, -ūs* (if polysyllabic), *-ns* (main exceptions: *dux* 'leader', m.; *fās* 'right', n.; *ōrdō* 'rank', m.; *mōns* 'mountain', *pōns* 'bridge', *fōns* 'fountain'; *dēns* 'tooth'; all m.)
>
> *Neuter*: nouns ending in *-us, -ūs* (if monosyllabic), *-en, -al, -ar, -re, -le*

2 Finding the nominative can be difficult with such nouns. Note the following clues:

  (i)   Gen. s. ending in *-cis, -gis*: nominative in *-x* (e.g. *pácis → pāx*)
  (ii) Gen. s. ending in *-tis, -dis*: nominative in *-s* (e.g. *uirtútis → uírtūs*)
  (iii) Gen. s. ending in *-pis*: nominative in *-ps* (e.g. *príncipis → prínceps*)
  (iv) Gen. s. ending in *-ris*: nominative in *-s, -r* (e.g. *témporis → témpus, mátris → máter*)
  (v)   Gen. s. ending in *-lis*: nominative in *-l* (e.g. *sólis → sōl*)

3 As a general rule (a) nouns with the *same* number of syllables in the nominative singular as in the genitive singular (parisyllabic) have genitive plurals in *-ium*, e.g. *cíuis*, gen. s. *cíuis*, gen. pl. *cíuium*. These are *i*-stem. (b) nouns with *more* syllables in the genitive singular than in the

nominative (imparisyllabic) have gen. pl. in -*um*, e.g. *uírtūs*, gen. s. *uirtútis*, gen. pl. *uirtútum*. These are consonant stem.

The major exceptions to (a) are *cánis cán-is* m. or f. 'dog', *iúuenis iúuen-is* m. 'young man', *sénex sén-is* m. 'old man', *sédēs séd-is* f. 'abode', *páter pátr-is* m. 'father', *máter mátr-is* f. 'mother', *fráter frátr-is* m. 'brother', *accípiter accípitr-is* m. 'hawk', all of which have gen. pl. in -*um*. The rule for major exceptions to (b) is given in the note under *fūr*.

H4 Nouns: fourth declension

(a) *mán-us ūs* 4f. 'hand'

	s.	pl.
nom.	mánus	mánūs
acc.	mánum	mánūs
gen.	mánūs	mánuum
dat.	mánuī	mánibus ⎫
abl.	mánū	mánibus ⎭ (mánubus)

Notes
1 Most 4th decl. nouns are *masculine*.
2 The gen. s. in -*ī* is found in early Latin.

(b) (Neuter) *cōrn-ū ūs* 4n. 'horn', 'wing of army'

	s.	pl.
nom.	córnū	córnua
acc.	córnū	córnua
gen.	córnūs	córnuum
dat.	córnū	córnibus
abl.	córnū	córnibus

(c) (Irregular) *dómus* 4f. 'house'

	s.	pl.
nom.	dómus	dómūs
acc.	dómum	dómūs *or* dómōs
gen.	dómūs *or* dómī	domórum *or* dómuum
dat.	dómuī *or* dómō	dómibus
abl.	dómō	dómibus

H5 Nouns: fifth declension

rēs rḗ-ī 5f. 'thing', 'matter', 'business', 'affair'

	s.	*pl.*
nom.	rēs	rēs
acc.	rem	rēs
gen.	rḗī (rē)	rḗrum
dat.	rḗī (rē)	rḗbus
abl.	rē	rḗbus

NB. 5th decl. nouns are mostly feminine, but *diēs* 'day' is usually m. (f. when it means the goddess 'Diēs', or a special day) and its compound *merīdiēs* 'midday', 'south' is always m.

H6 Greek declensions

Roman poets often use the Greek forms of Greek nouns, especially for names. Mostly only nom., acc. and gen. s., nom. and acc. pl. are found. The other cases have the normal Latin forms. Here are some examples.

1st declension Aenḗ-ās ae m. 'Aeneas', Priámid-ēs ae m. 'son of Priam', Eurýdic-ē ēs f. 'Eurydice'

nom.	Aenḗ-ās	Priámid-ēs	Eurýdic-ē
voc.	Aenḗ-ā	Priámid-ē	Eurýdic-ē
acc.	Aenḗ-ān	Priámid-ēn	Eurýdic-ēn
gen.	Aenḗ-ae	Priámid-ae	Eurýdic-ēs
dat.	Aenḗ-ae	Priámid-ae	Eurýdic-ae
abl.	Aenḗ-ā	Priámid-ē (-ā)	Eurýdic-ē

Notes

1 The pl. of such nouns is as for *sérv-a*, except that nouns in *-dēs* have gen. pl. in *-um*, e.g. *Aenéad-um* 'of the followers of Aeneas'.
2 The Latin form of names like *Eurýdicē* is often found e.g. *Cýbel-a Cýbel-am* etc. 'Cybele'.

2nd declension *Dél-os* ī f. 'Delos', *Péli-on* ī n. 'Pelion'

nom.	Dél-os	Péli-on
acc.	Dél-on	Péli-on
gen.	Dél-ī	Péli-ī
dat./abl.	Dél-ō	Péli-ō

3rd declension *crátēr crātḗr-os/crātḗr-is* m. 'mixing-bowl'

	s.	*pl.*
nom./voc.	crátēr	crātḗr-es
acc.	crātḗr-a/-em	crātḗr-as
gen.	crātḗr-os/-is	crātḗr-um
dat.	crātḗr-ī	crātḗr-ibus
abl.	crātḗr-e	crātḗr-ibus

NB.   Other 3rd declension forms are e.g. 'hero' m.: nom. *hḗrōs*, acc. *hērṓ-a*; 'Orpheus' m.: nom. *Órpheus*, voc. *Órpheu*, acc. *Órphea*, gen. *Órpheos*; 'Paris' m.: nom. *Páris*, voc. *Pári*, acc. *Párin/Párida*, gen. *Páridos*; 'Socrates' m.: nom. *Sṓcratēs*, voc. *Sṓcratē*, acc. *Sṓcratem*.

I1   Personal pronouns

(a) *ego* 'I', *tū* 'you'

	s.		*pl.*		*s.*		*pl.*
nom.	égo	'I'	nōs	'we'	tū	'you'	uōs	'you'
acc.	mē		nōs		tē		uōs	
gen.	méī		nóstrum/nóstrī		túī		uéstrum/uéstrī
dat.	míhi (mī)		nṓbīs		tíbi		uṓbīs
abl.	mē		nṓbīs		tē		uṓbīs

(b) Reflexive pronoun *sē* 'himself', 'herself', 'itself', 'themselves'

	s./pl.
nom.	—
acc.	sē (sḗsē) 'himself', 'herself', 'itself', 'themselves'
gen.	súī
dat.	síbi
abl.	sē (sḗsē)

Notes

1 Possessive adjectives based on personal pronouns are:

> *mé-us a um* 'my', 'mine' ⎫ declining like *lóng-us a um* **J1(a)** (but
> *tú-us a um* 'your', 'yours' ⎭ note *mī* voc. s. m. of *mé-us*)
> *nóster nóstr-a um* 'our', 'ours' ⎫ declining like *púlcher púlchr-a*
> *uéster uéstr-a um* 'your', 'yours' ⎬ *um* **J1(b)**
> *sú-us a um* 'his', 'hers', 'its', 'theirs' (reflexive – i.e. the 'he', 'she',
> 'it', 'them' being referred to are the same person as the subject
> of the clause in which they stand, but see 'reflexives' in the
> *Index of Grammar* for five important exceptions.)

> These usually follow their noun (unless emphatic). But *mī* (vocative s.
> of *méus*) usually precedes.

2 *cum* 'with' is linked with the ablative on the pattern *mḗcum*, *tḗcum*,
sḗcum etc.

---

12 Demonstrative pronouns

(a) *is ea id* 'that', 'those', 'that person', 'he', 'she', 'it'

	s.			*pl.*		
	m.	*f.*	*n.*	*m.*	*f.*	*n.*
nom.	is	éa	id	éī (íī)	éae	éa
acc.	éum	éam	id	éōs	éās	éā
gen.	←——éius →→			eórum	eárum	eórum
dat.	←——éī ——→			←——— éīs (íīs) ———→		
abl.	éō	éā	éō	←——— éīs (íīs) ———→		

Compare the definitive pronoun *ī́dem éadem ídem* 'the same':

	s.			*pl.*		
	m.	*f.*	*n.*	*m.*	*f.*	*n.*
nom.	ī́dem	éadem	ídem	eídem (ídem)	eaédem	éadem
acc.	eúndem	eándem	ídem	eósdem	eásdem	éadem
gen.	←——eiúsdem —→			eōrúndem	eārúndem	eōrúndem
dat.	←——eídem——→			←———eísdem (ísdem) ———→		
abl.	eódem	eádem	eódem	←———eísdem (ísdem) ———→		

(b) *hic haec hoc* 'this', 'this person', 'this thing', 'the latter', pl. 'these'

	s.			pl.		
	m.	*f.*	*n.*	*m.*	*f.*	*n.*
nom.	hic	haec	hoc	hī	hae	haec
acc.	hunc	hanc	hoc	hōs	hās	haec
gen.	←—— húius —→			hốrum	hãrum	hốrum
dat.	←— huic —→			←——— hīs ———→		
abl.	hōc	hāc	hōc	←——— hīs ———→		

NB. Originally *hi-ce, hae-ce, hod-ce* etc. The strengthened forms *huiúsce, hốsce, hãsce,* and *hísce* are reasonably common.

(c) *ille illa illud* 'that', 'that person', 'that thing' 'the former', pl. 'those'

	s.			pl.		
	m.	*f.*	*n.*	*m.*	*f.*	*n.*
nom.	ílle	ílla	íllud	íllī	íllae	ílla
acc.	íllum	íllam	íllud	íllōs	íllās	ílla
gen.	←—— illíus —→			illốrum	illãrum	illốrum
dat.	←— íllī —→			←——— íllīs ———→		
abl.	íllō	íllā	íllō	←——— íllīs ———→		

(d) *iste ista istud* 'that (of yours)'

	s.			pl.		
	m.	*f.*	*n.*	*m.*	*f.*	*n.*
nom.	íste	ísta	ístud	ístī	ístae	ísta
acc.	ístum	ístam	ístud	ístōs	ístās	ísta
gen.	←—— istíus —→			istốrum	istãrum	istốrum
dat.	←— ístī —→			←——— ístīs ———→		
abl.	ístō	ístā	ístō	←——— ístīs ———→		

(e) *ipse ipsa ipsum* 'very', 'actual', 'self'

	s.			pl.		
	m.	*f.*	*n.*	*m.*	*f.*	*n.*
nom.	ípse	ípsa	ípsum	ípsī	ípsae	ípsa
acc.	ípsum	ípsam	ípsum	ípsōs	ípsās	ípsa
gen.	←—— ipsíus —→			ipsốrum	ipsãrum	ipsốrum
dat.	←— ípsī —→			←——— ípsīs ———→		
abl.	ípsō	ípsā	ípsō	←——— ípsīs ———→		

I3 Relative pronoun

quī quae quod 'who', 'which', 'what'

	s.			*pl.*		
	m.	*f.*	*n.*	*m.*	*f.*	*n.*
nom.	quī	quae	quod	quī	quae	quae
acc.	quem	quam	quod	quōs	quās	quae
gen.	←——cúius——→			quốrum	quárum	quốrum
dat.	←——cui——→			←——quíbus (quīs)——→		
abl.	quō	quā	quō	←——quíbus (quīs)——→		

Notes

1 *quốcum, quácum, quíbuscum* 'with whom/which'.
2 *quī* as an old abl. form is found mostly in the word *quícum* 'with whom', where it is m. f. or n. s., and even occasionally pl.

I4 Interrogative (indefinite) pronoun/adjective

quis/quī, quae/quis, quid/quod 'who?', 'which?', 'what?'

		s.			*pl.*		
		m.	*f.*	*n.*	*m.*	*f.*	*n.*
nom.	*pron.*	quis	quis	quid ⎫	quī	quae	quae (qua)
	adj.	quī	quae (qua)	quod ⎭			
acc.	*pron.* ⎰	quem	quam	⎰ quid ⎱	quōs	quās	quae (qua)
	adj. ⎱			⎰ quod ⎱			
gen.		←——cúius——→			quốrum	quárum	quốrum
dat.		←——cui——→			←——quíbus (quīs)——→		
abl.		quō	quā	quō	←——quíbus (quīs)——→		

Notes

1 After *sī, nē, nisi, num*, the meaning of *quis* (Indefinite) is 'any', 'anyone', and nom. s. f. and n. pl. nom./acc. are always *qua*.
2 *quis* is quite often used for *quī* (adj.) e.g. *quis . . . púer*? 'What boy?' (Horace) Cf. *áliquis* **I5(b) Note 2** below.
3 *quī*, an old ablative form, as an interrogative means 'how?', e.g. *quī fit, Maecḗnas*? 'How does it come about, Maecenas?' (Horace).

I5   Compound pronouns

(a) *quīdam quaédam quóddam* 'a', 'a certain'

s.

	m.	*f.*	*n.*
nom.	quīdam	quáedam	quóddam (quíddam)
acc.	quéndam	quándam	quóddam (quíddam)
gen.	←——— cuiúsdam ———→		
dat.	←——— cúidam ———→		
abl.	quódam	quádam	quódam

pl.

	m.	*f.*	*n.*
nom.	quīdam	quaédam	quaédam
acc.	quósdam	quásdam	quaédam
gen.	quōrúndam	quārúndam	quōrúndam
dat.	←——— quíbusdam ———→		
abl.	←——— quíbusdam ———→		

(b) *áliquis áliqua áliquid* 'someone' and *áliquī áliqua áliquod* 'some'

	áliquis 'someone'			*áliquī* 'some' *(adj.)*		
	m.	*f.*	*n.*	*m.*	*f.*	*n.*
nom.	áliquis	áliqua	áliquid	áliquī	áliqua	áliquod
acc.	áliquem	áliquam	áliquid	áliquam	áliquam	áliquod
gen.	←—— alicúius ——→			←—— alicúius ——→		
dat.	←—— álicui ——→			←—— álicui ——→		
abl.	áliquō	áliquā	áliquō	áliquō	áliquā	áliquō

Notes

1 The pl. is the same as for *ali-* + *quī* (**I4** above), except that the n. pl. is *áliqua*.

2 *áliquis* is quite often used for *áliquī* (adj.). e.g. *num ígitur áliquis dólor in córpore est* 'Surely there isn't <u>any pain</u> in your body?' (Cicero). Cf. *quis*, **I4 Note 2**.

(c) Other compound pronouns

(i) *quísque quaéque quódque* 'each and every', 'everyone'.
quísque is very often used to mean 'every(one)', e.g. *súa cuíque natiōnī relígiō est, nóstra nōbīs* 'every nation has its own religion, and we have ours' (Cicero). Note *óptimus quísque* 'all the best men' and *quótus quísque* 'how few!'

(ii) *quísquam quísquam quícquam* 'anyone', 'any'.
quísquam is normally found in negative contexts (or in questions where a negative is implied, e.g. *quid quísquam suspicārī áliud pótest?* 'what else can anyone suspect?' (Cicero)).

(iii) *quísquis* 'whoever' *quídquid* or *quícquid* 'whatever'; *quīcúmque quaecúmque quodcúmque* 'whoever', 'whatever'.
quísquis and *quīcúmque* are used to introduce relative clauses; e.g. *férreus est, heu, heu, quísquis in úrbe mánet* 'anyone who stays in Rome (oh dear, oh dear) is made of iron' (Tibullus). *dī tíbi dent quaecúmque óptēs* 'may the gods give you whatever you want' (Plautus).

(iv) *écquis* 'anyone?' adj. *écquī écqua/écquae écquod* 'any?'
ecquis introduces questions and means 'Is there anyone (who)?', e.g. *heus, écquis hīc est?* 'Hey, is there anyone here?' (Plautus).

NB.   Compounds of *quis* decline like *quis*. See above **I4**. Compounds of *quī* decline like *quī*. See above **I3**. But not all forms are found in all of these pronoun/adjectives.

I6   Special pronoun–adjectives

(a) *álius ália áliud* 'other', 'another'

	s.			pl.		
	m.	*f.*	*n.*	*m.*	*f.*	*n.*
nom.	álius	ália	áliud	áliī	áliae	ália
acc.	álium	áliam	áliud	áliōs	áliās	ália
gen.	←—— álíus ——→			aliórum	aliárum	aliórum
dat.	←—— álíī ——→			←——— áliīs ———→		
abl.	áliō	áliā	áliō	←——— áliīs ———→		

NB.   Genitive and dative s. are not common, and occasionally the 2nd declension forms (gen. s. m./n. *áliī* f. *áliae*; dat. s. m. *áliō* f. *áliae*) are found. *alteríus* (gen. s. of *álter*) is also used for gen. s.

(b) *nū́ll-us a um* 'no(one)', 'not any', 'no man'

	s.			pl.		
	m.	*f.*	*n.*	*m.*	*f.*	*n.*
nom.	nū́llus	nū́lla	nū́llum	nū́llī	nū́llae	nū́lla
acc.	nū́llum	nū́llam	nū́llum	nū́llōs	nū́llās	nū́lla
gen.	←——— nūllī́us ———→			nūllṓrum	nūllā́rum	nūllṓrum
dat.	←——— nū́llī ———→			←——— nū́llīs ———→		
abl.	nū́llō	nū́llā	nū́llō	←——— nū́llīs ———→		

(c) *álter álter-a álter-um* 'one (of two)', 'the one . . . the other'

	s.			pl.		
	m.	*f.*	*n.*	*m.*	*f.*	*n.*
nom.	álter	áltera	álterum	álterī	álterae	áltera
acc.	álterum	álteram	álterum	álterōs	álterās	áltera
gen.	←——— alterī́us ———→			alterṓrum	alterā́rum	alterṓrum
dat.	←——— álterī ———→			←——— álterīs ———→		
abl.	álterō	álterā	álterō	←——— álterīs ———→		

(d) *utérque* 'both', 'each (of two)'

	s.			pl.		
	m.	*f.*	*n.*	*m.*	*f.*	*n.*
nom.	utérque	útraque	utrúmque	utrī́que	utraéque	útraque
acc.	utrúmque	utrámque	utrúmque	utrṓsque	utrā́sque	útraque
gen.	←——— utriū́sque ———→			utrōrúmque	utrārúmque	utrōrúmque
dat.	←——— utrī́que ———→			←——— utrī́sque ———→		
abl.	utrṓque	utrā́que	utrṓque	←——— utrī́sque ———→		

NB.   The following special pronoun/adjectives also decline like *lóng-us a um* elsewhere, but have gen. s. in *-íus* and dat. s. in *-ī̄*: *ū́n-us a um* 'one', *sṓl-us a um* 'alone', *tṓt-us a um* 'the whole', *ū́ll-us a um* 'any', *úter útr-a um* 'which of two?', 'whichever of two', *neúter neútr-a um* 'neither'.

I7   Numerals

Cardinal						*Ordinal*[1]	
			m.	*f.*	*n.*		
1	I		ū́nus	ū́na	ū́num[2]	*1st*	prímus (príor)
2	II	*nom.*	dúo	dúae	dúo	*2nd*	secúndus (álter)
		acc.	dúōs/dúo	dúās	dúo		
		gen.	duṓrum	duā́rum	duṓrum		
		dat./abl.	duṓbus	duā́bus	duṓbus		

			m./f.	n.		
3	III	*nom.*	trēs	tría	*3rd*	tértius
		acc.	trēs (trīs)	tría		
		gen.	←tríum→			
		dat.	←tríbus→			
		abl.	←tríbus→			
4	IV/IIII		quáttuor		*4th*	quártus
5	V		quínque		*5th*	quíntus
6	VI		sex		*6th*	séxtus
7	VII		séptem		*7th*	séptimus
8	VIII		óctō		*8th*	octáuus
9	IX/VIIII		nóuem		*9th*	nōnus
10	X		décem		*10th*	décimus
11	XI		úndecim		*11th*	ūndécimus
12	XII		duódecim		*12th*	duodécimus
13	XIII		trédecim		*13th*	tértius décimus
14	XIV		quattuórdecim		*14th*	quártus décimus
15	XV		quíndecim		*15th*	quíntus décimus
16	XVI		sédecim		*16th*	séxtus décimus
17	XVII		septéndecim		*17th*	séptimus décimus
18	XVIII		duodēuigíntī		*18th*	duodēuīcénsimus
19	XIX		ūndēuigíntī		*19th*	ūndēuīcénsimus
20	XX		uigíntī		*20th*	uīcénsimus
30	XXX		trīgíntā		*30th*	trīcénsimus
40	XL		quādrāgíntā		*40th*	quādrāgénsimus
50	L		quīnquāgíntā		*50th*	quīnquāgénsimus
60	LX		sexāgíntā		*60th*	sexāgénsimus
70	LXX		septuāgíntā		*70th*	septuāgénsimus
80	LXXX		octōgíntā		*80th*	octōgénsimus
90	XC		nōnāgíntā		*90th*	nōnāgénsimus
100	C		céntum		*100th*	centénsimus
200	CC		ducént-ī ae a (*like pl. of* lóng-us)		*200th*	ducenténsimus
300	CCC		trecént-ī ae a		*300th*	trēcenténsimus
500	D		quīngént-ī ae a		*500th*	quīngenténsimus
1,000	M		mílle (*indecl. adj.*) *pl.* mília *gen.* mílium *dat./abl.* mílibus (*see* Note 1)		*1,000th*	mīllénsimus

[1] These decline like *lóng-us a um*.
[2] Like *tótus* i.e. gen. s. *ūníus*, dat. s. *ūnī́*; pl. *ūnī́*, *ūnae*, *ūna*, like pl. of *lóngus* (**I6(d) Note**).

Notes

1 Normally, *mílle* is used as an adjective and *mília* as a noun, e.g.

> *mílle mílitēs* = one thousand soldiers
> *dúo mília mílitum* = two thousand(s) (of) soldiers
> *tría mília mílitum* = three thousand(s) (of) soldiers etc.

2 Latin has three other sets of numerals. One answers the question 'How many each?', e.g. *síngul-ī ae a* 'one each', then *-nī.* e.g. *bĩn-ī ae a* 'two each' (distributive adjectives). A second answers the question 'How many times?', e.g. *sémel* 'once', *bis* 'twice', *ter* 'three times', *quáter*, then *-iēns*, e.g. *mīliēns* 'a thousand times' (numeral adverbs). A third answers the question 'Of how many parts?', e.g. *tríplex tríplic-is* 'threefold' (multiplicative adjectives).

3 The ending *-ēnsimus* was, after the Augustan period, often written *-ēsimus.*

J–K   Adjectives, adverbs and prepositions

J   Introduction

(a) Adjectives agree with the word they describe in *gender* (m., f. or n.), *case* (nom., acc., gen., dat., abl.) and *number* (s. or pl.). Thus an adjective which is genitive plural masculine can only agree with a noun which is genitive plural masculine.

(b) Adjectives in agreement with no nouns will take their meaning from context. They will usually refer to a person or thing, e.g.

> *bónī* (nom. pl. m.) 'good *men*'.
> *bónae* (nom. pl. f.) 'good *women*'.
> *bóna* (nom. pl. n.) 'good *things*' 'goods'.
> *fugiéntēs* (nom. pl. m. or f.) '*people* as they are fleeing'
> *rogántī* (dat. s. m. or f.) 'to the *person* asking'.
> *mors málum est* 'death is a bad *thing*'.

(c) Some adjectives are often used predicatively. That is, instead of being best translated as adjectives (e.g. *uir bónus* 'a good man'), they should be translated as adverbs (e.g. *uir laétus ábiit* 'the man went away happily') or nouns (e.g. *súmmō mónte* 'at the top of the mountain'). The words most commonly used thus include those denoting position (e.g. *súmmus, médius, próximus*), quantity or order (e.g. *prīmus, sólus, tótus*), and attitude of mind or manner (e.g. *laétus* 'happily', *inuītus* 'unwillingly').

(d) Some words commonly double as nouns or adjectives, e.g. *hic, ílle, is* (etc.). Note that *uétus* 'old', 'old man', *paúper* 'poor', 'poor man', *díues* 'rich', 'rich man' are like this. They decline like third declension *nouns*, but they often perform as *adjectives*, e.g.

> *úbi paúper est?* 'where is the poor man?'
> *cum díuite senātóre ámbulat* 'he walks with the rich senator'

J1 Adjectives: first/second declension

(a) *lóng-us a um* 'long'

	s.			pl.		
	m.	*f.*	*n.*	*m.*	*f.*	*n.*
nom.	lóngus	lónga	lóngum	lóngī	lóngae	lónga
acc.	lóngum	lóngam	lóngum	lóngōs	lóngās	lónga
gen.	lóngī	lóngae	lóngī	longórum	longárum	longórum
dat.	lóngō	lóngae	lóngō	lóngīs	lóngīs	lóngīs
abl.	lóngō	lóngā	lóngō	lóngīs	lóngīs	lóngīs

(b) *púlcher púlchr-a um* 'beautiful', 'handsome'

	s.			pl.		
	m.	*f.*	*n.*	*m.*	*f.*	*n.*
nom.	púlcher	púlchra	púlchrum	púlchrī	púlchrae	púlchra
acc.	púlchrum	púlchram	púlchrum	púlchrōs	púlchrās	púlchra
gen.	púlchrī	púlchrae	púlchrī	pulchrórum	pulchrárum	pulchrórum
dat.	púlchrō	púlchrae	púlchrō	←—— púlchrīs ——→		
abl.	púlchrō	púlchrā	púlchrō	←—— púlchrīs ——→		

(c) *míser míser-a míser-um* 'unhappy'

	s.			pl.		
	m.	*f.*	*n.*	*m.*	*f.*	*n.*
nom.	míser	mísera	míserum	míserī	míserae	mísera
acc.	míserum	míseram	míserum	míserōs	míserās	mísera
gen.	míserī	míserae	míserī	miserórum	miserárum	miserórum
dat.	míserō	míserae	míserō	←—— míserīs ——→		
abl.	míserō	míserā	míserō	←—— míserīs ——→		

J2   Adjectives: third declension

(a) *ómnis ómne* 'all', 'every'

	s.		*pl.*	
	m./f.	*n.*	*m./f.*	*n.*
nom.	ómnis	ómne	ómnēs	ómnia
acc.	ómnem	ómne	ómnīs (ómnēs)	ómnia
gen.	←ómnis→		←ómnium→	
dat.	←ómnī→		←ómnibus→	
abl.	←ómnī→		←ómnibus→	

(b) *ingḗns ingḗns (ingént-)* 'huge'

	s.		*pl.*	
	m./f.	*n.*	*m./f.*	*n.*
nom.	ingḗns	ingḗns	ingéntēs	ingéntia
acc.	ingéntem	ingḗns	ingéntīs (ingéntēs)	ingéntia
gen.	←ingéntis→		←ingéntium→	
dat.	←ingéntī→		←ingéntibus→	
abl.	←ingéntī→		←ingéntibus→	

(c) *céler céler-is céler-e* 'swift', 'fast'

	s.			*pl.*	
	m.	*f.*	*n.*	*m./f.*	*n.*
nom.	céler	céleris	célere	célerēs	céléria
acc.	célerem	célerem	célere	célerīs (célerēs)	céléria
gen.	←—— céleris ——→			←celérium→	
dat.	←—— célerī ——→			←celéribus→	
abl.	←—— célerī ——→			←celéribus→	

(d) *ā́cer ā́cris ā́cre* 'keen', 'sharp'

	s.			*pl.*	
	m.	*f.*	*n.*	*m./f.*	*n.*
nom.	ā́cer	ā́cris	ā́cre	ā́crēs	ā́cria
acc.	ā́crem	ā́crem	ā́cre	ā́crīs (ā́crēs)	ā́cria
gen.	←—— ā́cris ——→			←ā́crium→	
dat.	←—— ā́crī ——→			←ā́cribus→	
abl.	←—— ā́crī ——→			←ā́cribus→	

NB.   All these are *i*-stems.

(e) Consonant-stem adjectives: *dīues* and *paúper*

	s.		*pl.*	
	m/f.	*n.*	*m/f.*	*n.*
nom.	dīues (dīs)	dīues (dīte)	dīuitēs (dītēs)	dīuita (dītia)
acc.	dīuitem (dītem)	dīues (dīte)	dīuites (dītēs)	dīuita (dītia)
gen.	←dīuitis (dītis)→		←dīuitum (dītium)→	
dat.	←dīuitī (dītī)→		←dīuítibus (dītibus)→	
abl.	←dīuite (dītī)→		←dīuítibus (dītibus)→	

	s.		*pl.*	
	m/f.	*n.*	*m/f.*	*n.*
nom.	paúper	paúper	paúperēs	paúpera
acc.	paúperem	paúper	paúperēs	paúpera
gen.	←paúperis→		←paúperum→	
dat.	←paúperī→		←paupéribus→	
abl.	←paúpere→		←paupéribus→	

Notes

1 *dīues* has also a set of *i*-stem endings (in brackets), which are commonly used. Both *dīues* and *paúper* are often used as nouns. See **47**.

2 Other consonant-stem adjectives are *caélebs caélib-is* 'unmarried', *cómpos cómpot-is* 'possessing', *ínops ínop-is* 'poor' (abl. s. -*ī*), *mémor mémor-is* 'mindful' (abl. s. -*ī*), *párticeps partícip-is* 'sharing', *sóspes sóspit-is* 'safe', *supérstes supérstit-is* 'surviving', *uétus uéter-is* 'old'.

J3 Comparative and superlative adjectives

These are formed as follows:

> Comparatives ('more —', 'rather —', 'quite —'): gen. s. stem + -*ior*, (neuter -*ius*)
>
> Superlatives ('very —', '—est', 'most —', 'extremely —'): gen. s. stem + -*íssimus*, or nom. s. + -*rimus* (in the case of adjectives which end in -*er* in the nominative, e.g. *púlcher*→ (comparative) *púlchrior*→(superlative) *pulchérrimus*)

Note also the irregular superlative, gen. s. stem + -*limus*, of six adjectives in –*ilis*, viz. *fácilis* 'easy', *diffícilis* 'difficult', *símilis* 'similar', *dissímilis* 'dissimilar', *grácilis* 'slender', *húmilis* 'lowly': e.g. *facíl-limus*.

The declension of comparative and superlative forms is as follows:

(a) Comparative adjectives: *lóngior lóngius* 'longer'

	s.		*pl.*	
	m./f.	*n.*	*m./f.*	*n.*
nom.	lóngior	lóngius	longiōrēs	longiōra
acc.	longiōrem	lóngius	longiōrēs	longiōra
gen.	←longiōris→		←longiōrum→	
dat.	←longiōrī→		←longiōribus→	
abl.	←longiōre→		←longiōribus→	

NB.   These adjectives are *consonant*-stems (cf. *dīues, paúper,* **J2(e)** above).

(b) Superlative adjectives: *longíssimus a um* 'longest' (sometimes *-íssumus*)

	s.		
	m.	*f.*	*n.*
nom.	longíssimus	longíssima	longíssimum
acc.	longíssimum	longíssimam	longíssimum
gen.	longíssimī	longíssimae	longíssimī
dat.	longíssimō	longíssimae	longíssimō
abl.	longíssimō	longíssimā	longíssimō

	pl.		
	m.	*f.*	*n.*
nom.	longíssimī	longíssimae	longíssima
acc.	longíssimōs	longíssimās	longíssima
gen.	longissimōrum	longissimārum	longissimōrum
dat.	←———— longíssimīs ————→		
abl.	←———— longíssimīs ————→		

(c) Irregular comparatives and superlatives: *bónus, málus, múltus, mágnus, páruus*

bón-us a um	mélior (meliōr-is)	óptim-us a um	'good', 'better', 'best' (*cf. ameliorate, optimise*)
mál-us a um	péior (peiōr-is)	péssim-us a um	'bad', 'worse', 'worst' (*cf. pejorative, pessimist*)

múlt-us a um	plūs (plŭr-is)	plūrim-us a um	'much', 'more', 'most' (*cf. plus* (+))
mágn-us a um	maíor (maiŏr-is)	máxim-us a um	'big', 'bigger', 'biggest' (*cf. major, maximise*)
páru-us a um	mínor (minŏr-is)	mínim-us a um	'small/few', 'smaller/fewer/less', 'smallest/fewest/least' (*cf. minor, minimise*)

NB. These decline quite regularly (see *lóngior longíssimus*) except for *plūs*:

	s.	pl.	
	(plūs *here* = *noun*)	m./f.	n.
nom.	plūs	plūrēs	plūra
acc.	plūs	plūrīs (plūrēs)	plūra
gen.	plŭris	plūrium	
dat.	–	plŭribus	
abl.	plŭre	plŭribus	

NB. *plūs* is really the comparative of the adverb *múltum* 'much', while *plūrēs* is the comparative of the plural *múlt-ī ae a*. The s. *múltus* has no true comparative.

J4 Adverbs

(a) Regular and irregular positive adverbs

1 Regular adverbs

A common way of forming adverbs in English is to add '—ly' to an adjective (e.g. 'slow-ly', 'quick-ly', 'passionate-ly'). In Latin, adverbs (which never change) are also regularly formed from adjectives as follows:

Adverbs based on 1st/2nd declension adjectives: add -ē to the stem, e.g. *stúltus→stúltē* 'foolishly'; *míser→míserē* 'unhappily'; *púlcher→púlchrē* 'beautifully'. A very few end in *-ter*, e.g. *hūmánus→hūmániter* 'gently', and some in *-ō*, e.g. *cértō* 'for a fact'.

Adverbs based on 3rd declension adjectives: add *-(i)ter* to the stem, e.g. *fórtis→fórtiter* 'bravely'; *aúdāx→audácter* 'boldly'; *céler→celériter* 'swiftly'. But note an important exception: *fácile* 'easily'

2 Irregular adverbs

bónus→béne 'well'.
páruus→paúlum '(a) little', 'slightly'.
múltus→múltum 'much'.
mágnus→magnópere 'greatly'.

NB.   *lóngē* (regularly formed from *lóngus* 'long') 'far'.

(b) Regular comparative and superlative adverbs 'more —ly', 'most —ly'

Comparative and superlative adverbs are formed from the comparative and superlative adjectives.

	'foolishly'	*'more foolishly'*	*'most foolishly'*
Adjective	stúlt-us	stúlt-ior	stultíssim-us
Adverb	stúlt-ē	stúlt-ius	stultíssim-ē
	'quickly'	*'more quickly'*	*'most quickly'*
Adjective	céler	celér-ior	celérrim-us
Adverb	celér-iter	celér-ius	celérrim-ē

NB.   The comparative adverb has the same form as the neuter of the comparative adjective.

(c) Irregular comparative and superlative adverbs

Most of these are only irregular in so far as the corresponding adjective has irregular comparative and superlative forms. If you already know the adjective forms, most of these adverbs are formed quite regularly from the adjective:

béne	'well'	mélius	'better'	óptimē	'best'.
mále	'badly'	péius	'worse'	péssimē	'worst', 'very badly'.
paúlum	'a little'	minus	'less'	mínimē	'very little'; 'no'.
múltum	'much'	plūs	'more'	plūrimum	'most'; 'a lot'.
magnópere	'greatly'	mágis	'more'	máximē	'very much'; 'most'; 'yes'.

J5 'Comparative' constructions

(a) Comparative

1   *quam* means 'than' when it is used with a comparative, e.g. *tū sānior es quam égo* 'you are saner than I'. Cf. *mālō pácem quam béllum* 'I prefer

513

peace to war' (*málō* = *mágis uólō* 'I want x more than y'). Observe that the two things compared are in the same case, e.g. *maiṓrem hábeō líbrum quam túum* (*líbrum*) 'I have a larger book than yours'.

2 But Latin can also compare two items by dropping *quam* and putting the item compared in the ablative, e.g.

> *tū mē sánior es* 'you are saner than I'
> *quis sapiéntior sapiénte est?* 'who is wiser than the wise?'

3 Note the use of the comparative + *quam quī* + subjunctive in the idiom 'too — to do something', e.g.

> *sapiéntior est quam quī hoc fáciat* '(lit.) he is wiser than one who would do that', i.e. 'he is too wise to do that'

4 Note the use of the ablative of the measure of difference (see **L(f)4(iv)**) with comparative adjectives or adverbs in sentences meaning 'the more . . . the more . . .', e.g.

> *quō própius éa conténtiō accédit . . . éō clárius id perículum appáret* 'the closer that fight comes, the more clearly that danger appears' (Caelius)
>
> *tántō bréuius ómne quántō félicius témpus* 'the happier a period (is), the shorter it (is)' (or 'seems to be') (Pliny) (lit. 'by so much shorter every (time is), by how much the happier the time (is)', i.e. 'time flies when you're enjoying yourself').

(b) Superlative

quam with the superlative means 'as — as possible', e.g.

> *cénam quam máximam hábeō* 'I have the largest dinner possible'

This usage applies equally to adverbs, e.g.

> *quam celérrimē* 'as fast as possible'

(c) Other 'comparative' constructions

1 átque/ac

átque/ac is used after adjectives or adverbs which express 'likeness' or 'unlikeness', such as *ídem* 'the same', *álius* 'different', 'other', *áliter*, 'differently', *cóntrā* 'opposite', 'contrary', *par* 'equal', *páriter* 'equally', *perínde* 'in like manner', *símilis* 'like', 'similar'. E.g.

iussérunt simulácrum Ióuis, cóntrā átque ánteā fúerat, ad oriéntem conuértere 'They ordered (them) to turn the statue of Jupiter towards the East, <u>contrary to what it had been before</u>' (Cicero).

perínde ēgit ac dīxit 'He acted <u>just as he said</u>'.

2 Correlatives

ut meaning 'as' acts as a 'correlative' to *sīc* or *íta* 'thus', e.g. *ut tū ímperās, sīc/íta égo fáciō* 'as you order, so I do'. In the same way, *tam* 'so' is answered by *quam* 'as', e.g.

> *tam beátus érat ílle quam míser égo* 'he was as (lit. so) happy as I unhappy'

tot 'so many' is answered by *quot* 'as many', e.g.

> *tot uírī sunt quot fḗminae* 'so many men there are as many (as) (there are) women', 'there are as many men as women'

Cf. *tántus* 'so great' . . . *quántus* 'as great', 'as'; *tális* 'of such a sort' . . . *quális* 'of which sort', 'as', e.g.

> *tánta sapiéntia ḗī ínest quánta uīs* 'there is so great wisdom in him as great (as there is) force', 'he has as much brain as brawn'
> *tálem uirtū́tem praebḗbat quálem Horátius* 'he showed bravery of such a sort as the sort (which) Horatius (showed)'

NB. See **J5(a)4** above for other correlative usages.

3 Unreal comparisons

quási, uélut, támquam mean 'as if', 'as though' and (with or without *sī* added) take a *subjunctive* where the comparison is unreal or hypothetical. Constructions under **J5(c)1** add *sī*. E.g.

> *íta sē gérit quási stúltus sit* 'he is behaving as though he were a fool' (but he is not).
> *perínde ágit ac sī hóstis sit* 'he acts just as though he were an enemy' (but he is not).

NB. *támquam, quási, uélut, sícut* and *ut* are all used with nouns to express 'like', 'as it were', e.g. *mónte dēcúrrēns* <u>*uélut ámnis*</u> '<u>like a river</u> as it runs down from the mountain' (Horace − speaking of Pindar).

515

K List of prepositions

This list is in alphabetical order and contains the most important prepositions (some of which have not been met in the course).

ā, *ab* or *abs* (+abl.) away from; by; on the side of

ábsque (+abl.) (=*sine*)

ad (+acc.) towards; at, near; for the purpose of; note *úsque ad* right up to

aduérsum/aduérsus (+acc.) opposite to; against

ánte (+acc.) before, in front of

ápud (+acc.) at the house of, in the hands of, in the works of; among

círcum/círcā/círciter (+acc.) around, about

cis/cítrā (+acc.) this side of

clam (+acc./abl.) unknown to

cóntrā (+acc.) against

cŏram (+abl.) in the presence of

cum (+abl.) with

dē (+abl.) about, concerning; from; down from

ē, ex (+abl.) out of, from; in accordance with; after

érgā (+acc.) towards

éxtrā (+acc.) outside

in (+acc.) into, onto; against; (+abl.) in, on

ínfrā (+acc.) below

ínter (+acc.) among; between

íntrā (+acc.) within

iúxtā (+acc.) close to, near

ob (+acc.) on account of, because of; before, so as to obstruct

pénes (+acc.) with, in the possession of

per (+acc.) through, by; in the name of, by the aid of

post (+acc.) behind, after

prae (+abl.) before; in comparison with; for, as a result of

praéter (+acc.) past; beyond; except

prō (+abl.) for, in return for; on behalf of; in front of; instead of; in accordance with

própe (+acc.) near

própter (+acc.) on account of

secúndum (+acc.) behind; along; after; according to

> *síne* (+ abl.) without
> *sub, súbter* (+ acc.) under, beneath; just after, just before; (+ abl.)
>   beneath, under; at
> *súper* (+ acc.) over, above; beyond; (+ abl.) over, above; about,
>   concerning
> *súprā* (+ acc.) above
> *ténus* (+ gen./abl.) as far as (placed *after* the word it governs)
> *trāns* (+ acc.) across
> *uérsus, uérsum* (+ acc.) towards, in the direction of (placed *after*
>   the word it governs)
> *última* (+ acc.) beyond
> *úsque* (+ acc.) all the way to

Note also the abl. nouns *caúsā* and *grātiā* (+ gen.), placed *after* the word
they govern, meaning 'for the sake of', 'for the purpose of'.

When prepositions are followed by the noun they govern, their accent
is determined by treating the two words as one, e.g. *ápud* (natural accent)
and *apúd mē* (as though it were *apudmē*).

L–V Constructions

Introduction

(a) Simple sentences

Simple sentences may be classified into four categories

1 *Statements (including exclamations)*: e.g. *Caésar ábit* 'Caesar leaves', *quam
   trístis est* 'how sad he is!'
   'Potential' statements ('would', 'should', 'could') are expressed by
   the subjunctive, e.g. *uélim* 'I should wish', *dícat/díxerit aliquis* 'someone
   would/may say', as are 'generalising' statements, e.g. *haud inuéniās*
   'you (i.e. one) would scarcely find', *créderēs* 'you would have believed'.
2 *Questions*: e.g. *abísne?* 'are you leaving?' (*-ne* turns a statement into a
   question.) *quis ábit* 'who is leaving?'

Double questions are asked with *útrum . . . an*, e.g. *útrum ábīs an mánēs?* 'are you going or staying?' *ánnōn* means 'or not' in direct speech; indirect uses *nécne* 'or not'. *útrum* is sometimes omitted (in direct and indirect speech), e.g. *ábīs an mánēs?*

an is very flexible. It can introduce a plain question (like *-ne*), or mean 'whether' or 'or'. *num* means 'surely not?', expecting the answer 'no' (*num* means 'if' 'whether' in indirect questions, e.g. *rógō num ábeās* 'I ask whether you depart'). *nōnne* means 'surely?', expecting the answer 'yes'. *écquis* means 'anyone' in a question, e.g. *écquis ábit?* 'is anyone leaving?' (See above **I5(c)(iv)** and **Note**.)

'Deliberative' questions take the form 'what am I to', 'should I –?' and are expressed by the subjunctive, e.g. *quid fáciam* 'what am I to do?' *quid fácerem* 'what was I to do?'

3 *Commands*: e.g. *ábī!* 'leave!'; *nōlī abīre* 'don't leave!'

nē + perfect subjunctive also expresses prohibitions, e.g. *nē trānsíerīs* 'do not cross'. *nē* + present subjunctive is used in general prohibitions, e.g. *nē pétās* 'you (i.e. one) should not seek'. *nē* + imperative is common in poetry, e.g. *nē fúgite hospítium* 'do not shun our hospitality' (Virgil).

Jussives ('let us', 'let him', 'let them') are expressed by the subjunctive (present), e.g. *abeámus* 'let us leave', *fīat* 'let there be'.

'Polite' subjunctives express 'please', e.g. *ábeās* 'kindly leave' (poetic), or general precepts, e.g. *sápiās* 'you (i.e. one) should be wise'. Often commands are made more polite by the use of *fac, uídē* 'see to it (that)', *cáuē* 'take care (not to)', *uélim* 'I would like (x to)' with subjunctive, e.g. *fac míhi scrībās* 'make sure you write to me'.

4 *Wishes*: e.g. *uólō abīre* 'I want to leave'. The subjunctive is also used to express wishes, e.g. *uáleant cīuēs* 'may the citizens flourish'. Sometimes *útinam* (negative *útinam nē*) precedes the wish, e.g. *útinam nē hoc scrīpsíssēs* 'would you had not written this'.

uólō + subjunctive sometimes combine, e.g. *uólō tū hoc fáciās* 'I wish (that) you would do this'.

NB. In general, the tenses are used as in subjunctive conditionals (see **S2(c)**), present referring to a wish for the future, imperfect to a wish for the present, pluperfect to a wish for the past.

(b) Agreement

1 A verb agrees with its subject in number and person, e.g.

> *Caésar ádest*

ádest is third person, singular, because *Caésar* (subject) is third person, singular.

2 An adjective agrees with the word it describes in number, gender and case, e.g.

> *fēminam trístem uídeō* 'I see the unhappy woman'

fēminam is accusative, singular, feminine, so *trístem* is accusative, singular, feminine (see **J Intro.**).

Notes

1 The verb 'to be' is often omitted in sentences, e.g. *níhil bónum nísi quod honéstum* 'nothing [is] good except what is honourable'.
2 A singular subject will sometimes take a plural verb, if the subject implies 'a number of people', e.g. *pars mílitum cáptī sunt* 'part of the soldiers was captured', 'some soldiers were captured'. Likewise, a list of subjects can be taken all together and the verb be singular, or the verb be singular because the last in the list is singular. Where there are both masculine and feminine subjects described by one adjective, the adjective will tend to agree with the masculine.
3 More information may be added about a noun or pronoun by further nouns or pronouns in the same case, e.g. *thésaurus Dēmaénetī, áuī Eucliónis* 'the treasure of Demaenetus, grandfather of Euclio'. *áuī* is genitive, because it refers to *Dēmaénetī*: it is said to be 'in apposition' to *Dēmaénetī*.

(c) Sequence of tenses

Primary sequence means that the main verb is present, future, future perfect, or perfect with 'have' (e.g. 'I have loved', not 'I loved'). In these cases, subjunctives used in subordinate clauses are restricted to the present, perfect and future participle + *sim*.

Secondary or *historic sequence* means that the main verb is imperfect, perfect without 'have' (e.g. 'I loved') or pluperfect. In these cases, subjunctives used in subordinate clauses are restricted to imperfect, pluperfect and future participle + *éssem*.

L The cases

(a) Nominative

The nominative case is used for:
1 The *subject* of a sentence or clause, e.g. *Eúcliō aúlam pórtat* 'Euclio carries the pot' (note that the subject of an indirect statement goes into the accusative – see **R1**).
2 The *complement*, especially with the verb 'to be', e.g. *Eúcliō sénex est* 'Euclio is an old man'; *Caésar cōnsul fit* 'Caesar becomes consul'.

(b) Vocative

The vocative case is used to indicate *the person or thing addressed* e.g. (ō) *Eúcliō, cūr aúlam pórtās?* 'Euclio, why are you carrying a pot?'; *et tū, Brúte?* 'you too, Brutus?'

(c) Accusative

The accusative case limits or defines. It is used in a number of ways.
1 For the *direct object* of a verb, e.g. *Eúcliō aúlam pórtat* 'Euclio carries a pot'.
   Some verbs take a double accusative. Some examples are:

   dóceō 'I teach x (acc.) y (acc.)'
   rógō 'I ask x (acc.) for y (acc.)'; cf. *ōrō* 'I beg x (acc.) for y (acc.)'
   cēlō 'I hide x (acc.) from y (acc.)'

   E.g. *Eúcliō Lycōnidem prūdéntiam dócet* 'Euclio teaches Lyconides wisdom'; *mē cōnsília cēlat* 'he hides his plans from me'.

   The 'cognate' accusative expresses the same idea as the verb, e.g. *uíam it* 'he travels on a road'; *lūdum lūdit* 'he plays a game'.

2 To express *motion towards*, often with *ad* or *in*, e.g.

   Eúcliō ad aédīs uénit 'Euclio comes to the house'
   Rōmam éunt 'they go to Rome'

3 To express *time throughout*, e.g.

   trēs diēs 'for three days'

4 To express *extent of space and its measurement*, e.g.

tría mília pássuum ambuláuērunt 'they walked for three miles'
céntum pédēs áltus 'one hundred feet high'

5 To express the idea '*in respect of*', e.g.

pédēs trémit 'he trembles in respect of his feet'
míhi símilis fáciem 'like me in respect of the face'

This is very common in poetry.

6 To express an adverbial idea, e.g.

dúlce 'sweetly'
quid? 'to what extent?'
múltum 'much'

7 To express exclamations, e.g.

mē míserum! 'unhappy me!'

(d) Genitive

The genitive often defines or completes the meaning of a noun. Its most frequent translation is 'of'. Note the different number of relationships that 'of' can indicate.

1 Possession, author or source ('belonging to', 'written by', 'derived from') e.g.

Euclíōnis aédēs 'the house of Euclio'
Vérgilī líber 'a book of Virgil' (i.e. written by Virgil)

Note that possession of a characteristic is indicated by the genitive in the following idiom:

stúltī est haec dícere 'it is (the mark) of a fool to say this'

2 Part of a whole, e.g.

mágna pars cíuium 'a great part of the citizens'

Cf. *nímis* 'too much', *sátis* 'enough', *párum* 'too little', *áliquid* 'some', *quid?* 'some', 'what?': all take the 'partitive' genitive.

3 Description of content or material ('consisting of', 'containing'), e.g.

pōculum áquae 'a cup of water'

521

4 Description of quality or character (always with an adjective), e.g.

   uir mágnae sapiéntiae 'a man of great wisdom'

5 Value, e.g.

   hómo níhilī 'a fellow of nothing' i.e. 'of no worth'
   fēmina plūrimī 'a woman of very great (worth)'

6 Subjective and objective genitives. Consider the ambiguity of *ámor pátris* 'the love of the father' – does it mean 'the love which the father shows' (i.e. 'father loves' – father is subject, so 'of the father' is subjective genitive) or 'the love which is shown to the father' (i.e. someone loves father, when father is the object, so 'of the father' is objective genitive)? The context will tell you, but you must be aware of both possibilities. Note that *méī, túī, súī, nóstrī, uéstrī*, are *objective* genitives, i.e. *ámor nóstrī* can only mean 'love which is shown to us', not 'love which we feel'.

7 Many verbs and adjectives control the genitive case, especially words involving:

   Remembering and forgetting (*mémini, oblīuīscor*)
   Pitying (*míseret*)
   Losing or lacking (*égeō*) (also with abl.)
   Filling (*plēnus*) (also with abl.)

   E.g.

   uerbōrum oblīuīscor 'I forget the words'
   mē míseret túī 'I feel pity for you'
   cíbī égeō 'I need food'
   plēnus áquae 'full of water'

8 *símilis* 'like', 'resembling' takes the genitive or dative, e.g.

   uir méī símilis 'a man like me'.

(e) Dative

The dative case is best dealt with in two parts.

1 People in the dative
The common idea behind all these usages is that the person in the dative will be interested or involved in the action, often to his advantage or

disadvantage. The action, in other words, has some consequence for the person in the dative. Often 'to', 'for' or 'from' will translate it adequately. In this sense, the dative case is used in the following ways.

(i)   To indicate the indirect object of the sentence – that is, the person *to whom* something is given, told, said, promised, shown, e.g.

aúlam tíbi dō 'I give you (= to you) the pot'
fábulam míhi nárrā! 'tell me (= to me) the story'
quid Caésarī dīxístī? 'what did you say to Caesar?'

(ii) To indicate the person *to whose advantage or disadvantage* something is done, e.g.

béne est míhi 'it's fine for me'

(iii) To indicate possession, with the verb 'to be', e.g.

est míhi pecūnia 'there is money to me', 'I have money'

See also **88.1**.

(iv) As agent, showing *by whom* something is done, e.g.

haec míhi dícta sunt 'these things have been said by me'
hoc míhi faciéndum est 'this is to be done by me'

(The dative of agent is most frequently used with gerundives.)

(v)   To indicate the person *interested* in the action (only personal pronouns, always used in lively way) e.g.

quid míhi Célsus ágit? 'what is Celsus doing? It interests me / I should like to know / please tell me' (Horace).

(vi) To indicate the person judging, *in whose eyes* something is the case, e.g.

Quíntia fōrmósa est múltīs 'Quintia is beautiful to many / in the eyes of many' (Catullus).

(vii) With certain verbs, and adjectives. Examples of verbs are:

crédō 'I believe'.
fáueō 'I favour'.
fídō 'I trust'.
ignóscō 'I pardon'.
ímperō 'I order'.
inuídeō 'I envy'.

īrắscor 'I am angry at'.
mínor 'I threaten'.
nóceō 'I harm'.
párcō 'I spare'.
pắreō 'I obey'.
persuắdeō 'I persuade'.
plắceō 'I please'.
resístō 'I resist'.
subuéniō 'I come to help'.

Many compound verbs, especially those compounded with *ob-*, *sub-*, *prae-*, *bene-*, *male-*, *satis-*, take the dative also.

Adjectives which imply advantage or disadvantage (e.g. nearness, likeness, helpfulness, kindness, trust etc.) take the dative, e.g.

próximus éī 'near (to) him'
Caésarī símilis 'resembling Caesar'
míhi ū̄tilis 'useful to me'

2 Nouns (often abstract) in the dative ('predicative' dative)

Nouns in the dative usually show that which a thing *serves for*, or what its *purpose is*, e.g.

ódiō sum Rōmắnīs 'I serve for a hatred to the Romans' i.e. 'am hated by the Romans'
uoluptắtī sum éī 'I serve for a pleasure to him/her'
mī̄litēs auxíliō mī̄sit 'he sent the soldiers to serve for / to be a help'

(f) Ablative

The ablative case has four basic usages. 'By', 'with', 'from', 'in' often translate it effectively.

1 The 'true' ablative denoting separation *away from*, e.g.

ex úrbe 'out of the city'
nắtus Ióue 'born from Jupiter'
dominātiốne lī̄berắtus 'freed from tyranny'

Under this heading we may list the ablative of comparison ('starting from a point of comparison with'), e.g.

quid móllius úndā? 'what is softer than water?'

2 The 'locative/temporal ablative'. This shows place/time in, on, or at, e.g.

> *in úrbe* 'in the city'
> *térrā maríque* 'on land and sea'
> *dextrā* 'on the right'
> *tríbus hórīs* '(with)in three hours'

3 The 'accompanying' ablative, e.g.

(i) Of description: *uir mágnā uirtū́te* 'a man (with) of great bravery'.

(ii) Of manner (how something is done): *súmmā (cum) celeritā́te uénit* 'he came with very great speed'.

(iii) The ablative absolute, e.g. *tē dúce uincḗmus* 'with you as leader, we shall win' (this shows the *accompanying* circumstances). Cf. **P Note 3**.

4 The 'instrumental' ablative, e.g.

(i) Of agent (*by whom* a thing is done): *ab hīs laudā́tur* 'he is praised by these people'.

(ii) Of instrument or means (*by which* something is carried out): *sáxīs sē dēféndunt* 'they defend themselves with rocks'.

(iii) Of cause (why something happens): *amṓre périit* 'he died (because) of love'.

(iv) Of measure of difference: *tū múltō áltior es* 'you are much taller' (lit. 'taller by much'). Note *éō* 'by so much'; *quō* 'by how much'; *tántō* 'by so much'; *quántō* 'by how much'; *paúlō* 'by a little'; *hōc* 'by this amount'; *aliquántō* 'by a certain amount'. See **J5(a)4**.

(v) Of price (cf. genitive of value at **L(d)5**): *múltō aúrō hanc aúlam ḗmī* 'I bought this pot at a price of much gold'; cf. *mágnō* 'at a high price', *páruō* 'at a small price', *uī́lī* 'at a cheap price'.

(vi) Of respect: *uir pietā́te gráuis* 'a man serious in respect of his piety' (Virgil). (This may also be classified as a *locative* ablative.)

5 Many verbs and some adjectives are followed by the ablative case. Some examples of verbs are:

> *fúngor* 'I perform'
> *frúor* 'I enjoy'
> *útor* 'I use'
> *pótior* 'I take possession of' (also genitive)
> *dṓnō* 'I present x (acc.) with y (abl.)'

abúndō 'I abound in'
ópus est 'there is a need of x (abl.) to y (dat.)'

Some adjectives are:

frēt-us a um 'relying on'
plēn-us a um 'full of' (also genitive)
díɡn-us a um 'worthy of'

6 Note the following phrases, all of which can be explained in the terms set out above:

siléntiō 'in silence'
iū̆re 'rightly'
mṓre maiṓrum 'in the fashion of our ancestors'
méā spónte 'on my own initiative'
ū̆sū̆ 'in practice'
fórte 'by chance'
uī 'by force'
nā̆tū̆ maíor 'older' (lit. 'greater *in respect of* birth')
aéquō ánimō 'with equanimity'
bónā fídē 'in good faith'
méā senténtiā 'in my opinion'
méā caúsā 'for my sake'

(g) Locative

The locative is the remnant of an old case. It is used to express 'at' with names of towns and one-town islands. It has the same form as the genitive in first and second declensions singular, and as the ablative in the first and second declensions plural; in third declension nouns it adopts a form in -*ī* in the s., -*ibus* in the pl. E.g.

> 1st decl. s. *Rṓmae* 'at Rome'
> 2nd decl. s. *Corínthī* 'at Corinth'
> 1st decl. pl. *Athḗnīs* 'at Athens'
> 3rd decl. s. *Carthā̆ginī* 'at Carthage'
> 3rd decl. pl. *Sárdibus* 'at Sardes'

Note also the following special usages:

> *dómī* 'at home'
> *húmī* 'on the ground'
> *rū̆rī* 'in the country' (or *rū̆re*)

> *bélli* 'at war'
> *mīlítiae* 'on military service'
> *ánimī* 'in the mind'

NB.   With towns and one-town islands 'to', 'into' are expressed by the plain accusative and '(away) from' by the plain ablative, e.g.

> *Rōmam* 'to Rome'
> *Rōmā* 'from Rome'
> *Syrācūsās* 'to Syracuse'

M The infinitive

The infinitive acts as a verb, when it is active or passive, has a present, future or past tense and can govern cases. The infinitive can also act as a noun, when it is neuter and stands in the nominative or accusative case.

(a) As a noun (= gerund)

The infinitive often acts as a nominative or accusative gerund, e.g.

> *hūmánum est erráre* 'to err is human', 'error is human'
> *erráre málum dúcimus* 'we consider error (lit. 'to do wrong') wicked'

(b) As a verb/noun (prolative infinitive)

The infinitive is used after certain verbs, e.g. *póssum* 'I am able to', *débeō* 'I ought to', *uólō* 'I wish to', *cónor* 'I try to', *incípiō* 'I begin to', *dúbitō* 'I hesitate to', *sóleō* 'I am accustomed to', etc.

It is common with verbs of being said or thought, e.g.

> *dícitur málus ésse* 'he is said to be wicked'
> *uidétur bónus ésse* 'he seems to be good'

(c) Indirect speech

The verb of indirect statements (see **R1**) is in the infinitive, e.g.

> *pútō tē abiísse* 'I think that you have gone away' (lit. 'I think you to have gone away')

(d) Historic infinitive

The 'historic' infinitive is used to describe vividly an action which would normally be in the imperfect indicative, e.g.

> *multī séquī, fúgere, occídī, cápī* 'many were following, fleeing, being killed and captured'

N Gerund

A gerund is a neuter noun, formed from a verb, with exactly the same form as the neuter s. of the gerundive (see **O**), e.g. *amánd-um ī* 2n. 'love', 'loving'. All such gerunds end in -ndum, e.g. *monéndum, capiéndum, regéndum* etc. This form is *never* nominative. It is most commonly used with a preposition or defining noun, e.g.

> *ad regéndum* 'with a view to ruling', 'in order to rule'
> *ars dīcéndī* 'the art of speaking'
> *regéndī grátiā* 'for the sake of ruling'
> *capiéndī caúsā* 'for the sake of taking', 'in order to take'.

It can take an object e.g. *nāuīs capiéndī caúsā* 'to capture the ships' (though some writers might express this by noun + gerundive + *caúsā* – *nāuium capiendārum caúsā*, see **O Note 3**). It can stand on its own in the dative and ablative, e.g.

> *docéndō et discéndō* 'by teaching and learning'
> *óperam legéndō dat* 'he pays attention to reading'

Infinitives also act as gerunds, in the nominative or accusative (without preposition). See **M**.

O Gerundive

The gerundive is a passive adjective, based on a verb, ending in -nd-us a um, meaning 'to be —ed', 'requiring to be —ed', 'needing to be —ed', 'must be —ed', e.g.

> *Rōma līberánda est* 'Rome is to be freed', 'Rome must be freed', 'Rome needs to be freed'
> *captíuōs necándōs trádidit* 'he handed over the captives to be slain'

Notes

1 The gerundive usually has the agent in the dative, e.g.

> *Rṓma Brū́tō līberā́nda est* 'Rome must be freed by Brutus'.

But verbs which take a dative object have the agent expressed by *ā/ ab* + abl., e.g. *míhi parcéndum est ā tē* 'it is to be spared to me by you', 'you must spare me'.

2 Where a verb is intransitive, the gerundive becomes impersonal, e.g.

> *eúndum est míhi* 'it is to be gone by me', 'I must go'.

3 In cases where a gerundive + noun, translated literally, sound odd, turn the phrase round into an active form, e.g.

> *ad mī́litēs capiéndōs* (lit.) 'with a view to soldiers to be captured' → 'with a view to capturing soldiers'
>
> *in līberā́ndā pátriā* (lit.) 'in the fatherland to be freed' → 'in freeing the fatherland'
>
> *rḗgī creándō* 'for a king to be made' → 'for making a king'

See **N** above for this construction expressed by the gerund.

P Participles

There are three tenses of participle in Latin:

(a) The present participle ACTIVE (see **A1**), meaning '—ing', 'while —ing'.

(b) The future participle ACTIVE (see **A2**), meaning 'about to —', 'on the point of —ing', 'with a view to —ing'.

(c) The perfect participle ACTIVE (used by deponent verbs), 'having —ed' (sometimes just '—ing': see also **C4 Note 2** for passive meaning in some verbs) and the perfect participle PASSIVE (used by transitive, active verbs), meaning 'having been -ed' (see **C4, B4**).

Participles are adjectives and agree in case, number and gender with the noun or pronoun to which they refer. Sometimes they are used as adjectives, merely to describe a noun, e.g. *áqua féruēns* 'boiling water'. But their commonest use is predicative, e.g. *Plátō scrī́bēns est mórtuus* 'Plato died while writing' (Cicero). Contrast *Plátō nóster est mórtuus* 'our Plato has died'. See under 'Predicative' in the Glossary of Latin – English Grammar, p. xxi.

Notes

1 A participle standing on its own either means 'a/the person —ing etc.',
e.g.

>*moritūrī* 'the (masculine plurals) about to die', 'those about to die'

or agrees with a noun or pronoun left out, and refers to a person
already mentioned e.g.

>*rogántī respóndit* 'to (him) as he was asking he replied', 'he replied
>to his question'

2 Participles indicate the *time* of the action in relation to the adjoining
verb, i.e. a present participle indicates the action is going on *at the same
time as the verb*, future participle that it will happen *after the verb*, perfect
that it has happened *before the verb*.

3 Participles, especially present and perfect passive, are often used with a
noun or pronoun in the ablative (*ablative absolute*) to form an
accompaniment to the action of a clause. E.g.

>*Cethḗgus, recitátīs lítterīs, repénte contícuit* 'when the letter had been
>read out, Cethegus suddenly fell silent' (Cicero)

>Cf. *tē dúce* 'under your leadership' (**L(f)3(iii)**).

4 The relationship between verb and participle can be more than merely
temporal and suggest cause, concession, or condition, e.g.

>*tímeō Dánaōs et dóna feréntīs* 'I fear the Greeks, even though
>bringing gifts'
>*nōn míhi nísi admónitō uēnísset in méntem* 'it wouldn't have entered
>my head if I hadn't been reminded' (Cicero)

5 The passive participle often expresses not the thing or person acted on,
but the very act itself, e.g.

>*uiolátī hóspitēs, lēgátī necátī, fána uexáta hanc tántam effēcḗrunt
>uāstitátem* lit. 'violated guests, slaughtered ambassadors, rav-
>aged shrines brought about this massive devastation', but
>better 'the violation of guests, the slaughter of ambassadors,
>the destruction of shrines . . .' etc.

Q1   Relative clauses: *quī* + indicative

A relative clause, introduced in Latin by some form of the relative pronoun *quī quae quod* 'who', 'which', 'what', 'that' (see **I4**) is an adjectival clause which describes a noun, e.g.

'The girls who are present'
'The book which I gave you is very old'

The word to which the relative pronoun refers is called the antecedent. In the above examples, the antecedent of 'who' is 'the girls', and the antecedent of 'which' is 'the book'.

The relative gets its *gender* (m., f. or n.) and its number (s. or pl.) from the *antecedent*; it gets its *case* from its *function* within the relative clause. Observe the following examples:

> *ámō puéllās quae ádsunt* 'I like the girls who are present'

quae: feminine, plural (because 'girls' is the antecedent); nominative, because 'who' is the subject of 'are present'.

> *ubi est fráter méus, quem uidére nōn póssum* 'where is my brother, whom I cannot see?'

quem: masculine, singular (because 'brother' is the antecedent); accusative, because 'whom' is the object of 'I cannot see'.

> *ábest rēx cúius mílitēs ádsunt* 'the king, whose soldiers are present, is absent'

cúius: masculine, singular (antecedent 'king'); genitive, because 'whose' means 'of whom', 'belonging to whom', so genitive of possession.

> *púerī quíbus pecúniam dédī effūgērunt* 'the boys to whom I gave the money have run off'

quíbus: masculine, plural ('boys'); dative, because I gave the money *to* them.

> *úbi est sáxum quō percússus sum* 'where is the rock by which I was hit?'

quō: neuter, singular ('rock'); ablative, because it was the instrument by which I was hit.

Notes

1 The 'connecting' relative joins the sentence closely to the previous one, e.g.

> *Caésar mílitēs mīsit. quōs úbi mīsit* . . . 'Caesar sent the soldiers. Whom when he had sent', i.e. 'when he had sent them'

2 Observe the following idioms:

> *mílitēs quōs habébat óptimōs mīsit* 'he sent the soldiers whom best he had', i.e. 'he sent the best soldiers he had'
> *quā es prūdéntiā, níhil tē effúgiet* lit. 'with what wisdom you are, nothing will escape you' i.e. 'such is your wisdom . . .'

Q2 Relative clauses: *quī* + subjunctive

When a relative clause 'hides' a clause of result, purpose, cause or concession, the verb is subjunctive:

(a) Hidden result clause, often called 'generic', e.g.

> *is est quī paupéribus nóceat* 'he is the sort of person who harms the poor'
> *sunt quī pútent* 'there are people (of the sort) who think . . .'
> *némo est quī hoc fáciat* 'there is no one who does this'
> *némo est quīn próbet* 'there is no one who does not approve' (note that here *quīn* = *ut nōn*)

> NB.   *est quī, sunt quī*, when they refer to a definite antecedent, take the indicative, e.g. *múltī sunt quī pútant* 'there are many who think . . .'

(b) Hidden purpose, e.g.

> *mílitēs mīsit quī hóstīs circúmdarent* 'he sent soldiers who would / to surround the enemy'

(c) Hidden cause, e.g.

> *ámō tē quī mē ámēs* 'I love you who (i.e. because you) love me'

> These clauses often occur with *útpote quī* or *quíppe quī*.

(d) Hidden concession, e.g.

Vérrēs, quī uísus múltīs diébus nōn ésset, támen sē in cōnspéctum dédit
'Verres, who had not been seen for many days, nevertheless presented himself to view', i.e. 'Verres, *although* he . . .'
(concessive)

Note

Observe the following idioms:

1 *dígnus est quī ímperet* 'he is worthy to govern'.
2 *quō* + comparative + subjunctive indicates purpose, e.g. *quō celérius effúgiat* 'in order that he may escape more quickly'.
3 *maíor est quam quem uíncere póssim* 'he is greater than one whom I can defeat', 'he is too great for me to defeat'.

R Indirect speech

When words are not quoted direct but given in reported form (e.g. 'he claimed that she was gone', 'we told him to leave at once', 'she asked where they were'), Latin

(a) Uses the accusative and infinitive to express indirect statements.
(b) Uses *ut*/*nē* + subjunctive (sometimes plain infinitive) to express indirect commands.
(c) Uses question word + subjunctive to express indirect questions.
(d) Puts all subordinate verbs into the subjunctive (except that *dum* 'at one point while' occasionally remains indicative).
(e) Makes all references to the speaker reflexive.

R1 Indirect statements

When you come across a verb of saying, thinking, reporting, etc., or even a noun implying these actions (e.g. *núntius*), be ready for an accusative and infinitive construction. This reports what is being said or thought, e.g.

Caésar dīxit hóstīs appropinquáre 'Caesar said <u>the enemy to be approaching</u>' i.e. 'that the enemy were approaching'.
púto tē púlchrum fuísse 'I consider <u>you to have been handsome</u>' i.e. 'that you were handsome'.
spḗrō tē mox discessū́rum ésse 'I hope <u>you to be about to go</u> soon' i.e. 'that you will go soon'.

Notes

1 Observe that the subject of the indirect statement is in the accusative, and the verb in the infinitive. The tense of the infinitive is the same as what was originally said.

2 Note how *English* changes in response to the tense of the introductory verb of saying or thinking, e.g.

> *Caésar dícit hóstīs appropinquáre* lit. 'Caesar says the enemy to be approaching' 'that the enemy *are* approaching'
> *Caésar díxit hóstīs appropinquáre* 'Caesar said the enemy to be approaching' 'that the enemy *were* approaching'.

3 *négō* means 'I say that . . . NOT'.

4 A reflexive refers to the speaker of the main verb, e.g.

> *Caésar díxit sē discessúrum ésse* 'Caesar said that he (i.e. Caesar) would leave'.

Cf. *Caésar díxit éum discessúrum* 'Caesar said that he (someone else) would leave'.

Note that *sē* and the other personal pronouns tend to come second in the clause unless emphatic.

5 *ésse* is sometimes dropped from the infinitive (see above example).

6 *fóre ut* + subjunctive 'that it should come about that' is often used in indirect statements to get round future passive expressions.

7 Remember to start your translation into English with the word 'THAT' – a word which does not appear in the Latin in these constructions at all.

R2 Indirect commands

Indirect commands are signposted by a word of ordering, persuading, commanding etc. followed by *ut* or *nē*. The verb is in the subjunctive – present in primary sequence, imperfect in secondary. E.g.

> *míhi imperáuit ut abírem* 'he ordered me that I should go / to go away'
> *éōs hortátī sunt nē trístēs éssent* 'they urged them that they should not be / not to be unhappy'

Notes

1 Observe *nē . . . quis* 'that no one' (see **I4** for declension of *quis* indefinite), *nē . . . ūllus* 'that not any', *nē . . . úmquam* 'that never'.
2 References in the indirect command to the subject of the ordering verb are reflexive, e.g.

> *Caésar mīlítibus imperáuit ut síbi pārērent* 'Caesar ordered the soldiėrs to obey him' (i.e. Caesar: *éī* would mean 'him', i.e. someone else)

3 Some verbs take an infinitive construction as in English, e.g. *iúbeō* 'I order', *uétō* 'I forbid', 'order not to', e.g.

> *iússit mē abíre* 'he ordered me to leave'
> *éōs prógredī uétuit* 'he forbade them / told them not to advance'.

4 In extended indirect speech, commands are sometimes introduced without *ut*, with just the plain subjunctive.

R3   Indirect questions

An indirect question puts the verb in the *subjunctive*. The rules are complex (see below), but the simplest thing to do is to translate the subjunctive as if it were the similar tense in the indicative, e.g.

> *rógat cūr uéneris* 'he asks <u>why you have come</u>'
> *nescíuit quid fácerēs* 'he did not know <u>what you were doing</u>'
> *petébam quid dictúrus ésset* 'I was asking <u>what he was about to say / would say</u>'

Notes

1 *num* and *an* in an indirect question mean 'if', 'whether'. *num quis* means 'if/whether anyone' (cf. *nē quis*, *sī quis*, *nísi quis*).
2 *útrum . . . nécne* in an indirect question means 'whether . . . or not'.
3 References to the subject of the verb of asking (etc.) will be reflexive, e.g.

> *Caésar rogáuit cūr ómnēs sē timérent* 'Caesar asked why everyone feared him (i.e. Caesar)'

4 Here are some examples from which you can deduce the chart, given below. They give the full picture of the exact relationship between the sequence, tense of verb and subjunctive required:

main verb primary	question word	subjunctive	main verb primary	question word	subjunctive
rógo	cūr	uénerit	I ask	why	he came / has come / was coming / had come
rógō	cūr	uéniat	I ask	why	he is coming
rógō	cūr	uentúrus sit	I ask	why	he will come / he is going to come

main verb secondary	question word	subjunctive	main verb secondary	question word	subjunctive
rogáuī	cūr	uēnísset	I asked	why	he had come
rogáuī	cūr	ueníret	I asked	why	he was coming
rogáuī	cūr	uentúrus esset	I asked	why	he would come / he was going to come

Summary chart

	Question refers to		
	Present	*Future*	*Past*
Introductory verb primary (e.g. *rógat* 'he asks')	Pres. subj. 'is — ing'	Fut. part. + *sim* 'will —', is going to —'	Perf. subj. '— ed' / 'has —ed' 'was —ing' 'had —ed'
Introductory verb secondary (e.g. *rogáuit* 'he asked')	Imperf. subj. 'was —ing'	Fut. part. + *éssem* 'would —', 'was going to —'	Plupf. subj. 'had —ed', 'had been —ing'

R4 Subjunctives in indirect speech

(a) All subordinate clauses in indirect speech (except occasionally *dum* 'at one point while') have their verbs in the subjunctive. The subjunctives follow the rule of sequence, i.e.

Primary main verb: subjunctives used are present (referring to present and future time) and perfect (referring to past time)

Secondary main verb: subjunctives used are imperfect (referring to present and future time) and pluperfect (referring to past time).

Occasionally future time will be referred to by means of the future participle + *sim* (primary) or *éssem* (*fórem*) secondary. See **142 Note**.

(b)   Conditional sentences in indirect speech have a subjunctive in the *sī/nísi* clause ('protasis'), and an accusative + infinitive in the other part ('apodosis'). The rules of sequence for the subjunctives are the same as those in **R4(a)** above. Note that only context will now allow you to distinguish between a future indicative condition and a subjunctive condition referring to the future, e.g. (he said that) *sī pácem pópulus Rōmánus cum Heluétiīs fáceret, in éam pártem itúrōs* could represent (Direct Speech) *either* (1) *or* (2):

(1)   *sī pácem . . . fáciat, in éam pártem eámus* 'if (the Roman people) were to make peace (with the Helvetii), we would go to that place . . .' Present subjunctive (referring to the future).

(2)   *sī pácem . . . fáciet, in éam pártem íbimus* 'if (the Roman people) is going to make peace (with the Helvetii), we shall go to that place . . .' Future indicative.

In the other subjunctive conditions (imperfect and pluperfect), 'would be —ing' and 'would have —ed' (the apodosis) are both represented by future participle + *fuisse*. E.g. *uidḗmur quiētúrī fuísse, nísi essḗmus lacessítī* 'It seems we would have kept quiet, had we not been provoked' (Cicero) (representing direct speech *sī* + pluperfect subjunctive, pluperfect subjunctive).

S   The subjunctive

The subjunctive originally expressed the will, desire, or hope *on the part of the speaker* that something should be (e.g. *uíuat rēx* 'may the king live' – this is the *speaker's* desire). It is used in main clauses and subordinate clauses. In subordinate clauses in classical Latin it is often used merely as a convention, and does not carry its original force (e.g. in indirect questions, see **R3**).

S1 Main clauses

(Cf. **L–V Intro.**)

(a) As an imperative

Expresses an order, or prohibition, e.g.

nē trānsíerīs 'do not cross'

or the 'jussive' subjunctive 'let us/him' etc, e.g.

eāmus 'let us go'
amēmus 'let us make love'

(b) 'Deliberative' subjunctive

This takes the form 'what am I to?', e.g.

quid fáciam 'what am I to do?'

(c) Wishes

Examples are:

sīs félīx 'may you be happy'
uólō tū scríbās 'I want you to write'

or, with *útinam* 'O that!':

útinam adéssēs 'O that you were present'

(See **L–V Intro. (a)4.**)

(d) Conditional/potential

Examples:

uélim 'I should like to'

$\left.\begin{array}{l}\textit{díxerit}\\\textit{dícat}\end{array}\right\}$ *áliquis* 'someone might/would say'

sī adfuísset, uīdísset 'if he had been there, he would have seen'

538

S2 Subordinate clauses

The subjunctive may be found in a number of clauses already dealt with elsewhere, i.e. indirect commands, indirect questions, and subordinate clauses in indirect speech (on all of which, see **R2** and **R3** and **R4**), relative clauses (see **Q2**), temporal clauses (see **T**), causal clauses (**U**) and concessive clauses (**V**).

(a) Result (or consecutive) clauses 'so . . . that', 'so . . . as to'

1 The 'that' clause is expressed by *ut* + subjunctive (negative *nōn*). The subjunctive is normally present, imperfect or perfect.
2 There are a number of different words for 'so'. These include: *ádeō*, *íta*, *tam*, *sīc*, *éō*.
   Note also *tántus* 'so great', *tot* 'so many', *tális* 'of such a sort', e.g.

   tántum est perículum ut nḗmo uénerit 'so great is the danger that no-one has come'
   tam fórtis érat ut uíncī nōn pósset 'he was so brave that he could not be defeated'
   íta ágere dēbḗmus ut ómnēs nōs laúdent 'we ought so to act that all praise us'

3 Consecutive constructions are also used in the following idioms:

   (i) *tántum ábest ut . . . ut* 'x is so far from . . . (*ut*) . . . THAT' (*ut* consecutive); *fácere nōn póssum quīn* 'I cannot do (a thing) but that . . .', 'I cannot help —ing'; *fíerī nōn pótest quīn* 'it cannot come about but that . . . not'.
   (ii) *quī* + subjunctive can mean 'of such a kind that' (generic), when it is followed by a consecutive construction, e.g. *nōn sum is quī quiḗscere póssim* 'I am not the <u>sort of person who can keep quiet</u>'.
       Cf. *nēmo est quīn próbet* 'there is no one of the sort who does not approve' (Cicero) (*quīn* = *quī nōn*).
   (iii) *áccidit ut* (*nōn*) + subjunctive 'it happens that . . .'; *perfíciō* / *effíciō* / *fáciō ut* (*nōn*) 'I bring it about that . . .'; *nōn múltum ábest quīn* 'it is not far from being the case that . . .'
   (iv) *númquam accḗdō <u>quīn ábeam</u> dóctior* 'I never approach (you) <u>without going away</u> more learned' (Cicero).

(b) Purpose (or final) clauses 'in order to / that', 'to'

Purpose clauses are commonly expressed by *ut* (negative *nē*) + subjunctive. The subjunctive is present in primary sequence, imperfect in secondary. E.g.

> *uénio ut uídeam* 'I come in order to / to / in order that I may see'
>
> *uḗnī ut uidḗrem* 'I came in order (etc.) to see'

Note that *nē quis* = 'that no-one' (see **I4** for declension of *quis* indefinite), *nē úmquam* 'that never', *nē úllus* 'that not . . . any', 'lest any'.

Notes

1 *quī* + subjunctive frequently expresses purpose, especially with verbs of movement, e.g.

> *lēgátōs mīsit quī pácem péterent* 'they sent ambassadors who should seek / to seek peace'

2 References in the purpose clause to the subject of the main verb are expressed by the reflexive, e.g.

> *Caésar uénit ut mīlitēs sē uidḗrent* 'Caesar arrived so that his soldiers should see him (i.e. Caesar)'.

3 *quō* + subjunctive expresses purpose when there is a comparative in the purpose clause, e.g.

> *quō celérius effúgiat* 'so that he may escape more quickly'

4 *perfíciō/efficiō/fáciō ut* (neg. *nē*) + subjunctive ('I bring it about that') may express purpose, as well as result (see **S2(a)3(iii)**).

5 Observe how many ways there are of expressing purpose in Latin:

(i)   *ut/nē* + subjunctive ⎫
                            ⎬ (see above).
(ii) *quī* + subjunctive ⎭

(iii) *ad* + gerund/gerundive 'with a view to —ing' ⎫
                                                     ⎬ (see **N, O**).
(iv) *caúsā* + gerund/gerundive   ⎭

(v)   The supine (see **A7** for formation): used especially with verbs of motion, e.g. *mīlitēs mīsit pácem petítum* 'he sent soldiers to seek peace'.

(c) Conditional sentences

The 'if' clause of a conditional sentence is often called the 'protasis', the main clause the 'apodosis'.

1 Indicative

Where a conditional sentence uses an indicative in both clauses, translate normally, e.g.

> *sī tū sápiēns es, égo stúltus* 'if you are wise, I am a fool'

(But see **Note 1** below.)

Note that English is less accurate about future and future perfects than Latin, e.g.

> *sī puélla discédet, laetus érō* 'if the girl departs (lit. 'will depart') I shall be delighted'
> *sī hoc féceris, habébō grátiam* 'if you do this (lit. 'will have done this') I shall be grateful'

2 Subjunctive

Where a conditional sentence has the subjunctive in both clauses, translate with 'would', 'should', 'were', as follows:

(i) Present subjunctive (refers to future time) 'If x were to happen y would happen'.

(ii) Imperfect subjunctive (refers to present time) 'If x were now happening, y would be happening'.

(iii) Pluperfect subjunctive (refers to past time) 'If x had happened, y would have happened'.

E.g.

> *sī puélla discédat, laétus sim* 'if the girl were to depart, I would be delighted'
> *sī puélla discéderet, laétus éssem* 'if the girl were (now) departing, I would (now) be happy'
> *sī puélla discessísset, laétus fuíssem* 'if the girl had departed, I would have been delighted'

Notes

1 Latin sometimes mixes indicatives and subjunctives in conditional sentences. Generally speaking, such conditions should be treated on the 'would/should' pattern, e.g.

> *pōns íter paéne hóstibus dédit, nísi únus uir fuísset* 'the bridge almost gave the enemy a way across (and would have done), if there had not been one man' (Livy)

2 The imperfect subjunctive can be used to refer to past time, e.g.

uidḗrēs 'you would have seen'

3 *nísi*, *nī* and *sī nōn* all mean 'if . . . not', 'unless'.

4 *sī/nísi quis* means 'if/unless *anyone*' (see **I4** for declension of *quis* indefinite). Cf. *sī/nísi quándō* 'if/unless at any time'.

5 *síue . . . síue* (*seu . . . seu*) means 'whether . . . or' and introduces alternative conditions, e.g.

> *síue haec uḗra síue fálsa sunt, profícīscar* 'whether these things are false or true, I shall set out'

6 The indicative is normal in the main clause (apodosis) of a condition using subjunctive, where it involves the ideas of possibility (e.g. *póssum*) or obligation (e.g. *dḗbeō* or gerundive), e.g.

> *nísi fēlícitās in socórdiam uertísset, exúere iúgum potuḗre* 'if their success had not turned to sloth, they would have been able to throw off the yoke' (Tacitus)
>
> *sī únum díem morā́tī essḗtis, moriéndum ómnibus fúit* 'if you had delayed for one day, you would all have had to die' (Livy)

7 For conditional sentences in indirect speech see **R4(b)**.

(d) Verbs of fearing

uéreor/tímeō meaning 'I fear *to*' take the infinitive as in English.

uéreor/tímeō meaning 'I fear *that/lest*' take the subjunctive, and are introduced by *nē* ('that', 'lest'), *ut* ('that . . . not') or *nē . . . nōn* ('that . . . not'). The subjunctive follows normal rules of sequence, e.g.

> *tímeō nē uéniat* 'I fear lest he (will) come'
> *timḗbam nē uēnísset* 'I was afraid that he had come'

NB. As with purpose clauses, any reference to the subject of the main verb inside the *nē/ut/nē nōn* clause will be reflexive.

(e) Verbs of doubting

nōn dúbitō 'I do not doubt', *nōn dúbium est* 'there is no doubt' and similar negative expressions of doubting are followed by *quīn* + subjunctive, e.g.

> *nōn dúbium est quīn érrēs* 'there is no doubt that you are wrong'

Notes

1 This amounts to an indirect question (see above **R3**), since it reports 'Are you not wrong?' *quīn* is composed from *quī* (old abl. of *quī quae quod*) and the negative *-ne*. The original meaning (common in Plautus) is 'How not?', 'Why not?'.

2 The affirmative (even more clearly an indirect question) is *dúbitō an* + subj. 'I doubt whether . . .'

(f) Verbs of hindering, preventing, forbidding

Verbs like *impédiō* 'I hinder', *dētérreō* 'I deter', *prohíbeō* 'I prevent', *óbstō* 'I stand in the way of (x doing something)' are followed by *nē* or *quóminus* with the subjunctive, unless negative, when they take *quóminus* or *quīn*. E.g.

> *tē impédiam nē/quóminus ábeās* 'I shall prevent you from leaving'

But

> *tē nōn impédiam quóminus/quīn ábeās* 'I shall *not* prevent you from leaving'

NB.   The infinitive or accusative and infinitive is common after *prohíbeō*, e.g. *prohíbeō tē íre* 'I prevent you from going'.

(g) 'Provided that'

dum, dúmmodo, módo can mean 'provided that' (negative *dum nē* etc.), when the verb is subjunctive, e.g.

> *óderint dum métuant* 'let them hate, provided that they fear' (Accius – Roman tragedian: a favourite quote of Caligula)

T Temporal clauses

These clauses indicate the time at which something takes place, e.g. 'when', 'as soon as', 'after', 'while', 'until', 'whenever', etc.

(a)   *úbi, ut* ('when'), *póstquam* 'after', *símulac, quam prímum* ('as soon as') take the indicative.

Note that when Latin uses the perfect indicative, English frequently translates with the pluperfect, e.g.

> *úbi Caésar peruénit* 'when Caesar arrived/had arrived'

(b) *dum, dṓnec*, 'while' take the indicative, e.g.

> *dum uī̆uō, spḗrō* 'while I live, I hope'

Note that when 'while' means 'at one point when', the indicative is *present*, e.g.

> *dum lóquor, hómo intrắuit* 'while I was speaking, the fellow entered'

(c) *dum, dṓnec* 'until' and *ántequam, priúsquam* 'before' take:

1 The indicative when the clause conveys nothing but the idea of pure time, e.g. *manḗbat dum Caésar peruḗnit* 'he waited till Caesar arrived'.

2 The subjunctive when the action is expected or waited for or intention is being expressed, e.g. *manḗbat dum Caésar ueníret* 'he waited until Caesar should come'; *ábiit priúsquam Caésar éum uidḗret* 'he left before Caesar should see him'.

(d) *cum* 'when' takes:

1 The indicative when referring to present or future, e.g. *cum uidḗbis, tum scíēs* 'when you (will) see, then you will know'.

2 The subjunctive (pluperfect or imperfect) when referring to past, e.g. *cum haec dīxísset, ábiit* 'when he had said this, he left'.

(e) An exception to **T(d)2** is that *cum* takes the indicative when referring to the past in the following circumstances:

1 When it expresses pure time, e.g. *cum égo Rṓmae éram, tū Londíniī érās* 'when I was at Rome, you were in London'

2 When it means 'whenever', e.g. *cum mē uíderat, laetābắtur* 'whenever he saw me, he rejoiced'

3 'Inverted' *cum*, e.g. *abíbam cum núntius peruḗnit* 'I was going away when a messenger arrived'.

U Causal clauses: 'because', 'since'

---

quod, quía, quóniam, quándō all mean 'since', 'because' and their verbs take the indicative when the speaker is vouching for the reason, e.g.

> *ádsunt quod offícium sequúntur* 'they are present because they follow their duty' (that is the speaker's explanation)

ádsunt quod officium sequántur would mean 'they are present on the grounds that (i.e. the reason is not the speaker's) they follow their duty'.

cum 'since' nearly always takes the subjunctive. After certain verbs, however, it can take the indicative, e.g.

> *dóleō cum aéger es* 'I grieve because you are ill'

Cf. *laúdō* 'I praise', *gaúdeō* 'I rejoice'.

Notes

1 *quī* + subjunctive can denote cause, e.g.

> *ámō tē quī mē ámēs* 'I love you who (= because you) love me'

quī in such utterances is often strengthened by the addition of *quíppe, útpote* or *ut*.

2 Causal clauses are often signposted or picked up by *éō* or *idcírcō* 'for this reason'.

V Concessive clauses

These are introduced by *étsī*, *etiámsī* 'even if'; *quámquam, quámuīs* 'although' and *quī* + subjunctive. *étsī* and *etiámsī* take indicative or subjunctive like conditional clauses, e.g.

> *etiámsī tácent, sátis dícunt* 'though they are silent, they say enough'
> *etiámsī táceant, sátis dícant* 'though they were to be silent, they would say enough'

quámquam 'although' takes indicative; *quámuīs* 'however' takes subjunctive, e.g.

> *quámquam inimícus es* 'although you are hostile'
> *quámuīs inimícus sīs* 'however hostile you may be'

quī 'who' can be used with concessive force, when it takes the subjunctive, e.g.

> *égo quī fórtis sim támen fúgiam* 'I, who am brave, nevertheless will flee' i.e. 'I, though brave . . .'

NB. *lícet* 'it is allowed' is quite often followed by a subjunctive verb. In this case it means 'though', e.g. *frémant ómnēs lícet, dícam quod séntiō.* 'Though they may all make a commotion, I will say what I think' (Cicero).

W Word-order

(a) Emphasis and scene-setting

1 *Caésar in Gálliam conténdit* 'Caesar marched into Gaul' may be called for convenience the 'normal' or 'narrative' order of that sentence in Latin. An 'emphatic' order would be *in Gálliam Caésar conténdit* 'it was into Gaul that Caesar marched' (answering the question 'Where was Caesar marching?'), or *conténdit in Gálliam Caésar* (answering the question 'What was it that Caesar was doing re Gaul?'). Putting the verb first is common in vivid or excited narrative, when we want to know what is happening at once or when there is no stated subject to the verb, so verb-ending is the only clue to it.

Observe how 'emphasis' affects the position of 'attributive' adjectives, normally placed *after* the noun (e.g. *uir bónus* 'good man'). They come first when they define it (emphatically) rather than merely add a description, e.g. *útram túnicam máuīs – álbam an purpúream? purpúream túnicam málō* 'Which tunic do you prefer – the white or the purple?' 'The purple's the one I prefer.'

2 *Gállia est ómnis dīuīsa in pártīs trēs* 'As for Gaul, the whole of it, it is divided into parts – how many? – Well, *three* actually.' Caesar 'sets the scene' – we are talking about the whole of Gaul – and leaves to the end the real importance of what he is to say: that it is divided into *three* parts. Observe how he continues: *quárum únam íncolunt Bélgae, áliam Aquitānī* 'of which, well, we have one part lived in by – Belgians – and the other by – Aquitanians'. Again, Caesar sets the scene and then gives the really important information: it was Belgians and Aquitanians who lived in two of the parts.

English also uses 'scene-setting' word-order to emphasise in this way, e.g. '*Talent*, Mr. Micawber *has*; *capital*, Mr. Micawber *hasn't*' (Dickens).

(b) Shadowing

1 Latin tends to alternate emphatic and unemphatic words or phrases within the sentence. In the example of the coloured tunics given above, the word *purpúream* in the answer is emphatic, and the word *túnicam* – less necessary, since we already know that tunics are what is being discussed – carries less emphasis. It is useful to think metaphorically of *túnicam* being cast into the shadow by the emphatic *purpúream* which precedes it.

2 Certain classes of words tend to be placed in the shadow of the first

important word in the sentence or clause (regardless of whether they are connected with it grammatically or logically). These are: (i) particles like *énim*, *aútem*, which connect the sentence they occur in with what precedes; (ii) unemphatic personal and demonstrative pronouns like *mē*, *tíbi*, *éum*, *nōs*: e.g. *hīs míhi rḗbus, Scípiō, léuis est senéctūs* (Cicero) 'it is because of these things, Scipio, that old age is no burden for me'. Note that *míhi* interposes itself between two grammatically connected words: *hīs* and *rḗbus*. (iii) The verb, when unemphatic, often gravitates to a position just after the first emphatic word: this happens especially with *est* as an auxiliary verb, e.g. *in Gálliam est Caésar proféctus* 'it was for Gaul that Caesar set out'.

3 Adverbial phrases may be 'shadowed' (or 'sandwiched') between two grammatically connected words when they are logically connected with the enclosing phrase: *mágnā in hāc rē prūdéntiā ūténdum est* 'great prudence must be used in this matter' (*in hāc rē* limits the application of the prudence to *this matter*); *clārṓrum uirṓrum post mórtem honṓrēs pérmanent* 'the honours paid to great men remain after death' (*post mórtem* warns us in good time that we are thinking of a special kind of honour – the sort that may be paid after death).

(c) Some consequences of emphasis, scene-setting and shadowing

1 The normal place for subordinating conjunctions is at the beginning of their clause, but when other words in the clause are used for 'scene-setting' (as often in temporal or conditional clauses), the conjunction often ends up immediately before the verb: *Caésar in Gálliam cum contendísset* 'when Caesar had marched into Gaul'.

2 In accusative and infinitive constructions, if there is no other word with more emphasis, the infinitive often comes at the very beginning, being often followed immediately by an unemphatic pronoun subject: (*dīxit míhi Caésar*) *uélle sē cōnsulátum pétere* 'Caesar told me he wanted to stand for the consulship'. On the other hand, if one of the other words is emphatic, it will naturally come first (the unemphatic pronoun remaining in second place): (*dīxit míhi Caésar*) *cōnsulátum sē uélle pétere* 'Caesar told me that it was the consulship he wanted to stand for'. When it is discovered for the first time that Britain is an island, Tacitus reports the event as follows: *hanc ṓram nouíssimī máris tunc prīmum Rōmāna clássis circumuécta ínsulam ésse Británniam adfirmāuit*, 'that was the first time a Roman fleet had rounded this shore of the furthest sea, and this confirmed that Britain was an island' – 'that it was an island Britain was'.

APPENDIX:
THE LATIN LANGUAGE

A brief history of the Latin language

The beginnings

Latin is one of the many languages belonging to the Indo-European family whose members extend from the Atlantic coasts of Europe to India. In Europe itself these languages can be divided into groups: Hellenic, represented by the various dialects of Greek; Italic, consisting of Latin and its close relatives in central Italy: Germanic, including English, German, and the Scandinavian languages; and Celtic, including Welsh and Irish (see Table). Latin is in the unique position of being not only a member of the Italic group but also the ancestor of the last European group, Romance (including Italian, Spanish, and French) which developed later than the rest, within historic times. Though Latin, settled in Latium, was only one of the members of the Italic group that also included Oscan and Umbrian, by the fourth century the energy of the Romans had reduced their neighbours to the status of subject allies, and their languages, known to us only from inscriptions and isolated words taken into Latin, never attained any recorded literary cultivation and succumbed to Latin during classical times.

Indo-European Languages			
European descendants (groups, then group-members)			
Celtic	Germanic	Italic	Hellenic
Irish	English	Latin	Greek
Welsh	German	↓	
	Scandinavian languages	*Romance languages*	
		Italian	
		Spanish	
		French	

548

Early Latin

The remains of early Latin consist of later quotations from the works of authors not preserved entire, and of inscriptions, beginning with a brooch from Praeneste (*c.* 600 B.C.) which reads in Greek letters MANIOS MED FHE FHAKED NUMASIOI (= *Mānius mē fēcit Numeriō*) 'Manius made me for Numerius'[1]. Between this date and the beginnings of surviving literary texts with the plays of Plautus (*c.* 254–184 B.C.) many changes in the language took place, as even these few words show: *-os* became *-us*, and *-om* became *-um* (see **H2(a) Note 2**); *-d* dropped in *med* (= *mē*) and the ablative singulars *Gnaiuod* (= *Gnaeō*), *sententiad*; *fhefhaked* shows a reduplicated perfect (*fhe fhaked*) in contrast to *fēcit*; the dative singular of the second declension is in *-oi* and distinct from the ablative; and single intervocalic *-s-* (*Numasioi*) becomes *-r-* (see **H3(d) Note**). Other evidence shows the early diphthongs *ei* becoming *i* (as *quei, sei*) and *oi, ou* becoming *u*, as *oinom* (= *ūnum*), *abdoucit*. Whereas classical Latin limits the position of the accent to the second or third syllable from the end of the word, at an early period the accent was on the first syllable of all words and was very strong; as a result the vowels in the syllables immediately after this accent were reduced, and these changes survived the later shift in the position of the accent and can still be seen in verbs compounded with prepositions, e.g. *capiō: incipiō; sedeō: obsideō; aestimō: exīstimō; caedō: incīdō; claudō: inclūdō*, and also in adjectives with the negative prefix *in-*, e.g. *aptus: ineptus; arma: inermis; aequus: inīquus*.

[1] There is controversy over this inscription – it *may* be a forgery – but the linguistic lessons it encapsulates are not affected.

The Empire

By the end of the Republic in 31 Roman rule extended to territories almost completely encircling the Mediterranean, with gaps only on the north coast of Africa, and including all the islands. In the eastern Mediterranean Greek was already established as the second language of the users of a great variety of tongues, but in the West Latin had no such competition, and passed with surprising rapidity from being a *lingua franca* to being adopted as the language of the country in the Iberian peninsula and Gaul. The conquest by the emperor Claudius in the first century A.D. introduced Latin to Britain but, as in other peripheral parts of the Empire, it did not long survive the collapse of central authority in the Western Empire in the fifth century.

The Middle Ages

From this point the history of Latin divides into two. (1) In the older Roman territories of Spain and Gaul, where it had ousted the native languages, it gradually developed in its spoken form into the various Romance languages. (2) As the medium of Western Christianity it continued, primarily as a *written* language of liturgy and administration throughout the old Roman lands and wherever Christianity became established, on the borders of the Empire as in Britain, or beyond them as in Germany and Scandinavia and among some of the Western Slavs. This Christian Latin, though open to local influences on vocabulary and idiom, was transmitted by education, and each generation of students learned it consciously and painfully in an unchanging form. Within communities of the educated such as monasteries and, later, universities, it became a spoken language also, as well as being the normal medium of teaching and writing on serious and technical subjects such as grammar, rhetoric, logic, mathematics, law, medicine, theology and history (though in Britain both Celtic and Anglo-Saxon, and in parts of Scandinavia the vernacular languages were cultivated in written form for learned purposes earlier than elsewhere). As the context of mediaeval Latin was first and foremost a religious one the language of St Jerome's late fourth-century revision of previous Latin translations of the Bible (the *ēditiō uulgāta*) was immensely influential, and sanctified late popular usages such as a simple sentence structure, changes in the use of cases and the subjunctive, and the abandonment of the accusative and infinitive construction in reported speech. At the same time the ancient practice, more appropriate to native speakers than to learners, of confining literary study to the poets, especially Virgil, was continued, though not without Christian misgivings about their pagan subject-matter, and thus constructions proper to verse found their way into medieval prose works.

The renascences

As the standard and even the continued existence of this mediaeval Christian Latin depended on the efficiency of educational institutions it fluctuated with the stability and prosperity of the region, and its history is marked by a series of renascences following periods of declining standards. One such was the Carolingian Renascence under the Emperor Charlemagne *c.* 800 A.D., who summoned to his court Alcuin of York to advise him and direct a reform of clerical education, and who made provision for cathedral and monastic schools. A good many classical Latin authors would have been lost to us if their works had not been collected and recopied at this time. A similar renascence took place in the twelfth century, more concerned with creation than conservation, and associated with a greater emphasis on secular learning and the first universities with their devotion to dialectic and professional training in medicine and law. The renascence to which the title 'Renaissance' is normally applied began in the late thirteenth and early fourteenth centuries in Northern Italy and at the papal court at Avignon. It was characterised by an eagerness to search out, copy, and edit new texts, and by an admiration for the style and a sympathetic appreciation of the virtues of the classical period, above all of Cicero, and it marked the beginning of the end of the Middle Ages, which it unfairly stigmatised as a period of barbarism and ignorance.

The Romance languages

Evolution

In one sense Latin is not a dead language but the unchanging *written* form that has survived down the centuries in parallel with the Romance languages, which represent the further evolution of its *spoken* form at various times and places. It took quite a long time for the magnitude of the difference to be appreciated: at first, Latin was the written norm and the spoken forms were regarded simply as less careful and less correct forms of the same language, and it is not until about the ninth century A.D. that the first attempts at writing the spoken forms continuously reveal that these had come to be perceived as different languages from Latin. Wherever Latin had become the ordinary language, by late classical times its differing local development created dialects distinct in small ways from their neighbours, and as new states came into being after the Dark Ages, in each a particular dialect, usually associated with the seat of government, acquired prestige; as the size of states increased these prestige dialects took the first steps toward becoming national languages. Thus, in addition to the well-known modern national languages of French, Spanish, Portuguese, Italian, and all their dialects, the Romance group includes languages representing cultural or former political units such as Provençal and Catalan, as well as the Romance dialects spoken in the Alpine regions and the various islands. Far to the east lies Romanian, first recorded in the sixteenth century, whose survival is something of a mystery. Dalmatian, in present-day Yugoslavia, died out about a century ago. Since the Middle Ages trade and colonisation have carried Romance languages all over the world, so that Portuguese became established in Brazil, Africa, and the Far East; Spanish in Mexico and the rest of South America (hence the term 'Latin America'); and French in North America and Africa.

Variety

While all these languages have diverged from Latin they have not done so in the same way or to the same degree, and the range of variation extends from French at the extreme of innovation to the Sardinian dialects at the conservative end of the spectrum. The process of differentiation must have begun long before the records and was probably detectable to the ear, though not in writing, before the fall of the Empire. To an undeterminable extent the changes as regards sounds represent the influence of the languages spoken before Latin was adopted (the 'substratum'), and as regards vocabulary the contact with other languages since then, e.g. with Frankish (a Germanic language) in France, Arabic in Spain, Magyar and Bulgarian in Romania.

Characteristics

We normally work backwards from the members of a language family in order to reconstruct their unrecorded common ancestor. When we do this with the Romance languages we do not produce a result which exactly tallies with classical Latin, but one which represents a more popular and less literary spoken style, unhappily called Vulgar Latin. While most of the detail is peculiar to each language and dialect, some general statements about the nature of the evolution from Latin to Romance can be made.

I. *Nouns and adjectives.* (A) All the languages (with the limited exception of Romanian) abandoned the Latin case system, reducing the noun to two forms, a singular and a plural. (1) The singular continues the Latin accusative singular minus the *-m* (which was already weak, perhaps only a nasalisation, in Latin), e.g. *corōna(m)*, It. *corona*, *annu(m)*, It. *anno*. (2) The plural either adds *-s* from the accusative plural (so in Fr., Sp., Port.) e.g. the Latin *corōnās* becomes Sp. *coronas*, the Latin *annōs*, becomes Sp. *anos*; or changes the final vowel (so in It., Rom.) as in the nominative plural of the first two declensions, e.g. *corōnae*, It. *corone*; *annī*, It. *anni*. (B) The three gender classes of Latin were reduced to two by the loss of the neuter, with neuter nouns generally becoming masculine. (C) The inflected forms of the degrees of comparison in adjectives and adverbs were replaced by phrases with *plūs* (It., Fr.) or *magis* (Sp., Port., Rom.), e.g. Latin *aqua calidissima*, It. *l'acqua più calda*, Fr. *l'eau la plus chaude*, Sp. *el* *agua más cálida*, with the comparative replacing the superlative. In place of the inflected adverb, e.g. *lentē*, the Romance languages formed phrases with the Latin ablative *mente*, e.g. *lentā mente*, It., Sp. *lentamente*, Fr. *lentement*. (D) The indefinite and definite articles were introduced, utilising *ūnus*, *ille*, e.g. Latin *ūnus homo*, *ūna domina/fēmina*, It. *un uomo, una donna*, Fr. *un homme, une femme*; Latin *ille homo*, It. *l'uomo*, Fr. *l'homme*; Latin *illī/illōs hominēs*, It. *gli uomini*, Fr. *les hommes*. (E) The insubstantial demonstratives *is* and *hic* were replaced by *iste, ipse*, and compounds of these with *ecce*, e.g. *iste*, Sp. *este*; *ipse*, Sp. *ese*; *eccu(m) istu(m)*, It. *questo*, Fr. *ce, cet*; *ecce illu(m)/illōs/illās*, Fr. *celui, celle(s), ceux*.

II. *Verbs.* (A) The four conjugations were sometimes reduced to three by the redistribution of the third between the second and fourth. (B) The whole inflected passive was lost, except for the participle, which combined with *esse* to form a new phrasal passive, e.g. Latin *amātur* but It. *è amato*, Fr. *il est aimé*. (C) The future and future perfect and, in most parts, the pluperfect indicative, disappeared, while the pluperfect subjunctive generally replaced the imperfect subjunctive, e.g. *cantāuisset/cantāsset*, It. *cantasse*, Fr. *il chantât*. (D) The Latin future was replaced by a combination of *habeō* (less frequently *uolō* or *dēbeō*) with the infinitive of the main verb to give a new Romance future, e.g. *cantāre-habet*, It. *canterà*, Fr. *il chantera*. (E) Beside the Latin perfect a new past tense was formed with the present of *habēre* or *tenēre* (in intransitive verbs sometimes with *esse*), plus the past participle, e.g. *habet cantātum*, It. *ha cantato*, Fr. *il a chanté*; and in parallel with this a new pluperfect was created using the imperfect of the auxiliary verb, e.g. *habēbat cantātum*, Fr. *il avait chanté*. (F) The other notable Romance creation was the conditional, formed like the new future but with the imperfect or perfect of *habeō* added to the infinitive, e.g. *cantāre-habēbat/habuit*, Fr. *il chanterait*, It. *canterebbe*; a parallel past conditional was then formed from the conditional of *habeō* plus the past participle, e.g. Fr. *il aurait chanté*. (G) The future participle did not survive, and the present one, except in purely adjectival use, was generally replaced by the ablative of the gerund, e.g. It. *cantando*.

Vocabulary

The vocabulary of the Latin that developed into Romance often differs from the literary terms for a variety of reasons: the classical word may be physically too slight to survive sound-change and so be expanded by prefixes or suffixes or be replaced by a more substantial approximate synonym, or the classical term may simply have gone out of fashion generally or at that particular social level. So, for example, *edō* 'eat' is replaced by *comedō* or *mandūcō; ōs (ōris)* 'mouth' by *bucca* (though *os, ossis* 'bone' survives); *ignis* 'fire' by *focus; magnus* 'great' by *grandis; apis* 'bee' by *apicella; auis* 'bird' by *auicellus* or *passer; ferre* 'to bring' by *portāre* or *leuāre; equus* 'horse' by *caballus; breuis* 'short' by *curtus; pulcher* 'beautiful' by *bellus* or *fōrmōsus;* and *domus* 'house' by *casa* or *mānsiō.* However, as the Romance languages never lost the sense of being connected in some way with Latin they continued to draw new vocabulary from book Latin, and from each other, as they developed into cultivated literary languages in the course of the Middle Ages. These later acquisitions can often be recognised because they are closer in form to their Latin source than the words that have shared the whole development of their particular Romance language.

The Latin element in English

First–fourth centuries A.D.
The Romans attempted the conquest of Britain unsuccessfully under Julius Caesar in 55 and successfully under the Emperor Claudius in A.D. 43, after which they remained in control of Britain (but not of Ireland) until about the end of the fourth century. During this period at least the town-dwelling Britons became familiar with Latin and many words were taken over into their own language and survive to the present day in its descendant, Welsh. At this time the Angles and Saxons, Germanic tribes speaking a language that was to be the ancestor of English, were still on the Continent, living along the North Sea coast of the present Netherlands, though some had already been introduced into Britain to act as a coastal defence force against other Germanic raiders. In the course of trade and service with the Roman army on the Continent some Latin words had been adopted by the Germanic peoples generally, and so were part of their language when the Angles and Saxons began in the fifth century to migrate to Britain and settle there. Some of these words were in fact Greek in origin but were already naturalised in Latin. A number of modern English words have survived from this early period, absorbed partly on the Continent and partly during their first century in Britain.

We have: ark (*arca*, chest; also the surname Ark-wright), bishop (*episcopus*), butter (*būtyrum*), candle (*candēla*), chalk (*calc-em*), cheap (*caupō;* place-names Cheapside, Chipping- 'market'; surname Chapman 'trader'), cheese (*cāseus*), Chester (*castra;* and names in –caster, -cester, -chester), church (*kyriakon*), copper (*cuprum*), coulter (*culter*), devil (*diabolus*), dish (*discus*), fever (*febris*), inch (*uncia*), kiln (*culīna*), kitchen (*coquīna*), line (*līnea*), mallow (*malua*), mile (*mīlle passūs*), mill (*molīna*), mint (coinage, *monēta*), mint (plant, *menta*), -monger, as fishmonger (*mangō*), pitch (tar, *pic-em*), purple (*purpura*), pillow (*puluīnus*), pile (as in pile-driver, *pīlum*), pin (*penna*), pine (tree, *pīnus*), port (*portus*), post (*postis*), priest (*presbyter*), plant (*planta*), pit (*puteus*), pound (weight, *pondō*), sack (*saccus*), sickle (*secula*), street (*strāta uia*), shrive (*scrībere*), shrine (*scrīnium*), tile (*tēgula*), toll (tax, *telōnium*), turtle (-dove, *turtur*), wall (*uallum*), wine (*uīnum*).

Many others have fallen out of use in the course of time while others survive in dialect, as *sikker* (*sēcūrus*) 'certain' (later taken over in its French form as 'sure', and then again from Latin as 'secure'), *neep* (*nāpus*) 'turnip', *soutar* (*sūtor*) 'shoemaker' (and as a surname), or have undergone a change of meaning which obscures the relationship, as 'shambles' (*scamellum*, originally 'butcher's stall'), 'pine' (*poena*, originally 'punish', 'torment').

Fifth–sixth centuries A.D.

A little later the English acquired more Latin words of a very similar kind from British speakers in the period immediately after the settlement and before their conversion to Christianity in the seventh century had made any of them familiar with Latin as a written language. Some examples are: anchor (*anchora*), cat (*cattus*), chervil (*cerefolium*), chest (*cista*), cowl (*cucullus*), fork (*furca*), minster (*monastērium*), monk (*monachus*), mortar (pestle and m., *mortārium*), mussel (*musculus*), nun (*nonna*), provost (*praepositus*), punt (*pontō*), relic (*reliquiae*), Satur-day (*Saturnus*; the other days of the week were given Germanic names on the pattern of the Latin ones), stop (up), (*stuppāre*, from *stuppa* 'tow'), strap (*stroppus*), trivet (*tripod-em*), trout (*tructa*).

A few others are now archaic or poetical, or of historical interest only: cockle (weed, *cocculus*), kirtle (tunic, *curtus*), lave (*lauāre*), soler (*sōlārium*; the sunny room or parlour in a medieval castle, now reintroduced in its Latin form in a new context).

Seventh–tenth centuries

During the remaining centuries before the Norman Conquest of 1066 many new Latin words appeared in English books but the majority of them were only superficially anglicised and never became widely used. Their survival rate is accordingly low. Some examples are: alms (*eleemosyna*), altar (*altāre*), apostle (*apostolus*), arch- (*archi-*), balsam (*balsamum*), beet (*bēta*), camel (*camēlus*), cole-wort, kail (*caulis*), cook (*coquus*), cope (garment, *cap*(*p*)*a*), creed (*crēdō*), idol (*īdōlum*), lily (*līlium*), martyr (*martyr*), mass (service; *missa*), offer (*offerre*), paradise (*paradīsus*), plaster (medical; (*em*)*plastrum*), part (*part-em*), pope (*papa*), psalm (*psalmus*), purse (*bursa*), school (*schola*), spend ((*e*)*xpendere*), title (*titulus*), and perhaps verse (*uersus*).

In some cases where the word has survived the original meaning is no longer current, as 'prime' and 'noon' (*prīma* and *nōna hōra*) the first and ninth hours of the monastic day, or 'scuttle' (*scutella*, diminutive of *scūtum*, originally 'dish', 'platter').

Some members of this late group are more likely to have been borrowed a second time from French than to have survived from pre-Conquest times, and this was certainly the case with many of the Latin loan-words found in Anglo-Saxon, when the modern forms show that they were lost and re-acquired in this way.

Eleventh–fifteenth centuries and after

From the Conquest to the Renaissance a very large number of words of ultimately Latin origin found their way into Middle English, but almost invariably they did so either through French or with the same modifications of endings as similar words had undergone in French, so that direct borrowings are hard to identify. From the sixteenth century this type of borrowing continues but at the same time a substantial number of words come into English as unmodified Latin and retaining such features as Latin plural formations. The largest number of these came in during the sixteenth and seventeenth centuries with a sharp decline thereafter, apart from the terminology of the natural sciences. A few examples from each century will illustrate the process.

Sixteenth century: alias, arbiter, area, circus, compendium, decorum, delirium, exit, genius, ignoramus, interim, interregnum, medium, peninsula, radius, species. *Seventeenth century*: affidavit, agenda, census, complex, curriculum, fulcrum, honorarium, lens, pendulum, premium, rabies, series, specimen, squalor, tedium. *Eighteenth century*: alibi, bonus, deficit, inertia, insomnia, propaganda, ultimatum, via. *Nineteenth century*: aquarium, consensus, omnibus, referendum.

TOTAL LATIN–ENGLISH LEARNING VOCABULARY

TOTAL ENGLISH–LATIN VOCABULARY FOR EXERCISES

Total Latin–English learning vocabulary

Note

This vocabulary contains all the words in the Learning Vocabularies, together with words learned in the Running Grammar. Words which appear in sections of *Text* in forms significantly different from the basic form are also entered, with a reference to the basic form, e.g. *ablāt-* see *auferō*; *cuius* gen. s. of *quī/quis*.

A

ā/ab (+abl.) away from 1D; by 4D(i)

abeō abīre abiī abitum I go / come away 1C

abiciō 3/4 abiēcī abiectus I throw down, throw away 4F(i)

ablāt-: see *auferō*

absēns absent-is absent, away 4C(ii)

abstul-: see *auferō*

absum abesse āfuī I am away from, am absent 4C(i); I am distant 5E(ii)

ac (or *atque*) and 2A(i)
aliter ac otherwise than
alius ac different from
contrā ac contrary to what
īdem ac the same as
pār ac equivalent to
pariter ac equally as
perinde ac in like

manner as, just as
similis ac similar to
(See 5G Gr.)

accēdō 3 accessī accessum I approach, reach 4E(iii)

access-: see *accēdō*

accidit 3 accidit it happens (*ut* / *ut nōn*+subj.) 4F(i)

accipiō 3/4 accēpī acceptus I receive, welcome; learn; obtain 2E; sustain, meet with 4E(ii)

accūsō 1 I accuse (x acc. of y gen.) 4A(iii)

ācer ācr-is e keen, sharp 2A Gr.

acerb-us a um bitter 5D(ii)

aci-ēs ēī 5f. battle-line; sharp edge, point; keenness (of sight) 5G(i)

āct-: see *agō*

ad (+acc.) towards; at 1A; for the purpose of 4F(i); *usque ad* right up to 6A(iv)

addō 3 addidī additus I add; increase 5F(i)

adeō adīre adiī aditum I go / come to, approach 1C

adeō to such an extent 5A(i)

adept-: see *adipīscor*

adferō adferre attulī allātus I bring to 2B

adgredior (aggredior) 3/4 dep. *adgressus* (*aggressus*) I go up to 2B; attack 4E(i)

adhūc up to now 6B(ii)

adipīscor 3 dep. *adeptus* I get, gain, acquire 3B

adiungō 3 adiūnxī adiūnctus I join (x acc. to y dat.) 5A(ii)

557

adiuuō 1 *adiūuī adiūtus* I help 2A

adloquor (alloquor) 3 dep. *adlocūtus (allocūtus)* I address 3B

adorior 4 dep. *adortus* I attack, rise up against 6C(ii)

adscrībō 3 *adscrīpsī adscrīptus* I write in addition 2A

adseruō 1 I keep, guard 2A

adsum adesse adfuī I am present, am at hand 2D

aduers-us a um hostile; opposite; unfavourable 5F(i); in front 5G(iii)

aduertō see *animaduertō*

adulēscēns adulēscent-is 3m. youth 6B(viii)

aduocō 1 I summon 5F(i)

aedis aed-is 3f. temple; pl. *aed-ēs aed-ium* house 1B

aeger aegr-a um ill 5G(i)

aegrē with difficulty 6D(iv)

aequor aequor-is 3n. plain; sea 6A(vii)

aequ-us a um fair, balanced, equal 1G; level 5E(ii)

aes aer-is 3n. bronze *aes aliēn-um aer-is aliēn-ī* debt (lit. 'someone else's bronze') 5A(ii)

aestimō 1 I value, estimate 6A(iv)

aetās aetāt-is 3f. age; lifetime; generation 5A(ii)

affirmō 1 I state strongly, assert 4A(iii)

age come! 1G

ager agr-ī 2m. land, field, territory 3B

aggredior: see *adgredior*

agitō 1 I stir up, incite 5A(i)

agmen agmin-is 3n. column 5E(ii)

agō 3 *ēgī āctus* I do, act 2B; drive, lead, direct 4F(ii); spend, pass 5F(ii); *(dē* + abl.) discuss 6C(iii) *grātiās agō* (+ dat.) I thank 3D

Agrigentīn-us ī 2m. person from Agrigentum 4A(i)

aiō irr. I say 6B(iv)

alibī somewhere else 4B Gr. and 5G(ii)

alicubī somewhere 4B Gr.

aliēn-us a um someone else's *aes aliēn-um aer-is aliēn-ī* debt (lit. 'someone else's bronze') 5A(ii)

aliquandō at some time 6B(viii)

aliquantō to some extent 4B Gr.

aliquī aliqua aliquod some (adj.) 4B

aliquis aliqua aliquid someone (pron.) 4B

aliquot several 5A(ii)

aliter ac otherwise than 5G Gr.

ali-us a ud other 4B(iii) (two different cases in same clause = 'different . . . different': see 4B Gr.) *aliī . . . aliī* some . . . others 4B Gr.

alius ac other than 5G Gr.

alloquor: see *adloquor*

alō 3 *aluī altus* I feed, nourish, rear; support; strengthen 6B(iv)

alter alter-a um one (or other) of two 2A (see also 2B Gr.)

alt-us a um high; deep 6A(vii)

ambō ambae ambō both 2E (declined as *duo*, see 2A Gr.)

ambulō 1 I walk 3A

amīc-a ae 1f. mistress 2A

amīciti-a ae 1f. friendship 6B(vii)

amīc-us ī 2m. friend, ally 4A(iii)

āmittō 3 *āmīsī āmissus* I lose 1F

amō 1 I love, like 1B

amor amōr-is 3m. love; pl. girl-friend, sexual intercourse 6A(i)

amplexor 1 dep. I embrace 2E

amplius more than 5G(i)

ampl-us a um large, great 5B(i)

an = *-ne* = ? (in direct questions); whether, if (in indirect questions: + subj. = *num*) 6D(iii) *utrum . . . an* = double question, i.e. A or B? (negative *annōn*) 5D(i) *utrum . . . an* (+ subj.) whether . . . or (Indirect question: negative *necne*) 5F Gr.

anim-a ae 1f. soul, life, breath 5G(iii)

animaduertō (or *animum*

Total learning vocabulary: Latin–English

aduertō) 3 *animaduertī animaduersus* I observe, take note of 6B(i)

anim-us ī 2m. mind, spirit, heart 1E

annōn or not? (see *an* or *utrum*) 5D(i)

ann-us ī 2m. year 2D

ante (+ acc.) before, in front of 2D; (adv.) earlier, before 4E(ii)

anteā (adv.) before 4G(i)

antequam (conjunction) before 5E Gr.

aperiō 4 *aperuī apertus* I open; reveal 5B(ii)

appellō 1 I address; name, call 5G(i)

appropinquō 1 (+ dat.) I approach 6C(ii)

apud (+ acc.) at the house of, in the hands of, in the works of 1F; among 4A(i)

aqu-a ae 1f. water 1C

ār-a ae 1f. altar 5D(iv)

arbitror 1 dep. I think, consider; give judgement 2C

arbor arbor-is 3f. tree 6D(iii)

arcessō 3 *arcessīuī arcessītus* I summon 5D(i)

ārdeō 2 *ārsī ārsūrus* I burn; am in love 6C(i)

argent-um ī 2n. silver; silver-plate; money 4C(i)

arm-a ōrum 2n. pl. arms; armed men 5A(i)

armāt-us a um armed 5A(iii)

ars art-is 3f. skill, art, accomplishment 6D(ii)

arx arc-is 3f. citadel 5D(i)

Asi-a ae 1f. Asia Minor 4B(i)

asper asper-a um rough 5E(ii)

astūti-a ae 1f. astuteness; pl. tricks 2A

at but 2B

atque (or *ac*) and 2A (see *ac* for list of comparative expressions learned in 5G Gr.)

atrōx atrōc-is fierce, unrelenting 6B(vii)

attribuō 3 *attribuī attribūtus* I assign, give 5D(i)

attul-: see *adferō*

auctōritās auctōritāt-is 3f. weight, authority 5B(i)

audāci-a ae 1f. boldness, cockiness 1G

audāx audāc-is brave, bold, resolute 1F

audeō 2 semi-dep. *ausus* I dare 2E (see 3A Gr.)

audiō 4 I hear, listen to 1D

auferō auferre abstulī ablātus I take away (x acc. from y dat.) 1F

augeō 2 *auxī auctus* I increase (trans.) 5D(iv)

aul-a ae 1f. pot 1B (NB. the normal Classical Latin form is *olla*, while *aula* generally means 'court' or 'palace')

aure-us a um golden 2C

aur-um ī 2n. gold 1A

aus-: see *audeō*

aut or 1F

aut . . . aut either . . . or 4D(ii)

autem but, however (2nd word) 1A

autumn-us ī 2m. autumn, fall 6D(ii)

auxili-um ī 2n. help 3D

B

bell-um ī 2n. war: *bellum gerō* I wage war 3A

bell-us a um pretty, beautiful 6B(ii)

bene well, thoroughly, rightly 1E; good! fine! 2A (see 3B Gr.)

bibō 3 *bibī* — I drink 4B(iii)

bon-a ōrum 2n. pl. goods 5F(ii)

bon-us a um good, brave, fit, honest 1E

breu-is e short, brief 3D

breuī (sc. *tempore*) shortly, soon 5C(i)

C

cadō 3 *cecidī cāsum* I fall; die 5G(ii)

caedēs caed-is 3f. slaughter, carnage 5B(iii)

caedō 3 *cecīdī caesus* I cut (down); flog, beat; kill 4B(iv)

caelest-is e in the heavens 6D(iii)

cael-um ī 2n. sky, heaven 6D(i)

caes-: see *caedō*

calamitās calamitāt-is 3f. disaster, calamity 4B(i)

camp-us ī 2m. field, plain 6D(iii)

candid-us a um white; bright, beautiful 6A(vi)

capiō 3/4 *cēpī captus* I take, capture 2A

caput capit-is 3n. head; source, fount 2B

carcer carcer-is 3m. prison; barrier 5E(i)

castīgō 1 I rebuke 2E

castr-a ōrum 2n. pl. camp 3B

cās-us ūs 4m. outcome; event, occurrence; disaster, death *cāsū* by accident; by chance 6B(viii)

caueō 2 *cāuī cautus* I am wary 2B

caus-a ae 1f. case; reason 4F(i); cause 4G(ii) *causā* (+ gen. – which precedes it) for the sake of 5D Gr.

cecid-: see *cadō*

cēdō 3 *cessī cessum* I yield; go 5F(i)

celer celer-is celer-e swift 2A

celeritās celeritāt-is 3f. speed 4B(iv)

celeriter quickly 3B

cēlō 1 I hide 1A

cēn-a ae 1f. dinner 1F

centum 100 2A Gr.

centuriō centuriōn-is 3m. centurion 5G(i)

cēp-: see *capiō*

cēr-a ae 1f. wax 2A

certē without doubt 1G

certior fīō (*fierī factus*) I am informed 6B(i)

certiōrem faciō (3/4 *fēcī*) I inform (x acc.) 6B(i)

certō for a fact 1G

certō 1 I struggle, fight; vie 5F(i)

cert-us a um sure, certain 5B(ii)

cess-: see *cēdō*

cēter-ī ae a the rest, the others 4B(i)

cib-us ī 2m. food 4E(i)

circiter (adv.) about 5E(ii)

circum (+ acc.) around 4C(ii)

circumeō circumīre circumiī circumitum I go around 4C(ii)

circumsedeō 2 *circumsēdī circumsessus* I besiege, blockade 6B(ii)

citō quickly 2C

cīuis cīu-is 3m. and f. citizen 1F

cīuitās cīuitāt-is 3f. state 4G(i)

clam secretly 1B

clāmitō 1 I keep on shouting 4G(i)

clāmō 1 I shout 1A

clāmor clāmōr-is 3m. shout; outcry; noise 4A(iv)

clār-us a um famous, well-known 4B(i); clear 6B(vi)

classis class-is 3f. fleet 4D(i)

coepī (perfect form: past participle active/ passive *coeptus*) I began 4B(ii)

cōgitō 1 I ponder, reflect, consider 1C

cognit-: see *cognōscō*

cognōscō 3 *cognōuī cognitus* I get to know, examine 2B (perf. tense = I know, plup. = I knew, fut. perf. = I shall know)

cōgō 3 *coēgī coāctus* I force, compel; gather 5F(ii)

cohors cohort-is 3f. governor's retinue; cohort 4D(i)

cohortor 1 dep. I encourage 5C(ii)

collēg-a ae 1m. colleague 6B(iv)

colligō 3 *collēgī collēctus* I collect, gather; gain, acquire 4C(ii)

collocō 1 I place, station 5A(iii)

coll-um ī 2n. neck 6D(iv)

colō 3 *coluī cultus* I worship; cultivate, till; inhabit 4A(ii)

com-a ae 1f. hair; foliage 6D(iii)

comes comit-is 3m. companion, friend; (pl.) retinue 4B(i)

committō 3 *commīsī commissus* I commit 5C(iii)

commod-us a um satisfactory, convenient 6B(i)

commoror 1 dep. I delay, wait 4E(iii)

commoueō 2 *commōuī commōtus* I move; remove; excite, disturb 4C(ii)

commūn-is e shared in, common, universal 5D(ii)

comparō 1 I prepare, provide, get ready, get 4B(iii)

complector 3 dep. *complexus* I embrace 6B(iii)

complūr-ēs complūr-ium several 6B(iii)

concidō 3 *concidī* — I fall, collapse; am killed 4F(i)

concordi-a ae 1f. harmony 5D(iii)

concurrō 3 *concurrī concursum* I run together 4B(iv)

condemnō 1 I condemn (x acc. for Y gen.) 6B(i)

Total learning vocabulary: Latin–English

condiciō condiciōn-is 3f.
condition, term
condiciōnem (condiciōnēs)
ferre to make terms
6B(vi)
cōnfect-: see cōnficiō
cōnficiō 3/4 cōnfēcī cōnfectus
I finish 5C(iii);
weaken 6C(iii)
cōnfirmō 1 I state clearly,
confirm 4A(iii)
cōnfiteor 2 dep. cōnfessus I
confess,
acknowledge 4G(i)
cōnflagrō 1 I burn
(intrans.) 4E(ii)
coniciō 3/4 coniēcī coniectus
I throw 4A(iv)
coniūrātiō coniūrātiōn-is 3f.
conspiracy 5A(i)
coniūrātor coniūrātōr-is 3m.
conspirator 5A(i)
cōnor 1 dep. I try 2C
cōnscrīptī: patrēs
cōnscrīptī = senators
5D(ii)
cōnseruō 1 I keep safe,
preserve 5D(ii)
cōnsīderō 1 I consider,
ponder 5B(ii)
cōnsīdō 3 cōnsēdī — I settle
down; encamp 5E(ii)
cōnsili-um ī 2n. plan;
advice; judgement 1E
cōnsistō 3 cōnstitī — I stop,
stand my ground
6C(ii)
cōnspicor 1 dep. I catch
sight of 2E
cōnstit-: see cōnsistō
cōnstituō 3 cōnstituī
cōnstitūtus I decide
4C(i)
cōnsul cōnsul-is 3m. consul
4B(ii)
cōnsulāt-us ūs 4m.
consulship 5A(i)

continenti-a ae 1f. self-
control, restraint 1G
contiō contiōn-is 3f.
meeting, assembly
5F(i)
contrā (+ acc.) against 5D(i)
contrā ac contrary to
what 5G Gr.
conueniō 4 conuēnī
conuentum I meet
4B(iii)
conuīui-um ī 2n. party
4B(iii)
conuocō 1 I summon, call
together 5A(iii)
cōpi-ae ārum 1f. pl. troops
3B
coquō 3 coxī coctus I cook
1F
coqu-us ī 2m. cook 1A
corn-ū ūs 4n. wing (of
army); horn 5G(i)
corpus corpor-is 3n. body
5G(iii)
cotīdiē daily 4D(ii)
crēber crēbr-a um frequent;
thick, close 6B(ii)
crēdō 3 crēdidī crēditum I
believe in (+ dat.);
entrust (x acc. to y
dat.) 1G
crūdēl-is e cruel 5D(i)
cui dat. s. of quī/quis
cuidam dat. s. of quīdam
cuiquam dat. of quisquam
cuius gen. s. of quī/quis
cuiusdam gen. s. of quīdam
culp-a ae 1f. fault; blame
(often of sexual
misconduct) 6A(vii)
culter cultr-ī 2m. knife 1D
Gr.
cum (+ abl.) with 2A
(+ subj.) when; since;
although 4E(iii)
cum semel as soon as
6A(iv)

cum . . . tum both . . . and
5D(ii)
cūnctor 1 dep. I delay;
hesitate (+ inf.) 5C(i)
cūnct-us a um all, the
whole of 6D(iii)
cupiditās cupiditāt-is 3f.
lust, greed, desire
4B(ii)
cupiō 3/4 cupīuī cupītus I
desire, yearn for;
want desperately
4B(i)
cūr why? 1A
cūr-a ae 1f. care; worry,
concern 1B
cūrō 1 I look after, care
for 1B; see to it that
5D Gr.
curs-us ūs 4m. running;
course; direction;
voyage 6C(ii)
custōs custōd-is 3m. and f.
guard 4A(i)

D

dat-: see dō
dē (+ abl.) about,
concerning 2A;
from, down from
4F(i)
dēbeō 2 I ought (+ inf.);
owe 2D
decem ten 2A Gr.
dēcēp-: see dēcipiō
decet 2 it befits (x acc. to
y inf.) 5C(iii) and
5C Gr.
decim-us a um tenth 5C Gr.
dēcipiō 3/4 dēcēpī dēceptus I
deceive 2A
decus decor-is 3n. honour;
beauty 5F(i)
ded-: see dō
dēdecet 2 it is unseemly
(for x acc. to y inf.)
5C Gr.

561

dēdecorī est it is a disgrace
(for x dat.) 5C(iii)
dēdō 3 *dēdidī dēditus* I hand
over, surrender 3B
dēdūcō 3 *dēdūxī dēductus* I
lead away, lead
down 3B
dēess-: see *dēsum*
dēfendō 3 *dēfendī dēfēnsus* I
defend 2C
dēferō dēferre dētulī dēlātus I
report, bring news
of; accuse, denounce;
transfer 4A(iii)
dēfu-: see *dēsum*
dein = deinde 6A(iv)
deinde then, next 1A
dēlāt-: see *dēferō*
dēleō 2 *dēlēuī dēlētus* I
destroy 2D
dēnique finally; in a word
4E(i)
dēscendō 3 *dēscendī*
dēscēnsum I descend
6C(iv)
dēsum dēesse dēfuī I am
missing, am lacking;
fail; abandon
(+ dat.) 4D(ii)
dētul-: see *dēferō*
de-us ī 2m. god 1B (see
also 1B Gr.)
dexter dextr-a um right;
favourable 5G(i)
dextr-a ae 1f. right hand
5F(i)
dī nom. pl. of *deus*
dīc imperative s. of *dīcō*
1D
dīcō 3 *dīxī dictus* I speak,
say 1D
diēs diē-ī 5m. and f. day
2B
  in diēs day by day
  5A(i)
difficil-is e difficult 2A
diffīdō 3 semi-dep. *diffīsus*

(+ dat.) I distrust
6C(iii)
dignitās dignitāt-is 3f.
distinction, position;
honour; rank, high
office 5D(iii)
dign-us a um worthy;
worthy of (+ abl.)
5E(i)
dīligenti-a ae 1f. care,
diligence 5D(iii)
dīligēns dīligent-is careful,
diligent 6B(i)
dīligō 3 *dīlēxī dīlēctus* I
love 2B
dīmicō 1 I fight 6B(vi)
dīmittō 3 *dīmīsī dīmissus* I
send away 5B(i)
discēdō 3 *discessī discessum* I
depart; (*in sententiam*
+ gen.) go over to
x's view 5E(i)
discordi-a ae 1f. strife,
quarrel 6B(vi)
dispōnō 3 *disposuī dispositus*
I set, place (in
different places) 5E(i)
diū for a long time 5B(ii)
comp. *diūtius* 5B(ii)
superl. *diūtissimē* 5B(ii)
dīuers-us a um different
5A(iii)
dīues dīuit-is rich (as noun
3m. rich man) 1D
dīuiti-ae ārum 1f. pl. riches
5F(i)
diūtius any longer 5F(i)
(see *diū*)
dīu-us ī 2m. god 6D(iii)
dō 1 *dedī datus* I give 1B
  operam dō I pay
  attention to (x dat.)
  3D
doct-us a um skilled (in x:
abl.); learned 5A(ii)
doleō 2 I suffer pain,
grieve 6A(vi)

dolor dolōr-is 3m. pain,
anguish 5D(i)
dol-us ī 2m. trick 3C
domī at home 1D
domin-us ī 2m. master 1C
domō from home 2B
domum to home,
homewards 1D
dom-us ūs 4f. (irr.) house,
home 2A Gr.
dōnō 1 I give 6A(i)
dormiō 4 I sleep 1F
dōs dōt-is 3f. dowry 1E
dubitō 1 I doubt; hesitate
(+ inf.) 6B(vi)
dubi-us a um doubtful 5F
Gr.
dūc imperative s. of *dūcō*
ducent-ī ae e 200 2A
dūcō 3 *dūxī ductus* I lead
1D; think, consider
6B(vii)
dulc-is e sweet 5D(iii)
dum (+ indic.) while 2A;
(+ indic./subj.) until;
(+ subj.) provided
that (also *dummodo*,
modo) 5E Gr.
duo duae duo two 2A Gr.
duodecim 12 2A Gr.
duodēuīgintī 18 5C Gr.
dūx-: see *dūcō*
dux duc-is 3m. leader 3A

E

ē (+ abl.) out of, from
(also *ex*) 1C
ea nom. s. f. or nom./acc.
pl. n. of *is*
eā abl. s. f. of *is*
eadem nom. s. f. or nom./
acc. pl. n. of *īdem*
eādem abl. s. f. of *īdem*
eae nom. pl. f. of *is*
eam acc. s. f. of *is*
eandem acc. s. f. of *īdem*
eārum gen. pl. f. of *īdem*

eās acc. pl. f. of *is*

eāsdem acc. pl. f. of *īdem*

ēbri-us a um drunk 4D(i)

ecce look! 2B

ēdūcō 3 *ēdūxī ēductus* I lead out 3B

efficiō 3/4 *effēcī effectus* I bring about (*ut* + subj.); cause, make; complete 5A(i)

effugiō 3/4 *effūgī* — I escape 4B(iii)

ēg-: see *agō*

egeō 2 I lack, need, am in want of (+ abl. or gen.) 4E(i)

ego I 1A

ēgredior 3/4 dep. *ēgressus* I go/come out 2B

ēgregi-us a um outstanding, excellent 6B(iii)

ēgress-: see *ēgredior*

eī dat. s. or nom. pl. m. of *is*

eīs dat./abl. pl. of *is*

eius gen. s. of *is*

enim for (2nd word) 1A

eō īre iī itum I go/come 1C

eō to that place 5C(i)

quō + comparative . . . *eō* + comparative 'the more x . . . the more y' 6B(vi)

eōdem abl. s. m. or n. of *īdem*

eōrum gen. pl. of *is*

eōs acc. pl. m. of *is*

eōsdem acc. pl. m. of *īdem*

eques equit-is 3m. horseman; pl. cavalry 3B; 'knight' (member of the Roman business class) 4G(ii)

equitāt-us ūs 4m. cavalry 6C(ii)

equus ī 2m. horse 2D

ergō therefore 2C

ēripiō 3/4 *ēripuī ēreptus* I snatch away, rescue (x acc. from y dat.) 5C(iii)

errō 1 I am wrong; wander 6B(vii)

et and; also, too; even Intro; *et . . . et* both . . . and 1E

etiam still, even, as well; yes indeed 3C

nōn sōlum (or *nōn modo*) . . . *sed etiam* not only . . . but also 4F(ii)

etiam atque etiam again and again 6B(vii)

etsī although, even though, even if 6C(iii)

Eucliō Eucliōn-is 3m. Euclio Intro.

ex (or *ē*) (+ abl.) out of, from 1C

excēdō 3 *excessī excessum* I depart, go out; surpass 6C(ii)

excipiō 3/4 *excēpī exceptus* I sustain, receive; welcome; catch; make an exception of 6C(ii)

excōgitō 1 I think up, devise 4C(ii)

excūsō 1 I excuse 6B(i)

exempl-um ī 2n. copy; example 5C(i)

exeō exīre exiī exitum I go/come out 1C

exercit-us ūs 4m. army 2D

exi-: see *exeō*

exīstimō 1 I think, consider 5B(i)

exiti-um ī 2n. death, destruction 1B Gr.

exorior 4 dep. *exortus* I arise 5C(ii)

explicō 1 I tell, explain 1B

expugnō 1 I storm 4A(i)

exsili-um ī 2n. exile 5F(ii)

exspectō 1 I await, wait for 4D(i)

extrēm-us a um furthest 6A(vii)

F

fābul-a ae 1f. story; play 6B(i)

fac imperative s. of *faciō* 1E Gr.

facēti-ae ārum 1f. pl. wit 6A(ii)

faciēs faci-ēī 5f. appearance; face 5E(i)

facil-is e easy 1F

facinus facinor-is 3n. deed; crime; endeavour 1E

faciō 3/4 *fēcī factus* I make, do 1E

certiōrem faciō I inform x (acc.) 6B(i)

faciō ut (+ subj.) I bring it about that (cf. *efficiō/perficiō ut*) 6C(i)

fact-: see *fīō*

fact-um ī 2n. deed 5E(i)

fām-a ae 1f. rumour, report; reputation 4A(i)

famili-a ae 1f. household Intro.

fān-um ī 2n. shrine 1G

faueō 2 *fāuī fautum* I am favourable to (+ dat.) 3D

fēc-: see *faciō*

fēmin-a ae 1f. woman 1D

fer imperative s. of *ferō* 1E Gr.

ferē almost 6B(iv)

feriō 4 I strike; beat; kill (perfect active and passive tenses supplied by *percussī percussus* – pf. and perf. part. of *percutiō* 3/4) 4D(ii)

ferō ferre tulī lātus I bear; lead 1E
mē ferō I charge 3B
condiciōnem (condiciōnēs) ferre to make terms 6B(vi)

ferōci-a ae 1f. fierceness 3B

ferōciter fiercely 3B

ferr-um ī 2n. sword; iron 5F(i)

festīnō 1 I hurry 4B(iii)

fidēs fid-eī 5f. loyalty, honour; trust; faith; promise; protection 6B(viii)

fīd-us a um faithful, loyal 6B(viii)

fīli-a ae 1f. daughter Intro.

fīli-us ī 2m. son 1D

fingō 3 *fīnxī fictus* I make up, fabricate 6B(ii)

fīō fierī factus I become; am done, am made (passive of *faciō*) 2D (see 3A Gr.)
certior fīō I am informed 6B(i)

flamm-a ae 1f. flame 6D(i)

fleō 2 *flēuī flētum* I weep 6C(iv)

flūmen flūmin-is 3n. river 6C(iii)

fore = futūrum esse to be about to be 4A Gr.
fore ut (+ subj.) that it will / would turn out that . . . 5B Gr.

foris for-is 3f. door 2E

fōrm-a ae 1f. shape, looks; beauty 3C

fōrmōs-us a um handsome, graceful, shapely 4D(ii)

fortasse perhaps 6B(viii)

forte by chance, perchance 6B(i)

fort-is e brave, courageous 3A; strong 3C

fortūn-a ae 1f. fortune, luck; pl. wealth 5B(ii)

fortunāt-us a um fortunate, lucky (in x: abl.) 5A(i)

for-um ī 2n. forum (main business centre) 2D

frangō 3 *frēgī frāctus* I break 5B(iii)

frāter frātr-is 3m. brother 1D

frīgus frīgor-is 3n. cold; pl. cold spells 6D(ii)

fruor 3 dep. *frūctus* I enjoy (+ abl.) 4B(i)

frūstrā in vain 5A(iii)

fu-: see *sum*

fug-a ae 1f. flight 5D(i)

fugiō 3/4 *fūgī fugitūrus* I escape, run off, flee 1F

fugō 1 I put to flight 6D(ii)

fulgeō 2 *fulsī* — I shine 6A(vi)

fūr fūr-is 3m. thief 1B

furor furōr-is 3m. rage, fury; madness 4F(ii)

G

gaudi-um ī 2n. joy 5G(iii)

gēns gent-is 3f. tribe; race; family; people 5B(i)

genus gener-is 3n. family; stock; tribe 4C(i); type, kind 5D(ii)

gerō 3 *gessī gestus* I do, conduct 2D
bellum gerō I wage war 3A

gladi-us ī 2m. sword 5C(ii)

glōri-a ae 1f. glory, renown, fame 4E(iii)

gradior 3/4 dep. *gressus* I step, walk, go (cf. compounds in -*gredior*) 6A(vii)

Graec-us a um Greek 4B(i)

grāti-a ae 1f. thanks, recompense 3D
grātiās agō (+ dat.) I thank 3D
grātiā (+ gen. – placed after the noun it qualifies) for the sake of 5D Gr.

grāt-us a um pleasing (to x dat.) 5A(i)

grau-is e serious, important, weighty; heavy 4E(ii)

grauitās grauitāt-is 3f. seriousness; solemnity; importance, authority 4B(iii)

H

habeō 2 I have 1A; hold, regard 1D
negōtium habeō I conduct business 1F
ōrātiōnem habeō I make a speech 5F(i)

habitō 1 I dwell Intro.

hāc this way 2E

harēn-a ae 1f. sand 6A(v)

haud not 2D

hic haec hoc this; this person, thing; pl. these 2C

hīc here 2D

hinc from here 2C Gr.
hodiē today 1E
homo homin-is 3m. man, fellow 1E
honor honōr-is 3m. respect 1B
hōr-a ae 1f. hour 2D
hortor 1 dep. I urge, encourage 3B
hospes hospit-is 3m. host; friend; guest; connection 4B(i)
hostis host-is 3m. enemy 3B
hūc to here 2E
hum-us ī 2f. ground
  humī on the ground (locative)
  humum to the ground 5E(i)

I

ī imperative s. of *eō* 1E Gr.
i-: see *eō*
iaceō 2 I lie 4D(i)
iactō 1 I discuss; throw; boast; toss about 6B(ii)
iam now, by now, already; presently 2C
iānu-a ae 1f. door 4B(iii)
ibi there 2E
idcircō therefore, for this/ that reason 5D(i)
īdem eadem idem the same 3C
  īdem ac the same as 5G Gr.
idōne-us a um suitable (for), qualified (for) (+ dat.) 5B(i)
igitur therefore 1A
ignāui-a ae 1f. laziness; cowardice 5F(i)
ignāu-us a um lazy; cowardly 5F(i)

ignis ign-is 3m. fire 1C
ignōscō 3 *ignōuī ignōtum* I forgive (+ dat.) 4G(i)
ille ill-a illud that; that person, thing; pl. those 2C
illīc there 2C Gr.
illinc from there 2C Gr.
illūc to there 2C Gr.
illūstr-is e famous 3B
imitor 1 dep. I imitate 6B(viii)
immō more precisely i.e. no *or* yes (a strong agreement or disagreement with what precedes) 2D
immortāl-is e immortal 4G(i)
impedīment-um ī 2n. hindrance 3D
  impedīmentō sum (+ dat.) I am a hindrance (to) 3D Gr.
impediō 4 I prevent, impede, hinder 5A(iii)
imperātor imperātōr-is 3m. leader, general, commander 4E(i)
imperi-um ī 2n. order, command 3A; power, authority; dominion 5D(ii)
imperō 1 I give orders (to), command (+ dat.: often followed by *ut*/ *nē* + subj. 'to / not to') 3D
impetrō 1 I gain by request 6C(iii)
impet-us ūs 4m. attack 4A(i)
  impetum faciō I make an attack 4A(i)

impi-us a um with no respect for gods, parents or fatherland 5D(iv)
impōnō 3 *imposuī impositus* I put x (acc.) on y (dat.) 6D(ii)
in (+ acc.) into, onto; (+ abl.) in, on 1A; (+ acc.) against 2D
incendi-um ī 2n. fire 4E(ii)
incendō 3 *incendī incēnsus* I set fire to; burn (trans.) 4E(ii)
incert-us a um uncertain 6B(ii)
ineō inīre iniī initum I enter, go in 1F
inerm-is e unarmed 6C(ii)
īnfest-us a um hostile; at the ready; indicating attack 6C(ii)
īnflammāt-us a um inflamed, on fire 4C(i)
ingeni-um ī 2n. talent, ability 1B Gr.
ingēns ingent-is huge, large, lavish 1F
ingredior 3/4 dep. *ingressus* I enter 2E
inimīc-us a um hostile, enemy 4G(ii)
innocēns innocent-is guiltless 4A(iii)
inquam I say (*inquis*, *inquit*; *inquiunt*) 3D
īnsidi-ae ārum 1f. pl. trap, ambush 5A(iii)
īnspiciō 3/4 *īnspexī īnspectus* I look into, inspect, examine 2B
īnstituō 3 *īnstituī īnstitūtus* I begin; construct; resolve 6C(iii)
īnstō 1 *īnstitī* — I press upon; urge, pursue;

am at hand, approach; strive after 5G(ii)

īnstruō 3 īnstrūxī īnstrūctus I draw up; prepare, equip 5E(ii)

īnsum inesse īnfuī I am in (+ dat.) 5A(i)

integer integr-a um whole, untouched 5G(ii)

intellegō 3 intellēxī intellēctus I perceive, understand, comprehend, grasp 4B(iii)

inter (+ acc.) among; between 4B(iii)

intereā meanwhile 4A(i)

interficiō 3/4 interfēcī interfectus I kill 5A(ii)

interrogō 1 I ask 3C

intrō 1 I enter 1A

intrō (adv.) inside 2B

inueniō 4 inuēnī inuentum I find 1F

inuideō 2 inuīdī inuīsum I envy, begrudge (+ dat.) 5F(ii)

inuīt-us a um unwilling 6A(vi)

ioc-us ī 2m. joke, joking, fun 6A(ii)

Iou-: see *Iuppiter*

ipse ips-a ips-um very, actual, self 4B Gr.

īrāscor 3 dep. īrātus I grow angry (with x: dat.) 2C

īrāt-us a um angry 2C

irrīdeō 2 irrīsī irrīsus I laugh at, mock 1E

is e-a id that; he/she/it 3A

iste ist-a istud that of yours 4A(iii)

it-: see *eō*

ita so, thus; yes 1D

Italia-a ae 1f. Italy 5A(iii)

itaque and so, therefore 5A(iii)

item likewise 5C(i)

iter itiner-is 3n. journey, route 5E(ii)

iterum again 2A

iubeō 2 iussī iussus I order, command, tell 1D

iūcund-us a um pleasant 5D(iii)

iūdex iūdic-is 3m. judge 4A(i)

iūdicō 1 I judge 4A(iii)

Iuppiter Iou-is 3m. Jupiter, Jove 3A

iūs iūr-is 3n. law, justice 4G(ii)

iūs iūrand-um iūr-is iūrand-ī 3n. oath 5C(i)

iuss-: see *iubeō*

iussū by the order (of x: gen.) 5C(iii)

iuuat 1 it pleases 6A(iii)

iuuen-is iuuen-is 3m. young man 1G

L

lābor 3 dep. lāpsus I slip, glide, fall down; make a mistake 6D(ii)

labor labōr-is 3m. toil, hard work; trouble 5D(iv)

lacert-us ī 2m. arm, upper arm 6D(iv)

laedō 3 laesī laesus I harm 6A(iii)

laetiti-a ae 1f. merriment, festivity, joy 4B(iii)

laet-us a um happy 4A(iv)

Lampsacēn-us ī 2m. person from Lampsacum 4B(i)

Lar Lar-is 3m. Lar, household god 1A

latebr-ae ārum 1f. pl. hiding-place, lair 6D(iv)

Latīn-us a um Latin 5A(ii)

latrō latrōn-is 3m. robber, bandit 5G(i)

latus later-is 3n. side; flank 5G(ii)

lect-us ī 2m. couch, bed 2B

lēgāt-us ī 2m. commander 5G(i); pl. ambassadors 3B

legiō legiōn-is 3f. legion 3B

legō 3 lēgī lēctus I read 2B

lepōs lepōr-is 3m. charm 6A(ii)

lēx lēg-is 3f. law 4A(iv)

līber lībera-a um free 3A

līber-ī ōrum 2m. pl. children 5A(ii)

līberō 1 I free, release 4D(i)

lībertās lībertāt-is 3f. freedom, liberty 4G(i)

libet 2 (perf. *libuit* or *libitum est*) it pleases (x dat. to y inf.), x chooses to y 5C Gr.

libīdō libīdin-is 3f. lust 5A(ii)

licet 2 it is permitted (to x dat. to y inf.) 3D

līctor līctōr-is 3m. magistrate's attendant, lictor 4F(i)

lingu-a ae 1f. tongue; language 6A(v)

litter-ae ārum 1f. pl. letter 2B; literature 5A(ii)

lītus lītor-is 3n. shore 4E(i)

loc-us ī 2m. place; pl. *loc-a ōrum* 2n. 4A(iii)

locūt-: see *loquor*

longē far 3B Gr.

long-us a um long 3A
loquor 3 dep. *locūtus* I am
  speaking, say 2B
lūct-us ūs 4m. grief,
  mourning 5G(iii)
lūdō 3 *lūsī lūsum* I play
  6A(iii)
lūmen lūmin-is 3n. light;
  pl. eyes 6D(ii)
lūn-a ae 1f. moon 2A
lūx lūc-is 3f. light 5D(i)

M
magis more 3C Gr.
magistrāt-us ūs 4m.
  magistrate, state
  official 4A(iii)
magnopere greatly 3B Gr.
magn-us a um great, large
  1D
maior maiōr-is greater,
  bigger 3A Gr.
mālō mālle māluī I prefer
  (x *quam* Y) 2A
mal-um ī 2n. trouble, evil
  2E
mal-us a um bad, evil,
  wicked 1C
mandō 1 I entrust (x acc.
  to Y dat.) 5A(i);
  order (x dat. to Y
  ut + subj.) 6B(iii)
maneō 2 *mānsī mānsum* I
  remain, wait 1C
manifest-us a um in the
  open; obvious, clear;
  caught in the act
  5B(ii)
man-us ūs 4f. hand 2A;
  band 3B
mare mar-is 3n. sea (abl.
  marī) 4E(ii)
mātrōn-a ae 1f. wife,
  mother; lady 5A(ii)
maximē very much; most;
  yes 3C Gr.

maxim-us a um very great,
  biggest 3A Gr.
mē acc. or abl. of *ego*
meditor 1 dep. I think,
  ponder on; practise
  3A
medi-us a um middle (of)
  4F(ii)
melior meliōr-is better 3A
  Gr.
melius (adv.) better 3C
  Gr.
membr-um ī 2n. limb
  6A(iii)
meminī (perfect form) I
  remember 5F(i)
memor memor-is
  remembering (x:
  gen.); mindful of (x:
  gen.) 5D(iv)
memori-a ae 1f.
  remembering,
  memory,
  recollection; record
  6B(i)
mendāx mendāc-is lying,
  untruthful 2A
mēns ment-is 3f. mind
  6D(i)
mentiō mentiōn-is 3f.
  mention 4E(iii)
mentior 4 dep. I lie 2B
meretrīx meretrīc-is 3f.
  prostitute 2C
mer-us a um unmixed,
  pure 6A(i)
met-us ūs 4m. fear, terror
  4E(iii)
me-us a um my, mine 1C
  (vocative s. m. *mī*)
mī = *mihi* (dat. s. of *ego*)
  6A(iv)
mī voc. s. m. of *meus* 1B
  Gr.
mihi dat. s. of *ego*
mīles mīlit-is 3m. soldier
  2C

mīlia mīl-ium 3n. pl.
  thousands (see *mīlle*)
  2A Gr.
mīlitār-is e military 5E(ii)
mīlle 1,000 (pl. *mīlia*) 2A
  Gr.
minimē very little; no 3C
  Gr.
minim-us a um smallest,
  fewest, least 3A Gr.
minor 1 dep. I threaten
  (+ dat.) 2B
minor minōr-is smaller,
  fewer, less 3A Gr.
minus (adv.) less 3C Gr.
mīr-us a um amazing,
  wonderful 6B(v)
mīs-: see *mittō*
miser miser-a um
  miserable, unhappy,
  wretched 1C
miserand-us a um to be
  pitied 5D(i)
miseret 2 it moves (x acc.)
  to pity (for Y gen.)
  5C Gr.
misericors misericord-is
  compassionate 5D(i)
miss-: see *mittō*
mittō 3 *mīsī missus* I send
  1F; throw 6C(ii)
modest-us a um chaste,
  modest, discreet
  5A(ii)
modo now 2A; only 4F(ii)
  nōn modo . . . sed etiam
  not only . . . but
  also 4F(ii)
  modo . . . modo at one
  time . . . at another
  5E(ii)
mod-us ī 2m. way,
  fashion, manner
  4C(ii)
moenia moen-ium 3n. pl.
  walls, fortifications
  4E(iii)

moneō 2 I advise, warn
1C
mōns mont-is 3m.
mountain 5A(i)
mor-a ae 1f. delay 4G(i)
mōre in the manner of,
like (+ gen.) 5F(ii)
morior 3/4 dep. *mortuus* I
die, am dying 4F(i)
mors mort-is 3f. death 2E
mōs mōr-is 3m. way,
habit, custom; pl.
character 2C
mōt-: see *moueō*
moueō 2 *mōuī mōtus* I
remove (from: abl.);
move; cause, begin
5A(i)
mox soon 2B
mulier mulier-is 3f.
woman, wife 2C
multitūdō multitūdin-is 3f.
mob, crowd,
number 4E(ii)
multō (by) much, far
4B(iv)
multum (adv.) much 3B
Gr.
mult-us a um much, many
1B
mūnus mūner-is 3n. gift;
duty 6A(ii)
mūtō 1 I change, alter,
exchange 6A(ii)

N
nam for 1A
nārrō 1 I tell, relate 5A(i)
nātūr-a ae 1f. nature 5B(i)
nāt-us a um born of/from
(abl.) 4C(i)
nāuigō 1 I sail 4E(i)
nāuis nāu-is 3f. ship 3B
naut-a ae 1m. sailor 4D(i)
-ne (added to the first
word of a
sentence) = ? 1E

nē (+ subj.) 'not to', 'that
x should not . . .' 4F
Gr.; 'lest', 'in order
that not', 'in order
not to. . .' 5A Gr.;
'that', 'lest' 5D Gr.;
(+ perf. subj.) 'don't'
5F Gr.
nē . . . quidem not even
(emphasising the
word in between)
6B(iii)
nē quis 'that no one' 4F
Gr.; 'in order that
no one . . .' 5A Gr.
nec and . . . not; neither;
nor 1D
necesse est it is necessary
(for x dat. to y inf.)
3D
necessitūdō necessitūdin-is
3f. necessity 5F(ii)
necō 1 I kill 2C
nefāri-us a um wicked,
vile, criminal 4D(ii)
neglegenti-a ae 1f.
carelessness 4G(i)
neglegō 3 *neglēxī neglēctus* I
ignore, overlook,
neglect 4B(ii)
negō 1 I deny, say that x
is not the case
(acc. + inf.) 4A(iii)
negōti-um ī 2n. business,
work, duty 4A(ii)
negōtium habeō I do
business 1F
quid negōtī? what (of)
business/problem/
trouble? 1F
nēmō nēmin-is 3m. no one,
nobody 3C
neque and . . . not;
neither; nor (also
nec) 1C
nēquiti-a ae 1f. wickedness
4E(ii)

nesciō 4 I do not know
2B
nesci-us a um ignorant (of:
gen.) 2B
neu = *nēue* 6C(iv)
nēue (+ subj.) 'and not
to', 'and that x
should not . . .' 4F(i)
niger nigr-a um black 3A
nihil (indecl. n.) nothing
1E
nihilī of no value,
worthless 3C
nihilōminus nevertheless
5C(iii)
nīl = *nihil* nothing 1F
nimis too much (of x:
gen.) 1D
nisi unless, if . . . not;
except 2E
nītor 3 dep. *nīxus* or *nīsus*
I lean on (+ abl.);
strive, exert myself
4E(i)
nix niu-is 3f. snow 6D(i)
nōbil-is e renowned,
distinguished; well-
born, noble 4B(i)
noceō 2 I harm (+ dat.)
5C(iii)
noctū by night 6C(iii)
nōlī (+ inf.) do not 2B
Gr.
nōlō nōlle nōluī I refuse,
am unwilling
(+ inf.) 2A
nōmen nōmin-is 3n. name
1D
nōminō 1 I name 5G(i)
nōn not 1A
nōn null-ī ae a some
6B(vii)
nōnāgintā 90 5C Gr.
nōndum not yet 5B(ii)
nōnne surely? 3C
nōn-us a um ninth 5C Gr.
nōs we 1F Gr.

nōscō 3 *nōuī nōtus* I get to know (perfect tenses = I know etc.) 5B(i)

noster nostr-a um our 2A

nōt-us a um known, well-known 5B(i)

nōu-: see *nōscō*

nou-us a um new 4G (ii)

nox noct-is 3f. night 2A

nūdō 1 I strip 4F(ii)

nūd-us a um naked 6D(iii)

nūll-us a um no, none 1B (gen. s. *nūllīus*; dat. s. *nūllī*) (see 2B Gr.) *nōn nūll-ī ae a* some 6B(vii)

num surely . . . not? 4A Gr.; (+ subj.) whether (indirect question) 5F Gr.

numer-us ī 2m. number 4D(ii)

numm-us ī 2m. coin; pl. money 2A

numquam never 1C

nunc now 1A

nūntiō 1 I announce, proclaim 3A

nūnti-us ī 2m. messenger 4A(i)

nūpti-ae ārum 1f. pl. marriage-rites 1E

O

ob (+ acc.) on account of, because of 3A

obdūrō 1 I am firm, hold out, persist 6A(vi)

oblīuīscor 3 dep. *oblītus* I forget 2B; (+ gen.) 5D(iv)

obscūr-us a um dark; obscure; mean, ignoble 6D(ii)

obsecrō 1 I beseech, beg 2A

obsess-: see *obsideō*

obsideō 2 *obsēdī obsessus* I besiege 5B(iii)

obstō 1 *obstitī* — I stand in the way of, obstruct (+ dat.) 3D

occāsiō occāsiōn-is 3f. opportunity 5E(ii)

occidī I'm done for! 1E

occidō 3 *occidī occāsum* I fall, die 5G(iii); set 6A(iv)

occīdō 3 *occīdī occīsus* I kill 4E(i)

occupō 1 I seize 5C(iii)

occurrō 3 *occurrī occursum* I run to meet, meet; attack (+ dat.) 6C(iv)

octāu-us a um eighth 5C Gr.

octō eight 2A Gr.

octōgintā 80 5C Gr.

ocul-us ī 2m. eye 1C

offendō 3 *offendī offēnsus* I meet with; offend 6B(ii)

offici-um ī 2n. duty, job 2A

omittō 3 *omīsī omissus* I give up; let fall; omit, leave aside 5G(ii)

omnīnō altogether, completely 6B(i)

omn-is e all, every; *omnia* everything 1F

onerī est it is a burden (to x: dat.) 5C(iii)

onus oner-is 3n. load, burden 1E

oper-a ae 1f. attention 3D; service 5A(iii) *operam dō* (+ dat.) I pay attention to 3D

opēs op-um 3f. pl. resources; wealth (s. *ops op-is* 3f. help, aid) 5B(ii)

opīnor 1 dep. I think 2B

oportet 2 it is right/fitting for x (acc.) to y (inf.), x (acc.) ought to y (inf.) 4B(iii)

oppid-um ī 2n. town 2A

opportūn-us a um strategic, suitable, favourable 5A (iii)

oppress-: see *opprimō*

opprimō 3 *oppressī oppressus* I surprise; catch; crush 2C

oppugnō 1 I attack 3B

optimē (adv.) best 3C Gr.

optim-us a um best 1D (see 3A Gr.)

opus oper-is 3n. job, work, task 2B; fortification 6C(iii)

opus est (+ abl.) there is need of 5F(ii)

ōrāc(u)l-um ī 2n. oracle 6A(v)

ōrātiō ōrātiōn-is 3f. speech 5F(i) *ōrātiōnem habeō* I make a speech 5F(i)

ōrdō ōrdin-is 3m. rank (i.e. section of society or line of soldiers) 5D(ii); order 6D(i)

orior 4 dep. *ortus* I rise; spring from, originate 6D(iv)

ōrō 1 I beg, pray 4B(iv)

ōs ōr-is 3n. face; mouth 4F(ii)

ostendō 3 *ostendī ostēnsus* (or *ostentus*) I show, reveal 1G

ōtiōs-us a um at leisure 6A(iii)

ōti-um ī 2n. cessation of conflict; leisure, inactivity 3B

ouis ou-is 3f. sheep 2E

P

paene almost 5D(iv)

paenitet 2 x (acc.) regrets
Y (gen.) 5C Gr.

palam openly 6B(ii)

pandō 3 *pandī pāssus* I
spread out, extend;
throw open, disclose
6D(i)

par par-is equal
par ac equivalent to
pariter ac equally as 5G
Gr.

parcō 3 *pepercī parsūrus* I
spare (+ dat.) 4B(iv)

parēns parent-is 3m. father,
parent; f. mother
5B(iii)

pāreō 2 I obey (+ dat.)
3D

pariō 3/4 *peperī partus* I
bring forth, bear,
produce; obtain,
acquire 6B(vii)

parō 1 I prepare, get
ready; provide,
obtain 5A(i)

pars part-is 3f. part 5A(iii);
side 6B(vi) *aliī* . . .
pars (or *pars* . . .
pars) some . . .
others 4B Gr.

paru-us a um small 3A Gr.

patefaciō 3/4 *patefēcī
patefactus* I reveal,
expose, throw open
5C(iii)

pater patr-is 3m. father 1D
patrēs cōnscrīptī =
senators 5D(ii)

patior 3/4 *passus* endure,
suffer; allow 2E

patri-a ae 1f. fatherland
5D(ii)

pauc-ī ae a a few 5B(i)

paulātim little by little,
gradually 5G(ii)

paulō slightly 4E(i)

paulum a little, slightly 3B
Gr.

pauper pauper-is 3m. poor
man 1D; (adj.) poor
1F Gr.

pāx pāc-is 3f. peace 3B

pecūni-a ae 1f. money 1D

peior peiōr-is worse 3A
Gr.

peper-: see *pariō*

per (+ acc.) through, by
2C; in the name of
4G(i)

percuss-: see *feriō*

perdō 3 *perdidī perditus* I
lose; destroy 6B(ii)

pereō perīre periī peritum I
perish, die 6A(vi)

perfēc-: ⎱ see *perficiō*
perfect-: ⎰

*perferō perferre pertulī
perlātus* I endure (to
the end); complete;
carry to; announce
6A(vi)

perficiō 3/4 *perfēcī perfectus*
I finish, complete,
carry out 2B; *perficiō
ut* (+ subj.) I bring it
about that 4F(ii)

pergō 3 *perrēxī perrēctum* I
go on, go ahead,
continue 2B

perīcul-um ī 2n. danger 1B
Gr.

peri-: see *pereō*

periī I'm lost 1E

perinde ac in like manner
as, just as 5G Gr.

perit-: see *pereō*

perlegō 3 *perlēgī perlēctus* I
read through, peruse
4C(i)

perscrībō 3 *perscrīpsī
perscrīptus* I write in
detail 6B(i)

persequor 3 dep. *persecūtus*
I pursue, follow after
5F(i)

persuādeō 2 *persuāsī
persuāsum* I persuade
(+ dat.) (to / not to
ut/nē + subj.) 4F(i)

perueniō 4 *peruēnī
peruentum* I reach,
arrive at, come to
(*ad* + acc.) 4A(i)

pēs ped-is 3m. foot 3C

pessimē worst, very badly
3C Gr.

pessim-us a um worst 3A
Gr.

petō 3 *petīuī petītus* I beg
4F Gr.; seek 4G(i);
proposition, court;
attack, make for
5A(ii); stand for
(public office) 5A(iii)

Phaedr-a ae 1f. Phaedra
Intro.

pietās pietāt-is 3f. respect
for the gods (also for
family, home and
native land) 6D(i)

pīl-um ī 2n. heavy javelin
5G(ii)

pīrāt-a ae 1m. pirate 4D(i)

placet 2 it is pleasing (to x
dat. to Y inf.); x
(dat.) votes (to Y
inf.) 3C

plānē clearly 2C

plān-us a um level, flat;
plain, distinct 6D(iv)

plēn-us a um full (of)
(+ gen. or abl.) 1A

plērīque plēraeque plēraque
the majority of 5B(i)

plūrēs plūr-ium more 3A Gr.

plūrimum (adv.) most, a
lot 3C Gr.

plūrim-us a um most, very
much 3A Gr.

plūs plūr-is 3n. more 3A Gr.; (adv.) more 3C Gr.

poen-a ae 1f. penalty 5C(iii)

polliceor 2 dep. I promise 2B

pōnō 3 *posuī positus* I place, position, put 4A(ii); lay aside (= *dēpōnō*) 6D(iv)

pōns pont-is 3m. bridge 5C(ii)

popul-us ī 2m. people 4E(i)

porrō besides, moreover 5C(iii)

portō 1 I carry 1A

port-us ūs 4m. harbour 4D(i)

poscō 3 *poposcī* — I demand 1E

posit-: see *pōnō*

possideō 2 *possēdī possessus* I have, hold, possess 1B

possum posse potuī I am able, can 2A; am powerful, have power (+ adv.) 4E (iii)

post (adv.) afterwards, later 2D; (+ acc.) behind, after 5G(i)

posteā afterwards 4A(ii)

postquam (conjunction) after 5A(iii)

postrēmō finally 4C(ii)

postrēm-us a um last 4E(i)

postulō 1 I demand 4F Gr.

posu-: see *pōnō*

pot-: see *possum*

potenti-a ae 1f. power 5F(i)

potior 4 dep. I control (+ gen.) 6B(vi); gain control of (+ abl.) 6C (iii)

potius quam rather than 4C(i)

potu-: see *possum*

praebeō 2 I show, display; *mē praebeō* I show myself (to be x: acc. adj./noun) 5C(iii); provide, offer 6D(iv)

praecept-: see *praecipiō*

praecipiō 3/4 *praecēpī praeceptus* I instruct, give orders to (+ dat.) (to / not to *ut*/*nē* + subj.) 5B(ii)

praeclār-us a um very famous, outstanding, brilliant 4D(ii)

praed-a ae 1f. booty 2D

praedō praedōn-is 3m. pirate; robber 4D(i)

praefect-us ī 2m. captain, prefect; (adj.) in charge of (+ dat.) 4D(i)

praeficiō 3/4 *praefēcī praefectus* I put (x acc.) in charge of (Y dat.) 5G(i)

praemi-um ī 2n. reward, prize 5B(ii)

praesēns praesent-is present 6B(iii)

praesidi-um ī 2n. protection, defence, guard 4G(i)

praesum praeesse praefuī I am in charge of (+ dat.) 3D

praetereā besides, moreover 4A(iv)

praetereō praeterīre praeteriī praeteritus I pass by; neglect, omit 6A(vii)

praetor praetōr-is 3m. praetor (Roman state official) 4B(iv)

precor 1 dep. I pray 2B

premō 3 *pressī pressus* I press; oppress 6D(iv)

prīmō at first 4A(iv)

prīmum (adv.) first *ubi prīmum* as soon as 5B(i) *quam prīmum* as soon as possible 5E(ii)

prīm-us a um first 4C (ii) *in prīmīs* especially 5A(i)

prīnceps prīncip-is 3m. leader, chieftain; (adj.) first 4E(i)

prīstin-us a um former; original 5G(ii)

prius (adv.) before, earlier; first 5A(iii)

priusquam (conjunction) before 5E Gr.

prō (+ abl.) for, in return for; on behalf of; in front of 2E; instead of 5B(ii); in accordance with 5G(i)

prōcurrō 3 *prōcucurrī prōcursum* I run forward, advance 6C(i)

proeli-um ī 2n. battle 3B

proficīscor 3 dep. *profectus* I set out 3B

profugiō 3/4 *profūgī* — I escape, flee away 4F(ii)

prōgredior 3/4 *prōgressus* I advance 2B

prohibeō 2 I prevent, hinder, keep x (acc.) from Y (abl. / *ā(ab)* + abl.) 5A(iii)

prōiciō 3/4 *prōiēcī prōiectus* I throw down 6C(iv)

prōmittō 3 *prōmīsī prōmissus* I promise 1E

prope (adv.) almost;
(+acc.) near 4B(i)
properō 1 I hurry, make
haste 5E(ii)
propius nearer 5C(i)
prōpōnō 3 *prōposuī*
prōpositus I set
before; imagine;
offer 5D(i)
propter (+acc.) on
account of 2E
prōuideō 2 *prōuīdī prōuīsus*
I take care of (that)
5D(ii)
prōuinci-a ae 1f. province
4C(ii)
proxim-us a um nearest,
next 4F(i)
pudet 2 x (acc.) is
ashamed at/for Y
(gen.) 5C Gr.
pudor pudōr-is 3m.
modesty, sense of
shame 6D(iv)
puell-a ae 1f. girl 1D
puer puer-ī 2m. boy 1D Gr.
pugn-a ae 1f. battle, fight
5E(ii)
pugnō 1 I fight 2D
pugn-us ī 2m. fist 3C
pulcher pulchr-a um
beautiful 1D; (sup.)
pulcherrimus a um 3A
Gr.; (comp.)
pulchrior pulchriōr-is
3A Gr.
pūniō 4 I punish 5C(iii)
pūtid-us a um rotten 2E
putō 1 I think 4A(iii)

Q

quā where 4F Gr.
quadrāgintā 40 5C Gr.
quadringent-ī ae a 400 2A
Gr.
quaerō 3 *quaesīuī quaesītus*
I seek, look for; ask
4G(i)

quāl-is e what sort of
6B(iii)
tālis . . . quālis of such
a kind as 5G Gr.
quam how! (+adj. or
adv.) 2C; (after
comp.) than 3A
tam . . . quam as . . . as
5G Gr.
(+superl. adv.) as . . .
as possible 5B(ii)
quam prīmum as soon as
possible 5E(ii)
quamquam although 2E
quamuīs (+subj.)
although 4G Gr.;
(+adj.) however
5A(i)
quandō since, when 3C
quantī: tantī . . . quantī of
as much value . . . as
2E Gr.
quantum as much as
5D(iii)
quant-us a um how much,
how great 5F(i)
tantus . . . quantus as
much . . . as 5G Gr.
quārē why? 1B; therefore
6A(ii)
quārt-us a um fourth 5C
Gr.
quasi as if, like 1E
quattuor four 2A Gr.
quattuordecim 14 5C Gr.
-que (added to the end of
the word) and 1D
quemadmodum how 6B(i)
queror 3 dep. *questus* I
complain 5B(i)
quī quae quod which?
what? 1D Gr.; who,
which 4C Gr.;
(+subj.) since (also
with *quippe*) 4G Gr.;
(+subj.) in order
that / to 5A Gr.
quia because 2B

quīcumque quaecumque
quodcumque whoever,
whatever 6A(vii)
quid what? 1C; why?
4A(ii)
quid cōnsilī? what (of)
plan? 1E
quid negōtī? what (of)
business? what
problem? what
trouble? 1F
quīdam quaedam quid-/
quod-dam a, a certain,
some 4A(i)
quidem indeed (places
emphasis on the
preceding word)
6B(viii)
nē . . . quidem not even
(emphasising the
enclosed word)
6B(iii)
quiēs quiēt-is 3f. sleep, rest
6A(iii)
quīn (+subj.) from —ing;
that . . . not; (but)
that 5F Gr.
quīndecim 15 5C Gr.
quīngent-ī ae a 500 2A Gr.
quīnquāgintā 50 5C Gr.
quīnt-us a um fifth 4E(i)
quippe quī (*quae quod*)
inasmuch as he (she,
it) 4G Gr.
quis quid who, what? 1D
Gr.
quis qua quid (after *sī, nisi,*
nē, num) anyone,
anything 4F and 4G
Gr.
quisquam quicquam (after
negatives) anyone
5G Gr.
quisque quaeque quodque
(*quidque*) each 5G Gr.
quisquis quidquid (or
quicquid) whoever,
whatever 6B(v)

quō to where? 1E; whither, to where 4E(ii); (see also 4F Gr. for *quō* as abl. s. of *quī, quae, quod*) (+ comp. + subj.) in order that . . . more 5B Gr.

quō + comp. . . . *eō* + comp. the more . . . the more 6B(vi)

quōcumque (to) wherever 5F(i)

quod because 1B

quod sī but if 6B(vii)

quōminus (+ subj.) so that . . . not; from —ing 5F Gr.

quoque also 1A

quot how many 5F(i)

tot . . . quot as many as 5G Gr.

R

rapiō 3/4 *rapuī raptus* I snatch, seize, carry away, plunder 6D(iii)

ratiō ratiōn-is 3f. plan, method; reason; count, list; calculation 4C(ii)

recēp-: see *recipiō*

recipiō 3/4 *recēpī receptus* I welcome, receive, take in 4B(ii); *mē recipiō* I retreat 6C(iii)

recordor 1 dep. I remember 2B

reddō 3 *reddidī redditus* I return, give back 1G

redeō redīre rediī reditum I return (intrans.) 1C

redūcō 3 *redūxī reductus* I lead back 3B

relict-: see *relinquō*

religiōs-us a um sacred,

revered, holy, awesome 4A(ii)

relinquō 3 *relīquī relictus* I leave, abandon 4A(ii)

reliqu-us a um remaining, left 4E(ii)

remaneō 2 *remānsī remānsum* I remain 6C(iii)

remittō 3 *remīsī remissus* I send back; remit 6C(iii)

reor 2 dep. *ratus* I think, believe, suppose 5G(ii)

repellō 3 *reppulī repulsus* I drive back, drive out 4A(i)

repente suddenly 4A(i)

reperiō 4 *repperī repertus* I find 4A(iii)

reprimō 3 *repressī repressus* I hold back, check 6C(ii)

requīrō 3 *requīsīuī requīsītus* I seek out; ask for 5B(i)

rēs rē-ī 5f. thing, matter, business; property; affair 2B

rēs pūblic-a rē-ī pūblic-ae state, republic 5A(i)

resistō 3 *restitī* — I resist (+ dat.); stand back; halt, pause 5G(ii)

respiciō 3/4 *respexī respectus* I look round (back) at, turn my gaze upon; reflect upon; care for 6C(i)

respondeō 2 *respondī respōnsum* I reply 2B

retineō 2 *retinuī retentus* I hold back, detain, restrain; maintain 4B(ii)

reuertor 3 dep. *reuersus* I return 6C(iv)

reuocō 1 I call back 4C(ii)

rēx rēg-is 3m. king 3A

rīp-a ae 1f. bank 6D(ii)

rogō 1 I ask 1C

Rōm-a ae 1f. Rome (*Rōmae*, locative, at Rome) 4C(ii)

Rōmān-us a um Roman 4B(iv)

rūmor rūmōr-is 3m. rumour, (piece of) gossip, unfavourable report 6A(iv)

S

sacer sacr-a um holy, sacred 4A(iii)

sacerdōs sacerdōt-is 3m. or f. priest, priestess 4A(iv)

sacr-a ōrum 2n. pl. rites 4A(iii)

saepe often 4E(iii)

saeu-us a um wild; angry 2B

saltem at least 6B(vii)

saluē welcome! 1E

salūs salūt-is 3f. safety 4F(i)

salūtem dīcit (*S.* or *S.D.* at a letter-head) 'he greets' (+ dat.) 6B(i)

salu-us a um safe 1C

sanguis sanguin-is 3m. blood 4F(i)

sapienti-a ae 1f. wisdom 2B

satis enough (of) (+ gen.) 1D

sauci-us a um wounded 5G(ii)

scaen-a ae 1f. stage 1A

scelest-us a um criminal 2B

scelus sceler-is 3n. crime, villainy; criminal, villain 1E *sciō* 4 I know 1F

scrībō 3 *scrīpsī scrīptus* I write 2A

scrīps-: ⎫
scrīpt-: ⎭ see *scrībō*

sē himself, herself, itself / themselves 3B Gr.

sēcum with/to himself/ herself 1E

secund-us a um second 5C Gr.

secūris secūr-is 3f. axe 4D(ii)

secūt-: see *sequor*

sed but 1A

sēdecim 16 5C Gr.

semel once

cum semel as soon as 6A(iv)

semper always 1A

senāt-us ūs 4m. senate 4A(iii)

senex sen-is 3m. old man 1B

sēns-: see *sentiō*

sententi-a ae 1f. opinion; judgement; sentence; maxim 5C(iii)

sentiō 4 *sēnsī sēnsus* I feel; understand; perceive, realise 4A(ii)

septem seven 2A Gr.

septendecim 17 5C Gr.

septim-us a um seventh 5C Gr.

septuāgintā 70 5C Gr.

sepulc(h)r-um ī 2n. tomb 6A(v)

sequor 3 dep. *secūtus* I follow 2B

sermō sermōn-is 3m. conversation, discussion 4B(iii)

seru-a ae 1f. slave-woman Intro.

seruō 1 I keep safe, preserve 4C(i)

seru-us ī 2m. slave 1A

sēsē = sē 5C(ii)

seu (or *sīue*) . . . *seu* (or *sīue*) whether . . . or 6A(vii)

seuēr-us a um strict, stern 5D(i)

sex six 2A Gr.

sexāgintā 60 5C Gr.

sext-us a um sixth 5C Gr.

sī if 1A

sī + pres. subj., pres. subj. 'if x were to happen, y would happen' 4G Gr.

sī + impf. subj., impf. subj. 'if x were happening (now), y would be happening' (sometimes: 'if x had happened, y would have happened') 4G Gr.

sī + plupf. subj., plupf. subj. 'if x had happened, y would have happened' 5F Gr.

quod sī but if 6B(vii)

sīc thus, in this way, so 2B

Sicili-a ae 1f. Sicily 4C(ii)

sīcutī (or *sīcut*) (just) as 5C(ii)

sīdus sīder-is 3n. star 6A(v)

sign-um ī 2n. seal, signal, sign 2D; statue 4A(iii); standard; trumpet-call 5G(i)

silu-a ae 1f. wood 6D(ii)

sim pres. subj. of *sum*

simil-is e alike, similar, like (+ gen.) 2E

similis ac similar to 5G Gr.

simul at the same time 4B(iii); together 6A(vii); = *simulatque* as soon as 6B(iv)

simulācr-um ī 2n. image 4A(i)

simulatque (or *simulac* or *simul*) as soon as 6B(iv)

simulō 1 I feign 5B(ii)

sīn but if 6B(viii)

sine (+ abl.) without 2D

singul-ī ae a individual, one by one 6D(iv)

sinister sinistr-a um left: unfavourable 5G(i)

sinō 3 *sīuī situs* I allow 3C

sīue (or *seu*) . . . *sīue* (or *seu*) whether . . . or 6A(vii)

soci-us ī 2m. ally, friend 5A(iii)

sōl sōl-is 3m. sun 2A

soleō 2 semi-dep. *solitus* I am accustomed, am used (+ inf.) 4A(iii)

solit-: see *soleō*

sollicitō 1 I bother, worry 2E

sōlum (adv.) only 4B(iii)

nōn sōlum . . . sed etiam not only . . . but also 4F(ii)

soluō 3 *soluī solūtus* I release, undo 2D

sōl-us a um (gen. s. *sōlīus*: dat. s. *sōlī*) alone 4B(iii); lonely 6D(ii)

somni-um ī 2n. dream 1B

somn-us ī 2m. sleep 6A(iii)

soror sorōr-is 3f. sister 1D

spati-um ī 2n. space; time 6B(vi)

spērō 1 I hope; expect 5E(ii)

spēs spē-ī 5f. hope(s); expectation 5B(i)

Staphyl-a ae 1f. Staphyla Intro.

statim at once 1C

stet-: see *stō*

stil-us ī 2m. stylus (for writing in wax) 2A

stō 1 *stetī statum* I stand 1C

studi-um ī 2n. enthusiasm, zeal 5B(ii)

stultē stupidly 4C(ii)

stult-us a um stupid 2B

suāu-is e sweet, pleasant, delightful 6A(i)

sub (+ abl.) beneath, under 1A

subitō suddenly 3D

sublāt-: see *tollō*

subsidi-um ī 2n. reserve; help 5G(i)

succurrō 3 *succurrī succursum* I run to help, assist (+ dat.) 5G(ii)

sum esse fuī futūrus I am Intro.

summ-us a um highest, top of 1G

  summum supplicium the death penalty 4G(ii)

sūmō 3 *sūmpsī sūmptus* I take; put on; eat

  supplicium sūmō (*dē* + abl.) I exact the penalty (from) 5D(i)

sūmpt-: see *sūmō*

sūmpt-us ūs 4m. expense(s) 2A

super (adv.) more than enough; above, over; (+ acc./abl.) over, above; (+ abl.) about 6A(v)

superior superiōr-is higher; earlier 6C(iv)

superō 1 I conquer, overcome; get the upper hand 3B

supplex supplic-is (adj.) suppliant (also as noun) 5D(iv)

supplici-um ī 2n. punishment

  summum supplicium the death penalty 4G(ii)

supplicium sūmō (*dē* + abl.) I exact the penalty (from) 5D(i)

supplicō 1 I make prayers (to) (+ dat.) 1B

surgō 3 *surrēxī surrēctum* I rise, arise, get up 6D(ii)

suspicor 1 dep. I suspect 2D

sustineo 2 *sustinuī sustentus* I withstand; support 6C(ii)

sustul-: see *tollō*

su-us a um his, hers / theirs 3B

Syrācūs-ae ārum 1f. pl. Syracuse 4D(i) (*Syrācūsīs* at Syracuse)

Syrācūsān-us ī 2m. person from Syracuse, Syracusan 4A(iv)

T

tabell-ae ārum 1f. pl. writing-tablets 2A

taceō 2 I am silent 1C

tacit-us a um silent 2D

tāct-: see *tangō*

tāl-is e of such a kind 5A Gr.

  tālis . . . quālis of such a kind as 5G Gr.

tam so 2B

  tam . . . quam as . . . as 5G Gr.

tamen however, but (second word) 1B

tamquam as though 5G Gr.

tandem at length 1B

tangō 3 *tetigī tāctus* 1 touch, lay hands on 1G

tantī . . . quantī of as much value . . . as 2E Gr.

tant-us a um so great, so much, so important 4B(iii)

  tantus . . . quantus as much . . . as 5G Gr.

tard-us a um slow 4E(ii)

tēcum with you/yourself 3C

tegō 3 *tēxī tēctus* I cover 5G(iii)

tēl-um ī 2n. weapon 5A(iii)

templ-um ī 2n. temple 4A(i)

temptō 1 I try, test, attempt; attack 5E(ii)

tempus tempor-is 3n. time 2D

tendō 3 *tetendī tentus* (or *tēnsus*) I stretch (out); offer; direct; travel 5D(iv); strive, fight 5G(ii)

tenebr-ae ārum 1f. pl. shadows, darkness 6D(iii)

teneō 3 *tenuī tentus* I hold 3D

terr-a ae 1f. land 3B

terreō 2 I frighten 6B(viii)

terribil-is e dreadful, frightening 5E(i)

terti-us a um third 5C Gr.

testis test-is 3m. witness 4F(i)

tetig-: see *tangō*

thalam-us ī 2m. chamber, bedchamber 6D(iv)

thēsaur-us ī 2m. treasure 1B

timeō 2 I fear, am afraid of 1A; (*nē* + subj.) am afraid that/lest 5D Gr.

timid-us a um frightened, fearful 5C(ii)

timor timōr-is 3m. fear 6B(vi)

tollō 3 *sustulī sublātus* I lift, remove, take away 4A(iii)

tor-us ī 2m. couch, bed 6D(iv)

tot so many 4E(iii)

tot . . . quot as many . . . as 5G Gr.

tōt-us a um (gen. s. *tōtīus*; dat. s. *tōtī*) whole, complete 4A(i)

trādō 3 *trādidī trāditus* I hand over 5C(ii)

trāns (+ acc.) across 6A(vii)

trecent-ī ae a 300 2A Gr.

trēdecim 13 5C Gr.

trēs tri-a three 2A Gr.

trīgintā 30 5C Gr.

trīst-is e sad, gloomy, unhappy 1F

trucīdō 1 I butcher 5F(ii)

tū you (s.) 1A

tueor 2 dep. *tuitus* (or *tūtus*) I look after, protect; look at 6B(viii)

tul-: see *ferō*

tum then 1D

cum . . . tum both . . . and 5D(ii)

tunic-a ae 1f. tunic 6D(iv)

turb-a ae 1f. crowd, mob 1F

turp-is e disgusting, filthy, outrageous, ugly 4B(i)

tūt-us a um safe 4G(i)

tu-us a um your(s) (s.) 1C

V

uacu-us a um empty; free (from: + abl. or *ā(ab)* + abl.) 6B(vii)

ualdē very much, strongly 6B(v)

ualē goodbye! 1D

ualeō 2 I am strong; am well, am powerful; am able (cf. *ualē* = 'Farewell!' 'Goodbye!') 6A(vii)

uari-us a um diverse, various 6D(i)

ubi where (at)? 1E; when? 1F

ubi primum as soon as 5A(i)

ubicumque wherever 6B(vii)

-ue (added onto the end of a word: cf. *-ne* and *-que*) or 6A(vii)

uehemēns uehement-is impetuous, violent 5D(i)

uehementer strongly 4F(i)

uel . . . uel either . . . or 5A(ii)

uel even 5D(iv)

uelim pres. subj. of *uolō*

uellem impf. subj. of *uolō*

uelut as, just as 5C(ii)

ueniō 4 *uēnī uentum* I come, arrive 3A

uent-: see *ueniō*

uent-us ī 2m. wind 6D(i)

uerber uerber-is 3n. blow; whip 4F(i)

uerberō 1 I flog, beat 1C

uerb-um ī 2n. word 2B

uereor 2 dep. *ueritus* I fear, am afraid 5D(ii) (*nē* + subj. that/lest 5D Gr.)

uerit-: see *uereor*

uērō indeed 2D

Verrēs Verr-is 3m. Verres 4A(i)

uersor 1 dep. I am occupied; stay, dwell; am in a certain condition 5G(ii)

uers-us ūs 4m. verse; pl. poetry 5A(ii)

uertō 3 *uertī uersus* I turn (trans.) 6C(ii)

uērum but 2D

uēr-us a um true 3C

uestāl-is e Vestal (belonging to the goddess Vesta) 5D(i)

uester uestr-a um your(s) (pl.) 2A

uestis uest-is 3f. clothes, clothing, dress 4D(ii)

uetō 1 *uetuī uetitus* I forbid 4A(iv)

uetus ueter-is old; long-established 5A(i)

uexō 1 I annoy, trouble, worry 1C

ui-a ae 1f. way, road 2A

uīc-: see *uincō*

uīcīn-us ī 2m. neighbour 1C

uict-: see *uincō*

uictōri-a ae 1f. victory 3A

uideō 2 *uīdī uīsus* I see 1B

uideor 2 passive *uīsus* I seem 2C; am seen 4D Gr.

uīgintī 20 5C Gr.

uinciō 4 *uīnxī uīnctus* I bind 2A

uincō 3 *uīcī uictus* I conquer 2D

uinc(u)l-um ī 2n. chain, bond 4F(ii)

uīn-um ī 2n. wine 6A(i)

uir uir-ī 2m. man, husband 1D

uirgō uirgin-is 3f. young girl, virgin 4A(iii)

uirtūs uirtūt-is 3f. manliness, courage; goodness 1G

uīs-: see *uideō/uideor*

uīs 2nd s. of *uolō*

uīs irr. force, violence

(acc. *uim*; abl. *uī*); pl.
uīrēs uīr-ium 3f.
strength; military
forces 4A(i)

uīt-a ae 1f. life 2E

uīuō 3 *uīxī uīctum* I am
alive, live 5A(iii)

uīu-us a um alive, living
5G(iii)

ūll-us a um (gen. s. *ūllīus*;
dat. s. *ūllī*) any (cf.
nūllus) 4B(i)

ultim-us a um furthest;
last; greatest 6A(vii)

umbr-a ae 1f. shadow,
darkness; shade,
ghost 6D(ii)

umer-us ī 2m. shoulder
6D(ii)

umquam ever 3A

und-a ae 1f. water, wave
6D(ii)

unde from where, whence
5G(ii)

undecim 11 5C Gr.

undēuīgintī 19 5C Gr.

unguent-um ī 2n. ointment
1B

ūniuers-us a um all
together; whole,
entire 6C(ii)

ūn-us a um (gen. s. *ūnīus*;
dat. s. *ūnī*) one 2A
Gr.

uōbīscum with you (pl.)
3C

uocō 1 I call 1A

uolō uelle uoluī I wish,
want 1E

uoluntās uoluntāt-is 3f.
will, wish 5D(ii)

uoluō 3 *uoluī uolūtus* I roll,
turn over (trans.)
5G(iii)

uoluptās uoluptāt-is 3f.
desire, love, passion
3D

uōs you (pl.) 1F Gr.

uōt-um ī 2n. vow, prayer
6D(i)

uōx uōc-is 3f. voice; word
2E

urbs urb-is 3f. city 2D

ūs-: see *ūtor*

usque continually,
without a break
usque ad (+ acc.) right
up to 6A(iv)

ut (+ indic.) how! 1C;
(+ indic.) as, when
1D; (+ subj.) to, that
. . . should 4F(i)
(and 4F Gr.);
(+ subj.) that (after
accidit, perficiō etc.)
4F Gr.; (+ subj.) that
(result) 5A Gr.;
(+ subj.) in order to/

that (purpose) 5A
Gr.; (+ subj.) that
. . . not (after verbs
of fearing) 5D Gr.

uterque utraque utrumque
each of two, both
5G Gr.

utī = *ut* 4B(i)

utinam I wish that 5C Gr.

ūtor 3 dep. *ūsus* I use,
make use of; adopt
(+ abl.) 4B(i)

utpote (*quī quae quod*) as is
natural (for one
who) (+ subj.) 5E
Gr.

utrimque on both sides 3B

utrum . . . an (double
question) A or B?
(negative *annōn* = or
not?) 5D(i); (+ subj.)
whether . . . or
(indirect question)
(negative *necne* = or
not) 5D(i)

uulnerō 1 I wound 5G(iii)

uulnus uulner-is 3n.
wound 5G(iii)

uult 3rd s. of *uolō*

uultis 2nd pl. of *uolō*

uult-us ūs 4m. face,
expression 5G(iii)

uxor uxōr-is 3f. wife 1D

English–Latin vocabulary

Note

This vocabulary is compiled specifically for the English–Latin exercises in the Grammar and contains only those words and forms required to complete these successfully.

A

a(n): simply use noun; see also 'a certain'
abandon *relinquō* 3
able, be *possum posse potuī*
about to: use future participle
absence, in x's absence: use *absēns absent-is* agreeing with x
absent (use with noun to tr. 'in x's absence') *absēns absent-is*
accordance: in accordance with *perinde ac* (+ indic.)
account (noun) *ratiō ratiōn-is* 3f.; I make an account *ratiōnem habeō*
accuse *accūsō* 1
accustomed, be *soleō* 2 (semi-dep.) *solitus*
a certain *quīdam quaedam quoddam*; see **92**
achieve one's object *rem perficiō* 3/4 *perfēcī perfectus*
act (verb) *agō* 3 *ēgī*; *faciō* 3/4 *fēcī*; (noun) *facinus facinor-is* 3n.
actual *ipse ipsa ipsum*
address *adloquor* 3 dep. *adlocūtus*
advance *prōgredior* 3/4 dep. *prōgressus*
advantage: to x's advantage: use dat. of x

affair(s) *rēs rē-ī* 5f.
affirm *affirmō* 1
afraid
 be . . . (of) *timeō* 2
 be . . . (that) *uereor* 2 dep. *ueritus*
 nē + subj.; *timeō* 2
 nē + subj.; *metuō* 3
 metuī nē + subj.
 (*ut* + subj. that . . . not)
 be . . . to: as above, but + inf.
after *postquam* + perf. indicative; if a deponent verb, use perfect participle
again *iterum*; (= after this) *posthāc*
against *in* (+ acc.), *ad* (+ acc.)
against: fighting against *cum* + abl.
against (= contrary to what) *contrā ac* (+ indic.)
agreement, be in *cōnsentiō* 4 *cōnsēnsī cōnsēnsus*
aid *oper-a ae* 1f.; *auxili-um ī* 2n.
Alcumena *Alcumēn-a ae* 1f.
alive, be *uīuō* 3
alive *uīu-us a um*
all *omn-is e*
all the best men *optimus quisque*
all the time = while

dum + same tense as main verb
Allobroges *Allobrog-ēs Allobrog-um* 3m. pl.
allowed, x is *licet* (x (dat.) *licet* + inf.)
ally *soci-us ī* 2m.
alone *sōl-us a um*
already *iam*
also *quoque*; *etiam*; *et*; not only . . . but also *nōn sōlum . . . sed etiam*
although *quamquam*; or use abl. abs. with present/perfect participle; *cum* + subj.; *quamuīs* + subj.
always *semper*
am: see 'be'
ambassador *lēgāt-us ī* 2m.
amid: use abl. (of attendant circumstances); or *inter* (+ acc.)
Amphitruo *Amphitruō Amphitruōn-is* 3m.
and *et*; *atque/ac*
announce *nūntiō* 1
Antonius *Antōni-us ī* 2m.
anxiety *cūr-a ae* 1f.
 anxiety in case *cūra nē* + subj.
anyone (after negatives) *quisquam*
anything (after negatives) *quicquam*

(= *quid* + *quam*)
appear *uideor* 2 dep.;
   appāreō 2
appearance *faciēs, faci-ēī*
   5f.
approach *adeō adīre*;
   adgredior 3/4 dep.
   (both use *ad* + acc.)
are: see 'be'
arise *exorior* 4 dep. *exortus*
   (gerund *exoriundum*)
armed men *arm-a ōrum*
   2n. pl.; *armāt-ī ōrum*
   2m. pl.
army *exercit-us ūs* 4m.
arrive (at) *perueniō* 4
   peruēnī peruentum ad
   (+ acc.) (except
   names of towns and
   one-town islands;
   there acc. only)
as: see 'consider'
   as much as: see 'worth
   as much as'
   as (e.g. as you ought)
   ut (+ indic.); just as
   ita . . . ut
   as x . . . as y *tam*
   (+ adj.) . . . *quam*
   as soon as possible
   quam prīmum
   as (time): use abl. abs.
   with present
   participle or any case
   of present participle,
   depending on
   construction of
   sentence
   as follows *sīc*
   as though *tamquam*
   (+ subj.)
ask *quaerō* 3 *quaesīuī*
   quaesītus
ask for *rogō* 1 (+ acc.)
asleep, be *dormiō* 4
assert *affirmō* 1
assist *succurrō* 3 (+ dat.)
astuteness *astūti-a ae* 1f.

at: in time phrases use
   abl. alone
   at home *domī*
   at once *statim*
   at the house of *apud*
   (+ acc.)
   at the same time *simul*
attack *adgredior* 3 dep.
   aggressus; *petō* 3 *petīuī*
   petītus
attempt *cōnor* 1 dep.
attention, pay *operam dō* 1
   (to x: dat.)
away from *ā(ab)* (+ abl.)
axe *secūris secūr-is* 3f.

B

back, be = come back
   redeō redīre
bad *mal-us a um*
battle *proeli-um ī* 2n.
be, to *sum esse*
   be accustomed *soleō* 2
   (semi-dep.) *solitus*
   sum
   be missing *dēsum dēesse*
   dēfuī
bear *ferō ferre*
beast, wild beast *bēsti-a ae*
   1f.
beat *uerberō* 1; *caedō* 3
   cecīdī caesus
beautiful *pulcher pulchra*
   pulchrum
beauty *pulchritūdō*
   pulchritūdin-is 3f.
because *quod, quia*
   (+ indic.);
   occasionally use abl.
   abs.
   because of *propter*
   (+ acc.); *ob* (+ acc.)
become *fīō fierī*
   become acquainted
   with *cognōscō* 3
   cognōuī
before (when the action
   of the main clause is

conditional on the
   completion of the
   before clause)
   antequam + subj.
beg *precor* 1 dep.; *ōrō* 1;
   obsecrō 1
believe *crēdō* 3 *crēdidī*
   crēditum (+ dat.); in
   passive used
   impersonally: x
   (dat.) is believed by
   y (*ā* + abl.)
belonging to x: use dat.
   or gen. of x
beseech *ōrō* 1; *obsecrō* 1
besiege *obsideō* 2 *obsēdī*
   obsessus
best *optimus a um*
   all the best men *optimus*
   quisque
bestow *dō dare*
better *meli-or meli-us*
   I'd better = *mihi melius*
   est + inf.
big *ingēns ingent-is*
black *niger nigra nigrum*
blame *castīgō* 1
bold *audāx audāc-is*
boldness *audāci-a ae* 1f.
booty *praed-a ae* 1f.
bore: x is a . . . to: x
   (nom.) *taediō est* to y
   (dat.)
born (of) *nāt-us a um*
   (+ abl. of origin)
both . . . and *et . . . et*
bother *sollicitō* 1
boy *puer puer-ī* 2m.
brave *fort-is e*
break *frangō* 3 *frēgī frāctus*
bring *portō* 1; *ferō ferre*
   bring to land (of a
   ship) *appellō* 3 *appulī*
   appulsus
   bring with *addūcō* 3
   addūxī adductus
brother *frāter frātr-is* 3m.
burden *onus oner-is* 3n.

be a . . . on *onerī esse*:
x (nom.) is a burden
on y (dat.)
burdensome, x is . . . to
y: x (nom.) *onerī est*
to y (dat.)
burn (intrans.) *cōnflagrō* 1
burn (trans.) *incendō* 3
incendī incēnsus
business *negōti-um ī* 2n.;
rēs rē-ī 5f.
do business: see 'do'
but *sed* (1st word); *autem*
(2nd word); *tamen*
(usu. 2nd word);
(= except) *nisi*
butcher *trucīdō* 1
by *ā* or *ab* + abl. (often
after passive verbs);
by —ing abl. of
gerund.

C

cadaver *cadāuer cadāuer-is*
3n.
call *uocō* 1
call back *reuocō* 1
called: use *nōmine* (abl. of
nōmen)
call together *conuocō* 1
calm *aequō animō*
camp *castr-a ōrum* 2n. pl.
can *possum posse*
captain *praefect-us ī* 2m.
capture *capiō* 3/4 *cēpī*
captus
care for *cūrō* 1
care, take *prōuideō* 2
carry *portō* 1; *ferō ferre tulī*
cast lots *sortior* 4 dep.
catch sight of *cōnspicor* 1
dep.
Catiline *Catilīn-a ae* 1m.
certain (= a) *quīdam*
quaedam quoddam
certainly *certē*
chain *uinc(u)l-um ī* 2n.

change (intransitive) *sē*
mutāre
chap: omit or use *uir uir-ī*
2m.; *homo homin-is*
3m.
charge, be in . . . of
praesum praeesse
(+ dat.)
character *mōr-ēs mōr-um*
3m. pl.
cheer up *bonum animum*
habeō 2
children *līber-ī ōrum* 2m.
pl.
Chrysalus *Chrȳsal-us ī*
2m.
Cicero *Cicerō Cicerōn-is*
3m.
citizen *cīuis cīu-is* 3m.
city *urbs urb-is* 3f. (city of
x: put x in same case
as *urbs*)
claim *arguō* 3 *arguī*
clearly *plānē*
Cleomenes *Cleomen-ēs*
Cleomen-is 3m.
clever *doct-us a um*
coins *numm-ī ōrum* 2m. pl.
collect *colligō* 3 *collēgī*
column *agmen agmin-is*
3n.
come *eō īre iī itum*; *ueniō*
4 *uēnī uentum*
come out *exeō exīre*;
ēgredior 3/4 dep.
come to *adeō adīre adiī*
aditum
come up to *accēdō* 3
accessī accessum
command (noun) *imperi-*
um ī 2n.; (vb) *iubeō*
2; *imperō* 1
commander *imperātor*
imperātōr-is 3m.; *dux*
duc-is 3m.
commit *committō* 3
commīsī commissus

compassionate *misericors*
misericord-is (3 adj.)
complain *queror* 3 dep.
questus
complete *perficiō* 3/4
perfēcī perfectus;
cōnficiō 3/4 *cōnfēcī*
cōnfectus
concerning *dē* (+ abl.)
confirm *cōnfirmō* 1
conquer *uincō* 3 *uīcī*
conscript *cōnscrīpt-us a um*
consider (x as y) *habeō* 2
(x acc., y acc.);
arbitror 1 dep. (same
construction)
conspiracy *coniūrātiō*
coniūrātiōn-is 3f.
conspirator *coniūrātor*
coniūrātōr-is 3m.
constellation *sign-um ī* 2n.
consul *cōnsul cōnsul-is* 3m.
consulship *cōnsulāt-us ūs* 4m.
stand for consulship
cōnsulātum petō 3
contrary: see 'on the
contrary'
conversation *sermō*
sermōn-is 3m.
cook (noun) *coqu-us ī*
2m.; (vb) *coquō* 3
corpse *corpus corpor-is* 3n.;
cadāuer cadāuer-is 3n.
courage *uirtūs uirtūt-is* 3f.
coward(ly) *ignāu-us a um*:
for 'coward' use as
noun
crime *scelus sceler-is* 3n.
criminal *scelest-us ī* 2m.
cross *crux cruc-is* 3f.
crowd *turb-a ae* 1f.;
multitūdō multitūdin-is
3f.
cup *pōcul-um ī* 2n.
Curius *Curi-us ī* 2m.
custom *mōs mōr-is* 3m.
cut (vb) *caedō* 3 *cecīdī*

D

danger *perīcul-um ī* 2n.

danger of x happening *perīculum nē* + subj.

dare *audeō* 2

daring *audāx audāc-is* (adj.); *audāci-a ae* 1f. (noun)

daughter *fīli-a ae* 1f.

day *di-ēs diēī* 5m.

dead *mortu-us a um*

dear me = *mē miserum/ miseram*

death *mors mort-is* 3f.

death penalty *summ-um supplici-um ī* 2n.

deceive *dēcipiō* 3/4 *dēcēpī dēceptus*

decide *placet* 2 *placuit*: x (dat.) decides to y (inf.); *cōnstituō* 3 *cōnstituī cōnstitūtus* (to: infinitive)

declare *affirmō* 1

deed *facinus facinor-is* 3n.; (= something already done) *fact-um ī* 2n.

defeat *uincō* 3 *uīcī*

defend *dēfendō* 3 *dēfendī dēfēnsus*

defendant: use *iste ista istum* (see **91**)

delay (vb) *moror* (1 dep.); *commoror* (1 dep.); (noun) *mor-a ae* 1f.

Demaenetus *Dēmaenet-us ī* 2m.

demand *poscō* 3; *postulō* 1

depart (= set out) *proficīscor* 3 dep. *profectus*

depart for *proficīscor ad* (+ acc.)

desire (vb) *cupiō* 4

destroy *dēleō* 2 *dēlēuī*

destruction *exiti-um ī* 2n.

devise *excōgitō* 1

die *morior* 3/4 dep. *mortuus*; (= fall in battle) *occidō* 3 *occidī occāsum*

differently from *aliter ac* (+ indic.)

difficult *difficil-is e*

dinner *cēn-a ae* 1f.

Diodorus *Diodōr-us ī* 2m.

disadvantage, to x's: use dat. of x

disembark *in terram exeō* (*exīre exiī exitum*)

disregard (for) *neglegenti-a ae* 1f. (+ gen.)

disturb *commoueō* 2 *commōuī*

do *faciō* 3/4 *fēcī factus*; *agō* 3 *ēgī āctus*; *gerō* 3 *gessī gestus*

do business *negōti-um agō* (3) or *gerō* (3)

done for, I'm *periī*

don't/do not (as command) *nōlī* + infin.; *nē* + perfect subj.

door *foris for-is* 3f.; *iānu-a ae* 1f.

doubt: use adj. *dubi-us a um* (rephrase 'there's no doubt', as 'it is not doubtful') there is no . . . that *nōn dubium est quīn* + subj. (see **174** for sequence)

dowry *dōs dōt-is* 3f.

drag back *retrahō* 3 *retrāxī retractus*

draw *ferō ferre*

draw up *īnstruō* 3 *īnstrūxī īnstrūctus*

drink *bibō* 3 *bibī*

drive back *repellō* 3 *reppulī*

drunk *ēbri-us a um*

duty *offici-um ī* 2n.

dwell *habitō* 1

E

each (man, woman, thing) *quisque quaeque quidque*

each individual *ūnus quisque*

each (of two) *uterque utraque utrumque*

easily *facile*

easy *facil-is e*

elect *creō* 1

embark *in nāuem ingredior* 3/4 *ingressus*

embrace *complector* 3 dep. *complexus*; *amplexor* 1 dep.

encourage *hortor* 1 dep.; x (acc.) to y (*ut* + subj. – neg. *nē*: see **134** for rules of sequence); (troops) *cohortor* 1 dep. (with acc. or *ut* + subj.)

endure *ferō ferre*

enemy *host-is host-is* 3m.

enjoin *iubeō* 2 (x acc. to y inf.)

enjoy *fruor* 3 dep. *frūctus* (+ abl.)

enough *satis* (+ gen.); or qualifying an adj.

enter *intrō* 1; *ingredior* 3/4 dep.

enthusiasm *studi-um ī* 2n.

enthusiasm for + gen.

entrust *mandō* 1 x (acc.) to y (dat.)

-er: use comparative adj.

escape *fugiō* 3/4; *profugiō* 3/4 *profūgī*

-est: use superlative adj.

estimate *coniciō* 3/4 *coniēcī coniectus*

Euclio *Eucliō Eucliōn-is*
3m.
even *etiam*
event *rēs rē-ī* 5f.
ever *umquam*
every *omn-is e*
everything: use n. pl.
of *omnis* or
omnis + *rēs*
everyone: use m. pl. of
omnis
evil *mal-us a um*
exact (the penalty)
supplici-um sūmō 3
examine *īnspiciō* 3/4
īnspexī īnspectus
excellence *uirtūs uirtūt-is*
3f.
excellent *optim-us a um*
except *nisi*
execute *necō* 1
exile *exsili-um ī* 2n.
expenses *sūmpt-us ūs* 4m.
expression *uult-us ūs* 4m.
extent, to such an *adeō*
extremely: use superlative
adj. or adv. or *summ-
us a um* with a noun
in abl. (e.g.
'extremely
beautiful' = 'of very
great beauty' abl.)
eye *ocul-us ī* 2m.

F

fail *dēsum dēesse
dēfuī* + dat.
fall (often = die) *cadō* 3
cecidī cāsum; *occidō* 3
occidī occāsum
family *famili-a ae* 1f.;
genus gener-is 3n.
famous *illūstr-is e*
far from *longē ā
(ab)* + abl.
father *pater patr-is* 3m.
fatherland *patri-a ae* 1f.
fear (vb) *timeō* 2; that . . .

not *ut* + subj.; (noun)
timor timōr-is 3m.;
met-us ūs 4m.
feign *simulō* 1
ferocity *ferōci-a ae* 1f.
fiercely *ferōciter*
fight *pugnō* 1; *certō* 1;
fight a war *bellum
gerō*
fighting *pugn-a ae* 1f.;
proeli-um ī 2n.; in
'fighting is going on'
use impersonal
passive of *pugnō* 1
finally *postrēmō*; *tandem*
(= at length)
find *inueniō* 4 *inuēnī
inuentus*; *reperiō* 4
repperī repertus
(= something that
was mislaid or lost)
find out *cognōscō* 3 *cognōuī
cognitus*
finish *cōnficiō* 3/4 *cōnfēcī
cōnfectus*
fire (noun) *ignis ign-is*
3m.; *incendi-um ī* 2n.;
(vb, = set alight)
accendō 3 *accendī
accēnsus*
fist *pugn-us ī* 2m.
fitting, it is *decet* (for x
acc. to y infin.)
flat-fish *mūrēn-a ae* 1f
flight *fug-a ae* 1f.
follow *sequor* 3 dep.
food *cib-us ī* 2m.
fool (noun) *stult-us ī* 2m.;
(vb) *dēcipiō* 3/4 *dēcēpī
dēceptus*
for: use dat.; (= because)
nam (1st word), *enim*
(2nd word); (= on
behalf of) *prō*
(+ abl.); for the sake
of *causā* (+ gen.);
grātiā (+ gen.) –
placed after the noun

or phrase they
qualify
forbid *uetō* 1 *uetuī uetitus*
force *cōgō* 3 *coēgī coāctus*
(x acc. to: inf.)
forces *cōpi-ae ārum* 1f. pl.;
exercit-us ūs 2m.
foresee *prōuideō* 2 *prōuīdī
prōuīsus*
forget *oblīuīscor* 3 dep.
oblītus
forum *for-um ī* 2n.
free (vb) *līberō* 1
freedom *lībertās lībertāt-is* 3f
friend *amīc-us ī* 2m.; *comes
comit-is* 3m.
from (= away)
ā(ab) + abl. or (= out
of) *ē(ex)* + abl.;
(= because of) use
abl. of cause
full (of) *plēn-us a um*
(+ gen.)
Fulvia *Fului-a ae* 1f.

G

Gabinius *Gabīni-us ī* 2m.
gain *adipīscor* 3 dep.
adeptus
garland *corōn-a ae* 1f.
Gaul *Galli-a ae* 1f.
Transalpine Gaul *Galli-
a Trānsalpīn-a Galli-
ae Trānsalpīn-ae* 1f.
Gavius *Gaui-us ī* 2m.
general *dux duc-is* 3m.
get in x's way *obstō* 1
(+ dat.)
get ready (trans.) *comparō*
1; *parō* 1
girl *puell-a ae* 1f.
give *dō dare dedī* (x acc. to
y dat.)
give back *reddō* 3
reddidī redditus
give oneself up *sē
trādere (trādidī
trāditus)* (the

English–Latin vocabulary

pronoun will change
with the person: *mē
trādō, tē trādis* etc.)
give orders *iubeō* 2
(+ acc.); *imperō* 1
(+ dat.)
give orders (that)
imperō ut + subj.
gladly *laet-us a um*
go *eō īre iī itum*
go around *circum-eo -īre
-iī -itum*
go away *abeō abīre abiī
abitum*; *ēgredior* 3/4
dep. *ēgressus*:
gerundives *abeundum,
ēgrediendum*
go back *redeō redīre*
go forward *prōgredior*
3/4 *prōgressus*
go in *ineō inīre*;
ingredior 3/4 dep.
go out *exeō exīre exiī*;
ēgredior (3/4 dep.)
go on *pergō* 3
go to *accēdō* 3 *accessī
accessum*
going to —: use future
participle
god *de-us ī* 2m. (pl. *dī*: see
16); household god
Lar Lar-is 3m.
gold *aur-um ī* 2n.
good *bon-us a um*
good! *bene*
goodbye! *ualē*
great *magn-us a um*; very
great *maxim-us a um,
summ-us a um*; so
great *tant-us a um*
greater *mai-or us*
greed *cupiditās cupiditāt-is*
3f.; greed for x: use
cupiditās + gen.
Greek *Graec-us a um*
guarantor *cognitor cognitōr-
is* 3m.
guard *custōs custōd-is* 3m.

H
hand *man-us ūs* 4f.
hand over *trādō* 3 *trādidī
trāditus*
happen *fīō fierī factus*; or
use passive of *gerō* 3
gessī gestus
it happens that *accidit* (3
accidit) *ut* + subj.
harbour *port-us ūs* 4m.
harm *noceō* 2 *nocuī
nocitum* + dat.; in
the passive use
impersonally: x
(dat.) is harmed by y
(*ā* + abl.)
harmony *concordi-a ae* 1f.
has: see 'have'
hated, x is . . . by y; x
(nom.) *odiō est* to y
(dat.)
have *habeō* 2; or use
sum + dat. of person
who has, nom. of
thing/person
possessed; I have
—ed: use perfect
tense
have/had to x: use
gerundive of the x
with *sum* (have to)
eram (had to). The
person who 'has to'
is in the dat. when
the verb is
intransitive
he: use verb in 3rd person
singular; in indirect
statement (acc. + inf.)
use *sē* if it refers to
subject of
introductory verb,
eum if to a different
person
head, be at the . . . of
praesum praeesse
(+ dat.)
hear (of) *audiō* 4

her: use parts of *ea*
here *hīc*; (= to here) *hūc*
hers: use gen. of *haec, illa*
or *ea*
hesitate *cūnctor* 1 dep. (to:
infin.)
hide *cēlō* 1
highest *summ-us a um*
him: use *hic, ille* or *is*; in
law-court speeches
iste is often used
when 'him' = 'the
defendant'
himself (acc.) *sē* (gen.) *suī*
(dat.) *sibi* (abl.) *sē*;
(speaks) to himself
sēcum
his: where it refers to the
subject and there is
no emphasis, use
noun alone: where it
refers to someone
other than the
subject, use gen. of
hic, ille or *is*; if
referring to subject
with some emphasis
use *su-us a um*
hold *teneō* 2
hold back *reprimō* 3
repressī repressus;
teneō 2 *tenuī tentus*;
retineō 2 *retinuī
retentus*; x acc. from
doing y: *quōminus* or
nē + subj.
home (= to home)
domum; (= at home)
domī; (= from home)
domō
honour *honor honōr-is* 3m.
hope *sp-ēs spē-ī* 3f.
horse *equ-us ī* 2m.
hospitable *hospitāl-is e*
hour *hōr-a ae* 1f.
house *aed-ēs aed-ium* 3f.
pl.; *dom-us ūs* 4f. (irr.
see **56**)

583

in the house *domī*
household *famili-a ae* 1f.
household god *Lar Lar-is* 3m.
how! *ut* (+ indic.); how
  the matter stands: see
  stands; how
  (qualifying an
  adjective) *quam*: may
  introduce indirect
  question (followed
  by subj. verb)
how many *quot*
  (introducing direct
  or indirect question:
  ind. questions have
  subj. verb)
how much *quant-us a
  um* (introduces both
  direct and indirect
  questions: ind.
  questions have subj.
  verb)
however *tamen* (usu. 2nd
  word); *autem* 2nd
  word or *sed* 1st
  word
huge *ingēns ingent-is*
hurry *properō* 1
husband *uir uir-ī* 2m.

I
I *ego* (only when
  emphatic: otherwise
  use 1st person
  singular of verb
  only)
idle *ignāu-us a um*
idleness *ignāui-a ae* 1f.
if *sī*; (very occasionally
  use abl. abs.); if . . .
  not *nisi*
ignorant of *nesci-us a
  um* + gen.
important, such an *tant-us
  a um*
in *in* (+ abl.)
  in case *nē* + subj.

in order (not) to
  ut + subj., negative
  nē; see **145** for rules
  of sequence
in order to . . . more
  quō + comp. adj./
  adv. + subj. (see **148**)
in x place: often just
  abl. without *in*.
  Some towns have a
  special locative (see
  under name of
  town)
in x's praetorship/
  consulship etc.: plain
  abl. name + abl. of
  praetor, cōnsul etc.
in x time: plain abl.
in x way *ita*; *sīc*; or a
  phrase in abl. with
  mod-us ī 2m.
in —ing: abl. of
  gerund
inasmuch as *quippe
  quī* + subj.
individual: each
  individual *ūnus
  quisque*
inflamed *īnflammāt-us a um*
innocent *innocēns innocent-
  is*
inside (= to inside) *intrō*
instruct *praecipiō* 3/4
  praecēpī praeceptus x
  (dat.) to / not to do
  y (*ut*/*nē* + subj.; see
  145 for rules of
  sequence)
instruction: in 'an
  instruction has been
  given' use
  impersonal passive of
  praecipiō 3/4 *praecēpī
  praeceptus*: give the
  instructions: see
  'instruct'
intend(ing) to: use future
  participle

into *in* + acc.
invite (someone to
  something) *inuītō* 1
  (x (acc.) to y
  (*ad* + acc.))
is see 'be'
it: use 3rd person singular
  of verb
Italy *Itali-a ae* 1f.

J
join *adiungō* 3 *adiūnxī
  adiūnctus* (transitive)
  x (acc.) to y (dat.)
join someone or
  something: *sē
  adiungere* (+ dat.)
join battle with
  proelium committō 3
  *commīsī commissus
  cum* + abl.
joy *laetiti-a ae* 1f.; *gaudi-
  um ī* 2n.
joyful *laet-us a um* (x was
  not a joyful event:
  use adj. on its own,
  or with *rēs*)
judge *iūdex iūdic-is* 3m.
Jupiter *Iuppiter Iou-is* 3m.
just as (. . . so) *ut* (. . . *ita*)

K
keep *adseruō* 1
  keep/kept —ing: use
  imperfect tense
  keep quiet *taceō* 2
  keep shouting *clāmitō* 1
kill *necō* 1; *interficiō* 3/4
  interfēcī interfectus
king *rēx rēg-is* 3m.
know *sciō* 4; *cognōuī,
  cognitus*;
  (= understand)
  intellegō 3 *intellēxī
  intellēctus*
known: well known *clār-
  us a um*

L

lack *egeō* 2 *eguī* (+ abl.)
lad: use adj. in
   appropriate case of
   masculine
   (alternatively *homo
   homin-is* 3m.; *puer
   puer-ī* 2m.)
Lampsacum, people of
   Lampsacēn-ī ōrum 2m.
   pl.
land *terr-a ae* 1f.;
   (= native land) *patri-
   a ae* 1f.
Lar *Lar Lar-is* 3m.
large *ingēns ingent-is*;
   magn-us a um
laugh *rīdeō* 2 *rīsī rīsus*
law *lēx lēg-is* 3f.
lead *dūcō* 3 *dūxī*
leader (= general) *dux
   duc-is* 3m.; *prīnceps
   prīncip-is* 3m.
leadership, under x's: use
   abl. of name and abl.
   of *dux duc-is* 3m.
learn *cognōscō* 3 *cognōuī
   cognitus*
leave
   (= go away) *abeō abīre*
   (= abandon) *relinquō* 3
   relīquī
   (= go out) *ēgredior* 3/4
   dep. *ēgressus*
leisure *ōti-um ī* 2n.
Lentulus *Lentul-us ī* 2m.
lest (esp. after verbs of
   fearing or
   apprehension)
   nē + subj.
let (x ... do y, or x be
   done): use 3rd s./pl.
   subj. present; let ...
   not *nē* + perf. subj.
   3rd s./pl.)
letter *litter-ae ārum* 1f. pl.
liberty *lībertās lībertāt-is*
   3f.

lictor *līctor līctōr-is* 3m.
lie *mentior* 4 dep.
life *uīt-a ae* 1f.
like (adj.) *simil-is e* (+ dat.
   or gen.); (vb) x
   likes: x (dat.) *placet*;
   (vb) *uolō uelle uoluī*
   (only in potential
   subj. usages: e.g. 'I
   would like')
Lilybaeum *Lilybae-um ī*
   2m.; locative
   Lilybaeī; use acc. for
   'to', abl. for 'from'
listen *audiō* 4
live *uīuō* 3 *uīxī uīctūrus*
   (no past participle)
   live one's life *aetātem
   agō* 3 *ēgī āctus*
long *long-us a um*
look after *cūrō* 1
looks *fōrm-a ae* 1f.
lot, a ... of: use *mult-us a
   um*
love (vb) *amō* 1
lover *amātor amātōr-is* 3m.
lust *cupiditās cupiditāt-is* 3f.
lying *mendāx mendāc-is*

M

madness *īnsani-ā ae* 1f.
magistrate *magistrāt-us ūs*
   4m.
make *faciō* 3/4 *fēcī factus*
   make a speech
   ōrātiōnem habeō 2
   make plans *cōnsilium
   capiō* 3/4 *cēpī captus*
   make one's way *iter
   faciō* 3/4
man: old man, see 'old':
   uir uir-ī 2m.; in
   military contexts,
   use *mīlitēs* for 'men'
   (= human being) *homo
   homin-is* 3m.
manage (to) *perficiō* 3/4
   perfēcī perfectus

ut + subj.; *efficiō* 3/4
   effēcī effectus ut + subj.
   (Rules of sequence in
   135)
many *mult-ī ae a* (pl.)
married *nūpt-us a um*
marry *in mātrimōnium
   dūcō* 3 *dūxī ductus* (x:
   acc.)
massive *ingēns ingent-is*
master *domin-us ī* 2m.
matter *rēs rē-ī* 5f.
may (x may do y): x dat.
   licet + inf.; sometimes
   occurs in subordinate
   clauses – check the
   construction; in
   main clause,
   'someone may —',
   use perfect
   subjunctive
   (potential)
mean (vb) *dīcō* 3 *dīxī
   dictus*
meanwhile *intereā*
mention *loquor* 3 dep.
   loquī locūtus
merriment *laetiti-a ae* 1f.
Messana *Messān-a ae* 1f.
Metellus *Metell-us ī* 2m.
middle (of) *medi-us a um*
mind *anim-us ī* 2m.
missing, be *dēsum dēesse
   dēfuī*
mistress *amīc-a ae* 1f.
Mnesilochus *Mnēsiloch-us
   ī* 2m.
money *pecūni-a ae* 1f.
moon *lūn-a ae* 1f.
more: normally use
   comparative form of
   adj. or adv.
more (adv.) *magis*
more (s.) *plūs* (+ gen.);
   (pl.) *plūrēs plūra* 3rd
   decl. adjective
mountain *mōns mont-is*
   3m.

move (= upset) *commoueō
2 commōuī commōtus*;
(= physically move)
moueō 2 mōuī mōtus
much (adj.) *mult-us a um*;
too much *nimis*
(+ gen.); much
(adv.) = (by) far
multō
murder *necō 1*
must: x (dat.) *necesse est* Y
(inf.); often use
gerundive (x must
do Y = Y nom. must
be done, gerundive
agreeing with Y, by
x dat. With
intransitive verbs x
must Y = Y nom. n.
gerundive + *est* x dat.)
my *me-us a um* (voc. s. m.
mī)
myself: use part of *ego*

N

name (noun) *nōmen
nōmin-is* 3n.; (vb)
name x as Y *nōminō
1* x acc. Y acc.
necessity *necessitūdō
necessitūdin-is* 3f.
neighbour *uīcīn-us ī* 2m.
never *numquam*
nevertheless *tamen* (2nd
word); *nihilōminus*
new *nou-us a um*
new man *nouus homo*
next (= and then) *deinde*
Nicobulus *Nīcobūl-us ī*
2m.
nigh, be *adsum adesse*
night *nox noct-is* 3f.
no (adj.) *nūll-us a um*
no! *immō*
no-one *nēmo nēmin-is*
3m.; after *nē* use *quis*
there is no-one who
. . . *nēmo est quī* . . .
+ subj. (generic)

noble *nōbil-is e*
nobles *nōbil-ēs nōbil-ium*
3m. pl.
nor *neque, nec*
not *nōn*
not to (indirect
command) *nē* + subj.
and not to *nēue* + subj.
not yet *nōndum*
nothing *nihil, nīl*
now *nunc*
number *numer-us ī* 2m.

O

O! *ō* (followed by voc. in
direct address, acc. if
an exclamation)
oar *rēm-us ī* 2m.
obey *pāreō 2* (+ dative)
object: see 'achieve one's
object'
obstruct *obsistō 3
obstitī* + dat.
obtain *adipīscor 3 dep.
adeptus*
obviously *plānē*
of: use genitive to denote
possession, source;
use ablative in
descriptions (e.g. a
man of great
courage), or genitive
often *saepe*
old: old man *senex sen-is*
3m.
on: in a time phrase, use
ablative
on account of *propter*
(+ acc.); *ob* (+ acc.)
on the point of: use
future participle
on the contrary *immō*;
minimē
on the say so (of) *iussū*
(+ gen.)
once x had been —ed:
use abl. abs.
one *ūnus ūna ūnum* (like
nūllus, **62**)

one of *ūnus ē(ex)* + abl.
only *sōlum*; not only . . .
but also *nōn sōlum
. . . sed etiam*
onto *in* (+ acc.)
or *aut* (where two things:
either . . . or *aut . . .
aut*)
ordain *dēcernō 3*
order, give an . . . to
iubeō 2 iussī iussus
(+ acc.); *imperō 1*
(+ dat.)
order x to Y *iubeō*
(+ acc. + inf.); *imperō*
(x dat. *ut* + subj.);
(noun) *imperi-um ī*
2n.
other *ali-us ali-a ali-ud*
(gen./dat. s. *alī-us
ali-ī*)
ought *dēbeō 2*; x ought to
Y: x acc. *oportet* + inf.
our *noster nostr-a um*
out of *ē(ex)* + abl.
over (of time) use plain
acc.
own, his: use *su-us a um* if
it refers to the
subject of the verb

P

part *pars part-is* 3f.
party *conuīui-um ī* 2n.
patron *patrōn-us ī* 2n.
pay attention to *operam dō
dare dedī datus*
(+ dat.)
peace *pāx pāc-is* 3f.
penalty *supplici-um ī* 2n.
exact the penalty
supplicium sūmō 3 dē
(+ abl.)
people: use *homo homin-is*
3m. in pl., or pl. of
adjective on its own;
(= nation) *popul-us ī*
2m.
perform (an act) *committō*

3 *commīsī commissus*
person: use m. of adj. or
   pronoun
persuade *persuādeō* 2
   persuāsī persuāsum;
   persuade . . . x (dat.)
   to y (*ut* + subj. –
   negative *nē*)
Petreius *Petrēi-us ī* 2m.
Phaedra *Phaedr-a ae* 1f.
Philodamus *Philodām-us ī*
   2m.
Philoxenus *Philoxen-us ī*
   2m.
Picenum *ager Pīcēn-us,*
   agr-ī Pīcēn-ī 2m.
piece (= coin) *numm-us ī*
   2m.
pirate *pīrāt-a ae* 1m.;
   praedō praedōn-is 3m.;
   (adj.) *pīrātic-us a um*
place (noun) *loc-us ī* 2m.
   in x's place *in locum*
   (+ gen.)
place (vb) *pōnō* 3 *posuī*
   positus; *collocō* 1
plan *cōnsili-um ī* 2n.
   plans, make *cōnsilium*
   capiō 3/4
pleasure *uoluptās uoluptāt-*
   is 3f.; x is a pleasure
   to y: x (nom.)
   uoluptātī est y (dat.)
poetry *uers-ūs uum* 4m.
   pl.
   write poetry *uersūs*
   facere
ponder *cōnsīderō* 1;
   excōgitō 1
poor, poor man *pauper*
   pauper-is 3m. or adj.;
   if = unhappy, *miser*
   miser-a um
possess *habeō* 2
possible, it is etc. *potest*
   (often uses a passive
   infin.)
pot *aul-a ae* 1f. (the usual
   Classical Latin form

is *olla; aula* usually
   means 'court',
   'palace')
pour scorn on *irrīdeō* 2
   irrīsī irrīsus
praetorship, in x's . . .:
   use abl. of name and
   abl. of *praetor praetōr-*
   is 3m.
pray (to), supplicate
   supplicō 1 (+ dat.);
   precor 1 dep.
prefer *mālō mālle māluī*;
   prefer x to y *mālō* x
   (acc.) *quam* y (acc.)
prepare *parō* 1
   prepared (to) *parāt-us a*
   um ad (+ acc.) (with
   a gerundive phrase)
present, be *adsum adesse*
   adfuī
preserve *cōnseruō* 1
pretty *pulcher pulchr-a um*
prevent *prohibeō* 2 (x acc.
   from doing y infin.);
   impediō 4 (x acc.
   from doing y: *nē* or
   quōminus if *impediō*
   positive, *quīn* or
   quōminus if *impediō*
   negative)
priest *sacerdōs sacerdōt-is*
   3m.
priesthood *sacerdōti-um ī*
   2n.
promise *polliceor* 2 dep.
prostitute *meretrīx*
   meretrīc-is 3f.
protect *dēfendō* 3 *dēfendī*
   dēfēnsus
protection *praesidi-um ī*
   2n.
provided (that) *dum*
   (*dummodo*) + subj.
province *prōuinci-a ae* 1f.
punish *pūniō* 4
punishment *supplici-um ī*
   2n.
   exact punishment from

supplicium sūmō 3
   dē + abl.
purpose, with the . . . of
   ut + subj.; *quī* + subj.:
   ut is in this case
   often preceded by *eō*
   cōnsiliō; for the
   purpose of —ing
   grātiā or *causā* + gen.
   gerund/gerundive
   phrase (e.g. *resistendī*
   causā for the purpose
   of resisting): note
   they are post-
   positions (i.e. come
   after the word they
   govern)
pursue *sequor* 3 dep.
   secūtus; *persequor* 3
   dep. *persecūtus*

Q

qualities *uirtūt-ēs uirtūt-um*
   3f. pl.
quick *celer celer-is e*
quickly *celeriter*
quiet, keep *taceō* 2

R

Raecius *Raeci-us ī* 2m.
rank *ōrdō ōrdin-is* 3m.
rather than *potius quam*
   rather than x: use comparative
   adjective
read *legō* 3 *lēgī lēctus*
   read through *perlegō* 3
   perlēgī perlēctus
ready, get (trans.) *comparō*
   1; *parō* 1
realise *sentiō* 4 *sēnsī sēnsus*
rebuke *castīgō* 1
recall *recordor* 1 dep.
refer *referō referre*
refuse *nōlō nōlle nōluī*;
   (= say no) *negō* 1
regret x (acc.) *paenitet*; I
   regret x *mē*
   paenitet + gen.
relate *nārrō* 1

relative (= blood-kin)
cognāt-us ī 2m.
rely upon *nītor* 3 dep.
nīsus/nīxus (+ abl.)
remember *recordor* 1 dep.;
meminī meminisse
(perfect form,
present meaning)
remove x's Y, Y from x
auferō Y (acc.) x
(dat.)
remove *tollō* 3 *sustulī*
sublātus; *auferō auferre*
abstulī ablātus; *moueō*
2 *mōuī mōtus* x (acc.)
from Y (abl.)
reply *respondeō* 2 *respondī*
report (= denounce)
dēferō (irr. 3) *dēferre*
dētulī; (= announce)
nūntiō 1
rescue *ēripiō* 3/4 *ēripuī*
ēreptus (x acc. from
Y dat.)
resist *resistō* 3 *restitī* —
(+ dat.)
resolute *audāx audāc-is*
resources *op-ēs op-um* 3f.
pl.
respect *honor honōr-is* 3m.
rest (of) *cēter-us a um*;
reliqu-us a um
retain *retineō* 2 *retinuī*
retentus
return (= go back) *redeō*
redīre rediī; *regredior*
3/4 *regressus*; (= give
back) *reddō* 3 *reddidī*
redditus
reveal *aperiō* 4 *aperuī*
apertus; *patefaciō* 3/4
patefēcī patefactus
reward *praemi-um ī* 2n.
rich (man) *dīues dīuit-is*
3m.; or adj.
Roman *Rōmān-us a um*
(for 'a Roman',
'Romans' use m.
forms as nouns)

Rome *Rōm-a ae* 1f.;
locative *Rōmae*; for
'to' use acc.; for
'from' use abl.
rotten *pūtid-us a um*
Rubrius *Rubri-us ī* 2m.
run:
run away *fugiō* 3/4 *fūgī*
run into *incurrō* 3
incurrī incursum
(in + acc.)
run together *concurrō* 2
concurrī
rush: in 'there was a rush'
use impersonal
passive of *concurrō* 3
concurrī concursum

S

safe (= saved) *salu-us a um*
safety *salūs salūt-is* 3f.
sail *nāuigō* 1
sailor *naut-a ae* 1 m.
sake, for the . . . of *causā*
(+ gen.); *grātiā*
(+ gen.) – placed
after the noun or
phrase they qualify;
for the sake of —ing
causā/grātiā + gen.
gerund/gerundive
phrase (place *causā/
grātiā* after noun or
phrase it governs)
same *īdem eadem idem*
at the same time *simul*
Sanga *Sang-a ae* 1m.
save (= keep safe)
seruō 1; save x from
Y *ēripiō* 3/4 *ēripuī*
ēreptus x acc. from Y
dat.
say *dīcō* 3 *dīxī dictus*
introducing direct
speech *inquam inquis*
inquit 3rd pl. *inquiunt*
say . . . not *negō* 1
(often with
acc. + inf.)

say so, on the . . . of
iussū + gen.
scene *tumult-us ūs* 4m.
scorn: see 'pour scorn on'
scoundrel *scelest-us a um* –
use as a noun
sea *mare mar-is* 3n.; abl.
marī = by sea
section of society *ōrdō*
ōrdin-is 3m.
see *uideō* 2 *uīdī uīsus*
seek *petō* 3; *quaerō* 3
seek out *requīrō* 3
requīsīuī requīsītus
seem *uideor* 2 pass. *uīsus*
seize *occupō* 1
senate *senāt-us ūs* 4m.
send *mittō* 3 *mīsī missus*
(x: acc., to Y:
ad + acc.)
send away *dīmittō* 3
dīmīsī dīmissus
seriously *grauiter*
seriousness *grauitās*
grauitāt-is 3f.
Sertorius, of *Sertōriān-us a*
um
Servilius *Seruīli-us ī* 2m.
set *occidō* 3 (intrans.)
set out *proficīscor* 3
profectus
set (a trap) *īnsidiās parō*
1 for x (dat.)
set free *līberō* 1
set (guards) *dispōnō* 3
disposuī dispositus
set on fire *incendō* 3
incendī incēnsus
shall: use future tense
shall have: use future
perf. tense
shame *pudor pudōr-is* 3m.
she: use 3rd s. of verb;
for emphasis use *illa*
or *haec*
ship *nāu-is nāu-is* 3f.
shore *lītus lītor-is* 3n.
should *dēbeō* 2;
occasionally subj.

alone is used (jussive): e.g. 'x should do Y'; gerundive is also used to express 'should' as obligation, x (dat.) should do Y (n. gerundive + *est*). Where 'should' occurs in subordinate clauses check whether the conjunction takes a subj.; if so, then nothing else is required to express should (e.g. until troops should be sent . . . *dum* + subj.)

shout *clāmō* 1
keep shouting *clāmitō* 1
shrine *fān-um ī* 2n.
shut in *claudō* 3 *claudī clausus*
Sicily *Sicili-a ae* 1f.
signal *sign-um ī* 2n.
silent, be *taceō* 2
silently *tacit-us a um*
silver *argent-um ī* 2n.
since *cum* + subj.
slave *seru-us ī* 2m.
slave-girl/woman *seru-a ae* 1f.
sleep (vb) *dormiō* 4
so x (adj./adv.) *tam*
so = to such an extent *adeō*
so as to / so that (purpose = in order that) *ut* + subj. (negative *nē*); see **145** for rules of sequence
so as to . . . more —ly / so that . . . more —ly (purpose) *quo* + comp. adverb + subj.; see **145** for rules of sequence

so great *tant-us a um*
society, section of *ordō ordin-is* 3m.
soldier *mīles mīlit-is* 3m.
someone *aliquis*
son *fīli-us ī* 2m. (voc. s. *fīlī*)
soon *mox; iam*
sorrow *lūct-us ūs* 4m.
sort (of person/people who) *is quī* + subj. (generic); sort of person that *tālis . . . quālis*
Sosia *Sōsi-a ae* 1m.
source, x is a . . . of pleasure to Y: x (nom.) *uoluptātī est* Y (dat.)
spare *parcō* 3 *pepercī parsūrus* (+ dat.); in passive used impersonally, x (dat.) will be spared (3rd s.) by Y (*ā*(*ab*) + abl.)
speak *dīcō* 3 *dīxī dictus; loquor* 3 dep. *locūtus*
speak to (= address) *alloquor* 3 dep. *allocūtus*
speech, make a *orātiōnem habeō* 2
spirits *anim-us ī* 2m. (often plural in this sense)
spot *loc-us ī* 2m.; pl. *loc-a ōrum* 2n.
stage *scaen-a ae* 1f.
stand (vb) *stō* 1 *stetī status;* how the matter stands *ita . . . ut rēs est*
stand in x's way *obstō* 1 *obstitī* (+ dat.)
stand (for consulship) (*cōnsulātum*) *petō* 3 *petīuī petītus*
Staphyla *Staphyl-a ae* 1f.

star *sign-um ī* 2n.
start *coepī coepisse* (past tenses only). Occasionally 'started to' can be expressed by either (a) historic infinitive or (b) imperfect indicative
state (strongly) *affirmō* 1; *dīcō* 3 *dīxī dictus*
state (noun) *rēs pūblic-a rē-ī pūblic-ae* 5f. + 1/ 2f. adj.; *cīuitās cīuitāt-is* 3f.
station *collocō* 1; *pōnō* 3 *posuī positus*
statue *simulācr-um ī* 2n.
stay *maneō* 2 *mānsī mānsum*
stop *prohibeō* 2 (x acc. from doing Y infin.); *impediō* 4 (x acc. from doing Y: *quōminus* or *nē* when *impediō* positive; *quōminus* or *quīn* when negative)
story *fām-a ae* 1f. 'The story is that . . .' *fāma est* followed by acc. + inf.; tell a story – use *rēs* or n. of *hic*
strategic *opportūn-us a um*
street *ui-a ae* 1f.
stretch forth *tendō* 3 *tetendī tēnsus*
strict *seuēr-us a um*
strike *feriō* 4
strip *nūdō* 1
strip (= rob corpses) *spoliō* 1
stupid *stult-us a um*
substitute *substituō* 3 *substituī substitūtus*
succeed *rem bene gerō* 3 *gessī gestus*
such
to such an extent *adeō*

such an important *tant-us a um*

suddenly *subitō*

suffer *patior* 3 dep. *passus*

summon *uocō* 1; *arcessō* 3 *arcessīuī arcessītus*

suppliant *supplex supplic-is* (adj.); also used as a noun

supporter *soci-us ī* 2m.

surely? *nōnne*; surely not? *num*; surely *certē*

swift *celer celer-is e*

Syracusans *Syrācūsān-ī ōrum* 2m. pl.

Syracuse *Syrācūs-ae ārum* 1f. pl.; locative *Syrācūsīs*

T

take (= capture) *capiō* 3/4 *cēpī captus*; (= lead off) *dēdūcō* 3 *dēdūxī dēductus*

take away *auferō auferre abstulī ablātus; tollō* 3 *sustulī sublātus*

take care lest/that *prōuideō* 2 *prōuīdī prōuīsus nē* + subj.

take from *auferō* (take x (acc.) from y (dat.))

talk *loquor* 3 dep. *locūtus*

Teleboans *Tēlebo-ae ārum* 1m. (pl.)

tell *loquor* 3 dep. *locūtus*; *dīcō* 3 *dīxī dictus*; (= relate) *nārrō* 1 (x acc. to y dat.); (= order) *iubeō* 2 *iussī iussus*

temple *templ-um ī* 2n.

than *quam*; or use abl. of comparison

that *ille illa illud; is ea id*

that (conjunction) use

acc. + infin. construction after verbs of saying thinking, perceiving; *ut* + subj. after verbs of command (neg. *nē*); so . . . that (as a result) *ut* + subj.; see **144**

the: simply use noun

their: referring to the subject, use noun alone

them: use pl. of *hic ille* or *is*

then (= next) *deinde*; (= at that point) *tum*

Theomnastus *Theomnāst-us ī* 2m.

there is *est*

there are *sunt*

there was *erat, fuit* or *factus est*

therefore *igitur* (2nd word)

these: see 'this'

they: use 3rd pl. verb

thief *fūr fūr-is* 3m.

thing *rēs rē-ī* 5f.; or use neut. adj.

think *opīnor* 1 dep.; *arbitror* 1 dep.; *putō* 1; think x (to be) y: *habeō/arbitror* x (acc.) y (acc.)

this *hic haec hoc*; sometimes possible to use part of *quī quae quod* at beginning of sentence

those: see 'that'

threaten *minor* 1 dep. (+ dat.); threaten x with y: *minor* x (dat.) y (acc.)

three *trēs tri-um*

through *per* (+ acc.); of

extent of time use acc. alone; = because of: use abl. of cause

throughout: use abl. of place (where the noun has an adjective); or *per* (+ acc.)

throw *coniciō* 3/4 *coniēcī coniectus*

thus *sīc; ita*

time *tempus tempor-is* 3n.

to (motion) *ad* (+ acc.), *in* (+ acc.); (gainer) plain dative

to x (vb): after *uolō, nōlō, mālō* use infinitive; prefer x to y: see 'prefer'

to (as in: order x to – indirect command) *ut* + subj.; see also 'manage (to)'

to: where this indicates purpose use *ut/nē* (not to) + subj. For sequence see **145**. In some cases it is possible to use *quī* + subj., see **145**[3]; also *ad* + gerundive + noun (acc.); or *ad* + gerund (acc.)

to such an extent (. . . that . . .) *adeō* . . . (*ut* + subj.)

today *hodiē*

too much *nimis* (+ gen.)

top *summ-us a um*

touch *tangō* 3 *tetigī tāctus*

towards *ad* (+ acc.)

town *oppid-um ī* 2n.

Transalpine Gaul *Galli-a ae Trānsalpīn-a ae* 1f.

trap (set a) *īnsidiās parō* 1 for x (dat.)

treasure *thēsaur-us ī* 2m.

trick *dol-us ī* 2m.

tricks *astūti-ae ārum* 1f. pl.
troops *cōpi-ae ārum* 1f. pl.
trouble *mal-um ī* 2n.
Troy *Trōi-a ae* 1f.
true *uēr-us a um*
truly *uērō*
try *cōnor* 1 dep.
turn, do a good *bene faciō*
3/4 (+ dat.)
turn over (transitive)
uoluō 3 *uoluī uolūtus*
two *du-o du-ae du-o*
two hundred *ducent-ī ae a*

U

Umbrenus *Umbrēn-us ī*
2m.
understand *intellegō* 3
intellēxī
unhappy *miser miser-a um*
until (with idea of
purpose) *dum* + subj.
up, what's . . .?: see
'what'
upbraid *castīgō* 1
urge *cohortor* 1 dep. (x
acc. to y: *ut* + subj.)
us: see 'we'
use *ūtor* 3 dep. *ūsus*
('using' = *ūs-us a um*)
used to — : use
imperfect indicative
utmost *summ-us a um*

V

value, of no *nihilī*
various *dīuers-us a um*
Verres *Verr-ēs Verr-is* 3m.
very: use superlative form
of adj. or adv. as
appropriate
very quickly: use
superlative adverb
(from *celer*); or abl.
phrase of manner,
summā celeritāte
via *per* (+ acc.)
victory *uictōri-a ae* 1f.

view, in my *ut opīnor*
vile *turp-is e*
visit *uīsō* 3
voice *uōx uōc-is* 3f.

W

wage (war) (*bellum*) *gerō* 3
gessī gestus; (*bellum*)
faciō 3/4
wait *exspectō* 1
walk *ambulō* 1
walls *moen-ia moen-ium*
3m. pl.
want *uolō uelle uoluī*; not
want *nōlō nōlle nōluī*
war *bell-um ī* 2n.
was/were —ing: use
imperfect indicative
watch *īnspiciō* 3/4 *īnspexī*
īnspectus
water *aqu-a ae* 1f.
way (= habit, custom)
mōs mōr-is 3m.;
(= manner) *mod-us ī*
2m.; (= journey) *iter*
itiner-is 3n.
make one's way *iter*
faciō 3/4
ways *mōr-ēs mōr-um*
3m. pl.
we *nōs* (if emphatic:
otherwise, use plain
1st person pl.)
wealth *dīuiti-ae ārum* 2f. pl.
weapon *tēl-um ī* 2n.
weight (= authority or
influence) *auctōritās*
auctōritāt-is 3f.
well known *clār-us a um*
were to . . . in
conditional
sentences: pres. subj.
what? *quid*?; or use
appropriate form of
the adjective *quī*?
what x? *quid* (+ gen.)
what's up? *quid negōtī*
est?

what a *ō* (+ acc. of
exclamation)
when *ubi* (+ perf. indic.);
with deponent verbs,
use past participle;
cum + plup. subj. Or
use abl. abs.
where to? *quō*
which?: use appropriate
form of *quī* to agree
with noun
which: use nom. of *quī*
quae quod; or use a
participle agreeing
with the noun
described
while *dum* + present
indicative (when the
main clause
interrupts the action
of the *dum* clause);
or use abl. abs. with
present participle
who? *quis*
who *quī quae quod*; see
106–7, 140; 145[3]
whole (of) *tōt-us a um*
(gen. s. *tōtīus*: dat. s.
tōtī)
whom?: use acc. s./pl. m./
f. of *quis* as
appropriate
whom: see 'who' (use
acc. s. or pl.)
whore *meretrīx meretrīc-is*
3f.
whose?: use gen. s./pl. of
quis as appropriate
whose: use gen. s. or pl.
of *quī quae quod*; or
dat. (with parts of
esse)
why? *cūr*; *quārē*; in
indirect questions
followed by subj.
verb
wicked *mal-us a um*;
scelest-us a um

591

wife *uxor uxōr-is* 3f.
wild beast *bēsti-a ae* 1f.
will: use fut. tense
will have: use fut. perf.
    tense
win *uincō* 3 *uīcī uictus*
wisdom *sapienti-a ae* 1f.
wish *uolō uelle uoluī*; not
    wish *nōlō nōlle nōluī*
with (= accompanied by)
    cum (+ abl.); (= by
    means of, or
    describing
    circumstances) plain
    abl.; with x —ing –
    use abl. abs. with
    pres. part.
without *sine* (+ abl.)
woman *fēmin-a ae* 1f.;
    mulier mulier-is 3f.
worry *cūr-a ae* 1f.
worse *pei-or pei-us*
worship *colō* 3 *coluī cultus*
worth as much as *tantī*
    . . . *quantī* . . .

worthy (of) *dign-us a*
    um + abl.
would: use fut. inf. (in
    acc. + inf.
    construction – 'that'
    clause – in secondary
    sequence); in
    conditional sentences
    use subj. (see rules in
    139, 173); in purpose
    clauses: use correct
    sequence (impf. subj.
    see **145**); I would
    like = *uelim* (pres.
    subj. – potential)
would be: in indirect
    statement past
    sequence use
    supine + *īrī* (e.g.
    captum īrī would be
    captured) or *fore*
    ut + subj. (pres. for
    primary, impf. for
    secondary sequence)
would have: in

conditional sentences
    use plupf. subj. or
    impf. subj.
wound (vb) *uulnerō* 1
wretched *miser miser-a um*
write (poetry) *faciō* (*uersūs*
    4m. pl.)

Y

year *ann-us ī* 2m.
ye gods! *prō dī immortālēs!*
yes *ita*
yet *tamen* (2nd word in
    clause)
yield *cēdō* 3 *cessī cessum*
    (to x: dat.)
you (s.) *tū*, (pl.) *uōs* (only
    if emphatic: if not,
    use 2nd person s./pl.
    of verb)
young man *iuuenis iuuen-*
    is 3m.
your *tu-us a um* (when
    'you' is one person)
yourself: use part of *tū*
yourselves *uōs*

Additional learning vocabulary

This list contains about 400 words which have been met in the course and are common in the most accessible parts of Latin literature, but have not been set for learning or used in exercises. For ease of reference, the place where each word first occurs is recorded. For principal parts of irregular verbs, consult the list in Reference Grammar **G**. (Note that where the prefix is followed by a hyphen compounds will be found under the simple form in that list: e.g. look up *per-tineō* under *teneō* and *con-tendō* under *tendō*, but *prōspiciō* under *prōspiciō*.) Prepositions are not included in the list, but may be found in Reference Grammar **K**.

A

ab-dūcō 3 I lead away 5E(ii)

adhibeō 2 I apply; employ 6C(iv)

adit-us ūs 4m. approach, entrance 5D(ii)

ad-mittō 3 I let in; commit 4E(ii)

ad-pellō 3 I bring to land 4E(i)

ad-pōnō 3 I place by 6D(iv)

ad-stō 1 I stand by 1D

aduent-us ūs 4m. approach, arrival 6B(vii)

aedifici-um ī 2n. building 6B(iii)

aedificō 1 I build 2D

aestās aestāt-is 3f. summer 6D(iii)

aest-us ūs 4m. heat; tide 6D(iv)

ancor-a ae 1f. anchor 4E(i)

antīqu-us a um old 2A

appāreō 2 I become visible; am evident 1B

arceō 2 I enclose; keep off, keep away 6D(ii)

arguō 3 I make clear, prove; accuse 4D(ii)

ariēs ariet-is 3m. ram; battering-ram 2E

ar-ripiō 3/4 I snatch up, seize 4A(i)

aspect-us ūs 4m. sight; appearance 5D(i)

āter ātr-a um black 6D(ii)

auāriti-a ae 1f. greed 5B(i)

auār-us a um greedy 1A

ā-uertō 3 I turn away (trans.) 4D(ii)

au-us ī 2m. grandfather 1B

B

bōs bou-is 3m. and f. ox, cow 1E

C

cadāuer cadāuer-is 3n. corpse 5G(iii)

caec-us a um blind; hidden; dark, obscure 1F

callid-us a um skilful, shrewd; cunning, crafty 3C

canō 3 I sing; play 5G(i)

cant-us ūs 4m. song 4E(ii)

cardō cardin-is 3m. hinge 3D

careō 2 (+ abl.) I am without, lack 4C(ii)

cār-us a um dear 3D

celebrō 1 I crowd, frequent; celebrate; extol 4B(iii)

cēnseō 2 I assess, value; propose; resolve; think 6B(vii)

censor cēnsōr-is 3m. censor (Roman magistrate) 5A(i)

cernō 3 I discern, distinguish 6D(i)

circum-dō 1 I put around; surround 4B(iv)

circum-sistō 3 I stand around, surround 4F(i)

cīuīl-is e civic, civil 6B(viii)

claudō 3 I close, shut 1A

clēmēns clēment-is gentle, mild; merciful 5D(i)

cognāt-us ī 2m. blood-relation 5G(iii)

col-loquor 3 dep. I converse, confer 2E

coll-um ī 2n. neck 3C

color colōr-is 3m. colour 6D(ii)

commemorō 1 I mention, relate, tell of 6C(i)

commendō 1 I entrust; recommend 5D(iv)

commūnicō 1 I share 5E(ii)

compleō 2 I fill up 4F(i)

com-pōnō 3 I put together, arrange; compose, construct; adjust 2A

com-prehendō 3 I grasp, seize; arrest; grasp mentally, understand; include (in narrative), describe 1F

concurs-us ūs 4m. running together, concourse; charge 6C(ii)

concutiō 3 I shake; shatter; terrify 5A(i)

con-dō 3 I build, found, establish; compose; put away, store; conceal, hide; bury 6D(ii)

cōnfert-us a um packed together, crowded, compact 5G(ii)

cōnflīgō 3 I come to blows 5E(ii)

con-gredior 3/4 dep. I come together, meet 2D

con-iungō 3 I join together, unite 4D(ii)

con-quīrō 3 I collect; search for 4C(ii)

cōn-sentiō 4 I am in agreement, agree 3B

cōnsōlor 1 dep. I comfort, console; alleviate 6C(iv)

cōnspiciō 3/4 I catch sight of; observe, gaze on 5B(i)

cōnstāns cōnstant-is stable, steadfast, consistent 5C(iii)

cōnstanti-a ae 1f. steadfastness, consistency 3A

cōnsuētūdō cōnsuētūdin-is 3f. custom, habit, wont; social intercourse, companionship 5A(i)

cōnsulār-is e consular 5E(i)

cōnsulō 3 I consult; (+ dat.) take thought for, consult the interests of 6B(vii)

cōnsult-um ī 2n. decree 6B(i)

cōn-sūmō 3 I use up; waste, squander 6C(ii)

cōn-surgō 3 I arise together 6C(iv)

con-tendō 3 I strain, exert; demand; affirm, insist; (intrans.) exert myself; push on, hasten; fight, struggle 6B(vii)

content-us a um satisfied, content 4G(i)

continēns continent-is adjacent; continuous 6C(iii)

con-uertō 3 I turn round, wheel; change (trans.: pass. supplies intrans. meanings) 6C(ii)

creō 1 I create, produce; appoint, choose, elect 4A(iv)

crīmen crīmin-is 3n. accusation, charge 4A(iii)

cruent-us a um gory, bloody 5F(ii)

cubō 1 I lie; lie in bed; sleep; recline at table 2C

currō 3 I run 1F

D

damn-um ī 2n. loss, damage 6D(iii)

dē-cēdō 3 I depart, retire, withdraw; die; abate, cease 6B(v)

dē-cernō 3 I decide, decree, determine 6B(vii)

dē-cidō 3 I fall down; perish 6D(iii)

dēfess-us a um tired out 6A(iii)

dēlectō 1 I delight, please 6B(i)

dēmenti-a ae 1f. madness 5F(ii)

dē-mittō 3 I let down 5E(i)

dēprecor 1 dep. I beg off, pray to avert 6B(i)

dē-prehendō 3 I catch in the act, surprise, intercept 5C(ii)

dē-rīdeō 2 I scoff at 2E

dē-serō 3 I abandon, desert 5C(ii)

dēsīderō 1 I long for; miss, feel the loss of 6C(iv)

dē-sinō 3 I cease 6A(vi)

dēspērāt-us a um abandoned, desperate 6B(vii)

dēspērō 1 I lose hope, despair 5F(ii)

dē-stituō 3 I leave in the lurch, abandon 6C(ii)

dict-um ī 2n. word; saying 2A

dif-fugiō 3/4 I scatter in flight 6D(iii)

dī-ripiō 3/4 I tear in pieces; plunder, sack 5D(i)

disciplīn-a ae 1f. instruction, training, learning; science; doctrine 4E(ii)

dis-tribuō 3 I distribute 4D(i)

dīuidō 3 I divide, separate 1C

doctrīn-a ae 1f. teaching, learning 4A(ii)

domestic-us a um home-, domestic; native, internal 6B(viii)

domicili-um ī 2n. abode, dwelling 5D(i)

Additional learning vocabulary: Latin–English

E

ēdict-um ī 2n. proclamation, manifesto 6B(i)

edō 3 I eat 3C

ef-fundō 3 I pour out (trans.) 6D(iii)

effūs-us a um outspread; slackened, dishevelled; extravagant, lavish 6D(ii)

ē-iciō 3/4 I cast out; cast ashore, wreck 4E(ii)

ē-ligō 3 I pick out, choose, select 6B(vi)

ē-rigō 3 I raise up; arouse; cheer up, encourage 4E(i)

ē-rumpō 3 I break out; burst forth 5B(iii)

ē-ueniō 4 I turn out, come to pass, happen, result 2E

ēuent-us ūs 4m. outcome, result 4A(iv)

ē-uertō 3 I overturn, overthrow, destroy 5D(i)

ēuocō 1 I call out, call forth 2E

excitō 1 I arouse, kindle 4B(i)

exercitāt-us a um well-trained, practised 6C(ii)

eximi-us a um exceptional, extraordinary 4B(ii)

exīstimātiō exīstimātiōn-is 3f. judgement, opinion; reputation 4B(ii)

expedīt-us a um unencumbered, free for action, in light marching order; convenient, ready to hand, uninterrupted 5G(ii)

ex-pellō 3 I drive out 1C

explōrō 1 I investigate, search out; reconnoitre 5G(ii)

ex-pōnō 3 I put out, set out; disembark (trans.); set forth, expound 6B(vii)

exspectātiō exspectātiōn-is 3f. awaiting, apprehension 6B(i)

exstinguō 3 I put out, extinguish; kill; blot out, wipe out 1C

F

facultās facultāt-is 3f. capability, skill; opportunity; supply, resources 6C(iii)

fallō 3 I deceive; escape the notice of 2A

fals-us a um false 1B

familiār-is e domestic; friendly, intimate 1B

fās indecl. n. divine law; right 4A(iv)

fateor 2 dep. I acknowledge, confess 1F

fax fac-is 3f. torch, firebrand 5D(iv)

fer-a ae 1f. wild animal 2D

ferōx ferōc-is spirited, courageous; fierce, savage 5A(i)

ferre-us a um made of iron; hard-hearted 5D(i)

flectō 3 I bend; turn; dissuade; prevail on, appease 6D(i)

flōs flōr-is 3m. flower, bloom 6A(vii)

fluō 3 I flow 4A(ii)

fluui-us ī 2m. river 4A(ii)

foc-us ī 2m. hearth 1A

foed-us a um filthy, foul; dishonourable, vile 5F(ii)

fremit-us ūs 4m. growling, murmuring 6D(i)

frīgid-us a um cold, chilly 6D(ii)

frōns front-is 3f. brow, forehead; front 5G(i)

frūgēs frūg-um 3f. pl. fruits of the earth 6D(iii)

fulmen fulmin-is 3n. thunderbolt; lightning 6D(i)

fūm-us ī 2m. smoke 1F

fundāment-um ī 2n. foundation 5D(i)

funditus from the foundations, completely 6B(vii)

fundō 1 I make firm, establish, fix 5D(iv)

fundō 3 I pour, shed; produce in abundance; scatter, rout; spread out, diffuse, display 5G(ii)

fūrt-um ī 2n. theft 6A(ii)

G

gemin-us a um twin; twofold 6D(iii)

gemit-us ūs 4m. groaning, groan 6D(i)

gurges gurgit-is 3m. gulf; sea, flood 6D(ii)

H

hērēs hērēd-is 3m. and f. heir; heiress 6D(iii)

horribil-is e dreadful 6A(vii)

hostīl-is e enemy's, hostile 5G(iii)

hūmānitās hūmānitāt-is 3f. human nature; humanity, kindliness; culture, refinement 4A(ii)

hūmān-us a um human; humane, kindly; civilised, cultured, refined 4D(ii)

595

I

ignōrō 1 I do not know, am ignorant (of) 1A

imāgō imāgin-is 3f. copy, likeness; image, picture, statue; echo; apparition, phantom; semblance, shadow; mental image, fancy, idea 1B

imber imbr-is 3m. rain, rain-storm 6D(i)

im-mittō 3 I send in, send against, let loose, hurl; set on, incite 6D(ii)

im-pellō 3 I drive on, urge on; excite, impel, instigate 5B(i)

im-pendeō 2 (+ dat.) I overhang; menace, threaten 5A(iii)

improb-us a um morally bad, depraved, shameless 2E

imprōuīs-us a um unforeseen, unexpected 5A(iii)

īm-us a um lowest, bottom of 1C

inān-is e empty, void; useless, vain 6D(ii)

in-cidō 3 I fall into, fall upon; fall in with, meet; light upon; befall, happen 5A(ii)

incitō 1 I set in quick motion, speed; arouse, spur on, stimulate 6B(vii)

in-clūdō 3 I shut in, enclose, imprison; include, insert 4E(ii)

incolumitās incolumitāt-is 3f. safety 6B(vii)

incommod-um ī 2n. trouble, setback 6B(vii)

incrēdibil-is e unbelievable 4E(i)

in-currō 3 I run into, run upon, charge; run up against, encounter 5G(ii)

indicō 1 I disclose, make known 2E

in-dūcō 3 I lead in, lead on; overspread; introduce; induce, persuade 5G(iii)

iners inert-is inactive, sluggish 6D(iii)

īnfēlīx īnfēlīc-is unfruitful; unlucky 6D(i)

īnfer-ī ōrum 2m. pl. inhabitants of the Underworld, the dead 1B

ingenu-us a um free-born; frank, open 5G(iii)

initi-um ī 2n. beginning 5A(iii)

iniūst-us a um unrighteous, wrongful 3B

īnsāni-a ae 1f. madness, frenzy 4C(ii)

īnsāniō 4 I am mad, rage, rave 4C(ii)

īnsān-us a um mad, frenzied; outrageous 1C

īn-scrībō 3 I write upon, inscribe 4A(ii)

integritās integritāt-is 3f. completeness; blamelessness 4B(ii)

intercessiō intercessiōn-is 3f. veto (of a tribune) 6B(vii)

inter-clūdō 3 I shut off; cut off, block; shut in, blockade 5E(ii)

inter-eō I perish, die 2E

inter-sum I am between; am different; (+ dat.) take part in 6B(viii)

intrō-dūcō 3 I bring inside, introduce 5C(iii)

intro-eō I enter 5A(iii)

in-uādō 3 I go in, enter; rush into; fall upon, assault, attack 2A

inuidi-a ae 1f. envy, ill-will; unpopularity 5A(i)

inuidiōs-us a um enviable; odious, unpopular 4C(ii)

inuītō 1 I invite; allure, attract 4B(iii)

īr-a ae 1f. anger, passion, wrath 6D(i)

iug-um ī 2n. yoke; pair; mountain ridge; summit; chain of mountains 6C(iii)

iūst-us a um righteous, upright; lawful, rightful; equitable, due, proper 3B

L

lac lact-is 3n. milk 2E

lacrim-a ae 1f. tear 2D

lacrimor 1 dep. I shed tears, weep 4E(ii)

laetor 1 dep. I rejoice 5C(iii)

lapis lapid-is 3m. stone; milestone; precious stone 6D(i)

lassitūdō lassitūdin-is 3f. faintness, weariness 6C(ii)

lass-us a um faint, tired, weary 6D(iv)

lateō 2 I lie hidden, lurk; am hidden from (trans.) 1A

lauō 1 I wash (trans.) 1F

laus laud-is 3f. praise; renown; credit, distinction 6B(viii)

lēniō 4 I soften; calm, soothe 2E

lēnitās lēnitāt-is 3f.
gentleness, mildness
6C(iv)
leuō 1 I lighten; lift;
console; relieve 6D(iv)

M

maeror maerōr-is 3m. grief,
sorrow 5G(iii)
mandāt-um ī 2n.
commission, injunction
5C(i)
mātūr-us a um ripe;
seasonable, timely;
early, speedy 4A(ii)
mediocr-is e middling,
moderate, ordinary 4C(ii)
metuō 3 I fear, dread 2E
min-ae ārum 1f. pl. threats
6D(i)
ministrō 1 I attend to,
manage; furnish,
supply 6D(ii)
minitor 1 dep. I keep on
threatening 4F(ii)
minuō 3 I diminish 5A(i)
miseri-a ae 1f.
wretchedness, distress
5B(i)
mīt-is e mellow, gentle,
mild 5D(i)
modesti-a ae 1f. discretion;
modesty 4B(ii)
molesti-a ae 1f.
irksomeness, trouble
6B(i)
molest-us a um irksome,
troublesome 2E
moll-is e soft; calm,
gentle; pliant, yielding;
irresolute; effeminate;
agreeable, pleasant
5A(ii)
mōnstrō 1 I point out,
show 1A
monument-um ī 2n.
memorial, monument
1D

moror 1 dep. I delay,
linger, tarry; (trans.)
delay, hinder 2E
mūnitiō mūnitiōn-is 3f.
fortifying; fortification,
entrenchment 6C(iii)

N

nāscor 3 dep. I am born;
arise, spring; am
produced, occur
naturally 4C(i)
neglegēns neglegent-is
careless, neglectful
6A(iv)
nimium = nimis too much
6B(i)
niteō 2 I glisten, glitter,
shine 2E
nōbilitās nōbilitāt-is 3f.
high birth; aristocracy;
excellence 5A(i)
nocēns nocent-is criminal,
guilty 5D(i)
nocturn-us a um by night;
nightly 4F(i)
nusquam nowhere 2C

O

ob-sistō 3 (+ dat.) I
obstruct, thwart 4A(i)
occult-us a um hidden,
secret 5C(ii)
odor odōr-is 3m. scent,
smell; stench 5E(i)
ōlim once (upon a time);
long ago; some time
(in the future) 3A
ōrātor ōrātōr-is 3m. orator,
speaker; spokesman 2D
orbis orb-is 3m. circle;
disc, hoop, ring, orbit:
orbis terrārum the world
4G(i)

P

pacīscor 3 dep. I bargain,
contract, covenant;

make an agreement;
(trans.) bargain for;
betroth 2C
palm-a ae 1f. palm of
hand; hand; palm-tree;
palm-branch,
palm,wreath; prize of
victory 4E(i)
pariēs pariet-is 3m. wall
(of house) 3C
pass-us ūs 4m. pace, step:
mīlle passūs (pl. *mīlia
passuum*) mile 6C(iii)
pāstor pāstōr-is 3m.
shepherd 2E
patrōn-us ī 2m. defender,
protector, patron;
counsel for defence,
advocate 4C(ii)
paucitās paucitāt-is 3f.
fewness, paucity 6B(v)
peccāt-um ī 2n. sin 4B(i)
pectus pector-is 3n. bosom,
breast; heart, soul
6D(iv)
pecus pecor-is 3n. herd of
animals, cattle 5F(ii)
pedes pedit-is on foot; 3m.
noun foot-soldier 5G(i)
pendeō 2 I hang; depend
3A
perdit-us a um desperate,
hopeless; abandoned,
profligate 1A
per-dūcō 3 I bring along,
conduct; prolong;
construct; win over 5B(i)
perfug-a ae 1m. deserter
5E(ii)
per-fugiō 3/4 I desert (to
the enemy) 5E(ii)
perfugi-um ī 2n. place of
refuge 6D(i)
perīculōs-us a um
dangerous 5A(i)
perīt-us a um experienced,
skilled, skilful; (+ gen.)
skilled in 4D(ii)

per-mittō 3 I entrust;
(+ dat.) allow, permit
5G(i)

perniciēs perniciē-ī 5f. utter
destruction, utter ruin
4B(i)

perpetu-us a um
continuous, unbroken
6A(iv)

perspicu-us a um evident
1E

perterreō 2 I frighten
thoroughly, demoralise
5A(iii)

per-tineō 2 I extend,
stretch; belong (to),
relate (to); lead (to),
tend (to) 4F(i)

perturbātiō perturbātiōn-is
3f. confusion, disorder
6B(viii)

perturbō 1 I throw into
confusion, confound
5E(ii)

plācō 1 I reconcile;
appease 6D(i)

plānitiēs plānitiē-ī 5f. plain
6C(iv)

pondus ponder-is 3n.
weight; load, mass 3C

pont-us ī 2m. (open) sea
6D(ii)

port-a ae 1f. gate 2A

possessiō possessiōn-is 3f.
holding, occupation,
possession 5D(iii)

poster-us a um next,
subsequent 6B(iii)

potestās potestāt-is 3f.
power; control;
magisterial power,
authority; opportunity
1D

pōtō 1 I drink; drink hard
4E(i)

prae-dīcō 3 I foretell; issue
warning 6B(vii)

prae-mittō 3 I send in

advance 5A(iii)

praeterit-us a um past
6B(iii)

praetōri-us a um praetor's;
general's 5G(ii)

prīuātim in a private
capacity 5B(i)

prīuāt-us a um personal,
private; not holding
office 6B(viii)

prīuō 1 I deprive, strip;
release 6C(i)

prob-us a um good,
honest, proper;
virtuous 2A

prō-cēdō 3 I advance, go
forward; (of time) pass;
make progress; come
off, turn out well
5A(iii)

procul far; from afar 2E

prōcumbō 3 I collapse, lie
down, sink to the
ground 6D(i)

prō-dō 3 I give forth;
publish; bequeath,
hand down; betray
5A(iii)

prō-dūcō 3 I lead forth;
drag out, protract 2E

profectō assuredly 6B(viii)

prō-ferō I bring forth;
bring to light; put
forward, cite, mention
1F

pro-fundō 3 I pour forth,
spill; lavish, squander
1F

propinqu-us a um near,
neighbouring; *propinqu-
us ī* 2m. (noun) near
relative 4B(iii)

prōspiciō 3/4 I look out;
(+ dat.) provide for;
(trans.) look out on;
foresee 6B(iii)

prūdēns prūdent-is discreet,
sensible 6B(vii)

pūblicē on behalf of the
state, at the state's
expense, officially 5B(i)

pūblic-us a um belonging
to the state, state-,
official; common,
public 4E(ii)

puluis puluer-is 3m. dust
6D(iii)

Q

quaest-us ūs 4m.
acquisition, gain,
profit; business, trade
5A(ii)

quiēt-us a um at rest,
quiet; peaceful, neutral
4B(i)

quondam once 6A(vi)

R

rādīx rādīc-is 3f. root;
foot-hill, (mountain)
spur 4E(i)

rār-us a um loose, thin;
here and there,
scattered, wide apart;
(pl.) in small groups;
scarce 6D(iv)

ratis rat-is 3f. raft; (in
poetry) ship, vessel
6D(ii)

re-cidō 3 I fall back;
relapse 6B(vi)

reciperō (or *recuperō*) 1 I
regain, recover 6C(i)

recitō 1 I read out, read
aloud 4A(iv)

re-currō 3 I run back;
recur 6D(iii)

recūsātiō recūsātiōn-is 3f.
objection 6C(iv)

red-imō 3 I buy back,
repurchase; ransom;
buy, purchase; contract
for, farm (taxes); buy
off; pay for, atone for
6B(viii)

re-*ferō* I bring back, carry back; repay; convey; repeat; reproduce; announce, relate, report; record, set down in writing; ascribe, refer; (intrans.) take back word, . report; put a motion (e.g. before senate) 1F

rēgnō 1 I reign, rule 5D(i)

rēgn-um ī 2n. kingship, sovereignty; despotism; kingdom, realm 4G(i)

regō 3 I direct, guide; govern, rule 6D(ii)

re-*gredior* 3/4 dep. I return; retreat 2E

religiō religiōn-is 3f. reverence, religious awe; religious scruple; superstition; conscientiousness; holiness, sanctity 4A(ii)

remedi-um ī 2n. cure, remedy 5B(i)

remissiō remissiōn-is 3f. slackening; abatement, relaxation 5D(ii)

re-*moueō* 2 I move back; remove 4D(ii)

rēm-us ī 2m. oar 4D(ii)

renouō 1 I renew, restore, revive 6C(ii)

renūntiō 1 I bring back word, report back; announce, report; announce the election of; disclaim, renounce 4A(iv)

repudiō 1 I reject, repudiate 5C(i)

re-*quiēscō* 3 I repose, rest

re-*stituō* 3 I set up again, replace; rebuild; re-establish, reform, restore, revive; restore, give back; reinstate 6D(iii)

reticeō 2 I keep silent; (trans.) keep silent about 5A(i)

re-*trahō* 3 I draw back, bring back; remove, withdraw 4F(ii)

rumpō 3 I break, burst; break off, cut short; break in on, interrupt 6A(vii)

ruō 3 I fall down, tumble down; dash, hurry, rush; (trans.) dash down; upheave 6D(ii)

rūrsus/rūrsum back again; again 1F

S

sagittāri-us ī 2m. archer 6C(ii)

sal sal-is 3m. salt; brine, sea; wit 6A(i)

sax-um ī 2n. rock, large stone 4B(iv)

scelerāt-us a um criminal, vicious 4B(iv)

sēcrētō in private 6B(ii)

sēdēs sēd-is 3f. seat; abode, habitation; base, foundation 6D(i)

sempitern-us a um everlasting, imperishable 5D(iv)

senātor senātōr-is 3m. senator 5A(iii)

senātōri-us a um senatorial 6C(iii)

sēns-us ūs 4m. feeling; perception, sense; emotion, opinion 4B(iv)

significō 1 I indicate, make known; betoken; mean, signify 6B(vii)

signō 1 I set a mark on; mark out; stamp (money); seal; indicate 5C(i)

singulār-is e one at a time; single; matchless, unique 4A(ii)

sit-us a um lying, placed, situated 1F

societās societāt-is 3f. alliance, association, confederacy, partnership 5B(i)

solitūdō solitūdin-is 3f. loneliness; lonely place, desert 6B(vii)

sors sort-is 3f. lot; casting of lots; allotted duty; oracular response; destiny, fate 4A(iv)

sortior 4 dep. I draw lots, assign by lot; select by lot; obtain by lot 4A(iv)

spargō 3 I scatter, strew; sprinkle; bedew, bespatter; disperse, spread abroad 6D(i)

spectācul-um ī 2n. sight, spectacle, show 4E(iii)

spectō 1 I look at, watch 1A

speculātor speculātōr-is 3m. spy, scout 4G(i)

spīrō 1 I breathe; blow; (trans.) breathe out, exhale 5G(iii)

splendid-us a um gleaming, shining; brilliant, illustrious, splendid 4C(i)

spoliō 1 I strip; despoil, plunder 2E

sponte of one's own accord, spontaneously 6C(ii)

stabiliō 4 I make firm, make steady, establish 5D(iv)

statuō 3 I erect, set up; establish, fix, settle; decide, determine 4E(iii)

statūr-a ae 1f. height,
stature 3C

stat-us ūs 4m. posture;
position; condition,
state; state of affairs;
constitution 5B(i)

strēnu-us a um active,
vigorous 5G(ii)

stringō 3 I bind, draw
tight; pull off, strip;
draw (sword); graze,
touch lightly 6C(ii)

stupeō 2 I am aghast,
astounded, dazed;
(trans.) am astonished
at 1B

suādeō 2 I advise,
recommend, urge (acc.
of thing, dat. of
person) 2D

sub-iciō 3/4 I thrust under;
put under; subdue,
subject; append,
subjoin; suggest;
substitute 6D(ii)

sub-igō 3 I bring under;
dig up, plough up;
conquer, subjugate;
compel 6D(ii)

sub-sum I am under; am
close at hand; am
under the surface, lie
concealed 6C(iii)

sum-moueō 2 I remove;
drive away 6C(ii)

superbi-a ae 1f. arrogance,
pride, haughtiness
5A(i)

superb-us a um arrogant,
haughty, proud 6D(ii)

super-ī ōrum 2m. pl. the
gods above 6D(iii)

super-sum I am over,
remain, survive;
(+ dat.) survive,
outlive; am in
abundance 6C(i)

sus-cipiō 3/4 I hold up,

support; take up,
undertake; beget; adopt
5A(iii)

suspiciō suspiciōn-is 3f.
mistrust, suspicion
4A(iii)

T

tametsī although 6B(i)

temere by accident, by
chance; at random;
heedlessly, rashly,
recklessly 6B(vii)

tenu-is e thin; slender,
slight; feeble, weak;
poor, trifling; fine,
subtle 4G(i)

tolerō 1 I bear, endure;
keep up, maintain
5A(ii)

tranquill-us a um calm,
still; at peace, serene,
undisturbed 2B

trāns-igō 3 I accomplish,
complete, perform;
(intrans.) make a
settlement, come to an
understanding 5D(ii)

trāns-mittō 3 I send across,
send over; hand over;
cross 6D(ii)

tribūn-us ī 2m. tribune
5D(iii)

tribuō 3 I allot, assign,
bestow; grant, render,
attribute 6B(vii)

trienni-um ī 2n. period of
three years 4C(ii)

triumphō 1 I celebrate a
triumph; exult,
triumph 2D

tub-a ae 1f. trumpet, war-
trumpet 3B

tumult-us ūs 4m.
commotion, disorder,
uproar; insurrection,
uprising 4B(i)

tunc then 4A(iv)

turbid-us a um boisterous;
disorderly; confused,
troubled 6D(ii)

turpitūdō turpitūdin-is 3f.
baseness, disgrace,
shamefulness 5F(ii)

turris turr-is 3f. tower,
turret; siege-tower 2A

V

uānitās uānitāt-is 3f.
emptiness;
deceptiveness, falsity;
vainglory 5A(i)

uās uās-is 3n. (pl. *uās-a
ōrum* 2n.) vessel; utensil
1F

uāstō 1 I desert, leave
empty; devastate, lay
waste 5D(i)

uāst-us a um empty;
desert, waste;
boundless; enormous,
prodigious, vast 6D(ii)

ueni-a ae 1f. favour,
grace; permission;
forgiveness, pardon
4G(i)

uēnor 1 dep. I hunt 6B(v)

uēr uēr-is 3n. spring 6D(iii)

uesper ī 2m. (and *uesper-is*
3m.) evening 2E

ueterān-us a um veteran
5G(i)

uetust-us a um old 2B

uexātiō uexātiōn-is 3f.
distress, trouble 5D(i)

uictor uictōr-is 3m.
conqueror, victor 3B

uindex uindic-is 3m.
defender, protector;
avenger 5E(i)

uiolō 1 I do violence to;
profane; break (law
etc.), outrage, violate
6C(iv)

uirid-is e green; blooming,
fresh 6D(ii)

uirīl-is e man's; of
manhood; manly 5A(ii)
uīsō 3 I look at, view; go
to see, visit 2C
uiti-um ī 2n. defect, fault,
flaw; crime, offence;
depravity 6B(viii)

uix scarcely 2E
ulcīscor 3 dep. I take
vengeance on; avenge
2E
ulterior ulteriōr-is further,
more remote 6D(ii)
uolō 1 I fly 6D(i)

urbān-us a um city–;
polished, refined; witty
5A(ii)
uulgō commonly,
generally 6B(ii)

INDEX OF GRAMMAR

Numbers alone refer to Running Grammar sections (adscript numbers refer to sections, superscript numbers to Notes within those e.g. 48.1, 89⁶). Letters A–W (with numbers/letters following) refer to the Reference Grammar (pp. 448ff.). Page numbers are given for grammar which occurs outside these parts. For a simplified definition of terms, see the Glossary of English–Latin Grammar pp. xvii–xxiii.

Table I.1 Active verbs

	Indicative	Infinitive	Imperative	Subjunctive	Participles
Present	amō, habeō, 2, 3; dīcō, 24; audiō, 25; capiō, 33	41	amō, 1; habeō, 2; dīcō, 24; audiō, 25; capiō, 36; irr., 37	127	120
Future	50	97	A2 Note 1	172⁴, A2 Note 2, L–V Intro.(c)	81–3
Imperfect	89			130	
Perfect	65	95		167	
Future perfect	156				
Pluperfect	104			121	

Table I.2 Deponents

	Indicative	Infinitive	Imperative	Subjunctive	Participles
Present	58	58	58	128	120
Future	68	97	A2 *Note* 1	172⁴, A2 *Note* 2, L–V Intro.(c)	81
Imperfect	90			131	
Perfect	75	96		168	77
Future perfect	157				
Pluperfect	105			122	

Index

Table I.3 Passive

	Indicative	Infinitive	Imperative	Subjunctive	Participles
Present	112	118	117	129	
Future	113	118	B2 *Note*		
Imperfect	114			132	
Perfect	115	118		169	82–3, 151, 163
Future perfect	158				
Pluperfect	116			123	
Gerundive					160